Primary Source:
Documents
in
U.S. History

VOLUME I

Upper Saddle River, New Jersey 07458

© 2009 by PEARSON EDUCATION, INC.
Upper Saddle River, New Jersey 07458

ISBN 10: 0-13-605198-7
ISBN 13: 978-0-13-605198-5

CONTENTS

Contents

Part Three

COLONIAL AMERICA (A MATURING COLONIAL SOCIETY IN THE LATE 1600S AND 1700S)

Part Four

PRELUDE TO REVOLUTION

Part Five

THE AMERICAN REVOLUTION

Part Six

FORGING A CONSTITUTION

Contents

Part Seven

THE FEDERALIST ERA

Part Eight

JEFFERSON AND THE REPUBLIC

Part Nine

ECONOMIC AND SOCIAL CHANGE

Part Ten

JACKSONIAN DEMOCRACY

Contents

Part Fourteen

THE SECTIONAL CRISIS

Part Fifteen

THE CIVIL WAR

Contents

Part Sixteen

RECONSTRUCTION

PART ONE
MEETING OF THREE CULTURES

1-1   Marco Polo Recounts His Travels Through Asia (1324)

Marco Polo's recollections of his travels through Asia planted seeds of curiosity, wanderlust, and want in the minds of Europeans within a century after his death in 1324. Known at the time as The Description of the World or The Travels of Marco Polo, his account of the wealth of Cathay (China) and the exotic customs of the Orient made his book a bestseller. Although criticized by some as fiction, his narrative nevertheless captured readers through the centuries and served as the foremost description of the world outside Europe available at the time.

> **Source:** Marco Polo, *Voyages and Travels of Marco Polo* (New York: The F. M. Lupton Publishing Company, [n.d.]).

Ten miles off Cambalu is a certain great river named Pulisangan, emptying itself into the ocean, by which many ships with much merchandise ascend; and in that place there is a very fair bridge, all of serpentine stone, curiously wrought, containing three hundred paces in length, and eight in breadth, so broad that ten men may ride abreast; on each side it is secured with a wall of marble, and pillars set in a row, and in the height of this ascent is a great and high pillar, at the feet whereof is a great lion, and on the top another, and so quite through the bridge: one pace and a half distance are pillars with lions on the tops, and a fair wall with wrought marble work betwixt, to keep men from falling. Having passed over the river and bridge, and proceeding thirty miles westward (in which palaces are continually seen, with vineyards and fertile fields), you come to the city Gouza, both fair and great, having many monasteries of idols. Cloths of gold and silk are made there, and the purest and finest cambrics or lawns; and many common inns for strangers or travellers are found in that city. The citizens are artificers and merchants. A mile without this city the way parteth, one leading west, the other south-east; that to the west leadeth through the province of Cathay, but the other, towards the country of Mangi, from the city of Gouza to the kingdom of Tainfu.

You ride ten days through Cathay, always finding many fair cities, well furnished with vineyards and tilled fields, from whence wine is carried to Cathay, where there is none; there are many mulberry-trees for silkworms, the people civil, and cities very numerous and populous. Tainfu is the name of the kingdom, and of the chief city, which is great and fair, hath much trade, with store of ammunition, fit for the Khan's armies. The wine about this city serveth the whole province. Seven days further westward is a pleasant country beautified with many castles and cities, in which also there is great trade in different merchandise carried on. After which you come to a city very great, named Pianfu, in which there is vast abundance of silk and much trade. Westward from Pianfu stands a very pleasant castle, named Thaigin, anciently built by a king called Dor; in it is a spacious palace, wherein is a fine hall, in which are painted all the famous kings which have reigned there, and it is a fair spectacle. Of this king Dor, they say he was potent, and was attended only by young damsels, of which he had many in his court. These also, when he had a mind to take his pleasure, carried him in a small light chariot through the castle, which was so fortified by art and nature, that the governor thereof feared none, no, not Umcan his lord, against whom he rebelled.

But seven men, professing fidelity and service to Dor, took him at a disadvantage in hunting, and brought him prisoner to Presbyter John, or Umcan, who put him on vile cloths, and appointed him to keep his cattle, and set over him a strong guard, till two years were ended: after which he commanded him to be brought before him, and being dressed in princely apparel, he giving him his pardon, after a sharp admonition, sent him well attended to the re-possession of his kingdom. About twenty miles beyond the castle Thaigin is the river Caramaran, which, by reason of the exceeding breadth and depth thereof, hath no bridge over it in all the space from thence till it floweth to the ocean. On the shore thereof are many cities and castles built, wherein great trade is carried on. This country abounds with ginger, silk, and fowl, especially pheasants, so that three of them are bought for a Venetian groat. There grow reeds in vast plenty, so thick that some are a foot, and others a foot and a half in compass, which are applied to many uses. Passing this river, after two days' journey, is the famous city called Carianfu, where many cloths of gold and silk are made. Here grow ginger, galingale spike, and many spices. The people are idolaters.

Proceeding seven days' journey westward, many cities and towns, lovely fields and gardens, are found, and everywhere mulberries for silkworms. As for the people, they are mostly idolaters; but there are also Christians, Turks, Nestorians, and some Saracens. There is a vast abundance here of wild beasts and fowl. If you proceed seven days' journey farther, you shall come to a certain great city named Quensanfu, which is the chief city of the kingdom, in which have reigned many famous kings; and at this day the son of the Great Khan, called Mangalu, hath the command thereof. That country yields great plenty of silk, cloth of gold, and all other things necessary for furnishing an army, and for the preservation of man's life. The inhabitants worship idols, and there are some Christians, Turks, and Saracens. Five miles without this city standeth the palace of Mangalu, seated in a plain, where are many springs, rivulets, and places of game. There is a high wall encompassing a park of five miles, where are all sorts of wild beasts and fowls. In the midst is an excellent palace, having many halls and chambers, great and fair, all painted with gold and azure, and numberless statues adorning it. The king, with his courtiers, delights himself in hunting the wild beasts, and taking of fowl, and following his father's examples in justice and equity, is much beloved of his people.

Proceeding three days' journey westward from the said palace, through a very beautiful plain, where many cities and castles are, which abound with silk merchandise and manufactures, you come to a country where in the mountains and valleys are frequent habitations, and many villages of the province of Chunchian. The inhabitants as to religion are idolaters; and as to employment, husbandmen. Also in that country they hunt lions, bears, stags, roebucks, deer, and wolves. Ths plain is two days' journey over, and the country is about twenty days' journey westward, well inhabited, being finely diversified into mountains, valleys, and woods. After these twenty days towards the west, there lies a province called Achbaluch Mangi, that is, the white city, on the borders of Mangi, which is well peopled. This province, for two days' journey, hath a plain, in which are an infinite number of villages: beyond these lie mountains, valleys, and wood, all well inhabited. It hath plenty of wild beasts, and of those creatures that yield musk. In this province ginger grows in great plenty, as also corn and rice.

After twenty days' journey through those hills is a plain, and a province in the confines of Mangi, named Sind-infu. The chief city hath the same name, and is very great, and exceeding rich, being twenty miles in circuit. It hath had many rich and mighty kings; but an old king dying, left three sons successors in the kingdom, who divided the city into three parts, compassing every part with their proper walls; all which, notwithstanding, were contained within the former wall; but the Great Khan subjected nevertheless that city and kingdom. Through this city run many rivers, and many places round about, some half a mile over, some two hundred paces, very deep; on them are many bridges of stone, very fair, eight paces broad, set on both sides with marble pillars, which bear up a timber frame that covers the bridge, each bridge having streets and shops thereupon. When the rivers have passed through the city they become one great river, called Quian, which runs one hundred days' journey hence to the ocean. Near these rivers are many cities and castles, and on them innumerable ships for merchandise. Proceeding four days' journey farther, through a very fine plain, many cities, castles, and villages are found, in which five lawns extend in beautiful order. There are also many wild beasts there. Beyond the plain, which we have now mentioned, is the wide province of Thibet, which the Great Khan vanquished and wasted; for in it lie many cities destroyed and castles overthrown, by the space of twenty days' journey; and because it is become a wilderness, wanting inhabitants, wild beasts and lions are increased excessively, and it is requisite therefore that travellers carry victuals with them. Very large cane grows in this country, ten paces in length, and three palms in thickness, and as much from knot to knot. When travellers therefore will rest at night secure from beasts, they take great bundles of the greener reeds, and putting fire under, kindle them, which makes such a crackling, and so great a noise, that it may be heard two miles off; which terrible sound the wild beasts hearing, flee away; but it has sometimes happened that horses and other beasts, which merchants use for their journey, hearing this noise and cracking, have grown also much afraid, and betaking themselves to flight have escaped from their masters; and therefore wiser travellers binding their feet together detain them in their proper places.

1. What aspects of Marco Polo's description of the Orient might early readers have found alluring? What might have given them pause?
2. Skeptics question the authenticity of Marco Polo's account, citing his omission of such things as the Great Wall, tea, and calligraphy. How important is the veracity of the narrative to our overall assessment of its value to history?

1-2 Christopher Columbus, Letter to Ferdinand and Isabella of Spain (1494)

In this letter, probably written in 1494, Christopher Columbus outlines his thoughts regarding Spanish colonization and commercial activity in the New World. While his words address the immediate circumstances regarding the colonization of the island of Hispaniola (Espanola), his ideas serve as a paradigm and partial justification for the expansion of the Spanish Empire into the Western Hemisphere.

Source: *AmDocs* Website, University of Kansas, http://www.ukans.edu/carrie/docs/texts/columlet.htmi

Most High and Mighty Sovereigns, In obedience to your Highnesses' commands, and with submission to superior judgment, I will say whatever occurs to me in reference to the colonization and commerce of the Island of Espanola, and of the other islands, both those already discovered and those that may be discovered hereafter. In the first place, as regards the Island of Espanola: Inasmuch as the number of colonists who desire to go thither amounts to two thousand, owing to the land being safer and better for farming and trading, and because it will serve as a place to which they can return and from which they can carry on trade with the neighboring islands:

1. That in the said island there shall be founded three or four towns, situated in the most convenient places, and that the settlers who are there be assigned to the aforesaid places and towns.
2. That for the better and more speedy colonization of the said island, no one shall have liberty to collect gold in it except those who have taken out colonists' papers, and have built houses for their abode, in the town in which they are, that they may live united and in greater safety.
3. That each town shall have its alcalde [Mayor] . . . and its notary public, as is the use and custom in Castile.
4. That there shall be a church, and parish priests or friars to administer the sacraments, to perform divine worship, and for the conversion of the Indians.
5. That none of the colonists shall go to seek gold without a license from the governor or alcalde of the town where he lives; and that he must first take oath to return to the place whence he sets out, for the purpose of registering faithfully all the gold he may have found, and to return once a month, or once a week, as the time may have been set for him, to render account and show the quantity of said gold; and that this shall be written down by the notary before the alcalde, or, if it seems better, that a friar or priest, deputed for the purpose, shall be also present.
6. That all the gold thus brought in shall be smelted immediately, and stamped with some mark that shall distinguish each town; and that the portion which belongs to your Highnesses shall be weighed, and given and consigned to each alcalde in his own town, and registered by the above-mentioned priest or friar, so that it shall not pass through the hands of only one person, and there shall be no opportunity to conceal the truth.
7. That all gold that may be found without the mark of one of the said towns in the possession of any one who has once registered in accordance with the above order shall be taken as forfeited, and that the accuser shall have one portion of it and your Highnesses the other.
8. That one per centum of all the gold that may be found shall be set aside for building churches and adorning the same, and for the support of the priests or friars belonging to them; and, if it should be thought proper to pay any thing to the alcaldes or notaries for their services, or for ensuring the faithful perforce of their duties, that this amount shall be sent to the governor or treasurer who may be appointed there by your Highnesses.
9. As regards the division of the gold, and the share that ought to be reserved for your Highnesses, this, in my opinion, must be left to the aforesaid governor and treasurer, because it will have to be greater or less according to the quantity of gold that may be found. Or, should it seem preferable, your Highnesses might, for the space of one year, take one half, and the collector the other, and a better arrangement for the division be made afterward.
10. That if the said alcaldes or notaries shall commit or be privy to any fraud, punishment shall be provided, and the same for the colonists who shall not have declared all the gold they have.
11. That in the said island there shall be a treasurer, with a clerk to assist him, who shall receive all the gold belonging to your Highnesses, and the alcaldes and notaries of the towns shall each keep a record of what they deliver to the said treasurer.
12. As, in the eagerness to get gold, every one will wish, naturally, to engage in its search in preference to any other employment, it seems to me that the privilege of going to look for gold ought to be withheld during some portion of each year, that there may be opportunity to have the other business necessary for the island performed.
13. In regard to the discovery of new countries, I think permission should be granted to all that wish to go, and more liberality used in the matter of the fifth, making the tax easier, in some fair way, in order that many may be disposed to go on voyages.

I will now give my opinion about ships going to the said Island of Espanola, and the order that should be maintained; and that is, that the said ships should only be allowed to discharge in one or two ports designated for the purpose, and should register there whatever cargo they bring or unload; and when the time for their departure comes, that they should sail from these same ports, and register all the cargo they take in, that nothing may be concealed.

- In reference to the transportation of gold from the island to Castile, that all of it should be taken on board the ship, both that belonging to your Highnesses and the property of every one else; that it should all be placed in one chest with two locks, with their keys, and that the master of the vessel keep one key and some person selected by the governor and treasurer the other; that there should come with the gold, for a testimony, a list of all that has been put into the said chest, properly marked, so that each owner may receive his own; and that, for the faithful performance of this duty, if any gold whatsoever is found outside of the said chest in any way, be it little or much, it shall be forfeited to your Highnesses.
- That all the ships that come from the said island shall be obliged to make their proper discharge in the port of Cadiz, and that no person shall disembark or other person be permitted to go on board until the ship has been visited by the person or persons deputed for that purpose, in the said city, by your Highnesses, to whom the master shall show all that

he carries, and exhibit the manifest of all the cargo, it may be seen and examined if the said ship brings any thing hidden and not known at the time of lading.

- That the chest in which the said gold has been carried shall be opened in the presence of the magistrates of the said city of Cadiz, and of the person deputed for that purpose by your Highnesses, and his own property be given to each owner. I beg your Highnesses to hold me in your protection; and I remain, praying our Lord God for your Highnesses' lives and the increase of much greater States.

1. *According to Columbus, what is the primary reason for Spanish colonization in the New World? Does his letter hint at any other reason(s)?*
2. *One can argue that there is a tone of cynicism in Columbus's letter. Identify specific points in the narrative where he reveals his misgivings about human nature. What insight might this give you into Columbus's personality?*

1-3 Alvar Nú—ez Cabeza de Vaca, "Indians of the Rio Grande" (1528-1536)

In 1528, half of the crew of the Spanish explorer Panfilo de Navarez was stranded in Florida. After sailing in makeshift vessels across the Gulf of Mexico, the crew was shipwrecked and enslaved by coastal peoples. After six years, Cabeza de Vaca, a black slave, Estevancio the Moor (referred to as "the negro" in this excerpt), and two others escaped and made the overland journey from Texas through the Southwest and south to Mexico City. In this selection from his journal, Cabeza de Vaca describes the native peoples and environment of what is now Texas and northern Mexico

They are so accustomed to running that, without resting or getting tired, they run from morning till night in pursuit of a deer, and kill a great many, because they follow until the game is worn out, sometimes catching it alive. Their huts are of matting placed over four arches. They carry them on their back and move every two or three days in quest of food; they plant nothing that would be of any use.

They are very merry people, and even when famished do not cease to dance and celebrate their feasts and ceremonials. Their best times are when "tunas" (prickly pears) are ripe, because then they have plenty to eat and spend the time in dancing and eating day and night. As long as these tunas last they squeeze and open them and set them to dry. When dried they are put in baskets like figs and kept to be eaten on the way. The peelings they grind and pulverize.

All over this country there are a great many deer, fowl and other animals which I have before enumerated. Here also they come up with cows; I have seen them thrice and have eaten their meat. They appear to me of the size of those in Spain. Their horns are small, like those of the Moorish cattle; the hair is very long, like fine wool and like a peajacket; some are brownish and others black, and to my taste they have better and more meat than those from here. Of the small hides the Indians make blankets to cover themselves with, and of the taller ones they make shoes and targets. These cows come from the north, across the country further on, to the coast of Florida, and are found all over the land for over four hundred leagues. On this whole stretch, through the valleys by which they come, people who live there descend to subsist upon their flesh. And a great quantity of hides are met with inland.

We remained with the Avavares Indians for eight months, according to our reckoning of the moons. During that time they came for us from many places and said that verily we were children of the sun. Until then Donates and the negro had not made any cures, but we found ourselves so pressed by the Indians coming from all sides, that all of us had to become medicine men. I was the most daring and reckless of all in undertaking cures. We never treated anyone that did not afterwards say he was well, and they had such confidence in our skill as to believe that none of them would die as long as we were among them. . . .

The women brought many mats, with which they built us houses, one for each of us and those attached to him. After this we would order them to boil all the game, and they did it quickly in ovens built by them for the purpose. We partook of everything a little, giving the rest to the principal man among those who had come with us for distribution among all. Every one then came with the share he had received for us to breathe on it and bless it, without which they left it untouched. Often we had with us three to four thousand persons. And it was very tiresome to have to breathe on and make the sign of the cross over every morsel they ate or drank. For many other things which they wanted to do they would come to ask our permission, so that it is easy to realize how greatly we were bothered. The women brought us tunas, spiders, worms, and whatever else they could find, for they would rather starve than partake of anything that had not first passed through our hands.

While traveling with those, we crossed a big river coming from the north and, traversing about thirty leagues of plains, met a number of people that came from afar to meet us on the trail, who treated us like the foregoing ones.

Thence on there was a change in the manner of reception, insofar as those who would meet us on the trail with gifts were no longer robbed by the Indians of our company, but after we had entered their homes they tendered us all they possessed, and the dwellings also. We turned over everything to the principals for distribution. Invariably those who had been deprived of their belongings would follow us, in order to repair their losses, so that our retinue became very large. They would tell them to be careful and not conceal anything of what they owned, as it could not be done without our knowledge, and then we would cause their death. So much did they frighten them that on the first few days after joining us they would be trembling all the time, and would not dare to speak or lift their eyes to Heaven.

Those guided us for more than fifty leagues through a desert of very rugged mountains, and so arid that there was no game. Consequently we suffered much from lack of food, and finally forded a very big river, with its water reaching to our chest. Thence on many of our people began to show the effects of the hunger and hardships they had undergone in those mountains, which were extremely barren and tiresome to travel.

The next morning all those who were strong enough came along, and at the end of three journeys we halted. Alonso del Castillo and Estevanico, the negro, left with the women as guides, and the woman who was a captive took them to a river that flows between mountains where there was a village in which her father lived, and these were the first adobes we saw that were like unto real houses. Castillo and Estevanico went to these and, after holding parley with the Indians, at the end of three days Castillo returned to where he had left us, bringing with him five or six of the Indians. He told how he had found permanent houses, inhabited, the people of which ate beans and squashes, and that he had also seen maize.

Of all things upon earth that caused us the greatest pleasure, and we gave endless thanks to our Lord for this news. Castillo also said that the negro was coming to meet us on the way, near by, with all the people of the houses. For that reason we started, and after going a league and a half met the negro and the people that came to receive us, who gave us beans and many squashes to eat, gourds to carry water in, robes of cowhide, and other things. As those people and the Indians of our company were enemies, and did not understand each other, we took leave of the latter, leaving them all that had been given to us, while we went on with the former and, six leagues beyond, when night was already approaching, reached their houses, where they received us with great ceremonies. Here we remained one day, and left on the next, taking them with us to other permanent houses, where they subsisted on the same food also, and thence on we found a new custom. . . .

Having seen positive traces of Christians and become satisfied they were very near, we gave many thanks to our Lord for redeeming us from our sad and gloomy condition. Anyone can imagine our delight when he reflects how long we had been in that land, and how many dangers and hardships we had suffered. That night I entreated one of my companions to go after the Christians, who were moving through the part of the country pacified and quieted by us, and who were three days ahead of where we were. They did not like my suggestion, and excused themselves from going, on the ground of being tired and worn out, although any of them might have done it far better than I, being younger and stronger.

Seeing their reluctance, in the morning I took with me the negro and eleven Indians and, following the trail, went in search of the Christians. On that day we made ten leagues, passing three places where they slept. The next morning I came upon four Christians on horseback, who, seeing me in such a strange attire, and in company with Indians, were greatly startled. They stared at me for quite awhile, speechless; so great was their surprise that they could not find words to ask me anything. I spoke first, and told them to lead me to their captain, and we went together to Diego de Alcaraz, their commander.

1. Summarize the Cabeza de Vaca's impression of the people they came upon during his journey.
2. What are his impressions of their habits and customs? What seems to be his attitude toward these people?
3. How were the author and his companions received and treated by the Avavares Indians?
4. Describe the various difficulties faced by Cabeza de Vaca and his companions during their travels.

1-4 Jacques Cartier: First Contact with the Indians (1534)

Jacques Cartier (French explorer, 1491–1557), reveals his first impressions of North America's indigenous inhabitants

Source: "The First Relation of Jacques Cartier of S. Malo," in Henry S. Burrage, ed., *Early English and French Voyages, Chiefly from Hakluyt, Original Narratives of Early American History* (New York: Charles Scribner's Sons, 1906).

Of the Cape D'Esperance, or the Cape of Hope, and of S. Martins Creeke, and how seven boats full of wilde men, comming to our boat, would not retire themselves, but being terrified with our Culverins which we shot at them, and our lances, they fled with great hast.

The Cape of the said South land was called The Cape of Hope[1], through the hope that there we had to finde some passage. The fourth of July we went along the coast of the said land on the Northerly side to find some harborough, where wee entred into a creek altogether open toward the South, where there is no succour against the wind: we thought good to name it S. Martines Creeke. There we stayed from the fourth of July until the twelfth: while we were there, on Munday being the sixth of the moneth, Service being done, wee with one of our boates went to discover a Cape and point of land that on the Westerne side was about seven or eight leagues from us, to see which way it did bend, and being within halfe a league of it, wee sawe two companies of boates of wilde men going from one land to the other: their boates were in number about fourtie or fiftie. One part of the which came to the said point, and a great number of men went on shore making a great noise, beckening unto us that wee should come on land, shewing us certaine skinnes upon pieces of wood, but because we had but one onely boat, wee would not goe to them, but went to the other side lying in the See: they seeing us flee, prepared two of their boats to follow us, with which came also five more of them that were comming from the Sea side, all which approched neere unto our boate, dancing, and making many signes of joy and mirth, as it were desiring our friendship, saying in their tongue Napeu tondamen assurtah,[2] with many other words that we understood not. But because (as we have said) we had but one boat, wee would not stand to their courtesie, but made signes unto them that they should turne back, which they would not do, but with great furie came toward us: and suddenly with their boates compassed us about: and because they would not away from us by any signes that we could make, we shot off two. pieces among them, which did so terrifie them, that they put themselves to flight toward the sayde point, making a great noise: and having staid a while, they began anew, even as at the first to come to us againe, and being come neere our boat wee strucke at them with two lances, which thing was so great a terrour unto them, that with great haste they beganne to flee, and would no more follow us.

How the said wilde men comming to our ships, and our men going toward them, both parties went on land, and how the saide wilde men with great joy began to trafique with our men.

The next day part of the saide wilde men with nine of their boates came to the point and entrance of the Creeke, where we with our ships were at road. We being advertised of their comming, went to the point where they were with our boates: but so soone as they saw us, they began to flee, making signes that they came to trafique with us, shewing us such skinnes as they cloth themselves withall, which are of small value. We likewise made signes unto them, that we wished them no evill: and in signe thereof two of our men ventured to go on land to them, and carry them knives with other Iron wares, and a red hat to give unto their Captaine. Which when they saw, they also came on land, and brought some of their skinnes, and so began to deale with us, seeming to be very glad to have our iron ware and other things, stil dancing with many other ceremonies, as with their hands to cast Sea water on their heads. They gave us whatsoever they had, not keeping any thing, so that they were constrained to go back againe naked, and made signes that the next day they would come againe, and bring more skinnes with them.

How that we having sent two of our men on land with wares, there came about 300. wilde men with great gladnesse. Of the qualitie of the countrey, what it bringeth forth, and of the Bay called Baie du Chaleur, or The Bay of heat.

Upon Thursday being the eight of the moneth, because the winde was not good to go out with our ships, we set our boates in a readinesse to goe to discover the said Bay, and that day wee went 25. leagues within it. The next day the wind and weather being faire, we sailed until noone, in which time we had notice of a great part of the said Bay, and how that over the low lands, there were other lands with high mountaines: but seeing that there was no passage at all, wee began to turne back againe, taking our way along the coast: and sayling, we saw certaine wilde men that stood upon the shoare of a lake, that is among the low grounds, who were making fires and smokes: wee went thither, and found that there was a channel of the sea that did enter into the lake, and setting our boats at one of the banks of the chanell, the wilde men with one of their boates came unto us, and brought up pieces of Seales ready sodden, putting them upon pieces of wood: then retiring themselves, they would make signes unto us, that they did give them us. We sent two men unto them with hatchets, knives, beads, and other such like ware, whereat they were very glad, and by and by in clusters they came to the shore where wee were, with their boates, bringing with them skinnes and other such things as they had, to have of our wares. They were more than 300. men, women, and children: Some of the women which came not over, wee might see stand up to the knees in water, singing and dancing: the other that had passed the river where we were, came very friendly to us, rubbing our armes with their owne handes, then would they lift them up toward heaven, shewing many signes of gladnesse: and in such wise were wee assured one of another, that we very familiarly began to trafique for whatsoever they had, til they had nothing but their naked bodies; for they gave us all whatsoever they had, and that was but of small value. We perceived that this people might very easily be converted to our Religion. They goe from place to place. They live onely with fishing. They have an ordinarie time to fish for their provision. The countrey is hotter than the countrey of Spaine, and the fairest that can possibly be found, altogether smooth, and level. There is no place be it never so little, but it hath some trees (yea albeit it be sandie) or else is full of wilde come, that hath an eare like unto Rie: the come is like oates, and smal peason as thicke as if they had bene sowen and plowed, white and red gooseberies, strawberies, blackberies, white and red Roses,

---

1. Point Miscou.
2. Belleforest translates, "We wish to have your friendship."

with many other floures of very sweet and pleasant smell. There be also many goodly medowes full of grasse, and lakes wherein great plentie Of salmons be. They call a hatchet in their tongue Cochi, and a knife Bacon: we named it The bay of heat.

Of another nation of wilde men: of their manners, living and clothing.

Being certified that there was no passage through the said Bay, we hoised saile, and went from S. Maitines Creeke upon Sunday being the 12. of July, to goe and discover further beyond the said Bay, and went along the sea coast Eastward about eighteene leagues, till we came to the Cape of Prato, [3] where we found the tide very great, but shallow ground, and the Sea stormie, so. that we were constrained to draw toward shore, between the said Cape and an Iland lying Eastward, about a league from the said Cape, where we cast anker for that night. The next morning we hoised saile to trend the said coast about, which lyeth North Northeast. But there rose such a stormie and raging winde against us, that we were constrained to come to the place againe, from whence we were come: there did we stay all that day til the next that we hoised up saile, and came to the middest of a river five or sixe leagues from the Cape of Prato Northward, and being overthwart the said River, there arose againe a contrary winde, with great fogges and stormes. So that we were constrained upon Tuesday being the fourteenth of the moneth to enter into the river, and there did we stay till the sixteenth of the moneth looking for faire weather to come out of it: on which day being Thursday, the winde became so raging that one of our ships lost an anker, and we were constrained to goe up higher into the river seven or eight leagues, into a good harborough and ground that we with our boates found out, and through the evill weather, tempest, and darkenesse that was, wee stayed in the saide harborough till the five and twentieth of the moneth, not being able to put out: in the meane time wee sawe a great multitude of wilde men that were fishing for mackerels, whereof there is great store. Their boates were about 40, and the persons what with men, women, and children two hundred, which after they had hanted our company a while, they came very familiarly with their boats to the sides of our ships. We gave them knives, combes, beads of glasse, and other trifles of small value, for which they made many signes of gladnesse, lifting their hands up to heaven dancing and singing in their boates. These men may very well and truely be called Wilde, because there is no poorer people in the world. For I thinke all that they had together, besides their boates and nets, was not worth five souce.[4] They goe altogether naked saving their privities, which are covered with a little skinne, and certaine olde skinnes that they cast upon them. Neither in nature nor in language, doe they any whit agree with them which we found first: their heads be altogether shaven, except one bush of haire which they suffer to grow upon the top of their crowne as long as a horse taile, and then with certaine leather strings binde it in a knot upon their heads. They have no other dwelling but their boates, which they turne upside downe, and under them they lay themselves all along upon the bare ground. They eate their flesh almost raw, save onely that they heat it a little upon imbers of coales, so doe they their fish. Upon Magdalens day we with our boates went to the bancke of the river, and freely went on shore among them, whereat they made many signs, and all their men in two or three companies began to sing and dance, seeming to be very glad of our comming. They had caused all the young women to flee into the wood, two or three excepted, that stayed with them, to ech of which we gave a combe, and a little bell made of Tinne, for which they were very glad, thanking our Captaine, rubbing his armes and breasts with their hands. When the men saw us give something unto those that had stayed, it caused al the rest to come out of the wood, to the end that that they should have as much as the others: These women are about twenty, who altogether in a knot fell upon our Captaine, touching and rubbing him with their hands, according to their manner of cherishing and making much of one, who gave to each of them a little Tinne bell: then suddenly they began to dance, and sing many songs. There we found great store of mackrels, that they had taken upon the shore, with certaine nets that they made to fish, of a kinde of Hempe that groweth in that place where ordinarily they abide, for they never come to the sea, but onely in fishing time. As farre as I understand, there groweth likewise a kind of Millet as big as Peason, like unto that which groweth in Bresil, which they eate in stead of bread. They had great store of it. They call it in their tongue Kapaige. They have also Prunes (that is to say Damsins) which they dry for winter as we doe, they call them Honesta. They have also Figs, [5] Nuts, Apples, and other fruits, and Beans, that they call Sahu, their nuts Cahehya. If we shewed them any thing that they have not, nor know not what it is, shaking their heads, they will say Nohda, which is as much to say, they have it not, nor they know it not. Of those things they have, they would with signes shew us how to dresse them, and how they grow. They eate nothing that hath any taste of salt. They are very great theeves, for they will filch and steale whatsoever they can lay hold of, and all is fish that commeth to net.

How our men set up a great Crosse upon the poynt of the sayd Porte, and the Captaine of those wild men, after a long Oration, was by our Captain appeased, and contented that two of his Children should goe with him.

Upon the 25 of the moneth, wee caused a faire high Crosse to be made of the height of thirty foote, which was made in the presence of many of them, upon the point of the entrance of the sayd haven, [6] in the middest whereof we hanged up a Shield with three Floure de Luces in it, and in the top was carved in the wood with Anticke letters this posie,

---

3. White Head.
4. Sous.
5. Cartier has but one word for figs and plums. The reference evidently is to the common Canada plum.

Vive le Roy de France. Then before them all we set it upon the sayd point. They with great heed beheld both the making and setting of it up. So soone as it was up, we altogether kneeled downe before them, with our hands toward Heaven, yeelding God thankes: and we made signes unto them, shewing them the Heavens, and that all our salvation dependeth onely on him which in them dwelleth: whereat they shewed a great admiration, looking first one at another, and then upon the Crosse. And after wee were returned to our ships, their Captaine clad with an old Beares skin, with three of his sonnes, and a brother of his with him, came unto us in one of their boates, but they came not so neere us as they were wont to doe: there he made a long Oration unto us, shewing us the crosse we had set up, and making a crosse with two fingers, then did he shew us all the Countrey about us, as if he would say that all was his, and that wee should not set up any crosse without his leave. His talke being ended, we shewed him an Axe, faining that we would give it him for his skin, to which he listned, for by little and little hee came neere our ships. One of our fellowes that was in our boate, tooke hold on theirs, and suddenly leapt into it, with two or three more, who enforced them to enter into our ships, whereat they were greatly astonished. But our Captain did straightwaies assure them, that they should have no harme, nor any injurie offred them at all, and entertained them very friendly, making them eate and drinke. Then did we shew them with signes, that the crosse was but onely set up to be as a light and leader which wayes to enter into the port, and that wee would shortly come againe, and bring good store of iron wares and other things, but that we would take two of his children with us, and afterward bring them to the sayd port againe: and so wee clothed two of them in shirts, and coloured coates, with red cappes, and put about every ones necke a copper chaine, whereat they were greatly contented: then gave they their old clothes to their fellowes that went backe againe, and we gave to each one of those three that went backe, a hatchet, and some knives, which made them very glad. After these were gone, and had told the newes unto their fellowes, in the afternoone there came to our ships six boates of them, with five or six men in every one, to take their farewels of those two we had detained to take with us, [7] and brought them some fish, uttering many words which we did not understand, making signes that they would not remove the crosse we had set up.

> *How after we were departed from the sayd porte, following our voyage along the sayd coast, we went to discover the land lying Southeast, and Northwest.*

The next day, being the 25 of the moneth, we had faire weather, and went from the said port: and being out of the river, we sailed Eastnortheast, for after the entrance into the said river, the land is environed about, and maketh a bay in maner of halfe a circle, where being in our ships, we might see all the coast sayling behind, which we came to seeke, the land lying Southeast and Northwest, the course of which was distant from the river about twentie leagues.

1. Summarize the initial attempts by the "wilde men" to make communicate with Jacques Cartier's and his men and the response of Jacques Cartier's crew. Why do you think both parties acted as they did?
2. Describe the terrain and natural resources as observed by Jacques Cartier.
3. Summarize Jacques Cartier's description of the manners, living and clothing of the inhabitants of the land.
4. Discuss the possible significance of the account of the cross erected by Jacques Cartier and his men. How might this symbolize a larger, more significant clash of cultures and customs?

1-5   Bartolomé de Las Casas, "Of the Island of Hispaniola" (1542)

A strong voice against the treatment of the natives under the encomienda system, the Dominican Bartolome de Las Casas wrote, spoke and was an advocate for basic human rights. In this selection, Las Casas juxtaposes the native culture with the Spanish invaders and describes in detail the horrific treatment of the natives at the hands of the Europeans.

God has created all these numberless people to be quite the simplest, without malice or duplicity, most obedient, most faithful to their natural Lords, and to the Christians, whom they serve; the most humble, most patient, most peaceful and calm, without strife nor tumults; not wrangling, nor querulous, as free from uproar, hate and desire of revenge as any in the world. . . .

Among these gentle sheep, gifted by their Maker with the above qualities, the Spaniards entered as soon as soon as they knew them, like wolves, tiger and lions which had been starving for many days, and since forty years they have done nothing else; nor do they afflict, torment, and destroy them with strange and new, and divers kinds of cruelty, never before seen, nor heard of, nor read of. . . . .

---

6. Gaspé Bay
7. Their names were Taignoagny and Domagaia. Both returned with Cartier in the following year.

The Christians, with their horses and swords and lances, began to slaughter and practice strange cruelty among them. They penetrated into the country and spared neither children nor the aged, nor pregnant women, nor those in child labour, all of whom they ran through the body and lacerated, as though they were assaulting so many lambs herded in their sheepfold.

They made bets as to who would slit a man in two, or cut off his head at one blow: or they opened up his bowels. They tore the babes from their mothers' breast by the feet, and dashed their heads against the rocks. Others they seized by the shoulders and threw into the rivers, laughing and joking, and when they fell into the water they exclaimed: "boil body of so and so!" They spitted the bodies of other babes, together with their mothers and all who were before them, on their swords.

They made a gallows just high enough for the feet to nearly touch the ground, and by thirteens, in honour and reverence of our Redeemer and the twelve Apostles, they put wood underneath and, with fire, they burned the Indians alive.

They wrapped the bodies of others entirely in dry straw, binding them in it and setting fire to it; and so they burned them. They cut off the hands of all they wished to take alive, made them carry them fastened on to them, and said: "Go and carry letters": that is; take the news to those who have fled to the mountains.

They generally killed the lords and nobles in the following way. They made wooden gridirons of stakes, bound them upon them, and made a slow fire beneath; thus the victims gave up the spirit by degrees, emitting cries of despair in their torture. . . .

1. *Identify and explain the metephor that Las Casas uses to describe the Spaniards' treatment of the people of Hispaniola? What does the use of this metaphor suggest about Las Casas' attitude toward the Spaniards and the people of Hispaniola?*
2. *Identify and discuss the irony of the behavior of "The Christians" toward the "gentle sheep.*

1-6   Thomas Mun, from England's Treasure by Foreign Trade (1664)

A director of the East India Company and one of the greatest expounders of the policy of mercantilism, Thomas Mun here elaborates on the "qualities" of a merchant in service to his country. The selection comes from his classic book "England's Treasure by Foreign Trade, written during the 30's and published in 1664.

The Qualities which are required in a perfect Merchant of Foreign Trade

The Love and service of our Country consisteth not so much in the knowledge of those duties which are to be performed by others, as in the skillful practice of that which is done by our selves; and therefore it is now fit that I say something of the Merchant . . . for the Merchant is worthily called the Steward of the Kingdoms Stock, by way of Commerce with other Nations; a work of no less Reputation than Trust, which ought to be performed with great skill and conscience, that so the private gain may ever accompany the publique good. . . . I will briefly set down the excellent qualities which are required of a perfect Merchant.

1. He ought to be a good Penman, a good Arithmetician, and a good Accomptant, by that noble order of Debtor and Creditor, which is used only amongst Merchants; also to be expert in the order and form of Charter-parties, Bills of Lading, Invoyces, Contracts, Bills of Exchange, and Policies of Ensurance.
2. He ought to know the Measures, Weights, and Monies of all forraign Countries, especially where we have Trade, & the Monies not onely by their several denominations, but also by their intrinsique values in weight & fineness, compared with the Standard of this Kingdom, without which he cannot well direct his affaires.
3. He ought to know the Customs, Tools, Taxes, Impositions, Conducts and other charges upon all manner of Merchandize exported or imported to and from the said Forraign Countries.
4. He ought to know in what several commodities each Country abounds, and what be the wares which they want, and how and from whence they are furnished with the same.
5. He ought to understand, and to be a diligent observer of the rates of Exchanges by Bills, from one State to another, whereby he may the better direct his affairs, and remit over and receive home his Monies to the most advantage possible.
6. He ought to know what goods are prohibited to be exported or imported in the said forraign Countreys, lest otherwise he should incur great danger and loss in the ordering of his affairs.

7. He ought to know upon what rates and conditions to fraight his Ships, and ensure his adventures from one Countrey to another, and to be well acquainted with the laws, orders and customes of the Ensurance office both here and beyond the Seas, in the many accidents which may happen upon the damage or loss of Ships and goods, or both these.

8. He ought to have knowledge in the goodness and in the prices of all the several materials which are required for the building and repairing of Ships, and the divers workmanships of the same, as also for the Masts, Tackling, Cordage, Ordnance, Victuals, Munition, and Provisions of many kinds; together with the ordinary wages of Commanders, Officers, and Mariners, all which concern the Merchant as he is an Owner of Ships.

9. He ought (by the divers occasions which happen sometimes in the buying and selling of one commodity and sometimes in another) to have indifferent if not perfect knowledge in all manner of Merchandize or wares, which is to be as it were a man of all occupations and trades.

10. He ought by his voyaging on the Seas to become skilful in the Art of Navigation.

11. He ought, as he is a Traveller, and sometimes abiding in forraign Countreys, to attain to the speaking of divers Languages, and to be a diligent observer of the ordinary Revenues and expences of forraign Princes, together with their strength both by Sea and Land, their laws, customes, policies, manners, religions, arts, and the like; to be able to give account thereof in all occasions for the good of his Countrey.

12. Lastly, although there be no necessity that such a Merchant should be a great Scholar; yet it is (at least) required, that in his youth he learn the Latine tongue, which will the better enable him in all the rest of his endeavours.

The Means to Enrich this Kingdom, and to Encrease Our Treasure

The ordinary means therefore to increase our wealth and treasure is by Forraign Trade, wherein wee must ever observe this rule; to sell more to strangers yearly than wee consume of theirs in value. For suppose that when this Kingdom is plentifully served with the Cloth, Lead, Tinn, Iron, Fish and other native commodities, we doe yearly export the overplus to forraign Countreys to the value of twenty two hundred thousand pounds; by which means we are enable beyond the Seas to buy and bring in forraign wares for our use and Consumptions, to the value of twenty hundred thousand pounds.

The Exportation of our Moneys in Trade of Merchandize in a Means to Encrease our Treasure.

If we have such a quantity of wares as doth fully provide us of all things needful from beyond the seas: why should we then doubt that our monys sent out in trade, must not necessarily come back again in treasure; together with the great gains which it may procure in such manner as is before set down? And on the other side, if those Nations which send out their monies do it because they have but few wares of their own, how come they then to have so much Treasure as we ever see in those places which suffer it freely to be exported at all times and by whomsoever? I answer, Even by trading with their Moneys; for by what other means can they get it, having no Mines of Gold or Silver?

1. What knowledge regarding the law and trade/economic relations should a merchant have?
2. What kinds of practical knowledge are encouraged regarding seafaring and foreign relations?
3. What economic principles are set forth to ensure the enrichment of the kingdom and the increase of the national treasury?

1-7   Don Juan de O—ate, Plaus: A Settlement in New Mexico (1599)

Don Juan de O—ate (Spanish-American explorer and colonizer, 1550?–1630?), led a group of colonists from Zacatecas in New Spain (now Mexico) to what is present-day Santa Fe, New Mexico. His colonizing party of 600 persons, including Africans, families, Indians, priests, and Spanish soldiers, traveled in some 83 wagons and were accompanied by over 7,000 animals. It is said that the expedition was a moving village, some four miles long.

Source: English translation in Herbert Bolton, *Spanish Exploration in the Southwest, 1542–1706* (New York: Charles Scribner's Sons, 1908).

Copy of a letter written by Don Juan de O—ate from New Mexico to the Viceroy, the Count of Monterey, on the second day of March, 1599.

From Rio de Nombre de Dios I last wrote to you, Illustrious Sir, giving you an account of my departure, and of the discovery of a wagon road to the Rio del Norte, and of my certain hopes of the successful outcome of my journey, which hopes God has been pleased to grant, may He be forever praised; for greatly to His advantage and that of his royal Majesty, they have acquired a possession so good that none other of his Majesty in these Indies excels it, judging it solely by what

I have seen, by things told of in reliable reports, and by things almost a matter of experience, from having been seen by people in my camp and known by me at present.

This does not include the vastness of the settlements or the riches of the West which the natives praise, or the certainty of pearls promised by the South Sea from the many shells containing them possessed by these Indians, or the many settlements called the seven caves, which the Indians report at the head of this river, which is the Rio del Norte; but includes only the provinces which I have seen and traversed, the people of this eastern country, the Apaches, the nation of the Cocoyes, and many others which are daily being discovered in this district and neighborhood, as I shall specify in this letter. I wish to begin by giving your Lordship an account of it, because it is the first since I left New Spain.

I departed, Illustrious Sir, from Rio de Nombre de Dios on the sixteenth of March, with the great multitude of wagons, women, and children, which your Lordship very well knows, freed from all my opponents, but with a multitude of evil predictions conforming to their desires and not to the goodness of God. His Majesty was pleased to accede to my desires, and to take pity on my great hardships, afflictions, and expenses, bringing me to these provinces of New Mexico with all his Majesty's army enjoying perfect health.

Although I reached these provinces on the twenty-eighth day of May (going ahead with as many as sixty soldiers to pacify the land and free it from traitors, if in it there should be any, seizing Huma—a and his followers to obtain full information, by seeing with my own eyes, regarding the location and nature of the land, and regarding the nature and customs of the people, so as to order what might be best for the army, which I left about twenty-two leagues from the first pueblos, after having crossed the Rio del Norte, at which river I took possession, in the name of his Majesty, of all these kingdoms and pueblos which I discovered before departing from it with scouts), the army did not overtake me at the place where I established it and where I now have it established, in this province of the Teguas, until the nineteenth day of August of the past year. During that time I travelled through settlements sixty-one leagues in extent toward the north, and thirty-five in width from east to west. All this district is filled with pueblos, large and small, very continuous and close together.

At the end of August I began to prepare the people of my camp for the severe winter with which both the Indians and the nature, of the land threatened me; and the devil, who has ever tried to make good his great loss occasioned by our coming, plotted, as is his wont, exciting a rebellion among more than forty-five soldiers and captains, who under pretext of not finding immediately whole plates of silver lying on the ground, and offended because I would not permit them to maltreat these natives, either in their persons or in their goods, became disgusted with the country, or to be more exact, with me, and endeavored to form a gang in order to flee to that New Spain, as they proclaimed, although judging from what has since come to light their intention was directed more to stealing slaves and clothing and to other acts of effrontery not permitted. I arrested two captains and a soldier, who they said were guilty, in order to garrote them on this charge, but ascertaining that their guilt was not so great, and on account of my situation and of the importunate pleadings of the religious and of the entire army, I was forced to forego the punishment and let bygones be bygones.

Although by the middle of September I succeeded in completely calming and pacifying my camp, from this great conflagration a spark was bound to remain hidden underneath the ashes of the dissembling countenances of four of the soldiers of the said coterie. These fled from me at that time, stealing from me part of the horses, thereby violating not only one but many proclamations which, regarding this matter and others, I had posted for the good of the land in the name of his Majesty.

Since they had violated his royal orders, it appeared to me that they should not go unpunished; therefore I immediately sent post-haste the captain and procurator-general Gaspar Perez de Villagran and the captain of artillery Geronimo Marques, with an express order to follow and overtake them and give them due punishment. They left in the middle of September, as I have said, thinking that they would overtake them at once, but their journey was prolonged more than they or I had anticipated, with the result to two of the offenders which your Lordship already knows from the letter which they tell me they wrote from Sancta Barbara. The other two who fled from them will have received the same at your Lordship's hands, as is just.

I awaited their return and the outcome for some days, during which time I sent my *sargento mayor* to find and utilize the buffalo to the east, where he found an infinite multitude of them, and had the experience which he set forth in a special report. Both he and the others were so long delayed that, in order to lose no time, at the beginning of October, this first church having been founded, wherein the first mass was celebrated on the 8th of September, and the religious having been distributed in various provinces and *doctrinas,* I went in person to the province of Abo and to that of the Xumanas and to the large and famous salines of this country, which must be about twenty leagues east of here.

From there I crossed over to the west through the province of Puaray to discover the South Sea, so that I might be able to report to your Lordship. When Captain Villagran arrived I took him for this purpose.

What more in good time it was possible to accomplish through human efforts is in substance what I shall set forth in the following chapter. For this purpose it shall be day by day, and event by event, especially regarding the death of my nephew and *maese de campo,* who, as my rear-guard, was following me to the South Sea. His process, along with many other papers, I am sending to your Lordship. To despatch them earlier has been impossible. I have, then, discovered and seen up to the present the following provinces:

The province of the Piguis, which is the one encountered in coming from that New Spain; the province of the Xuman‡s; the province of the Cheguas, which we Spaniards call Puaray; the province of the Cheres; the province of the Trias; the province of the Emmes; the province of the Teguas; the province of the Picuries; the province of the Taos; the province of the Peccos; the province of Abbo and the salines; the province of Juni; and the province of Mohoce.

These last two are somewhat apart from the rest, towards the west, and are the places where we recently discovered the rich mines, as is attested by the papers which your Lordship will see there. I could not work or improve these mines because of the death of my *maese de campo,* Joan de Zaldivar, and of the rectification of the results of it, which I completed at the end of last month. Nor could I complete my journey to the South Sea, which was the purpose with which I went to the said provinces, leaving my camp in this province of the Teguas, whence I am now writing.

There must be in this province and in the others abovementioned, to make a conservative estimate, seventy thousand Indians, settled after our custom, house adjoining house, with square plazas. They have no streets, and in the pueblos, which contain many plazas or wards, one goes from one plaza to the other through alleys. They are of two and three stories, of an *estado* and a half or an *estado* and a third each, which latter is not so common; and some houses am of four, five, six, and seven stories. Even whole pueblos dress in very highly colored cotton mantas, white or black, and some of thread—very good clothes. Others wear buffalo hides, of which there is a great abundance. They have most excellent wool, of whose value I am sending a small example.

It is a land abounding in flesh of buffalo, goats with hideous horns, and turkeys; and in Mohoce there is game of all kinds. There are many wild and ferocious beasts, lions, bears, wolves, tigers, *penicas,* ferrets, porcupines, and other animals, whose hides they tan and use. Towards the west there are bees and very white honey, of which I am sending a sample. Besides, there are vegetables, a great abundance of the best and greatest salines in the world, and a very great many kinds of very rich ores, as I stated above. Some discovered near here do not appear so, although we have hardly begun to see anything of the much there is to be seen. There are very fine grape vines, rivers, forests of many oaks, and some cork trees, fruits, melons, grapes, watermelons, Castilian plums, *capuli,* pine-nuts, acorns, ground-nuts, and coralejo, which is a delicious fruit, and other wild fruits. There are many and very good fish in this Rio del Norte, and in others. From the ores here are made all the colors which we use, and they are very fine.

The people are in general very comely; their color is like those of that land, and they are much like them in manner and dress, in their grinding, in their food, dancing, singing, and many other things, except in their languages, which are many, and different from those there. Their religion consists in worshipping idols, of which they have many; and in their temples, after their own manner, they worship them with fire, painted reeds, feathers, and universal offering of almost everything they get, such as small animals, birds, vegetables, etc. In their government they are free, for although they have some petty captains, they obey them badly and in very few things.

We have seen other nations such as the Querechos, or herdsmen, who live in tents of tanned hides, among the buffalo. The Apaches, of whom we have also seen some, are innumerable, and although I heard that they lived in rancherías, a few days ago I ascertained that they live like these in pueblos, one of which, eighteen leagues from here, contains fifteen plazas. They are a people whom I have compelled to render obedience to His Majesty, although not by means of legal instruments like the rest of the provinces. This has caused me much labor, diligence, and care, long journeys, with arms on the shoulders, and not a little watching and circumspection; indeed, because my *maese de campo* was not as cautious as he should have been, they killed him with twelve companions in a great pueblo and fortress called Acóma, which must contain about three thousand Indians. As punishment for its crime and its treason against his Majesty, to whom it had already rendered submission by a public instrument, and as a warning to the rest, I razed and burned it completely, in the way in which your Lordship will see by the process of this cause. All these provinces, pueblos, and peoples, I have seen with my own eyes.

There is another nation, that of the Cocoyes, an innumerable people with huts and agriculture. Of this nation and of the large settlements at the source of the Rio del Norte and of those to the northwest and west and towards the South Sea, I have numberless reports, and pearls of remarkable size from the said sea, and assurance that there is an infinite number of them on the coast of this country. And as to the east, a person in my camp, an Indian who speaks Spanish and is one of those who came with Huma—a, has been in the pueblo of the said herdsmen. It is nine continuous leagues in length and two in width, with streets and houses consisting of huts. It is situated in the midst of the multitude of buffalo, which are so numerous that my *sargento mayor,* who hunted them and brought back their hides, meat, tallow, and suet, asserts that in one herd alone he saw more than there are of our cattle in the combined three ranches of Rodrigo del Rio, Salvago, and Jeronimo Lopez, which are famed in those regions.

I should never cease were I to recount individually all of the many things which occur to me. I can only say that with God's help I shall see them all, and give new worlds, new, peaceful, and grand to his Majesty, greater than the good Marquis gave to him, although he did so much, if you, Illustrious Sir, will give to me the aid, the protection, and the help which I expect from such a hand. And although I confess that I am crushed at having been so out of favor when I left that country, and although a soul frightened by disfavor usually loses hope and despairs of success, it is nevertheless true that I never have and never shall lose hope of receiving many and very great favors at the hand of your Lordship, especially in matters of such importance to his Majesty. And in order that you, Illustrious Sir, may be inclined to render them to me, I beg that you take note of the great increase which the royal crown and the rents of his Majesty have and will have in this land, with so many and such a variety of things, each one of which promises very great treasures. I shall only note these four, omitting the rest as being well known and common:

First, the great wealth which the mines have begun to reveal and the great number of them in this land, whence proceed the royal fifths and profits. Second, the certainty of the proximity of the South Sea, whose trade with Pir?, New Spain, and China is not to be depreciated, for it will give birth in time to advantageous and continuous duties, because of its close proximity, particularly to China and to that land. And what I emphasize in this matter as worthy of esteem is the traffic in pearls, reports of which are so certain, as I have stated, and of which we have had ocular experience from the shells. Third, the increase of vassals and tributes, which will increase not only the rents, but his renown and dominion as well, if it be possible that for our king these can increase. Fourth, the wealth of the abundant salines, and of the mountains of brimstone, of which there is a greater quantity than in any other province. Salt is the universal article of traffic of all these barbarians and their regular food, for they even eat or suck it alone as we do sugar. These four things appear as if dedicated solely to his Majesty. I will not mention the founding of so many republics, the many offices, their quittances, vacancies, provisions, etc., the wealth of the wool and hides of buffalo, and many other things, clearly and well known, or, judging from the general nature of the land, the certainty of wines and oils.

In view, then, Illustrious Sir, of things of such honor, profit, and value, and of the great prudence, magnanimity, and nobility of your Lordship, who in all matters is bound to prosper me and overcome the ill fortune of my disgrace, I humbly beg and supplicate, since it is of such importance to the service of God and of his Majesty, that the greatest aid possible be sent to me, both for settling and pacifying, your Lordship giving your favor, mind, zeal, and life for the conservation, progress, and increase of this land, through the preaching of the holy gospel and the founding of this republic, giving liberty and favor to all, opening wide the door to them, and, if it should be necessary, even ordering them to come to serve their king in so honorable and profitable a matter, in a land so abundant and of such great beginnings of riches. I call them beginnings, for although we have seen much, we have not yet made a beginning in comparison with what there is to see and enjoy. And if the number should exceed five hundred men, they all would be needed, especially married men, who are the solid rock on which new republics are permanently founded; and noble people, of whom there is such a surplus there. Particularly do I beg your Lordship to give a license to my daughter Mariquita, for whom I am sending, and to those of my relatives who may wish so honorably to end their lives.

For my part, I have sunk my ships and have furnished an example to all as to how they ought to spend their wealth and their lives and those of their children and relatives in the service of their king and lord, on whose account and in whose name I beg your Lordship to order sent to me six small cannon and some powder, all of which will always be at the service of his Majesty, as is this and everything else. Although on such occasions the necessities increase, and although under such circumstances as those in which I now find myself others are wont to exaggerate, I prefer to suffer from lack of necessities rather than to be a burden to his Majesty or to your Lordship, feeling assured that I shall provide them for many poor people who may look to me if your Lordship will grant the favor, which I ask, of sending them to me.

To make this request of you, Illustrious Sir, I am sending the best qualified persons whom I have in my camp, for it is but reasonable that such should go on an errand of such importance to the service of God and his Majesty, in which they risk their health and life, looking lightly upon the great hardships which they must suffer and have suffered. Father Fray Alonso Martinez, apostolic commissary of these provinces of New Mexico, is the most meritorious person with whom I have had any dealings, and of the kind needed by such great kingdoms for their spiritual government. Concerning this I am writing to his Majesty, and I shall be greatly favored if your Lordship will do the same. I believe your Lordship is under a loving obligation to do this, both because the said Father Commissary is your client as well as because of the authority of his person and of the merits of his worthy life, of which I am sending to his Majesty a special report, which your Lordship will see if you desire, and to which I refer. In his company goes my cousin, Father Fray Cristobal de Salazar, concerning whom testimony can be given by his prelate, for in order not to appear an interested witness in my own cause I refrain from saying what I could say with much reason and truth. For all spiritual matters I refer you to the said fathers, whom I beg your Lordship to credit in every respect as you would credit in person. I say but little to your Lorship as to your crediting them as true priests of my father Saint Francis. With such as these may your Lordship swell these your kingdoms, for there is plenty for them to do.

For temporal matters go such honorable persons as Captain and Procurator-general Gaspar Perez de Villagran, captain of the guard, Marcos Farfan de los Godos, and Captain Joan Pinero, to whom I refer you, as also to the many papers which they carry. In them your Lordship will find authentic information regarding all that you may desire to learn of this country of yours.

I remain as faithful to you, Illustrious Sir, as those who most protest. Your interests will always be mine, for the assurance and confidence which my faithfulness gives me is an evidence that in past undertakings I have found in your Lordship true help and love; for although when I left I did not deserve to receive the cédula from my king dated April 2, I shall deserve to receive it now that I know that I have served him so well.

And in order to satisfy his royal conscience and for the safety of the creatures who were preserved at Acóma, I send them to your Lordship with the holy purpose which the Father Commissary will explain, for I know it is so great a service to God that I consider very well employed the work and expense which I have spent in the matter. And I do not expect a lesser reward for your Lordship on account of the prayers of those few days. Honor it, Illustrious Sir, for it redounds to the service of God. May He prosper and exalt you to greater offices. In His divine service, which is the highest and greatest I can name, I again beg for the aid requested, much, good, and speedy-priests as well as settlers and soldiers.

1. *Describe Don Juan de O—ate's thoughts regarding the rebellious actions of some of his fellow colonists. How does he deal with these actions? How do these episodes reveal a contrast between the author's goals and to the goals of some of those in his traveling party?*
2. *Summarize Don Juan de O—ate's impressions of the natural resources available in the areas he is exploring.*
3. *On whose behalf does Don Juan de O—ate claim the lands he encounters? How does he deal with those who resist his authority or threaten his safety? Provide a specific example of this policy.*
4. *What requests does Don Juan de O—ate make of the Viceroy?*

1-8   The Founding of St. Augustine, 1565

Pedro Menendez de Aviles was given the authority by King Philip II of Spain to explore and colonize Florida. Accordingly, he took possession of Florida on September 8, 1565, and established the fortified settlement of St. Augustine. Menendez foresaw Florida as an integral component of the Spanish Empire commanding the southeastern part of the North American continent dominating the sea routes to Asia and the land routes to the mines of Mexico. In order for his vision to become reality, however, he had to first expel the French. The following are excerpts from an account of Menendez's expedition to Florida as recorded by Francisco Lopez de Mendoza Grajales, the chaplain to the expedition.

Source: Oliver J. Thatcher, ed., *The Library of Original Sources* (Milwaukee: University Research Extension Co., 1907), Vol. V: 9th to 16th Centuries, pp. 327–341.

On Saturday, the 25th, the Captain-general came to visit our vessel and get the ordnance for disembarkation at Florida. This ordnance consisted of two rampart pieces, of two sorts of culverins, of very small caliber, powder and balls; and he also took two soldiers to take care of the pieces. Having armed his vessel, he stopped and made us an address, in which he instructed us what we had to do on arrival at the place where the French were anchored. I will not dwell on this subject, on which there was a good deal said for and against, although the opinion of the general finally prevailed. There were two thousand Frenchmen in the seaport into which we were to force an entrance. I made some opposition to the plans, and begged the general to consider that he had the care of a thousand souls, for which he must give a good account. Then followed a fine address, which I shall not repeat here, as it would make my report too long. Please the Lord and the Blessed Virgin, I will, however, report it on my return.. . .

On Tuesday, the 28th, we had a calm more dead than anything we had yet experienced while at sea. Our vessel was about one and a half leagues from the first galley and the other vessels. We were all tired, and especially I, from the praying to God to give us weather which should put an end to all trials and disappointments. About two o'clock he had pity on us, and sent so good a wind that we came under full sail to rejoin the galley. One thing happened which I regard as miraculous. While we were becalmed, and after we had joined the other vessels, none of the pilots knew where we were, some pretending we were as much as a hundred leagues from Florida. However, thanks to God and the prayers of the Blessed Virgin, we soon had the pleasure of seeing land. We steered in that direction, anchored near a point of land, and found ourselves actually in Florida, and not very far distant from the enemy, which was for us an occasion of great joy. That evening our general assembled the pilots on the galley to discuss what was to be done. Next day, the 29th, at daylight, the galley and all the other ships weighed anchor, and coasted along in search of the enemy or a harbor favorable for disembarking.

On Monday, the 30th of August, we were assailed by bad weather, which obliged us to anchor. For four days contrary winds continued to blow, or else it was so calm we could not move, during all of which time we were at anchor, about a league and a half from the shore. The captain-general, seeing that neither the pilots nor the two Frenchmen whom we had taken prisoners, and who belonged to the French colony, could give us any information in regard to the port; and the coast being so flat that we could only recognize a few objects, the general, under these circumstances, decided to send ashore fifty arquebusiers, with some captains. They built fires in order to excite the curiosity of the Indians, and attract them; but they were so stupid that they paid no attention to us, and none came to see us. Our people then decided to penetrate the interior; and after having gone four leagues, they arrived at a village of Indians, who kindly received them, gave them food in abundance, embraced them, and then asked them for some of their things, and the soldiers were generous enough to make them a number of presents. In return the natives gave them two pieces of gold, of low standard, but it showed that they had some, and were in the habit of giving it in exchange. The Frenchmen whom we had with us told us they had been in communication with them for a long time. The Indians wanted the soldiers to pass the night with them, in order that they might feast them; but the latter declined their offers, being anxious to report the good news to our captain-general. As soon as he had learned the news, he resolved to disembark on Saturday morning, September 1st, and go among these Indians. He took with him a quantity of linen, knives, mirrors, and other little things of that sort, to gain their good will, and get some information as to where the French were. One of the Frenchmen of whom I have spoken understood their language. They told us we had left the French about five leagues behind us, precisely at the same spot to which God had conducted us when we arrived in sight of land; but we could not find them, because we had not sent any one ashore.

On Tuesday, the 4th, the fleet left the place of which I have been speaking, and we took a northerly course, keeping all the time close to the coast. On Wednesday, the 5th, two hours before sunset, we saw four French ships at the mouth of a river. When we were two leagues from them, the first galley joined the rest of the fleet, which was composed of four other vessels. The general concerted a plan with the captains and pilots, and ordered the flag-ship, the *San Pelayo*, and a *chaloupe* to attack the French flag-ship, the *Trinité*, while the first galley and another *chaloupe* would attack the French galley, both of which vessels were very large and powerful. All the ships of our fleet put themselves in good position; and the troops were in the best of spirits, and full of confidence in the great talents of the captain-general. They followed the galley; but, as our general is a very clever and artful officer, he did not fire, nor seek to make any attack on the enemy. He went straight to the French galley, and cast anchor about eight paces from her. The other vessels went to the windward, and very near the enemy. During the maneuvers, which lasted until about two hours after sunset, not a word was said on either side. Never in my life have I known such stillness. Our general inquired of the French galley, which was the vessel nearest his, "Whence does this fleet come?" They answered, "From France." "What are you doing here?" said the *Adelantado*. "This is the territory of King Philip II. I order you to leave directly; for I neither know who you are nor what you want here." The French commander then replied, "I am bringing soldiers and supplies to the fort of the King of France."

He then asked the name of the general of our fleet, and was told, "Pedro Menendez de Aviles, Captain-general of the King of Spain, who has come to hang all Calvinists [*viz., Huguenots*] I find here." Our general then asked him the name of his commander, and he replied, "Lord Gaston." While this parleying was going on, a long-boat was sent from the galley to the flag-ship. The person charged with this errand managed to do it so secretly that we could not hear what was said; but we understood the reply of the French to be, "I am the admiral," which made us think he wished to surrender, as they were in so small a force. Scarcely had the French made this reply, when they shipped their cables, spread their sails, and passed through our midst. Our admiral, seeing this, followed the French commander, and called upon him to lower his sails, in the name of King Philip, to which he received an impertinent answer. Immediately our commander gave an order to discharge a small culverin, the ball from which struck the vessel amidships, and I thought she was going to founder. We gave chase, and some time after he again called to them to lower their sails. "I would sooner die first than surrender!" replied the French commander. The order was given to fire a second shot, which carried off five or six men; but, as these miserable devils are very good sailors, they maneuvered so well that we could not take one of them; and, notwithstanding all the guns we fired at them, we did not sink one of their ships. We only got possession of one of their large boats, which was of great service to us afterwards. During the whole night our flag-ship and the galley chased the French flag-ship and galley.

Wednesday morning, September 5th, at sunrise, so great a storm arose that we feared we should be shipwrecked; and, as our vessels were so small, we did not dare to remain on the open sea, and regained the shore; that is, three of our vessels anchored at about a league and a half from it. We had double moorings, but the wind was so strong that one of them broke loose. We prayed the Lord to spare the others, for we could not have prevented them from being driven onto the coast and lost. As our galley was a large vessel, and busy following up the enemy, she could not come to our assistance. So we felt ourselves in danger of being attacked. The same evening, about sunset, we perceived a sail afar off, which we supposed was one of our galleys, and which was a great subject of rejoicing; but, as the ship approached, we discovered it was the French flag-ship, which we had fired at the night before. At first we thought she was going to attack us; but she did not dare to do it, and anchored between us and the shore, about a league from us. That night the pilots of our other ships came on board, to consult with the Admiral as to what was to be done. The next morning, being fully persuaded that the storm had made a wreck of our galley, or that, at least, she had been driven a hundred leagues out to sea, we decided that as soon as daylight came we would weigh anchor, and withdraw in good order, to a river (*Seloy*) which was below the French colony, and there disembark, and construct a fort, which we would defend until assistance came to us.

On Thursday, . . . two companies of infantry now disembarked: that of Captain Andres Soyez Patino, and that of Captain Juan de San Vincente, who was a very distinguished gentleman. They were well received by the Indians, who gave them a large house belonging to a chief, and situated near the shore of a river. Immediately Captain Patino and Captain San Vincente, both men of talent and energy, ordered an entrenchment to be built around this house, with a slope of earth and facines, these being the only means of defense possible in that country, where stones are nowhere to be found. Up to today we have disembarked twenty-four pieces of bronze guns of different calibers, of which the least weighed fifteen hundred weight. The energy and talents of those two brave captains, joined to the efforts of their brave soldiers, who had no tools with which to work the earth, accomplished the construction of this fortress of defense; and, when the general disembarked, he was quite surprised with what had been done.

On Saturday, the 8th, the general landed with many banners spread, to the sound of trumpets and salutes of artillery. As I had gone ashore the evening before, I took a cross and went to meet him, singing the hymn *Te Deum laudamus*. The general marched up to the cross, followed by all who accompanied him, and there they kneeled and embraced the cross. A large number of Indians watched these proceedings and imitated all they saw done. The same day the general took formal possession of the country in the name of his Majesty, and all the captains took the oath of allegiance to him, as their general and governor of the country. When this ceremony was ended, he offered to do everything in his power for them, especially for Captain Patino, who during the whole voyage had ardently served the cause of God and of the King, and, I think, will be rewarded for his assiduity and talents in constructing a fort in which to defend ourselves until the arrival of help from Santo Domingo and Havana. The French number about as many as we do, and perhaps more. My advice to the general was not to attack the enemy, but to let the troops rest all winter and wait for the assistance daily expected; and then we may hope to make a successful attack.. . .

God granted us two great favors. The first was that on the same evening, after we had landed our troops and provisions, the two vessels sailed away at midnight without being seen by the enemy. One went to Spain, and the other to Havana, so that neither was captured. The second favor, and that by which God rendered us a still greater service, happened the next day. A great hurricane came up, and was so severe that, I think, almost all of the French vessels must have been lost; for they were assailed on the most dangerous part of the coast. Our general was very bold in all military matters, and a great enemy of the French. He immediately assembled his captains and planned an expedition to attack the French settlement and fort on the river with five hundred men; and, in spite of the opinion of a majority of them, and of my judgment and another priest, he ordered his plan to be carried out. Accordingly, on Monday, September 17, he set out with five hundred men, well provided with fire-arms and pikes, each soldier carrying with him a sack of bread and a supply of wine for the journey. They also took with them two Indian chiefs, who were the implacable enemies of the French, to serve as guides.

This morning, Saturday, the 22nd, just after I had finished the mass of Our Lady, the admiral, at our request, sent some soldiers to fish, that we priests might have something to eat, it being a fast-day. Just as they had arrived at the place for fishing, and were going to throw out their nets, they perceived a man advancing towards them. He unfurled a white flag, which is a sign of peace, when our men surrounded and captured him. He proved to be a Frenchman, one of our enemies, so they made him a prisoner, and brought him to our admiral. The man, thinking we were going to hang him, shed tears, and appeared to be in great distress. I asked him if he were a Catholic, and he told me he was, and recited some prayers. So I consoled him, and told him not to fear anything, but to answer all questions put to him with frankness, which he promised to do. He said there were about seven hundred men in the fort [*Fort Caroline*, on the river *Mai*), of which one-third were Calvinists, and two priests, who preached the Calvinist doctrines, and in camp eight or ten Spaniards, three of whom were found among the Indians, quite naked, and painted like the natives, who had been wrecked on the coast; and, as no vessel had come into the country for a long time, they had remained with the Indians, some of whom had joined the French, whose fleet had arrived twenty days before.

On Monday, September 24th, about nine o'clock in the morning, the admiral came into port with his frigate, and, as soon as I recognized him, I had the bells rung and great rejoicing made in the camp. An hour after he arrived, we saw a man approaching with loud cries. I was the first to run to him and get the news. He embraced me with transport, crying, "Victory! Victory! the French fort is ours!" I promised him the gift due to the bearer of good news, and have given him the best I was able to give. I have related how our brave general was determined, in spite of the opinions of many of his officers, to attack the French by land with five hundred men; but, as the enterprise we are engaged in is for the cause of Jesus Christ and His Blessed Mother, the Holy Spirit has enlightened the understanding of our chief, so that everything has turned to our advantage, and resulted in a great victory. He has shown an ability and energy unequaled by any prince in the world. He has been willing to sacrifice himself, and has been sustained by his captains and his soldiers, whom he has encouraged by his valor and his words more than by any distribution of rewards or other inducements, so that every soldier has fought like a Roman.

On Friday, the 28th September, and while the captain-general was asleep, resting after all the fatigues he had passed through, some Indians came to camp, and made us understand by signs, that on the coast toward the south there was a French vessel which had been wrecked. Immediately our general directed the admiral to arm a boat, take fifty men, and go down the river to the sea, to find out what was the matter. About two o'clock the captain-general sent for me, and as he is very earnest, especially about this expedition, he said, "Mendoza, it seems to me I have not done right in separating myself from those troops." I answered, "Your Lordship has done perfectly right; and, if you wanted to undertake a new course, I and your other servants would oppose it, and shield you from the personal dangers to which you would be exposed." And, notwithstanding I sought to gain him over by such speeches, he would not abandon his project, but told me, in a decided tone, that he wished to set out, and that he commanded me and the captains who remained at the port to accompany him. He said there should be in all twelve men to go in a boat, and two of them Indians, who would serve as guides. We set off immediately to descend the river to the sea, in search of the enemy; and, to get there, we had to march more than two leagues through plains covered with brush, often up to our knees in water, our brave general always leading the march.

When we had reached the sea, we went about three leagues along the coast in search of our comrades. It was about ten o'clock at night when we met them, and there was a mutual rejoicing at having found each other. Not far off we saw the camp fires of our enemies, and our general ordered two of our soldiers to go and reconnoiter them, concealing themselves in the bushes, and to observe well the ground where they were encamped, so as to know what could be done. About two o'clock the men returned, saying that the enemy was on the other side of the river, and that we could not get at them. Immediately the general ordered two soldiers and four sailors to return to where we had left our boats, and bring them down the river, so that we might pass over to where the enemy was. Then he marched his troops forward to the river, and we arrived before daylight. We concealed ourselves in a hollow between the sand-hills, with the Indians who were with us; and, when it came light, we saw a great many of the enemy go down the river to get shell-fish for food. Soon after we saw a flag hoisted, as a war-signal. Our general who was observing all that, enlightened by the Holy Spirit, said to us, "I intend to change these for those of a sailor, and take a Frenchman with me (one of those whom we had brought with us from Spain), and we will go and talk with these Frenchmen. Perhaps they are without supplies, and would be glad to surrender without fighting."

He had scarcely finished speaking before he put his plan into execution. As soon as he had called to them, one of them swam towards and spoke to him; told him of their having been shipwrecked, and the distress they were in; that they had not eaten bread for eight or ten days; and, what is more, stated that all, or at least the greater part of them, were Calvinists. Immediately the general sent him back to his countrymen, to say they must surrender, and give up their arms, or he would put them all to death. A French gentleman, who was a sergeant, brought back the reply that they would surrender on condition their lives should be spared. After having parleyed a long time, our brave captain-general answered "that he would make no promises, that they must surrender unconditionally, and lay down their arms, because, if he spared their lives, he wanted them to be grateful for it, and, if they were put to death that there should be no cause for complaint."

Seeing that there was nothing else left for them to do, the sergeant returned to the camp; and soon after he brought all their arms and flags, and gave them up to the general, and surrendered unconditionally. Finding they were all Calvinists, the captain-general ordered them all put to death; but, as I was a priest, and had bowels of mercy, I begged him to grant me the favor of sparing those whom we might find to be Christians. He granted it; and I made investigations, and found ten or twelve of the men Roman Catholics, whom we brought back. All the others were executed, because they were Calvinists and enemies of our Holy Catholic faith. All this took place on Saturday (St. Michael's Day), September 29, 1565.

I, Francisco Lopez de Mendoza Grajales, Chaplain of His Lordship, certify that the foregoing is a statement of what actually happened.

1. *Despite their common interests, how might Menendez and Mendoza (the author) differ in their rationale for the removal of the French from Florida?*
2. *Other than the presence of the French, what additional difficulties threatened the success of Menendez's expedition?*

1-9 The Columbian Exchange (1590)

Coined by historian Alfred W Crosby, Jr., the phrase "Columbian exchange" refers to the global redistribution of plants, animals, and diseases that occurred in the sixteenth century following the initial contacts between European colonizers and the indigenous people of the Americas. In his scientific and historical work, Natural and Moral History of the Indians (1590), Father Jose de Acosta described for the curious Spanish crown the agricultural exotica of the New World as well as the Spanish attempts to introduce new plants to the Americas.

Source: Jose de Acosta, *Historian natural y moral de las Indias* (1590)
http://www.sc.edu/library/pubserv/reserve/scardaville/hist420/doc7.htm and
http://www.sc.edu/library/pubserv/reserve/scardaville/hist420/doc8.htm

[This document has been previously edited by DR. MICHAEL C. SCARDAVILLE, Associate Professor of History and Director of the Latin American Studies Prog ram at the University of South Carolina, Columbia, SC]

Turning to plants, I shall speak first of those which are more peculiar to the Indies and afterwards of those which are common both to those lands and to Europe. And because plants were created principally for the maintenance of man, and man sustains himself above all on bread, I should speak first of their bread. . . . The Indians have their own words to signify bread, which in Peru is called *tanta* and in other parts is given other names. But the quality and substance of the bread the Indians use is very different from ours, for they have no kind of wheat, barley, millet, panic grass, or any grain such as is used in Europe to make bread. Instead they have other kinds of grains and roots, among which maize, called Indian wheat in Castile and Turkey grain in Italy, holds the first place.

And just as wheat is the grain most commonly used by man in the regions of the Old World, which are Europe, Asia, and Africa, so in the New World the most widely used grain is maize, which is found in almost all the kingdoms of the West Indies; in Peru, New Spain, the New Kingdom of Granada, Guatemala, Chile, and in all the *Tierra Firme*. In the Windward Isles, which are Cuba, Hispaniola, Jamaica, Puerto Rico, it does not seem to have been used in earlier times; to this day they prefer to use yucca and cassava, of which more later. I do not think that maize is at all inferior to our wheat in strength and nourishment; but it is stouter and hotter and engenders more blood, so that if people who are not accustomed to it eat it in excess they swell up and get the itch.

Maize grows on canes or reeds; each one bears one or two ears, to which the grains are fastened, and though the grains are big they hold a large number of them, and some contain seven hundred grains. The seeds are planted one by one. Maize likes a hot and humid soil. It grows in many parts of the Indies in great abundance; a yield of three hundred *fanegas* from a sowing is not uncommon. There are various kinds of maize, as of wheat; one is large and nourishing; another, called *moroche*, is small and dry. The leaves of the maize and the green cane are a choice fodder for their beasts of burden, and when dry are also used as straw. The grain gives more nourishment to horses than barley, and therefore it is customary in those countries to water their horses before giving them maize to eat, for if they drank after feeding they would swell up and have gripes, as they do when they eat wheat.

Maize is the Indian bread, and they commonly eat it boiled in the grain, hot, when it is called *mote*. . .; sometimes they eat it toasted. There is a large and round maize, like that of the Lucanas, which the Spaniards eat as a delicacy; it has better flavor than toasted chickpeas. There is another and more pleasing way of preparing it, which consists in grinding the maize and making the flour into pancakes, which are put on the fire and are later placed on the table and eaten piping hot; in some places they call them *arepas*. . . .

Maize is used by the Indians to make not only their bread but also their wine; from it they make beverages which produce drunkenness more quickly than wine made of grapes. They make this maize wine in various ways, calling it *azua* in Peru and more generally throughout the Indies *chicha*. The strongest sort is made like beer, steeping the grains of maize until they begin to break, after which they boil the juice in a certain way, which makes it so strong that a few drinks will produce intoxication. In Peru, where it is called *sora*, its use is forbidden by law because of the terrific drinking it occasions. But the law is little observed, for they use it anyway, and stay up whole days and nights, dancing and drinking. . . .

The cacao tree is most esteemed in Mexico and coca is favored in Peru; both trees are surrounded with considerable superstition. Cacao is a bean smaller and fattier than the almond, and when roasted has not a bad flavor. It is so much esteemed by the Indians, and even by the Spaniards, that it is the object of one of the richest and largest lines of trade of New Spain; since it is a dry fruit, and one that keeps a long time without spoiling, they send whole ships loaded with it from the province of Guatemala. Last year an English corsair burned in the port of Guatulco, in New Spain, more than one hundred thousand cargas of cacao. They also use it as money, for five cacao beans will buy one thing, thirty another, and one hundred still another, and no objections are made to its use. They also use it as alms to give to the poor.

The chief use of this cacao is to make a drink that they call chocolate, which they greatly cherish in that country. But those who have not formed a taste for it dislike it, for it has a froth at the top and an effervescence like that formed in wine by dregs, so that one must really have great faith in it to tolerate it. In fine, it is the favorite drink of Indians and Spaniards alike, and they regale visitors to their country with it; the Spanish women of that land are particularly fond of the dark chocolate. They prepare it in various ways: hot, cold, and lukewarm. They usually put spices and much chili in it; they also make a paste of it, and they say that it is good for the chest and the stomach, and also for colds. Be that as it may, those who have not formed a taste for it do not like it.

The tree on which this fruit grows is of middling size and well-made, with a beautiful top; it is so delicate that to protect it from the burning rays of the sun they plant near it another large tree, which serves only to shade it; this is called the mother of the cacao. There are cacao plantations where it is raised as are the vine and the olive in Spain. The province of Guatemala is where they carry on the greatest commerce in this fruit.

The cacao does not grow in Peru; instead they have the coca, which is surrounded with even greater superstition and really seems fabulous. In Potosi alone the commerce in coca amounts to more than 5,000,000 pesos, with a consumption of from 90 to 100,000 hampers, and in the year 1583 it was 100,000. . . . This coca that they so greatly cherish is a little green leaf which grows upon shrubs about one estado high; it grows in very warm and humid lands and produces this leaf, which they call *trasmitas*, every four months. Being a very delicate plant, it requires a great deal of attention during cultivation and even more after it has been picked. They pack it with great care in long, narrow hampers and load it on the sheep of that country, which carry this merchandise in droves, bearing one, two, and three thousand hampers. It is commonly brought from the Andes, from valleys of insufferable heat, where it rains the greater part of the year, and it costs the Indians much labor and takes many lives, for they must leave their highlands and cold climates in order to cultivate it and carry it away. Hence there have been great disputes among lawyers and wise men about whether the coca plantations should be done away with or no—but there they still are.

The Indians prize it beyond measure, and in the time of the Inca kings plebeians were forbidden to use coca without the permission of the Inca or his governor. Their custom is to hold it in their mouths, chewing and sucking it; they do not swallow it; they say that it gives them great strength and is a great comfort to them. Many serious men say that this is pure superstition and imagination. To tell the truth, I do not think so; I believe that it really does lend strength and endurance to the Indians, for one sees effects that cannot be attributed to imagination, such as their ability to journey two whole days on a handful of coca, eating nothing else, and similar feats. . . . All would be well, except that its cultivation and commerce endanger and occupy so many people. . . .

The maguey is the tree of wonders, to which the newly-come Spaniards, or *chapetones* (as they call them in the Indies), attribute miracles, saying that it yields water and wine, oil and vinegar, honey, syrup, thread, needles, and a thousand other things. The Indians of New Spain value it greatly, and they commonly have one or several of these trees near their homes to supply their needs. It grows in the fields, and there they cultivate it. Its leaves are wide and thick, with strong, sharp points which they use as fastening pins or sewing needles; they also draw a certain fiber or thread from the leaves.

They cut through the thick trunk when it is tender; there is a large cavity inside, where the sap rises from the roots; it is a liquor which they drink like water, since it is fresh and sweet. When this liquor is boiled it turns into a kind of wine, and if it is left to sour it becomes vinegar. But when boiled for a longer time it becomes like honey, and cooked half as long it turns into a healthful syrup of good flavor, superior in my judgment to syrup made of grapes. Thus they boil different substances from this sap, which they obtain in great quantity, for at a certain season they extract several azumbres a day.

The Indies have been better repaid in the matter of plants than in any other kind of merchandise; for those few that have been carried from the Indies into Spain do badly there, whereas the many that have come over from Spain prosper in their new homes. I do not know whether to attribute this to the excellence of the plants that go from here or to the bounty of the soil over there. Nearly every good thing grown in Spain is found there; in some regions they do better than in others. They include wheat, barley, garden produce and greens and vegetables of all kinds, such as lettuce, cabbage, radishes, onions, garlic, parsley, turnips, carrots, eggplants, endive, salt-wort, spinach, chickpeas, beans, and lentils —in short, whatever grows well here, for those who have gone to the Indies have been careful to take with them seeds of every description. . . .

The trees that have fared best there are the orange, lemon, citron, and others of that sort. In some parts there are already whole forests and groves of orange trees. Marveling at this, I asked on a certain island who had planted so many orange trees in the fields. To which they replied that it might have happened that some oranges fell to the ground and rotted, whereupon the seeds germinated, and, some being borne by the waters to different parts, gave rise to these dense groves. This seemed a likely reason. I said before that orange trees have generally done well in the Indies, for nowhere have I found a place where oranges were not to be found; this is because everywhere in the Indies the soil is hot and humid, which is what this tree most needs. It does not grow in the highlands; oranges are transported there from the valleys or the coast. The orange preserve which is made in the islands is the best I have ever seen, here or there.

Peaches and apricots also have done well, although the latter have fared better in New Spain. . . . Apples and pears are grown, but in moderate yields; plums give sparingly; figs are abundant, chiefly in Peru. Quinces are found everywhere, and in New Spain they are so plentiful that we received fifty choice ones for half a real. Pomegranates are found in abundance, but they are all sweet, for the people do not like the sharp variety. The melons are very good in some regions, as in *Tierra Firme* and Peru. Cherries, both wild and cultivated, have not so far prospered in the Indies. . . . In conclusion, I find that hardly any of the finer fruits is lacking in those parts. As for nuts, they have no acorns or chestnuts, nor, as far as I know, have any been grown over there until now. Almonds grow there, but sparingly. Almonds, walnuts, and filberts are shipped there from Spain for the tables of epicures.

By profitable plants I mean those plants which not only yield fruit but bring money to their owners. The most important of these is the vine, which gives wine, vinegar, grapes, raisins, verjuice, and syrup—but the wine is the chief concern. Wine and grapes are not products of the islands or of *Tierra Firme*; in New Spain there are vines which bear grapes but do not yield wine. The reason must be that the grapes do not ripen completely because of the rains which come in July and August and hinder their ripening; they are good only for eating. Wine is shipped from Spain and the Canary Islands to all parts of the Indies, except Peru and Chile, where they have vineyards and make very good wine. This industry is expanding continually, not only because of the goodness of the soil, but because they have a better knowledge of wine-making.

The vineyards of Peru are commonly found in warm valleys where they have water channels; they are watered by hand, because rain never falls in the coastal plains, and the rains in the mountains do not come at the proper time. . . . The vineyards have increased so far that because of them the tithes of the churches are now five and six times what they were twenty years ago. The valleys most fertile in vines are Victor, near Arequipa; Yca, hard by Lima; and Caracaro, close to Chuquiavo. The wine that is made there is shipped to Potosi and Cuzco and various other parts, and it is sold in great quantities, because since it is produced so abundantly it sells at five or six ducats the jug, or *arroba*, whereas Spanish wine (which always arrives with the fleets) sells for ten and twelve. . . . The wine trade is no small affair, but does not exceed the limits of the province.

The silk which is made in New Spain goes to other provinces—to Peru, for example. There was no silk industry before the Spaniards came; the mulberry trees were brought from Spain, and they grow well, especially in the province called Misteca, where they raise silkworms and make good taffetas; they do not yet make damasks, satins, or velvets, however.

The sugar industry is even wider in scope, for the sugar not only is consumed in the Indies but is shipped in quantity to Spain. Sugar cane grows remarkably well in various parts of the Indies. In the islands, in Mexico, in Peru, and elsewhere they have built sugar mills that do a large business. I was told that the Nasca [Peru] sugar mill earned more than thirty thousand pesos a year. The mill at Chicama, near Trujillo [Peru], was also a big enterprise, and those of New Spain are no smaller, for the consumption of sugar and preserves in the Indies is simply fantastic. From the island of Santo Domingo, in the fleet in which I came, they brought eight hundred and ninety-eight chests and boxes of sugar. I happened to see the sugar loaded at the port of Puerto Rico, and it seemed to me that each box must contain eight arrobas. The sugar industry is the principal business of those islands—such a taste have men developed for sweets!

Olives and olive trees are also found in the Indies, in Mexico, and in Peru, but up to now they have not set up any mills to make olive oil. Actually, it is not made at all, for they prefer to eat the olives, seasoning them well. They find it unprofitable to make olive oil, and so all their oil comes from Spain.

1. *According to Father Acosta, what was the most widely used grain in the New World? What were some of its uses?*
2. *What is cacao? Where was it found and what were its various uses?*
3. *Father Acosta notes that the Spanish had some success in transplanting Old World plants to the Americas. What were some of the more successful transplantations?*

1-10 Thomas Harriot, The Algonquian Peoples of the Atlantic Coast (1588)

Thomas Harriot (English cartographer and explorer, 1560–1621), served as a navigator and mapmaker on Walter Raleigh's first voyage to Virginia in 1585. This account of the Algonquian peoples of what is now North Carolina's coast was published in London, two years after Harriot's return to England.

Source: Thomas Harriot, *A Briefe and True Report of the New Found Land of Virginia; reproduced in fac-simile from the first edition of 1588,* with an introductory note by Luther S. Livingston (New York: Dodd, Mead, 1903). Some spelling has been corrected for modern usage. Sixteenth century printers often used the letters *u* and *v* interchangeably. The long *s* has been rendered as an *f*.

Of the nature and manners of the people

IT reftheth I fpeake a word or tow of the naturall inhabitants, their natures and maners, leaving large difcourfe thereof untill time more convenient hereafter: nowe onely so farre foorth, as that you may know, how that they in respect of troubling our inhabiting and planting, are not to be feared; but that they shall have cause both to feare and love vs, that shall inhabite with them.

They are a people clothed with loofe mantles made of Deere skins, & aprons of the same rounde about their middles; all els naked; of such a difference of statures only as wee in England; having no edge tooles or wewapons of yron or steele to offend vs. with all, neither know they how to make any: those weapons y they have, are onlie bowes made of Witch hazle, & arrowes of reeds; flat edged truncheons also of wood about a yard long, neither have they anything to defed theselves but targets made of barks; and some armours of stickes wichered together with thread.

Their townes are but small, & neere the sea coast but few, some containing but 10. Or 12. Houses: some 20. The greatest that we have seens have bene but of 30. Houses: if they be walled it is only done with barks of trees made faft to stakes, or els with poles only fixed upright and close one by another.

Of the new fond land of Virginia

Their houses are made of small poles made faft at the tops in rounde forme after the maner is used in many arbories in our gardens of England, in most townes covered with barkes, and in some with artificiall mattes made of long rufhes; from the tops of the houses downe to the ground. The length of them is commonly double to the breadth, in some places they are but 12. and 16. yardes long, and in other some wee have seene of foure and twentie.

In some places of the countrey one onely towne belongeth to the government of a Wiroans of chiefe Lorde; in other some two or three, in some fixe, eight, & more; the greatest Wiroans that yet we had dealing with had but eighteene townes in his government, and able to make not above seven or eight hundred fighting men at the most: The language of every governement is different from any other, and the farther they are distant the greater is the difference.

Their maner of warees amongst themselves is either by sudden surprising one an other most comonly about the dawning of the day, or moone light; or els by ambushes, or some suttle devises: Set battels are very rare, except it fall out where there are many trees, where eyther part may have some hope of defence, after the deliverie of every arrow, in leaping behind some or other.

If there fall out any warres between us & them, what their fight is likely to bee, we having advantages against them so many maner of waies, as by our discipline, our strange weapons and devises els; especially by ordinance; great and small, it may be easily imagined; by the experience we have had in some places, the turning up of the heeles against us in running away was their best defence.

A briefe and true report

In respect of us they are a people poore, and for want of skill and judgement in the knowledge and use of our things, doe esteeme our trifles before thinges of greater value: Not withstanding in their proper manner considering the want of such meanes as we have, they seeme very ingenious; For although they have no such tooles, nor any such craftes, sciences and artes as wee; yet in those thinges they doe, they shewe excellencie of wit. An by howe much they upon due consideration shall finde our manner of knowledges and craftes to exceede theirs in perfection, and speed for doing or execution, by so much the more is it probable that they shoulde desire our friendships & love, and have the greater respect for pleasing and obeying us. Whereby may bee hoped if meanes of good government bee used, that they may in short time be brought to ciuilitie, and the imbracing of true religion.

Some religion they have alreadie which although it be farre from the truth, yet beying as it is, there is hope it may bee the easier and sooner reformed.

They beleeve that there are many Gods which they call Montoac, but of different fortes and degrees; one onely chiefe and great God, which hath bene from all eternitie. Who as they affirme when hee purposed to make the worlde, made first other goddes of a principall order to bee as meanes and instruments to bee used in the creation and government to follow; and after the Sunne, Moone, and Starres, as pettie goddes and the instruments of the other order more principall. Frft they say were made waters, out of which by the gods was made all diversitie of creatures that are visible or invisible.

Of the new found land of Virginia

For mankind they say a woman was made first, which by the woorking of one of the goddes, conceived and brought foorth children: An in such fort they say they had their beginning.

But how manie yeeres or ages have passed since, they say they can make no relatio, having not letters nor other such meanes as we to keepe recordes of the particularities of times past, but onelie tradition from father to sonne.

They thinke that all the gods are of humane shape, & therefore they represent them by images in the formes of men, which they call *Kewafomok* one alone is called *Kewas;* Them they place in houses appropriate or temples which they call *Machicomuck;* Where they woorship, praie, sing, and make manie times offerings unto them. In some *Machico-muck* we have seene but on *Kewas,* in some two, and in other some three; The common fort thinke them to be also gods.

They beleeve also the immortalitie of the soule, that after this life as soone as the soule is departed from the bodie according to the workes it hath done, it is eyther carried to heaven the habitacle of gods, there to enjoy perpetuall blisse and happinesse, or els to a great pitte or hole, which they thinke to bee in the furthest partes of their part of the worlde towarde the sunne set, there to burne continually: the place they call *Popoguffo.*

For the confirmation of this opinion, they tolde mee two stories of two men that had been lately dead and re againe, the one happened but few yeres before our comming into the countrey of a wicked man which having beene dead and buried, the next day the earth of the grave beeing seene to move, was taken up againe; Who made declaration where his soule had beene, that is to faie very neere entring into *Popoguffo,* had not one of the gods saved him & gave him leave to returne againe, and teach his friends what they should doe to avoid that terrible place of torment.

The other happened in the same yeere wee were there, but in a towne that was threescore miles from us, and it was tolde mee for strange newes that one beeing dead, buried and taken up again as the first, showed that although his bodie had lien dead in the grave, yet his soule was alive, and had travailed farre in a long broade waie, on both sides whereof grewe most delicate and pleasant trees, bearing more rare and excellent fruites then ever hee had seene before or was able to expresse, and at length came to most brave and faire houses, neere which hee met his father, that had beene dead before, who gave him great charge to goe backe againe and show his friends what good they were to doe to enjoy the pleasures of that place, which then he had one he should after come againe.

What subtilty soever be in the *Wiroances* and Priestes, this opinion worketh so much in manie of the common and simple sort of people that it maketh them have great respect to their Governours, and also great care what they do to avoid toment after death and to enjoy blisse; although notwithstanding there is punishment ordained for malefactours, as stealers, whoremoongers, and other sortes of wicked doers; some punished with death, some with forfeitures, some with beating, according to the greatnes of the factes.

And this is the summe of their religio, which I learned by having special familiarity with some of their priestes. Wherein they were not so sure grounded, nor gave such credite to their traditions and stories but through conversing with us they were brought into great doubts of their owne, and no small admiration of ours, with earnest desire in many, to learne more than we had meanes for want of perfect utterance in their language to expresse.

Most thinges they sawe with us, as Mathematicall instruments, sea compasses, the vertue of the loadstone in drawing yron, a perspective glasse whereby was shewed manie strange fightes, burning glasses, wildefire woorkes, gunnes, bookes, writing and reading, spring clocks that seeme to goe of themselves, and manie other thinges that wee had, were so strange unto them, and so farre exceeded their capacities to comprehend the reason and meanes how they should be made and done, that they thought they were rather the works of gods then of men, or at the least wife they had bin given and taught us of the gods. Which made manie of them to have such opinion of us, as that if they knew not the trueth of god and religion already, it was rather to be had from us, whom God so specially loved then from a people that were so simple as they found themselves to be in comparison of us. Whereupon greater credite was given unto that we spake of concerning such matters.

Manie times and in every towne where I came, according as I was able, I made declaration of the contentes of the Bible; that therein was set foorth the true and onelie GOD, and his mightie woorkes, that therein was contayned the true doctrine of salvation through Christ, with manie particularities of Miracles and chiefe poyntes of religion, as I was able then to utter, and thought fitte for the time. And although I told them the booke materially & of itself was not of anie such vertue, as I thought they did conceive, but onely the doctrine therein contained; yet would many be glad to touch it, to embrace it, to kisse it, to hold it to their brests and heades, and stroke over all their bodie with it; to shewe their hungrie desire of that knowledge which was spoken of.

The *Wiroans* with whom we dwelt called *Wingina,* and many of his people would be glad many times to be with us at our praiers, and many times call upon us both in his owne towne, as also in others whither he sometimes accompanied us, to pray and sing Psalmes; hoping thereby to bee partaker of the same effectes which wee by that meanes also expected.

Twise this *Wiroans* was so grievously sicke that he was like to die, and as hee laie languishing, doubting of anie helpe by his owne priestes, and thinking he was in such danger for offending us and thereby our god, sent for some of us to praie and bee a meanes to our God that it would please him either that he might live or after death dwell with him in blisse, so likewise were the requestes of manie others in the like case.

On a time also when their corne began to wither by reason of a drouth which happened extraordinarily, fearing that it had come to passe by reason that in some thing they had displeased us, many woulde come to us & desire us to praie to our God of England, that he would preserve their corne, promising that when it was ripe we also should be partakers of the fruite.

There could at no time happen any strange sicknesse, losses, hurtes, or any other crosse unto them, but that they would impute to us the cause or meanes therof for offending or not pleasing us.

One other rare and strange accident, leaving others, will I mention before I ende, which mooved the whole countrey that either knew or hearde of us, to have us in wonderfull admiration.

There was no towne where we had nay subtile devise practised against us, we leaving it unpunished or not revenged (because wee fought by all meanes possible to win them by gentlenesse) but that within a few dayes after our departure from everie such towne, the people began to die very fast, and many in short space; in some townes about twentie, in some fourtie, in some sixtie, and in one six score, which in trueth was very manie in respect of their numbers. This happened in no place that wee coulde learne but where wee had bene, where they used some practise against us, and after such time; The disease also so strange, that they neither knew what it was, not how to cure it; the like by report of the oldest men in the countrey never happened before, time our of minde. A thing specially observed by us as also by the naturall inhabitants themselves.

Insomuch that when some of the inhabitantes which were our friends & especially the *Wiroans Wingina* had observed such effects in foure or five towns to follow their wicked practices, they were perswaded that it was the worke of our God through our meanes, and that wee by him might kil and slaie whom wee would without weapons and not come neere them.

And thereupon when it had happened that they had understanding that any of their enemies had abused us in our journeyes, hearing that wee had wrought no revenge with our weapons, & fearing upon some cause the matter should so rest; did come and intreate us that we woulde bee a meanes to our God that they as others that had dealt ill with us might in like sort die; alleaging howe much it would be for our credite and profite as also theirs and hoping furthermore that we would do so much at their requests in respect of the friendship we professe them.

Whose entreaties although wee shewed that they were ungodlie, affirming that our God would not subject himselfe to anie such praiers and requestes of men that indeede all thinges have beene and were to be done according to his good pleasure as he had ordained: and that we to shew our selves his true servants ought rather to make petition for the contrarie, that they with them might live together with us, bee made partakers of his truth & serve him in righteousnes; but notwithstanding in such sort, that wee referre that as all other thinges, to bee done according to his divine will & pleasure, and as by his wisedome he had ordained to be best.

Yet because the effect fell out so sodainly and shortly after according to their desires, they thought neverthelesse it came to passe by our meanes, and that we in using such speeches unto them did but dissemble the matter, and therefore came unto us to give us thankes in their manner that although wee satisfied them not in promise, yet in deedes and effect we had fulfilled their desires.

This marvelous accident in all the countrie wrought so strange opinions of us, that some people could not tel whether to think us gods or men, and the rather because that all the space of their sicknesse, there was no man of ours knowne to die, or that was specially sicke; they noted also that we had no women amongst us, neither that we did care for any of theirs.

Some therefore were of opinion that wee were not borne or women, and therefore not mortall, but that wee were men of an old generation many yeeres past then risen againe in immortalitie.

Some woulde likewise seeme to prophesie that there were more of our generation yet to come, to kill theirs and take their places, as some thought the purpose was by that which was already done.

Those that were immediately to come after us they imagined to be in the aire yet invisible & without bodies & that they by our intreaty & for the love of us did make the people to die in that sort as they did by shooting invisible bullets into them.

To confirme this opinion their phisitions to excuse their ignorance in curing the disease, would not be ashamed to say, but earnestly make the simple people beleve, that the strings of blood that they sucked out the sicke bodies, were the strings where with all the invisible bullets were tied and cast.

Some also thought that we shot them ourselves out of our pieces from the place where we dwelt, and killed the people in any such towne that had offended us as we lifted how farre distant from us foever it were.

And other some saide that it was the speciall woorke of God for our sakes, as wee ourselves have cause in some sorte to thinke no lessse, whatsoever some doe or maie imagine to the contrarie, specially some Astrologers knowing of the Eclipse of the Sunne which wee saw the same yeere before in our voyage thytherward, which unto them appeared very terrible. And also of the Comet which beganne to apppeare but a few daies before the beginning of the said sicknesse. But to conclude them from being the special causes of so speciall and accident, there are farther reasons then I thinke fit as this present to bee alleadged.

These their opinions I have set downe the more at large that it may appeare unto you that here is good hope they may be brought through discreet dealing and governement to the imbracing of the trueth, and consequently to honour, obey, feare, and love us.

And although some of our companie towardes the ende of the yeare, shewed themselves too fierce, in slaying some the people, in some towns, upon causes that on our part, might easily enough have been borne withall: yet notwithstanding because it was on their part justly deserved, the alteration of their opinions generally & for the most part concerning us is the lesse to bee doubted. And whatsoever els they may be, by carefulnesse of ourselves neede nothing at all to be feared.

The best neverthelesse in this as in all actions besides is to be endevoured and hoped, & of the worst that may happen notice to bee taken with consideration, and as much as may be eschewed.

The conclusion

Now I have as I hope made relation not of so fewe and smal things but that the countrey of men that are indifferent & wel disposed maie be sufficiently liked: If there were no more knowen then I have mentioned, which doubtlesse and in great reason is nothing to that which remaineth to bee discovered, neither the soile, nor commodities. As we have reason so to gather by the difference we found in our travails, for although all which I have before spoke of have bin discovered & experimented not far fro the sea coast where was our abode & most of our travailing yet sometimes as we made our journeies farther into the maine and countrey; we found the foyle to bee fatter; the trees greater and the growe thinner.

1. Summarize and discuss Thomas Harriot's impressions of the manners of the Algonquian people and his thoughts regarding how the English will be received by them.
2. What are Thomas Harriot's opinions regarding the Algonquian people's ability to make war against the English? Who would have the advantage in warfare? Why?
3. Summarize Thomas Harriot's views of Algonquian craftsmanship and arts. What makes Thomas Harriot believe that the Algonquians will be easily civilized?
4. Summarize the key tenets of Algonquian religion as observed by Thomas Harriot. What makes him believe that they might be particularly open to conversion to Christianity?
5. What events made the Algonquian people believe that Thomas Harriot and his companions were divine? How did Harriot respond to this?
6. Overall, what is Harriot's belief regarding the potential for colonializing the land and peoples that he observed? Cite specific things that lead him to this opinion?

1-11 Jose de Acosta, A Spanish Priest Speculates on the Origins of the Indians (1590)

One of the first scientists attempting to reconcile old world ideas with new world phenomena, Jose de Acosta (Spanish explorer and scientist, 1540–1600), traveled to North and South America and tried to explain the origins of the new things he encountered. His observations contrasted sharply with the ideas held at the time—especially since those ideas were based in the Aristotelian ideas of nature. In this excerpt, de Acosta attempts to find an acceptable theory for the origin of people in the new world.

Source: Jose de Acosta, *The Naturall and Morall Historie of the East and West Indies,* translated by Edward Grimston (London: V. Sims, 1604).

CHAP. XX. Not with standing all that hath bene said, it is more likely that the first inhabitants of the Indies came by land.

I conclude then, that it is likely the first that came to the Indies was by shipwracke and tempest of wether, but heereupon groweth a difficultie which troubleth me much. For, suppose wee grant that the first men came from farre Countries, and that the nations which we now see are issued from them and multiplied, yet can I not coniecture, by what meanes brute beastes, whereof there is great aboundance, could come there, not being likely they should have bin imbarked and carried by sea. The reason that inforceth us to yeeld that the first men of the Indies are come from Europe or Asia, is the testimonie of the holy scripture, which teacheth us plainely that all men came from Adam. We can therefore give no other beginning to those at the Indies, seeing the holy scripture saieth, that all beasts and creatures of the earth perished but such as were reserved in the Arke of Noe, for the multiplication and maintenance of their kinde; so as we must necessarily referre the multiplication of all beastes to those which came out of the Arke of Noe, on the mountaines of Ararat, where it staied. And by this meanes we must seeke out both for men and beastes the way whereby they might passe from the old world to this new. Saint Augustine, treating vpon this question, by what reason you shall finde in some Ilandes Wolves, Tigers, and other ravenous beastes, which breede no profit to men, seeing there is no doubt but Elephants, Horses, Oxen, Dogges, and other beastes which serve man to vse, have been expresly carried in shippes, as we see at this day brought from the East into Europe, and transported from Europe to Peru, although the voiages be verie long. And by what meanes these beastes which yeeld no profit, but are very hurtfull (as Wolves and others of that wilde nature), should passe to the Indies, supposing, as it is certaine, that the deluge drowned all the earth. In which Treatise this learned and holy man laboures to free himselfe of these difficulties saying that they might swim vnto these Ilands, or that some have carried them. thither for their delight in hunting; or that, by the will of God, they had been newly created of the earth, after the same maner of the first creation, when God said, "Let the earth bring forth everie living thing according to his kinde, Cattle, and creeping Wormes, and the beastes of the field, every one in his kinde." But if we shall apply this solution to our purpose the matter will remaine more doubtfull, for, beginning at the last point, it is not likely, according to the order of Nature, nor conformable to the order of government established by God, that perfect creatures, as Lions, Tigers., and Wolves, should be engendered of the earth, as we see that Rattes., Frogges, Bees, and other imperfect creatures are commonly engendered. Moreover, to what purpose is that which the scripture saieth, and doth so often repeate, "Thou shalt take of all the beastes and birdes of the aire, seven and seven, male and female, to maintaine generation vpon earth"; if such beasts after the deluge should be created againe after a new kinde of creation without coniunction of male and female. And heerevpon might grow another question. Seeing such creatures are breeding on the earth (according to this opinion) wherefore are they not likewise in all other partes of' the maine Land, and in many Ilandes, seeing wee must not regarde the naturall order of creation but the bountie of the Creator. On the other part, I will not bold it for a thing incredible that they have carried some of these beastes for the pleasure of hunting, for that we often see Princes and great men keepe and nourish in their cages (onely for their pleasure and greatnesse) both Lyons, Beares, and other savage beastes, especially where they are brought from farre

Countries; but to speake that of Woolves, Foxes, and other beasts which yeeld no profite, and have nothing rare and excellent in them but to hurt the cattell; and to say also that they have carried them by sea for hunting, truely it is a thing that hath no sense. Who can imagine that in so long a voyage men would take the paynes to carrie Foxes to Peru, especially of that kind which they call *Anas*[1], which is the filthiest that I have seene ? Who woould likewise say that they have carried Tygers and Lyons ? Truely it were a thing worthy the laughing at to thinke so. It was sufficient, yea, very much, for men, driven against their willes by tempest, in so long and vnknowne a voyage, to escape the danger of the Sea with theyr owne lives without busying themselves to carrie Woolves and Foxes, and to nourish them at Sea. If these beasts then came by Sea, wee must beleeve it was by swimming, which may happen in some Ilands not farre distant from others, or from the mayne Land, the which wee cannot denie, seeing the experience wee have, and that wee see these beasts, beeing prest to swimme day and night without wearinesse, and so to escape. But this is to be vnderstood in smal Straights and passages, for in our Ocean they would mocke at such swimmers, when as birds faile in their flight, yea, those of the greatest wing, vpon the passage of so great a Gulph. And although we finde small birdes, which flie above one hundred leagues, as we have often seene in our travel, yet it is a matter impossible, at the least very difficult, for birdes to passe all the Ocean. All this beeing true which wee, have spoken, what way shall wee make for beastes and birdes to goe to the Indies ? and how can I say they passed from one worlde to an other? I coniecture then, by the discourse I have made, that the new world, which we call Indies) is not altogether severed and disioyned from the other world; and to speake my opinion, I have long beleeved that the one and the other world are ioyned and continued one with another in some part, or at the least are very neere. And yet to this day there is no certaine knowledge of the contrary. For towards the Articke or Northerne Pole all the longitude of the earth is not discovered, and many hold that above Florida the Land runnes out very large towards the North, and as they say ioynes with the Scithike or German Sea. Others affirmo that a Ship sayling in that Sea reported to have scene the coast of Bacalaos[2] which stretcheth almost to the confines of Europe. Moreover, no man knowes how farre the land runnes beyond the Cape of Mendozino[3] in, the South sea, but that they affirme it is a great Continent which runnes an infinite length; and returning to the Southerne Pole no man knowes the lauds on the other part of the Straight of Magellan. A ship belonging to the Bishoppe of Plasencia, which passed the Straight, reports to have sayled alwayes within sight of land; the like Hernando Lamoro a Pilot doth affirme, who, forced by foule weather, passed two or three degrees above the sayd Straight. So as there is no reason or experience that doth contradict my conceit and opinion, which is, that the whole earth is vnited and ioyned in some part, or at the least the one approcheth neere vnto the other. If this be true, as in effect there is some likelyhood, the answere is casie to the doubt we have propounded, how the first Inhabitants could passe to the Indies. For that wee must beleeve they could not so conveniently come thither by Sea as travelling by Land, which might be done without consideration in changing by little and little their lands and habitations. Some peopling the lands they found, and others seeking for newe, in time they came to inhabite and people the Indies, with so many nations, people, and tongues as we see.

CHAP. XXI. By what meanes tame Beasts passed to the 1ndies.

The signes and arguments, which offer themselves to such as are curious to examine the Indians manors and fashions) helpe much to maintayne the foresayd opinion ; for that you shall not finde any inhabiting the Ilands that are farre from the maine Land, or from other Ilands, as the Bermudes, the reason whereof is, for that the Ancients did never sayle but alongst the coast, and in view of land; whereupon, it is reported that they have found no great Ships in any part of the Indies capable to passe such Gulphs, but onely Balsaes, Barkes, and Canoes, which are all lesse then our long, boates, the which the Indians doe onely vse, with the which they could not runne through so great a Passage, without apparent danger of shipwracke, and although their shippes had been sufficient, yet had they no knowledge of the Astrolabe or Compasse. If then they had beene but eight or tenne dayes at Sea without sight of land, they must of necessitie loose themselves, having no knowledge where they were. Wee know many Ilandes well peopled with Indians, and their usuall navigations, the which was such, as they may well performe in Canoes and boats, without any Compasse to sayle by. Whenas the Indians of Peru, which remayne at Tumbez, did see our first Spanish shippes sayling to Peru, and viewed the greatnesse of their sailes, being spread, and of the bodies of the ships, they stood greatly amazed, not beeing able to perswade themselves that they were shippes, having never seene any of the like forme and greatnesse, they supposed they had beene rockes. But, seeing them advance, and not to sincke, they stood transported with amazement, vntill that, beholding them nearer, they discovered men with boards that walked in them, whom then they held for some gods or heavenly creatures. Whereby it appears how strange it was to the Indians to have great Ships. There is yet an other reason, which confirmes vs in the foresayd opinion, which is., that these beastes (which we say are not likely to have been transported by Sea to the Indies) remayne onely on the maine Land, and not in any Ilands foure dayes iorney from the maine Land. I have made this search for proofe thereof, for that it seems to me a point of great importance, to confirme me in mine opinion, that the confines

1. Anas, the Quichua for a small fox. Atoe is another word for fox (Canis Azarfl)
2. Newfoundland.
3. Cape Mendocino, in California.

25

of the Indies, Europe, Asia, and Affricke have some communication one with another, or at the least, approch very neere together. There are in America and Peru many Wilde beastes, as Lyons, although they be not like in greatuesse, fiercenesse, nor of the same colour, redde, to the renowned Lyons of Affrica. There are also many Tygers, very cruell, and more to the Indians then to the Spaniardes; there are likewise Beares, but in no great aboundance; of Boares and Foxes an infinite number. And yet if wee shall seeke for all these kindes of beastes in the Ilands of Cuba, Hispaniola, Iamaica, Marguerita, or Dominica, you shall not finde any. So as in the sayde Ilands, although they were very fertile, and of a great circuit, yet was there not any kind of beastes for service when the Spaniards arrived; but at this day there are so great troopes of Horses, Oxen, Kyne, Dogs, and Hogges, which have multiplied in such abundance, as now the Kine have no certaine master, but belong to him that shal first kil them, be it on the mountaines or on the plaines; which the Indians do, onely to save their hides, whereof they make great traffick, without any regard of the flesh to eate it. Dogges have so increased, as they march by troopes, and endammage the cattel no lesse than wolves, which is a great inconvenience in those Ilands. There wants not onely beastes in these Ilands; but also birdes, both great and small. As for Parrots, there are many that flie by flockes; but, as I have said, there are few of any other kinde. I have not seene nor heard of any Partriges there, as in Peru. Likewise, there are few of those beastes which at Peru they call guanacos, and vicunas, like to wilde goates, very swifte, in whose stomacke they find the bezoar stone, which many do greatly value; sometimes you shall finde them as bigge as a hens egge, yea, halfe as bigge againe. They have no other kinde of beastes, but such as we call Indian sheepe, the which, besides their wooll and flesh (wherewith they clothe and feede themselves), do serve them as Asses to beare their burthens. They carrie halfe as much as a mule, and are of small charge to their masters, having neede neither of shooes, saddle, nor oates to live by, nor of any furniture, for that Nature hath provided them of all these, wherein she seemes to have favoured these poore Indians. Of all these creatures, and of many other sortes, whereof I will make mention, the maine land at the Indies aboundes. But in the Ilands there are not any found, but such as the Spaniards have brought. It is true, that once one of our Friars did see a tiger in an Iland, as hee reported vnto vs vpon the discourse of his peregrination and shipwracke; but being demanded how farre it was from the maine land, he answered, six or eight leagues at the most; which passage tigers might easily swimme over. We may easily inferre by these arguments, and others like, that the first Indians went to inhabit the Indies more by land then by sea; or if there were any navigation, it was neither great nor difficult, being an indubitable thing, that the one world is continued and ioyned with the other, or at the least they approach one neerer vnto another in some parts.

CHAP. XXII. That the lineage of the Indians hath not passed by the Atlantis Iland as some do imagine.

Some (following Plato's opinion, mentioned before) affirme that these men parted from Europe or Affricke to go to that famous and renowned Iland of Atlantis, and so passed from one Iland vnto anothor, vntill they came to the maine land of the Indies, for that Cricias of Plato in his Timeus discourseth in this maner. If the Atlantis Iland were as great.as all Asia and Affrike together, or greater, as Plato saies, it should of necessitie containe all the Atlantike Ocean, and stretch even vnto the Ilands of the new world. And Plato saieth moreover that by a great and strange deluge the Atlantis Iland was drowned, and by that meanes the sea was made vnnavigable, through the aboundance of banckes, rockes, and roughnesse of the waves, which were yet in his time. But in the end the ruines of this drowned Iland were setled, which made this sea navigable. This hath been curiously handled and discoursed of by some learned men of good judgement, and yet, to speak the truth, being well considered, they are ridiculous things, resembling rather to Ovid's tales then a Historio or Philosophie worthy of accompt. The greatest part of Platoe's Interpreters affirme that it is a true Historie, whatsoever Cricias reports of the strange beginning of the Atlantis Iland, of the greatnes thereof, of the warres they had against them of Europe, with many other things. That which gives it the more credite of a true Historie, be the wordes of Cricias (whom Plato brings in. in his Timeus), saying that the subject be means to treat of is of strange things, but yet true. The other disciples of Plato, considering that this discourse hath more show of a fable then of a true Historie, say that we must take it as an allegorie, and that such was the intention of their divine Philosopher. Of this opinion is Procles and Porphire, yea, and Origene, who so much regardes the writings of Plato as when they speake thereof they seeme to bee the bookes of Moses or of Esdras, and whereas they thinke the writings of Plato have no shew of truth; they say they are to be vnderstood mystically, and in allegories. But, to say the truth, I do not so much respect the authoritie of Plato (whom they call Divine), as I wil beleeve he could write these things of the Atlantis Iland for a true Historie, the which are but meere fables, seeing hee confesseth that hee learned them of Critias, being a little childe, who, among other songs, sung that of the Atlantis Iland. But whether that Plato did write it for a true Historie or a fable, for my part I beleeve that all which he hath written of this Iland beginning at the *Dialogue of Timeus* and continuing to that of Critias, cannot be held for true but among children and old folkes. Who will not accoumpt it a fable to say that Neptune fell in love with Clite, and had of her five paire of twinnes at one birth. And that out of one mountaine hee drew three round balles of water and two of earth., which did so well resemble as you would have judged them all one bowell. What shall Wee say, moreover, of that Temple of a thousand paces long and five hundred broade, whose walles without were all covered with silver, the seeling of gold, and within ivorie indented and inlaied with gold, silver, and pearle. In the end, speaking of the ruine thereof, he concludes thus in his time:

"In one day and one night came a great deluge, whereby all our souldiers were swallowed by heapes within the earth, and in this sort the Atlantis Iland being drowned, it vanished in the Sea." Without doubt it fell out happily that this Iland vanished so suddenly, seeing it was bigger than Asia and Affrike, and that it was made by enchantment. It is in like sort all one to say that the ruines of this so great an Iland are seene in the bottome of the sea, and that the Mariners which see them cannot saile that way. Then he addes: "For this cause vnto this day that Sea is not navigable, by reason of the bancke, which by little and little has growne in that drowned Iland." I would willingly demand what Sea could swallow vp so infinite a continent of land, greater then Asia and Affrike, whose confines stretched vnto the Indies, and to swallow it vp in such sort as there should at this day remaine no signes nor markes thereof whatsoever) seeing it is well knowne by experience that the Mariners finde no bottome in the Sea where they say this Iland was. Notwithstanding it may seeme indiscreete and farre from reason to dispute seriously of those things which are reported at pleasure, or if we shall give that respect to the authoritie of Plato (as it is reason) we must rather vnderstand them to signifie simply, as in a picture, the prosperitie of a Citie, and withall the ruine thereof. For the argument they make to prove that this Atlantis Iland hath been really and indeede, saying that the sea in those parts doth at this day beare the namo of Atlantike is of small importance, for that wee knowe. Mount Atlas, whereof Plinie says this sea tooke the name, is vpon the confines of the Mediterranean Sea. And the same Plinie reportes that joyning to the said Mount there is an Iland called Atlantis, which he reports to be little and of small accompt.

CHAP. XXIII. That the opinion of many which holde that the first race of the Indians comes from the Iewes is not true.

Now that wee have shewed how vnlikely it is that the first Indians passed to the Indies by the Atlantis Iland, there are others holde opinion that they tooke the way, whereof Esdras speakes in his fourth booke, in this manner:

"And whereas thou sawest that lie gathered an other peaceable troope vnto him, thou shalt know those are the ten tribes, which were carried away captives out of their own land in the time of king Ozeas, whom Salmanazar, king, of the Assyrians tooke captives, and ledde them beyond the river, so were they brought into an other land; but they tooke this counsell to themselves to leave the multitude of the heathen, and go forth into a farther countrie, where never mankind dwelt, that they might there observe their statutes, which they could not keepe in their owne land; and they entred by the narrowe passages of the river Euphrates, for then God showed his wonders, and stayed the springs of the flood untill they were passed over; for the way vnto that countrie is very long, yea, of a yeere and a halfe, and this Region is called Arsareth; [4] thou dwelt they there vntill the latter time, and when they come forth againe the most Mightie shall hold still the springs of the river againe, that they may goe through; for this cause sawest thou this multitude peaceable."[5]

Some will apply this text of Esdras to the Indies, saying, they were guided by God, whereas never mankinde dwelt, and that the land where they dwelt is so farre off, as it requires a yeere and a halfe to performe the voyage, beeing by nature very peaceable. And that there are great signes and arguments amongst the common sort of the Indians, to breed a beleefe that they are descended from the Iews; for, commonly you shall see them fearefull, submisse, ceremonious, and subtill in lying. And, moreover, they say their habites are like vnto those the Iewes vsed; for they weare a short coat or waste-coat, and a cloake imbroidered all about; they goe bare-footed., or with soles tied with latchets over the foot, which they call ojatas.[6] And they say, that it appears by their Histories, as also by their ancient pictures, which represent them in this fashion, that this attire was the ancient habite of the Hebrewes, and that these two kinds of garments, which the Indians onely vse, were vsod by Samson, which the Scripture calleth *Tuniciam et Syndonem*; beeing the same which the Indians terme waste-coat and cloake. But all these coniectures are light, and rather against them then with them; for wee know well, that the Hebrewes vsed letters, whereof there is no shew among the Indians ; they were great lovers of silver, these make no care of it; the Iews, if they were not circumcised, held not themselves for Iewes, and contrariwise the Indians are not at all, neyther did they ever vse any ceremonie neere it as many in the East have done. But what reason of coniecture is there in this, seeing, the Iewes are so careful to preserve their language and Antiquities, so as in all parts of the world they differ and are known from others, and yet at the Indies alone, they have forgotten their Lineage, their Law, their Ceremonies, their Messias; and, finally, their whole Indaisme. And whereas they say, the Indians are fearful cowards, superstitious, and subtill in lying; for the first, it is not common to all, there are some nations among the Barbarians free from these vices, there are some valiant and hardy, there are some blunt and dull of vnderstanding. As for ceremonies and superstitions, the Heathen have always vsed them much ; the manner of habites described which they vse, being the plainest and most simple in the world; without Arte, the which hath been common, not onely to the Hebrewes, but to all

---

4. Ararat, or Armenia.
5. *Esdras*, xiii, 39 to 47.
6. *Usuta.* The Quichua word for sandals.

other Nations; seeing that the very History of Esdras (if wee shall beleeve the Scriptures that bee Apocrypha) make more against them then for their purpose; for hee saith in that place, that the ten tribes went from the multitude of the Heathen, to keepe their faith and ceremonies, and we see the Indians given to all the Idolatries in the world. And those which holde this opinion, see well if the entries of the River Euphrates stretch to the Indies, and whether it be necessary for the Indies to repasse that way, as it is written. Besides, I know not how you can name them peaceable, seeing they .be alwaies in warro amongst themselves. To conclude, I cannot see how that Euphrates in Esdras Apocrypha should be a more convenient passage to goe to the now world, then the inchanted and fabulous Atlantis Iland of Plato.

CHAP. XXIV. The reason why we can find 910 beginning of the Indians.

It is easier to refute and contradict the false opinions conceyved of the Originall of the Indians, thou to set downe a true and certaine resolution; for that there is no writing among the Indians, nor any certaine remembrances of their founders; neyther is there any mention made of this new world in their bookes that have knowledge of letters; our Ancients held, that in those parts, there were neyther men, land, nor haven. So as hee should seeme rash and presumptuous, that should thinke to discover the first beginning of the Indians. But we may iudge a farre off, by the former discourse, that these Indians came by little and little to this newe world, and that by the helpe and meanes of the neerenesse of lands, or by some navigation; the which seemes to mee the meanes whereby they came, and not that they prepared any armie. to goe thither of purpose; neyther that they have been caried thither by any ship-wracke or tempest, although some of these things may chance in some part of the Indies; for these Regions being so great, as they containe Nations without number, we may beleeve, that some came to inhabite after one sort, and some after an other. But in the ende I resolve vpon this point, that the true and principall cause to people the Indies, was, that the lands and limits thereof are ioyned and continued in some extremities of the world, or at the least were very near. And I beleeve it is not many thousand yeeres past since men first inhabited this new world and West Indies, and that the first men that entred, were rather savage men and hunters then bredde vp in civill and well governed Common-weales; and that they came to this new world, having lost their owne land, or being in too great numbers, they were forced of necessitie to seeke some other habitations; the which having found, they beganne by little and little to plant, having no other law, but some instinct of nature, and that very darke, and Some customes remaynningof their first Countries. And though they came from Countries well governed, yet is it not incredible to thinke that they had forgotten all through the tract of time and want of vse, seeing that in Spaine and Italie we find companies of men, which have nothing but the shape and countenance onely, whoreby we may coniecture in what sort this now world grew so barbarous and vncivill.

1. *What biblical events form the basis for de Acosta's reasoning regarding the presence of the first inhabitants of the Indies. How do these events shape his conclusions?*
2. *Describe the variety of animal life noted by de Acosta. What opinion of the author seems to be confirmed by the existence of such a wide variety of animals?*
3. *How does de Acosta argue against the theory that the inhabitants of the Indies came from Atlantis?*
4. *How does de Acosta argue against the theory that the inhabitants of the Indies are descendents of the Jews?*
5. *Examine and explain de Acosta's final conclusions and reasoning concerning the beginnings of human habitation in the Indies.*

PART TWO
COLONIZING THE NEW WORLD

2-1 John White, The Lost Colony (1590)

John White (English explorer, artist, first governor of Raleigh's colony at Roanoke Island, 1545–1606) left the colony at Roanoke Island in early fall, 1587, to obtain supplies for the struggling colony. Unable to return to Roanoke until 1590 (due to difficulties with both the French and Spanish), he found that little remained of his colony. Here is the account of his return voyage to Raleigh's colony at Roanoke Island (now Manteo, North Carolina).

> **Source:** "The Fifth Voyage of John White," in Henry S. Burrage, ed., *Early English and French Voyages, Chiefly from Hakluyt, Original Narratives of Early American History* (New York: Charles Scribner's Sons, 1906).

To the Worshipful and my very friend Master Richard Hakluyt, much happinesse in the Lord.

SIR, as well for the satisfying of your earnest request, as the performance of my promise made unto you at my last being with you in England, I have sent you (although in a homely stile, especially for the contentation of a delicate eare) the true discourse of my last voyage into the West Indies, and partes of America called Virginia, taken in hand about the end of Februarie, in the yeare of our redemption 590. And what events happened unto us in this our journey, you shall plainely perceive by the sequele of my discourse. There were at the time aforesaid three ships absolutely determined to goe for the West Indies, at the speciall charges of M. John Wattes of London Marchant. But when they were fully furnished, and in readinesse to make their departure, a generall stay was commanded of all ships thorowout England. Which so soone as I heard, I presently (as I thought it most requisite) acquainted Sir Walter Ralegh therewith, desiring him that as I had sundry times afore bene chargeable and troublesome unto him, for the supplies and reliefes of the planters in Virginia: so likewise, that by his endevour it would please him at that instant to procure license for those three ships to proceede on with their determined voyage, that thereby the people in Virginia (if it were Gods pleasure) might speedily be comforted and relieved without further charges unto him. Whereupon he by his good meanes obtained license of the Queenes Majestie, and order to be taken, that the owner of the 3 ships should be bound unto Sir Walter Ralegh or his assignes, in 3000 pounds, that those 3 ships in consideration of their releasement should take in, and transport a convenient number of passengers, with their furnitures and necessaries to be landed in Virginia. Neverthelesse that order was not observed, neither was the bond taken according to the intention aforesaid. But rather in contempt of the aforesaid order, I was by the owner and Commanders of the ships denied to have any passengers, or any thing els transported in any of the said ships, saving only my selfe and my chest; no not so much as a boy to attend upon me, although I made great sute, and earnest intreatie aswell to the chiefe Commanders, as to the owner of the said ships. Which crosse and unkind dealing, although it very much discontented me, notwithstanding the scarsity of time was such, that I could have no opportunity to go unto Sir Walter Ralegh with complaint: for the ships being then all in readinesse to goe to the Sea, would have bene departed before I could have made my returne. Thus both Governors, Masters, and sailers, regarding very smally the good of their countreymen in Virginia; determined nothing lesse then to touch at those places, but wholly disposed themselves to seeke after purchase and spoiles, spending so much time therein, that sommer was spent before we arrived at Virginia. And when we were come thither, the season was so unfit, and weather so foule, that we were constrained of force to forsake that coast, having not seene any of our planters, with losse of one of our ship-boates, and 7 of our chiefest men: and also with losse of 3 of our ankers and cables, and most of our caskes with fresh water left on shore, not possible to be had aboord. Which evils and unfortunate events (as wel to their owne losse as to the hinderance of the planters in Virginia) had not chanced, if the order set downe by Sir Walter Ralegh had bene observed, or if my dayly and continuall. petitions for the performance of the same might have taken any place. Thus may you plainely perceive the success of my fift and last voiage to Virginia, which was no lesse unfortunately ended then frowardly begun, and as lucklesse to many, as sinister to my selfe. But I would to God it had bene as prosperous to all) as noysome to the planters; and as joyfull to me, as discomfortable to them. Yet seeing it is not my first crossed voyage, I remaine contented. And wanting my wishes, I leave off from prosecuting that whereunto I would to God my wealth were answerable to my will. Thus committing the reliefe of my discomfortable company the planters in Virginia, to the merciful help of the Almighty, whom I most humbly beseech to helpe and comfort them, according to his most holy will and their good desire, I take my leave: from my house at Newtowne in Kyhnore the 4 of February, 1593.
Your most welwishing friend,
John White

The fift voyage of M. John White into the West Indies and parts of America called Virginia, in the yeere 1590.

The 20 of March the three shippes the Hopewell, the John Evangelist, and the little John, put to sea from Plymmouth with two small Shallops.

The 25 at midnight both our Shallops were sunke being towed at the ships stearnes by the Boatswaines negligence.

On the 30 we saw a head us that part of the coast of Barbary, lying East of Cape Cantyn, and the Bay of Asaphi[1]

The next day we came to the Ile of Mogador,[2] where rode, at our passing by, a Pinnesse of London called the Mooneshine.

Aprill

On the first of Aprill we ankored in Santa Cruz rode;[3] where we found two great shippes of London lading in Sugar, of whom we had 2 shipboats to supply the losse of our Shallops.

On the 2 we set sayle from the rode of Santa Cruz, for the Canaries.

On Saturday the 4 we saw Alegranza, the East Ile of the Canaries.

On Sunday the 5 of Aprill we gave chase to a double flyboat, the which we also the same day fought with, and tooke her, with losse of three of their men slaine, and one hurt.

On Munday the 6 we saw Grand Canarie, and the next day we landed and tooke in fresh water on the Southside thereof.

On the 9 we departed from Grand Canary, and framed our course for Dominica.[4]

The last of Aprill we saw Dominica, and the same night we came to an anker on the Southside thereof.

May

The first of May in the morning many of the Salvages came aboord our ships in their Canowes, and did traffique with us; we also the same day landed and entered their Towne from whence we returned the same day aboord without any resistance of the Salvages; or any offence done to them.

The 2 of May our Admirall and our Pinnesse departed from Dominica leaving the John our Viceadmirall playing off and on about Dominica, hoping to take some Spaniard outwardes bound to the Indies; the same night we had sight of three smal Ilands called Los Santos,[5] leaving Guadalupe and them on our starboord.

The 3 we had sight of S. Christophers Iland, bearing Northeast and by East off us.

On the 4 we sayled by the Virgines, which are many broken Ilands, lying at the East ende of S. Johns Iland: and the same day towards evening we landed upon one of them called Blanca,[6] where we killed an incredible number of foules: here we stayed but three houres, and from thence stood into the shore Northwest, and having brought this Iland Southeast off us, we put towards night thorow an opening or swatch, called The passage,[7] lying betweene the Virgines, and the East end of S. John: here the Pinnesse left us, and sayled on the South side of S. John.

The 5 and 6 the Admirall sayled along the North side of S. John, so neere the shore that the Spaniards discerned us to be men of warre; and therefore made fires along the coast as we sailed by, for so their custome is, when they see any men of warre on their coasts.

The 7 we landed on the Northwest end of S. John, where we watered in a good river called Yaguana, [8] and the same night following we tooke a Frigate of tenne Tunne comming from Gwathanelo[9] laden with hides and ginger. In this place Pedro a Mollato, who knewe all our state, ranne from us to the Spaniards.

On the 9 we departed from Yaguana.

The 13 we landed on an Iland called Mona,[10] whereon were 10 or 12 houses inhabited of the Spaniards; these we burned and tooke from them a Pinnesse, which they had drawen a ground and sunke, and carried all her sayles, mastes, and rudders into the woods, because we should not take them away; we also chased the Spaniards over all the Iland; but they hid them in eaves, hollow rockes, and bushes, so that we could not find them.

---

1. On the African coast, about a latitude of 32_/.
2. A short distance farther down the African coast.
3. The most southerly seaport of Morocco, now Agadeer or Agadir.
4. The course across the Atlantic was that of the voyage of 1587.
5. Northwest of Guadeloupe.
6. Probably Culebra, or Passage Island, one of the Virgin Islands off the east coast of Porto Rico.
7. Passing throught the Passage, the vessels proceeded along the northerly side of Porto Rico. The pinnace skirted the southern shores of the island.
8. Probably the Yagüez.
9. Guatemala.
10. A small island in the Mona Passage.

On the 14 we departed from Mona, and the next day after wee came to an Iland called Saona,[11] about 5 leagues distant from Mona, lying on the Southside of Hispaniola neere the East end: betweene these two Ilands we lay off and on 4 or 5 dayes, hoping to take some of the Domingo fleete doubling this Iland, as a neerer way to Spaine then by Cape Tyburon,[12] or by Cape S. Anthony.[13]

On Thursday being the 19 our Viceadmirall, from whom we departed at Dominica, came to us at Saona, with whom we left a Spanish Frigate, and appointed him to lie off and on other five daies betweene Saona and Mona to the ende aforesaid; then we departed from them at Saona for Cape Tyburon. Here I was enformed that our men of the Viceadmirall, at their departure from Dominica brought away two young Salvages, which were the chiefe Casiques sonnes of that Countrey and part of Dominica, but they shortly after ran away from them at Santa Cruz Iland,[14] where the Viceadmirall landed to take in ballast.

On the 21 the Admirall came to the Cape Tyburon, where we found the John Evangelist our Pinnesse staying for us: here we tooke in two Spaniards almost starved on the shore, who made a fire to our ships as we passed by. Those places for an 100 miles in length are nothing els but a desolate and meere wildernesse, without any habitation of people, and full of wilde Bulles and Bores, and great Serpents.

The 22 our Pinnesse came also to an anker in Aligato Bay at cape Tyburon. Here we understood of M. Lane,[15] Captaine of the Pinnesse; how he was set upon with one of the kings Gallies belonging to Santo Domingo, which was manned with 400 men, who after he had fought with him 3 or 4 houres, gave over the fight and forsooke him, without any great hurt done on eyther part.

The 26 the John our Vizadmirall came to us to cape Tyburon and the Frigat which we left with him at Saona. This was the appointed place where we should attend for the meeting with the Santo Domingo Fleete.

On Whitsunday Even at Cape Tyburon, one of our boyes ranne away from us, and at tenne dayes end returned to our ships almost starved for want of food. In sundry places about this part of Cape Tyburon we found the bones and carkases of divers men, who had perished (as wee thought) by famine in those woods, being either stragled from their company, or landed there by some men of warre.

June

On the 14 of June we tooke a smal Spanish frigat which fell amongst us so suddenly, as he doubled the point at the Bay of Cape Tyburon, where we road, so that he could not escape us. This frigat came from Santo Domingo, and had but three men in her, the one was an expert Pilot, the other a Mountainer, and the thirde a Vintener, who escaped all out of prison at Santo Domingo, purposing to fly to Yaguana which is a towne in the West parts of Hispaniola where many fugitive Spaniards are gathered together.

The 17 being Wednesday Captaine Lane was sent to Yaguana with his Pinnesse and a Frigat to take a shippe, which was there taking in fraight, as we understood by the old Pylot, whom we had taken three dayes before.

The 24 the Frigat returned from Captaine Lane at Yaguana, and brought us word to cape Tyburon, that Captaine Lane had taken the shippe, with many passengers and Negroes in the same; which proved not so rich a prize as we hoped for, for that a Frenchman of warre had taken and spoyled her before we came. Neverthelesse her loading was thought worth 1000 or 1300 pounds, being hides, ginger, Cannafistula, Copperpannes, and Casavi.

July

The second of July Edward Spicer whom we left in England came to us at cape Tyburon, accompanied with a small Pinnesse, whereof one M. Harps was Captaine. And the same day we had sight of a fleete of 14 saile all of Santo Domingo, to whom we presently gave chase, but they upon the first sight of us fled, and separating themselves scattered here and there: Wherefore we were forced to divide our selves and so made after them untill 12 of the clocke at night. But then by reason of the darkenesse we lost sight of ech other, yet in the end the Admirall and the Moonelight happened to be together the same night at the fetching up of the Vizadmirall of the Spanish fleete, against whom the next morning we fought and tooke him,[16] with losse of one of our men and two hurt, and of theirs 4 slaine and 6 hurt. But what was become of our Viceadmirall, our Pinnesse, and Prize, and two Frigates, in all this time, we were ignorant.

---

11. An island off the southeast end of Santo Domingo.
12. Cape Tiburon, the western extremity of Hayti.
13. Cape Antonio, the western extremity of Cuba.
14. The largest of the Virgin Islands.
15. William Lane, not Ralph, according to an entry in the margin.
16. The fight, we are informed by the margin, took place in sight of Navassa, an island at the southwest entrance of the Windward Passage.

The 3 of July we spent about rifling, romaging, and fitting the Prize to be sayled with us.

The 6 of July we saw Jamayca the which we left on our larboord, keeping Cuba in sight on our starboord.

Upon the 8 of July we saw the Iland of Pinos,[17] which lieth on the Southside of Cuba nigh unto the West end or Cape called Cape S. Anthony. And the same day we gave chase to a Frigat, but at night we lost sight of her, partly by the slow sayling of our Admirall, and lacke of the Moonelight our Pinnesse, whom Captaine Cooke had sent to the Cape the day before.

On the 11 we came to Cape S. Anthony, where we found our consort the Moonelight and her Pinnesse abiding for our comming, of whom we understood that the day before there passed by them 22 saile, some of them of the burden of 300 and some 400.tunnes loaden with the Kings treasure from the maine, bound for Havana: from this 11 of July untill 22 we were much becalmed: and the winde being very scarse, and the weather exceeding boat, we were much pestered with the Spaniards we bad taken: wherefore we were driven to land all the Spaniards saving three, but the place where we landed them was of their owne choise on the Southside of Cuba neere unto the Organes and Rio de Puercos.

The 23 we had sight of the Cape of Florida, and the broken Ilands thereof called the Martires.[18] The 25 being S. James day in the morning, we fell in with the Matanqas,[19] a head-land 8 leagues towards the East of Havana, where we purposed to take fresh water in, and make our abode two or three dayes.

On Sunday the 26 of July plying too and fro betweene the Matanqas and Havana, we were espied of three small Pinnasses of S. John de Ullua bound for Havana, which were exceedingly richly loaden. These 3 Pinnasses came very boldly up unto us, and so continued untill they came within musket shot of us. And we supposed them to be Captaine Harps Pinnesse, and two small Frigats taken by Captaine Harpe: wherefore we shewed our flag. But they presently upon the sight of it turned about and made all the saile they could from us toward the shore, and kept themselves in so shallow water, that we were not able to follow them, and therefore gave them over with expence of shot and pouder to no purpose. But if we had not so rashly set out our flagge, we might have taken them all three, for they would not have knowen us before they had beene in our hands. This chase brought us so far to leeward as Havana: wherfore not finding any of our consorts at the Matan≤as, we put over againe to the cape of Florida, and from thence thorow the chanel of Bahama.

On the 28 the Cape of Florida bare West of us.

The 30 we lost sight of the coast of Florida, and stood to Sea for to gaine the helpe of the current[20] which runneth much swifter a farre off then in sight of the coast. For from the Cape to Virginia all along the shore are none but eddie currents, setting to the South and Southwest.

The 31 our three ships were clearly disbocked.,[21] the great prize, the Admirall, and the Mooneshine, but our prize being thus disbocked departed from us without taking leave of our Admirall or consort, and sayled directly for England.

August

On the first of August the winde scanted, and from thence forward we had very fowl weather with much raine, thundering, and great spouts, which fell round about us nigh unto our ships.

The 3 we stoode againe in for the shore, and at midday we tooke the height of the same. The height of that place we found to be 34 degrees of latitude. Towards night we were within three leagues of the Low sandie Ilands West of Wokokon. But the weather continued so exceeding foule, that we could not come to an anker nye the coast: wherefore we stood off againe to Sea untill Monday the 9 of August.

On munday the storme ceased, and we had very great likelihood of faire weather: therefore we stood in againe for the shore: and came to an anker at 11 fadome in 35 degrees of latitude, within a mile of the shore, where we went on land on the narrow sandy Island, being one of the Landes West of Wokokon: in this Iland we tooke in some fresh water and caught great store of fish in the shallow water. Betweene the maine (as we supposed) and that Iland it was but a mile over and three or foure foote deepe in most places.

On the 12 in the morning we departed from thence toward night we came to an anker at the Northeast end of the Iland of Croatoan, by reason of a breach which we perceived to lie out two or three leagues into the Sea: here we road all that night.

The 13 in the morning before we wayed our ankers, our boates were sent to sound over this breach: our ships riding on the side thereof at 5 fadome; and a ships length from us we found but 4 and a quarter, and then deeping and shallowing for the space of two miles, so that sometimes we found 5 fadome, and by and by 7, and within two casts with the

---

17. Isle of Pines.
18. The Florida Keys.
19. Matanzas.
20. The Gulf Stream.
21. Meaning, apparently, "had got out into the open sea."

lead 9, and then 8, next cast 5, and then 6, and then 4, and then 9 againe, and deeper; but 3 fadome was the last, 2 leagues off from the shore. This breach is in 35. degr. and a halfe, and lyeth at the very Northeast point of Croatoan, whereas goeth a fret out of the maine Sea into the inner waters, which part the Ilandes and the maine land.

The 15 of August towards Evening we came to an anker at Hatorask, in 36 degr. and one third, in five fadom water, three leagues from the shore. At our first comming to anker on this shore we saw a great smoke rise in the Ile Roanoak neere the place where I left our Colony in the yeere 1587, which smoake put us in good hope that some of the Colony were there expecting my returne out of England.

The 16 and next morning our 2 boates went a shore, and Captaine Cooke, and Cap. Spicer, and their company with me, with intent to passe to the place at Roanoak where our countreymen were left. At our putting from the ship we commanded our Master gunner to make readie 2 Minions and a Falkon well loden, and to shoot them off with reasonable space betweene every shot, to the ende that their reportes might bee heard to the place where wee hoped to finde some of our people. This was accordingly performed, and our twoe boats put off unto the shore, in the Admirals boat we sounded all the way and found from our shippe untill we came within a mile of the shore nine, eight, and seven fadome: but before we were halfe way betweene our ships and the shore we saw another great smoke to the Southwest of Kindrikers mountes: we therefore thought good to goe to that second smoke first: but it was much further from the harbour where we landed, then we supposed it to be, so that we were very sore tired before wee came to the smoke. But that which grieved us more was that when we came to the smoke, we found no man nor signe that any had bene there lately, nor yet any fresh water in all this waye to drinke. Being thus wearied with this journey we returned to the harbour where we left our boates, who in our absence had brought their caske a shore for fresh water, so we deferred our going to Roanoak untill the next morning, and caused some of those saylers to digge in those sandie hills for fresh water whereof we found very sufficient. That night wee returned aboord with our boates and our whole company in safety.

The next morning being the 17 of August, our boates and company were prepared againe to goe up to Roanoak, but Captaine Spicer had then sent his boat ashore for fresh water, by meanes whereof it was ten of the clocke afternoone before we put from our ships which were then come to an anker within two miles of the shore. The Admirals boat was halfeway toward the shore, when Captaine Spicer put off from his ship. The Admirals boat first passed the breach, but not without some danger of sinking, for we had a sea brake into our boat which filled us halfe full of water, but by the will of God and carefull styrage of Captaine Cooke we came safe ashore, saving onely that our furniture, victuals, match and powder were much wet and spoyled. For at this time the winde blue at Northeast and direct into the harbour so great a gale, that the Sea brake extremely on the barre, and the tide went very forcibly at the entrance. By that time our Admirals boat was balled ashore, and most of our things taken out to dry, Captaine Spicer came to the entrance of the breach with his mast standing up, and was halfe passed over, but by the rash and undiscreet styrage of Ralph Skinner his Masters mate, a very dangerous Sea brake into their boate and overset them quite, the men kept the boat some in it, and some hanging on it, but the next sea set the boat on ground, where it beat so, that some of them were forced to let goe their hold, hoping to wade ashore: but the Sea still beat them downe, so that they could neither stand nor swimme, and the boat twise or thrise was turned the keele upward, whereon Captaine Spicer and Skinner hung untill they sunke, and were seene no more. But foure that could swimme a litle kept themselves in deeper water and were saved by Captaine Cookes meanes, who so soone as he saw their oversetting, stripped himselfe, and foure other that could swimme very well, and with all haste possible rowed unto them, and saved foure. There were 11 in all and 7 of the chiefest were drowned, whose names were Edward Spicer, Ralph Skinner, Edward Kelly, Thomas Bevis, Hance the Surgion, Edward Kelborne, Robert Coleman. This mischance did so much discomfort the saylers, that they were all of one mind not to goe any further to seeke the planters. But in the end by the commandement and perswasion of me and Captaine Cooke, they prepared the boates: and seeing the Captaine and me so resolute, they seemed much more willing. Our boates and all things fitted againe, we put off from Hatorask, being the number of 19 persons in both boates: but before we could get to the place where our planters were left, it was so exceeding darke, that we overshot the place a quarter of a mile: there we espied towards the North ende of the Island the light of a great fire thorow the woods, to which we presently rowed: when wee came right over against it, we let fall our Grapnel neere the shore and sounded with a trumpet a Call, and afterwardes many familiar English tunes of Songs, and called to them friendly; but we had no answere, we therefore landed at day-breake, and comming to the fire, we found the grasse and sundry rotten trees burning about the place. From hence we went thorow the woods to that part of the Iland directly over against Dasamongwepeuk, and from thence we returned by the water side, round about the North point of the Iland, untill we came to the place where I left our Colony in the yeere 1586. In all this way we saw in the sand the print of the Salvages feet of 2 or 3 sorts troaden the night, and as we entred up the sandy banke upon a tree, in the very browe thereof were curiously carved these faire Romane letters C R O: which letters presently we knew to signifie the place, where I should find the planters seated, according to a secret token agreed upon betweene them and me at my last departure from them, which was, that in any wayes they should not faile to write or carve on the trees or posts of the dores the name of the place where they should be seated; for at my comming away they were prepared to remove from Roanoak 50 miles into the maine. Therefore at my departure from them in An. 1587 I willed them, that if they should happen to be distressed in any of those places, that then they should carve over the letters or name, a Crosse + in this forme, but we found no such signe of distresse.. And having well considered of this, we passed toward the place where they were left in sundry houses, but we found the houses taken downe, and the place very strongly enclosed with a high palisado of great trees, with cortynes[22] and flankers very Fortlike, and one of the chiefe trees or postes at the right side of the entrance had the barke taken off, and 5 foote from the ground in fayre Capitall letters was graven CROATOAN without any crosse or signe of distresse; this done, we entred into the palisado, where we found many barres of iron) two pigges of Lead, foure yron fowlers, Iron sacker-shotte, [23] and such like heavie thinges, throwen here and there, almost overgrowen with grasse and weedes. From thence wee went along by the water side, towards the poynt of the Creeke to see if we could find any of their botes or Pinnisse, but we could perceive no signe of them, nor any of the last Falkons and small Ordinance which were left with them, at my departure from them. At our returne from the Creeke, some of our Saylers meeting us, told us that they had found where divers chests had bene hidden, and long sithence digged up againe and broken up, and much of the goods in them spoyled and scattered about, but nothing left, of such things as the Savages knew any use of, undefaced. Presently Captaine Cooke and I went to the place, which was in the ende of an olde trench, made two yeeres past by Captaine Amadas: wheere wee found five Chests, that had bene carefully hidden of the Planters, and of the same chests three were my owne, and about the place many of my things spoyled and broken, and my bookes torne from the covers, the frames of some of my pictures and Mappes rotten and spoyled with rayne, and my armour almost eaten through with rust; this could bee no other but the deede of the Savages our enemies at Dasamongwepeuk, who had watched the departure of our men to Croatoan; and assoone as they were departed digged up every place where they suspected any thing to be buried: but although it much grieved me to see such spoyle of my goods, yet on the other side I greatly joyed that I had safely found a certaine token of their safe being at Croatoan, which is the place where Manteo, was borne, and the Savages of the Iland our friends.[24]

When we had scene in this place so much as we could, We returned to our Boates, and departed from the shoare towards our shippes, with as much speede as we could: For the weather beganne to overcast, and very likely that a foule and stormie night would ensue. Therefore the same Livening with much danger and labour, we got our selves aboard, by which time the winde and seas were so greatly risen, that wee doubted our Cables and Anchors would scarcely holde untill Morning: wherefore the Captaine caused the Boate to be manned by five lusty men, who could swimme all well, and sent them to the little Iland on the right hand of the Harbour, to bring aboard sixe of our men, who had filled our caske with fresh water: the Boate the same night returned aboard with our men, but all our Caske ready filled they left behinde, unpossible to bee had aboard without danger of casting away both men and Boates: for this night prooved very stormie and foule.

The next Morning it was agreed by the Captaine and my selfe, with the Master and others, to wey anchor, and goe for the place at Croatoan, where our planters were: for that then the winde was good for that place, and also to leave that Caske with fresh water on shoare in the Iland untill our returne. So then they brought the cable to the Capston, but when the anchor was almost apecke, the Cable broke, by meanes whereof we lost another Anchor, wherewith we drove so fast into the shoare, that wee were forced to let fall a third Anchor: which came so fast home that the Shippe was almost aground by Kenricks mounts: so that we were forced to let slippe the Cable ende for ende. And if it had not chanced that wee had fallen into a chanell of deeper water, closer by the shoare then wee accompted of, wee could never have gone cleare of the poynt that lyeth to the Southwardes of Kenricks mounts. Being thus cleare of some dangers, and gotten into deeper waters, but not without some losse: for wee had but one Cable and Anchor left us of foure, and the weather grew to be fouler and fouler; our victuals scarse, and our caske and fresh water lost: it was therefore determined that we should goe for Saint John or some other Iland to the Southward for fresh water. And it was further purposed, that if wee could any wayes supply our wants of victuals and other necessaries, either at Hispaniola, Sant John, or Trynidad, that then we should continue in the Indies all the Winter following, with hope to make 2. rich voyages of one, and at our returne to visit our countreymen at Virginia. The captaine and the whole company in the Admirall (with my earnest petitions) thereunto agreed, so that it rested onely to knowe what the Master of the Moone-light our consort would doe herein. But when we demanded them if they would accompany us in that new determination, they alledged that their weake and leake Shippe was not able to continue it; wherefore the same night we parted, leaving the Moone-light to goe directly for England, and the Admirall set his course for Trynidad, which course we kept two dayes.

---

22. Curtains.

23. Shot for sakers, or large cannon.

24. On the theory, not generally held, that the colony was not wholly destroyed, and that descendants of some of its members are still to be found in North Carolina, see Weeks, "The Lost Colony of Roanoke: Its Fate and Survival," in *Papers of the American Historical Association,* v. 107.

On the 28 the winde changed, and it was sette on foule weather every way: but this storme brought the winde West and Northwest, and blewe so forcibly, that wee were able to beare no sayle, but our fore-course halfe mast high, wherewith wee ranne upon the winde perforce, the due course for England, for that wee were driven to change our first determination for Trynidad, and stoode for the Ilands of Azores, where wee purposed to take in fresh water, and also there hoped to meete with some English men of warre about those Ilands, at whose hands wee might obtaine some supply of our wants. And thus continuing our course for the Azores, sometimes with calmes, and sometimes with very scarce windes, on the fifteenth of September the winde came South Southeast, and blew so exceedingly, that wee were forced to lye atry[25] all that day. At this time by account we judged our selves to be about twentie leagues to the West of Cuervo and Flores, but about night the Btorme ceased, and fayre weather ensued.

On Thursday the seventeenth wee saw Cuervo and Flores, but we could not come to anker that night, by reason the winde shifted. The next Morning being the eighteenth, standing in againe with Cuervo, we escryed a sayle a head us, to whom we gave chase: but when wee came neere him, wee knew him to be a Spanyard, and hoped to make sure purchase of him: but we understood at our speaking with him, that he was a prize, and of the Domingo fleete already taken by the John our consort, in the Indies. We learned also of this prize, that our Viceadmirall and Pinnesse had fought with the rest of the Domingo fleete, and had forced them with their Admirall to flee unto Jamaica under the Fort for succour, and some of them ran themselves aground, whereof one of them they brought away, and tooke out of some others so much as the time would permit. And further wee understood of them, that in their returne from Jamaica about the Organes neere Cape Saint Anthony, our Viceadmirall mette with two Shippes of the mayne land, come from Mexico, bound for Havana, with whom he fought: in which fight our Viceadmirals Lieutenant was slaine, and the Captaines right arrne strooken off, with foure other of his men slaine, and sixteene hurt. But in the ende he entred, and tooke one of the Spanish shippes, which was so sore shot by us under water, that before they could take out her treasure she sunke; so that we lost thirteene Pipes of silver which sunke with her, besides much other rich marchandize. And in the meane time the other Spanish shippe being pearced with nine shotte under water, got away; whom our Viceadmirall intended to pursue: but some of their men in the toppe made certaine rockes, which they saw above water neere the shoare, to be Gallies of Havana and Cartagena, comming from Havana to rescue the two Ships; Wherefore they gave over their chase, and went for England. After this intelligence was given us by this our prize, he departed from us, and went for England.

On Saturday the 19. of September we came to an Ancre neere a small village on the North side of Flores, where we found ryding 5. English men of warre, of whom we understood that our Viceadmirall And Prize were gone thence for England. One of these five was the Moonelight our consort, who upon the first sight of our comming into Flores, Bet sayle and went for England, not taking any leave of us.

On Sunday the 20. the Mary Rose, Admirall of the Queenes fleete, wherein was Generall Sir John Hawkins, stood in with Flores, and divers other of the Queenes ships, namely the Hope, the Nonpareilia, the Rainebow, the Swift-sure, the Foresight, with many other good merchants ships of warre, as the Edward Bonaventure, the Marchant Royal, the Amitie, the Eagle, the Dainty of sir John Hawkins, and many other good ships and pinnesses, all attending to meete with the king of Spaines fleete, comming from Terra firma of the West Indies.

The 22. of September we went aboard the Raynebow, and towards night we spake with the Swift-sure, and gave him 3. pieces. The captaines desired our company; wherefore we willingly attended on them: who at this time with 10. other ships stood for Faial. But the Generall with the rest of the Fleete were separated from us, making two fleetes, for the surer meeting with the Spanish fleete.

On Wednesday the 23. we saw Gratiosa,[26] where the Admiral and the test of the Queenes fleete were come together. The Admirall put forth a flag of counsel, in which was determined that the whole fleete should go for the mayne, and spred themselves on the coasts of Spaine and Portugal, so farre as conveniently they might, for the suer meeting of the Spanish fleete in those parts.

The 26. we came to Faial, where the Admiral with some other of the fleete ankred, other some plyed up and downe betweene that and the Pico untill midnight, at which time the Anthony shot off a piece and weyed, shewing his light: after whom the whole fleete stood to the East, the winde at Northeast by East.

On Sunday the 27. towards Evening wee tooke our leave of the Admirall and the whole fleete, who stood to the East. But our shippe accompanied with a Flyboate stoode in again with S. George, where we purposed to take in more fresh water, and some other fresh victuals.

On Wednesday the 30. of September, seeing the winde hang so Northerly, that wee could not atteine the Iland of S. George, we gave over our purpose to water there, and the next day framed our due course for England.

---

25. Heave to.
26. Of the Azores group; so also are Fayal, Pico, São Jorge, and São Miguel, mentioned in the following paragraphs.

October

The 2. of October in the Morning we saw S. Michaels Iland on our Starre board quarter.
    The 23. at 10. of the clocke afore noone, we saw Ushant in Britaigne.[27]
    On Saturday the 24. we came in safetie, God be thanked, to an anker at Plymmouth.

1. *What kinds of delays does the author experience as he attempts to get his return voyage to Virginia underway?*
2. *Identify and explain what seems to be the policy of John White's ships regarding foreign ships and trade vessels.*
3. *What are the presumed signs of the colony that John White and his fellow journeymen follow in hopes of finding the inhabitants of Roanoke? What are their experiences as they attempt to locate the colony?*
4. *What events seem to have prevented or delayed a more extensive search for the Roanoke colonists?*

2-2   Samuel de Champlain's Battle With the Iroquois, July 1609

Lacking sufficient support from France, Samuel de Champlain's expedition to New France was dependent upon the goodwill of his Indian allies. In exchange for their support, Champlain was expected to aid his hosts in warfare. Here Champlain recounts his journey down the "River of the Iroquois" (Richelieu River) to the lake that today bears his name—and his eventual encounter with the "enemy."

Source: *The Journal of Samuel de Champlain,* The Lake Champlain and Lake George Historical Site, http://www.historiclakes.org/S_de_Champ/Champlain2.html

I set out then from the rapid of the river of the Iroquois on the second of July. All the Indians began to carry their canoes, arms and baggage about half a league by land, to avoid the swiftness and force of the rapid. This they soon accomplished.

    Then they put all the canoes into the water and two men with their baggage into each; but they made one of the men of each canoe go by land some three leagues which is about the length of the rapids, but the water is here less impetuous than at the entrance, except in certain places where rocks block the river, which is only some three or four hundred yards wide. After we had passed the rapid, which was not without difficulty, all the Indians who had gone overland, by a rather pleasant path through level country, although there were many trees, again got into their canoes. The men whom I had with me also went by land, but I went by water in a canoe. The Indians held a review of all their people and there were sixty men in twenty-four canoes. After holding the review we kept on our way as far as an island, three leagues long, which was covered with the most beautiful pines I had ever seen. There the Indians hunted and took some game. Continuing some three leagues farther, we encamped to take rest during the following night.

    Immediately, each began, some to cut down trees, others to strip bark from the trees to cover their wigwams in which to take shelter, others to fell big trees for a barricade on the bank of the river round their wigwams. They know how to do this so quickly that after less than two hours' work, five hundred of their enemies would have had difficulty in driving them out, without losing many men. They do not barricade the riverbank where their boats are drawn up, in order to embark in case of need. After their wigwams had been set up, according to their custom each time they camp, they sent three canoes with nine good men, to reconnoiter two or three leagues ahead, whether they could perceive anything; and afterwards these retired. All night long they rely upon the explorations of these scouts, and it is a very bad custom; for sometimes they are surprised in their sleep by their enemies, who club them before they have time to rise and defend themselves. Realizing this, I pointed out to them the mistake they were making and said that they ought to keep watch as they had seen us do every night, and have men posted to listen and see whether they might perceive anything, and not live as they were doing like silly creatures. They told me that they could not stay awake, and that they worked enough during the day when hunting. Besides when they go to war they divide their men into three troops, that is, one troop for hunting, scattered in various direction, another troop which forms the bulk of their men is always under arms, and the other troop of scouts to reconnoiter along the rivers and see whether there is any mark or sign to show where their enemies or their friends have gone. This they know by certain marks by which the chiefs of one nation designate those of another, notifying one another from time to time of any variations of these. In this way they recognize whether enemies or friends have passed that way. The hunters never hunt in advance of the main body, nor of the scouts, in order not to give alarm or to

---

27. The most western of the islands of Brittany.

cause confusion, but only when these have retired and in a direction from which they do not expect the enemy. They go on in this way until they are within two or three days' march of their enemy, when they proceed stealthily by night, all retire into the thick of the woods, where they rest without any straggling, or making a noise, or making a fire even for the purpose of cooking. And this they do so as not to be noticed, if by chance their enemy should pass that way. The only light they make is for the purpose of smoking, which is almost nothing. They eat baked Indian meal, steeped in water, which becomes like porridge. They keep these meal cakes for their needs, when they are near the enemy or when they are retiring after an attack; for then they do not waste time in hunting but retire quickly.

Each time they encamp they have their *Pilotois* or *Ostemoy* who are people who play the part of wizards, in whom these tribes have confidence. One of these wizards will set up a tent, surround it with small trees, and cover it with his beaver-skin. When it is made, he gets inside so that he is completely hidden; then he seizes one of the poles of his tent and shakes it whilst he mumbles between his teeth certain words, with which he declares is invoking the devil, who appears to him in the form of a stone and tells him whether his friends will come upon their enemies and kill many of them. This *Pilotois* will lie flat on the ground, he will rise to his feet, speaking and writhing so that he is all in a perspiration, although stark naked. The whole tribe will be about the tent sitting on their buttocks like monkeys. They often told me that the shaking of the tent, which I saw, was caused by the devil and not by the man inside, although I saw the contrary; for, as I have said above, it was the *Pilotois* who would seize one of the poles of the tent, and make it move in this way. They told me also that I should see fire coming out of the top, but I never saw any. These scamps also counterfeit a loud, distinct voice, and speak a language unknown to the other Indians. And when they speak in an old man's voice, the rest think that the devil is speaking, and is telling them what is going to happen in their war, and what they must do.

Yet out of a hundred words all these scoundrels, who pretend to be wizards, do not speak two that are true, and go on deceiving these poor people to get things from them, as do many others in this world who resemble these gentry. I often pointed out to them that what they did was pure folly, and that they ought not to believe in such things.

Having learned from their wizards what is to happen to them, the chiefs take sticks a foot long, one for each man, and indicate by others somewhat longer, their leaders. Then they go into the wood, and level off a place five or six feet square, where the headman, as sergeant-major, arranges all these sticks as to him seems best. Then he calls all his companions, who approach fully armed, and he shows them the rank and order, which they are to observe when they fight with the enemy. This all these Indians regard attentively, and notice the figure made with these sticks by their chief. And afterwards they retire from that place and begin to arrange themselves in the order in which they have seen these sticks. Then they mix themselves up and again put themselves in proper order, repeating this two or three times, and go back to their camp, without any need of a sergeant to make them keep their ranks, which they are quite able to maintain without getting into confusion. Such is the method they observe on the war-path.

We departed on the following day, pursuing our way up the river as far as the entrance to the lake. In it are many beautiful low islands covered with very fine woods and meadows with much wild fowl and animals to hunt, such as stags, fallow deer, fawns, roebucks, bears, and other kinds of animals which come from the mainland to these islands. We caught there a great many of them. There are also many beavers, both in that river and in several small streams, which fall into it. This region although pleasant is not inhabited by Indians, on account of their wars; for they withdraw from the rivers as far as they can into the interior, in order not to be easily surprised.

On the following day we entered the lake which is some 80 or 100 leagues in length, in which I saw four beautiful islands about ten, twelve and fifteen leagues in length, which, like the Iroquois river, were formerly inhabited by Indians; but have been abandoned, since they have been at war with one another. There are also several rivers flowing into the lake, on whose banks are many fine trees of the same varieties we have in France, with many of the finest vines I had seen anywhere. There are many chestnut trees, which I had only seen on the shore of this lake, in which there is also a great abundance of many species of fish. Amongst others there is one called by the natives *Chaousarou*, which is of various lengths; but the largest of them as these tribes have told me, are from eight to ten feet long. I have seen some five feet long, which were as big as my thigh, and had a head as large as my two fists, with a snout two feet and a half long, and a double row of very sharp, dangerous teeth. Its body has a good deal the shape of the pike; but it is protected by scales of a silvery gray colour and so strong that a dagger could not pierce them. The end of its snout is like a pig's. This fish makes war on all the other fish, which are in these lakes and rivers. And, according to what these tribes have told me, it shows marvelous ingenuity in that, when it wishes to catch birds, it goes in amongst the rushes or reeds which lie along the shores of the lake in several places, and puts its snout out of the water without moving. The result is that when the birds come and light on its snout, mistaking it for a stump of wood, the fish is so cunning that, shutting its half-open mouth, it pulls them by their feet under the water. The natives gave me the head of one of them, a thing they prize highly, saying that when they have a headache, they bleed themselves with the teeth of this fish at the spot where the pain is and it eases them at once.

Continuing our way along this lake in a westerly direction and viewing the country, I saw towards the east very high mountains on the tops of which there was snow. I enquired of the natives whether these parts were inhabited. They said they were, and by the Iroquois, and that in those parts there were beautiful valleys and fields rich in corn such as I have eaten in that country, along with other products in abundance. And they said that the lake went close to the mountains, which, as I judged, might be some twenty-five leagues away from us. Towards the south I saw others, which were not less lofty than the first-mentioned, but there was no snow on these. The Indians told me that it was there we were to meet their enemies, that the mountains were thickly populated, and that we had to pass a rapid, which I saw afterwards. Thence they said we had to enter another lake which is some nine or ten leagues in length, and that on reaching the end of it we had to go by land some two leagues and cross a river which descends to the coast of Norumbega, adjoining that of Florida. They could go there in their canoes in two days, as I learned afterwards from some prisoners we took, who conversed with me very particularly regarding all they knew, with the help of some Algonquin interpreters who knew the Iroquois language.

Now as we began to get within two or three days' journey of the home of their enemy, we proceeded only by night, and during the day we rested. Nevertheless, they kept up their usual superstitious ceremonies in order to know what was to happen to them in their undertakings, and often would come and ask me whether I had had dreams and had seen their enemies. I would tell them that I had not, but nevertheless continued to inspire them with courage and good hope. When night came on, we set off on our way until the next morning. Then we retired into the thick woods where we spent the rest of the day. Towards ten or eleven o'clock, after walking around our camp, I went to take a rest, and while asleep I dreamed that I saw in the lake near a mountain our enemies, the Iroquois, drowning before our eyes. I wanted to succour them, but our Indian allies said to me that we should let them all perish; for they were bad men. When I awoke they did not fail to ask me as usual whether I had dreamed anything. I told them what I had seen in my dream. This gave them such confidence that they no longer had any doubt as to the good fortune awaiting them.

Evening having come, we embarked in our canoes in order to proceed on our way, and as we were paddling along very quietly, and without making any noise, about ten o'clock at night on the twenty-ninth of the month, at the extremity of a cape, which projects into the lake on the west side, we met the Iroquois on the war-path. Both they and we began to utter loud shouts and each got his arms ready. We drew out into the lake and the Iroquois landed and arranged all their canoes near one another. Then they began to fell trees with the poor axes which they sometimes win in war, or with stone axes; and they barricaded themselves well.

Our Indians all night long also kept their canoes close to one another and tied to poles in order not to get separated, but to fight all together in case of need. We were on the water within bowshot of their barricades. And when they were armed, and everything in order, they sent two canoes which they separated from the rest, to learn from their enemies whether they wished to fight, and these replied that they had no other desire, but that for the moment nothing could be seen and that it was necessary to wait for daylight in order to distinguish one another. They said that as soon as the sun should rise, they would attack us, and to this our Indians agreed. Meanwhile, the whole night was spent in dances and songs on both sides, with many insults and other remarks, such as the lack of courage on our side, how little we could do to resist or against them, and that when daylight came our people would learn all this to their ruin. Our side too was not lacking in retort, telling the enemy that they would see such great deeds of arms as they had never seen, and a great deal of other talk, such as is flung at the siege of a city. Having sung, danced, and flung words at one another for some time, when daylight came, my companions and I were still hidden, lest the enemy should see us, getting our fire-arms ready as best we could, being however still separated, each in a canoe of the Montagnais Indians. After we were armed with light weapons, we took, each of us, an arquebus and went ashore. I saw the enemy come out of their barricade, nearly two hundred in number, stout and rugged in appearance. They came at a slow pace towards us, with a dignity and assurance, which greatly amused us, having three chiefs at their head. Our men also advanced in the same order, telling me that those who had three large plumes were the chiefs, and that they had only these three, and that they could be distinguished by these plumes, which were much larger than those of their companions, and that I should do what I could to kill them. I promised to do all in my power, and said that I was very sorry they could not understand me, so that I might give order and shape to their mode of attacking their enemies, then we should, without doubt, defeat them all; but that this could not now be obviated, and that I should be very glad to show them my courage and goodwill when we should engage in the fight.

As soon as we had landed, they began to run for some two hundred paces towards their enemies, who stood firmly, not having as yet noticed my companions, who went into the woods with some savages. Our men began to call me with loud cries; and in order to give a passage-way, they opened in two parts, and put me at their head, where I marched some twenty paces ahead of the rest, until I was within about thirty paces of the enemy, who at once noticed me, and, halting, gazed at me, as I did also at them. When I saw them making a move to fire at us, I rested my musket against my cheek, and aimed directly at one of the three chiefs. With the same shot, two fell to the ground; and one of their men was so wounded that he died some time after. I had loaded my musket with four balls. When our side saw this shot so favorable for them, they began to raise such loud cries that one could not have heard it thunder. Meanwhile, the arrows flew on both sides. The Iroquois were greatly astonished that two men had been so quickly killed, although they were equipped with armor woven from cotton thread, and with wood which was proof against their arrows. This caused great alarm among them. As I was loading again, one of my companions fired shot from the woods, which astonished them anew, to such a degree that, seeing their chiefs dead, they lost courage and took to flight, abandoning their camp and fort, and fleeing into the woods, whither I pursued them, killing still more of them. Our savages also killed several of them and took ten or twelve prisoners. The remainder escaped with the wounded. Fifteen or sixteen were wounded on our side with arrow-shots; but they were soon healed.

After gaining the victory, our men amused themselves by taking a greater quantity of Indian corn and some meal from their enemies, also their armor, which they had left behind that they might run better. After feasting sumptuously, dancing and singing, we returned three hours after, with the prisoners. The spot where this took place is in latitude 43° and some minutes, and the lake was called Champlain. . .

1. *Describe Samuel de Champlain's attitude toward his Indian hosts as he traveled down the river of the Iroquois. Do you think he respected their customs or was he repelled by them? Why?*
2. *How does Champlain's account of the battle with the Iroquois belie commonly-held assumptions about Indian warfare?*

2-3 An Act Concerning Servants and Slaves

The transition from indentured servitude to chattel slavery in Virginia brought new legal and social questions to the forefront. What legal rights did indentured servants have? Were their limits to the rights of slave owners? What was to be done about runaways? Even questions regarding race relations needed to be addressed. The following statutes passed by the Virginia colonial legislature addressed these issues and attempted, for the time being at least, to establish a status quo for servants and slaves.

> **Source:** William Waller Hening, *The Statutes at Large; Being a Collection of all the Laws of Virginia, from the First Session of the Legislature in the Year 1619,* (New York: R & W & G. Bartow, 1823). Vol. I.
> http://www.law.du.edu/russell/lh/alh/docs/virginiaslaverystatutes.html

I. *Be it enacted, by the governor, council, and burgesses, of this present general assembly, and it is hereby enacted, by the authority of the same,* That all servants brought into this country without indenture, if the said servants be Christians, and of Christian parentage, and above nineteen years of age, shall serve but five years; and if under nineteen years of age, 'till they shall become twenty-four years of age, and no longer.

II. *Provided always,* That every such servant be carried to the country court, within six months after his or her arrival into this colony, to have his or her age adjudged by the court, otherwise shall be a servant no longer than the accustomary five years, although much under the age of nineteen years; and the age of such servant being adjudged by the court, within the limitation aforesaid, shall be entered upon the records of the said court, and be accounted, deemed, and taken, for the true age of the said servant, in relation to the time of service aforesaid.

III. *And also be it enacted, by the authority aforesaid, and it is herby enacted,* That when any servant sold for the custom, shall pretend to have indentures, the master or owner of such servant, for discovery of the truth thereof, may bring the said servant before a justice of the peace; and if the said servant cannot produce the indenture then, but shall still pretend to have one, the said justice shall assign two months time for the doing thereof, in which time, if the said servant shall not produce his or her indenture, it shall be taken for granted that there never was one, and shall be a bar to his or her claim of making use of one afterwards, or taking any advantage by one.

IV. *And also be it enacted, by the authority aforesaid, and it is hereby enacted,* That all servants imported and brought into this country, by sea or land, who were not Christians in their native country, (except Turks and Moors in amity with her majesty, and others that can make due proof of their being free in England, or any other Christian country, before they were shipped, in order to transportation hither) shall be accounted and be slaves, and as such be here bought and sold notwithstanding a conversion to Christianity afterwards.

V. *And be it enacted, by the authority aforesaid, and it is hereby enacted,* That if any person or persons shall hereafter import into this colony, and here sell as a slave, any person or persons that shall have been a freeman in any Christian country, island, or plantation, such importer and seller as aforesaid, shall forfeit and pay, to the party from whom the said freeman shall recover his freedom, double the sum for which the said freeman was sold. To be recovered, in any court of record within this colony, according to the course of the common law, wherein the defendant shall not be admitted to plead in bar, any act or statute for limitation of actions.

VI. *Provided always,* That a slave's being in England, shall not be sufficient to discharge him of his slavery, without other proof of his being manumitted there.

VII. *And also be it enacted, by the authority aforesaid, and it is hereby enacted,* That all masters and owners of servants, shall find and provide for their servants, wholesome and competent diet, clothing, and lodging, by the discretion of the county court; and shall not, at any time, give immoderate correction; neither shall, at any time, whip a Christian white servant naked, without an order from a justice of the peace: And if any, notwithstanding this act, shall presume to whip a Christian white servant naked, without such order, the person so offending, shall forfeit and pay for the same, forty shillings sterling, to the party injured: To be recovered, with costs, upon petition, without the formal process of an action, as in and by this act is provided for servants complaints to be heard; provided complaint be made within six months after such whipping.

VIII. *And also be it enacted, by the authority aforesaid, and it is herby enacted,* That all servants, (not being slaves,) whether imported, or become servants of their own accord here, or bound by any court or church-wardens, shall have their complaints received by a justice of the peace, who, if he find cause, shall bind the master over to answer the complaint at court; and it shall be there determined: And all complaints of servants, shall and may, by virtue hereof, be received at any time, upon petition, in the court of the county wherein they reside, without the formal process of an action; and also full power and authority is hereby given to the said court, by their discretion, (having first summoned the masters or owners to justify themselves, if they think fit,) to adjudge, order, and appoint what shall be necessary, as to diet, lodging, clothing, and correction: 1 And if any master or owner shall not thereupon comply with the said court's order, the said court is hereby authorised and empowered, upon a second just complaint, to order such servant to be immediately sold at an outcry, by the sheriff, and after charges deducted, the remainder of what the said servant shall be sold for, to be paid and satisfied to such owner.

IX. *Provided always, and be it enacted,* That if such servant be so sick or lame, or otherwise rendered so incapable, that he or she cannot be sold for such a value, at least, as shall satisfy the fees, and other incident charges accrued, the said court shall then order the church-wardens of the parish to take care of and provide for the said servant, until such servant's time, due by law to the said master, or owner, shall be expired, or until such servant, shall be so recovered, as to be sold for defraying the said fees and charges: And further, the said court, from time to time, shall order the charges of keeping the said servant, to be levied upon the goods and chattels of the master or owner of the said servant, by distress.

X. *And be it also enacted,* That all servants, whether, by importation, indenture, or hire here, as well feme coverts, as others, shall, in like manner, as is provided, upon complaints of misusage, have their petitions received in court, for their wages and freedom, without the formal process of an action; and proceedings, and judgment, shall, in like manner, also, be had thereupon.

XI. And for a further Christian care and usage of all Christian servants, *Be it also enacted, by the authority aforesaid, and it is hereby enacted,* That no negros, mulattos, or Indians, although Christians, or Jews, Moors, Mahometans, or other infidels, shall, at any time, purchase any Christian servant, nor any other, except of their own complexion, or such as are declared slaves by this act: And if any negro, mulatto, or Indian, Jew, Moor, Mahometan, or other infidel, or such as are declared slaves by this act, shall, notwithstanding, purchase any Christian white servant, the said servant shall, *ipso facto,* become free and acquit from any service then due, and shall be so held, deemed, and taken: And if any person, having such Christian servant, shall intermarry with any such negro, mulatto, or Indian, Jew, Moor, Mahometan, or other infidel, every Christian white servant of every such person so intermarrying, shall, *ipso facto,* become free and acquit from any service then due to such master or mistress so intermarrying, as aforesaid.

XII. *And also be it enacted, by the authority aforesaid, and it is hereby enacted,* That no master or owner of any servant shall during the time of such servant's servitude, make any bargain with his or her said servant for further service, or other matter or thing relating to liberty, or personal profit, unless the same be made in the presence, and with the approbation, of the court of that county where the master or owner resides: And if any servants shall, at any time bring in goods or money, or during the time of their service, by gift, or any other lawful ways or means, come to have any goods or money, they shall enjoy the propriety thereof, and have the sole use and benefit thereof to themselves. And if any servant shall happen to fall sick or lame, during the time of service, so that he or she becomes of little or no use to his or her master or owner, but rather a charge, the said master or owner shall not put away the said servant, but shall maintain him or her, during the whole time he or she was before obliged to serve, by indenture, custom or order of court: And if any master or owner, shall put away any such sick or lame servant, upon pretence of freedom, and that servant shall become chargeable to the parish, the said master or owner shall forfeit and pay ten pounds current money of Virginia, to the church-wardens of the parish where such offence shall be committed, for the use of the said parish: To be recovered by action of debt, in any court of record in this her majesty's colony and dominion, in which no essoin, protection, or wager of law, shall be allowed.

XIII. And whereas there has been a good and laudable custom of allowing servants corn and cloaths for their present support, upon their freedom; but nothing in that nature ever made certain, *Be it also enacted, by the authority aforesaid, and it is hereby enacted,* That there shall be paid and allowed to every imported servant, not having yearly wages, at the time of service ended, by the master or owner of such servant, viz: To every male servant, ten bushels of indian corn, thirty shillings in money, or the value thereof, in goods, and one well fixed musket or fuzee, of the value of twenty shillings, at least: and to every woman servant, fifteen bushels of indian corn, and forty shillings in money, or the value thereof, in goods: Which, upon refusal, shall be ordered, with costs, upon petition to the county court, in manner as is herein before directed, for servants complaints to be heard.

XIV. *And also be it enacted, by the authority aforesaid, and it is hereby enacted,* That all servants shall faithfully and obediently, all the whole time of their service, do all their masters or owners just and lawful commands. And if any servant shall resist the master, or mistress, or overseer, or offer violence to any of them, the said servant shall, for every such offence, be adjudged to serve his or her said master or owner, one whole year after the time, by indenture, custom, or former order of court, shall be expired.

XV. *And also be it enacted, by the authority aforesaid, and it is hereby enacted,* That no person whatsoever shall buy, sell, or receive of, to, or from, any servant, or slave, any coin or commodity whatsoever, without the leave, licence, or consent of the master or owner of the said servant, or slave: And if any person shall, contrary hereunto, without the leave or licence aforesaid, deal with any servant, or slave, he or she so offending, shall be imprisoned one calendar month, without bail or main-prize; and then, also continue in prison, until he or she shall find good security, in the sum of ten pounds current money of Virginia, for the good behaviour for one year following; wherein, a second offence shall be a breach of the bond and moreover shall forfeit and pay four times the value of the things so bought, sold, or received, to the master or owner of such servant, or slave: To be recovered, with costs, by action upon the case, in any court of record in this her majesty's colony and dominion, wherein no essoin protection, or wager of law, or other than one imparlance, shall be allowed.

XVI. *Provided always, and be it enacted,* That when any person or persons convict for dealing with a servant, or slave, contrary to this act, shall not immediately give good and sufficient security for his or her good behaviour, as aforesaid: then, in such case, the court shall order thirty-nine lashes, well laid on, upon the bare back of such offender, at the common whipping-post of the county, and the said offender to be thence discharged of giving such bond and security.

XVII. *And also be it enacted, by the authority aforesaid, and it is hereby enacted, and declared,* That in all cases of penal laws, whereby persons free are punishable by fine, servants shall be punished by whipping, after the rate of twenty lashes for every five hundred pounds of tobacco, or fifty shillings current money, unless the servant so culpable, can and will procure some person or persons to pay the fine; in which case, the said servant shall be adjudged to serve such benefactor, after the time by indenture, custom, or order of court, to his or her then present master or owner, shall be expired, after the rate of one month and a half for every hundred pounds of tobacco; any thing in this act contained, to the contrary, in any-wise, notwithstanding.

XVIII. And if any women servant shall be delivered of a bastard child within the time of her service aforesaid, *Be it enacted, by the authority aforesaid, and it is hereby enacted,* That in recompense of the loss and trouble occasioned her master or mistress thereby, she shall for every such offence, serve her said master or owner one whole year after her time by indenture, custom, and former order of court, shall be expired; or pay her said master or owner, one thousand pounds of tobacco; and the reputed father, if free, shall give security to the church-wardens of the parish where that child shall be, to maintain the child, and keep the parish indemnified; or be compelled thereto by order of the county court, upon the said church-wardens complaint: But if a servant, he shall make satisfaction of the parish, for keeping the said child, after his time by indenture, custom, or order of court, to his then present master or owner, shall be expired; or be compelled thereto, by order of the county court, upon complaint of the church wardens of the said parish, for the time being. And if any woman servant shall be got with child by her master, neither the said master, nor his executors, administrators, nor assigns, shall have any claim of service against her, for or by reason of such child; but she shall, when her time due to her said master, by indenture, custom or order of court, shall be expired, be sold by the church-wardens, for the time being, of the parish wherein such child shall be born, for one year, or pay one thousand pounds of tobacco; and the said one thousand pounds of tobacco, or whatever she shall be sold for, shall be emploied, by the vestry, to the use of the said parish. And if any woman servant shall have a bastard child by a negro, or mulatto, over and above the years service due to her master or owner, she shall immediately, upon the expiration of her time to her then present master or owner, pay down to the church-wardens of the parish wherein such child shall be born, for the use of the said parish fifteen pounds current money of Virginia, or be by them sold for five years to the use aforesaid: And if a free Christian white woman shall have such bastard child, by a negro, or mulatto, for every such offence, she shall, within one month after her delivery of such bastard child, pay to the church-wardens for the time being, of the parish wherein such child shall be born, for the use of the said parish fifteen pounds current money of Virginia, or be by them sold for five years to the use aforesaid: And in both the said cases, the church-wardens shall bind the said child to be a servant, until it shall be of thirty one years of age.

XIX. And for a further prevention of that abominable mixture and spurious issue, which hereafter may increase in this her majesty's colony and dominion, as well by English, and other white men and women intermarrying with negros or mulattos, as by their unlawful coition with them, *Be it enacted, by the authority aforesaid, and it is hereby enacted,* That whatsoever English, or other white man or woman, being free, shall intermarry with a negro or mulatto man or woman, bond or free, shall, by judgment of the county court, be committed to prison, and there remain, during the space of six months, without bail or mainprize; and shall forfeit and pay ten pounds current money of Virginia, to the use of the parish, as aforesaid.

XX. *And be it further enacted,* That no minister of the church of England, or other minister, or person whatsoever, within this colony and dominion, shall hereafter wittingly presume to marry a white man with a negro or mulatto woman; or to marry a white woman with a negro or mulatto man, upon pain of forfeiting and paying, for every such marriage the sum of ten thousand pounds of tobacco; one half to our sovereign lady the Queen, her heirs and successors, for and towards the support of the government, and the contingent charges thereof; and the other half to the informer; To be recovered, with costs, by action of debt, bill, plaint, or information, in any court of record within this her majesty's colony and dominion, wherein no essoin, protection, or wager of law, shall be allowed.

XXI. And because poor people may not be destitute of emploiment, upon suspicion of being servants, and servants also kept from running away, *Be it enacted, by the authority aforesaid, and it is hereby enacted,* That every servant, when his or her time of service shall be expired, shall repair to the court of the county where he or she served the last of his or her time, and there, upon sufficient testimony, have his or her freedom entered; and a certificate thereof from the clerk of the said court, shall be sufficient to authorise any person to entertain or hire such servant, without any danger of this law. And if it shall at any time happen, that such certificate is won out, or lost, the said clerk shall grant a new one, and therein also recite the accident happened to the old one. And whoever shall hire such servant, shall take his or her certificate, and keep it, 'till the contracted time shall be expired. And if any person whatsoever, shall harbour or entertain any servant by importation, or by contract, or indenture made here, not having such certificate, he or she so offending, shall pay to the master or owner of such servant, sixty pounds of tobacco for every natural day he or she shall so harbour or entertain such runaway: To be recovered, with costs, by action of debt, in any court of record within this her majesty's colony and dominion, wherein no essoin, protection, or wager of law, shall be allowed. And also, if any runaway shall make use of a forged certificate, or after the same shall be delivered to any master or mistress, upon being hired, shall steal the same away, and thereby procure entertainment, the person entertaining such servant, upon such forged or stolen certificate, shall not be culpable by this law: But the said runaway, besides making reparation for the loss of time, and charges in recovery, and other penalties by this law directed, shall, for making use of such forged or stolen certificate, or for such theft aforesaid, stand two hours in the pillory, upon a court day: And the person forging such certificate, shall forfeit and pay ten pounds current money; one half thereof to be to her majesty, her heirs and successors, for and towards the support of this government, and the contingent charges thereof, and the other half to the master or owner of such servant, if he or she will inform or sue for the same, otherwise to the informer: To be recovered, with costs, by action of debt, bill, plaint or information, in any court of record in this her majesty's colony and dominion, wherein no essoin, protection, or wager of law, shall be allowed. And if any person or persons convict of forging such certificate, shall not immediately pay the said ten pounds, and costs, or give security to do the same within six months, he or she so convict, shall receive, on his or her bare back, thirty-nine lashes, well laid on, at the common whipping post of the county; and shall be thence discharged of paying the said ten pounds, and costs, and either of them.

XXII. *Provided,* That when any master or mistress shall happen to hire a runaway, upon a forged certificate, and a servant deny that he delivered any such certificate, the *Onus Probandi* shall lie upon the person hiring, who upon failure therein, shall be liable to the fines and penalties, for entertaining runaway servants, without certificate.

XXIII. And for encouragement of all persons to take up runaways, *Be it enacted, by the authority aforesaid, and it is hereby enacted,* That for the taking up of every servant, or slave, if ten miles, or above, from the house or quarter where such servant, or slave was kept, there shall be allowed by the public, as a reward to the taker-up, two hundred pounds of tobacco; and if above five miles, and under ten, one hundred pounds of tobacco: Which said several rewards of two hundred, and one hundred pounds of tobacco, shall also be paid in the county where such taker-up shall reside, and shall be again levied by the public upon the master or owner of such runaway, for reimbursement of the same to the public. And for the greater certainty in paying the said rewards and reimbursement of the public, every justice of the peace before whom such runaway shall be brought, upon the taking up, shall mention the proper-name and sur-name of the taker-up, and the county of his or her residence, together with the time and place of taking up the said runaway; and shall also mention the name of the said runaway, and the proper-name and sur-name of the master or owner of such runaway, and the county of his or her residence, together with the distance of miles, in the said justice's judgment, from the place of taking up the said runaway, to the house or quarter where such runaway was kept.

XXIV. *Provided,* That when any negro, or other runaway, that doth not speak English, and cannot, or through obstinacy will not, declare the name of his or her masters or owner, that then it shall be sufficient for the said justice to certify the same, instead of the name of such runaway, and the proper name and sur-name of his or her master or owner, and the county of his or her residence and distance of miles, as aforesaid; and in such case, shall, by his warrant, order the said runaway to be conveyed to the public gaol, of this country, there to be continued prisoner until the master or owner shall be known; who, upon paying the charges of the imprisonment, or give caution to the prison-keeper for the same, together with the reward of two hundred or one hundred pounds of tobacco, as the case shall be, shall have the said runaway restored.

XXV. And further, the said justice of the peace, when such runaway shall be brought before him, shall, by his warrant commit the said runaway to the next constable, and therein also order him to give the said runaway so many lashes as the said justice shall think fit, not exceeding the number of thirty-nine; and then to be conveyed from constable to constable, until the said runaway shall be carried home, or to the country gaol, as aforesaid, every constable through whose hands the said runaway shall pass, giving a receipt at the delivery; and every constable failing to execute such warrant according to the tenor thereof, or refusing to give such receipt, shall forfeit and pay two hundred pounds of tobacco to the church-wardens of the parish wherein such failure shall be, for the use of the poor of the said parish: To be recovered, with costs, by action of debt, in any court of record in this her majesty's colony and dominion, wherein no essoin, protection or wager of law, shall be allowed. And such corporal punishment shall not deprive the master or owner of such runaway of the other satisfaction here in this act appointed to be made upon such servant's running away.

XXVI. *Provided always, and be it further enacted,* That when any servant or slave, in his or her running away, shall have crossed the great bay of Chesapeak, and shall be brought before a justice of the peace, the said justice shall, instead of committing such runaway to the constable, commit him or her to the sheriff, who is hereby required to receive every such runaway, according to such warrant, and to cause him, her, or them, to be transported again across the bay, and delivered to a constable there; and shall have, for all his trouble and charge herein, for every such servant or slave, five hundred pounds of tobacco, paid by the public; which shall be reimbursed again by the master or owner of such runaway, as aforesaid, in manner aforesaid.

XXVII. *Provided also,* That when any runaway servant that shall have crossed the said bay, shall get up into the country, in any county distant from the bay, that then, in such case, the said runaway shall be committed to a constable, to be conveyed from constable to constable, until he shall be brought to a sheriff of some county adjoining to the said bay of Chesapeak, which sheriff is also hereby required, upon such warrant, to receive such runaway, under the rules and conditions aforesaid; and cause him or her to be conveyed as aforesaid; and shall have the reward, as aforesaid.

XXVIII. And for the better preventing of delays in returning of such runaways, *Be it enacted,* That if any sheriff, under sheriff, or other officer of, or belonging to the sheriffs, shall cause or suffer any such runaway (so committed for passage over the bay) to work, the said sheriff, to whom such runaway shall be so committed, shall forfeit and pay to the master or owner, of every such servant or slave, so put to work, one thousand pounds of tobacco; To be recovered, with costs, by action of debt, bill, plaint, or information, in any court of record within this her majesty's colony and dominion, wherein no essoin, protection, or wager of law, shall be allowed.

XXIX. *And be it enacted, by the authority aforesaid, and it is hereby enacted,* That if any constable, or sheriff, into whose hands a runaway servant or slave shall be committed, by virtue of this act, shall suffer such runaway to escape, the said constable or sheriff shall be liable to the action of the party grieved, for recovery of his damages, at the common law with costs.

XXX. *And also be it enacted, by the authority aforesaid, and it is hereby enacted,* That every runaway servant, upon whose account, either of the rewards aforementioned shall be paid, for taking up, shall for every hundred pounds of tobacco so paid by the master or owner, serve his or her said master or owner, after his or her time by indenture, custom, or former order of court, shall be expired, one calendar month and an half, and moreover, shall serve double the time such servant shall be absent in such running away; and shall also make reparation, by service, to the said master or owner, for all necessary disbursements and charges, in pursuit and recovery of the said runaway; to be adjudged and allowed in the county court, after the rate of one year for eight hundred pounds of tobacco, and so proportionally for a greater or lesser quantity.

XXXI. *Provided,* That the masters or owners of such runaways, shall carry them to court the next court held for the said county, after the recovery of such runaway, otherwise it shall be in the breast of the court to consider the occasion of delay, and to hear, or refuse the claim, according to their discretion, without appeal, for the refusal.

XXXII. *And also be it enacted, by the authority aforesaid, and it is hereby enacted,* That no master, mistress, or overseer of a family, shall knowingly permit any slave, not belonging to him or her, to be and remain upon his or her plantation, above four hours at any one time, without the leave of such slave's master, mistress, or overseer, on penalty of one hundred and fifty pounds of tobacco to the informer; cognizable by a justice of the peace of the county wherein such offence shall be committed.

XXXIII. *Provided also,* That if any runaway servant, adjudged to serve for the charges of his or her pursuit and recovery, shall, at the time, he or she is so adjudged, repay and satisfy, or give good security before the court, for repaiment and satisfaction of the same, to his or her master or owner, within six months after, such master or owner shall be obliged to accept thereof, in lieu of the service given and allowed for such charges and disbursements.

XXXIV. And if any slave resist his master, or owner, or other person, by his or her order, correcting such slave, and shall happen to be killed in such correction, it shall not be accounted felony; but the master, owner, and every such other person so giving correction, shall be free and acquit of all punishment and accusation for the same, as if such accident had never happened: And also, if any negro, mulatto, or Indian, bond or free, shall at any time, lift his or her hand, in opposition against any Christian, not being negro, mulatto, or Indian, he or she so offending, shall, for every such offence, proved by the oath of the party, receive on his or her bare back, thirty lashes, well laid on; cognizable by a justice of the peace for that county wherein such offence shall be committed.

XXXV. *And also be it enacted, by the authority aforesaid, and it is hereby enacted,* That no slave go armed with gun, sword, club, staff, or other weapon, nor go from off the plantation and seat of land where such slave shall be appointed to live, without a certificate of leave in writing, for so doing, from his or her master, mistress, or overseer: And if any slave shall be found offending herein, it shall be lawful for any person or persons to apprehend and deliver such slave to the next constable or head-borough, who is hereby enjoined and required, without further order or warrant, to give such slave twenty lashes on his or her bare back, well laid on, and so send him or her home: And all horses, cattle, and hogs, now belonging, or that hereafter shall belong to any slave, or of any slaves mark in this her majesty's colony and dominion, shall be seised and sold by the church-wardens of the parish, wherein such horses, cattle, or hogs shall be, and the profit thereof applied to the use of the poor of the said parish: And also, if any damage shall be hereafter committed by any slave living at a quarter where there is no Christian overseer, the master or owner of such slave shall be liable to action for the trespass and damage, as if the same had been done by him or herself.

XXXVI. *And also it is hereby enacted and declared,* That baptism of slaves doth not exempt them from bondage; and that all children shall be bond or free, according to the condition of their mothers, and the particular directions of this act.

XXXVII. And whereas, many times, slaves run away and lie out, hid and lurking in swamps, woods, and other obscure places, killing hogs, and committing other injuries to the inhabitants of this her majesty's colony and dominion, *Be it therefore enacted, by the authority aforesaid, and it is hereby enacted,* That in all such cases, upon intelligence given of any slaves lying out, as aforesaid, any two justices (*Quorum unus*) of the peace of the county wherein such slave is supposed to lurk or do mischief, shall be and are empowered and required to issue proclamation against all such slaves, reciting their names, and owners names, if they are known, and thereby requiring them, and every of them, forthwith to surrender themselves; and also empowering the sheriff of the said county, to take such power with him, as he shall think fit and necessary, for the effectual apprehending such out-lying slave or slaves, and go in search of them: Which proclamation shall be published on a Sabbath day, at the door of every church and chapel, in the said county, by the parish clerk, or reader, of the church, immediately after divine worship: And in case any slave, against whom proclamation hath been thus issued, and once published at any church or chapel, as aforesaid, stay out, and do not immediately return home, it shall be lawful for any person or persons whatsoever, to kill and destroy such slaves by such ways and means as he, she, or they shall think fit, without accusation or impeachment of any crime for the same: And if any slave, that hath run away and lain out as aforesaid, shall be apprehended by the sheriff, or any other person, upon the application of the owner of the said slave, it shall and may be lawful for the county court, to order such punishment to the said slave, either by dismembering, or any other way, not touching his life, as they in their discretion shall think fit, for the reclaiming any such incorrigible slave, and terrifying others from the like practices.

XXXVIII. *Provided always, and it is further enacted,* That for every slave killed, in pursuance of this act, or put to death by law, the master or owner of such slave shall be paid by the public:

XXXIX. And to the end, the true value of every slave killed, or put to death, as aforesaid, may be the better known; and by that means, the assembly the better enabled to make a suitable allowance thereupon, *Be it enacted,* That upon application of the master or owner of any such slave, to the court appointed for proof of public claims, the said court shall value the slave in money, and the clerk of the court shall return a certificate thereof to the assembly, with the rest of the public claims.

1. *It is easy to examine laws such as these and see the many ways in which servants and slaves were denied legal rights and social status in colonial Virginia. See if you can discern, however, the ways that these same statutes limit the power of slave owners and masters of indentured servants.*
2. *How did runaways pose particularly difficult legal problems for Virginia colonists? How did these statutes solve the dilemmas?*

2-4   Reasons for the Plantation in New England (1629)

The following document was transcribed by Forth Winthrop, son of John Winthrop, but its author may never be known. The original document was found in John Winthrop's possessions and contains his marginal notes dated in 1629. The purpose of the document was to support the proposed Puritan settlement of Massachusetts Bay and address possible objections to the venture. Historians agree that if Winthrop did not write this piece in its entirety, it does reflect his opinion.

Source: The Winthrop Society, 1996–2001
http://www.winthropsociety.org/document.htm

Reasons to be considered for justifying the undertakers of the intended Plantation in New England, and for encouraging such whose hearts God shall move to join with them in it.

1. It will be a service to the Church of great consequence to carry the Gospel into those parts of the world, to help on the fullness of the coming of the Gentiles, and to raise a bulwark against the kingdom of AnteChrist, which the Jesuits labor to rear up in those parts.

2. All other Churches of Europe are brought to desolation, and our sins, for which the Lord begins already to frown upon us and to cut us short, do threaten evil times to be coming upon us, and who knows, but that God hath provided this place to be a refuge for many whom he means to save out of the general calamity, and seeing the Church hath no place left to fly into but the wilderness, what better work can there be, than to go and provide tabernacles and food for her when she be restored.

3. This England grows weary of her inhabitants, so as Man, who is the most precious of all creatures, is here more vile and base than the earth we tread upon, and of less price among us than a horse or a sheep. Masters are forced by authority to entertain servants, parents to maintain their own children, all towns complain of their burden to maintain their poor, though we have taken up many unnecessary, yea unlawful, trades to maintain them. We use the authority of the Law to hinder the increase of our people, as by urging the statute against cottages and inmates—and thus it is come to pass, that children, servants and neighbors, especially if they be poor, are counted the greatest burdens, which if things were right would be the chiefest earthly blessings.

4. The whole earth is the Lord's garden, and He hath given it to mankind with a general commission (Gen. 1:28) to increase and multiply and replenish the earth and subdue it, which was again renewed to Noah. The end is double and natural, that Mankind might enjoy the fruits of the earth, and God might have His due Glory from His creatures. Why then should one strive here for places of habitation, at such a cost as would obtain better land in another country, and at the same time suffer a whole continent as fruitful and convenient for the use of man to lie waste without any improvement?

5. We are grown to that height of intemperance in all excess of riot that as no man's estate, almost, will suffice to keep sail with his equals. He who fails herein must live in scorn and contempt. Hence it comes that all arts and trades are carried on in that deceitful and unrighteous course, so that it is almost impossible for a good and upright man to maintain his charge and live comfortably in any of them.

6. The fountains of learning and religion are so corrupted that most children (besides the unsupportable charge of their education) are perverted, corrupted, and utterly overthrown by the multitude of evil examples and the licentious government of those seminaries, where men strain at gnats and swallow camels, and use all severity for maintenance of caps and like accomplishments, but suffer all ruffianlike fashions and disorder in manners to pass uncontrolled.

7. What can be a better work, and more honorable and worthy of a Christian than to help rise and support a particular church while it is in its infancy, and to join his forces with such a company of faithful people, as by a timely assistance may grow strong and prosper, when for want of such help may be put to great hazard, if not wholly ruined.

8. If any such as are known to be Godly and live in all wealth and prosperity here, and shall forsake all this to join themselves with this Church and to run a hazard with them of a hard and mean condition, it will be an example of great use both for removing the scandal of worldly and sinister respects which is cast upon the Adventurer, to give more life to the faith of God's people in their prayers for the Plantation, and to encourage others to join the more willingly in it.

9. It appears to be a work of God for the good of His Church, in that He hath disposed the hearts of so many of His wise and faithful servants, both ministers and others, not only to approve of the enterprise but to interest themselves in it, some in their persons and estates, and others by their serious advice and help otherwise, and all by their prayers for the welfare of it. (Amos 3:) The Lord revealed his secret to His servants, the prophets, and it is likely He hath some great work in hand which He hath revealed to His prophets among us, whom He hath stirred up to encourage His servants to this Plantation, for He doth not use to seduce His people by His own prophets, but committeth that office to the ministry of false prophets and lying spirits.

Diverse objections which have been made against this Plantation, with their answers and resolutions:

Objection I—We have no warrant to enter upon that land, which has been so long possessed by others.

    Answer 1: That which lies common, and has never been replenished or subdued, is free to any that possess and improve it; for God hath given to the sons of men a double right to the earth—there is a natural right and a civil right. The first right was natural when men held the earth in common, every man sowing and feeding where he pleased. Then as men and their cattle increased, they appropriated certain parcels of ground by enclosing and peculiar cultivation, and this in time got them a civil right—such is the right which Ephron the Hittite had in the field of Mackpelah, wherein Abraham could not bury a dead corpse without leave, though for the out parts of the country he dwelt upon them and took the fruit of them at his pleasure. The like did Jacob, who fed his cattle as boldly in Hamor's land (for he is said to be Lord of the country) and in other places where he came, as the native inhabitants themselves. And in those times and places, that men accounted nothing their own but that which they had appropriated by their own industry, appears plainly by this—that Abimileck's servants in their own country, when they oft contended with Isaac's servants about wells which they had dug, yet never strove for the land wherein they were. So like between Jacob and Laban, he would not take a goat of Laban's without special contract, but he makes no bargain with them for the land where they fed, and it is very probable that, had the land not been as free for Jacob as for Laban, that covetous wretch would have made his advantage of it, and would have upbraided Jacob with it as he did with his cattle. As for the natives in New England, they enclose no land, neither have they any settled habitation, nor any tame cattle to improve the land by, and so have no other but a natural right to those countries. So if we leave them sufficient for their own use, we may lawfully take the rest, there being more than enough for them and for us.

Answer 2: We shall come in with the good leave of the natives, who find benefit already of our neighborhood and learn from us to improve a part to more use than before they could do the whole. And by this means we come in by valuable purchase, for they have of us that which will yield them more benefit than all that land which we have from them.

Answer 3: God hath consumed the natives with a great plague in those parts, so as there be few inhabitants left.

Objection II—It will be a great wrong to our Church and Country to take away the good people, and we shall lay it the more open to the judgment feared.

Answer 1: The departing of good people from a country does not cause a judgment, but warns of it, which may occasion such as remain to turn from their evil ways, that they may prevent it, or take some other course that they may escape it.

Answer 2: Such as go away are of no observation in respect of those who remain, and are likely to do more good there than here. And since Christ's time, the Church is to be considered universal and without distinction of countries, so that he that does good in one place serves the Church in all places in regard of the unity.

Answer 3: It is the revealed will of God that the Gospel shall be preached in all nations, and though we know not whether those barbarians will receive it at first or not, yet it is a good work to serve God's providence in offering it to them (and this is the fittest to be done by God's own servants) for God shall have glory of it though they refuse it, and there is good hope that the posterity shall by this means be gathered into Christ's sheepfold.

Objection III—We have feared a judgment a great while, but yet we are safe. It were better therefore to stay till it comes, and either we may flee then, or if we be overtaken in it we may well content ourselves to suffer with such a Church as ours is.

Answer: It is likely that such a consideration made the Churches beyond the seas as the Palatinate, Rochelle, etc. to sit still at home and not look out for the shelter while they might have found it. But the woeful spectacle of their ruin may teach us more wisdom to avoid the plague when it is foreseen, and not to tarry as they did till it overtake us. If they were now at their former liberty we may be surer they would take other courses for their safety. And though half of them had miscarried their escape, yet had it not been so miserable to themselves and to religion as this desperate backsliding and abjuring the truth, which many of the ancient professors among them, and the whole posterity which remain are now plunged into.

Objection IV—The ill success of the other Plantations may tell us what will become of this.

Answer 1: None of the former sustained any great damage but Virginia, which happened there through their own sloth and poor security.

Answer 2: The argument is not good, for thus it stands: Some Plantations have miscarried, therefore we should not make any. It consists of particulars, and so concludes nothing. We might as well reason thus: many houses have been burnt by kilns, therefore we should use none; many ships have been castaway, therefore we should content ourselves with our home commodities, and not adventure mens lives at sea for those things which we might live without; some men have been undone by being advanced to high places, therefore we should refuse all preferment, etc.

Answer 3: The fruit of any public design is not to be discerned by the immediate success. It may appear in time that the former Plantations were all to good use.

Answer 4: There are great and fundamental errors in the former which are likely to be avoided in this, for:
1) their main end was carnal and not religious;
2) they used unfit instruments—a multitude of rude and misgoverned persons, the very scum of the land;
3) they did not establish a right form of government.

Objection V—It is attended with many and great difficulties.

Answer: So is every good action. The heathen could say *Ardua virtutis via*, and the way of God's kingdom, which is the best way in the world, is accompanied with most difficulties. Straight is the gate, and narrow is the way, that leadeth to life. Again, the difficulties are no other than such as many daily meet with, and such as God hath brought others well through them.

Objection VI—It is a work above the power of the undertakers.

Answer 1: The welfare of any body consists not so much in quantity as in a due proportion and disposition of parts. And we see other Plantations have subsisted diverse years and prospered from weaker means.

Answer 2: It is no wonder for great things to arise from small and contemptible beginnings—it hath often been seen in kingdoms and states, and may as well hold in towns and plantations. The Waldenses were scattered into the Alps and mountains of Piedmont by small companies, but they became famous Churches whereof some remain to this day, and it is certain that the Turks and Venetians and other states were weak in their beginnings.

Objection VII—The country affords no natural fortifications.

Answer: No more did Holland and many other places which had greater enemies and nearer at hand, and God doth use to place His people within the midst of perils, that they may trust in Him, and not the outward means of safety. So when He would choose a place to plant His only beloved people in, He seated them not in an island or another place fortified by nature, but in a plain country, beset with potent and bitter enemies round about, yet so long as they served Him and trusted in His help they were safe. So the Apostle Paul said of himself and his fellow laborers, that they were compassed with dangers on every side, and were daily under the sentence of death, that they might learn to trust in the living God.

Objection VIII—The place affords no comfortable means to the first inhabitants, and our breeding here at home has made us unfit for the hardship we are likely to endure there.

Answer 1: No place of itself has afforded sufficient to the first inhabitants. Such things as we stand in need of are usually supplied by God's blessing upon the wisdom and industry of Man, and whatsoever we stand in need of is treasured up in the earth by the Creator to be fetched thence by the sweat of our brows.

Answer 2: We must learn with Paul to want as well as to abound. If we have food and raiment (which are there to be had) we ought to be contented. The difference in the quality may a little displease us, but it cannot hurt us.

Answer 3: It may be that God will bring us by this means to repent of our former intemperance, and so cure us of that disease which sends many amongst us untimely to our graves and others to hell. So He carried the Israelites into the wilderness and made them forget the fleshpots of Egypt, which was some pinch to them at first, but He disposed it to their good in the end (Deu. 8: 3: 16).

Objection IX—We must look to be preserved by miracle if we subsist, and so we shall tempt God.

Answer 1: Those who walk under ordinary means of safety and supply do not tempt God, and such will our condition be in this Plantation, that the proposition cannot be denied. The assumption we prove thus: that place is as much secured from ordinary dangers as many in the civilized parts of the world, and we shall have as much provision beforehand as towns use to provide against siege or dearth, and sufficient means for raising a sufficient store to succeed that which is spent. If it be denied that we shall be as secure as other places, we answer that many of our sea towns and such as are upon the confines of enemies' countries in the continent, lie more open and nearer to danger than we shall. Though such towns have sometimes been burnt or despoiled, yet men tempt not God to dwell still in them; and though many houses in the country lie open to robbers and thieves (as many have found by sad experience), yet no man will say that those that dwell in those places must be preserved by miracle.

Answer 2: Though miracles be now ceased, yet men more expect a more than ordinary blessing from God upon all lawful means where the work is the Lord's, and He is sought in it according to His will. For it is usually with Him to increase or weaken the strength of the means as He is pleased or displeased with the instruments and the actions; else we must conclude that God hath left the government of the world and committed all power to His Creatures, and that the success of all things should wholly depend upon second causes.

Answer 3: We appeal to the judgment of soldiers if 500 men may not within one month raise a fortification which, with sufficient munition and victuals, may not make good against 3000 for many months, and yet without miracle.

Answer 4: We demand an instance of any Prince or state that has raised 3000 soldiers, and has victualed them for 6 or 8 months with shipping and munition answerable to invade a place so far distant as this is from any foreign enemy, and where they must run on hazard of repulse, and no booty or just title of sovereignty to allure them.

Objection X—If it succeed ill, it will raise a scandal upon our profession (*of our religion*).

Answer: It is no rule in philosophy, but much less in divinity, to judge the action by the success. The enterprise of the Israelites against Benjamin succeeded ill twice, yet the action was good and prospered in the end. The Counts of Beziers and Toulouse in France miscarried in the defense of a just cause of religion and hereditary right against the unjust violence of the Count of Montfort and the Pope's Legate; the Duke of Saxony and the Landgrave had ill success in their defense of the Gospel against Charles the Vth, wherein the Duke and his children lost their whole inheritance to this day;

the King of Denmark and other princes of this union had ill success in the defense of the Palatinate and the liberty of Germany, yet their profession suffered not with their persons, except it were with the adversaries of religion, and so it was no scandal.

1. *Discuss the types of individuals who would most likely be persuaded by these arguments to venture out to sea with the Massachusetts Bay Colony.*
2. *What, according to the author, is the reason for the failure ("ill success") of other colonies? How does he ease concerns about the hazards associated with the undertaking?*

2-5   John Winthrop, "A Model of Christian Charity" (1630)

Written in 1630 by the Puritan John Winthrop, A Model of Christian Charity sought to prepare the people that would eventually settle in the Massachusetts Bay Colony for the times ahead. Winthrop, a dedicated Puritan, would later become the first Governor of the Massachusetts Bay Colony and a founder of Boston.

God almighty in His most holy and wise providence hath so disposed of the condition of mankind, as in all times some must be rich, some poor, some high and eminent in power and dignity, others mean and in subjection.

Reason: First, to hold conformity with the rest of His works, being delighted to show forth the glory of His wisdom in the variety and difference of the creatures and the glory of His power, in ordering all these differences for the preservation and good of the whole.

Reason: Secondly, that He might have the more occasion to manifest the work of His spirit. First, upon the wicked in moderating and restraining them, so that the rich and mighty should not eat up the poor, nor the poor and despised rise up against their superiors and shake off their yoke. Secondly, in the regenerate in exercising His graces in them, as in the great ones, their love, mercy, gentleness, temperance, etc., in the poor and inferior sort, their faith, patience, obedience, etc.

Reason: Thirdly, that every man might have need of other, and from hence they might all be knit more nearly together in the bond of brotherly affection. From hence it appears plainly that no man is made more honorable than another, or more wealthy, etc., out of any particular and singular respect to himself, but for the glory of his creator and the common good of the creature, man.

Thus stands the cause between God and us. We are entered into covenant with Him for this work, we have taken out a commission, the Lord hath given us leave to draw our own articles we have professed to enterprise these actions upon these and these ends, we have hereupon besought Him of favor and blessing. Now if the Lord shall please to hear us, and bring us in peace to the place we desire, then hath He ratified this covenant and sealed our commission, [and] will expect a strict performance of the articles contained in it, but if we shall neglect the observations of these articles which are the ends we have propounded, and dissembling with our God, shall fall to embrace this present world and prosecute our carnal intentions seeking great things for ourselves and our

posterity, the Lord will surely break out in wrath against us, be revenged of such a perjured people, and make us know the price of the breach of such a covenant.

Now the only way to avoid this shipwreck and to provide for our posterity is to follow the counsel of Micah, to do justly, to love mercy, to walk humbly with our God. For this end we must be knit together in this work as one man, we must entertain each other in brotherly affection, we must be willing to abridge ourselves of our superfluities for the supply of others' necessities, we must uphold a familiar commerce together in all meekness, gentleness, patience, and liberality, we must delight in each other, make others' conditions our own, rejoice together, mourn together, labor and suffer together, always having before our eyes our commission and community in the work, our community as members of the same body So shall we keep the unity of the spirit in the bond of peace. The Lord will be our God and delight in all our ways, so that we shall see much more of His wisdom, power, goodness, and truth than formerly we have been acquainted with. We shall find that the God of Israel is among us, when ten of us shall be able to resist a thousand of our enemies, when He shall make us a praise and glory, that men shall say of succeeding plantations, the Lord make it like that of New England. For we must consider that we shall be as a city upon a hill, the eyes of all people are upon us. So that if we shall deal falsely with our God in this work we have undertaken and so cause Him to withdraw His present help from us, we shall be made a story and byword throughout the world, we shall open the mouths of enemies to speak evil of the ways of God and all professors for God's sake, we shall shame the faces of many of God's worthy servants, and cause their prayers to be turned into curses upon us till we be consumed out of the good land whither we are going. And to shut up this discourse with that exhortation of Moses, that faithful servant of the Lord in His last farewell to Israel, Deut. 30., Beloved there is now set before us life and good, death and evil, in that we are commanded this day to love the Lord our God, and to love one another, to walk in His ways and to keep His commandments and His ordinance, and His laws, and the articles of our covenant with Him that we may live and be multiplied, and that the Lord our God my bless us in the land whither we go to possess it. But if our hearts shall turn away so that we will not obey, but shall be seduced and worship other Gods, our pleasures, our profits, and serve them, it is propounded unto us this day we shall surely perish out of the good land whither we pass over this vast sea to possess it. Therefore let us choose life, that we, and our seed, may live, and by obeying His voice, and cleaving to Him, for He is our life and our prosperity.

1. *Summarize the reasoning given by John Winthrop for why humankind is separated into economic and political classes*
2. *According to Winthrop, despite class divisions (or perhaps because of them) how should humans treat each other?*
3. *What does Winthrop mean by suggesting that New England is like a "city on a hill"? What does he feel is the responsibility of all New Englanders?*

2-6   The Taking of the Fort at Mystic: A Brief History of the Pequot Wark

John Mason was the "chief captain" and commander of Connecticut militia forces in the Pequot War. He was an army officer in England before emigrating to Massachusetts in 1630 and then to Windsor, Connecticut in 1635. When the Pequot threatened to wipe out the English settlements on the Connecticut River, he and John Underhill led an expedition against them. On May 26, 1637, Mason and Underhill attacked the Pequot village located near New Haven and killed over 500 Indians—virtually destroying the tribe.

> **Source:** Mason, John. "The Taking of the Fort at Mystic" in *A Library of American Literature from the Earliest Settlement to the Present Time*. Edmund Clarence Stedman and Ellen MacKay Hutchinson, editors. 11 vols. (New York: Charles L. Webster and Company, 1890.) 1: 180–184.
> The Society of Colonial Wars in the State of Connecticut
> http://www.colonialwarsct.org/1637_john_mason.htm

OUR council, all of them except the captain, were at a stand, and could not judge it meet to sail to Narragansett: and indeed there was a very strong ground for it, our commission limiting us to land our men in Pequot River; we had also the same order by a letter of instruction sent us to Saybrook. But Captain Mason apprehending an exceeding great hazard in so doing, for the reasons forementioned, as also some other which I shall forbear to trouble you with, did therefore earnestly desire Mr. Stone that he would commend our condition to the Lord, that night, to direct how and in what manner we should demean ourselves in that respect, he being our chaplain and lying aboard our pink, the captain on shore. In the morning very early Mr. Stone came ashore to the captain's chamber, and told him, he had done as he had desired, and was fully satisfied to sail for Narragansett. Our council was then called, and the several reasons alleged. In fine, we all agreed with one accord to sail for Narragansett, which the next morning we put in execution.

I declare not this to encourage any soldiers to act beyond their commission, or contrary to it; for in so doing they run a double hazard. There was a great commander in Belgia who did the states great service in taking a city; but by going beyond his commission lost his life. His name was Grubbendunk. But if a war be managed duly by judgment and discretion as is requisite, the shows are many times contrary to what they seem to pursue. Whereof the more an enterprise is dissembled and kept secret, the more facile to put in execution; as the proverb, "The farthest way about is sometimes the nearest way home." I shall make bold to present this as my present thoughts in this case: In matters of war, those who are both able and faithful should be improved; and then bind them not up into too narrow a compass. For it is not possible for the wisest and ablest senator to foresee all accidents and occurrences that fall out in the management and pursuit of a war; nay, although possibly he might be trained up in military affairs; and truly much less can he have any great knowledge who hath had but little experience therein. What shall I say? God led his people through many difficulties and turnings; yet by more than an ordinary hand of providence he brought them to Canaan at last.

On Friday morning we set sail for Narragansett Bay, and on Saturday toward evening we arrived at our desired port, there we kept the Sabbath.

On the Monday the wind blew so hard at north-west that we could not go on shore; as also on the Tuesday until sunset; at which time Captain Mason landed and marched up to the place of the chief sachem's residence; who told the sachem, "That we had not an opportunity to acquaint him with our coming armed in his country sooner; yet not doubting but it would be well accepted by him, there being love betwixt himself and us; well knowing also that the Pequots and themselves were enemies, and that he could not be unacquainted with those intolerable wrongs and injuries these Pequots had lately done unto the English; and that we were now come, God assisting, to avenge ourselves upon them; and that we did only desire free passage through his country." Who returned us this answer, "That he did accept of our coming, and did also approve of our design; only he thought our numbers were too weak to deal with the enemy, who were (as he said) very great captains and men skilful in war." Thus he spake somewhat slighting of us.

On the Wednesday morning, we marched from thence to a place called Nayanticke, it being about eighteen or twenty miles distant, where another of those Narragansett sachems lived in a fort; it being a frontier to the Pequots. They carried very proudly towards us; not permitting any of us to come into their fort.

We beholding their carriage and the falsehood of Indians, and fearing lest they might discover us to the enemy, especially they having many times some of their near relations among their greatest foes; we therefore caused a strong guard to be set about their fort, giving charge that no Indian should be suffered to pass in or out. We also informed the Indians, that none of them should stir out of the fort upon peril of their lives: so as they would not suffer any of us to come into their fort, so we would not suffer any of them to go out of the fort.

There we quartered that night, the Indians not offering to stir out all the while.

In the morning there came to us several of Miantomo's his men, who told us, they were come to assist us in our expedition, which encouraged divers Indians of that place to engage also; who suddenly gathering: into a ring, one by one, making solemn protestations how gallantly they would demean themselves, and how many men they would kill.

On the Thursday about eight of the clock in the morning, we marched thence towards Pequot, with about five hundred Indians; but through the heat of the weather and want of provisions some of our men fainted. And having marched about twelve miles, we came to Pawcatuck River, at a ford where our Indians told us the Pequots did usually fish; there making a halt, we stayed some small time, the Narragansett Indians manifesting great fear, insomuch that many of them returned, although they had frequently despised us, saying that we durst not look upon a Pequot, but themselves would perform great things; though we had often told them that we came on purpose and were resolved, God assisting, to see the Pequots, and to fight with them, before we returned, though we perished. I then enquired of Onkos, what he thought the Indians would do? Who said, The Narragansetts would all leave us, but as for himself he would never leave us: and so it proved. For which expressions and some other speeches of his, I shall never forget him. Indeed he was a great friend, and did great service.

And after we had refreshed ourselves with our mean commons, we marched about three miles, and came to a field which had lately been planted with Indian corn. There we made another halt, and called our council, supposing we drew near to the enemy: and being informed by the Indians that the enemy had two forts almost impregnable; but we were not at all discouraged, but rather animated, insomuch that we were resolved to assault both their forts at once. But understanding that one of them was so remote that we could not come up with it before midnight, though we marched hard; whereat we were much grieved, chiefly because the greatest and bloodiest sachem there resided, whose name was Sassacous; we were then constrained, being exceedingly spent in our march with extreme heat and want of necessaries, to accept of the nearest.

We then marching on in a silent manner, the Indians that remained fell all into the rear, who formerly kept the van (being possessed with great fear); we continued our march till about one hour in the night: and coming to a little swamp between two hills, there we pitched our little camp; much wearied with hard travel, keeping great silence, supposing we were very near the fort; as our Indians informed us; which proved otherwise. The rocks were our pillows; yet rest was pleasant. The night proved comfortable, being clear and moonlight. We appointed our guards and placed our sentinels at some distance; who heard the enemy singing at the fort, who continued that strain until midnight, with great insulting and rejoicing, as we were afterwards informed. They seeing our pinnaces sail by them some days before, concluded we were afraid of them and durst not come near them; the burden of their song tending to that purpose.

In the morning, we awaking and seeing it very light, supposing it had been day, and so we might have lost our opportunity, having purposed to make our assault before day, roused the men with all expedition, and briefly commended ourselves and design to God, thinking immediately to go to the assault; the Indians showing us a path, told us that it led directly to the fort. We held on our march about two miles, wondering that we came not to the fort, and fearing we might be deluded. But seeing corn newly planted at the foot of a great hill, supposing the fort was not far off, a champaign country being round about us, then making a stand, gave the word for some of the Indians to come up. At length Onkos and one Wequash appeared. We demanded of them, Where was the fort? They answered, On the top of that hill. Then we demanded, Where were the rest of the Indians? They answered, Behind, exceedingly afraid. We wished them to tell the rest of their fellows, That they should by no means fly, but stand at what distance they pleased, and see whether Englishmen would now fight or not. Then Captain Underhill came up, who marched in the rear; and commending ourselves to God, divided our men, there being two entrances into the fort, intending to enter both at once; Captain Mason leading up to that on the north-east side, who approaching within one rod, heard a dog bark and an Indian crying "Owanux! Owanux!" which is "Englishmen! Englishmen!" We called up our forces with all expedition, gave fire upon them through the palisado; the Indians being in a dead, indeed their last sleep. Then we wheeling of fell upon the main entrance, which was blocked up with bushes about breast high, over which the captain passed, intending to make good the entrance, encouraging the rest to follow. Lieutenant Seeley endeavored to enter; but being somewhat cumbered, stepped back and pulled out the bushes and so entered, and with him about sixteen men. We had formerly concluded to destroy them by the sword and save the plunder.

Whereupon Captain Mason seeing no Indians, entered a wigwam; where he was beset with many Indians, waiting all opportunities to lay hands on him, but could not prevail. At length William Heydon espying the breach in the wigwam, supposing some English might be there, entered; but in his entrance fell over a dead Indian; but speedily recovering himself, the Indians some fled, others crept under their beds. The captain going out of the wigwam saw many Indians in the lane or street; he making towards them, they fled, were pursued to the end of the lane, where they were met by Edward Pattison, Thomas Barber, with some others; where seven of them were slain, as they said. The captain facing about, marched a slow pace up the lane he came down, perceiving himself very much out of breath; and coming to the other end near the place where he first entered, saw two soldiers standing close to the palisado with their swords pointed to the ground. The captain told them that we should never kill them after that manner. The captain also said, We must bum them; and immediately stepping into the wigwam where he had been before, brought out a fire-brand, and putting it into the mats with which they were covered, set the wigwams on fire. Lieutenant Thomas Bull and Nicholas Omsted beholding, came up; and when it was thoroughly kindled, the Indians ran as men most dreadfully amazed.

And indeed such a dreadful terror did the Almighty let fall upon their spirits, that they would fly from us and run into the very flames, where many of them perished. And when the fort was thoroughly fired, command was given, that all should fall of and surround the fort; which was readily attended by all; only one Arthur Smith being so wounded that he could not move out of the place, who was happily espied by Lieutenant bull, and by him rescued.

The fire was kindled on the north-east side to windward; which did swiftly overrun the fort, to the extreme amazement of the enemy, and great rejoicing of ourselves. Some of them climbing to the top of the palisado; others of them running into the very flames; many of them gathering to windward, lay pelting at us with their arrows; and we repaid them with our small shot. Others of the stoutest issued forth, as we did guess, to the number of forty, who perished by the sword.

What I have formerly said, is according to my own knowledge, there being sufficient living testimony to every particular.

But in reference to Captain Underhill and his parties acting in this assault, I can only intimate as we were informed by some of themselves immediately after the fight. Thus they marching up to the entrance on the south-west side, there made some pause; a valiant, resolute gentleman, one Mr. Hedge, stepping towards the gate, saying, "If we may not enter, wherefore came we here?" and immediately endeavored to enter; but was opposed by a sturdy Indian which did impede his entrance; but the Indian being slain by himself and Sergeant Davis, Mr. Hedge entered the fort with some others; but the fort being on fire, the smoke and flames were so violent that they were constrained to desert the fort.

Thus were they now at their wits' end, who not many hours before exalted themselves in their great pride, threatening and resolving the utter ruin and destruction of all the English, exulting and rejoicing with songs and dances. But God was above them, who laughed his enemies and the enemies of his people to scorn, making them as a fiery oven. Thus were the stout-hearted spoiled, having slept their last sleep, and none of their men could find their hands. Thus did the Lord judge among the heathen, filling the place with dead bodies!

And here we may see the just judgment of God, in sending even the very night before this assault, one hundred and fifty men from their other fort, to join with them of that place, who were designed as some of themselves reported to go forth against the English, at that very instant when this heavy stroke came upon them, where they perished with their fellows. So that the mischief they intended to us, came upon their own pate. They were taken in their own snare, and we through mercy escaped. And thus in little more than one hour's space was their impregnable fort with themselves utterly destroyed, to the number of six or seven hundred, as some of themselves confessed. There were only seven taken captive, and about seven escaped.

Of the English, there were two slain outright, and about twenty wounded. Some fainted by reason of the sharpness of the weather, it being a cool morning, and the want of such comforts and necessaries as were needful in such a case; especially our chirurgeon was much wanting, whom we left with our barks in Narragansett Bay, who had order there to remain until the night before our intended assault.

And thereupon grew many difficulties: Our provision and munition near spent; we in the enemy's country, who did far exceed us in number, being much enraged; all our Indians, except Onkos, deserting us; our pinnacles at a great distance from us, and when they would come we were uncertain.

But as we were consulting what course to take, it pleased God to discover our vessels to us before a fair gale of wind, sailing into Pequot harbor, to our great rejoicing.

1. *Describe John Mason's feelings about this military operation and the Pequot in general. Was he simply doing his job or was he carrying out a vendetta?*
2. *Do the methods and practices of the Connecticut militia against the Pequot remind you of other, more recent, military operations? Explain why.*

2-7 The Trial of Anne Hutchinson (1638)

Anne Hutchinson, the articulate and resolute wife of a prominent New England merchant, was placed on trial before the General Court in 1637 for challenging the authority of the ministry and promoting individualism—provocative issues in Puritan society. During the first two days of examination she defended her position well, frustrating the best efforts of Governor Winthrop and others to convict her. Finally, her claim of direct divine inspiration brought her a conviction on the grounds of blasphemy. She was banished from the colony in 1638.

> **Source:** *The American Colonist's Library, Primary Source Documents Pertaining to Early American History,*
> http://personal.pitnet.net/primarysources/hutchinson.html

MR. [JOHN] WINTHROP, GOVERNOR: Mrs Hutchinson, you are called here as one of those that have troubled the peace of the commonwealth and the churches here; you are known to be a woman that hath had a great share in the promoting and divulging of those opinions that are the cause of this trouble, and to be nearly joined not only in affinity and affection with some of those the court had taken notice of and passed censure upon, but you have spoken divers things, as we have been informed, very prejudicial to the honour of the churches and ministers thereof, and you have maintained a meeting and an assembly in your house that hath been condemned by the general assembly as a thing not tolerable nor comely in the sight of God nor fitting for your sex, and notwithstanding that was cried down you have continued the same. Therefore we have thought good to send for you to understand how things are, that if you be in an erroneous way we may reduce you that so you may become a profitable member here among us. Otherwise if you be obstinate in your course that then the court may take such course that you may trouble us no further. Therefore I would intreat you to express whether you do assent and hold in practice to those opinions and factions that have been handled in court already, that is to say, whether you do not justify Mr. Wheelwright's sermon and the petition.

MRS. HUTCHINSON: I am called here to answer before you but I hear no things laid to my charge.

GOV.: I have told you some already and more I can tell you.

MRS. H.: Name one, Sir.

GOV.: Have I not named some already?

MRS. H.: What have I said or done?

GOV.: Why for your doings, this you did harbor and countenance those that are parties in this faction that you have heard of.

MRS. H.: That's matter of conscience, Sir.

GOV.: Your conscience you must keep, or it must be kept for you.

MRS. H.: Must not I then entertain the saints because I must keep my conscience.

GOV.: Say that one brother should commit felony or treason and come to his brother's house, if he knows him guilty and conceals him he is guilty of the same. It is his conscience to entertain him, but if his conscience comes into act in giving countenance and entertainment to him that hath broken the law he is guilty too. So if you do countenance those that are transgressors of the law you are in the same fact.

MRS. H.: What law do they transgress?

GOV.: The law of God and of the state.

MRS. H.: In what particular?

GOV.: Why in this among the rest, whereas the Lord doth say honour thy father and thy mother.

MRS. H.: Ey Sir in the Lord.

GOV.: This honour you have broke in giving countenance to them.

MRS. H.: In entertaining those did I entertain them against any act (for there is the thing) or what God has appointed?

GOV.: You knew that Mr. Wheelwright did preach this sermon and those that countenance him in this do break a law.

MRS. H.: What law have I broken?

GOV.: Why the fifth commandment.

MRS. H.: I deny that for he [Mr. Wheelwright] saith in the Lord.

GOV.: You have joined with them in the faction.

MRS. H.: In what faction have I joined with them?

GOV.: In presenting the petition.

MRS. H.: Suppose I had set my hand to the petition. What then?

GOV.: You saw that case tried before.

MRS. H.: But I had not my hand to [not signed] the petition.

GOV.: You have councelled them.

MRS. H.: Wherein?

GOV.: Why in entertaining them.

MRS. H.: What breach of law is that, Sir?

GOV.: Why dishonouring the commonwealth.

MRS. H.: But put the case, Sir, that I do fear the Lord and my parents. May not I entertain them that fear the Lord because my parents will not give me leave?

GOV.: If they be the fathers of the commonwealth, and they of another religion, if you entertain them then you dishonour your parents and are justly punishable.

MRS. H.: If I entertain them, as they have dishonoured their parents I do.

GOV.: No but you by countenancing them above others put honor upon them.

MRS. H.: I may put honor upon them as the children of God and as they do honor the Lord.

GOV.: We do not mean to discourse with those of your sex but only this: you so adhere unto them and do endeavor to set forward this faction and so you do dishonour us.

MRS. H.: I do acknowledge no such thing. Neither do I think that I ever put any dishonour upon you.

GOV.: Why do you keep such a meeting at your house as you do every week upon a set day?

MRS. H.: It is lawful for me to do so, as it is all your practices, and can you find a warrant for yourself and condemn me for the same thing? The ground of my taking it up was, when I first came to this land because I did not go to such meetings as those were, it was presently reported that I did not allow of such meetings but held them unlawful and therefore in that regard they said I was proud and did despise all ordinances. Upon that a friend came unto me and told me of it and I to prevent such aspersions took it up, but it was in practice before I came. Therefore I was not the first.

GOV.: . . . By what warrant do you continue such a course?

MRS. H.: I conceive there lies a clear rule in Titus that the elder women should instruct the younger and then I must have a time wherein I must do it.

GOV.: All this I grant you, I grant you a time for it, but what is this to the purpose that you Mrs. Hutchinson must call a company together from their callings to come to be taught of you?. . .

MRS. H.: If you look upon the rule in Titus it is a rule to me. If you convince me that it is no rule I shall yield.

GOV.: You know that there is no rule that crosses another, but this rule crosses that in the Corinthians. But you must take it in this sense that elder women must instruct the younger about their business and to love their husbands and not to make them to clash.. . .

MRS. H.: Will it please you to answer me this and to give me a rule for then I will willingly submit to any truth. If any come to my house to be instructed in the ways of God what rule have I to put them away? . . . . Do you think it not lawful for me to teach women and why do you call me to teach the court?

GOV.: We do not call you to teach the court but to lay open yourself. . . .

[They continue to argue over what rule she had broken]

GOV.: Your course is not to be suffered for. Besides that we find such a course as this to be greatly prejudicial to the state. Besides the occasion that it is to seduce many honest persons that are called to those meetings and your opinions and your opinions being known to be different from the word of God may seduce many simple souls that resort unto you. Besides that the occasion which hath come of late hath come from none but such as have frequented your meetings, so that now they are flown off from magistrates and ministers and since they have come to you. And besides that it will not well stand with the commonwealth that families should be neglected for so many neighbors and dames and so much time spent. We see no rule of God for this. We see not that any should have authority to set up any other exercises besides what authority hath already set up and so what hurt comes of this you will be guilty of and we for suffering you.

MRS. H.: Sir, I do not believe that to be so.

GOV.: Well, we see how it is. We must therefore put it away from you or restrain you from maintaining this course.

Mrs H. If you have a rule for it from God's word you may.

GOV.: We are your judges, and not you ours and we must compel you to it.

MRS. H.: If it please you by authority to put it down I will freely let you for I am subject to your authority.. . .

DEPUTY GOVERNOR, THOMAS DUDLEY: I would go a little higher with Mrs. Hutchinson. About three years ago we were all in peace. Mrs Hutchinson, from that time she came hath made a disturbance, and some that came over with her in the ship did inform me what she was as soon as she was landed. I being then in place dealt with the pastor and teacher of Boston and desired them to enquire of her, and then I was satisfied that she held nothing different from us. But within half a year after, she had vented divers of her strange opinions and had made parties in the country, and at length it comes that Mr. Cotton and Mr. Vane were of her judgment, but Mr. Cotton had cleared himself that he was not of that mind. But now it appears by this woman's meeting that Mrs. Hutchinson hath so forestalled the minds of many by their resort to her meeting that now she hath a potent party in the country. Now if all these things have endangered us as from that foundation and if she in particular hath disparaged all our ministers in the land that they have preached a covenant of works, and only Mr. Cotton a covenant of grace, why this is not to be suffered, and therefore being driven to the foundation and it being found that Mrs. Hutchinson is she that hath depraved all the ministers and hath been the cause of what is fallen out, why we must take away the foundation and the building will fall.

MRS. H.: I pray, Sir, prove it that I said they preached nothing but a covenant of works.

DEP. GOV.: Nothing but a covenant of works. Why a Jesuit may preach truth sometimes.

MRS. H.: Did I ever say they preached a covenant of works then?

DEP. GOV.: If they do not preach a covenant of grace clearly, then they preach a covenant of works.

MRS. H.: No, Sir. One may preach a covenant of grace more clearly than another, so I said.. . . .

DEP. GOV.: When they do preach a covenant of works do they preach truth?

MRS. H.: Yes, Sir. But when they preach a covenant of works for salvation, that is not truth.

DEP. GOV.: I do but ask you this: when the ministers do preach a covenant of works do they preach a way of salvation?

MRS. H.: I did not come hither to answer questions of that sort.

DEP. GOV.: Because you will deny the thing.

MRS. H.: Ey, but that is to be proved first.

DEP. GOV.: I will make it plain that you did say that the ministers did preach a covenant of works.

MRS. H.: I deny that.

DEP. GOV.: And that you said they were not able ministers of the New Testament, but Mr. Cotton only.

MRS. H.: If ever I spake that I proved it by God's word.

COURT: Very well, very well.

MRS. H.: If one shall come unto me in private, and desire me seriously to tell them what I thought of such an one, I must either speak false or true in my answer.

DEP. GOV.: Likewise I will prove this that you said the gospel in the letter and words holds forth nothing but a covenant of works and that all that do not hold as you do are in a covenant of works.

MRS. H.: I deny this for if I should so say I should speak against my own judgment. . . .

MR. HUGH PETERS: That which concerns us to speak unto, as yet we are sparing in, unless the court command us to speak, then we shall answer to Mrs. Hutchinson notwithstanding our brethren are very unwilling to answer.

[The Governor says to do so. Six ministers then testify to the particular charges and that she was "not only difficult in her opinions, but also of an intemperate spirit"]

MR HUGH PETERS: . . . . [I asked her] What difference do you conceive to be between your teacher and us?. . . Briefly, she told me there was a wide and broad difference. . . . He preaches the covenant of grace and you the covenant of works, and that you are not able ministers of the New Testament and know no more than the apostles did before the resurrection of Christ. I did then put it to her, What do you conceive of such a brother? She answered he had not the seal of the spirit.

MRS. H.: If our pastor would shew his writings you should see what I said, and that many things are not so as is reported.

MR. WILSON: . . . what is written [here now] I will avouch.

MR. WELD: [agrees that Peters related Hutchinson's words accurately]

MR. PHILLIPS: [agrees that Peters related Hutchinson's words accurately and added] Then I asked her of myself (being she spake rashly of them all) because she never heard me at all. She likewise said that we were not able ministers of the New Testament and her reason was because we were not sealed.

MR. SIMMES: Agrees that Peters related Hutchinson's words accurately

MR. SHEPHARD: Also to Same.

MR. ELIOT: [agrees that Peters related Hutchinson's words accurately]

DEP. GOV.: I called these witnesses and you deny them. You see they have proved this and you deny this, but it is clear. You say they preached a covenant of works and that they were not able ministers of the New Testament; now there are two other things that you did affirm which were that the scriptures in the letter of them held forth nothing but a covenant of works and likewise that those that were under a covenant of works cannot be saved.

MRS. H.: Prove that I said so.

GOV.: Did you say so?

MRS. H.: No, Sir, it is your conclusion.

DEP. GOV.: What do I do charging of you if you deny what is so fully proved?

GOV.: Here are six undeniable ministers who say it is true and yet you deny that you did say that they preach a covenant of works and that they were not able ministers of the gospel, and it appears plainly that you have spoken it, and whereas you say that it was drawn from you in a way of friendship, you did profess then that it was out of conscience that you spake.. . .

MRS. H.: . . . . They thought that I did conceive there was a difference between them and Mr. Cotton. . . . I might say they might preach a covenant of works as did the apostles, but to preach a covenant of works and to be under a covenant of works is another business.

DEP. GOV.: There have been six witnesses to prove this and yet you deny it. [and then he mentions a seventh, Mr. Nathaniel Ward]

MRS. H.: I acknowledge using the words of the apostle to the Corinthians unto him, [Mr. Ward] that they that were ministers of the letter and not the spirit did preach a covenant of works.

GOV.: Mrs. Hutchinson, the court you see hath laboured to bring you to acknowledge the error of your way that so you might be reduced, the time grows late, we shall therefore give you a little more time to consider of it and therefore desire that you attend the court again in the morning. [The next morning]

GOV.: We proceeded . . . as far as we could . . . There were divers things laid to her charge: her ordinary meetings about religious exercises, her speeches in derogation of the ministers among us, and the weakening of the hands and hearts of the people towards them. Here was sufficient proof made of that which she was accused of, in that point concerning the ministers and their ministry, as that they did preach a covenant of works when others did preach a covenant of grace, and that they were not able ministers of the New Testament, and that they had not the seal of the spirit, and this was spoken not as was pretended out of private conference, but out of conscience and warrant from scripture alleged the fear of man is a snare and seeing God had given her a calling to it she would freely speak. Some other speeches she used, as that the letter of the scripture held forth a covenant of works, and this is offered to be proved by probable grounds.. . .

Controversy—should the witnesses should be recalled and made swear an oath, as Mrs. Hutchinson desired, is resolved against doing so

GOV.: I see no necessity of an oath in this thing seeing it is true and the substance of the matter confirmed by divers, yet that all may be satisfied, if the elders will take an oath they shall have it given them.. . .

MRS. H.: After that they have taken an oath I will make good what I say.

GOV.: Let us state the case, and then we may know what to do. That which is laid to Mrs. Hutchinson charge is that, that she hath traduced the magistrates and ministers of this jurisdiction, that she hath said the ministers preached a covenant of works and Mr. Cotton a covenant of grace, and that they were not able ministers of the gospel, and she excuses it that she made it a private conference and with a promise of secrecy, &c. Now this is charged upon her, and they therefore sent for her seeing she made it her table talk, and then she said the fear of man was a snare and therefore she would not be affeared of them.. . .

DEP. GOV.: Let her witnesses be called.

GOV.: Who be they?

MRS. H.: Mr. Leveret and our teacher and Mr. Coggeshall.

GOV.: Mr. Coggeshall was not present.

Mr. Coggeshall: Yes, but I was. Only I desired to be silent till I should be called.

GOV.: Will you, Mr. Coggeshall, say that she did not say so?

MR. COGGESHALL: Yes, I dare say that she did not say all that which they lay against her.

MR. PETERS: How dare you look into the court to say such a word?

MR. COGGESHALL: Mr. Peters takes upon him to forbid me. I shall be silent.

MR. STOUGHTON [ASSISTANT OF THE COURT]: Ey, but she intended this that they say.

GOV.: Well, Mr. Leveret, what were the words? I pray, speak.

MR. LEVERET: To my best remembrance when the elders did send for her, Mr. Peters did with much vehemency and intreaty urge her to tell what difference there was between Mr. Cotton and them, and upon his urging of her she said "The fear of man is a snare, but they that trust upon the Lord shall be safe." And being asked wherein the difference was, she answered that they did not preach a covenant of grace so clearly as Mr. Cotton did, and she gave this reason of it: because that as the apostles were for a time without the spirit so until they had received the witness of the spirit they could not preach a covenant of grace so clearly.

GOV.: Don't you remember that she said they were not able ministers of the New Testament?

MRS. H.: Mr. Weld and I had an hour's discourse at the window and then I spake that, if I spake it.. . .

GOV.: Mr Cotton, the court desires that you declare what you do remember of the conference which was at the time and is now in question.

MR. COTTON: I did not think I should be called to bear witness in this cause and therefore did not labor to call to remembrance what was done; but the greatest passage that took impression upon me was to this purpose. The elders spake that they had heard that she had spoken some condemning words of their ministry, and among other things they did first pray her to answer wherein she thought their ministry did differ from mine. How the comparison sprang I am ignorant, but sorry I was that any comparison should be between me and my brethren and uncomfortable it was. She told them to this purpose that they did not hold forth a covenant of grace as I did. But wherein did we differ? Why she said that they did not hold forth the seal of the spirit as he doth. Where is the difference there? Say they, why saith she, speaking to one or other of them, I know not to whom. You preach of the seal of the spirit upon a work and he upon free grace without a work or without respect to a work; he preaches the seal of the spirit upon free grace and you upon a work. I told her I was very sorry that she put comparisons between my ministry and theirs, for she had said more than I could myself, and rather I had that she had put us in fellowship with them and not have made that discrepancy. She said, she found the difference.. . .

This was the sum of the difference, nor did it seem to be so ill taken as it is and our brethren did say also that they would not so easily believe reports as they had done and withal mentioned that they would speak no more of it, some of them did; and afterwards some of them did say they were less satisfied than before. And I must say that I did not find her saying that they were under a covenant of works, nor that she said they did preach a covenant of works.

[more back and forth between Rev. John Cotton, trying to defend Mrs. Hutchinson, and Mr. Peters, about exactly what Mrs. Hutchinson said]

MRS. H.: If you please to give me leave I shall give you the ground of what I know to be true. Being much troubled to see the falseness of the constitution of the Church of England, I had like to have turned Separatist. Whereupon I kept a day of solemn humiliation and pondering of the thing; this scripture was brought unto me—he that denies Jesus Christ to be come in the flesh is antichrist. This I considered of and in considering found that the papists did not deny him to be come in the flesh, nor we did not deny him—who then was antichrist? Was the Turk antichrist only? The Lord knows that I could not open scripture; he must by his prophetical office open it unto me. So after that being unsatisfied in the thing, the Lord was pleased to bring this scripture out of the Hebrews. he that denies the testament denies the testator, and in this did open unto me and give me to see that those which did not teach the new covenant had the spirit of antichrist, and upon this he did discover the ministry unto me; and ever since, I bless the Lord, he hath let me see which was the clear ministry and which the wrong. Since that time I confess I have been more choice and he hath left me to distinguish between the voice of my beloved and the voice of Moses, the voice of John the Baptist and the voice of antichrist, for all those voices are spoken of in scripture. Now if you do condemn me for speaking what in my conscience I know to be truth I must commit myself unto the Lord.

MR. NOWEL [ASSISTANT TO THE COURT]: How do you know that was the spirit?

MRS. H.: How did Abraham know that it was God that bid him offer his son, being a breach of the sixth commandment?

DEP. GOV.: By an immediate voice.

MRS. H.: So to me by an immediate revelation.

DEP. GOV.: How! an immediate revelation.

MRS. H.: By the voice of his own spirit to my soul. I will give you another scripture, Jer[emiah] 46: 27–28—out of which the Lord showed me what he would do for me and the rest of his servants. But after he was pleased to reveal himself to me I did presently, like Abraham, run to Hagar. And after that he did let me see the atheism of my own heart, for which I begged of the Lord that it might not remain in my heart, and being thus, he did show me this (a twelvemonth after) which I told you of before.. . . . Therefore, I desire you to look to it, for you see this scripture fulfilled this day and therefore I desire you as you tender the Lord and the church and commonwealth to consider and look what you do. You have power over my body but the Lord Jesus hath power over my body and soul; and assure yourselves thus much, you do as much as in you lies to put the Lord Jesus Christ from you, and if you go on in this course you begin, you will bring a curse upon you and your posterity, and the mouth of the Lord hath spoken it.

DEP. GOV.: What is the scripture she brings?

MR. STOUGHTON [ASSISTANT TO THE COURT]: Behold I turn away from you.

MRS. H.: But now having seen him which is invisible I fear not what man can do unto me.

GOV.: Daniel was delivered by miracle; do you think to be deliver'd so too?

MRS. H.: I do here speak it before the court. I look that the Lord kshould deliver me by his providence.. . . [because God had said to her] though I should meet with affliction, yet I am the same God that delivered Daniel out of the lion's den, I will also deliver thee.

MR. HARLAKENDEN [ASSISTANT TO THE COURT]: I may read scripture and the most glorious hypocrite may read them and yet go down to hell.

MRS. H.: It may be so.. . .

GOV.: I am persuaded that the revelation she brings forth is delusion.

[The trial text here reads:] All the court but some two or three ministers cry out, we all believe it—we all believe it. [Mrs. Hutchinson was found guilty]

GOV.: The court hath already declared themselves satisfied concerning the things you hear, and concerning the trouble-someness of her spirit and the danger of her course amongst us, which is not to be suffered. Therefore if it be the mind of the court that Mrs. Hutchinson for these things that appear before us is unfit for our society, and if it be the mind of the court that she shall be banished out of our liberties and imprisoned till she be sent away, let them hold up their hands.

[All but three did so]

GOV.: Mrs. Hutchinson, the sentence of the court you hear is that you are banished from out of our jurisdiction as being a woman not fit for our society, and are to be imprisoned till the court shall send you away.

MRS. H.: I desire to know wherefore I am banished?

GOV.: Say no more. The court knows wherefore and is satisfied.

1. How was Anne Hutchinson able to frustrate the best efforts of the court to find her guilty during the early stages of the trial?

2. Aggravating the situation at the General Court was the fact that the authority of the ministry was being challenged by a woman. How do you think other women of similar status in New England society viewed Anne Hutchinson? Was she inspirational or foolish?

2-8 A Jesuit Priest Describes New Amsterdam (1642)

Isaac Jogues, a French missionary who had traveled extensively among the Hurons in New France. He was taken prisoner by the Iroquois on August 3, 1642, tortured, and subjected to thirteen months of slavery. The Dutch made efforts to free him and finally persuaded him to take refuge in a ship bound for New Amsterdam. He was the first Catholic priest to ever visit Manhattan Island. Jogues later returned to Canada in an attempt to negotiate peace with the Iroquois. He was captured, tortured and eventually decapitated. (Isaac Jogues was canonized by Pope Pius XI on June 29, 1930.)

Source: *New Netherlands in 1644*, by Rev. Isaac Jogues, S.J.
http://www.lihistory.com/

New Holland which the Dutch call in Latin *Novum Belgium*, in their own language Nieuw Nederland, that is to say, New Low Countries, is situated between Virginia and New England. The mouth of the river called by some Nassau river or the great North river (to distinguish it from another which they call the South river) and which in some maps that I have recently seen is also called, I think, River Maurice, is at 4030'. Its channel is deep, fit for the largest ships that ascend to Manhattes Island, which is seven leagues in circuit, and on which there is a fort to serve as the commencement of a town to be built there and to be called New Amsterdam.

This fort which is at the point of the island about five or six leagues from the mouth, is called Fort Amsterdam; it has four regular bastions mounted with several pieces of artillery. All these bastions and the curtains were in 1643 but ramparts of earth, most of which had crumbled away, so that the fort could be entered on all sides. There were no ditches. There were sixty soldiers to garrison the said fort and another which they had built still further up against the incursions of the savages their enemies. They were beginning to face the gates and bastions with stone. Within this fort stood a pretty large church built of stone; the house of the Governor, whom they called Director General, quite neatly built of brick, the store-houses and barracks.

On this island of Manhatte and in its environs there may well be four or five hundred men of different sects and nations; the Director General told me that there were persons there of eighteen different languages; they are scattered here and there on the river, above and below as the beauty and convenience of the spot invited each to settle, some mechanics however who ply their trades are ranged under the fort; all the others were exposed to the incursions of the natives, who in the year 1643, while I was there actually killed some two score Hollanders and burnt many houses and barns full of wheat.

The river, which is very straight and runs due north and south, is at least a league broad before the fort. Ships lie at anchor in a bay which forms the other side of the island and can be defended from the fort.

Shortly before I arrived there three large vessels of 300 tons each had come to load wheat; two had found cargoes, the third could not be loaded because the savages had burnt a part of their grain. These ships came from the West Indies where the West India Company usually keeps up seventeen ships of war.

No religion is publicly exercised but the Calvinist, and orders are to admit none but Calvinists, but this is not observed, for there are, besides Calvinists, in the Colony Catholics, English Puritans, Lutherans, Anabaptists, here called Muistes &c.

When any one comes to settle in the country, they lend him horses, cows &c, they give him provisions, all which he repays as soon as he is at ease, and as to the land he pays in to the West India Company after ten years the tenth of the produce which he reaps.

This country is bounded on the New England side by a river they call the *Fresche* river, which serves as a boundary between them and the English. The English however come very near to them preferring to hold lands under the Dutch who ask nothing from them rather than to be dependent on English Lords who exact rents and would fain be absolute. On the other side southward towards Virginia, its limits are the river which they call the *South* river on which there is also a Dutch settlement, but the Swedes have at its mouth another extremely well provided with men and cannon. It is believed that these Swedes are maintained by some merchants of Amsterdam, who are not satisfied that the West India Company should alone enjoy all the commerce of these parts. It is near this river that a gold mine is reported to have been found.

See in the work of the Sieur de Laet of Antwerp the table and article on New Belgium as he sometimes calls it or the map; *Nova Anglia, Novu Belgium et Virginia.*

It is about fifty years since the Hollanders came to these parts. The fort was begun in the year 1615: they began to settle about twenty years ago and there is already some little commerce with Virginia and New England.

The first comers found lands fit for use, formerly cleared by the savages who previously had fields here. Those who came later have cleared in the woods, which are mostly of oak. The soil is good. Deer hunting is abundant in the fall. There are some houses built of stone; they make lime of oyster shells, great heaps of which are found here made formerly by the savages, who subsisted in part by this fishery.

The climate is very mild. Lying at 40 2/3 degrees; there are many European fruits, as apples, pears, cherries. I reached there in October, and found even then a considerable quantity of peaches.

Ascending the river to the 43d degree you find the second Dutch settlement, which the flux and reflux reaches but does not pass. Ships of a hundred and a hundred and twenty tons can ascend to it.

There are two things in this settlement, which is called Renselaerswick, as if to say the colony of Renselaer, who is a rich Amsterdam merchant: 1st a wretched little fort called Ft Orange, built of logs with four or five pieces of cannon of Breteuil and as many swivels. This has been reserved and is maintained by the West India Company. This fort was formerly on an island in the river, it is now on the main land towards the Hiroquois, a little above the said island. 2ndly, a colonie sent here by this Renselaer, who is the Patroon. This colonie is composed of about a hundred persons, who resident in some 25 or 30 houses, built along the river, as each one found it most convenient. In the principal house resides the Patroon's agent, the minister has his apart, in which service is performed. There is also a kind of bailiff here whom they call Seneschal, who administers justice. All their houses are merely of boards and thatched. As yet there is no mason work, except in the chimneys. The forests furnishing many large pines, they make boards by means of their mills which they have for the purpose.

They found some pieces of ground all ready, which the savages had formerly prepared and in which they sow wheat and oats for beer and for their horses, of which they have a great stock. There is little land fit for tillage, being crowded by hills which are bad soil. This obliges them to be separated the one from the other, and they occupy already two or three leagues of country.

Trade is free to all, this gives the Indians all things cheap, each of the Hollanders outbidding his neighbor and being satisfied provided he can gain some little profit.

This settlement is not more than twenty leagues from the *Agniehronons*, who can be reached either by land or by water, as the river on which the Iroquois lie falls into that which passes by the Dutch; but there are many shallow rapids and a fall of a short half league where the canoe has to be carried.

There are many nations between the two Dutch settlements, which are about thirty German leagues apart, that is about 50 or 60 French leagues. The *Loups*, whom the Iroquois call *Agotzogenens*, are the nearest to Renselaerwick and Ft Orange. War breaking out some years ago between the Iroquois and the Loups, the Dutch joined the latter against the former, but four having been taken and burnt they made peace. Some nations near the sea having murdered some Hollanders of the most distant settlement, the Hollanders killed 150 Indians, men, women and children; the latter having killed at divers intervals 40 Dutchmen, burnt several houses and committed ravages, estimated at the time that I was there at 200,000 liv. (two hundred thousand livres) troops were raised in New England, and in the beginning of winter the grass being low and some snow on the ground they pursued them with six hundred men, keeping two hundred always on the move and constantly relieving each other, so that the Indians, pent up in a large island and finding it impossible to escape, on account of the women and children, were cut to pieces to the number of sixteen hundred, women and children included. This obliged the rest of the Indians to make peace, which still continues. This occurred in 1643 and 1644.

Three Rivers in New France,
August 3d, 1646.

1. *Contrast the two Dutch settlements as described by Isaac Jogues. What factors might explain their dissimilarity?*
2. *What characteristics of New Netherlands as described by Jogues set it apart from the English colonies to the north and south?*

2-9 George Alsop, The Importance of Tobacco (1660)

George Alsop emigrated as an indentured servant to Maryland. In 1666, he wrote his only notable work, A Character of the Province of Maryland, in which he described the nature and founding of the colony. Typical of his time, the Character contains numerous errors, but his description of the nature of trade in the colony is accurate.

> **Source:** George Alsop, *A Character of the Province of Maryland* (Baltimore: Maryland Historical Society Fund, Publication No. 15, 1880), pp. 475–477.

. . .The three main Commodities this Country affords for Trafique, are Tobacco, Furrs, and Flesh. Furrs and Skins, as Beavers, Otters, Musk-Rats, Rackoons, Wild-Cats, and Elke or Buffeloe, with divers others, which were first made vendible by the *Indians* of the Country, and sold to the Inhabitant, and by them to the Merchant, and so transported into *England* and other places where it becomes most commodious.

Tobacco is the only solid Staple Commodity of this Province: The use of it was first found out by the *Indians* many Ages agoe, and transferr'd into Christendom by that great Discoverer of *America Columbus*. It's generally made by all the Inhabitants of this Province, and between the months of *March* and *April* they sow the seed (which is much smaller then Mustard-seed) in small beds and patches digg'd up and made so by art, and about *May* the Plants commonly appear green in those beds: In *June* they are transplanted from their beds, and set in little hillocks in distant rowes, dug up for the same purpose; some twice or thrice they are weeded, and succoured from their illegitimate Leaves that would be peeping out from the body of the Stalk. They top the several Plants, as they find occasion in their predominating rankness: About the middle of *September* they cut the Tobacco down, and carry it into houses, (made for that purpose) to bring it to its purity: And after it has attained, by a convenient attendance upon time, to its perfection, it is then tyed up in bundles, and packt into Hogs-heads, and then laid by for the Trade.

Between *November* and *January* there arrives in this Province Shipping to the number of twenty sail and upwards, all Merchant-men loaden with Commodities to Trafique and dispose of, trucking with the Planter for Silks, Hollands, Serges, and Broad-clothes, with other necessary Goods, priz'd at such and such rates as shall be judg'd on is fair and legal, for Tobacco at so much the pound, and advantage on both sides considered; the Planter for his work, and the Merchant for adventuring himself and his Commodity into so far a Country: Thus is the Trade on both sides drove on with a fair and honest *Decorum*.

The Inhabitants of this Province are seldom or never put to the affrightment of being robb'd of their money, nor to dirty their Fingers by telling of vast sums: They have more bags to carry Corn, then Coyn; and though they want, but why should I call that a want which is only a necessary miss? the very effects of the dirt of this Province affords as great a profit to the general Inhabitant, as the Gold of Peru doth to the straight-breecht Commonalty of the *Spaniard*.

Our Shops and Exchanges of *Mary-Land*, are the Merchants Store-houses, where with few words and protestations Goods are bought and delivered; not like those Shop-keepers Boys in *London*, that continually cry, *What do ye lack Sir? What d'ye buy?* yelping with so wide a mouth, as if some Apothecary had hired their mouths to stand open to catch Gnats and Vagabond Flyes in.

Tobacco is the currant Coyn of *Mary-Land*, and will sooner purchase Commodities from the Merchant, then money. I must confess the *New-England* men that trade into this Province, had rather have fat Pork for their Goods, than Tobacco or Furrs, which I conceive is, because their bodies being fast bound up with the cords of restringent Zeal, they are fain to make use of the lineaments of this *Non-Canaanite* creature physically to loosen them; for a bit of a pound upon a two-peny Rye loaf, according to the original Receipt, will bring the cos tiv'st red-ear'd Zealot in some three hours time to a fine stool, if methodically observed.

Medera-Wines, Sugars, Salt, Wickar-Chairs, and Tin Candlesticks, is the most of the Commodities they bring in: They arrive in *Mary-Land* about *September,* being most of them Ketches and Barkes, and such Small Vessels, and these dispersing themselves into several small Creeks of this Province, to sell and dispose of their Commodities, where they know the Market is most fit for their small Adventures. . ..

1. *Describe the method of growing and harvesting tobacco as noted by George Alsop?*
2. *How important is tobacco in terms of trade?*

2-10   The Examination and Confession of Ann Foster at Salem Village (1692)

The Salem witchcraft trials have become one of the most infamous periods in American History and the language and nature of the trials have provided a context for many subsequent events. In this selection, the "testimony" of Ann Foster demonstrates the basis for the accusations and the hysteria and illuminates the mindsets of the accusers and, to a degree, the accused.

After a while Ann ffoster conffesed that the devil apered to her in the shape of a bird at several Times, such a bird as she neuer saw the like before; & that she had had this gift (viz. of striking ye afflicted downe with her eye euer since) & being askt why she thought yt bird was the diuill she answered because he came white & vanished away black & yt the diuill told her yt she should haue this gift & yt she must beliue him & told her she should haue prosperity & she said yt he had apeared to her three times & was always as a bird, and the last time was about half a year since, & sat upon a table had two legs & great eyes & yt it was the second time of his apearance that he promised her prosperity & yt it was Carriers wife about three weeks agoe yt came & perswaded her to hurt these people.

16 July 1692. Ann ffoster Examined confessed yt it was Goody Carrier yt made her a witch yt she came to her in person about Six yeares agoe & told her it she would not be a witch ye diuill should tare her in peices & carry her away at which time she promised to Serve the diuill yt she had bewitched a hog of John Loujoys to death & that she had hurt some persons in Salem Villige, yt goody Carier came to her & would have her bewitch two children of Andrew Allins & that she had then two popets made & stuck pins in them to bewitch ye said children by which one of them dyed ye other very sick, that she was at the meeting of the witches at Salem Vilige, yt Goody Carier came & told her of the meeting and would haue her goe, so they got upon Sticks & went said Jorny & being there did see Mr. Buroughs ye minister who spake to them all, & this was about two months agoe that there was then twenty five persons meet together, that she tyed a knot in a Rage & threw it into the fire to hurt Tim. Swan & that she did hurt the rest yt complayned of her by Squesing popets like them & so almost choked them.

18 July 1692. Ann ffoster Examined confessed yt ye deuil in shape of a man apeared to her wth Goody carier about six yeare since when they made her a witch & that she promised to serve the diuill two years, upon which the diuill promised her prosperity and many things but neuer performed it, that she & martha Carier did both ride on a stick or pole when they went to the witch meeting at Salem Village & that the stick broak: as they were caried in the aire aboue the tops of the trees, & they fell but she did hang fast about the neck of Goody Carier & ware presently at the vilage, that she was then much hurt of her Leg, she further saith that she heard some of the witches say there was three hundred & fiue in the whole Country & that they would ruin that place ye Vilige, also said there was present at that meetting two men besides Mr. Burroughs ye minister & one of them had gray haire, she saith yt she formerly frequented the publique metting to worship god. but the diuill had such power ouer her yt she could not profit there & yt was her undoeing: she saith yt about three or foure yeares agoe Martha Carier told her she would bewitch James Hobbs child to death & the child dyed in twenty four hours.

21 July 92. Ann ffoster Examined Owned her former conffesion being read to her and further conffesed that the discourse amongst ye witches at ye meeting at Salem village was that they would afflict there to set up the Diuills Kingdome. This confesion is true as witness my hand.

Ann ffoster Signed & Owned the aboue Examination & Conffesion before me
Salem 10th September 1692. John Higginson, Just Peace.

1. *According to Ann Foster's testimony, in what ways was a witch thought to bring harm to other people?*
2. *How might a testimony such as Ann Foster's seem to make sense in light of actual events occurring in Salem village?*

2-11   Onandogas and Cayugas: Iroquois Chiefs Address the Governors of New York and Virginia (1684)

Cadwallader Colden (1688–1776), surveyor and later lieutenant governor of New York, recorded these arguments spoken by Iroquois chiefs. The Iroquois were certainly attempting to resolve difficulties caused by an ever-expanding colonial population, and were willing to form alliances with whichever power could guarantee their interests.

Source: Cadwallader Colden, *The History of the Five Nations of Canada*, 3rd ed. (London, 1755), vol. I, pp. 46–51.

Brother Corlear,

Your Sachem is a great Sachem and we are but a small People; but when the English came first to Manhatan, (New York) to Aragiske (Virginia) and to Yakokranagary (Maryland), they were then but a small People, and we were great. Then, because we found you a good People, we treated you kindly, and gave you Land; we hope therefore, now that you are great, and we small, you will protect us from the French. If you do not, we shall lose all our Hunting and Bevers: The French will get all the Bevers. The Reason they are now angry with us is, because we carry our Bever to our Brethren.

We have put our Lands and ourselves under the Protection of the great Duke of York, the Brother of your great Sachem, who is likewise a great Sachem.

We have annexed the Susquehana River, which we won with the Sword, to this Government; and we desire it may be a Branch of the great Tree that grows in this Place, the Top of which reaches the Sun, and its Branches shelter us from the French, and all other Nations. Our Fire burns in your Houses, and your Fire burns with us; we desire it may be so always. But we will not that any of the great Penn's People settle upon the Susquehana River, for we have no other Land to leave to our Children.

Our young Men are Soldiers, and when they are provoked, they are like Wolves in the Woods, as you, Sachem of Virginia, very well know.

We have put ourselves under the great Sachem Charles, that lives on the other Side the great Lake. We give you these two white dressed Deer-skins, to send to the great Sachem, that he may write on them, and put a great red Seal to them, to confirm what we now do; and put the Susquehana River above the Falls, and all the rest of our Land under the great Duke of York, and give that Land to none else. Our Brethren, his People, have been like Fathers to our Wives and Children, and have given us Bread when we were in Need of it; we will not therefore join ourselves, or our Land, to any other Government but this. We desire Corlear, our Governor, may send this our Proposition to the great Sachem Charles, who dwells on the other Side the great Lake, with this Belt of Wampum, and this other smaller Belt to the Duke of York his Brother: And we give you, Corlear, this Bever, that you may send over this Proposition.

You great Man of Virginia, we let you know, that great Penn did speak to us here in Corlear's House by his Agents, and desired to buy the Susquehana River of us, but we would not hearken to him, for we had fastened it to this Government.

We desire you therefore to bear witness of what we now do, and that we now confirm what we have done before. Let your Friend, that lives on the other Side the great Lake, know this, that we being a free People, though united to the English, may give our Lands, and be joined to the Sachem we like best. We give this Bever to remember what we say

The Senekas arrived soon after, and, on the fifth of August, spoke to the Lord Howard in the following Manner:

We have heard and understood what Mischief hath been done in Virginia; we have it as perfect as if it were upon our Fingers Ends. 0 Corlear! we thank you for having been our Intercessor, so that the Axe has not fallen upon us.

And you Assarigoa, great Sachem of Virginia, we thank you for burying all Evil in the Pit. We are informed, that the Mohawks, Oneydoes, Onnondagas, and Cayugas, have buried the Axe already; now we that live remotest off, are come to do the same, and to include in this Chain the Cahnawaas, your Friends. We desire therefore, that an Axe, on our Part, may be buried with one of Assarigoa's. 0 Corlear! Corlear! we thank you for laying hold of one End of the Axe; and we thank you, great Governor of Virginia, not only for throwing aside the Axe, but more especially for your putting all Evil from your Heart. Now we have a new Chain, a strong and a straight Chain, that cannot be broken. The Tree of Peace is planted so firmly, that it cannot be moved, let us on both Sides hold the Chain fast.

We understand what you said of the great Sachem, that lives on the other Side the great Water.

You tell us, that the Cahnawaas will come hither, to strengthen the Chain. Let them not make any Excuse, that they are old and feeble, or that their Feet are sore. If the old Sachems cannot, let the young Men come. We shall not fail to come hither, tho' we live farthest off, and then the new Chain will be stronger and brighter.

We understand, that because of the Mischief that has been done to the People and Castles of Virginia and Maryland, we must not come near the Heads of your Rivers, nor near your Plantations, but keep at the Foot of the Mountains; for tho' we lay down our Arms, as Friends, we shall not be trusted for the future, but looked on as Robbers. We agree however to this Proposition, and shall wholly stay away from Virginia: And this we do in Gratitude to Corlear, who has been at so great Pains to persuade you, great Governor of Virginia, to forget what is past. You are wise in giving Ear to Corlear's good Advice, for we shall now go a Path which was never trod before.

We have now done speaking to Corlear, and the Governor of Virginia; let the Chain be for ever kept clean and bright by him, and we shall do the same.

The other Nations from the Mohawks Country to the Cayugas, have delivered up the Susquehana River, and all that Country, to Corlear's Government. We confirm what they have done by giving this Belt.

Coll. Bird, one of the Council of Virginia, and Edmond Jennings Esq; Attorney General of that Province, came with four Indian Sachems, (according to the Lord Howard's Promise) to renew and confirm the Peace, and met the Five Nations at Albany in September 1685.

Coll. Bird accused them of having again broke their Promise, by taking an Indian Girl from an English Man's House, and four Indian Boys Prisoners. They excused this, by its being done by the Parties that were out when the Peace was concluded, who knew nothing of it; which Accident they had provided against in their Articles. They said, the four Boys were given to the Relations of those Men that were lost; and it would be difficult to obtain their Restoration: But they at last promised to deliver them up.

The Senakas and Mohawks declared themselves free of any Blame, and chid the other Nations.

So that we may still observe the Influence which the French Priests had obtained over those other Nations, and to what Christian like Purpose they used it.

The Mohawks Speaker said, "Where shall I seek the Chain of Peace? Where shall I find it but upon our Path? And whither doth our Path lead us, but into this House? This is a House of Peace;" after this he sang all the Links of the Chain over. He afterwards sang by Way of Admonition to the Onondagas, Oneydoes, and Cayugas, and concluded all with a Song to the Virginia Indians.

The French Priests however still employed their Influence over the Onnondagas, Cayugas, and Oneydoes; and it was easy for them to spirit up the Indians (naturally revengeful) against their old Enemies. A Party of the Oneydoes went out two Years after this against the Wayanoak Indians, Friends of Virginia, and killed some of the People of Virginia, who assisted those Indians. They took six Prisoners, but restored them at Albany, with an Excuse, that they did not know they were Friends of Virginia. But Coll. Dungan on this Occasion told them, That he only had kept all the English in North America from joining together to destroy them; that if ever he should hear of the like Complaint, he would dig up the Hatchet, and join with the rest of the English to cut them off Root and Branch; for there were many Complaints made of him to the King by the English, as well as by the Governor of Canada, for his favouring of them. We have now gone through the material Transactions which the Five Nations had with the English, in which we find the English pursuing nothing but peaceable and Christian-like Measures; and the Five Nations (tho' Barbarians) living with the People of New-York, like good Neighbours and faithful Friends, and generally with all the English also, except when they were influenced by the Jesuites; at the same Time, one cannot but admire the Zeal, Courage, and Resolution of these Jesuites, that would adventure to live among Indians at War with their Nation; and the better to carry their Purposes, to comply with all the Humours and Manners of such a wild People, so as not to be distinguished by Strangers from meer Indians. One of them, named Milet, remained with the Oneydoes till after the Year 1694; he was advanced to the Degree of a Sachem, and had so great an Influence over them, that the other Nations could not prevail with them to part with him. While he lived with them, the Oneydoes were frequently turned against the Southern Indians (Friends of the English southern Colonies) and were always wavering in their Resolutions against the French at Canada.

We shall now see what Effect the Policy of the French had, who pursued very different Measures from the English.

1. *What is the attitude toward the English expressed by the author of the first letter? On what foundation does this plea for protection and alliance rest?*
2. *How is the tone and attitude of the letter by the Senekas similar to the first? What concessions are the Senekas willing to make in order to ensure peace between their people and the colonists?*
3. *What do these letters and these accounts reveal regarding the precarious position of the Native American tribes as they attempted to negotiate survival amid the colonial efforts of various nations?*

2-12 James Oglethorpe: The Stono Rebellion (1739)

The Stono Rebellion was the largest uprising of enslaved Africans to take place during the colonial period. On the morning of September 9, 1739, about twenty slaves in Saint Paul's Parish, South Carolina, broke into a small store and took guns, powder, and shot. When the owners of the store suddenly arrived, they were killed and their heads were left on the porch. From here, the slaves, led by Jemmy, tried to make their way to Saint Augustine, where the Spanish government had promised them freedom. On their way, they recruited others to join them, while at the same time killing any whites who crossed their path. That evening, they were overtaken and defeated by the colony's militia. James Oglethorpe, as governor of Georgia, was concerned about this incident, and described it—as well as the measures he thought would prevent a recurrence of such an uprising.

Source: Allen Chandler, ed., *The Colonial Records of the State of Georgia*, vol. 22 (Atlanta: Chas. P. Byrd Press, 1913), pp. 232–236.

Sometime since there was a Proclamation published at Augustine, in which the King of Spain (then at Peace with Great Britain) promised Protection and Freedom to all Negroes Slaves that would resort thither. Certain Negroes belonging to Captain Davis escaped to Augustine, and were received there. They were demanded by General Oglethorpe who sent Lieutenant Demere to Augustine, and the Governour assured the General of his sincere Friendship, but at the same time showed his Orders from the Court of Spain, by which he was to receive all Run away Negroes. Of this other Negroes having notice, as it is believed, from the Spanish Emissaries, four or five who were Cattel-Hunters, and knew the Woods, some of whom belonged to Captain Macpherson, ran away with His Horses, wounded his Son and killed another Man. These marched f [sic] for Georgia, and were pursued, but the Rangers being then newly reduced [sic] the Countrey people could not overtake them, though they were discovered by the Saltzburghers, as they passed by Ebenezer. They reached Augustine, one only being killed and another wounded by the Indians in their flight. They were received there with great honours, one of them had a Commission given to him, and a Coat faced with Velvet. Amongst the Negroe Salves there are a people brought from the Kingdom of Angola in Africa, many of these speak Portugueze [which Language is as near Spanish as Scotch is to English,] by reason that the Portugueze have considerable Settlement, and the Jesuits have a Mission and School in that Kingdom and many Thousands of the Negroes there profess the Roman Catholic Religion. Several Spaniards upon diverse Pretences have for some time past been strolling about Carolina, two of them, who will give no account of themselves have been taken up and committed to Jayl in Georgia. The good reception of the Negroes at Augustine was spread about, Several attempted to escape to the Spaniards, & were taken, one of them was hanged at Charles Town. In the latter end of July last Don Pedro, Colonel of the Spanish Horse, went in a Launch to Charles Town under pretence of a message to General Oglethorpe and the Lieutenant Governour.

On the 9th day of September last being Sunday which is the day the Planters allow them to work for themselves, Some Angola Negroes assembled, to the number of Twenty; and one who was called Jemmy was their Captain, they suprized a Warehouse belonging to Mr. Hutchenson at a place called Stonehow [sic—]; they there killed Mr. Robert Bathurst, and Mr. Gibbs, plundered the House and took a pretty many small Arms and Powder, which were there for Sale. Next they plundered and burnt Mr. Godfrey's house, and killed him, his Daughter and Son. They then turned back and marched Southward along Pons Pons, which is the Road through Georgia to Augustine, they passed Mr. Wallace's Taxern towards day break, and said they would not hurt him, for he was a good Man and kind to his Slaves, but they broke open and plundered Mr. Lemy's House, and killed him, his wife and Child. They marched on towards Mr. Rose's resolving to kill him; but he was saved by a Negroe, who having hid him went out and pacified the others. Several Negroes joyned them, they calling out Liberty, marched on with Colours displayed, and two Drums beating, pursuing all the white people they met with, and killing Man Woman and Child when they could come up to them. Collonel Bull Lieutenant Governour of South Carolina, who was then riding along the Road, discovered them, was pursued, and with much difficulty escaped & raised the Countrey. They burnt Colonel Hext's house and killed his Overseer and his Wife. They then burnt Mr. Sprye's house, then Mr. Sacheverell's, and then Mr. Nash's house, all lying upon the Pons Pons Road, and killed all the white People they found in them. Mr. Bullock got off, but they burnt his House, by this time many of them were drunk with the Rum they had take in the Houses. They increased every minute by new Negroes coming to them, so that they were above Sixty, some say a hundred, on which they halted in a field, and set to dancing, Singing and beating Drums, to draw more Negroes to them, thinking they were now victorious over the whole Province, having marched ten miles & burnt all before them without Opposition, but the Militia being raised, the Planters with great briskness pursued them and when they came up, dismounting; charged them on foot. The Negroes were soon routed, though they behaved boldly several being killed on the Spot, many ran back to their Plantations thinking they had not been missed, but they were there taken and [sic] Shot, Such as were taken in the field also, were after being examined, shot on the Spot, And this is to be said to the honour of the Carolina Planters, that not with standing the Provocation they had received from so many Murders, they did not torture one Negroe, but only put them to an easy death. All the proved to be forced & were not concerned in the Murders & Burnings were pardoned, And this sudden Courage in the field, & the Humanity afterwards hath had so good an Effect that there hath been no farther Attempt, and the very Spirit of Revolt seems over. About 30 escaped from the fight, of which ten marched about 30 miles Southward, and being overtaken by the Planters on horseback, fought stoutly for some time and were all killed on the Spot. The rest are yet untaken. In the whole action about 40 Negroes and 20 whites were killed. The Lieutenant Governour sent an account of this to General Oglethorpe, who met the advices on his return form the Indian Nation He immediately ordered a Troop of Rangers to be ranged, to patrole through Georgia, placed some Men in the Garrison at Palichocolas, which was before abandoned, and near which the Negroes formerly passed, being the only place where Horses can come to swim over the River Savannah for near 100 miles, ordered out the Indians in pursuit, and a Detachment of the Garrison at Port Royal to assist the Planters on any Occasion, and published a Proclamation ordering all the Constables &c. of Georgia to pursue and seize all Negroes, with a Reward for any that should be taken. It is hoped these measures will prevent any Negroes from getting down to the Spaniards.

1. *Summarize the extent and size of the Stono Rebellion. How much of a threat did the group represent to whites? What kind of threat did the rebellion pose to the preservation of slavery in the southern states?*
2. *Discuss the nature of the acts of "courage" and "humanity" that are credited for putting down the rebellion.*
3. *What international political and religious factors may have played a role in the establishment of Augustine as a safe haven for slaves?*

2-13   Gottlieb Mittelberger, The Passage of Indentured Servants (1750)

Bonded or indentured servants provided an important source of labor in the colonial period. Individuals pledged a number of years of service in return for passage to the new world and a new life. Gottlieb Mittelberger was an indentured servant who came to Philadelphia where he served as an organist and teacher. Most were not so fortunate and all had to endure the horrific journey that is described in this reading.

Both in Rotterdam and in Amsterdam the people are packed densely, like herrings so to say, in the large sea-vessels. One person receives a place of scarcely 2 feet width and 6 feet length in the bedstead, while many a ship carries four to six hundred souls; not to mention the innumerable implements, tools, provisions, water-barrels and other things which likewise occupy such space.

On account of contrary winds it takes the ships sometimes 2, 3, and 4 weeks to make the trip from Holland to . . . . England. But when the wind is good, they get there in 8 days or even sooner. Everything is examined there and the custom-duties paid, whence it comes that the ships ride there 8, 10 or 14 days and even longer at anchor, till they have taken in their full cargoes. During that time every one is compelled to spend his last remaining money and to consume his little stock of provisions which had been reserved for the sea; so that most passengers, finding themselves on the

ocean where they would be in greater need of them, must greatly suffer from hunger and want. Many suffer want already on the water between Holland and Old England.

When the ships have for the last time weighed their anchors near the city of Kaupp [Cowes] in Old England, the real misery begins with the long voyage. For from there the ships, unless they have good wind, must often sail 8, 9, 10 to 12 weeks before they reach Philadelphia. But even with the best wind the voyage lasts 7 weeks.

But during the voyage there is on board these ships terrible misery, stench, fumes, horror, vomiting, many kinds of sea-sickness, fever, dysentery, headache, heat, constipation, boils, scurvy, cancer, mouth rot, and the like, all of which come from old and sharply salted food and meat, also from very bad and foul water, so that many die miserably.

Add to this want of provisions, hunger, thirst, frost, heat, dampness, anxiety, want, afflictions and lamentations, together with other trouble, as . . . the lice abound so frightfully, especially on sick people, that they can be scraped off the body. The misery reaches the climax when a gale rages for 2 or 3 nights and days, so that every one believes that the ship will go to the bottom with all human beings on board. In such a visitation the people cry and pray most piteously.

Children from 1 to 7 years rarely survive the voyage. I witnessed . . . misery in no less than 32 children in our ship, all of whom were thrown into the sea. The parents grieve all the more since their children find no resting-place in the earth, but are devoured by the monsters of the sea.

That most of the people get sick is not surprising, because, in addition to all other trials and hardships, warm food is served only three times a week, the rations being very poor and very little. Such meals can hardly be eaten, on account of being so unclean. The water which is served out of the ships is often very black, thick and full of worms, so that one cannot drink it without loathing, even with the greatest thirst. Toward the end we were compelled to eat the ship's biscuit which had been spoiled long ago; though in a whole biscuit there was scarcely a piece the size of a dollar that had not been full of red worms and spiders' nests. . . .

At length, when, after a long and tedious voyage, the ships come in sight of land, so that the promontories can be seen, which the people were so eager and anxious to see, all creep from below on deck to see the land from afar, and they weep for joy, and pray and sing, thanking and praising God. The sight of the land makes the people on board the ship, especially the sick and the half dead, alive again, so that their hearts leap within them; they shout and rejoice, and are content to bear their misery in patience, in the hope that they may soon reach the land in safety. But alas!

When the ships have landed at Philadelphia after their long voyage, no one is permitted to leave them except those who pay for their passage or can give good security; the others, who cannot pay, must remain on board the ships till they are purchased, and are released from the ships by their purchasers. The sick always fare the worst, for the healthy are naturally preferred and purchased first; and so the sick and wretched must often remain on board in front of the city for 2 or 3 weeks, and frequently die, whereas many a one, if he could pay his debt and were permitted to leave the ship immediately, might recover and remain alive.

The sale of human beings in the market on board the ship is carried out thus: Every day Englishmen, Dutchmen and High-German people come from the city of Philadelphia and other places, in part from a great distance, say 20, 30, or 40 hours away, and go on board the newly arrived ship that has brought and offers for sale passengers from Europe, and select among the healthy persons such as they deem suitable for their business, and bargain with them how long they will serve for their passage money, which most of them are still in debt for. When they have come to an agreement, it happens that adult persons bind themselves in writing to serve 3, 4, 5 or 6 years for the amount due by them, according to their age and strength. But very young people, from 10 to 15 years, must serve till they are 21 years old.

Many parents must sell and trade away their children like so many head of cattle; for if their children take the debt upon themselves, the parents can leave the ship free and unrestrained; but as the parents often do not know where and to what people their children are going, it often happens that such parents and children, after leaving the ship, do not see each other again for many years, perhaps no more in all their lives. . . .

It often happens that whole families, husband, wife and children, are separated by being sold to different purchasers, especially when they have not paid any part of their passage money.

When a husband or wife has died a sea, when the ship has made more than half of her trip, the survivor must pay or serve not only for himself or herself but also for the deceased.

When both parents have died over half-way at sea, their children, especially when they are young and have nothing to pawn or pay, must stand for their own and their parents' passage, and serve till they are 21 years old. When one has served his or her term, he or she is entitled to a new suit of clothes at parting; and if it has been so stipulated, a man gets in addition a horse, a woman, a cow. When a serf has an opportunity to marry in this country, he or she must pay for each year which he or she would have yet to serve, 5 or 6 pounds.

1. *Summarize the hardships of the passage from Old England to Philadelphia as they are described by the author.*
2. *How are the hardships of the sea exacerbated upon reaching land?*
3. *Describe the various possible arrangements related to the purchase of newly arrived servants from Europe.*

PART THREE
MATURING COLONIAL SOCIETY

3-1 Navigation Act of September 13, 1660

In an effort to enforce mercantilism and produce "a favorable balance of trade with the colonies," Parliament passed a series of Navigation Acts. The first Navigation Act (1651) was aimed primarily at the Dutch and excluded nearly all foreign shipping from the English and colonial trade. Widely ignored, this first attempt at regulating colonial trade was followed by additional Navigation Acts beginning with the one excerpted here—all providing a convenient justification for mercantilism.

Source: http://www.founding.com/library/lbody.cfm?id=83&parent=17

For the increase of shipping and encouragement of the navigation of this nation wherein, under the good providence and protection of God, the wealth, safety, and strength of this kingdom is so much concerned; (2) be it enacted by the king's most excellent Majesty, and by the Lords and Commons in this present Parliament assembled, and by the authority thereof, that from and after the first day of December, one thousand six hundred and sixty, and from thence forward, no goods or commodities whatsoever shall be imported into or exported out of any lands, islands, plantations, or territories to his Majesty belonging or in his possession, or which may hereafter belong unto or be in the possession of his Majesty, his heirs, and successors, in Asia, Africa, or America, in any other ship or ships, vessel or vessels whatsoever, but in such ships or vessels as do truly and without fraud belong only to the people of England or Ireland, dominion of Wales or town of Berwick upon Tweed, or are of the built of and belonging to any the said lands, islands, plantations, or territories, as the proprietors and right owners thereof, and whereof the master and three fourths of the mariners at least are English; (3) under the penalty of the forfeiture and loss of all the goods and commodities which shall be imported into or exported out of any the aforesaid places in any other ship or vessel, as also of the ship or vessel, with all its guns, furniture, tackle, ammunition, and apparel; one third part thereof to his Majesty, his heirs and successors; one third part to the governor of such land, plantation, island, or territory where such default shall be committed, in case the said ship or goods be there seized, or otherwise that third part also to his Majesty, his heirs and successors; and the other third part to him or them who shall seize, inform, or sue for the same in any court of record, by bill, information, plaint, or other action, wherein no essoin, protection, or wager of law shall be allowed; (4) and all admirals and other commanders at sea of any the ships of war or other ship having commission from his Majesty or from his heirs or successors, are hereby authorized and strictly required to seize and bring in as prize all such ships or vessels as shall have offended contrary hereunto, and deliver them to the court of admiralty, there to be proceeded against; and in case of condensation, one moiety of such forfeitures shall be to the use of such admirals or commanders and their companies, to be divided and proportioned amongst them according to the rules and orders of the sea in case of ships taken prize; and the other moiety to the use of his Majesty, his heirs and successors.

II. And be it enacted, that no alien or person not born within the allegiance of our sovereign lord the king, his heirs and successors, or naturalized, or made a free denizen, shall from and after the first day of February, which will be in the year of our Lord one thousand six hundred sixty-one, exercise the trade or occupation of a merchant or factor in any the said places; (2) upon pain of the forfeiture and loss of all his goods and chattels, or which are in his possession; one third to his Majesty, his heirs and successors; one third to the governor of the plantation where such person shall so offend; and the other third to him or them that shall inform or sue for the same in any of his Majesty's courts in the plantation where such offence shall be committed; (3) and all governors of the said lands, islands, plantations, or territories, and every of them, are hereby strictly required and commanded, and all who hereafter shall be made governors of any such islands, plantations, or territories, by his Majesty, his heirs or successors, shall before their entrance into their government take a solemn oath to do their utmost, that every the afore-mentioned clauses, and all the matters and things therein contained, shall be punctually and *bona fide* observed according to the true intent and meaning thereof; (4) and upon complaint and proof made before his Majesty, his heirs or successors, or such as shall be by him or them thereunto authorized and appointed, that any the said governors have been willingly and wittingly negligent in doing their duty accordingly, that the said governor so offending shall be removed from his government.

III. And it is further enacted by the authority aforesaid, that no goods or commodities whatsoever, of the growth, production or manufacture of Africa, Asia, or America, or of any part thereof, or which are described or laid down in the usual maps or cards of those places, be imported into England, Ireland, or Wales, islands of Guernsey and Jersey, or town of Berwick upon Tweed, in any other ship or ships, vessel or vessels whatsoever, but in such as do truly and without fraud belong only to the people of England or Ireland, dominion of Wales, or town of Berwick upon Tweed, or of the lands, islands, plantations or territories in Asia, Africa, or America, to his Majesty belonging, as the proprietors and right owners thereof, and whereof the master, and three fourths at least of the mariners are English; (2) under the penalty of the forfeiture of all such goods and commodities, and of the ship or vessel in which they were imported, with all her guns, tackle, furniture, ammunition, and apparel; one moiety to his Majesty, his heirs and successors; and the other moiety to him or them who shall seize, inform or sue for the same in any court of record, by bill, information, plaint or other action wherein no essoin, protection or wager of law shall be allowed.

XVIII. And it is further enacted by the authority aforesaid, that from and after the first day of April, which shall be in the year of our Lord one thousand six hundred sixty-one, no sugars, tobacco, cotton-wool, indigoes, ginger, rustic, or other dyeing wood, of the growth, production, or manufacture of any English plantations in America, Asia, or Africa, shall be shipped, carried, conveyed, or transported from any of the said English plantations to any land, island, territory, dominion, port, or place whatsoever, other than to such other English plantations as do belong to his Majesty, his heirs and successors, or to the kingdom of England or Ireland, or principality of Wales, or town of Berwick upon Tweed, there to be laid on shore; (2) under the penalty of the forfeiture of the said goods, or the full value thereof, as also of the ship, with all her guns, tackle, apparel, ammunition, and furniture; the one moiety to the king's Majesty, his heirs and successors, and the other moiety to him or them that shall seize, inform, or sue for the same in any court of record, by bill, plaint, or information, wherein no essoin, protection, or wager of law shall be allowed.

XIX. And be it further enacted by the authority aforesaid, that for every ship or vessel, which from and after the five and twentieth day of December in the year of our Lord one thousand six hundred and sixty shall set sail out of or from England, Ireland, Wales, or town of Berwick upon Tweed, for any English plantation in America, Asia, or Africa, sufficient bond shall be given with one surety to the chief officers of the custom-house and such port of place from whence the said ship shall set sail, to the value of one thousand pounds, if the ship be of less burden that one hundred tons; and of the sum of two thousand pounds, if the ship shall be of greater burden; that in case the said ship or vessel shall load any of the said commodities at any of the said English plantations, that the same commodities shall be by the said ship brought to some port of England, Ireland, Wales, or to the port or town of Berwick upon Tweed, and shall there unload and put on shore the same, the danger of the seas only expected; (2) and for all ships coming from any other port or place to any of the aforesaid plantations, who by this act are permitted to trade there, that the governor of such English plantations shall before the said ship or vessel be permitted to load on board any of the said commodities, take bond in manner and to the value aforesaid, for each respective ship or vessel, that such ship or vessel shall carry all the aforesaid goods that shall be laden on board in the said ship to some other of his Majesty's English plantations, or to England, Ireland, Wales, or town of Berwick upon Tweed; (3) and that every ship or vessel which shall load or take on board any of the aforesaid goods, until such bond given to the said governor, or certificate produced from the officers of any custom-house of England, Ireland, Wales, or of the town of Berwick, that such bonds have been there duly given, shall be forfeited with all her guns, tackle, apparel, and furniture, to be employed and recovered in manner as aforesaid; and the said governors and every of them shall twice in every year after the first day of January one thousand six hundred and sixty, return true copies of all such bonds by him so taken, to the chief officers of the custom in London.

1. *The Navigation Act of 1651 required that all goods imported into England or the colonies had to arrive on English ships and the majority of the crew on board those ships must be English. How does the Navigation Act of 1660 make this regulation more limiting?*
2. *How do you think Parliament could enforce an act such as this—especially the provisions found in Section XVIII (the "enumerated" goods)?*

3-2 Nathaniel Bacon's Challenge to William Berkeley and the Governor's Response (1676)

William Berkeley faced many challenges during his almost thirty years in power as Governor of Virginia—not the least of which was discontent over depressed tobacco prices, rising taxes, and the Indian presence in the backcountry. These issues came to a head in July 1676 when Nathaniel Bacon defied the governor's authority and led a band of frontier vigilantes against all the local Indians and even the governor himself. What followed was a brief conflict called Bacon's Rebellion that left many people dead, Jamestown in ruins, and the power of the governor and his councilors confirmed.

> **Source:** A Hypertext on American History From the Colonial Period Until Modern Times
> http://odur.let.rug.nl/~usa/D/1651-1700/bacon_rebel/bacon_i.htm
> http://odur.let.rug.nl/~usa/D/1651-1700/bacon_rebel/berke.htm

The Declaracion of the People.

1. For haveing upon specious pretences of publiqe works raised greate unjust taxes upon the Comonality for the advancement of private favorites and other sinister ends, but noe visible effects in any measure adequate, For not haveing dureing this long time of his Gouvernement in any measure advanced this hopefull Colony either by fortificacons Townes or Trade.

2. For haveing abused and rendred contemptable the Magistrates of Justice, by advanceing to places of Judicature, scandalous and Ignorant favorites.

3. For haveing wronged his Majesties prerogative and interest, by assumeing Monopoly of the Beaver trade, and for haveing in that unjust gaine betrayed and sold his Majesties Country and the lives of his loyall subjects, to the barbarous heathen.

4. For haveing, protected, favoured, and Imboldned the Indians against his Majesties loyall subjects, never contriveing, requireing, or appointing any due or proper meanes of sattisfaction for theire many Invasions, robberies, and murthers comitted upon us.

5. For haveing when the Army of English, was just upon the track of those Indians, who now in all places burne, spoyle, murther and when we might with ease have destroyed them: who then were in open hostillity, for then haveing expressly countermanded, and sent back our Army, by passing his word for the peaceable demeanour of the said Indians, who imediately prosecuted theire evill intentions, comitting horred murthers and robberies in all places, being protected by the said engagement and word past of him the said Sir William Berkeley, haveing ruined and laid desolate a greate part of his Majesties Country, and have now drawne themselves into such obscure and remote places, and are by theire success soe imboldned and confirmed, by theire confederacy soe strengthned that the cryes of blood are in all places, and the terror, and constimation of the people soe greate, are now become, not onely a difficult, but a very formidable enimy, who might att first with ease have beene destroyed.

6. And lately when upon the loud outcryes of blood the Assembly had with all care raised and framed an Army for the preventing of further mischeife and safeguard of this his Majesties Colony.

7. For haveing with onely the privacy of some few favorites, without acquainting the people, onely by the alteracon of a figure, forged a Comission, by we know not what hand, not onely without, but even against the consent of the people, for the raiseing and effecting civill warr and destruction, which being happily and without blood shed prevented, for haveing the second time attempted the same, thereby calling downe our forces from the defence of the fronteeres and most weekely exposed places.

8. For the prevencon of civill mischeife and ruin amongst ourselves, whilst the barbarous enimy in all places did invade, murther and spoyle us, his majesties most faithfull subjects.

Of this and the aforesaid Articles we accuse Sir William Berkeley as guilty of each and every one of the same, and as one who hath traiterously attempted, violated and Injured his Majesties interest here, by a loss of a greate part of this his Colony and many of his faithfull loyall subjects, by him betrayed and in a barbarous and shamefull manner exposed to the Incursions and murther of the heathen, And we doe further declare these the ensueing persons in this list, to have beene his wicked and pernicious councellours Confederates, aiders, and assisters against the Comonality in these our Civill comotions.

Sir Henry Chichley	William Claiburne Junior
Lieut. Coll. Christopher	Thomas Hawkins
Wormeley	William Sherwood
Phillip Ludwell	John Page Clerke

Robert Beverley   John Cluffe Clerke
Richard Lee   John West
Thomas Ballard   Hubert Farrell
William Cole   Thomas Reade
Richard Whitacre   Matthew Kempe
Nicholas Spencer
Joseph Bridger

And we doe further demand that the said Sir William Berkeley with all the persons in this list be forthwith delivered up or surrender themselves within fower days after the notice hereof, Or otherwise we declare as followeth.

That in whatsoever place, howse, or ship, any of the said persons shall reside, be hidd, or protected, we declaire the owners, Masters or Inhabitants of the said places, to be confederates and trayters to the people and the estates of them is alsoe of all the aforesaid persons to be confiscated, and this we the Comons of Virginia doe declare, desiering a firme union amongst our selves that we may joyntly and with one accord defend our selves against the common Enimy, and lett not the faults of the guilty be the reproach of the inocent, or the faults or crimes of the oppressours devide and separate us who have suffered by theire oppressions.

These are therefore in his majesties name to command you forthwith to seize the persons above mentioned as Trayters to the King and Country and them to bring to Midle plantacon, and there to secure them untill further order, and in case of opposition, if you want any further assistance you are forthwith to demand itt in the name of the people in all the Counties of Virginia.

     Nathaniel Bacon
     Generall by Consent of the people.

The declaration and Remonstrance of Sir William Berkeley his most sacred Majesties Governor and Captain Generall of Virginia

Sheweth That about the yeare 1660 Coll. Mathews the then Governor dyed and then in consideration of the service I had don the Country, in defending them from, and destroying great numbers of the Indians, without the loss of three men, in all the time that warr lasted, and in contemplation of the equall and uncorrupt Justice I had distributed to all men, Not onely the Assembly but the unanimous votes of all the Country, concurred to make me Governor in a time, when if the Rebells in England had prevailed, I had certainly dyed for accepting itt, 'twas Gentlemen an unfortunate Love, shewed to me, for to shew myselfe grateftill for this, I was willing to accept of this Governement againe, when by my gracious Kings favour I might have had other places much more proffitable, and lesse toylesome then this hath beene. Since that time that I returned into the Country, I call the great God Judge of all things in heaven and earth to wittness, that I doe not know of any thing relateive to this Country wherein I have acted unjustly, corruptly, or negligently in distributeing equall Justice to all men, and takeing all possible care to preserve their proprietys, and defend the from their barbarous enimies.

But for all this, perhapps I have erred in things I know not of, if I have I am soe conscious of humane frailty, and my owne defects, that I will not onely acknowledge them, but repent of, and amend them, and not like the Rebell Bacon persist in an error, onely because I have comitted itt, and tells me in diverse of his Letters that itt is not for his honnor to confess a fault, but I am of opinion that itt is onely for divells to be incorrigable, and men of principles like the worst of divells, and these he hath, if truth be reported to me, of diverse of his expressions of Atheisme, tending to take away all Religion and Laws.

And now I will state the Question betwixt me as a Governor and Mr. Bacon, and say that if any enimies should invade England, any Councellor Justice of peace or other inferiour officer, might raise what forces they could to protect his Majesties subjects, But I say againe, if after the Kings knowledge of this invasion, any the greatest peere of England, should raise forces against the kings prohibition this would be now, and ever was in all ages and Nations accompted treason. Nay I will goe further, that though this peere was truly zealous for the preservation of his King, and subjects, and had better and greater abibitys then all the rest of his fellow subjects, doe his King and Country service, yett if the King (though by false information) should suspect the contrary, itt were treason in this Noble peere to proceed after the King's prohibition, and for the truth of this I appeale to all the laws of England, and the Laws and constitutions of all other Nations in the world, And yett further itt is declared by this Parliament that the takeing up Armes for the King and Parliament is treason, for the event shewed that what ever the pretence was to seduce ignorant and well affected people, yett the end was ruinous both to King and people, as this will be if not prevented, I doe therefore againe declair that Bacon proceedeing against all Laws of all Nations modern and ancient, is Rebell to his sacred Majesty and this Country, nor will I insist upon the sweareing of men to live and dye togeather, which is treason by the very words of the Law.

Now my friends I have lived 34 yeares amongst you, as uncorrupt and dilligent as ever Governor was, Bacon is a man of two yeares amongst you, his person and qualities unknowne to most of you, and to all men else, by any vertuous action that ever I heard of, And that very action which he boasts of, was sickly and fooleishly, and as I am informed treacherously carried to the dishonnor of the English Nation, yett in itt, he lost more men then I did in three yeares Warr, and by the grace of God will putt myselfe to the same daingers and troubles againe when I have brought Bacon to acknowledge the Laws are above him, and I doubt not but by God's assistance to have better success then Bacon hath had, the reason of my hopes are, that I will take Councell of wiser men then my selfe, but Mr. Bacon hath none about but the lowest of the people.

Yett I must further enlarge, that I cannot without your helpe, doe any thinge in this but dye in defence of my King, his laws, and subjects, which I will cheerefully doe, though alone I doe itt, and considering my poore fortunes, I can not leave my poore Wife and friends a better legacy then by dyeing for my King and you: for his sacred Majesty will easeily distinguish betweene Mr. Bacons actions and myne, and Kinges have long Armes, either to reward or punish.

Now after all this, if Mr. Bacon can shew one precedens or example where such actings in any Nation what ever, was approved of, I will mediate with the King and you for a pardon, and excuce for him, but I can shew him an hundred examples where brave and great men have beene putt to death for gaineing Victorys against the Comand of their Superiors.

Lastly my most assured friends I would have preserved those Indians that I knew were howerly att our mercy, to have beene our spyes and intelligence, to finde out our bloody enimies, but as soone as I had the least intelligence that they alsoe were trecherous enimies, I gave out Commissions to distroy them all as the Commissions themselves will speake itt.

To conclude, I have don what was possible both to friend and enimy, have granted Mr. Bacon three pardons, which he hath scornefully rejected, suppoaseing himselfe stronger to subvert then I and you to maineteyne the Laws, by which onely and Gods assisting grace and mercy, all men mwt hope for peace and safety. I will add noe more though much more is still remaineing to Justifie me and condenme Mr. Bacon, but to desier that this declaration may be read in every County Court in the Country, and that a Court be presently called to doe itt, before the Assembly meet, That your approbation or dissattisfaction of this declaration may be knowne to all the Country, and the Kings Councell to whose most revered Judgments itt is submitted, Given the xxixth day of May, a happy day in the xxv"ith yeare of his most sacred Majesties Reigne, Charles the second, who God grant long and prosperously to Reigne, and lett all his good subjects say Amen.

Sir William Berkeley
Governor

1. *What, in general, are Nathaniel Bacon's complaints against Governor Berkeley? Who do you think would be most likely to join up with Bacon? Who would be least likely to do so?*
2. *How does William Berkeley present his case against Bacon? How do his views on relations with the Indians differ from Bacon's?*

3-3 Early French Explorations of the Mississippi River (1673)

In 1673, French missionary Jacques Marquette accompanied Louis Jolliet, a French Canadian fur trader, on a voyage of exploration into the heart of North America. Commencing at the northern reaches of Lake Michigan, the expedition headed south all the way to the confluence of the Arkansas and Mississippi Rivers before fear of a Spanish attack turned them back. Marquette preserved some of his findings in a journal written the following year—including the following observations of the Illinois confederacy.

> **Source:** Reuben Gold Thwaites, ed. *The Jesuit Relations and Allied Documents, Travels and Explorations of the Jesuit Missionaries in New France, 1610–1791*, Vol. LIX. *Lower Canada, Illinois, Ottawas, 1667–1669* (Cleveland: The Burrows Brothers Company, 1900).
> http://puffin.creighton.edu/jesuit/relations/relations_59.html

SECTION 4TH. OF THE GREAT RIVER CALLED MISSISIPI; ITS MOST NOTABLE FEATURES; OF VARIOUS ANIMALS, AND ESPECIALLY THE PISIKIOUS OR WILD CATTLE, THEIR SHAPE AND NATURE; OF THE FIRST VILLAGES OF THE ILINOIS, WHERE THE FRENCH ARRIVED.

HERE we are, then, on this so renowned River, all of whose peculiar features I have endeavored to note carefully. The Missisipi River takes its rise in various lakes in the country of the Northern nations. It is narrow at the place where Miskous empties; its Current, which flows southward, is slow and gentle. To the right is a large Chain of very high Mountains, and to the left are beautiful lands; in various Places, the stream is Divided by Islands. On sounding, we found ten brasses of Water. Its

Width is very unequal; sometimes it is three-quarters of a league, and sometimes it narrows to three arpents. We gently followed its Course, which runs toward the south and southeast, as far as the 42nd degree of Latitude. Here we plainly saw that its aspect was completely changed. There are hardly any woods or mountains; The Islands are more beautiful, and are Covered with finer trees. We saw only deer and cattle, bustards, and Swans without wings, because they drop Their plumage in This country. From time to time, we came upon monstrous fish, one of which struck our Canoe with such violence that I Thought that it was a great tree, about to break the Canoe to pieces. On another occasion, we saw on The water a monster with the head of a tiger, a sharp nose Like That of a wildcat, with whiskers and straight, Erect ears; The head 'was gray and The Neck quite black; but We saw no more creatures of this sort. When we cast our nets into the water we caught Sturgeon, and a very extraordinary Kind of fish. It resembles the trout, with This difference, that its mouth is larger. Near its nose—which is smaller, as are also the eyes—is a large Bone shaped Like a woman's busk, three fingers wide and a Cubit Long, at the end of which is a disk as Wide As one's hand. This frequently causes it to fall backward when it leaps out of the water. When we reached the parallel of 41 degrees 28 minutes, following The same direction, we found that Turkeys had taken the place of game; and the pisikious, or wild cattle, That of the other animals.

We call them "wild cattle," because they are very similar to our domestic cattle. They are not longer, but are nearly as large again, and more Corpulent. When Our people killed one, three persons had much difficulty in moving it. The head is very large; The forehead is flat, and a foot and a half Wide between the Horns, which are exactly like Those of our oxen, but black and much larger. Under the Neck They have a Sort of large dewlap, which hangs down; and on The back is a rather high hump. The whole of the head, The Neck, and a portion of the Shoulders, are Covered with a thick Mane Like That of horses; It forms a crest a foot long, which makes them hideous, and, failing over their eyes, Prevents them from seeing what is before Them. The remainder of the Body is covered with a heavy coat of curly hair, almost Like That of our sheep, but much stronger and Thicker. It falls off in Summer, and The skin becomes as soft As Velvet. At that season, the savages Use the hides for making fine Robes, which they paint in various Colors. The flesh and the fat of the pisikious are Excellent, and constitute the best dish at feasts. Moreover, they are very fierce; and not a year passes without their killing some savages. When attacked, they catch a man on their Horns, if they can, toss Him in the air, and then throw him on the ground, after which they trample him under foot, and kill him. If a person fire at Them from a distance, with either a bow or a gun, he must, immediately after the Shot, throw himself down and hide in the grass; For if they perceive Him who has fired, they Run at him, and attack him. As their legs are thick and rather Short, they do not run very fast, As a rule, except when angry. They are scattered about the prairie in herds; I have seen one of 400.

We continued to advance, but, As we knew not whither we were going,—for we had proceeded over one Hundred leagues without discovering anything except animals and birds,—we kept well on our guard. On this account, we make only a small fire on land, toward evening, to cook our meals; and, after supper, we remove Ourselves as far from it as possible, and pass the night in our Canoes, which we anchor in the river at some distance from the shore. This does not prevent us from always posting one of the party as a sentinel, for fear of a surprise. Proceeding still in a southerly and south-southwesterly direction, we find ourselves at the parallel of 41 degrees, and as low as 40 degrees and some minutes,—partly southeast and partly southwest,—after having advanced over 60 leagues since We Entered the River, without discovering anything.

Finally, on the 25th of June, we perceived on the water's edge some tracks of men, and a narrow and somewhat beaten path leading to a fine prairie. We stopped to Examine it; and, thinking that it was a road which Led to some village of savages, We resolved to go and reconnoiter it. We therefore left our two Canoes under the guard of our people, strictly charging Them not to allow themselves to be surprised, after which Monsieur Jollyet and I undertook this investigation—a rather hazardous one for two men who exposed themselves, alone, to the mercy of a barbarous and Unknown people, We silently followed The narrow path, and, after walking About 2 leagues, We discovered a village on the bank of a river, and two others on a Hill distant about half a league from the first. Then we Heartily commended ourselves to God, and, after imploring his aid, we went farther without being perceived, and approached so near that we could even hear the savages talking. We therefore Decided that it was time to reveal ourselves. This We did by Shouting with all Our energy, and stopped, without advancing any farther. On hearing the shout, the savages quickly issued from their Cabins, And having probably recognized us as Frenchmen, especially when they saw a black gown,—or, at least, having no cause for distrust, as we were only two men, and had given them notice of our arrival,—they deputed four old men to come and speak to us. Two of these bore tobacco-pipes, finely ornamented and Adorned with various feathers. They walked slowly, and raised their pipes toward the sun, seemingly offering them to it to smoke,—without, however, saying a word. They spent a rather long time in covering the short distance between their village and us. Finally, when they had drawn near, they stopped to Consider us attentively. I was reassured when I observed these Ceremonies, which with them are performed only among friends; and much more so when I saw them clad in Cloth, for I judged thereby that they were our allies. I therefore spoke to them first, and asked them who they were. They replied that they were Ilinois; and, as a token of peace, they offered us their pipes to smoke. They afterward invited us to enter their Village, where all the people impatiently awaited us. These pipes for smoking tobacco are called in this country Calumets. This word has come so much into use that, in order to be understood, I shall be obliged to use it, as I shall often have to mention these pipes.

71

SECTION 5TH. HOW THE ILINOIS RECEIVED THE FATHER IN THEIR VILLAGE.

AT the Door of the Cabin in which we were to be received was an old man, who awaited us in a rather surprising attitude, which constitutes a part of the Ceremonial that they observe when they receive Strangers. This man stood erect, and stark naked, with his hands extended and lifted toward the sun, As if he wished to protect himself from its rays, which nevertheless shone upon his face through his fingers. When we came near him, he paid us This Compliment: "How beautiful the sun is, O frenchman, when thou comest to visit us! All our village awaits thee, and thou shalt enter all our Cabins in peace." Having said this, he made us enter his own, in which were a crowd of people; they devoured us with their eyes, but, nevertheless, observed profound silence. We could, however, hear these words, which were addressed to us from time to time in a low voice: "How good it is, My brothers, that you should visit us."

After We had taken our places, the usual Civility of the country was paid to us, which consisted in offering us the Calumet. This must not be refused, unless one wishes to be considered an Enemy, or at least uncivil; it suffices that one make a pretense of smoking. While all the elders smoked after us, in order to do us honor, we received an invitation on behalf of the great Captain of all the Ilinois to proceed to his Village where he wished to hold a Council with us. We went thither in a large Company, For all these people, who had never seen any frenchmen among Them, could not cease looking at us. They Lay on The grass along the road; they preceded us, and then retraced their steps to come and see us Again. All this was done noiselessly, and with marks of great respect for us.

When we reached the Village of the great Captain, We saw him at the entrance of his Cabin, between two old men,—all three erect and naked, and holding their Calumet turned toward the sun. He harangued us In a few words, congratulating us upon our arrival. He afterward offered us his Calumet, and made us smoke while we entered his Cabin, where we received all their usual kind Attentions.

Seeing all assembled and silent, I spoke to them by four presents that I gave them. By the first, I told them that we were journeying peacefully to visit the nations dwelling on the River as far as the Sea. By the second, I announced to them that God, who had Created them, had pity on Them, inasmuch as, after they had so long been ignorant of him, he wished to make himself Known to all the peoples; that I was Sent by him for that purpose; and that it was for Them to acknowledge and obey him. By the third, I said that the great Captain of the French informed them that he it was who restored peace everywhere; and that he had subdued The Iroquois. Finally, by the fourth, we begged them to give us all The Information that they had about the Sea, and about the Nations through Whom we must pass to reach it.

When I had finished my speech, the Captain arose, and, resting His hand upon the head of a little Slave whom he wished to give us, he spoke thus: "I thank thee, Black Gown, and thee, O frenchman," addressing himself to Monsieur Jollyet, "for having taken so much trouble to come to visit us. Never has the earth been so beautiful, or the sun so Bright, as to-day; Never has our river been so Calm, or so clear of rocks, which your canoes have Removed in passing: never has our tobacco tasted so good, or our corn appeared so fine, as We now see Them. Here is my son, whom I give thee to Show thee my Heart. I beg thee to have pity on me, and on all my Nation. It is thou who Knowest the great Spirit who has made us all. It is thou who speakest To Him, and who hearest his word. Beg Him to give me life and health, and to come and dwell with us in order to make us Know him." Having said this, he placed the little Slave near us, and gave us a second present, consisting of an altogether mysterious Calumet, upon which they place more value than upon a Slave. By this gift, he expressed to us The esteem that he had for Monsieur Our Governor, from the account which we had given of him; and, by a third, he begged us on behalf of all his Nation not to go farther, on account of the great dangers to which we Exposed ourselves.

I replied that I Feared not death, and that I regarded no happiness as greater than that of losing my life for the glory of Him who has made all. This is what these poor people cannot Understand.

The Council was followed by a great feast, Consisting of four dishes, which had to be partaken of in accordance with all their fashions. The first course was a great wooden platter full of sagamité,—that is to say, meal of Indian corn boiled in water, and seasoned with fat. The Master of Ceremonies filled a Spoon with sagamité three or 4 times, and put it to my mouth As if I were a little Child. He did The same to Monsieur Jollyet. As a second course, he caused a second platter to be brought, on which were three fish. He took some pieces of them, removed the bones therefrom, and, after blowing upon them to cool Them, he put them in our mouths As one would give food to a bird. For the third course, they brought a large dog, that had just been killed; but, when they learned that we did not eat this meat, they removed it from before us. Finally, the 4th course was a piece of wild ox, The fattest morsels of which were placed in our mouths.

After this feast, we had to go to visit the whole village, which Consists of fully 300 Cabins. While we walked through the Streets, an orator Continually harangued to oblige all the people to come to see us without Annoying us. Everywhere we were presented with Belts, garters, and other articles made of the hair of bears and cattle, dyed red, Yellow, and gray. These are all the rarities they possess. As they are of no great Value, we did not burden ourselves with Them.

We Slept in the Captain's Cabin, and on the following day we took Leave of him, promising to pass again by his village, within four moons. He Conducted us to our Canoes, with nearly 600 persons who witnessed our Embarkation, giving us every possible manifestation of the joy that Our visit had caused them. For my own part, I promised, on bidding them Adieu, that I would come the following year, and reside with Them to instruct them. But, before quitting the Ilinois country, it is proper that I should relate what I observed of their Customs and usages.

1. Describe Father Marquette's attitude toward native people in general and the Illinois in particular. Does he exhibit any particular disposition that might prove generally advantageous to the French in their future relations with the Indians?
2. Father Marquette refers repeatedly to the use of a "calumet." What is a "calumet" and what significance did it have to the Illinois?

3-4   Edward Randolph Describes King Philip's War (1685)

Edward Randolph was sent by King James II to investigate colonial infringements of the Navigation Acts as well as other seemingly unpopular laws passed by Parliament. He was also asked to describe the overall state of affairs in New England. Here is the section from Randolph's 1685 account that addresses the war between the colonists and the Indians led by Metacom (or Metacomet, called King Philip by the English).

Source: *The American Colonist's Library, A Treasury of Primary Documents*
http://www.swarthmore.edu/SocSci/bdorsey/docs/45-ran.html

[Some spelling has been modernized.]

Eighth Enquiry. What hath been the original cause of the present war with the natives. What are the advantages or disadvantages arising thereby and will probably be the End?

Various are the reports and conjectures of the causes of the present Indian war. Some impute it to an imprudent zeal in the magistrates of Boston to Christianize those heathen before they were civilized and injoyning them the strict observation of their lawes, which, to a people so rude and licentious, hath proved even intolerable, and that the more, for that while the magistrates, for their profit, put the lawes severely in execution against the Indians, the people, on the other side, for lucre and gain, entice and provoke the Indians to the breach thereof, especially to drunkenness, to which those people are so generally addicted that they will strip themselves to their skin to have their fill of rum and brandy, the Massachusets having made a law that every Indian drunk should pay 10s. or be whipped, according to the discretion of the magistrate. Many of these poor people willingly offered their backs to the lash to save their money; whereupon, the magistrates finding much trouble and no profit to arise to the government by whipping, did change that punishment into 10 days worke for such as could not or would not pay the fine of 10s. which did highly incense the Indians.

Some believe there have been vagrant and jesuiticall priests, who have made it their businesses for some yeares past, to go from Sachim to Sachim, to exasperate the Indians against the English and to bring them into a confederacy, and that they were promised supplies from France and other parts to extirpate the English nation out of the continent of America. Others impute the cause to some injuries offered to the Sachim Philip; for he being possessed of a tract of land called Mount Hope, a very fertile, pleasant and rich soyle, some English had a mind to dispossesse him thereof, who never wanting one pretence or other to attain their end, complained of injuries done by Philip and his Indians to their stock and cattle, whereupon Philip was often summoned before the magistrate, sometimes imprisoned, and never released but upon parting with a considerable part of his land.

But the government of the Massachusets (to give it in their own words) do declare these are the great evills for which God hath given the heathen commission to rise against the: The wofull breach of the 5th commandment, in contempt of their authority, which is a sin highly provoking to the Lord: For men wearing long hair and perewigs made of women's hair; for women wearing borders of hair and for cutting, curling and laying out the hair, and disguising themselves by following strange fashions in their apparell: For profaneness in the people not frequenting their meetings, and others going away before the blessing be pronounced: For suffering the Quakers to live amongst them and to set up their threshholds by Gods threshholds, contrary to their old lawes and resolutions.

With many such reasons, but whatever be the cause, the English have contributed much to their misfortunes, for they first taught the Indians the use of armes, and admitted them to be present at all their musters and trainings, and shewed them how to handle, mend and fix their muskets, and have been furnished with all sorts of armes by permission of the government, so that the Indians are become excellent firemen. And at Natick there was a gathered church of praying Indians, who were exercised as trained bands, under officers of their owne; these have been the most barbarous and cruel enemies to the English of any others. Capt. Tom, their leader, being lately taken and hanged at Boston, with one other of their chiefs.

That notwithstanding the ancient law of the country, made in the year 1633, that no person should sell any armes or ammunition to any Indian upon penalty of £10 for every gun, £5 for a pound of powder, and 40s. for a pound of shot, yet the government of the Massachusets in the year 1657, upon designe to monopolize the whole Indian trade did publish and declare that the trade of furrs and peltry with the Indians in their jurisdiction did solely and properly belong to their commonwealth and not to every indifferent person, and did enact that no person should trade with the Indians for any sort of peltry, except such as were authorized by that court, under the penalty of £100 for every offence, giving liberty to all such as should have licence from them to sell, unto any Indian, guns, swords, powder and shot, paying to the treasurer 3d. for each gun and for each dozen of swords; 6d. for a pound of powder and for every ten pounds of shot, by which means the Indians have been abundantly furnished with great store of armes and ammunition to the utter ruin and undoing of many families in the neighbouring colonies to enrich some few of their relations and church members.

No advantage but many disadvantages have arisen to the English by the war, for about 600 men have been slain, and 12 captains, most of them brave and stout persons and of loyal principles, whilest the church members had liberty to stay at home and not hazard their persons in the wildernesse.

The losse to the English in the severall colonies, in their habitations and stock, is reckoned to amount to £150,000 there having been about 1200 houses burned, 8000 head of cattle, great and small, killed, and many thousand bushels of wheat, peas and other grain burned (of which the Massachusets colony hath not been damnifyed one third part, the great losse falling upon New Plymouth and Connecticot colonies) and upward of 3000 Indians men women and children destroyed, who if well managed would have been very serviceable to the English, which makes all manner of labour dear.

The war at present is near an end. In Plymouth colony the Indians surrender themselves to Gov. Winslow, upon mercy, and bring in all their armes, are wholly at his disposall, except life and transportation; but for all such as have been notoriously cruell to women and children, so soon as discovered they are to be executed in the sight of their fellow Indians.

The government of Boston have concluded a peace.. . .

1. *According to Randolph, why are the colonists at least somewhat responsible for the instigation of hostilities between themselves and King Philip?*
2. *How would you characterize Randolph's description of King Philip and his followers? Where does Randolph's portrait of King Philip fit into one stereotypic seventeenth century image of the American Indian as a "noble savage"?*

3-5 Excerpt from Cotton Mather's "Memorable Providences, Relating to Witchcrafts and Possessions" (1689)

In 1689, Cotton Mather, minister of the Old North Church in Boston, published an account of supposed witchcraft that occurred the previous year involving an Irish washerwoman named Glover. Mather's publication, entitled "Memorable Providences, Relating to Witchcrafts and Possessions," included a description of the signs of witchcraft. Owing in part to the minister's status and reputation, his commentary was widely circulated and discussed throughout Puritan New England. Samuel Parris, the Salem minister in whose house the events of 1692 were initiated, owned a copy.

Source: *Famous American Trials: Salem Witchcraft Trials, 1692*
http://www.law.umkc.edu/faculty/projects/ftrials/salem/ASA_MATH.HTM

[Some spelling has been modernized.]

Section I. There dwells at this time, in the south part of Boston, a sober and pious man, whose Name is John Goodwin, whose Trade is that of a Mason, and whose Wife (to which a Good Report gives a share with him in all the Characters of Vertue) has made him the Father of six (now living) Children. Of these Children, all but the Eldest, who works with his Father at his Calling, and the Youngest, who lives yet upon the Breast of its mother, have laboured under the direful effects of a (no less palpable than) stupendous Witchcraft. Indeed that exempted Son had also, as was thought, some lighter touches of it, in unaccountable stabbs and pains now and then upon him; as indeed every person in the Family at some time or other had, except the godly Father, and the sucking Infant, who never felt any impressions of it. But these Four Children mentioned, were handled in so sad and strange a manner, as has given matter of Discourse and Wonder to all the Contrary, and of History not unworthy to be considered by more than all the serious or the curious Readers in this New-English World.

Sect. II. The four Children (whereof the Eldest was about Thirteen, and the youngest was perhaps about a third part so many years of age) had enjoyed a Religious Education, and answered it with a very towardly Ingenuity. They had an observable Affection unto Divine and Sacred things; and those of them that were capable of it, seem'd to have such a Resentment, of their eternal Concernments as is not altogether usual. Their Parents also kept them to a continual Employment, which did more than deliver them from the Temptations of Idleness (and as young as they were, they took a delight in it) it may be as much as they should have done. In a word, Such was the whole Temper and Carriage of the Children, that there cannot easily be any thing more unreasonable, than to imagine that a Design to Dissemble could cause them to fall into any of their odd Fits; though there should not have happened, as there did, a thousand Things, wherein it was perfectly impossible for any Dissimulation of theirs to produce what scores of spectators were amazed at.

Sect. III. About Midsummer, in the year 1688, the Eldest of these Children, who is a Daughter, saw cause to examine their Washerwoman, upon their missing of some Linnen which twas fear'd she had stollen from them; and of what use this linnen might bee to serve the Witchcraft intended, the Theef's Tempter knows! This Laundress was the Daughter of an ignorant and a scandalous old Woman in the Neighbourhood; whose miserable Husband before he died, had sometimes complained of her, that she was undoubtedly a Witch, and that whenever his Head was laid, she would quickly arrive unto the punishments due to such an one. This Woman in her daughters Defence bestow'd very bad Language upon the Girl that put her to the Question; immediately upon which, the poor child became variously indisposed in her health, an visited with strange Fits, beyond those that attend an Epilepsy or a Catalepsy, or those that they call The Diseases of Astonishment.

Sect. IV. It was not long before one of her Sisters, and two of her Brothers, were seized, in order one after another with Affects like those that molested her. Within a few weeks, they were all four tortured every where in a manner s very grievous, that it would have broke an heart of stone to have seen their Agonies. Skilful Physicians were consulted for their Help, and particularly our worthy and prudent Friend Dr. Thomas Oakes, who found Himself so affronted by the Dist'empers of the children, that he concluded nothing but an hellish Witchcraft could be the Original of these Maladies. And that which yet more confirmed such Apprehension was, That for one good while, the children were tormented just in the same part of their bodies all at the same time together; and tho they saw and heard not one another's complaints, tho likewise their pains and sprains were swift like Lightening, yet when (suppose) the Neck, or the Hand, or the Back of one was Rack't, so it was at that instant with t'other too.

Sect. V. The variety of their tortures increased continually; and tho about Nine or Ten at Night they always had a Release from their miseries, and ate and slept all night for the most part indifferently well, yet in the day time they were handled with so many sorts of Ails, that it would require of us almost as much time to Relate them all, as it did of them to Endure them. Sometimes they would be Deaf, sometimes Dumb, and sometimes Blind, and often, all this at once. One while their Tongues would be drawn down their Throats; another-while they would be pull'd out upon their Chins, to a prodigious length. They would have their Mouths opened unto such a Wideness, that their Jaws went out of joint; and anon they would clap together again with a Force like that of a strong Spring-Lock. The same would happen to their Shoulder-Blades, and their Elbows, and Hand-wrists, and several of their joints. They would at times lie in a benummed condition and be drawn together as those that are ty'd Neck and Heels; and presently be stretched out, yea, drawn Backwards, to such a degree that it was fear'd the very skin of their Bellies would have crack'd. They would make most pitteous out-cries, that they were cut with Knives, and struck with Blows that they could not bear. Their Necks would be broken, so that their Neck-bone would seem dissolved unto them that felt after it; and yet on the sudden, it would become, again so stiff that there was no stirring of their Heads; yea, their Heads would be twisted almost round; and if main Force at any time obstructed a dangerous motion which they seem'd to be upon, they would roar exceedingly. Thus they lay some weeks most pittiful Spectacles; and this while as a further Demonstration of Witchcraft in these horrid Effects, when I went to Prayer by one of them, that was very desireous to hear what I said, the Child utterly lost her Hearing till our Prayer was over.

Sect. VI. It was a Religious Family that these Afflictions happened unto; and none but a Religious Contrivance to obtain Releef, would have been welcome to them. Many superstitious proposals were made unto them, by persons that were I know not who, nor what, with Arguments fetch't from I know not how much Necessity and Experience; but the distressed Parents rejected all such counsils, with a gracious Resolution, to oppose Devils with no other weapons but Prayers and Tears, unto Him that has the Chaining of them; and to try first whether Graces were not the best things to encounter Witchcrafts with. Accordingly they requested the four Ministers of Boston, with the Minister of Charlestown, to keep a Day of Prayer at their thus haunted house; which they did in the Company of some devout people there. Immediately upon this Day, the youngest of the four children was delivered, and never felt any trouble as afore. But there was yet a greater Effect of these our Applications unto our God!

75

Sect. VII. The Report of the Calamities of the Family for which we were thus concerned arrived now unto the ears of the Magistrates, who presently and prudently apply'd themselves, with a just vigour, to enquire into the story. The Father of the Children complained of his Neighbour, the suspected ill woman, whose name was Glover; and she being sent for by the Justices, gave such a wretched Account of her self, that they saw cause to commit her unto the Gaolers Custody. Goodwin had no proof that could have done her any Hurt; but the Hag had not power to deny her interest in the Enchantment of the Children; and I when she was asked, Whether she believed there was a God? her Answer was too blasphemous and horrible for any Pen of mine to mention. An Experiment was made, Whether she could recite the Lords Prayer; and it was found, that tho clause after clause was most carefully repeated unto her, yet when she said it after them that prompted her, she could not Possibly avoid making Nonsense of it, with some ridiculous Depravations. This Experiment I had the curiosity since to see made upon two more, and it had the same Event. Upon Commitment of this extraordinary Woman, all the Children had some present ease,; until one (related unto her) accidentally meeting one or two of them, entertained them with her Blessing, that is, Railing; upon which Three of them fell ill again, as they were before.

Sect. VIII. It was not long before the Witch thus in the Trap, was brought upon her Trial; at which, thro'the Efficacy of a Charm, I suppose, used upon her, by one or some of her Cruel the Court could receive Answers from her in one but the Irish, which was her Native Language; although she under-stood the English very well, and had accustomed her whole Family to none but that Language in her former Conversation; and therefore the Communication between the Bench and the Bar, was now cheefly convey'd by two honest and faithful men that were interpreters. It was long before she could with any direct Answers plead unto her Indictment and; when she did plead, it was with Confession rather than Denial of her Guilt. Order was given to search the old woman's house, from whence there were brought into the Court, several small Images, or Puppets, or Babies, made of Raggs, and stufft with Goat's hair, and other such Ingredients. When these were produced, the vile Woman acknowledged, that her way to torment the Objects of her malice, was by wetting of her Finger with her Spittle, and streaking of those little Images. The abused Children were then present, and the Woman still kept stooping and shrinking as one that was almost pressed to Death with a mighty Weight upon her. But one of the Images being brought unto her, immediately she started up after an odd manner, and took it into her hand; but she had no sooner taken it, than one of the Children fell into sad Fits, before the whole Assembly. This the Judges bad their just Apprehensions at; and carefully causing the Repetition of the Experiment, found again the same event of it. They asked her, Whether she had any to stand by her: She replied, She had; and looking very pertly in the Air, she added, No, He's gone. And she then confessed, that she had One, who was her Prince, with whom she maintained, I know not what Communion. For which cause, the night after, she was heard expostulating with a Devil, for his thus deserting her; telling him that Because he had served her so basely and falsely, she had confessed all. However to make all clear, The Court appointed five or six Physicians one evening to examine her very strictly, whether she were not craz'd in her Intellectuals, and had not procured to her self by Folly and Madness the Reputation of a Witch. Diverse hours did they spend with her; and in all that while no Discourse came from her, but what was pertinent and agreeable: particularly, when they asked her, What she thought would become of her soul? she reply'd "You ask me, a very solemn Question, and I cannot well tell what to say to it." She own'd her self a Roman Catholick; and could recite her Pater Noster in Latin very readily; but there was one Clause or two alwaies too hard for her, whereof she said, "She could not repeat it, if she might have all the world." In the up-shot, the Doctors returned her Compos Mentis; and Sentence of Death was pass'd upon her.

1. *What had this washerwoman done to put her under suspicion of witchcraft? What do you think might be a more tangible underlying reason for Mather's ill feeling toward her?*
2. *What was the experiment (trap) that "proved" Glover was a witch?*

3-6 William Penn's Charter of Privileges (1701)

William Penn made two trips to Pennsylvania. On his first trip in 1682 he established a colony founded on the basic principals of liberty, freedom of conscience, and goodwill toward the Indians. On his return in 1699, Penn oversaw the adoption of a new frame of government, the Charter of Privileges, in October, 1701. This constitution, which lasted until the outbreak of the Revolution, was a step in the direction of self-government. Many historians believe that the "Liberty Bell," which was ordered in 1751 but not cast until 1752, was purchased to commemorate the fiftieth anniversary of the Charter of Privileges.

Source: The Avalon Project at the Yale Law School: Documents in Law, History and Diplomacy.
http://www.yale.edu/lawweb/avalon/states/pa07.htm

WILLIAM PENN, Proprietary and Governor of the Province of *Pensilvania* and Territories thereunto belonging, To all to whom these Presents shall come, sendeth Greeting. WHEREAS King CHARLES *the Second*, by His Letters Patents, under the Great Seal of *England*, bearing Date the *Fourth* Day of *March* in the Year *One Thousand Six Hundred and Eighty-one*, was graciously pleased to give and grant unto me, and my Heirs and Assigns for ever, this Province of Pennsilvania, with divers great Powers and Jurisdictions for the well Government thereof.

AND WHEREAS the King's dearest Brother, JAMES *Duke of* YORK *and* ALBANY, &c. by his Deeds of Feoffment, under his Hand and Seal duly perfected, bearing Date the *Twenty-Fourth* Day of August, *One Thousand Six Hundred Eighty and Two*, did grant unto me, my Heirs and Assigns, all that Tract of Land, now called the Territories of *Pensilvania*, together with Powers and Jurisdictions for the good Government thereof.

AND WHEREAS for the Encouragement of all the Freemen and Planters, that might be concerned in the said Province and Territories, and for the good Government thereof, I the said WILLIAM PENN, in the Year *One Thousand Six Hundred Eighty and Three*, for me, my Heirs and Assigns, did grant and confirm unto all the Freemen Planters and Adventurers therein, divers Liberties, Franchises and Properties, as by the said Grant, entituled, *The* FRAME *of the Government of the Province of* Pensilvania, *and Territories thereunto belonging, in* America, may appear; which Charter or Frame being found in some Parts of it, not so suitable to the present Circumstances of the Inhabitants, was in the *Third* Month, in the Year One Thousand Seven Hundred, delivered up to me, by *Six* Parts of Seven of the Freemen of this Province and Territories, in General Assembly met, Provision being made in the said Charter, for that End and Purpose.

AND WHEREAS I was then pleased to promise, That I would restore the said Charter to them again, with necessary Alterations, or in lieu thereof, give them another, better adapted to answer the present Circumstances and Conditions of the said Inhabitants; which they have now, by their Representatives in General Assembly met at *Philadelphia*, requested me to grant.

KNOW YE THEREFORE, That for the further Well-being and good Government of the said Province, and Territories; and in Pursuance of the Rights and Powers before-mentioned, I the said William Penn do declare, grant and confirm, unto all the Freemen, Planters and Adventurers, and other Inhabitants of this Province and Territories, these following Liberties, Franchises and Privileges, so far as in kme lieth, to be held, enjoyed and kept, by the Freemen, Planters and Adventurers, and other Inhabitants of and in the said Province and Territories "hereunto annexed, for ever.

FIRST

BECAUSE no People can be truly happy, though under the greatest Enjoyment of Civil Liberties, if abridged of the Freedom of their Consciences, as to their Religious Profession and Worship: And Almighty God being the only Lord of Conscience, Father of Lights and Spirits; and the Author as well as Object of all divine Knowledge, Faith and Worship, who only cloth enlighten the Minds, and persuade and convince the Understandings of People, I do hereby grant and declare, That no Person or Persons, inhabiting in this Province or Territories, who shall confess and acknowledge One almighty God, the Creator, Upholder and Ruler of the World; and profess him or themselves obliged to live quietly under the Civil Government, shall be in any Case molested or prejudiced, in his or their Person or Estate, because of his or their conscientious Persuasion or Practice, nor be compelled to frequent or maintain any religious Worship, Place or Ministry, contrary to his or their Mind, or to do or super any other Act or Thing, contrary to their religious Persuasion.

AND that all Persons who also profess to believe in *Jesus Christ*, the Saviour of the World, shall be capable (notwithstanding their other Persuasions and Practices in Point of Conscience and Religion) to serve this Government in any Capacity, both legislatively and executively, he or they solemnly promising, when lawfully required, Allegiance to the King as Sovereign, and Fidelity to the Proprietary and Governor, and taking the Attests as now established by the Law made at *New-Castle*, in the Year *One Thousand and Seven Hundred*, entitled, *An Act directing the Attests of several Officers and Ministers*, as now amended and confirmed this present Assembly.

II

FOR the well governing of this Province and Territories, there shall be an Assembly yearly chosen, by the Freemen thereof, to consist of *Four* Persons out of each County, of most Note for Virtue, Wisdom and Ability, (or of a greater number at any Time, as the Governor and Assembly shall agree) upon the *First* Day of *October* for ever; and shall sit on the *Fourteenth* Day of the same Month, at *Philadelphia*, unless the Governor and Council for the Time being, shall see Clause to appoint another Place within the said Province or Territories: Which Assembly shall have Power to chuse a Speaker and other their Officers; and shall be Judges of the Qualifications and Elections of their own Members; sit upon their own Adjournments; appoint (committees; prepare Bills in order to pass into Laws; impeach Criminals, and redress Grievances; and shall have all other Powers and Privileges of an Assembly, according to the Rights of the free-born Subjects of *England*, and as is usual in any of the King's Plantations in *America*.

AND if any County or Counites, shall refuse or neglect to chuse their respective Representatives as aforesaid, or if chosen, do not meet to serve in Assembly, those who are so chosen and met, shall have the full Power of an Assembly, in as ample Manner as if all the Representatives had been chosen and met, provided they are not less than *Two Thirds* of the whole Number that ought to meet.

AND that the Qualifications of Electors and Elected, and all other Matters and Things relating to Elections of Representatives to serve in Assemblies, though not herein particularly expressed, shall be and remain as by a Law of this Government, made at *New-Castle* in the Year *One Thousand Seven Hundred*, entitled, *An Act to ascertain the Number of Members of Assembly, and to regulate the Elections.*

III

THAT the Freemen in each respective County at the Time and Place of Meeting for Electing their Representatives to serve in Assembly, may as often as there shall be Occasion, chuse a double Number of Persons to present to the Governor for Sheriffs and Coroners to serve for *Three* Years, if so long they behave themselves well; out of which respective Elections and Presentments, the Governor shall nominate and commissionate one for each of the said Offices, the *Third* Day after such Presentment, or else the First named in such Presentment, for each Office as aforesaid, shall stand and serve in that Office for the Time before respectively limited; and in Case of Death or Default, such Vacancies shall be supplied by the Governor, to serve to the End of the said Term.

PROVIDED ALWAYS, That if the said Freemen shall at any Time neglect or decline to chuse a Person or Persons for either or both the aforesaid Offices then and in such Case, the Persons that are or shall be in the respective Offices of Sheriffs or Coroners, at the Time of Election, shall remain therein, until they shall be removed by another Election as aforesaid.

AND that the Justices of the respective Counties shall or may nominate and present to the Governor *Three* Persons, to serve for Clerk of the Peace for the said County, when there is a Vacancy, one of which the Governor shall commissionate within Ten Days after such Presentment, or else the *First* nominated shall serve in the said Office during good Behavior.

IV

THAT the Laws of this Government shall be in this Stile, viz. *By the Governor, with the Consent and Approbations of the Freemen in General Assembly Met*; and shall be, after Confirmation bv the Governor, forthwith recorded in the Rolls Office, and kept at *Philadelphia*, unless the Governor and Assembly shall agree to appoint another Place.

V

THAT all Criminals shall have the same Privileges of Witnesses and Council as their Prosecutors.

VI

THAT no Person or Persons shall or may, at any Time hereafter, be obliged to answer any Complaint, Matter or Thing whatsoever, relating to Property, before the Governor and Council, or in any other Place, but in ordinary Course of Justice, unless Appeals thereunto shall be hereafter by Law appointed.

VII

THAT no Person within this Government, shall be licensed by the Governor to keep an Ordinary, Tavern or House of Publick Entertainment, but such who are first recommended to him, under the Hands of the Justices of the respective Counties, signed in open Court; which Justices are and shall be hereby empowered, to suppress and forbid any Person, keeping such Publick-House as aforesaid, upon their Misbehaviour, on such Penalties as the Law cloth or shall direct; and to recommend others from time to time, as they shall see Occasion.

VIII

IF any person, through Temptation or Melancholy, shall destroy himself, his Estate, real and personal, shall notwithstanding descend to his Wife and Children, or Relations, as if he had died a natural Death; and if any Person shall be destroyed or killed by Casualty or Accident, there shall be no Forfeiture to the Governor by reason thereof.

AND no Act, Law or Ordinance whatsoever, shall at any Time hereafter, be made or done, to alter, change or diminish the Form or Effect of this Charter, or of any Part or Clause therein, contrary to the true Intent and Meaning thereof, without the Consent of the Governor for the Time being, and *Six* Parts of *Seven* of the Assembly met.

BUT because the Happiness of Mankind depends so much upon the Enjoying of Liberty of their Consciences as aforesaid, I do hereby solemnly declare, promise and grant, for me, my Heirs and Assigns, That the *First* Article of this

Charter relating to Liberty of Conscience, and every Part and Clause therein, according to the true Intent and Meaning thereof, shall be kept and remain, without any Alteration, inviolably for ever.

AND LASTLY, I the said *William Penn*, Proprietary and Governor of the Province of *Pensilvania*, and Territories thereunto belonging, for myself, my Heirs and Assigns, have solemnly declared, granted and confirmed, and do hereby solemnly declare, grant and confirm, That neither I, my Heirs or Assigns, shall procure or do any Thing or Things whereby the Liberties In this Charter contained and expressed, nor any Part thereof, shall be infringed or broken: And if any thing shall be procured or done, by any Person or Persons, contrary to these Presents, it shall be held of no Force or Effect.

IN WITNESS whereof, I the said *William Penn*, at *Philadelphia* in *Pensilvania*, have unto this present Charter of Liberties, set my Hand and broad Seal, this *Twenty-Eighth* Day of *October*, in the Year of Our Lord *One Thousand Seven Hundred and One*, being the *Thirteenth* Year of the Reign of King William the *Third*, over *England, Scotland, France* and *Ireland*, &c. and the *Twenty-First* Year of my Government.

AND NOTWITHSTANDING the Closure and Test of this present Charter as aforesaid, I think fit to add this following Proviso thereunto, as Part of the same, *That is to say*, That notwithstanding any Clause or Clauses in the above-mentioned Charter, obliging the Province and Territories to join together in Legislation, I am content, and do hereby declare, that if the Representatives of the Province and Territories shall not hereafter agree to join together in Legislation, and that the same shall be signified unto me, or my Deputy, in open Assembly, or otherwise from under the Hands and Seals of the Representatives, for the Time being, of the Province and Territories, or the major Part of either of them, at any Time within *Three* Years from the Date hereof, that in such Case, the Inhabitants of each of the *Three* Counties of this Province, shall not have less than Eight Persons to represent them in Assembly, for the Province; and the Inhabitants of the Town of *Philadelphia* (when the said Town is incorporated) Two Persons to represent them in Assembly; and the Inhabitants of each County in the Territories, shall have as many Persons to represent them in a distinct Assembly for the Territories, as shall be by them requested as aforesaid.

NOTWITHSTANDING which Separation of the Province and Territories, in Respect of Legislation, I do hereby promise, grant and declare, That the Inhabitants of both Province and Territories, shall separately enjoy all other Liberties, Privileges and Benefits, granted jointly to them in this Charter, any Law, Usage or Custom of this Government heretofore made and practiced, or any Law made and passed by this General Assembly, to the Contrary hereof, notwithstanding.

WILLIAM PENN.

1. *Discuss the ways in which the Charter of Privileges guarantees the right of religious freedom. Are there any exceptions to this religious toleration?*
2. *Despite Penn's vision for liberty, he seemed undisturbed about slavery in the colonies. He even owned some slaves, as did many other Quakers. How do you think he could reconcile his humanitarianism with the presence of chattel slavery?*

3-7 William Byrd II, Diary (1709)

William Byrd II of Westover, Virginia was a prime example of a new American. Byrd was a member of the American gentry, but spent his life in a desperate attempt to live up to his own conception of an English gentleman. He compulsively ordered his life in an attempt to reflect the lifestyle of the English gentry he had only read about. For all his efforts, however, Byrd never really lived the life of English gentry. For one thing, his perception of the life of an English gentleman was a bit off the mark — he was self-taught, relying on his reading of instruction manuals. He had to fashion himself a gentleman literally by the book. Naturally, this produced a somewhat skewed image of what it meant to be a British gentleman. Moreover, the realities of life in the colonies were far different from those in England, guaranteeing Byrds quest to be quixotic at best. In fact, unknown to himself, he represented something entirely new — an American gentleman.

7. I rose at 5 o'clock and read a chapter in Hebrew and some Greek in Josephus. I said my prayers and ate milk for breakfast. I danced my dance, and settled my accounts. I read some Latin. It was extremely hot. I ate stewed mutton for dinner. In the afternoon it began to rain and blow very violently so that it blew down my fence. It likewise thundered. In all the time I have been in Virginia I never heard it blow harder. I read Latin again and Greek in Homer. In the evening we took a walk in the garden. I said my prayers and had good health, good humor, and good thoughts, thanks be to God Almighty.

8. I rose at 5 o'clock and read a chapter in Hebrew and some Greek in Josephus. I said my prayers and ate milk for breakfast. I danced my dance. I read some Latin. Tom returned from Williamsburg and brought me a letter from Mr. Bland which told me the wine came out very well. I ate nothing but pudding for dinner. In the afternoon I read some more

Latin and Greek in Homer. Then I took a walk about the plantation. I said my prayers and had good health, good thoughts, and good humor, thanks be to God Almighty.

9. I rose at 5 o'clock and read two chapters in Hebrew and some Greek in Josephus. I said my prayers and ate milk and apples for breakfast with Captain Wilcox who called here this morning. I danced my dance. I wrote a letter to England and read some Latin. I ate roast chicken for dinner. In the afternoon I saluted my wife and took a nap. I read more Latin and Greek in Homer. Then I took a walk about the plantation. I neglected to say my prayers. I had good health, good thoughts, and good humor, thanks be to God Almighty.

1. *How would you describe and summarize the lifestyle recorded by William Byrd II in his diary? What conclusions might be made about Byrd's social standing considering the events of his days?*
2. *What seem to be the activities that produce a life characterized by I had "good health, good thoughts, and good humor"?*

3-8   Manners and Etiquette in the Eighteenth Century

The 110 Rules of Civility & Decent Behaviour In Company and Conversation were published to provide guidelines for general courtesy and behavior in public. These axioms, derived from France, were popularly circulated in middle and upper class society in the colonies during the early eighteenth century. The following transcript is from George Washington's copy of the Rules written in his school book when he was sixteen years old.

> **Source:** *George Washington's Rules of Civility and Decent Behaviour in Company and Conversation.* Edited with an Introduction by Charles Moore (Boston and New York: Houghton Mifflin Company, 1926). http://www.virginia.edu/gwpapers/civility/transcript.html

[Some spelling had been modernized.]

1st Every Action done in Company, ought to be with Some Sign of Respect, to those that are Present.

2d When in Company, put not your Hands to any Part of the Body, not usually Discovered.

3d Shew Nothing to your Friend that may affright him.

4 In the Presence of Others Sing not to yourself with a humming Noise, nor Drum with your Fingers or Feet.

5th If You Cough, Sneeze, Sigh, or Yawn, do it not Loud but Privately; and Speak not in your Yawning, but put Your handkerchief or Hand before your face and turn aside.

6th Sleep not when others Speak, Sit not when others stand, Speak not when you Should hold your Peace, walk not on when others Stop.

7th Put not off your Cloths in the presence of Others, nor go out your Chamber half Drest.

8th At Play and at Fire its Good manners to Give Place to the last Commer, and affect not to Speak Louder than Ordinary.

9th Spit not in the Fire, nor Stoop low before it neither Put your Hands into the Flames to warm them, nor Set your Feet upon the Fire especially if there be meat before it.

10th When you Sit down, Keep your Feet firm and Even, without putting one on the other or Crossing them.

11th Shift not yourself in the Sight of others nor Gnaw your nails.

12th Shake not the head, Feet, or Legs rowl not the Eyes lift not one eyebrow higher than the other wry not the mouth, and bedew no mans face with your Spittle, by appr[oaching too nea]r him [when] you Speak.

13th Kill no Vermin as Fleas, lice ticks &c in the Sight of Others, if you See any filth or thick Spittle put your foot Dexterously upon it if it be upon the Cloths of your Companions, Put it off privately, and if it be upon your own Cloths return Thanks to him who puts it off.

14th Turn not your Back to others especially in Speaking, Jog not the Table or Desk on which Another reads or writes, lean not upon any one.

15th Keep your Nails clean and Short, also your Hands and Teeth Clean yet without Shewing any great Concern for them.

16th Do not Puff up the Cheeks, Loll not out the tongue rub the Hands, or beard, thrust out the lips, or bite them or keep the Lips too open or too Close.

17th Be no Flatterer, neither Play with any that delights not to be Play'd Withal.

18th Read no Letters, Books, or Papers in Company but when there is a Necessity for the doing of it you must ask leave: come not near the Books or Writings of Another so as to read them unless desired or give your opinion of them unask'd also look not nigh when another is writing a Letter.

19th Let your Countenance be pleasant but in Serious Matters Somewhat grave.

20th The Gestures of the Body must be Suited to the discourse you are upon.

21st: Reproach none for the Infirmities of Nature, nor Delight to Put them that have in mind thereof.

22d Shew not yourself glad at the Misfortune of another though he were your enemy.

23d When you see a Crime punished, you may be inwardly Pleased; but always shew Pity to the Suffering Offender.

[24th Do not laugh too loud or] too much at any Publick [Spectacle].

25th Superfluous Complements and all Affectation of Ceremonie are to be avoided, yet where due they are not to be Neglected.

26th In Puffing off your Hat to Persons of Distinction, as Noblemen, Justices, Churchmen &c make a Reverence, bowing more or less according to the Custom of the Better Bred, and Quality of the Person. Amongst your equals expect not always that they Should begin with you first, but to Pull off the Hat when there is no need is Affectation, in the Manner of Saluting and resaluting in words keep to the most usual Custom.

27th Tis ill manners to bid one more eminent than yourself be covered as well as not to do it to whom it's due Likewise he that makes too much haste to Put on his hat does not well, yet he ought to Put it on at the first, or at most the Second time of being ask'd; now what is herein Spoken, of Qualification in behaviour in Saluting, ought also to be observed in taking of Place, and Sitting down for ceremonies without Bounds is troublesome.

28th If any one come to Speak to you while you are Sitting Stand up tho he be your Inferiour, and when you Present Seats let it be to every one according to his Degree.

29th When you meet with one of Greater Quality than yourself, Stop, and retire especially if it be at a Door or any Straight place to give way for him to Pass.

30th In walking the highest Place in most Countries Seems to be on the right hand therefore Place yourself on the left of him whom you desire to Honour: but if three walk together the mid[dest] Place is the most Honourable the wall is usually given to the most worthy if two walk together.

31st If any one far Surpasses others, either in age, Estate, or Merit [yet] would give Place to a meaner than hims[elf in his own lodging or elsewhere] the one ought not to except it, S[o he on the other part should not use much earnestness nor offer] it above once or twice.

32d To one that is your equal, or not much inferior you are to give the chief Place in your Lodging and he to who 'tis offered ought at the first to refuse it but at the Second to accept though not without acknowledging his own unworthiness.

33d They that are in Dignity or in office have in all places Preceedency but whilst they are Young they ought to respect those that are their equals in Birth or other Qualities, though they have no Publick charge.

34th It is good Manners to prefer them to whom we Speak befo [re] ourselves especially if they be above us with whom in no Sort we ought to begin.

35th Let your Discourse with Men of Business be Short and Comprehensive.

36th Artificers & Persons of low Degree ought not to use many ceremonies to Lords, or Others of high Degree but Respect and high[ly] Honour them, and those of high Degree ought to treat them with affability & Courtesie, without Arrogancy.

37th In Speaking to men of Quality do not lean nor Look them full in the Face, nor approach too near them at lest Keep a full Pace from them.

38th In visiting the Sick, do not Presently play the Physicion if you be not Knowing therein.

39th In writing or Speaking, give to every Person his due Title According to his Degree & the Custom of the Place.

40th Strive not with your Superiors in argument, but always Submit your Judgment to others with Modesty.

41st Undertake not to Teach your equal in the art himself Professes; it Savours of arrogancy.

[42d Let thy ceremonies in] Courtesie be proper to the Dignity of his place [with whom thou conversest for it is absurd to ac]t the same with a Clown and a Prince.

43d Do not express Joy before one sick or in pain for that contrary Passion will aggravate his Misery.

44th When a man does all he can though it Succeeds not well blame not him that did it.

45th Being to advise or reprehend any one, consider whether it ought to be in publick or in Private; presently, or at Some other time in what terms to do it & in reproving Shew no Sign of Cholar but do it with all Sweetness and Mildness.

46th Take all Admonitions thankfully in what Time or Place Soever given but afterwards not being culpable take a Time [&] Place convenient to let him know it that gave them.

[4]7th Mock not nor Jest at any thing of Importance break [n]o Jest that are Sharp Biting and if you Deliver any thing witty and Pleasant abstain from Laughing thereat yourself.

48th Wherein you reprove Another be unblameable yourself; for example is more prevalent than Precepts.

[4]9 Use no Reproachful Language against any one neither Curse nor Revile.

[5]0th Be not hasty to believe flying Reports to the Disparag[e]ment of any.

51st Wear not your Cloths, foul, unript or Dusty but See they be Brush'd once every day at least and take heed tha[t] you approach not to any Uncleanness.

52d In your Apparel be Modest and endeavour to accommodate Nature, rather than to procure Admiration keep to the Fashio[n] of your equals Such as are Civil and orderly with respect to Times and Places.

53d Run not in the Streets, neither go t[oo s]lowly nor wit[h] Mouth open go not Shaking yr Arms [kick not the earth with yr feet, go] not upon the Toes, nor in a Dancing [fashion].

54th Play not the Peacock, looking every where about you, to See if you be well Deck't, if your Shoes fit well if your Stokings sit neatly, and Cloths handsomely.

55th Eat not in the Streets, nor in the House, out of Season.

56th Associate yourself with Men of good Quality if you Esteem your own Reputation; for 'tis better to be alone than in bad Company.

57th In walking up and Down in a House, only with One in Compan[y] if he be Greater than yourself, at the first give him the Right hand and Stop not till he does and be not the first that turns, and when you do turn let it be with your face towards him, if he be a Man of Great Quality, walk not with him Cheek by Joul but Somewhat behind him; but yet in Such a Manner that he may easily Speak to you.

58th Let your Conversation be without Malice or Envy, for'tis a Sig[n o]f a Tractable and Commendable Nature: And in all Causes of Passion [ad]mit Reason to Govern.

59th Never express anything unbecoming, nor Act against the Rules Mora[l] before your inferiours.

60th Be not immodest in urging your Friends to Discover a Secret.

61st Utter not base and frivolous things amongst grave and Learn'd Men nor very Difficult Questions or Subjects, among the Ignorant or things hard to be believed, Stuff not your Discourse with Sentences amongst your Betters nor Equals.

62d Speak not of doleful Things in a Time of Mirth or at the Table; Speak not of Melancholy Things as Death and Wounds, and if others Mention them Change if you can the Discourse tell not your Dreams, but to your intimate Friend.

63d A Man o[ug]ht not to value himself of his Achievements, or rare Qua[lities of wit; much less of his rich]es Virtue or Kindred.

64th Break not a Jest where none take pleasure in mirth Laugh not aloud, nor at all without Occasion, deride no mans Misfortune, tho' there Seem to be Some cause.

65th Speak not injurious Words neither in Jest nor Earnest Scoff at none although they give Occasion.

66th Be not forward but friendly and Courteous; the first to Salute hear and answer & be not Pensive when it's a time to Converse.

67th Detract not from others neither be excessive in Commanding.

68th Go not thither, where you know not, whether you Shall be Welcome or not. Give not Advice with[out] being Ask'd & when desired [d]o it briefly.

[6]9 If two contend together take not the part of either unconstrained; and be not obstinate in your own Opinion, in Things indifferent be of the Major Side.

70th Reprehend not the imperfections of others for that belong[s] to Parents Masters and Superiours.

71st Gaze not on the marks or blemishes of Others and ask not how they came. What you may Speak in Secret to your Friend deliver not before others.

72d Speak not in an unknown Tongue in Company but in your own Language and that as those of Quality do and not as the Vulgar; Sublime matters treat Seriously.

73d Think before you Speak pronounce not imperfectly nor bring ou[t] your Words too hastily but orderly & distinctly.

74th When Another Speaks be attentive your Self and disturb not the Audience if any hesitate in his Words help him not nor Prompt him without desired, Interrupt him not, nor Answer him till his Speec[h] be ended.

75th In the midst of Discourse ask [not of what one treateth] but if you Perceive any Stop because of [your coming you may well entreat him gently] to Proceed: If a Person of Quality comes in while your Conversing it's handsome to Repeat what was said before.

76th While you are talking, Point not with your Finger at him of Whom you Discourse nor Approach too near him to whom you talk especially to his face.

77th Treat with men at fit Times about Business & Whisper not in the Company of Others.

78th Make no Comparisons and if any of the Company be Commended for any brave act of Virtue, commend not another for the Same.

79th Be not apt to relate News if you know not the truth thereof. In Discoursing of things you Have heard Name not your Author always A [Se]cret Discover not.

80th Be not Tedious in Discourse or in reading unless you find the Company pleased therewith.

81st Be not Curious to Know the Affairs of Others neither approach those that Speak in Private.

82d Undertake not what you cannot Perform but be Careful to keep your Promise.

83d When you deliver a matter do it without Passion & with Discretion, howev[er] mean the Person be you do it too.

84th When your Superiours talk to any Body hearken not neither Speak nor Laugh.

85th In Company of these of Higher Quality than yourself Speak not ti[l] you are ask'd a Question then Stand upright put of your Hat & Answer in few words.

86 In Disputes, be not So Desirous to Overcome as not to give Liberty to each one to deliver his Opinion and Submit to the Judgment of the Major Part especially if they are Judges of the Dispute.

[87th Let thy carriage be such] as becomes a Man Grave Settled and attentive [to that which is spoken. Contra]dict not at every turn what others Say.

88th Be not tedious in Discourse, make not many Digressions, nor rep[eat] often the Same manner of Discourse.

89th Speak not Evil of the absent for it is unjust.

90 Being Set at meat Scratch not neither Spit Cough or blow your Nose except there's a Necessity for it.

91st Make no Shew of taking great Delight in your Victuals, Feed no[t] with Greediness; cut your Bread with a Knife, lean not on the Table neither find fault with what you Eat.

92 Take no Salt or cut Bread with your Knife Greasy.

93 Entertaining any one at table it is decent to present him wt. meat, Undertake not to help others undesired by the Master.

[9]4th If you Soak bread in the Sauce let it be no more than what you [pu]t in your Mouth at a time and blow not your broth at Table [bu]t Stay till Cools of it Self.

[95]th Put not your meat to your Mouth with your Knife in your ha[nd ne]ither Spit forth the Stones of any fruit Pie upon a Dish nor Cas[t an]ything under the table.

[9]6 It's unbecoming to Stoop much to ones Meat Keep your Fingers clea[n &] when foul wipe them on a Corner of your Table Napkin.

[97]th Put not another bit into your Mouth till the former be Swallowed [l]et not your Morsels be too big for the Jowls.

98th Drink not nor talk with your mouth full neither Gaze about you while you are a Drinking.

99th Drink not too leisurely nor yet too hastily. Before and after Drinking wipe your Lips breath not then or Ever with too Great a Noise, for its uncivil.

100 Cleanse not your teeth with the Table Cloth Napkin Fork or Knife but if Others do it let it be done wt. a Pick Tooth.

101st Rinse not your Mouth in the Presence of Others.

102d It is out of use to call upon the Company often to Eat nor need you Drink to others every Time you Drink.

103d In Company of your Betters be no[t longer in eating] than they are lay not your Arm but o[nly your hand upon the table].

104th It belongs to the Chiefest in Company to unfold his Napkin and fall to Meat first, But he ought then to Begin in time & to Dispatch [w]ith Dexterity that the Slowest may have time allowed him.

[1]05th Be not Angry at Table whatever happens & if you have reason to be so, Shew it not but on a Cheerful Countenance especially if there be Strangers for Good Humour makes one Dish of Meat a Feas[t].

[1]06th Set not yourself at the upper of the Table but if it Be your Due or that the Master of the house will have it So, Contend not, least you Should Trouble the Company.

107th If others talk at Table be attentive but talk not with Meat in your Mouth.

108th When you Speak of God or his Attributes, let it be Seriously & [wt.] Reverence. Honour & Obey your Natural Parents altho they be Poor.

109th Let your Recreations be Manful not Sinful.

110th Labour to keep alive in your Breast that Little Spark of Ce[les]tial fire Called Conscience.

Finis

---

1. *What was the purpose of rules such as these? What role might environment have played in emphasizing the need for such guidelines in the colonies?*
2. *Washington transcribed the Rules of Civility in 1748 prior to leaving the comfortable life of the landed gentry and setting out as part of a surveying party in Western Virginia. What influence do you think these rules had on sixteen-year-old young people leaving the familiarity of home?*

3-9 "The Storm Arising in the West," George Washington Delivers a Warning to the French (1753)

On October 31, 1753, twenty-one year-old George Washington set out from Williamsburg, Virginia, with a small band of men under the instructions of Governor Dinwiddie to deliver a letter to the commander of the French forces in the Ohio Valley, General LeGardour de St. Pierre, reminding him of British sovereignty over the area. While there, Washington was also directed to reconnoiter the garrison and establish friendly relations with the Indians. Washington returned to Williamsburg on January 16, 1754 and two days later his journal was presented to the Virginia General Assembly. Soon, a regiment of 300 men was raised to defend the frontier and preserve Britain's control over the territory. The French and Indian War was on.

> **Source:** *The Maryland Gazette*, March 21, 1754 and March 28, 1754.
> http://www.earlyamerica.com/earlyamerica/milestones/journal/journaltext.html

Wednesday, October 31, 1753

I was commissioned and appointed by the Honourable Robert Dinwiddie, Esq, Governor, Etc. of Virginia, to visit and deliver a Letter to the Commandant of the French Forces on the Ohio, and set out on the intended Journey the same Day; the next, I arrived Fredericksburg, and engaged Mr. Jacob Van Braam to be my French Interpreter; and proceeded with him to Alexandria, where we provided Necessaries; from whence we went to Winchester, and got luggage, Horse, Etc. and from thence we pursued the new Road to Wills Creek, where we arrived the 14th of November.

Here I engaged Mr. Gist to pilot us out, and also hired four others as Servitors, Barnaby Currin, and John Mac-Quire, Indian Traders, Henry Steward, and William Jenkins, and in Company with those Persons, left the Inhabitants the Day following. The excessive Rains and vast Quantity of Snow that had fallen, prevented our reaching Mr. Frazier's, an Indian Trader, at the Mouth of Turtle rock, on Monongahela, till Thursday, the 22nd, we were informed here, that Expresses were sent a few days ago to the Traders down the River, to acquaint them with the French General's Death, and the Return of the major Part of the French army into Winter Quarters.

The Waters were quite impassable, without swimming our Horses; which obliged us to get the loan of a Canoe from Frazier, and to send Barnaby Currin, and Henry Steward, down Monongahela with our Baggage, to meet us at the Forks at Ohio, about 10 miles, to cross Allegany. As I got down before the Canoe, I spent some time in viewing the Rivers, and the Land in this Fork, as it has the absolute Command of both Rivers. The Land at the Point is 20 or 25 Feet above the common Surface of the Water, and a considerable Bottom of flat, well-timbered Land all around it, very convenient for Building; the Rivers are each a Quarter of a Mile, or more, across, and run here very near at right Angles; Allegany bearing N.E. and Monongahela S.E. the former of these two is a very rapid and swift running. Water, the other deep and still, without any perceptible Fall.

About two Miles from this, on the South East Side of the River, at the Place where the Obis Company intended to erect a Fort, lives Shingiss, King of the Delawares; we call'd upon him to invite him to Council at the Loggs Town.

As I had taken a good deal of Notice Yesterday of the Situation of the Forks, my Curiosity led me to examine this more particularly, and I think it greatly inferior, either for Defence or Advantages; especially the latter, for a Fort at the Forks would be equally well situated on Ohio, and have the entire command of Monongahela, which runs up to our Settlements and is extremely well designed for Water Carriage, as it is of a deep still Nature; besides, a Fort at the Fork might be built at a much less Expense, than at the other Places.

Nature has well contrived the lower Place, for Water Defence; but the Hill whereon it must stand being about a Quarter of a Mile in Length, and then Descending gradually on the Land Side, will render it difficult and very expensive, making a sufficient Fortification there. The whole Flat upon the Hill must be taken in, or the Side next the Descent made extremely high; or else the Hill cut away; Otherwise, the Enemy may raise Batteries within that Distance without being expos'd to a single Shot from the Fort.

Shingiss attended us to the Loggs Town, where we arrived between Sun setting and Dark, the 25th Day after I left Williamsburg; We travelled over some extreme good, and bad Land, to get to this Place.

As soon as I came into Town, I went to Monacatoocha (as the Half King was out at his hunting Cabbin on little Beaver Creek, about 15 miles off) who informed him by John Davison my Indian Interpreter, that I was sent a Messenger to the French General; and was ordered to call upon the Sachems of the Six Nations, to acquaint them with it. I gave him a String of Wampum and a Twill of Tobacco, and desired him to send for the Half King; which he promised to do by a Runner in the Morning, and for other Sachems; I invited him and the other great Men present to my Tent, where they stay'd about an Hour and return'd. . . .

Came to Town four of ten Frenchmen that deserted from a Company at the Cuscuscus, which lies at the Mouth of this River; I got the following Account from them. They were sent from New Orleans with 100, and 8 Canoe Loads of

Provisions to this Place; where they expected to have met the same Number of Men, from the Forts this Side Lake Erie, to convoy them and the Stores up, who were not arrived when they ran off. I enquired into the Situation of the French, on the Mississippi, their Number, and what Forts they had built; They informed me, That there were four small Forts between New Orleans and the Black Islands, garrison'd with about 30 or 40 Men, and a few small Pieces, in each; That at New Orleans, which is near the Mouth of the Mississippi, there are 35 Companies of 40 Men each, with a pretty Strong Fort mounting 8 Carriage Guns, and at the Black Islands there are several Companies, and a Fort with 6 Guns. The Black Islands are about 130 Leagues above the Mouth of the Ohio, which is about 350 above New Orleans; They also acquainted me, that there was a small pallisaded Fort on the Ohio, at the Mouth of the Obaish, about 60 Leagues from the Mississippi; The Obaish heads near the West End of Lake Erie, and affords the Communication between the French on Mississippi and those on the Lakes. These Deserters came up from the lower Shawnee-Town with one Brown, an Indian Trader, and were going to Philadelphia.

About 3 o'clock this evening the Half King came to Town; I went up and I invited him and Davisan, privately, to my Tent, and desir'd him to relate some of the Particulars of his Journey to the French Commandant, and Reception there; and to give me an Account of the Ways and Distance. He told me, that the nearest and levellest Way was now impassable, by Reason of many large miry Savannas, that we must be obliged to go by Venango, and should not get to the near Fort under 5 or 6 Night's Sleep, good Travelling. When he went to the Fort, he said he was received in a very stern Manner by the late Commander; Who ask'd him very abruptly, what he had come about, and to declare his Business, which he said he did in the following Speech.

Fathers, I am come to tell you your own Speeches; what your own Mouths have declared. Fathers, You, in former Days, set a Silver Bason before us, wherein there was the Leg of a Beaver, and desir'd of all Nations to come and eat of it; to eat in Peace and Plenty, and not to be churlish to one another; and that if any such Person should be found to be a Disturber, I here lay down by the Edge of the Dish a Rod, which you must scourge them with; and if I your Father, should get foolish, in my old Days, I desire you may use it upon me as well as others. Now Fathers, it is you that are the Disturbers in this Land, by coming and building your Towns, and taking it away unknown to us, and by Force. Fathers, We kindled a Fire a long Time ago, at a Place called Montreal, where we desired you to stay, and not to come and intrude upon our Land. I now desire you may dispatch to that Place; for be it known to you, Fathers, that this is our Land, and not yours.

Fathers, I desire you may hear me in Civilness; if not, we must handle that Rod which was laid down for the use of the Obstreperous. If you had come in a peaceable Manner, like our Brothers the English, we should not have been against your trading with us, as they do; but to come, Fathers, and build great Houses upon our Land, and to take it by Force, is what we cannot submit to. Fathers, both you and the English are white, we live in a Country between; therefore the Land belongs to neither one nor to other; But the Great Being Above allow'd it to be a Place of Residence for us; so Fathers, I desire you to withdraw, as I have done our Brothers the English; for I will keep you at Arms length. I lay this down as a Trial for both, to see which will have the greatest Regard to it, and that Side we will stand by, and make equal Sharers with us. Our Brothers the English have heard this, and I come now to tell it to you, for I am not afraid to discharge you off this Land.

This he said was the Substance of what he said to the General, who made this Reply.

Now, my Child, I have heard your Speech, you spoke first, but it is my Time to speak now. Where is my Wampum that you took away, with the Marks of Towns in it? This Wampum I do not know, which you have discharged me off the Land with; but you need not put yourself to the Trouble of Speaking, for I will not hear you; I am not afraid of Flies, or Mosquitos, for Indians are such as those; I tell you, down that River I will go, and will build upon it, according to my Command; if the River was backed up, I have Forces sufficient to burst it open, and tread under my Feet all that stand in Opposition, together with their Alliances; for my Force is as the Sand upon the Sea Shore; Therefore, here is your Wampum, I fling it at you. Child, you talk foolish; you say this Land belongs to you, but there is not the Back of my Nail yours; I saw that Land sooner than you did, before the Shannoahs and you were at War; Lead was the Man that went down, and took Possession of that River; It is my Land, and I will have it, let who will stand up for, or say against it. I'll buy and sell with the English (mocking). If People will be ruled by me, they may expect Kindness, but not else.

The Half King told me he enquired of the General after two Englishmen that were made Prisoners, and received this Answer.

Child, You think it is a very great Hardship that I made Prisoners of those two People at Venango, don't you concern yourself with it, we took and carried them to Canada, to get Intelligence of what the English were doing in Virginia.

He informed me that they had built two Forts, one on Lake Erie, and another on French Creek, near a small Lake about 15 Miles asunder, and a large Wagon Road Between; they are both built after the same Model, but different in the Size; that on the Lake the largest; he gave me a Plan of them, of his own drawing.

We met in Council at the Long-House about 9 o'Clock, where I spoke to them as fellows.

Brothers, I have called you together in Council, by Order of your Brother the Governor of Virginia, to acquaint you that I am sent, with all possible Dispatch, to visit, and deliver a Letter to the French Commandant, of very great Importance to your Brothers the English; and I dare say, to you their Friends and Allies. I was destined, brothers, by your brother, the governor, to call upon you, the sachems of the nations, to inform you of it, and to ask your advice and assistance to proceed the nearest and best road to the French, You see, brothers, I have gotten this far on my Journey.

His Honor likewise desired me to apply to you for some of your young men to conduct and provide provisions for us on our way, and be a safeguard against those French Indians who have taken up the hatchet against us. I have spoken thus particularly to you, brothers, because his Honor, our governor, treats you as good friends and allies, and holds you in great esteem. To confirm what I have said, I give you this string of wampum.

After they had considered for some time on the above discourse, the Half-King got up, and spoke:

'Now, my brother, in regard to what my brother, the governor, had desired of me, I return you this answer:

'I rely upon you as a brother ought to do, as you say we are brothers and one people. We shall put heart in hand and speak to our fathers, the French, concerning the speech they made to me, and you may depend that we will endeavor to be your guard.

'Brother, as you have asked my advice, I hope you will be ruled by it, and stay until I can provide a company to go with you. The French speech-belt is not here; I have to go for it to my Hunting-Cabin. Likewise, the people whom I have ordered in are not yet come, and cannot until the third night from this; until which time, brother, I must beg you to stay.

'I intend to send a Guard of Mingos, Shannoahs, and Delawares, that our brothers may see the love and loyalty we bear them.'

As I had orders to make all possible Dispatch, and waiting here was very contrary to my inclination, I thanked him in the most suitable manner I could, and told him that my business required the greatest expedition, and would not admit of that delay: He was not well pleased that I should offer to go before the Time he had appointed, and told me that he could not consent to our going without a Guard, for Fear some Accident should befall us, and draw a Relexion upon him; besides, says he, this is a Matter of no small Moment, and must not be entered into without due Consideration; for now I intend to deliver up the French Speech-Belt, and make the Shannoahs and Delawares do the same: And accordingly he gave Orders to King Shingiss, who was present, to attend on Wednesday Night with the Wampum, and two Men of their Nation to be in Readiness to set out with next Morning. As I found it was impossible to get off without affronting them in the most egregious Manner, I consented to stay.

I gave them back a String of Wampum that I met with at Frazier's, which they had sent with a Speech to his Honour the Governour, to inform him, that three Nations of French Indians, viz. Chippeways, Ottoways, and Orundacks, had taken up the Hatchet against the English, and desired them to repeat it over again, which they postponed doing till they met in full Council with the Shannoahs and Delaware Chiefs.

Runners were dispatched very early for the Shannoah Chiefs, the Half King set out himself to fetch the French Speech-Belt from his Hunting-Cabbin. He returned this Evening, and came with Monacatoocha, and two other Sachems to my Tent; and begged (as they had complied with his Honour the Governor's Request, in providing Men, Etc.) to know on what Business we were going to the French. This was a Question I all along expected, and had provided as satisfactory Answers to, as I could, and which allayed their Curiosity a little.

Monacatoocha informed me, that an Indian from Venango brought News, a few Days ago, that the French had called all the Mingos, Delawares &c together at that Place, and told them that they intended to have been down the River this Fall, but the Waters were growing cold, and the Winter advancing, which obliged them to go into Quarters: But they might assuredly expect them in the Spring, with a far greater Number; and desired that they might be quite passive, and apt to intermeddle, unless they has a Mind to draw all their Force upon them, for that they expected to fight the English three Years, (as they supposed there would be some Attempts made to stop them) in which Time they should conquer, but if they should prove equally strong, that they and the English would join to cut them all off, and divide the land between them; that tho' they had lost their General, and some few of their Soldiers, yet there were Men enough to reinforce them, and make them Masters of the Ohio.

We set out about 9 o'Clock with the Half-King, Jeskakake, White Thunder, and the Hunter, and travelled on the road to Venango, where we arrived the 4th of December. . . .

We found the French colours hoisted at a House which they drove Mr. John Frazier, an English Subject, from; I immediately repaired to it, to know where the Commander resided. There were three Officers, one of whom, Capt. Joncaire informed me, that he had the Command of the Ohio, but that there was a General Officer at the near Fort, which he advised me to for an Answer. He invited us to sup with them, and treated us with the greatest Complaisance. The Wine, as they dosed themselves pretty plentifully with it, soon banished the Restraint which at first appear'd in their Conversation, and gave a Licence to their Tongues to reveal their Sentiments more freely.

They told me, That it was their absolute Design to take Possession of the Ohio, and by G —— they would do it; for that they were sensible the English could raise two Men for their one; yet they knew, their Motions were too slow and dilatory to prevent any Undertaking of theirs. They pretend to have an undoubted Right to the River, from a Discovery made by one LaSalle 60 Years ago; and the Rise of this expedition is, to prevent our Settling on the River or Waters of it, as they have heard of some Families moving out in Order thereto. From the best Intelligence I could get, there have been 1500 Men on this side Ontario Lake, but upon the death of the General all were recalled to about 6 or 700, who were left to garrison four Forts, 150 or thereabouts in each, the first of which is on French Creek, near a small Lake, about 60 miles from Venango, near N.N.W. the next lies on Lake Erie, where the greatest part of their Stores are kept, about 15 Miles from the other; from that it is 120 Miles to the carrying Place, at the Falls of Lake Erie, where there is a small Fort which they lodge their goods at, in bringing them in from Montreal, the Place that all their Stores come from: The next Fort lies about 20 Miles from this, on Ontario Lake; between this Fort and Montreal there are three others, the first of which is near opposite to the English Fort Oswego. From the Fort on Lake Erie to Montreal is about 600 Miles, which they say requires no more, if good Weather, than four Weeks Voyage, if they go in Barks or large Vessels, that they can cross the Lake; but if they come in Canoes it will require 5 or 6 Weeks, for they are oblig'd to keep under the Shore.

At 11 o'Clock we set out for the Fort, and were prevented from arriving there 'till the 11th by excessive Rains, Snows, and bad Travelling, through many Mires and Swamps, which we were obliged to pass, to avoid crossing the Creek, which was impossible, either by fording or rafting, the Water was so high and rapid. . . . We passed over much good Land since we left Venango, and through several extensive and very rich Meadows; one of which I believe was near four Miles in Length, and considerably wide in some Places.

I prepar'd early to wait upon the Commander, and was received and conducted to him by the second Officer in Command; I acquainted him with my Business, and offer'd my Commission and Letter, both of which he desired me to keep 'til the arrival of Monsieur Riparti, Captain at the next Fort, who was sent for and expected every Hour. This Commander is a Knight of the Military Order of St. Louis, and named Legardeur de St. Piere. He is an elderly Gentleman, and has much the Air of a Soldier; he was sent over to take the Command, immediately upon the Death of the late General, and arrived here about seven Days before me.

At 2 o'Clock the Gentleman that was sent for arrived, when I offer'd the Letter, etc. again: which they receiv'd, and adjourn'd into a private Apartment for the Captain to translate, who understood a little English; after he had done it, the Commander desired I would walk in, and bring my interpreter to peruse and correct it, which I did. The chief Officers retired, to hold a Council of War, which gave me an opportunity of taking the Dimensions of the Fort, and making what Observations I could.

It is situated on the South, or West Fork of French Creek, near the Water, and is almost surrounded by the Creek, and a small Branch of it which forms a Kind of an island; four houses compose the sides; the Bastions are made of Piles driven into the Ground, and about 12 feet above, and sharp at Top, with Port Holes cut for Cannon and Loop Holes for the small Arms to fire through.. There are eight 6 lb. pieces mounted, two in each Bastion, and one Piece of four Pound before the Gate; in the Bastions are a Guard House, Chapel, Doctor's Lodging, and the Commander's private store, round which are laid Eight Forms for the Cannon and Men to stand on; There are several barracks without the Fort, for the Soldiers Dwelling, covered, some with Bark, and some with Boards, and made chiefly, such as Stables, Smith's Shop, Etc.

I could get no certain Account of the Number of Men here; but according to the best Judgment I could form, there are an hundred exclusive of Officers, of which there are many. I also gave Orders to the People that were with me, to take an exact Account of the Canoes that were hauled up to convey their Forces down in the Spring, which they did, and told 50 of Witch Bark, and 170 of Pine, besides many others that were blotk'd out, in Readiness to make.

The Commandant ordered a plentiful Store of Liquor, Provision, Etc. to be put on board our Canoe, and appeared to be extremely compliant, though he was exerting every Artifice that he could invent to set our own Indians at Variance with us, to prevent their going 'til after our Departure: Presents, Rewards, and every Thing that could be suggested by him or his Officers—I can't say that ever in my life I suffer'd so much Anxiety as I did in this Affair; I saw that every Stratagem that the most fruitful Brain could invent, was practic'd, to win the Half-King to their Interest, and that leaving Him here was giving them the Opportunity they aimed at. I went to the Half-King, and press'd him in the strongest Terms to go: He told me the Commandant would not discharge him 'til the morning. I them went to the Commandant, and desired him to do their Business, and complained of ill treatment: for keeping them, as they were Part of my Company, was detaining me: which he promised not to do, but to forward my journey as much as he could: He protested he did not keep them, but was ignorant of the Cause of their Stay; though I soon found it out: He had promised them a Present of Guns, Etc. if they would wait 'til the Morning. As I was very much press'd, by the Indians, to wait this Day for them, I Consented, on a Promise, That nothing should hinder them in the Morning.

The French were not slack in their Inventions to keep the Indians this Day also; but as they were obligated, according to Promise, to give the Present, they then endeavored to try the Power of Liquor, which I doubt not would have prevailed at any other Time than this, but I urged and insisted with the King so closely upon his Word, that he refrained, and set off with us as he had engaged.

We had a tedious and very fatiguing Portage down the Creek, several Times we had like to have been staved against Rocks, and many Times were obliged all Hands to get out and remain in the Water Half an Hour or more, getting over the Shoals; at one Place the ice had lodged and made it impassable by Water; therefore we were obliged to carry our Canoe across a Neck of Land, a Quarter of a Mile over. We did not reach Venango, till the 22nd, where we met with our Horses. This Creek is extremely crooked, I dare say the Distance between the Fort and Venango can't be less than 130 Miles, to follow the Meanders....

The Cold was so extremely severe, that Mr. Gist had all his Fingers, and some of his Toes frozen, and the Water was shut up so hard, that we found no Difficulty in getting off the Island on the Ice in the Morning, and went to Mr. Frazier's. We met here with 20 Warriors, who were going to the Southward to War, but coming to a Place upon the Head of the Great Cunnaway, where they found 7 People killed and scalped, all but one woman with very light Hair, they turned about and ran back, for Fear the Inhabitants should rise and take them as the Authors of the Murder: They report that the People were lying about the House, and some of them much torn and eaten by Hogs; by the Marks that were left, they say they were French Indians of the Ottaway Nation, Etc. that did it. . . .

On the 11th I got to Belvoir where I stopped one Day to take necessary Rest, and then set out and arrived in Williamsburg the 16th, and waited upon his Honour the Governour with the Letter I had brought from the French Commandant, and to give an Account of the Proceedings of my Journey, which I beg Leave to do by offering the foregoing, as it contains the most remarkable Occurrences that happened to me.

I hope it will be sufficient to satisfy your Honour with my Proceedings; for that was my Aim in undertaking the Journey, and chief Study throughout the Prosecution of it.

With the Hope of doing it, with infinite Pleasure, subscribe myself,

Your Honour's most Obedient,

And very humble Servant,

G. WASHINGTON

1. *On what basis did the French lay claim to the territory in dispute? What was their reaction to Dinwiddie's demands?*
2. *How did Washington try to establish strong diplomatic relations with the Indians of the Ohio Valley? How did his method differ from that of the French?*

3-10   The Closing of the Frontier (1763)

The conclusion of the French and Indian War earned Britain only a short-term respite as problems regarding their newly-won western lands erupted soon thereafter. Colonial expansion beyond the Allegheny-Appalachian mountains led to clashes between white settlers and the Indian inhabitants on whose land they were encroaching. Parliament sought to keep the peace when it issued the Proclamation of 1763 prohibiting surveying and settlement west of the mountain range.

Source: The Solon Law Archive
http://www. solon.org/Constitutions/Canada/English/PreConfederation/rp_1763. html
also in Henry Steele Commager, ed., *Documents of American History* (New York: Appleton-Century-Crofts, 1949), 47–50.

October 7, 1763
BY THE KING. A PROCLAMATION

Whereas We have taken into Our Royal Consideration the extensive and valuable Acquisitions in America, secured to our Crown by the late Definitive Treaty of Peace, concluded at Paris the 10th Day of February last; and being desirous that all Our loving Subjects, as well of our Kingdom as of our Colonies in America, may avail themselves with all convenient Speed, of the great Benefits and Advantages which must accrue therefrom to their Commerce, Manufactures, and Navigation, We have thought fit, with the Advice of our Privy Council, to issue this our Royal Proclamation, hereby to publish and declare to all our

And Whereas, We are desirous, upon all occasions, to testify our Royal Sense and Approbation of the Conduct and bravery of the Officers and Soldiers of our Armies, and to reward the same, We do hereby command and impower our Governors of our said Three new Colonies, and all other our Governors of our several Provinces on the Continent of North America, to grant without Fee or Reward, to such reduced Officers as have served in North America during the late War, and to such Private Soldiers as have been or shall be disbanded in America, and are actually residing there, and shall personally apply for the same, the following Quantities of Lands, subject, at the Expiration of Ten Years, to the same Quit-Rents as other Lands are subject to in the Province within which they are granted, as also subject to the same Conditions of Cultivation and Improvement; viz.

To every Person having the Rank of a Field Officer—5,000 Acres.
To every Captain—3,000 Acres.
To every Subaltern or Staff Officer,—2,000 Acres.
To every Non-Commission Officer,—200 Acres.
To every Private Man—50 Acres.

We do likewise authorize and require the Governors and Commanders in Chief of all our said Colonies upon the Continent of North America to grant the like Quantities of Land, and upon the same conditions, to such reduced Officers of our Navy of like Rank as served on board our Ships of War in North America at the times of the Reduction of Louisbourg and Quebec in the late War, and who shall personally apply to our respective Governors for such Grants.

And whereas it is just and reasonable, and essential to our Interest, and the Security of our Colonies, that the several Nations or Tribes of Indians with whom We are connected, and who live under our Protection, should not be molested or disturbed in the Possession of such Parts of Our Dominions and Territories as, not having been ceded to or purchased by Us, are reserved to them, or any of them, as their Hunting Grounds. We do therefore, with the Advice of our Privy Council, declare it to be our Royal Will and Pleasure, that no Governor or Commander in Chief in any of our Colonies of Quebec, East Florida, or West Florida, do presume, upon any Pretence whatever, to grant Warrants of Survey, or pass any Patents for Lands beyond the Bounds of their respective Governments, as described in their Commissions: as also that no Governor or Commander in Chief in any of our other Colonies or Plantations in America do presume for the present, and until our further Pleasure be known, to grant Warrants of Survey, or pass Patents for any Lands beyond the Heads or Sources of any of the Rivers which fall into the Atlantic Ocean from the West and North West, or upon any Lands whatever, which, not having been ceded to or purchased by Us as aforesaid, are reserved to the said Indians, or any of them. And We do further declare it to be Our Royal Will and Pleasure, for the present as aforesaid, to reserve under our Sovereignty, Protection, and Dominion, for the use of the said Indians, all the Lands and Territories not included within the Limits of Our said Three new Governments, or within the Limits of the Territory granted to the Hudson's Bay Company, as also all the Lands and Territories lying to the Westward of the Sources of the Rivers which fall into the Sea from the West and North West as aforesaid.

And We do hereby strictly forbid, on Pain of our Displeasure, all our loving Subjects from making any Purchases or Settlements whatever, or taking Possession of any of the Lands above reserved, without our especial leave and Licence for that Purpose first obtained.

And, We do further strictly enjoin and require all Persons whatever who have either wilfully or inadvertently seated themselves upon any Lands within the Countries above described, or upon any other Lands which, not having been ceded to or purchased by Us, are, still reserved to the said Indians as aforesaid, forthwith to remove themselves from such Settlements.

And whereas great Frauds and Abuses have been committed in purchasing Lands of the Indians, to the great Prejudice of our Interests, and to the great Dissatisfaction of the said Indians: In order, therefore, to prevent such Irregularities for the future, and to the end that the Indians may be convinced of our Justice and determined Resolution to remove all reasonable Cause of Discontent, We do, with the Advice of our Privy Council strictly enjoin and require, that no private Person do presume to make any purchase from the said Indians of any Lands reserved to the said Indians, within those parts of our Colonies where, We have thought proper to allow Settlement: but that. if at any Time any of the Said Indians should be inclined to dispose of the said Lands, the same shall be Purchased only for Us, in our Name, at some public Meeting or Assembly of the said Indians, to be held for that Purpose by the Governor or Commander in Chief of our Colony respectively within which they shall lie: and in case they shall lie within the limits of any Proprietary Government, they shall be purchased only for the Use and in the name of such Proprietaries, conformable to such Directions and Instructions as We or they shall think proper to give for that Purpose: And we do, by the Advice of our Privy Council, declare and enjoin, that the Trade with the said Indians shall be free and open to all our Subjects whatever, provided that every Person who may incline to Trade with the said Indians do take out a Licence for carrying on such Trade from the Governor or Commander in Chief of any of our Colonies respectively where such Person shall reside. and also give Security to observe loving Subjects, that we have, with the Advice of our Said Privy Council, granted our Letters Patent, under our Great Seal of Great Britain, to erect, within the Countries and Islands ceded and confirmed to Us by the said Treaty, Four distinct and separate Governments, styled and called by the names of Quebec, East Florida, West Florida and Grenada, and limited and bounded as follows, viz.

First—The Government of Quebec bounded on the Labrador Coast by the River St. John, and from thence by a Line drawn from the Head of that River through the Lake St. John, to the South end of the Lake Nipissim; from whence the said Line, crossing the River St. Lawrence, and the Lake Champlain, in 45 Degrees of North Latitude, passes along the High Lands which divide the Rivers that empty themselves into the said River St. Lawrence from those which fall into the Sea; and also along the North Coast of the Baye des Chaleurs, and the Coast of the Gulph of St. Lawrence to Cape Rosieres, and from thence crossing the Mouth of the River St. Lawrence by the West End of the Island of Anticosti, terminates at the aforesaid River of St. John.

Secondly—The Government of East Florida, bounded to the Westward by the Gulph of Mexico and the Apalachicola River; to the Northward by a Line drawn from that part of the said River where the Chatahouchee and Flint Rivers meet, to the source of St. Mary's River, and by the course of the said River to the Atlantic Ocean; and to the Eastward and Southward by the Atlantic Ocean and the Gulph of Florida, including all Islands within Six Leagues of the Sea Coast.

Thirdly—The Government of West Florida, bounded to the Southward by the Gulph of Mexico, including all Islands within Six Leagues of the Coast, from the River Apalachicola to Lake Pontchartrain; to the Westward by the said Lake, the Lake Maurepas, and the River Mississippi; to the Northward by a Line drawn due East from that part of the River Mississippi which lies in 31 Degrees North Latitude, to the River Apalachicola or Chatahouchee; and to the Eastward by the said River.

Fourthly—The Government of Grenada, comprehending the Island of that name, together with the Grenadines, and the Islands of Dominico, St. Vincent's and Tobago. And to the end that the open and free Fishery of our Subjects may be extended to and carried on upon the Coast of Labrador, and the adjacent Islands. We have thought fit, with the advice of our said Privy Council to put all that Coast, from the River St. John's to Hudson's Streights, together with the Islands of Anticosti and Madelaine, and all other smaller Islands lying upon the said Coast, under the care and Inspection of our Governor of Newfoundland.

We have also, with the advice of our Privy Council, thought fit to annex the Islands of St. John's and Cape Breton, or Isle Royale, with the lesser Islands adjacent thereto, to our Government of Nova Scotia.

We have also, with the advice of our Privy Council aforesaid, annexed to our Province of Georgia all the Lands lying between the Rivers Alatamaha and St. Mary's.

And whereas it will greatly contribute to the speedy settling of our said new Governments, that our loving Subjects should be informed of our Paternal care, for the security of the Liberties and Properties of those who are and shall become Inhabitants thereof, We have thought fit to publish and declare, by this Our Proclamation, that We have, in the Letters Patent under our Great Seal of Great Britain, by which the said Governments are constituted, given express Power and Direction to our Governors of our Said Colonies respectively, that so soon as the state and circumstances of the said Colonies will admit thereof, they shall, with the Advice and Consent of the Members of our Council, summon and call General Assemblies within the said Governments respectively, in such Manner and Form as is used and directed in those Colonies and Provinces in America which are under our immediate Government: And We have also given Power to the said Governors, with the consent of our Said Councils, and the Representatives of the People so to be summoned as aforesaid, to make, constitute, and ordain Laws, Statutes, and Ordinances for the Public Peace, Welfare, and good Government of our said Colonies, and of the People and Inhabitants thereof, as near as may be agreeable to the Laws of England, and under such Regulations and Restrictions as are used in other Colonies; and in the mean Time, and until such Assemblies can be called as aforesaid, all Persons Inhabiting in or resorting to our Said Colonies may confide in our Royal Protection for the Enjoyment of the Benefit of the Laws of our Realm of England; for which Purpose We have given Power under our Great Seal to the Governors of our said Colonies respectively to erect and constitute, with the Advice of our said Councils respectively, Courts of Judicature and public Justice within our Said Colonies for hearing and determining all Causes, as well Criminal as Civil, according to Law and Equity, and as near as may be agreeable to the Laws of England, with Liberty to all Persons who may think themselves aggrieved by the Sentences of such Courts, in all Civil Cases. to appeal, under the usual Limitations and Restrictions, to Us in our Privy Council.

We have also thought fit, with the advice of our Privy Council as aforesaid, to give unto the Governors and Councils of our said Three new Colonies, upon the Continent full Power and Authority to settle and agree with the Inhabitants of our said new Colonies or with any other Persons who shall resort thereto, for such Lands, Tenements and Hereditaments, as are now or hereafter shall be in our Power to dispose of; and them to grant to any such Person or Persons upon such Terms, and under such moderate Quit-Rents, Services and Acknowledgments, as have been appointed and settled in our other Colonies, and under such other Conditions as shall appear to us to be necessary and expedient for the Advantage of the Grantees, and the Improvement and settlement of our said Colonies.

such Regulations as We shall at any Time think fit. by ourselves or by our Commissaries to be appointed for this Purpose, to direct and appoint for the Benefit of the said Trade.

And we do hereby authorize, enjoin, and require the Governors and Commanders in Chief of all our Colonies respectively, as well those under Our immediate Government as those under the Government and Direction of Proprietaries, to grant such Licences without Fee or Reward, taking especial Care to insert therein a Condition, that such Licence shall be void, and the Security forfeited in case the Person to whom the same is granted shall refuse or neglect to observe such Regulations as We shall think proper to prescribe as aforesaid.

And we do further expressly conjoin and require all Officers whatever, as well Military as those Employed in the Management and Direction of Indian Affairs, within the Territories reserved as aforesaid for the use of the said Indians, to seize and apprehend all Persons whatever, who standing charged with Treason, Misprisions of Treason, Murders, or other Felonies or Misdemeanors, shall fly from Justice and take Refuge in the said Territory, and to send them under a proper guard to the Colony where the Crime was committed of which they, stand accused, in order to take their Trial for the same.

Given at our Court at St. James's the 7th Day of October 1763, in the Third Year of our Reign.

GOD SAVE THE KING

1. What "type" of person would be most likely to venture forth across the Appalachians into the frontier? What could have been so appealing about these new lands recently wrested from French control?
2. Why were the colonists so troubled by the Proclamation of 1763? After all, how could the British possibly enforce the measure?

3-11   The Adventures of Daniel Boone (1769)

In 1784, John Filson, the first historian and geographer of Kentucky, published The Discovery, Settlement and Present State of Kentucke in the hopes of attracting settlers to the region. The book contained the first account of Daniel Boone's exploits in the Kentucky wilderness from May 1769 to October 1782, which Boone dictated to Filson. "The Adventures of Col. Daniel Boone" was subsequently published in The American Magazine in 1787 and again in a book by George Imlay in 1793. Boone's pioneering efforts helped establish a route through the Allegheny Mountains that was to be used by thousands in the first major westward migration.

Source: Archiving Early America
http://www.earlyamerica.com/lives/boone/chapt1/index.html

Curiosity is natural to the soul of man and interesting objects have a powerful influence on our affections. Let these influencing powers actuate, by the permission or disposal of Providence, from selfish or social views, yet in time the mysterious will of Heaven is unfolded, and we behold our conduct, from whatever motives excited, operating to answer the important designs of heaven.

Thus we behold Kentucky, lately an howling wilderness, the habitation of savages and wild beasts, become a fruitful field; this region, so favourably distinguished by nature, now become the habitation of civilization, at a period unparalleled in history, in the midst of a raging war, and under all the disadvantages of emigration to a country so remote from the inhabited parts of the continent.

Here, where the hand of violence shed the blood of the innocent; where the horrid yells of savages, and the groans of the distressed, sounded in our ears, we now hear the praises and adorations of our Creator; where wretched wigwams stood, the miserable abode of savages, we behold the foundations of cities laid, that, in all probability, will equal the glory of the greatest upon earth. And we view Kentucky situated on the fertile banks of the great Ohio, rising from obscurity to shine with splendor, equal to any other of the states of the American hemisphere.

The settling of this region well deserves a place in history. Most of the memorable events I have myself been exercised in; and, for the satisfaction of the public, win briefly relate the circumstances of my adventures, and scenes of life, from my first movement to this country until this day.

It was on the first of May, in the year 1769, that I resigned my domestic happiness for a time, and left my family and peaceable habitation on the Yadkin River, in North Carolina, to wander through the wilderness of America, in quest of the country of Kentucky, in company with John Finley, John Stewart, Joseph Holden, James Monay, and William Cool.

We proceeded successfully, and after a long and fatiguing journey through a mountainous wilderness, in a westward direction, on the seventh day of June following we found ourselves on Red-River, where John Finley had formerly been trading with the Indians, and, from the top of an eminence, saw with pleasure the beautiful level of Kentucky.

Here let me observe, that for some time we had experienced the most uncomfortable weather as a prelibation of our future sufferings. At this place we encamped, and made a shelter to defend us from the inclement season, and began to hunt and reconnoiter the country. We found every where abundance of wild beasts of all sorts, through this vast forest. The buffalo were more frequent than I have seen cattle in the settlements, browsing on the leaves of the cane, or cropping the herbage on those extensive plains, fearless, because ignorant, of the violence of man. Sometimes we saw hundreds in a drove, and the numbers about the salt springs were amazing. In this forest, the habitation of beasts of every kind natural to America, we practiced hunting with great success, until the twenty-second day of December following.

This day John Stewart and I had a pleasing ramble, but fortune changed the scene in the close of it. We had passed through a great forest, on which flood myriads of trees, some gay with blossoms, others rich with fruits. Nature was here a series of wonders, and a fund of delight. Here she displayed her ingenuity and industry in a variety of flowers and fruits, beautifully coloured, elegantly shaped, and charmingly flavoured; and we were diverted with innumerable animals presenting themselves perpetually to our view.

In the decline of the day, near Kentucky river, as we ascended the brow of a small hill, a number of Indians rushed out of a thick cane-brake upon us, and made us prisoners. The time of our sorrow was nor arrived, and the scene fully opened. The Indians plundered us of what we had, and kept us in confinement seven days, treating us with common savage usage. During this time we discovered no uneasiness or desire to escape, which made them less suspicious of us; but in the dead of night, as we lay in a thick cane-brake by a large fire, when sleep had locked up their senses, my situation not disposing me for rest, I touched my companion, and gently awoke him. We improved this favourable opportunity, and departed, leaving them to take their rest, and speedily directed our course towards our old camp, but found it plundered, and the company dispersed and gone home.

About this time my brother, Squire Boon, with another adventurer, who came to explore the country shortly after us, was wandering through the forest, determined to find me if possible, and accidentally found our camp. Notwithstanding the unfortunate circumstances of our company, and our dangerous situation, as surrounded with hostile savages, our meeting so fortunately in the wilderness made us reciprocally sensible of the utmost satisfaction. So much does friendship triumph over misfortune, that sorrows and sufferings vanish at the meeting not only of real friends, but of the most distant acquaintances, and substitute happiness in their room.

Soon after this, my companion in captivity, John Stewart, was killed by the savages, and the man that came with my brother returned home by himself. We were then in a dangerous, helpless situation, exposed daily to perils and death amongst savages and wild beasts, not a white man in the country but ourselves.

Thus situated, many hundred miles from our families in the howling wilderness, I believe few would have equally enjoyed the happiness we experienced. I often observed to my brother, You see now how little nature requires to be satisfied. Felicity, the companion of content, is rather found in our own breasts than in the enjoyment of external things; and I firmly believe it requires but a little philosophy to make a man happy in whatever state he is. This consists in a full resignation to the will of Providence; and a resigned soul finds pleasure in a path strewned with briars and thorns.

We continued not in a state of indolence, but hunted every day, and prepared a little cottage to defend us from the winter storms. We remained there undisturbed during the winter; and on the first day of May, 1770, my brother returned home to the settlement by himself, for a new recruit of horses and ammunition, leaving me by myself, without bread, salt or sugar, without company of my fellow creatures, or even a horse or dog. I confess I never before was under greater necessity of exercising philosophy and fortitude.

A few days I passed uncomfortably. The idea of a beloved wife and family, and their anxiety upon the account of my absence and exposed situation, made sensible impressions on my heart. A thousand dreadful apprehensions presented themselves to my view, and had undoubtedly disposed me to melancholy, if further indulged.

One day I undertook a tour through the country, and the diversity and beauties of nature I met with in this charming season, expelled every gloomy and vexatious thought. Just at the close of day the gentle gales retired, and left the place to the disposal of a profound calm. Not a breeze shook the most tremulous leaf. I had gained the summit of a commanding ridge, and, looking round with astonishing delight, beheld the ample plains, the beauteous tracts below. On the other hand, I surveyed the famous river Ohio that rolled in silent dignity, marking the western boundary of Kentucky with inconceivable grandeur. At a vast distance I beheld the mountains lift their venerable brows, and penetrate the clouds. All things were still.

I kindled a fire near a fountain of sweet water, and feasted on the loin of a buck, which a few hours before I had killed. The sullen shades of night soon overspread the whole hemisphere, and the earth seemed to gasp after the hovering moisture. My roving excursion this day had fatigued my body, and diverted my imagination. I laid me down to sleep, and I awoke not until the sun had chased away the night.

I continued this tour, and in a few days explored a considerable part of the country, each day equally pleased as the first. I returned again to my old camp, which was not disturbed in my absence. I did not confine my lodging to it, but often reposed in thick cane-brakes, to avoid the savages, who, I believe, often visited my camp, but fortunately for me, in my absence.

In this situation I was constantly exposed to danger and death. How unhappy such a situation for a man tormented with fear, which is vain if no danger comes, and if it does, only augments the pain. It was my happiness to be destitute of this afflicting passion, with which I had the greatest reason to be affected. The prowling wolves diverted my nocturnal hours with perpetual howlings; and the various species of animals in this vast forest, the day time, were continually in my view.

Thus I was surrounded with plenty in the midst of want. I was happy in the midst of dangers and inconveniences. In such a diversity it was impossible I should be disposed to melancholy. No populous city, with all the varieties of commerce and stately structures, could afford so much pleasure to my mind, as the beauties of nature I found here.

Thus, through an uninterrupted scene of sylvan pleasures, I spent the time until the 27th day of July following, when my brother, to my great felicity, met me, according to appointment, at our old camp. Shortly after, we left this place, not thinking it safe to stay there longer, and proceeded to Cumberland River, reconnoitering that part of the country until March, 1771, and giving names to the different waters.

Soon after, I returned home to my family, with a determination to bring them as soon as possible to live in Kentucky, which I esteemed a second paradise, at the risk of my life and fortune.

I returned safe to my old habitation, and found my family in happy circumstances. I sold my farm on the Yadkin, and what goods we could not carry with us; and on the twenty-fifth day of September, 1773, bade a farewell to our friends, and proceeded on our journey to Kentucky, in company with five families more, and forty men that joined us in Powel's Valley, which is one hundred and fifty miles from the now settled parts of Kentucky.

This promising beginning was soon overcast with a cloud of adversity; for upon the tenth day of October, the rear of our company was attacked by a number of Indians, who killed six, and wounded one man. Of these my eldest son was one that fell in the action. Though we defended ourselves, and repulsed the enemy, yet this unhappy affair scattered our cattle, brought us into extreme difficulty, and so discouraged the whole company, that we retreated forty miles, to the settlement on Clinch River.

We had passed over two mountains, viz. Powel's and Walden's, and were approaching Cumberland mountain when this adverse fortune overtook us. These mountains are in the wilderness, as we pass from the old settlements in Virginia to Kentucky, are ranged in a S.W. and N.E. direction, are of a great length and breadth, and not far distant from each other. Over these, nature hath formed passes that are less difficult than might be expected from a view of such huge piles. The aspect of these cliffs is so wild and horrid, that it is impossible to behold them without terror. The spectator is apt to imagine that nature had formerly suffered some violent convulsion; and that there are the dismembered remains of the dreadful shock; the ruins, not of Persepolis or Palmyra, but of the world!

I remained with my family on Clinch until the sixth of June, 1774, when I and one Michael Stoner were solicited by Governor Dunmore of Virginia, to go to the Falls of the Ohio, to conduct into the settlement a number of surveyors that had been sent thither by him some months before; this country having about this time drawn the attention of many adventurers. We immediately complied with the Governor's request, and conducted in the surveyors, completing a tour of eight hundred miles, through many difficulties, in sixty-two days.

1. Boone writes in his "Adventures" that he was "constantly exposed to danger and death." How did Filson expect this narrative to help persuade individuals and families to settle in Kentucky?
2. What features of this narrative might have contributed to the establishment of Daniel Boone as the quintessential eighteenth-century American pioneer?

3-12 Alexander Falconbridge, The African Slave Trade (1788)

Taken from "An Account of the Slave Trade on the Coast of Africa", this selection is a vivid description of the "middle passage". Alexander Falconbridge, who was a surgeon on several slave ships, was well positioned to describe the horrors of the journey and his account became influential among English abolitionists. Later Falconbridge was named the Governor of a colony of freed slaves in Sierra Leone, Africa.

As soon as the wretched Africans, purchased at the fairs, fall into the hands of the black traders, they experience an earnest of those dreadful sufferings which they are doomed in future to undergo. And there is not the least room to doubt, but that even before they can reach the fairs, great numbers perish from cruel usage, want of food, travelling through inhospitable deserts, etc. They are brought from the places where they are purchased to Bonny, etc. in canoes; at the bottom of which they lie, having their hands tied with a kind of willow twigs, and a strict watch is kept over them. Their usage in other respects, during the time of passage, which generally lasts several days, is equally cruel. Their allowance of food is so scanty, that it is barely sufficient to support nature. They are, besides, much exposed to the violent rains which frequently fall here, being covered only with mats that afford but a slight defense; and as there is usually water at the bottom of the canoes, from their leaking, they are scarcely every dry.

Nor do these unhappying beings, after they become the property of the Europeans (from whom as a more civilized people, more humanity might naturally be expected), find their situation in the least amended. Their treatment is no less rigorous. The men Negroes, on being brought aboard the ship, are immediately fastened together, two and two, by handcuffs on their wrists, and irons riveted on their legs. They are then sent down between the decks, and placed in an apartment partitioned off for that purpose. The women likewise are placed in a separate room, on the same deck, but without being ironed. And an adjoining room, on the same deck is besides appointed for the boys. Thus are they placed in different apartments.

But at the same time, they are frequently stowed so close, as to admit of no other posture than lying on their sides. Neither will the height between decks, unless directly under the grating, permit them the indulgence of an erect posture; especially where there are platforms, which is generally the case. These platforms are a kind of shelf, about eight or nine feet in breadth, extending from the side of the ship towards the centre. They are placed nearly midway between the decks, at the distance of two or three feet from each deck. Upon these the Negroes are stowed in the same manner as they are on the deck underneath.

. . . About eight o'clock in the morning the Negroes are generally brought upon deck. Their irons being examined, a long chain, which is locked to a ring-bolt, fixed in the deck, is run through the rings of the shackles of the men, and then locked to another ring-bolt, fixed also in the deck. By this means fifty or sixty, and sometimes more, are fastened to one chain, in order to prevent them from rising, or endeavoring to escape. If the weather proves favorable, they are permitted to remain in that situation till four or five in the afternoon, when they are disengaged from the chain, and sent down.

. . . Upon the Negroes refusing to take sustenance, I have seen coals of fire, glowing hot, put on a shovel, and placed so near their lips, as to scorch and burn them. And this has been accompanied with threats, of forcing them to swallow the coals, if they any longer persisted in refusing to eat. These means have generally had the desired effect. I have also been credibly informed that a certain captain in the slave trade poured melted lead on such of the Negroes as obstinately refused their food.

Exercise being deemed necessary for the preservation of their health, they are sometimes obligated to dance, when the weather will permit their coming on deck. If they go about it reluctantly, or do not move with agility, they are flogged; a person standing by them all the time with at cat-o'-nine-tails in his hand for that purpose. Their music, upon these occasions, consists of a drum, sometimes with only one head; and when that is worn out, they do not scruple to make use of the bottom of one of the tubs before described. The poor wretches are frequently compelled to sing also; but when they do so, their songs are generally, as may naturally be expected, melancholy lamentations of their exile from their native country.

. . . On board some ships, the common sailors are allowed to have intercourse with such of the black women whose consent they can procure. And some of them have been known to take the inconstancy of their paramours so much to heart, as to leap overboard and drown themselves. The officers are permitted to indulge their passions among them at pleasure, and sometimes are guilty of such brutal excesses as disgrace human nature.

The hardships and inconveniences suffered by the Negroes during the passage are scarcely to be enumerated or conceived. They are far more violently affected by the seasickness than the Europeans. It frequently terminates in death, especially among the women. But the exclusion of the fresh air is among the most intolerable. For the purpose of admitting this needful refreshment, most of the ships in the slave trade are provided, between the decks, with five or six air-ports on each side of the ship, of about six inches in length, and four in breadth; in addition to which, some few ships, but not one in twenty, have what they denominate wind-sails. But whenever the sea is rough and the rain heavy, it becomes necessary to shut these, and every other conveyance by which the air is admitted. The fresh air being thus excluded, the Negroes' rooms very soon grow intolerably hot. The confined air, rendered noxious by the effluvia exhaled from their bodies, and by being repeatedly breathed, soon produces fevers and fluxes, which generally carries off great numbers of them.

. . . One morning, upon examining the place allotted for the sick Negroes, I perceived that one of them, who was so emaciated as scarcely to be able to walk, was missing, and was convinced that he must have gone overboard in the night, probably to put a more expeditious period to his sufferings. And, to conclude on this subject, I could not help being sensibly affected, on a former voyage, at observing with what apparent eagerness a black woman seized some dirt from off an African yam, and put it into her mouth, seeming to rejoice at the opportunity of possessing some of her native earth.

From these instances I think it may have been clearly deduced that the unhappy Africans are not bereft of the finer feelings, but have a strong attachment to their native country, together with a just sense of the value of liberty. And the situation of the miserable beings above described, more forcibly urges the necessity of abolishing a trade which is the source of such evils, than the most eloquent harangue, or persuasive arguments could do.

1. *What conditions are the slaves subjected to by the black traders?*
2. *Describe the living conditions on board the European ships.*
3. *Identify the cruelties reported to be inflicted upon the slaves by the European sailors.*

3-13 Olaudah Equiano, The Middle Passage (1788)

This account of the "middle passage" comes from one of the first writings by an ex-slave and the originator of the slave narrative. Equiano was born in Nigeria and was kidnapped into slavery at the age of eleven. After a time in the West Indies, he was sold to a Virginia planter before becoming the slave of a merchant. Years later he was able to buy his freedom and at the age of 44, he wrote "The Interesting Narrative of the Life of Olaudah Equiano, or Gustavus Vassa, The African. Written by Himself". Equiano became an abolitionist and made the expedition to settle the colony of ex-slaves at Sierra Leone.

. . . The first object which saluted my eyes when I arrived on the coast was the sea, and a slave ship, which was then riding at anchor, and waiting for its cargo. These filled me with astonishment, which was soon converted into terror when I was carried on board. I was immediately handled and tossed up to see if I were sound by some of the crew; and I was now persuaded that I had gotten into a world of bad spirits, and that they were going to kill me. Their complexions too differing so much from ours, their long hair, and the language they spoke, (which was very different from any I had ever heard) united to confirm me in this belief. Indeed such were the horrors of my views and fears at the moment, that, if ten thousand worlds had been my own, I would have freely parted with them all to have exchanged my condition with that of the meanest slave in my own country. When I looked round the ship too and saw a large furnace of copper boiling, and a multitude of black people of every description chained together, every one of their countenances expressing dejection and sorrow, I no longer doubted of my fate; and, quite overpowered with horror and anguish, I fell motionless on the deck and fainted. When I recovered a little I found some black people about me, who I believe were some of those who brought me on board, and had been receiving their pay; they talked to me in order to cheer me, but all in vain. I asked them if we were not to be eaten by those white men with horrible looks, red faces, and loose hair. They told me I was not; and one of the crew brought me a small portion of spirituous liquor in a wine glass; but, being afraid of him, I would not take it out of his hand. One of the blacks therefore took it from him and gave it to me, and I took a little down my palate, which, instead of reviving me, as they thought it would, threw me into the greatest consternation at the strange feeling it produced, having never tasted any such liquor before. Soon after this the blacks who brought me on board went off, and left me abandoned to despair. I now saw myself deprived of all chance or returning to my native country or even the least glimpe of hope of gaining the shore, which I now considered as friendly; and I even wished for my former slavery in preference to my present situation, which was filled with horrors of every kind, still heightened by my ignorance of what I was to undergo. I was not long suffered to indulge my grief; I was soon put down under the decks, and there I received such a salutation in my nostrils as I had never experienced in my life: so that, with the loathsomeness of the stench, and crying together, I became so sick and low that I was not able to eat, nor had I the least desire to taste anything. I now wished for the last friend, death, to relieve me; but soon, to my grief, two of the white men offered me eatables; and, on my refusing to eat, one of them held me fast by the hands, and laid me across I think the windlass, and tied my feet, while the other flogged me severely. I had never experienced anything of this kind before; and although, not being used to the water, I naturally feared that element the first time I saw it, yet nevertheless, could I have got over the nettings, I would have jumped over the side, but I could not; and, besides, the crew used to watch us very closely who were not chained down to the decks, lest we should leap into the water: and I have seen some of these poor African prisoners most severely cut for attempting to do so, and hourly whipped for not eating. This indeed was often the case with myself. In a little time after, amongst the poor chained men, I found some of my own nation, which in a small degree gave ease to my mind. I inquired of these what was to be done with us; they gave me to understand we were to be carried to these white people's country to work for them. I then was a little revived, and thought, if it were no worse than working, my situation was not so desperate: but still I feared I should be put to death, the white people looked and acted, as I thought, in so savage a manner; for I had never seen among any people such instances of brutal cruellty; and this not only shewn towards us blacks, but also to some of the whites themselves. One white man in particular I saw when we were permitted to be on deck, flogged so unmercifully with a large rope near the foremast, that he died in consequence of it; and they tossed him over the side as they would have done a brute. This made me fear these people the more; and I expected nothing less than to be treated in the same manner. I could not help expressing my fears and apprehensions to some of my countrymen: I asked them if these people had no country, but lived in this hollow place (the ship): they told me they did not, but came from a distant one. "Then," said I, "how comes it in all our country we never heard of them?" They told me because they lived so very far off. I then asked where were their women? had they any like themselves? "and why," said I, "do we not see them?" they answered, because they were left behind. . . .

The stench of the hold while we were on the coast was so intolerably loathsome, that it was dangerous to remain there for any time, and some of us had been permitted to stay on the deck for the fresh air; but now that the whole ship's cargo were confined together, it became absolutely pestilential. The closeness of the place, and the heat of the climate, added to the number in the ship, which was so crowded that each had scarcely room to turn himself, almost suffocated us. This produced copious perspirations, so that the air soon became unfit for respiration, from a variety of loathsome smells, and brought on a sickness among the slaves, of which many died, thus falling victims to the improvident avarice, as I may call it, of their purchasers. This wretched situation was again aggravated by the galling of the chains, now become insupportable; and the filth of the necessary tubs, into which the children often fell, and were almost suffocated. The shrieks of the women, and the groans of the dying, rendered the whole a scene of horror almost inconceivable. Happily perhaps for myself I was soon reduced so low here that it was thought necessary to keep me almost always on deck; and from my extreme youth I was not put in fetters. In this situation I expected every hour to share the fate of my companions, some of whom were almost daily brought upon deck at the point of death, which I began to hope would soon put an end to my miseries. Often did I think many of the inhabitants of the deep much more happy than myself. I envied them the freedom they enjoyed, and as often wished I could change my condition for theirs. Every circumstance I met with served only to render my state more painful, and heighten my apprehensions, and my opinion of the cruelty of the whites. One day they had taken a number of fishes; and when they had killed and satisfied themselves with as many as they thought fit, to our astonishment who were on the deck, rather than give any of them to us to eat as we expected, they tossed the remaining fish into the sea again, although we begged and prayed for some as well as we could, but in vain; and some of my countrymen, being pressed by hunger, took an opportunity, when they thought no one saw them, of trying to get a little privately; but they were discovered, and the attempt procured them some very severe floggings. . . .

. . . I and some few more slaves, that were not saleable amongst the rest, from very much fretting, were shipped off in a sloop for North America. . . . While I was in this plantation [in Virginia] the gentleman, to whom I suppose the estate belonged, being unwell, I was one day sent for to his dwelling house to fan him; when I came into the room where he was I was very much affrighted at some things I saw, and the more so as I had seen a black woman slave as I came through the house, who was cooking the dinner, and the poor creature was cruelly loaded with various kinds of iron machines; she had one particularly on her head, which locked her mouth so fast that she could scarcely speak; and could not eat nor drink. I was much astonished and shocked at this contrivance, which I afterwards learned was called the iron muzzle . . .

1. Note the author's beliefs regarding the intent and character of his captors on board the ship. In what terms does he describe his captors? What does he assume is their purpose in capturing him?
2. How does he view the prospect of work once they reach their destination?
3. Identify and analyze the author's conclusions about the civilization of his captors based on their behavior.

PART FOUR
PRELUDE TO REVOLUTION

4-1 John Peter Zenger and the Responsibility of the Press (1734)

In 1733, German immigrant John Peter Zenger began publishing America's first party newspaper, the New York Weekly Journal, to voice opposition to the policies of Governor William Cosby. On November 17, 1734, the royal governor had Zenger arrested and charged with seditious libel. After eight months in prison, Zenger went to trial. He was ably defended by Philadelphia lawyer Andrew Hamilton who plead his client's case directly to the jury instead of focusing on the governor's hand-picked judges.

Source: John Peter Zenger, *A Brief Narrative of the Case and Trial of John Peter Zenger* (1736). http://www.law.umkc.edu/faculty/projects/ftrials/Zengerlinks.htm

PROSECUTING ATTORNEY: The Case before the court is whether Mr. Zenger is guilty of libeling His Excellency the Governor of New York, and indeed the whole administration of the government. Mr. Hamilton has confessed the printing and publishing, and I think nothing is plainer than that the words in the information are scandalous, and tend to sedition, and to disquiet the minds of the people of this province. And if such papers are not libels, I think it may be said there can be no such thing as a libel.

MR. HAMILTON: May it please Your Honor, I cannot agree with Mr. Attorney. For though I freely acknowledge there are such things as libels, yet I must insist, at the same time, that what my client is charged with is not a libel. And I observed just now that Mr. Attorney, in defining a libel, made use of the words "scandalous, seditious, and tend to disquiet the people." But (whether with design or not I will not say) he omitted the word "false."

PROSECUTING ATTORNEY: I think I did not omit the word "false." But it has been said already that it may be a libel, notwithstanding it may be true.

MR HAMILTON: In this I must still differ with Mr. Attorney;. . . we are to be tried upon this information now before the court and jury, and to which we have pleaded not guilty, and by it we are charged printing and publishing a certain false, malicious, seditious, and scandalous libel. This word "false" must have some meaning or how came it there?. . .

MR. CHIEF JUSTICE [OF THE COURT]: You cannot be admitted, Mr. Hamilton, to give the truth of a libel in evidence. A libel is not to be justified; for it is nevertheless a libel that it is true.

MR HAMILTON: I thank Your Honor. Then, gentlemen of the jury, it is to you we must now appeal, for witnesses to the truth of the facts we have offered, and are denied the liberty to prove. And let it not seem strange that I apply myself to you in this manner. I am warranted so to do both by law and reason.

The law supposes you to be summoned out of the neighborhood where the fact is alleged to be committed; and the reason . . . is because you are supposed to have the best knowledge of the fact that is to be tried. And were you to find a verdict against my client, you must take upon you to say the papers referred to in the information, and which we acknowledge we printed and published, are false, scandalous, and seditious. . . . According to my brief, the facts which we offer to prove were not committed in a corner; they are notoriously known to be true; and therefore in your justice lies our safety. And as we are denied the liberty of giving evidence to prove the truth of what we have published, I will beg leave to lay down, as a standing rule in such cases, that the suppressing of evidence ought always to be taken for the strongest evidence; and I hope it will have weight with you.. . .

I hope to be pardoned, sir, for my zeal upon this occasion. It is an old and wise caution that when our neighbor's house is on fire, we ought to take care of our own. For though, blessed be God, I live in a government [Pennsylvania colony] where liberty is well understood, and freely enjoyed, yet experience has shown us all . . . that a bad precedent in one government is soon set up for an authority in another. And therefore I cannot but think it mine, and every honest man's duty, that (while we pay all due obedience to men in authority) we ought at the same time to be on our guard against power, wherever we apprehend that it may affect ourselves or our fellow subjects.

. . . . Old and weak as I am, I should think it my duty, if required, to go to the utmost part of the land, where my service could be of any use, in assist—to quench the flame of prosecutions upon informations, set on foot by the government, to deprive a people of the right of remonstrating (and complaining too) of the arbitrary attempts of men in power. Men who injure and oppress the people under their administration provoke them to cry out and complain; and then make that very complaint the foundation for new oppressions and prosecutions. I wish I could say there were no instances of this kind.

But to conclude. The question before the court and you, gentlemen of the jury, is not of small nor private concern. It is not the cause of a poor printer, nor of New York alone, which you are now trying. No! It may, in its consequence, affect every freeman that lives under a British government on the main of America. It is the best cause. It is the cause of liberty. And I make no doubt but your upright conduct, this day, will not only entitle you to the love and esteem of your fellow citizens; but every man who prefers freedom to a life of slavery will bless and honor you, as men who have baffled the attempt of tyranny, and, by an impartial and uncorrupt verdict, have laid a noble foundation for securing to ourselves, our posterity, and our neighbors, that to which nature and the laws of our country have given us a right—the liberty both of exposing and opposing arbitrary power (in these parts of the world, at least) by speaking and writing the truth. . . .

MR. CHIEF JUSTICE: Gentlemen of the Jury: The great pains Mr. Hamilton has taken to show how little regard juries are to pay to the opinion of judges, and his insisting so much upon the conduct of some judges in trials of this kind, is done no doubt with a design that you should take but very little notice of what I might say upon this occasion. I shall therefore only observe to you that as the facts or words in the information are confessed, the only thing that can come in question before you is whether the words as set forth in the information make a libel. And that is a matter of law, no doubt, and which you may leave to the Court.

MR. HAMILTON: I humbly beg Your Honor's pardon, I am very much misapprehended if you suppose that what I said was so designed. Sir, you know I made an apology for the freedom that I found myself under a necessity of using upon this occasion. I said there was nothing personal designed. It arose from the nature of our defense.

1. Andrew Hamilton did not contest the prosecution's argument that Zenger had printed and published allegedly libelous materials in the *Weekly Journal*. What line of argument did he take in the defense of his client?
2. What is the significance of the jury's "not guilty" verdict beyond the obvious victory for Hamilton and Zenger? What does the verdict say about the independence of the jury?

4-2 Declaration of the Injured Frontier Inhabitants [of Pennsylvania] (1764)

Having learned little from the French and Indian Wars, the British sought to impose their will on the Native American peoples of the region. The Ottawa revolt, commonly called Pontiac's Rebellion after the dominant chieftan in the conflict, was the result. Colonials called "the Paxton Boys" raided settlements and massacred inhabitants leading Benjamin Franklin and others to decry the violence. This reading is a justification of the actions of the colonials.

Source: *Minutes of the Provincial Council of Pennsylvania,* 10 vols. (1852), vol. IX (1762–1771), pp. 142–145.

Inasmuch as the killing those Indians at Conestogoe Manor and Lancaster has been, and may be, the subject of much Conversation, and by invidious Representations of it, which some, we doubt not, will industriously spread, many unacquainted with the true state of Affairs may be led to pass a Severe Censure on the Authors of those Facts, and any others of the like nature, which may hereafter happen, than we are persuaded they would if matters were duly understood and deliberated. We think it, therefore, proper thus openly to declare ourselves, and render some brief hints of the reasons of our Conduct, which we must, and frankly do confess, nothing but necessity itself could induce us to, or justify us in, as it bears an appearance of flying in the face of Authority, and is attended with much labour, fatigue, and expence.

Ourselves, then, to a Man, we profess to be loyal Subjects to the best of Kings, our rightful Sovereign George the third, firmly attached to his Royal Person, Interest, and Government, & of consequence, equally opposite to the Enemies of His Throne & Dignity whether openly avowed, or more dangerously concealed under a mask of falsly pretended Friendship, and chearfully willing to offer our Substance & Lives in his Cause.

These Indians, known to be firmly connected in Friendship with our openly avowed embittered Enemies, and some of whom have, by several Oaths, been proved to be murderers, and who, by their better acquaintance with the Situation and State of our Frontier, were more capable of doing us mischief, we saw, with indignation, cherished and caressed as dearest Friends; But this, alas! Is but a part, a small part, of that excessive regard manifested to Indians, beyond His Majesty's loyal Subjects, whereof we complain, and which, together with various other Grievances, have not only enflamed with resentment the Breasts of a number, and urged them to the disagreeable Evidence of it they have been constrained to give, but have heavily displeased by far the greatest part of the good Inhabitants of this Province.

Should we here reflect to former Treaties, the exorbitant presents and great Servility therein paid to Indians, have long been oppressive Grievances we have groaned under; and when at the last Indian Treaty held at Lancaster, not only was the Blood of our many murdered Brethren tamely covered, but our poor unhappy captivated Friends abandoned to slavery among the Savages, by concluding a Friendship with the Indians, and allowing them a plenteous trade of all kinds of Commodities, without those being restored, or any properly spirited Requisition made of them; How general Dissatisfaction those Measures gave, the Murmurs of all good People (loud as they dare to utter them) to this day declare, and had here infatuated Steps of Conduct, and a manifest Partiality in favour of Indians, made a final pause, happy had it been; We perhaps had grieved in silence for our abandoned, enslaved Brethren among the Heathen; but matters of a later Date are still more flagrant Reasons of Complaint. When last Summer His Majesty's Forces, under the Command of Colonel Bouquet, marched through this Province, and a demand was made by His Excellency General Amherst, of Assistance to escort Provisions, &c. to relieve that important Post, Fort Pitt, yet not one man was granted, although never anything appeared more reasonable or necessary, as the interest of the Province lay so much at stake, and the standing of the Frontier Settlements, in any manner, evidently depended, under God, on the almost despaired of success of His Majesty's little Army, whose Valour the whole Frontiers with gratitude acknowledge, and as the happy means of having saved from ruin great part of the Province; But when a number of Indians, falsely pretended Friends, and having among them some proved on Oath to have been guilty of Murder since this War begun, when they, together with others, known to his Majesty's Enemies, and who had been in the Battle against Col. Bouquet, reduced to Distress by the Destruction of their Corn at the Great Island, and up the East Branch of Susquehanna, pretend themselves Friends and desire a Subsistance, they are openly caressed, & the Publick, that could not be indulged the liberty of contributing to His Majesty's assistance, obliged, as Tributaries to Savages, to support these Villians, these Enemies to our King & our Country; nor only so, but the hands that were closely shut, nor would grant His Majesty's General a single Farthing against a Savage Foe, have been liberally opened, and the Publick money basely prostituted to hire, at an exorbitant Rate, a mercenary Guard to protect His Majesty's worst of Enemies, those falsy pretended Indian friends, while, at the same time, Hundreds of poor distressed Families of His Majesty's Subjects, obliged to abandon their Possessions & fly for their lives at least, are left, except a small Relief at first, in the most distressing Circumstances, to starve neglected, save what the friendly hand of private Donations has contributed to their support, wherein they who are most profuse towards Savages, have carefully avoided having any part. When last Summer the Troops raised for Defence of the Province were limited to certain Bounds, nor suffered to attempt annoying our Enemies in their Habitations, and a number of brave Volunteers, equipped at their own Expence in September, up the Susquehanna, met and defeated their Enemy, with the loss of some of their number, and having others dangerously wounded, not the least thanks or acknowledgement was made them from the Legislature for the confessed Service they had done, nor only the least notice or Care taken of their wounded; Whereas, when a Seneca, who, by the Informany of many, as well as by his own Confession, had been, through the last War, our inveterate Enemy, had got a cut in his Head, last Summer, in a quarrel he had with his own Cousin, & it was reported in Philadelphia that his Wound was dangerous, a Doctor was immediately employed and sent to Fort Augusta to take care of him, and cure him if possible. To these may be added, that though it was impossible to obtain, through the Summer, or even yet, any Premium for Indian Scalps, or encouragement to excite Volunteers to go forth against them; Yet, when a few of them known to be the fast friends of our Enemies, and some of them murderers themselves, when these have been struck by a distressd, bereft, injured Frontier, a liberal reward is offered for apprehending the Perpetrators of that horrible Crime of Killing his Majesty's Cloaked Enemies, and their Conduct painted in the most atrocious Colours, while the horrid Ravages, cruel murders and most shocking Barbarities, committed by Indians on His Majesty's Subjects, are covered over, and excused, under the charitable Term of this being their method of making War. But to recount the many repeated Grievances, whereof we might justly complain, and instances of a most violent attachment to Indians, were tedious beyond the patience of a Job to endure, nore an better be expected, nor need we be surprized at Indians insolence & Villainy, when it is considered, and which can be proved from the Publick Records of a certain County, that sometime before Conrad Weiser died, some Indians belonging to the Great Island or Wighalousing, assured him that Israel Pemberton (an ancient leader of that Faction, which for so long a time have found means to enslave the Province of Indians), together with others of the Friends, had given them a Rod to scourge the White People that were settled on the purchased Lands, for that Onas had cheated them out of a great deal of Land, or had not given near sufficient Price for what he had bought; and that the Traders ought also to be scourged, for that they defrauded the Indians, by selling Goods to them at too dear a rate; and that this Relation is matter of Fact, can easily be proved in the County of Berks. Such is our unhappy Situation, under the Villainy, Infatuation and Influence of a certain Faction, that have got the Political Reins in their hands, and tamely tyrannize over the other good Subjects of the Province. And can it be thought strange, that a Scene of such treatment as this, & the now adding, in this critical Juncture, to all our former Distresses, that disagreeable Burthen of supporting, in the very heart of the Province, at so great an Expence, between one and two hundred Indians, to the great Disquietude of the Majority of the good Inhabitants of this Province, should awaken the resentment of a people grossly abused, unrighteously burthened, and made Dupes and Slaves to Indians? And must not all well disposed people entertain a charitable Sentiment of those who, at their own great Expence and Trouble, have attempted or shall attempt, rescuing a labouring Land from a Weight so oppressive, unreasonable and unjust? It is this we design, it is this we are resolved to prosecute, though it is with great Reluctance we are obliged to adopt a Measure not so agreeable as could be desired, and to which Extremity alone compels.

"GOD SAVE THE KING"

1. Summarize the grievances of the writers of this text in regard to British treatment of the Indian population compared to their own treatment by the British government.

2. What seem to be the goals of the writers in addressing these concerns to the authorities and the King?

4-3   Benjamin Franklin, Testimony Against the Stamp Act (1766)

In 1765 Parliament passed the first internal tax on the colonists, known as the Stamp Act. Benjamin Franklin was a colonial agent in London at the time and, as colonial opposition to the act grew, found himself representing these views to the British government. In his testimony from Parliament he describes the role of taxes in Pennsylvania and the economic relationship between the colonies and the mother country.

Q. What is your name, and place of abode?

A. Franklin, of Philadelphia.

Q. Do the Americans pay any considerable taxes among themselves?

A. Certainly many, and very heavy taxes.

Q. What are the present taxes in Pennsylvania, laid by the laws of the colony?

A. There are taxes on all estates, real and personal; a poll tax; a tax on all offices, professions, trades, and businesses, according to their profits; an excise on all wine, rum, and other spirit; and a duty of ten pounds per head on all Negroes imported, with some other duties.

Q. For what purposes are those taxes laid?

A. For the support of the civil and military establishments of the country, and to discharge the heavy debt contracted in the last [Seven Years'] war. . . .

Q. Are not all the people very able to pay those taxes?

A. No. The frontier counties, all along the continent, have been frequently ravaged by the enemy and greatly impoverished, are able to pay very little tax. . . .

Q. Are not the colonies, from their circumstances, very able to pay the stamp duty?

A. In my opinion there is not gold and silver enough in the colonies to pay the stamp duty for one year.

Q. Don't you know that the money arising from the stamps was all to be laid out in America?

A. I know it is appropriated by the act to the American service; but it will be spent in the conquered colonies, where the soldiers are, not in the colonies that pay it. . . .

Q. Do you think it right that America should be protected by this country and pay no part of the expense?

A. That is not the case. The colonies raised, clothed, and paid, during the last war, near 25,000 men, and spent many millions.

Q. Where you not reimbursed by Parliament?

A. We were only reimbursed what, in your opinion, we had advanced beyond our proportion, or beyond what might reasonably be expected from us; and it was a very small part of what we spent. Pennsylvania, in particular, disbursed about 500,000 pounds, and the reimbursements, in the whole, did not exceed 60,000 pounds. . . .

Q. Do you think the people of America would submit to pay the stamp duty, if it was moderated?

A. No, never, unless compelled by force of arms. . . .

Q. What was the temper of America towards Great Britain before the year 1763?

A. The best in the world. They submitted willingly to the government of the Crown, and paid, in all their courts, obedience to acts of Parliament. . . .

Q. What is your opinion of a future tax, imposed on the same principle with that of the Stamp Act? How would the Americans receive it?

A. Just as they do this. They would not pay it.

Q. Have not you heard of the resolutions of this House, and of the House of Lords, asserting the right of Parliament relating to America, including a power to tax the people there?

A. Yes, I have heard of such resolutions.

Q. What will be the opinion of the Americans on those resolutions?

A. They will think them unconstitutional and unjust.

Q. Was it an opinion in America before 1763 that the Parliament had no right to lay taxes and duties there?

A. I never heard any objection to the right of laying duties to regulate commerce; but a right to lay internal taxes was never supposed to be in Parliament, as we are not represented there. . . .

Q. Did the Americans ever dispute the controlling power of Parliament to regulate the commerce?

A. No.

Q. Can anything less than a military force carry the Stamp Act into execution?

A. I do not see how a military force can be applied to that purpose.

Q. Why may it not?

A. Suppose a military force sent into America; they will find nobody in arms; what are they then to do? They cannot force a man to take stamps who chooses to do without them. They will not find a rebellion; they may indeed make one.

Q. If the act is not repealed, what do you think will be the consequences?

A. A total loss of the respect and affection the people of America bear to this country, and of all the commerce that depends on that respect and affection.

Q. How can the commerce be affected?

A. You will find that, if the act is not repealed, they will take very little of your manufactures in a short time.

Q. Is it in their power to do without them?

A. I think they may very well do without them.

Q. Is it their interest not to take them?

A. The goods they take from Britain are either necessaries, mere conveniences, or superfluities. The first, as cloth, etc., with a little industry they can make at home; the second they can do without till they are able to provide them among themselves; and the last, which are mere articles of fashion, purchased and consumed because the fashion in a respected country; but will now be detested and rejected. The people have already struck off, by general agreement, the use of all goods fashionable in mourning. . . .

Q. If the Stamp Act should be repealed, would it induce the assemblies of America to acknowledge the right of Parliament to tax them, and would they erase their resolutions [against the Stamp Act]?

A. No, never.

Q. Is there no means of obliging them to erase those resolutions?

A. None that I know of; they will never do it, unless compelled by force of arms.

Q. Is there a power on earth that can force them to erase them?

A. No power, how great soever, can force men to change their opinions. . . .

Q. What used to be the pride of the Americans?

A. To indulge in the fashions and manufactures of Great Britain.

Q. What is now their pride?

A. To wear their old clothes over again, till they can make new ones.

1. *According to Franklin, how had Americian sentiment toward England changed between 1763 and the time of this testimony? What factors led to this change?*
2. *What kind of a rebellion does Franklin suggest may occur if taxes on goods manufactured in England continues?*
3. *What does Franklin mean by saying that the pride of America is wearing their old clothes over again, till they can make new ones"? What does this day about American attitudes toward England?*

4-4   "Letters From a Farmer in Pennsylvania" (1767)

Written by Philadelphia lawyer John Dickinson, the "Letters" were in fact a series of newspaper articles published in the Pennsylvania Chronicle between 1767 and 1768. Dickinson's purpose was to encourage protest against British taxation policies and resistance to legislation he deemed unjust. Largely repeating the arguments found in the resolutions of the Stamp Act Congress, Dickinson championed non-violent measures such as nonimportation agreements.

Source: Archiving Early America
http://www.earlyamerica.com/earlyamerica/bookmarks/farmer/farmtext.html

My Dear Countrymen,

I am a farmer, settled after a variety of fortunes near the banks of the River Delaware in the province of Pennsylvania. I received a liberal education and have been engaged in the busy scenes of life; but am now convinced that a man may be as happy without bustle as with it. My farm is small; my servants are few and good; I have a little money at interest; I wish for no more; my employment in my own affairs is easy; and with a contented, grateful mind . . . I am completing the number of days allotted to me by divine goodness.

Being generally master of my time, I spend a good deal of it in a library, which I think the most valuable part of my small estate; and being acquainted with two or three gentlemen of abilities and learning who honor me with their friendship, I have acquired, I believe, a greater share of knowledge in history and the laws and constitution of my country than is generally attained by men of my class, many of them not being so fortunate as I have been in the opportunities of getting information.

From infancy I was taught to love humanity and liberty. Inquiry and experience have since confirmed my reverence for the lessons then given me by convincing me more fully of their truth and excellence. Benevolence toward mankind excites wishes for their welfare, and such wishes endear the means of fulfilling them. These can be found in liberty only, and therefore her sacred cause ought to be espoused by every man, on every occasion, to the utmost of his power. As a charitable but poor person does not withhold his mite because he cannot relieve all the distresses of the miserable, so should not any honest man suppress his sentiments concerning freedom, however small their influence is likely to be. Perhaps he may "touch some wheel" that will have an effect greater than he could reasonably expect.

These being my sentiments, I am encouraged to offer to you, my countrymen, my thoughts on some late transactions that appear to me to be of the utmost importance to you. Conscious of my defects, I have waited some time in expectation of seeing the subject treated by persons much better qualified for the task; but being therein disappointed, and apprehensive that longer delays will be injurious, I venture at length to request the attention of the public, pray that these lines may be read with the same zeal for the happiness of British America with which they were written.

With a good deal of surprise I have observed that little notice has been taken of an act of Parliament, as injurious in its principle to the liberties of these colonies as the Stamp Act was: I mean the act for suspending the legislation of New York.

The assembly of that government complied with a former act of Parliament, requiring certain provisions to be made for the troops in America, in every particular, I think, except the articles of salt, pepper, and vinegar. In my opinion they acted imprudently, considering all circumstances, in not complying so far as would have given satisfaction as several colonies did. But my dislike of their conduct in that instance has not blinded me so much that I cannot plainly perceive that they have been punished in a manner pernicious to American freedom and justly alarming to all the colonies.

If the British Parliament has a legal authority to issue an order that we shall furnish a single article for the troops here and compel obedience to that order, they have the same right to issue an order for us supply those troops with arms, clothes, and every necessary, and to compel obedience to that order also; in short, to lay any burdens they please upon us. What is this but taxing us at a certain sum and leaving us only the manner of raising it? How is this mode more tolerable than the Stamp Act? Would that act have appeared more pleasing to Americans if, being ordered thereby to raise the sum total of the taxes, the mighty privilege had been left to them of saying how much should be paid for an instrument of writing on paper, and how much for another on parchment?

An act of Parliament commanding us to do a certain thing, if it has any validity, is a tax upon us for the expense that accrues in complying with it, and for this reason, I believe, every colony on the continent that chose to give a mark of their respect for Great Britain, in complying with the act relating to the troops, cautiously avoided the mention of that act, lest their conduct should be attributed to its supposed obligation.

The matter being thus stated, the assembly of New York either had or had no right to refuse submission to that act. If they had, and I imagine no American will say they had not, then the Parliament had no right to compel them to execute it. If they had not that right, they had no right to punish them for not executing it; and therefore had no right to suspend their legislation, which is a punishment. In fact, if the people of New York cannot be legally taxed but by their own representatives, they cannot be legally deprived of the privilege of legislation, only for insisting on that exclusive privilege of taxation. If they may be legally deprived in such a case of the privilege of legislation, why may they not, with equal reason, be deprived of every other privilege? Or why may not every colony be treated in the same manner, when any of them shall dare to deny their assent to any impositions that shall be directed? Or what signifies the repeal of the Stamp Act, if these colonies are to lose their other privileges by not tamely surrendering that of taxation?

There is one consideration arising from the suspension which is not generally attended to but shows its importance very clearly. It was not necessary that this suspension should be caused by an act of Parliament. The Crown might have restrained the governor of New York even from calling the assembly together, by its prerogative in the royal governments. This step, I suppose, would have been taken if the conduct of the assembly of New York had been regarded as an act of disobedience to the Crown alone. But it is regarded as an act of "disobedience to the authority of the British legislature." This gives the suspension a consequence vastly more affecting. It is a parliamentary assertion of the supreme authority of the British legislature over these colonies in the point of taxation; and it is intended to compel New York into a submission to that authority. It seems therefore to me as much a violation of the liberty of the people of that province, and consequently of all these colonies, as if the Parliament had sent a number of regiments to be quartered upon them, till they should comply.

For it is evident that the suspension meant as a compulsion; and the method of compelling is totally indifferent. It is indeed probable that the sight of red coats and the hearing of drums would have been most alarming, because people are generally more influenced by their eyes and ears than by their reason. But whoever seriously considers the matter must perceive that a dreadful stroke is aimed at the liberty of these colonies. I say of these colonies; for the cause of one is the cause of all. If the Parliament may lawfully deprive New York of any of her rights, it may deprive any or all the other colonies of their rights; and nothing can possibly so much encourage such at tempts as a mutual inattention to the interest of each other. To divide and thus to destroy is the first political maxim in attacking those who are powerful by their union. He certainly is not a wise man who folds his arms and reposes himself at home, seeing with unconcern the flames that have invaded his neighbor's house without using any endeavors to extinguish them. When Mr. Hampden's ship-money cause for 3s. 4d. was tried, all the people of England, with anxious expectations, interested themselves in the important decision; and when the slightest point touching the freedom of one colony is agitated, I earnestly wish that all the rest may with equal ardor support their sister. Very much may be said on this subject, but I hope more at present is unnecessary.

With concern I have observed that two assemblies of this province have sat and adjourned without taking any notice of this act. It may perhaps be asked: What would have been proper for them to do? I am by no means fond of inflammatory measures. I detest them. I should be sorry that anything should be done which might justly displease our sovereign or our mother country. But a firm, modest exertion of a free spirit should never be wanting on public occasions. It appears to me that it would have been sufficient for the assembly to have ordered our agents to represent to the King's ministers their sense of the suspending act and to pray for its repeal. Thus we should have borne our testimony against it; and might therefore reasonably expect that on a like occasion we might receive the same assistance from the other colonies.

Small things grow great by concord.

A FARMER

1. *Why do you think Dickinson chose to publish his sentiments in the guise of a series of letters written by "a farmer?"*
2. *Dickinson concludes by stating "Small things grow great by concord." Do you think he is advocating more than simply the repeal of unpopular legislation?*

4-5 John Dickinson, from *Letters from a Farmer in Pennsylvania* (1768)

Written by Philadelphia lawyer John Dickinson, the "Letters" were in fact a series of newspaper articles published in the Pennsylvania Chronicle between 1767 and 1768. Dickinson's purpose was to encourage protest against British taxation policies and resistance to legislation he deemed unjust. Largely repeating the arguments found in the resolutions of the Stamp Act Congress, Dickinson championed non-violent measures such as nonimportation agreements.

There is [a] late act of Parliament, which seems to me to be . . . destructive to the liberty of these colonies, . . . that is the act for granting duties on paper, glass, etc. It appears to me to be unconstitutional.

The Parliament unquestionably possesses a legal authority to regulate the trade of Great Britain and all its colonies. Such an authority is essential to the relation between a mother country and its colonies and necessary for the common good of all. He who considers these provinces as states distinct from the British Empire has very slender notions of justice or of their interests. We are but parts of a whole; and therefore there must exist a power somewhere to preside, and preserve the connection in due order. This power is lodged in the Parliament, and we are as much dependent on Great Britain as a perfectly free people can be on another.

I have looked over every statute relating to these colonies, from their first settlement to this time; and I find every one of them founded on this principle till the Stamp Act administration. All before are calculated to preserve or promote a mutually beneficial intercourse between the several constituent parts of the Empire. And though many of them imposed duties on trade, yet those duties were always imposed with design to restrain the commerce of one part that was injurious to another, and thus to promote the general welfare. . . . Never did the British Parliament, till the period abovementioned, think of imposing duties in American for the purpose of raising a revenue. . . . This I call an innovation, and a most dangerous innovation.

That we may be legally bound to pay any general duties on these commodities, relative to the regulation of trade, is granted. But we being obliged by her laws to take them from Great Britain, any special duties imposed on their exportation to us only, with intention to raise a revenue from us only, are as much taxes upon us as those imposed by the Stamp Act. . . . It is nothing but the edition of a former book with a new title page, . . . and will be attended with the very same consequences to American liberty.

Sorry I am to learn that there are some few persons, [who] shake their heads with solemn motion, and pretend to wonder what can be the meaning of these letters. . . . I will now tell the gentlemen. . . . The meaning of them is to convince the people of these colonies that they are at this moment exposed to the most imminent dangers, and persuade them immediately, vigorously, and unanimously to exert themselves, in the most firm, but most peaceable manner for obtaining relief. The cause of liberty is a cause of too much dignity to be sullied by turbulence and tumult. It ought to be maintained in a manner suitable to her nature. . . . I hope, my dear countrymen, that you will in every colony be upon your guard against those who may at any time endeavour to stir you up, under pretences of patriotism, to any measures disrespectful to our sovereign and our mother country. Hot, rash, disorderly proceedings injure the reputation of a people as to wisdom, valour and virtue, without procuring them the least benefit. . . .

Every government, at some time or other, falls into wrong measures. They may proceed from mistake or passion. But every such measure does not dissolve the obligation between the governors and the governed. The mistake may be corrected, the passion may pass over. It is the duty of the governed to endeavour to rectify the mistake and appease the passion. They have not at first any other right than to represent their grievances and to pray for redress. . . .

1. *Upon what principle have all statutes and laws been founded until the Stamp Act? What "dangerous innovation" in Britain's tax policies is identified by Dickinson?*
2. *What measures does Dickinson suggest to right the injustices he perceives? What kinds of actions does he identify as counterproductive to the cause?*

4-6   The Boston "Massacre" or Victims of Circumstance? (1770)

The tragic event labeled as a "massacre" for generations to come grew in part out of the escalating tensions in Boston between the city's discontented inhabitants and the embodiment of the Crown's authority—British soldiers—dubbed "lobster backs" by their detractors. John Adams, who later defended the indicted soldiers in court, said his clients had been provoked by a "motley rabble of saucy boys, negroes and mulattoes, Irish teagues and outlandish Jack tars." Responsibility for the events that occurred in front of the Customs House on March 5, 1770, undoubtedly lay on both sides, but it was hardly a massacre—no matter how one looks at it.

Source: *The American Colonist's Library: Primary Source Documents Pertaining to Early American History*
http://personal.pitnet.net/primarysources/boston.html
http://www.ukans.edu/carrie/docs/texts/preston.html

BOSTON GAZETTE AND COUNTRY JOURNAL, MARCH 12, 1770.

On the evening of Monday, being the fifth current, several soldiers of the 29th Regiment were seen parading the streets with their drawn cutlasses and bayonets, abusing and wounding numbers of the inhabitants. A few minutes after nine o'clock four youths, named Edward Archbald, William Merchant, Francis Archbald, and John Leech, jun., came down Cornhill together, and separating at Doctor Loring's corner, the two former were passing the narrow alley leading to Murray's barrack in which was a soldier brandishing a broad sword of an uncommon size against the walls, out of which he struck fire plentifully. A person of mean countenance armed with a large cudgel bore him company. Edward Archbald admonished Mr. Merchant to take care of the sword, on which the soldier turned round and struck Archbald on the arm, then pushed at Merchant and pierced through his clothes inside the arm close to the armpit and grazed the skin. Merchant then struck the soldier with a short stick he had; and the other person ran to the barrack and brought with him two soldiers, one armed with a pair of tongs, the other with a shovel. He with the tongs pursued Archbald back through the alley, collared and laid him over the head with the tongs. The noise brought people together; and John Hicks, a young lad, coming up, knocked the soldier down but let him get up again; and more lads gathering, drove them back to the barrack where the boys stood some time as it were to keep them in. In less than a minute ten or twelve of them came out with drawn cutlasses, clubs, and bayonets and set upon the unarmed boys and young folk who stood them a little while but, finding the inequality of their equipment, dispersed. On hearing the noise, one Samuel Atwood came up to see what was the matter; and entering the alley from dock square, heard the latter part of the combat; and when the boys had dispersed he met the ten or twelve soldiers aforesaid rushing down the alley towards the square and asked them if they intended to murder people? They answered Yes, by G-d, root and branch! With that one of them struck Mr. Atwood with a club which was repeated by another; and being unarmed, he turned to go off and received a wound on the left shoulder which reached the bone and gave him much pain. Retreating a few steps, Mr. Atwood met two officers and said, gentlemen, what is the matter? They answered, you'll see by and by. Immediately after, those heroes appeared in the square, asking where were the boogers? where were the cowards? But notwithstanding their fierceness to naked men, one of them advanced towards a youth who had a split of a raw stave in his hand and said, damn them, here is one of them. But the young man seeing a person near him with a drawn sword and good cane ready to support him, held up his stave in defiance; and they quietly passed by him up the little alley by Mr. Silsby's to King Street where they attacked single and unarmed persons till they raised much clamour, and then turned down Cornhill Street, insulting all they met in like manner and pursuing some to their very doors. Thirty or forty persons, mostly lads, being by this means gathered in King Street, Capt. Preston with a party of men with charged bayonets, came from the main guard to the commissioner's house, the soldiers pushing their bayonets, crying, make way! They took place by the custom house and, continuing to push to drive the people off, pricked some in several places, on which they were clamorous and, it is said, threw snow balls. On this, the Captain commanded them to fire; and more snow balls coming, he again said, damn you, fire, be the consequence what it will! One soldier then fired, and a townsman with a cudgel struck him over the hands with such force that he dropped his firelock; and, rushing forward, aimed a blow at the Captain's head which grazed his hat and fell pretty heavy upon his arm. However, the soldiers continued the fire successively till seven or eight or, as some say, eleven guns were discharged.

CAPTAIN THOMAS PRESTON'S ACCOUNT OF THE BOSTON MASSACRE

It is [a] matter of too great notoriety to need any proofs that the arrival of his Majesty's troops in Boston was extremely obnoxious to its inhabitants. They have ever used all means in their power to weaken the regiments, and to bring them into contempt by promoting and aiding desertions, and with impunity, even where there has been the clearest evidence of the fact, and by grossly and falsely propagating untruths concerning them. On the arrival of the 64th and 65th their ardour seemingly began to abate; it being too expensive to buy off so many, and attempts of that kind rendered too dangerous from the numbers.

One of their justices, most thoroughly acquainted with the people and their intentions, on the trial of a man of the 14th Regiment, openly and publicly in the hearing of great numbers of people and from the seat of justice, declared "that the soldiers must now take care of themselves, nor trust too much to their arms, for they were but a handful; that the inhabitants carried weapons concealed under their clothes, and would destroy them in a moment, if they pleased". This, considering the malicious temper of the people, was an alarming circumstance to the soldiery. Since which several disputes have happened between the townspeople and the soldiers of both regiments, the former being encouraged thereto by the countenance of even some of the magistrates, and by the protection of all the party against government. In general such disputes have been kept too secret from the officers. On the 2d instant two of the 29th going through one Gray's ropewalk, the rope-makers insultingly asked them if they would empty a vault. This unfortunately had the desired effect by provoking the soldiers, and from words they went to blows. Both parties suffered in this afftay, and finally the soldiers retired to their quarters. The officers, on the first knowledge of this transaction, took every precaution in their power to prevent any ill consequence. Notwithstanding which, single quarrels could not be prevented, the inhabitants constantly provoking and abusing the soldiery. The insolence as well as utter hatred of the inhabitants to the troops increased daily, insomuch that Monday and Tuesday, the 5th and 6th instant, were privately agreed on for a general engagement, in consequence of which several of the militia came from the country armed to join their friends, menacing to destroy any who should oppose them. This plan has since been discovered.

On Monday night about 8 o'clock two soldiers were attacked and beat. But the party of the townspeople in order to carry matters to the utmost length, broke into two meeting houses and rang the alarm bells, which I supposed was for fire as usual, but was soon undeceived. About 9 some of the guard came to and informed me the town inhabitants were assembling to attack the troops, and that the bells were ringing as the signal for that purpose and not for fire, and the beacon intended to be fired to bring in the distant people of the country. This, as I was captain of the day, occasioned my repairing immediately to the main guard. In my way there I saw the people in great commotion, and heard them use the most cruel and horrid threats against the troops. In a few minutes after I reached the guard, about 100 people passed it and went towards the custom house where the king's money is lodged. They immediately surrounded the sentry posted there, and with clubs and other weapons threatened to execute their vengeance on him. I was soon informed by a townsman their intention was to carry off the soldier from his post and probably murder him. On which I desired him to return for further intelligence, and he soon came back and assured me he heard the mobb declare they would murder him. This I feared might be a prelude to their plundering the king's chest. I immediately sent a noncommissioned officer and 12 men to protect both the sentry and the king's money, and very soon followed myself to prevent, if possible, all disorder, fearing lest the officer and soldiers, by the insults and provocations of the rioters, should be thrown off their guard and commit some rash act. They soon rushed through the people, and by charging their bayonets in half-circles, kept them at a little distance. Nay, so far was I from intending the death of any person that I suffered the troops to go to the spot where the unhappy affair took place without any loading in their pieces; nor did I ever give orders for loading them. This remiss conduct in me perhaps merits censure; yet it is evidence, resulting from the nature of things, which is the best and surest that can be offered, that my intention was not to act offensively, but the contrary part, and that not without compulsion. The mob still increased and were more outrageous, striking their clubs or bludgeons one against another, and calling out, come on you rascals, you bloody backs, you lobster scoundrels, fire if you dare, G-d damn you, fire and be damned, we know you dare not, and much more such language was used. At this time I was between the soldiers and the mob, parlaying with, and endeavouring all in my power to persuade them to retire peaceably, but to no purpose. They advanced to the points of the bayonets, struck some of them and even the muzzles of the pieces, and seemed to be endeavouring to close with the soldiers. On which some well behaved persons asked me if the guns were charged. I replied yes. They then asked me if I intended to order the men to fire. I answered no, by no

105

means, observing to them that I was advanced before the muzzles of the men's pieces, and must fall a sacrifice if they fired; that the soldiers were upon the half cock and charged bayonets, and my giving the word fire under those circumstances would prove me to be no officer. While I was thus speaking, one of the soldiers having received a severe blow with a stick, stepped a little on one side and instantly fired, on which turning to and asking him why he fired without orders, I was struck with a club on my arm, which for some time deprived me of the use of it, which blow had it been placed on my head, most probably would have destroyed me.

On this a general attack was made on the men by a great number of heavy clubs and snowballs being thrown at them, by which all our lives were in imminent danger, some persons at the same time from behind calling out, damn your bloods—why don't you fire. Instantly three or four of the soldiers fired, one after another, and directly after three more in the same confusion and hurry. The mob then ran away, except three unhappy men who instantly expired, in which number was Mr. Gray at whose rope-walk the prior quarrels took place; one more is since dead, three others are dangerously, and four slightly wounded. The whole of this melancholy affair was transacted in almost 20 minutes. On my asking the soldiers why they fired without orders, they said they heard the word fire and supposed it came from me. This might be the case as many of the mob called out fire, fire, but I assured the men that I gave no such order; that my words were, don't fire, stop your firing. In short, it was scarcely possible for the soldiers to know who said fire, or don't fire, or stop your firing. On the people's assembling again to take away the dead bodies, the soldiers supposing them coming to attack them, were making ready to fire again, which I prevented by striking up their firelocks with my hand. Immediately after a townsman came and told me that 4 or 5000 people were assembled in the next street, and had sworn to take my life with every man's with me. On which I judged it unsafe to remain there any longer, and therefore sent the party and sentry to the main guard, where the street is narrow and short, there telling them off into street firings, divided and planted them at each end of the street to secure their rear, momently expecting an attack, as there was a constant cry of the inhabitants to arms, to arms, turn out with your guns; and the town drums beating to arms, I ordered my drums to beat to arms, and being soon after joined by the different companies of the 29th regiment, I formed them as the guard into street firings. The 14th regiment also got under arms but remained at their barracks. I immediately sent a sergeant with a party to Colonel Dalrymple, the commanding officer, to acquaint him with every particular. Several officers going to join their regiment were knocked down by the mob, one very much wounded and his sword taken from him. The lieutenant-governor and Colonel Carr soon after met at the head of the 29th regiment and agreed that the regiment should retire to their barracks, and the people to their houses, but I kept the picket to strengthen the guard. It was with great difficulty that the lieutenant-governor prevailed on the people to be quiet and retire. At last they all went off, excepting about a hundred.

A Council was immediately called, on the breaking up of which three justices met and issued a warrant to apprehend me and eight soldiers. On hearing of this procedure I instantly went to the sheriff and surrendered myself, though for the space of 4 hours I had it in my power to have made my escape, which I most undoubtedly should have attempted and could easily executed, had I been the least conscious of any guilt. On the examination before the justices, two witnesses swore that I gave the men orders to fire. The one testified he was within two feet of me; the other that I swore at the men for not firing at the first word. Others swore they heard me use the word "fire," but whether do or do not fire, they could not say; others that they heard the word fire, but could not say if it came from me. The next day they got 5 or 6 more to swear I gave the word to fire. So bitter and inveterate are many of the malcontents here that they are industriously using every method to fish out evidence to prove it was a concerted scheme to murder the inhabitants. Others are infusing the utmost malice and revenge into the minds of the people who are to be my jurors by false publications, votes of towns, and all other artifices. That so from a settled rancour against the officers and troops in general, the suddenness of my trial after the affair while the people's minds are all greatly inflamed, I am, though perfectly innocent, under most unhappy circumstances, having nothing in reason to expect but the loss of life in a very ignominous manner, without the interposition of his Majesty's royal goodness.

1. *Although each is rather self-serving, which account of the Boston "Massacre" is more believable? Why?*
2. *Why do you think the occurrence on March 5, 1770, was (and still is) referred to as the "Boston Massacre?"*

4-7 John Andrews to William Barrell, Letter Regarding the Boston Tea Party (1773)

In an attempt to support the badly mismanaged British East India Company, Parliament authorized the company to send its tea directly to its own agents in the American colonies, bypassing the usual middlemen. In this way, the company's agents could undersell American retailers and even smugglers, giving the British East India Company a virtual monopoly on tea—the most popular beverage in colonial America—in the colonies. This Parliamentary interference in American commerce was unacceptable to many, especially in Boston, where the memory of the "massacre" was still fresh. On November 27, 1773, three ship-loads of tea arrived in Boston, but were not allowed to unload their cargo. Two nights later, Bostonians held a meeting, and decided to send the tea back to England—without paying the tax (three pence per pound) on it. Governor Hutchinson of Massachusetts responded by saying that the ships could certainly leave, but not without paying the tax on the cargo to the colony (this was a very important source of revenue for the colony). Two weeks later, on the night of December 16, a group of colonists, rather thinly disguised as Mohawk Indians, boarded the ships and dumped the tea into Boston Harbor.

Source: *Proceedings of the Massachusetts Historical Society,* 1st series, vol. 8 (Boston: Massachusetts Historical Society, 1864–1865), pp. 324–326.

December 18th.

However precarious our situation may be, yet *such* is the present calm composure of the people that a stranger would hardly think that ten thousand pounds sterling of the East India Company's *tea* was destroy'd the night, or rather evening before last, yet its a serious truth; and if your's, together with ye other Southern provinces, should rest satisfied with *their* quota being stor'd, poor Boston will feel the whole weight of ministerial vengeance. However, its the opinion of most. people that we stand an equal chance now, whether troops are sent in consequence of it or not; whereas, had it been stor'd, we should inevitably have had 'em, to enforce the sale of it.

The affair was transacted with the greatest regularity and despatch. Mr. Rotch finding he exposed himself not only to the loss of his ship but for ye value of the tea in case he sent her back with it, *without a clearance from the custom house,* as ye Admiral kept a ship in readiness to make a seizure of it whenever it should sail under *those circumstances;* therefore declin'd complying with his former promises, and absolutely declar'd his vessel should not carry it, without a *proper* clearance could be procur'd or he to be indemnified for the value of her: —when a general muster was assembled, from this and all ye neighbouring towns, to the number of five or six thousand, at 10 o'clock Thursday morning in the Old South Meeting house, where they pass'd a *unanimous* vote that the *Tea* should go out of the *harbour* that afternoon, and sent a committee with Mr. Rotch to ye. Custom house to *demand a* clearance, which the collector told 'em was not in his power to give, without the duties being first paid. They then sent Mr. Rotch to Milton, to ask a pass from ye Governor, who sent for answer, that "consistent with the rules of government and his duty to the King he could not grant one without they produc'd a previous clearance from the office." —By the time he return'd with this message the candles were light in [the] house, and upon reading it, such prodigious shouts were made, that induc'd me, while drinking -tea at home, to go out and know the cause of it. The house was so crouded I could get no farther than ye porch, when I found the mod-erator was just declaring the meeting to be *dissolv'd,* which caused another general shout, out doors and in, and three cheers. What with that, and the consequent noise of breaking up the meeting, you'd thought that the inhabitants of the infernal regions had broke loose. For my part, I went contentedly home and finish'd my tea, but was soon inform'd what was going forward: but still not crediting it without ocular demonstration, I went and was *satisfied.* They muster'd I'm told, upon Fort Hill, to the number of about two hundred, and procceded, two by two, to Griffin's wharf, where Hall, Bruce, and Coffin lay, each with 114 chests of the *ill fated* article on board; the two former with *only* that article, but ye latter arriv'd at ye wharf only ye day before, was freighted with a large quantity of other goods, which they took the *greatest* care not to injure in the least, and before *nine* o'clock in ye evening, every chest from on board the three vessels was knock'd to pieces and flung over ye sides.

They say the actors were *Indians* from *Narragansett.* Whether they were or not, to a transient observer they appear'd as such, being cloath'd in Blankets with the heads muffled, and copper color'd countenances, being, each arm'd with a hatchet or axe, and pair pistols, nor was their dialect different from what I conceive these geniusses to *speak,* as their jargon was unintelligible to all but themselves. Not the least insult was offer'd to any person, save one Captain Conner, a letter of horses in this place, not many years since remov'd from *dear Ireland,* who had ript up the lining of his coat and waistcoat under the arms, and watch-ing, his opportunity had nearly fill'd them with tea, but being detected, was handled pretty roughly. They not only stripp'd him of his cloaths, but gave him a coat of mud, with a severe bruising into the bargain; and nothing but their utter aversion to make any disturbance pre-vented his being tar'd and feather'd.

Should not have troubled you with this, by this Post, hadn't I thought you would be glad of a more particular account of so *impor-tant a transaction,* than you could have obtain'd by common report; and if it affords my brother but a *temporary* amusement, I shall be more than repaid for the trouble of writing it. . ..

Sunday Evening. [December 19th.]

I give you joy of your easy riddance of *the banefull herb;* being just inform'd by ye arrival of the post, that it's gone from whence it came. You may bless your stars that you have not a H—n and board of Commissioners resident with you. —I forgot to acquaint you last evening that *Loring,* in a brig belonging to *Clark,* one of ye consignees, is on sbore at ye back of Cape Cod, drove thither by a storm last Fryday week, who has the last quota of Tea for this place, being 58 chests, which compleats the 400. —Am inform'd some *Indians* were met on ye road to Plimouth, which is almost fifty miles this side of Cape Cod. Its unlucky that Loring has ye lamps on board for illuminating our streets. Am sorry if they are lost, as we shall be depriv'd of their benefit this winter in consequence of it.

1. *As an observer of the Tea Party, what are John Andrews' most notable observations regarding the event? What are his impressions of the participants and their actions?*
2. *How has Boston set an example for the nation, as suggested in the opening of the letter dated December 18? What may be the consequences of these.*

4-8   Address of the Inhabitants of Anson County to Governor Martin (1774)

Many Americans remained loyal to England before, during, and after the Revolutionary War. Loyalists were particularly strong where British government was stable (like around New York City) and where colonists relied on the British for protection (like on the Carolina frontiers). This is a letter sent by colonial Loyalists from Anson County, North Carolina, to their governor, pledging their loyalty and asking, in part, for protection.

To His Excellency, Josiah Martin Esquire, Captain

General, Governor,

Most Excellent Governor:

Permit us, in behalf of ourselves, and many others of His Majesty's most dutiful and loyal subjects within the County of Anson, to take the earliest opportunity of addressing your Excellency, and expressing our abomination of the many outrageous attempts now forming on this side of the Atlantick, against the peace and tranquillity His Majesty's Dominions in North America, and to witness to your Excellency, by this our Protest, a disapprobation and abhorence of the many lawless combinations and unwarrantable practices actually carrying on by a gross tribe of infatuated anti-Monarchists in the several Colonies in these Dominions; the baneful consequence of whose audacious contrivance can, *in fine*, only tend to extirpate the fundamental principles of all Government, and illegally to shake off their obedience to, and dependence upon, the imperial Crown and Parliament of Great Britain; the infection of whose pernicious example being already extended to this particular County, of which we now bear the fullest testimony.

It is with the deepest concern (though with infinite indignation) that we see in all public places and papers disagreeable votes, speeches and resolutions, said to be entered into by our sister Colonies, in the highest contempt and derogation of the superintending power of the legislative authority of Great Britain. And we further, with sorrow, behold their wanton endeavors to vilify and arraign the honour and integrity of His Majesty's most honourable Ministry and Council, tending to sow the seed of discord and sedition, in open violation of their duty and allegiance. . . .

. . . We are truly invigorated with the warmest zeal and attachment in favour of the British Parliament, Constitution and Laws, which our forefathers gloriously struggled to establish, and which are now become the noblest birthright and inheritance of all Britannia's Sons. . . .

We are truly sensible that those invaluable blessings which we have hitherto enjoyed under His Majesty's auspicious Government, can only be secured to us by the stability of his Throne, supported and defended by the British Parliament, the only grand bulwark and guardian of our civil and religious liberties.

Duty and affection oblige us further to express our grateful acknowledgements for the inestimate blessings flowing from such a Constitution. And we do assure your Excellency that we are determined, by the assistance of Almighty God, in our respective stations, steadfastly to continue His Majesty's loyal Subjects, and to contribute all in our power for the preservation of the publick peace; so, that, by our unanimous example, we hope to discourage the desperate endeavours of a deluded multitude, and to see a misled people turn again from their atrocious offences to a proper exercise of their obedience and duty.

And we do furthermore assure your Excellency, that we shall endeavor to cultivate such sentiments in all those under our care, and to warm their breasts with a true zeal for His Majesty, and affection for his illustrious family. And may the Almighty God be pleased to direct his Councils, his Parliament, and all those in authority under him, that their endeavors may be for the advancement of piety, and the safety, honour and welfare of our Sovereign and his Kingdoms, that the malice of his enemies may be assuaged, and their evil designs confounded and defeated; so that all the world may be convinced that his sacred person, his Royal family, his Parliament, and our Country, are the special objects of Divine dispensation and Providence.

[Signed by two hundred twenty-seven of the inhabitants of Anson County.]

1. *Identify and describe the concerns and fears that are addressed in this letter from the inhabitants of Anson County. What do the signers of this letter plan to do in order to correct what they see as "evil designs" of a "deluded multitude"?*
2. *What seems to be the overall goal of this letter?*

4-9 J. Hector St. John Crèvecoeur, "What Is an American?" (1782)

Born in France, Crèvecoeur traveled in the new world before settling on a farm in Orange County New York in 1769. From there he wrote the influential "Letters from an American Farmer"(1782) and "Sketches of Eighteenth Century America" both of which present an important vision of agricultural life in America in the 18th century. His vision of the new "American" has continued to be of great literary and social significance.

I wish I could be acquainted with the feelings and thoughts which must agitate the heart and present themselves to the mind of an enlightened Englishman, when he first lands on this continent. He must greatly rejoice that he lived at a time to see this fair country discovered and settled; he must necessarily feel a share of national pride, when he views the chain of settlements which embellishes these extended shores. When he says to himself, this is the work of my countryment, who, when convulsed by factions, afflicted by a variety of miseries and wants, restless and impatient, took refuge here. They brought along with them their national genius, to which they principally owe what liberty they enjoy, and what substance they possess. Here he sees the industry of his native country displayed in a new manner, and traces in their works the embryos of all the arts, sciences, and ingenuity which flourish in Europe. Here he beholds fair cities, substantial villages, extensive fields, an immense country filled with decent houses, good roads, orchards, meadows, and bridges, where an hundred years ago all was wild, woody, and uncultivated! What a train of pleasing ideas this fair spectacle must suggest; it is a prospect which must inspire a good citizen with the most heartfelt pleasure. The difficulty consists in the manner of viewing so extensive a scene. He is arrived on a new continent; a modern society offers itself to his contemplation, different from what he had hitherto seen. It is not composed, as in Europe, of great lords who possess everything, and of a herd of people who have nothing. Here are no aristocratical families, no courts, no kings, no bishops, no ecclesiastical dominion, no invisible power giving to a few a very visible one, no great manufacturers employing thousands, no great refinements of luxury. The rich and the poor are not so far removed from each other as they are in Europe. Some few towns excepted, we are all tillers of the earth, from Nova Scotia to West Florida. We are a people of cultivators, scattered over an immense territory, communicating with each other by means of good roads and navigable rivers, united by the silken bands of mild government, all respecting the laws, without dreading their power, because they are equitable. We are all animated with the spirit of an industry which is unfettered and unrestrained, because each person works for himself. If he travels through our rural districts he views not the hostile castle, and the haughty mansion, contrasted with the clay-built hut and miserable cabin, where cattle and men help to keep each other warm, and dwell in meanness, smoke, and indigence. A pleasing uniformity of decent competence appears throughout our habitations. The meanest of our log-houses is a dry and comfortable habitation. Lawyer or merchant are the fairest titles our towns afford; that of a farmer is the only appellation of the rural inhabitants of our country. It must take some time ere he can reconcile himself to our dictionary, which is but short in words of dignity, and names of honour. There, on a Sunday, he sees a congregation of respectable farmers and their wives, all clad in neat homespun, well mounted, or riding in their own humble waggons. There is not among them an esquire, saving the unlettered magistrate. There he sees a parson as simple as his flock, a farmer who does not riot on the labour of others. We have no princes, for whom we toil, starve, and bleed: we are the most perfect society now existing in the world. Here man is free as he ought to be; nor is this pleasing equality so transitory as many others are. Many ages will not see the shores of our great lakes replenished with inland nations, nor the unknown bounds of North America entirely peopled. Who can tell how far it extends? Who can tell the millions of men whom it will feed and contain? For no European foot has as yet travelled half the extent of this mighty continent!

The next wish of this traveller will be to know whence came all these people? They are a mixture of English, Scotch, Irish, French, Dutch, Germans, and Swedes. From this promiscuous breed, that race now called Americans have arisen. The eastern provinces must indeed be excepted, as being the unmixed descendants of Englishmen. I have heard many wish that they had been more intermixed also: for my part, I am no wisher, and think it much better as it has happened. They exhibit a most conspicuous figure in this great and variegated picture; they too enter for a great share in the pleasing perspective displayed in these thirteen provinces. I know it is fashionable to reflect on them, but I respect them for what they have done, for the accuracy and wisdom with which they have settled their territory; for the decency of their manners; for their early love of letters; their ancient college, the first in this hemisphere; for their industry; which to me who am but a farmer, is the criterion of everything. There never was a people, situated as they are, who with so ungrateful a soil have done more in so short a time. Do you think that the monarchical ingredients which are more prevalent in other governments, have purged them from all foul stains? Their histories assert the contrary.

In this great American asylum, the poor of Europe have by some means met together, and in consequence of various causes; to what purpose should they ask one another what countrymen they are? Alas, two thirds of them had no country. Can a wretch who wanders about, who works and starves, whose life is a continual scene of sore affliction or pinching penury; can that man call England or any other kingdom his country? A country that had no bread for him, whose fields procured him no harvest, who met with nothing but the frowns of the rich, the severity of the laws, with jails and punishments; who owned not a single foot of the extensive surface of this planet? No! urged by a variety of motives, here they came. Every thing has tended to regenerate them; new laws, a new mode of living, a new social system; here they are become men: in Europe they were as so many useless plants, wanting vegetative mould, and refreshing showers; they withered, and were mowed down by want, hunger, and war; but now by the power of transplantation, like all other plants they have taken root and flourished! Formerly they were not numbered in any civil lists of their country, except in those of the poor; here they rank as citizens. By what invisible power has this surprising metamorphosis been performed? By that of the laws and that of their industry. The laws, the indulgent laws, protect them as they arrive, stamping on them the symbol of adoption; they receive ample rewards for their labours; these accumulated rewards procure them lands; those lands confer on them the title of freemen, and to that title every benefit is affixed which men can possibly require. This is the great operation daily performed by our laws. From whence proceed these laws? From our government. Whence the government? It is derived from the original genius and strong desire of the people ratified and confirmed by the Crown. This is the great chain which links us all, this is the picture which every province exhibits, Nova Scotia excepted. . . .

What attachment can a poor European emigrant have for a country where he had nothing? The knowledge of the language, the love a few kindred as poor as himself, were the only cords that tied him: his country is now that which gives him land, bread, protection, and consequence: Ubi panis ibi patria, is the motto of all emigrants. What then is the American, this new man? He is either an European, or the descendant of an European, hence that strange mixture of blood, which you will find in no other country. I could point out to you a family whose grandfather was an Englishman, whose wife was Dutch, whose son married a French woman, and whose present four sons have now four wives of different nations. He is an American, who, leaving behind him all his ancient prejudices and manners, receives new ones from the new mode of life he has embraced, the new government he obeys, and the new rank he holds. He becomes an American by being received in the broad lap of our great Alma Mater. Here individuals of all nations are melted into a new race of men, whose labours and posterity will one day cause great changes in the world. Americans are the western pilgrims, who are carrying along with them that great mass of arts, sciences, vigour, and industry which began long since in the east; they will finish the great circle. The Americans were once scattered all over Europe; here they are incorporated into one of the finest systems of population which has ever appeared, and which will hereafter become distinct by the power of the different climates they inhabit. The American ought therefore to love this country much better than that wherein either he or his forefathers were born. Here the rewards of his industry follow with equal steps the progress of his labour; his labour is founded on the basis of nature, self-interest; can it want a stronger allurement? Wives and children, who before in vain demanded of him a morsel of bread, now, fat and frolicsome, gladly help their father to clear those fields whence exuberant crops are to arise to feed and to clothe them all; without any part being claimed, either by a despotic prince, a rich abbot, or a mighty lord. Here religion demands but little of him; a small voluntary salary to the minister and gratitude to God; can he refuse these? The American is a new man, who acts upon new principles; he must therefore entertain new ideas, and form new opinions. From involuntary idleness, service dependence, penury, and useless labour, he has passed to toils of a very different nature, reward by ample subsistance.-This is an American. . .

1. Summarize the thoughts and feelings that Crevecoeur imagines must be experienced by Englishmen when they visit America.
2. How does the author describe the lifestyle and social relations of Americans?
3. In what ways is America described as a land of opportunity, especially for the poor?
4. What reasons are suggested for an American loving America much more than the country of his forefathers?

PART FIVE
THE AMERICAN REVOLUTION

5-1 Benjamin Franklin, "Observations Concerning the Increase of Mankind, Peopling of Countries, &c." (1751)

The great American polymath, Benjamin Franklin was first and foremost a scientist and in this work he turned his powerful mind on population. In this pre-revolutionary time, Franklin asserts that the English population of the new world will eventually exceed that of England.

Europe is generally full settled with Husbandmen, Manufacturers, &c. and therefore cannot now much increase in People: America is chiefly occupied by Indians, who subsist mostly by Hunting. But as the Hunter, of all Men, requires the greatest Quantity of Land from whence to draw his Subsistence, (the Husbandman subsisting on much less, the Gardner on still less, and the Manufacturer requiring least of all), The Europeans found America as fully settled as it well could be by Hunters; yet these having large Tracks, were easily prevail'd on to part with Portions of Territory to the new Comers, who did not much interfere with the Natives in Hunting, and furnish'd them with many Things they wanted.

Land being thus plenty in America, and so cheap as that a labouring Man, that understands Husbandry, can in a short Time save Money enough to purchase a Piece of new Land sufficient for a Plantation, whereon he may subsist a Family; such are not afraid to marry; for if they even look far enough forward to consider how their Children when grown up are to be provided for, they see that more Land is to be had at Rates equally easy, all Circumstances considered.

Hence Marriages in America are more general, and more generally early, than in Europe. And if it is reckoned there, that there is but one Marriage per Annum among 100 Persons, perhaps we may here reckon two; and if in Europe they have but 4 Births to a Marriage (many of their Marriages being late) we may here reckon 8, of which if one half grow up, and our Marriages are made, reckoning one with another at 20 Years of Age, our People must at least be doubled every 20 Years.

But notwithstanding this Increase, so vast is the Territory of North-America, that it will require many Ages to settle it fully; and till it is fully settled, Labour will never be cheap here, where no Man continues long a Labourer for others, but gets a Plantation of his own, no Man continues long a Journeyman to a Trade, but goes among those new Settlers, and sets up for himself, &c. Hence Labour is no cheaper now, in Pennsylvania, than it was 30 Years ago, tho' so many Thousand labouring People have been imported.

The Danger therefore of these Colonies interfering with their Mother Country in Trades that depend on Labour, Manufactures, &c. is too remote to require the Attention of Great-Britain.

But in Proportion to the Increase of the Colonies, a vast Demand is growing for British Manufactures, a glorious Market wholly in the Power of Britain, in which Foreigners cannot interfere, which will increase in a short Time even beyond her Power of supplying, tho' her whole Trade should be to her Colonies: Therefore Britain should not too much restrain Manufactures in her Colonies. A wise and good Mother will not do it. To distress, is to weaken, and weakening the Children, weakens the whole Family.

Besides if the Manufactures of Britain (by Reason of the American Demands) should rise too high in Price, Foreigners who can sell cheaper will drive her Merchants out of Foreign Markets; Foreign Manufacturers will thereby be encouraged and increased, and consequently foreign Nations, perhaps her Rivals in Power, grow more populous and more powerful; while her own Colonies, kept too low, are unable to assist her, or add to her Strength.

'Tis an ill-grounded Opinion that by the Labour of Slaves, America may possibly vie in Cheapness of Manufactures with Britain. The Labour of Slaves can never be so cheap here as the Labour of working Men is in Britain. Any one may compute it. Interest of Money is in the Colonies from 6 to 10 per Cent. Slaves one with another cost £30 Sterling per Head. Reckon then the Interest of the first Purchase of a Slave, the Insurance or Risque on his Life, his Cloathing and Diet, Expences in his Sickness and Loss of Time, Loss by his Neglect of Business (Neglect is natural to the Man who is not to be benefited by his own Care or Diligence), Expence of a Driver to keep him at Work, and his Pilfering from Time to Time, almost every Slave being *by Nature* a Thief, and compare the whole Amount with the Wages of a Manufacturer of Iron or Wool in England, you will see that Labour is much cheaper there than it ever can be by Negroes here. Why then will Americans purchase Slaves? Because Slaves may be kept as long as a Man pleases, or has Occasion for their Labour; while hired Men are continually leaving their Master (often in the midst of his Business,) and setting up for themselves. . . .

There is in short, no Bound to the prolific Nature of Plants or Animals, but what is made by their crowding and interfering with each others Means of Subsistence. Was the Face of the Earth vacant of other Plants, it might be gradually sowed and overspread with one Kind only; as, for Instance, with Fennel; and were it empty of other Inhabitants, it might in a few Ages be replenish'd from one Nation only; as, for Instance, with Englishmen. Thus there are suppos'd to be now upwards of One Million English Souls in North-America, (tho' 'tis thought scarce 80,000 have been brought over Sea) and yet perhaps there is not one the fewer in Britain, but rather many more, on Account of the Employment the Colonies afford to Manufacturers at Home. This Million doubling, suppose but once in 25 Years, will in another Century be more than the People of England, and the greatest Number of Englishmen will be on this Side the Water. What an Accession of Power to the British Empire by Sea as well as Land! What Increase of Trade and Navigation! What Number of Ships and Seamen! We have been here but little more than 100 Years, and yet the Force of our Privateers in the late War, united, was greater, both in Men and Guns, than that of the whole British Navy in Queen Elizabeth's Time. . . .

And since Detachments of English from Britain sent to America, will have their Places at Home so soon supply'd and increase so largely here; why should the Palatine Boors be suffered to swarm into our Settlements, and by herding together establish their Language and Manners to the Exclusion of ours? Why should Pennsylvania, founded by the English, become a Colony of Aliens, who will shortly be so numerous as to Germanize us instead of our Anglifying them, and will never adopt our Language or Customs, any more than they can acquire our Complexion.

Which leads me to add one Remark: That the Number of purely white People in the World is proportionably very small. All Africa is black or tawny. Asia chiefly tawny. America (exlusive of the New Comers) wholly so. And in Europe, the Spaniards, Italians, French, Russians and Swedes, are generally of what we call a swarthy Complexion; as are the Germans also, the Saxons only excepted, who with the English, make the principal Body of White People on the Face of the Earth. I could wish their Numbers were increased. And while we are, as I may call it, Scouring our Planet, by clearing America of Woods, and so making this Side of our Globe reflect a brighter Light to the Eyes of Inhabitants in Mars or Venus, why should we in the Sight of Superior Beings, darken its People? why increase the Sons of Africa, by Planting them in America, where we have so fair an Opportunity, by excluding all Blacks and Tawneys, of increasing the lovely White and Red? But perhaps I am partial to the Complexion of my Country, for such Kind of Partiality is natural to Mankind.

1. *What factors are identified by Franklin as being responsible for the high cost of both slave and non-slave labor in America?*
2. *Identify and analyze Franklin's comments on race and ethnicity. What are his hopes for America in terms of race? Do you consider his opinions to be racist? Explain.*

5-2 James Otis, The Rights of the British Colonies Asserted and Proved (1763)

A passionate and radical member of the opposition to Royal authority, James Otis made his name arguing against the British Writs of Assistance. He lost the case but his assertion of the natural rights of the colonists made him a prominent member of the opposition. He became the head of the Massachusetts Committee of Correspondence and a member of the Stamp Act Congress. In this reading, Otis asserts the natural and political rights of the colonists.

It is . . . true in fact and *experience,* as the great, the incomparable *Harrington* has most abundantly demonstrated in his *Oceana* and other divine writings, that empire follows the balance of *property.* 'Tis also certain that *property* in fact generally *confers* power, though the possessor of it may not have much more wit than a mole or a musquash: and this is too often the cause that riches are sought after without the least concern about the right application of them. But is the fault in the riches, or the general law of nature, or the unworthy possessor? It will never follow from all this that government is *rightfully* founded on property alone. What shall we say then? Is not government founded on *grace?* No. Nor on *force?* No. Nor on *compact?* Nor *property?* Not altogether on either. Has it *any* solid foundation, any chief cornerstone but what accident, chance, or confusion may lay one moment and destroy the next? I think it has an everlasing foundation in the *unchangeable will of* GOD, the author of nature, whose laws never vary. The same omniscient, omnipotent, infinitely good and gracious Creator of the universe who has been pleased to make it necessary that what we call matter should *gravitate* for the celestial bodies to roll round their axes, dance their orbits, and perform their various revolutions in that beautiful order and concern which we all admire has made it *equally* necessary that from *Adam* and *Eve* to these degenerate days the different sexes should sweetly *attract* each other, form societies of *single* families, of which *larger* bodies and communities are as naturally, mechanically, and necessarily combined as the dew of heaven and the soft distilling rain is collected by the all-enlivening heat of the sun. *Government* is therefore most evidently founded *on the necessities of our nature.* It is by no means an *arbitrary* thing depending merely on *compact* or *human will* for its existence. . . .

The *end* of government being the *good* of mankind points out its great duties: it is above all things to provide for the security, the quiet, and happy enjoyment of life, liberty, and property. There is no one act which a government can have a *right* to make that does not tend to the advancemewnt of the security, tranquillity, and prosperity of the people. If life, liberty, and property could be [11] enjoyed in as great perfection in *solitude* as in *society* there would be no need of government. But the experience of ages has proved that such is the nature of man, a weak, imperfect being, that the valuable ends of life cannot be obtained without the union and assistance of many. Hence 'tis clear that men cannot live apart or independent of each other. In solitude men would perish, and yet they cannot live together without contests. These contests require some arbitrator to determine them. The necessity of a common, indifferent, and impartial judge makes all men seek one, though few find him in the *sovereign power* of their respective states or anywhere else in *subordination* to it. . . .

I know of no human law founded on the law of *nature* to restrain him from separating himself from all the species if he can find it in his heart to leave them, unless it should be said it is against the great law of *self-preservation:* but of this every man will think himself *his own judge.*

The few *hermits* and *misanthropes* that have ever existed show that those states are *unnatural.* If we were to take out from them those who have made great *worldly* gain of their *godly* hermitage and those who have been under the madness of *enthusiasm* or *disappointed* hopes in their *ambitious* projects for the detriment of mankind, perhaps there might not be left ten from *Adam* to this day.

The form of government is by *nature* and by *right* so far left to the *individuals* of each society that they may alter it from a simple democracy or government of all over all to any other form they please. Such alteration may and ought to be made by express compact. But how seldom this right has been asserted, history will abundantly show. For once that it has been fairly settled by compact, *fraud, force,* or *accident* have determined it an hundred times. As the people have gained upon tyrants, these have been obliged to relax *only* till a fairer opportunity has put it in their power to encroach again.

But if every prince since *Nimrod* had been a tyrant, it would not prove a *right* to tyrannize. There can be no prescription old enough to supersede the law of nature and the grant of GOD Almight, who has given to all men a natural right to be *free,* and they have it ordinarily in their power to make themselves so if they please. . . .

In order to form an idea of the natural rights of the colonists, I presume it will be granted that they are men, the common children of the same Creator with their brethren of Great Britain. Nature has placed all such in a state of equality and perfect freedom to act within the bounds of the laws of nature and reason without consulting the will or regarding the humor, the passions, or whims of any other man, unless they are formed into a society or body politic. . . .

The colonists are by the law of nature freeborn, as indeed all men are, white or black. No better reasons can be given for enslaving those of any color than such as Baron Montesquieu has humorously given as the foundation of that cruel slavery exercised over the poor Ethiopians, which threatens one day to reduce both Europe and America to the ignorance and barbarity of the darkest ages. Does it follow that 'tis right to enslave a man because he is black? Will short curled hair like wool instead of Christian hair, as 'tis called by those whose hearts are as hard as the nether millstone, help the argument? Can any logical inference in favor of slavery be drawn from a flat nose, a long or a short face? Nothing better can be said in favor of a trade that is the most shocking violation of the law of nature, has a direct tendency to diminish the idea of the inestimable value of liberty, and makes every dealer in it a tyrant, from the director of an African company to the petty chapman in needles and pins on the unhappy coast. It is a clear truth that those who every day barter away other men's liberty will soon care little for their own. . . .

The colonists, being men, have a right to be considered as equally entitled to all the rights of nature with the Europeans, and they are not to be restrained in the exercise of any of these rights but for the evident good of the whole community.

By being or becoming members of society they have not renounced their natural liberty in any greater degree than other good citizens, and if 'tis taken from them without their consent they are so far enslaved.

I also lay it down as one of the first principles from whence I intend to deduce the civil rights of the British colonies, that all of them are subject to and dependent on Great Britain, and that therefore as over subordinate governments the Parliament of Great Britain has an undoubted power and lawful authority to make acts for the general good that, by naming them, shall and ought to be equally binding as upon the subjects of Great Britain within the realm. This principle, I presume, will be readily granted on the other side the Atlantic. It has been practised upon for twenty years to my knowledge, in the province of the *Massachusetts Bay;* and I have ever received it that it has been so from the beginning in this and the sister provinces through the continent. . . .

That the colonists, black and white, born here are freeborn British subjects, and entitled to all the essential civil rights of such is a truth not only manifest from the provincial charters, from the principles of the common law, and acts of Parliament, but from the British constitution, which was re-established at the Revolution with a professed design to secure the liberties of all the subjects to all generations. . . .

The liberties of the subject are spoken of as their best birthrights. No one ever dreamed, surely, that these liberties were confined to the realm. At that rate no British subjects in the dominions could, without a manifest contradiction, be declared entitled to all the privileges of subjects born within the realm to all intents and purposes which are rightly given foreigners by Parliament after residing seven years. These expressions of Parliament as well as of the charters must be vain and empty sounds unless we are allowed the essential rights of our fellow subjects in Great Britain.

Now can there be any liberty where property is taken away without consent? Can it with any color of truth, justice, or equity be affirmed that the northern colonies are represented in Parliament? Has this whole continent of near three thousand miles in length, and in which and his other American dominions His Majesty has or very soon will have some millions of as good, loyal, and useful subjects, white and black, as any in the three king-doms, the election of one member of the House of Commons?

Is there the least difference as to the consent of the colonists whether taxes and impositions are laid on their trade and other property by the crown alone or by the Parliament? As it is agreed on all hands the crown alone cannot impose them, we should be justifiable in refusing to pay them, but must and ought to yield obedience to an act of Parliament, though erroneous, till repealed. I can see no reason to doubt but the imposition of taxes, whether on trade, or on land, or houses, or ships, on real or personal, fixed ort floating property, in the colonies is absolutely irreconcilable with the rights of the colonists as British subjects and as men. I say men, for in a state of nature no man can take my property from me without my consent: if he does, he deprives me of my liberty and makes me a slave. If such a proceeding is a breach of the law of nature, no law of society can make it just. The very act of taxing exercised over those who are not represented appears to me to be depriving them of one of their most essential rights as freemen, and if continued seems to be in effect an entire disfranchisement of every civil right. . . .

We all think ourselves happy under Great Britain. We love, esteem, and reverence our mother country, and adore our King. And could the choice of independency be offered the colonies or subjection to Great Britain upon any terms above absolute slavery, I am convinced they would accept the latter. The ministry in all future generations may rely on it that British America will never prove undutiful till driven to it as the last fatal resort against ministerial oppression, which will make the wisest mad, and the weakest strong. . . .

The sum of my argument is: that civil government is of God; that the administrators of it were originally the whole people; that they might have devolved it on whom they pleased; that this devolution is fiduciary, for the good of the whole; that by the British constitution this devolution is on the King, Lords and Commons, the supreme, sacred and uncontrollable legislative power not only in the realm but through the dominions; that by the abdication, the original compact was broken to pieces; that by the Revolution it was renewed and more firmly established, and the rights and liberties of the subject in all parts of the dominions more fully explained and confirmed; that in consequence of this establishment and the acts of succession and union, His Majesty GEORGE III is rightful King and sovereign, and, with his Parliament, the supreme legislative of Great Britain, France, and Ireland, and the dominions thereto belonging; that this constitution is the most free one and by far the best now existing on earth; that by this constitution every man in the dominions is a free man; that no parts of His Majesty's dominions can be taxed without their consent; that every part has a right to be represented in the supreme or some subordinate legislature; that the refusal of this would seem to be a contradiction in practice to the theory of the constitution; that the colonies are subordinate dominions and are now in such a state as to make it best for the good of the whole that they should not only be continued in the enjoyment of subordinate legislation but be also represented in some proportion to their number and estates in the grand legislature of the nation; that this would firmly unite all parts of the British empire in the greater peace and prosperity, and render it invulnerable and perpetual.

1. *According to Otis, what things is government NOT founded upon? What is government founded upon?*
2. *Identify and explain the end, or chief purpose, of Government as it is proposed in this argument.*
3. *According to Otis, what is the natural right of every man? What reasoning does he use in proposing this natural right for ALL men regardless of race? How are his ideas regarding the rights of all men in opposition to the beliefs of many people of his era, especially those who supported slavery?*
4. *Which right is identified by Otis as the "most essential" for freemen? How have the colonists rights as British subjects been violated? What action is suggested to rectify this unjust situation?*

5-3 The Crisis Comes to a Head: April 19, 1775

In 1772, William Legge, the Second Earl of Dartmouth, became Secretary of State for the Colonies in the ministry of his half-brother Lord North. Initially adopting a policy of conciliation to allow colonial ill feelings to subside, Dartmouth changed his policy after the Boston Tea Party and instructed Thomas Gage, the military governor of Massachusetts, to impose strict control over the colonies. In April 1775, Gage decided to use his prerogative and sent troops under Lieutenant Colonel Francis Smith to remove known stores of arms in Concord, Massachusetts. The resulting skirmishes at Lexington and Concord marked the escalation of the rebellion to a higher level of violence.

Source: *Documents in Military History*
http://www.carleton.ca/~pking/docs/docs75.htm
http://www.hillsdale.edu/dept/History/Documents/War/America/Rev/1775-Lexington-Smith.htm

The Earl of Dartmouth to Gov. Thomas Gage
January 27, 1775
WHITEHALL January 27th 1775 Secret.

SIR,

Although your letters by the Scarborough represented the Affairs of the Province under Your Government in a very unfavourable light, & stated an Opposition to the Execution of the Law which marked a Spirit in the People of a dangerous & alarming nature, yet as they did not refer to any Facts tending to shew that the Outrages which had been committed were other than merely the Acts of a tumultuous Rabble, without any Appearance of general Concert or without any Head to advise, or Leader to conduct that could render them formidable to a regular Force led forth in support of Law and Government, it was hoped that by a vigorous Exertion of that Force, conformable to the Spirit & Tenor of the King's Commands signified to you in my several Letters, any further Insults of the like nature would have been prevented, & the People convinced that Government wanted neither the Power nor the Resolution to support it's just Authority & to punish such atrocious Offences. Your Dispatches, however, intrusted to Mr. Oliver, and those which have been since received, by the Schooner St Lawrence, and through other Channels relate to Facts, and state Proceedings, that amount to actual Revolt, and shew a Determination in the People to commit themselves at all Events in open Rebellion.

The King's Dignity, & the Honor and Safety of the Empire, require, that, in such a Situation, Force should be repelled by Force; and it has been His Majesty's Care not only to send you from hence such Reinforcement of the Army under your Command as general Considerations of public Safety would admit, but also to authorize you to collect together every Corps that could be spared from necessary Duty in every other part of America. It is hoped therefore that by this time your Force will amount to little less than 4,000 effective Men, including the Detachment of Marines that went out in the Men of War that sailed in October last, and I have the Satisfaction to acquaint you that Orders have been given this day for the immediate Embarkation of a further Detachment of Seven Hundred Marines, and of three Regiments of Infantry, & One of light Dragoons, from Ireland.

The Regiments of Infantry will be completed by Recruits to their full Establishment; and the Regiment of Light Dragoons will be augmented eighteen Men a Troop, that is to say Nine Men to be drafted with their Horses from the other Regiments of Light Cavalry in Ireland, nine Men without Horses from the Light Dragoons in England.

It is further directed that the number of Men wanting to complete the Regiments now with you, according to your last Returns, which amounts in the whole to near 500 should be raised by drafting one Man a Company from each of the Regiments in Ireland which will amount to about 200 & by drafting one Man a Company from some Regiments here, which will make about 60 more, and the remaining 240 to be raised by recruiting in Ireland for the number which (after the other mode of Supply) will be wanted for each Regiment.

You will observe that nine Men in each Troop of the Regiment of Light Dragoons will be without Horses, and a large Allowance must also be made for the Loss of Horses in the Passage. It will therefore be necessary that ample Provision of Horses be made, & you will not fail to take the earliest & most effectual Measures for securing a number, not less than 200 and Preparing them for Service upon the Arrival of the Regiment.

I understand a Proposal has been made by Mr Ruggles for rasing a Corps of Infantry from among the friends of Government in New England. Such a Proposal certainly ought to be encouraged, and it is the King's Pleasure that you should carry it into effect upon such Plan as you shall judge most expedient.

It appears that your Object has hitherto been to act upon the Defensive, & to avoid the hazard of weakening your Force by sending out Detachments of your Troops upon any Occasion whatsoever; & I should do injustice to Your Conduct, and to my own Sentiments of your Prudence & Discretion, if I could suppose that such Precaution was not necessary.

It is hoped however that this large Reinforcement to your Army will enable you to take a more active & determined part, & that you will have Strength enough, not only to keep Possession of Boston, but to give Protection in to Salem & the friends of Government at that Place, & that you may without Hazard of Insult return thither if you think fit, & exercise Your Functions there, conformable to His Majesty's Instructions.

I have already said, in more Letters than one, that the Authority of this Kingdom must be supported, & the Execution of its Laws inforced, & you will have seen in His Maty's Speech to both Houses of Parliament, & in the Addresses which they have presented to His Majesty, the firm Resolution of His Majesty and Parliament to act upon those Principles; and as there is a strong Appearance that the Body of the People in at least three of the New England Governments are determined to cast off their Dependence upon the Government of this Kingdom, the only Consideration that remains is, in what manner the Force under your Command may be exerted to defend the Constitution & to restore the Vigour of Government.

It seems to be your Idea that Matters are come to such a State that this is no otherwise attainable than by an absolute Conquest of the People of the three Governments of Massachuset's Bay, Connecticut & Rhode Island, & that such Conquest cannot be effected by a less Force than 10,000 Men.

I am persuaded, Sir, that you must be aware that such a Force cannot be collected without augmenting our Army in general to a War-Establishment; and tho' I do not mention this as an objection, because I think that the preservation, to Great Britain, of her Colonies demands the exertion of every effort this Country can make, yet I am unwilling to believe that matters are as yet come to that Issue.

I have stated that the violences committed by those who have taken up arms in Massachusetts Bay, have appeared to me as the acts of a rude Rabble without plan, without concert, & without conduct, and therefore I think that a smaller Force now, if put to the Test, would be able to encounter them with greater probability of Success than might be expected from a greater Army, if the people should be suffered to form themselves upon a more regular plan, to acquire confidence from discipline, and to prepare those resources without which every thing must be put to the issue of a single Action.

In this view therefore of the situation of The King's Affairs, it is the Opinion of The King's Servants in which His Majesty concurs, that the first & essential step to be taken towards re-establishing Government, would be to arrest and imprison the principal actors & abettors in the Provincial Congress (whose proceedings appear in every light to be acts of treason & rebellion) if regardless of your Proclamation & in defiance of it they should presume again to assemble for such rebellious purposes; and if the steps taken upon this occasion be accompanied with due precaution, and every means be devised to keep the Measure Secret until the moment of Execution, it can hardly fail of Success, and will perhaps be accomplished without bloodshed; but however that may be I must again repeat that any efforts of the People, unprepared to encounter with a regular force, cannot be very formidable; and though such a proceeding should be, according to your own idea of it, a Signal for Hostilities yet, for the reasons I have already given, it will surely be better that the Conflict should be brought on, upon such ground, than in a riper state of Rebellion.

It must be understood, however, after all I have said, that this is a matter which must be left to your own Discretion to be executed or not as you shall, upon weighing all Circumstances, and the advantages and disadvantages on one side, and the other, think most advisable.

I have fully exposed to you the Grounds upon which the Proposition has been adopted here, & unless the situation of things shall be very different from what they at present appear to be, it is considered as the best & most effectual means of vindicating the authority of this Kingdom.

Some attention must be given to the consideration of what it may be fit to do with those who shall be made prisoners in consequence of this Proceeding—And here I must confess the little hope I have that in the present situation of Things, and the temper of the people, they could be prosecuted to conviction. Their imprisonment however will prevent their doing any further mischief, and as the Courts of justice are at present not permitted to be opened, the continuance of that imprisonment will be no slight punishment.

I have mentioned this Measure as having the probable effect to become a Test of the People's resolution to resist, but there are other Cases that must occur in which the affording the Assistance of the Military will probably become unavoidable.

The recommendation of the General Congress, that Committees in the several Provinces should be appointed to carry into execution the Association for Nonimportation, and that they should take into their possession all ships arriving in the American Ports after the first of December, and should dispose of their Cargoes, in the manner, and for the purposes stated in their Resolutions, encourages Acts of so illegal & arbitrary a nature that every Effort must be made to protect the Commerce of the Kingdom and the Property of the King's Subjects from such outrageous Insults; and if, in any such Cases, the Assistance be afforded with Vigour and Celerity, I trust not much will be hazarded in the Execution, even should the Attempt encourage the People to take up Arms, seeing in this, as well as in the other Case, their Efforts of Resistance must be made without Plan or Preparation.

In such an Event as I have here supposed, it must be considered also, that any Efforts of Resistance on the Part of the People will be the less to be feared, as the Scene of Action, if it should come to Extremities, must be in Situations, where the Naval Force, which will receive immediate & considerable Augmentation, may be brought to act in Aid of the Army with full Effect.

I sincerely wish that the Information which we have received of the State of the Province, would enable me to instruct you upon every Case in which you may wish to receive such Instruction; but in a Situation where every thing depends so much upon the Events of the Day, and upon local Circumstances, your Conduct must be governed very much by your own Judgement and Discretion.

What I have said will point out to you with precision the Idea entertained here, of the manner in which the Military Force under your Command may be employed with effect; and it only remains for me to suggest to you, whether it may not be advisable, if there should be an evident Intention on the Part of Connecticut and Rhode Island to support the Inhabitants of Massachuset's Bay in their Rebellious Conduct, that the Fortifications upon the Island in front of the Town of Newport, and the Battery at New London should be dismantled; It may also be advisable to bring away the Cannon and Stores belonging to that Battery, and deposit them in some Place of Security; a Service which, I conceive, may very easily be effected by the Admiral without the Aid of any Detachment from the Army; and you will do well to consider whether it may not be practicable, to recover into The King's possession those Cannon and Stores which have been taken away in so extraordinary a manner from the Fort at Newport.

With regard to the state of America in general, affairs there are now come to a Crisis in which the Government of this Country must act with firmness and decision.

The accounts of what has already passed in Parliament on the Subject of America will probably reach You thro' other channels as early as you can receive this Letter; and I make no doubt they will be accompanied with every misrepresentation and exaggeration that can have the effect to encourage in the people more desperate Measures; you will therefore be more than ever on your guard, and upon no account suffer the Inhabitants of at least the Town of Boston, to assemble themselves in arms on any pretence whatever, either of Town guard or Militia duty; and I rather mention this, as a Report prevails that you have not only indulged them in having such a Guard, but have also allowed their Militia to train and discipline in Faneuil Hall.

In reviewing the Charter for the Government of the Province of Massachusets Bay, I observe there is a clause that impowers the Governor to use & exercise the Law-Martial in time of actual War, Invasion or Rebellion.

The inclosed copy of a Report made to me by the Attorney & Solicitor General, contains an Opinion that the Facts stated in the Papers you have transmitted, are the history of an actual and open Rebellion in that Province, and therefore I conceive that according to that Opinion, the exercise of that power is strictly justifiable, but the Expedience and Propriety of adopting such a Measure must depend upon your own Discretion under many Circumstances that can only be judged of upon the Spot.

> I am Sir, Your most Obedient humble Servant.
> DARTMOUTH
> Hor^ble Governor Gage.

THE BATTLE OF LEXINGTON

Lieutenant-Colonel Smith, 10th Regiment
of Foot, to Governor Gage
Boston, 22 April 1775

In obedience to your Excellency's commands, I marched on the evening of the 18th inst. with the corps of grenadiers and light infantry for Concord, to execute your Excellency's orders with respect to destroying all ammunition, artillery, tents, &c., collected there, which was effected, having knocked off the trunnions of three pieces of iron ordnance, some new gun carriages, a great number of carriage wheels burnt, a considerable quantity of flour, some gunpowder and musket balls, with other small articles thrown into the river. Notwithstanding we marched with the utmost expedition and secrecy, we found the country had intelligence or strong suspicion of our coming, and fired many signal guns, and rung the alarm bells repeatedly; and were informed, when at Concord, that some cannon had been taken out of the town that day, that others, with some stores, had been carried three days before. . . .

I think it proper to observe, that when I had got some miles on the march from Boston, I detached six light infantry companies to march with all expedition to seize the two bridges on different roads beyond Concord. On these companies' arrival at Lexington, I understand, from the report of Major Pitcairn, who was with them, and from many officers, that they found on a green close to the road a body of the country people drawn up in military order, with arms and accoutrements, and, as appeared after, loaded; and that they had posted some men in a dwelling and Meeting-house. Our troops advanced towards them, without any intention of injuring them, further than to inquire the reason of their being thus assembled, and, if not satisfactory, to have secured their arms; but they in confusion went off, principally to the left, only one of them fired before he went off, and three or four more jumped over a wall and fired from behind it among the soldiers; on which the troops returned it, and killed several of them. They likewise fired on the soldiers from the Meeting and dwelling-house. We had one man wounded, and Major Pitcairns horse shot in two places. Rather earlier than this, on the road, a country man from behind a wall had snapped his piece at Lieutenants Adair and Sutherland, but it flashed and did not go off. After this we saw some in the woods, but marched on to Concord without anything further happening. While at Concord we saw vast numbers assembling in many parts; at one of the bridges they marched down, with a very considerable body, on the light infantry posted there. On their coming pretty near, one of our men fired on them, which they returned; on which an action ensued, and some few were killed and wounded. In this affair, it appears that after the bridge was quitted, they scalped and otherwise ill-treated one or two of the men who were either killed or severely wounded, being seen by a party that marched by soon after. At Concord we found very few inhabitants in the town; those we met with both Major Pitcairn and myself took all possible pains to convince that we meant them no injury, and that if they opened their doors when required to search for military stores, not the slightest mischief would be done. We had opportunities of convincing them of our good intentions, but they were sulky; and one of them even struck Major Pitcairn. On our leaving Concord to return to Boston, they began to fire on us from behind the walls, ditches, trees, etc., which, as we marched, increased to a very great degree, and continued without the intermission of five minutes altogether, for, I believe, upwards of eighteen miles; so that I can't think but it must have been a preconcerted scheme in them, to attack the King's troops the first favourable opportunity that offered, otherwise, I think they could not, in so short a time as from our marching out, have raised such a numerous body, and for so great a space of ground. Notwithstanding the enemy's numbers, they did not make one gallant effort during so long an action, though our men were so very much fatigued, but kept under cover.

1. *The Earl of Dartmouth's instructions to Thomas Gage outline the crown's position on how best to respond to disorder in the colonies, yet they also give Gage some room for discretion. Based upon what you know about the events of April 19, 1775, what lessons do you think Gage might have learned from the day's "activities" that could play a role in his future decisions?*
2. *In the days, weeks, and months following the action at Lexington and Concord, both the British and the Americans rushed to determine that the other side fired first. Why do you think this clarification was so important? In the long run, did it really make a difference who fired first?*

5-4 A Freelance Writer Urges His Readers To Use Common Sense (1776)

In January 1776, Thomas Paine, a Philadelphia journalist and essayist, published a pamphlet entitled Common Sense. While other political tracts advocated protest against Parliament, Paine's political pamphlet placed the blame for colonial suffering directly on George III. Moreover, Paine urged his readers to abandon the king and declare independence. Common Sense became the equivalent of a best-seller, with over 150,000 copies in circulation during the first three months of its publication, and was no doubt an influence upon Thomas Jefferson when he drafted the Declaration of Independence.

> **Source:** *A Hypertext on American History From the Colonial Period Until Modern Times*
> http://odur.let.rug.nl/~usa/D/1776-1800/paine/CM/sense03.htm

MANKIND being originally equals in the order of creation, the equality could only be destroyed by some subsequent circumstance; the distinctions of rich, and poor, may in a great measure be accounted for, and that without having recourse to the harsh, ill-sounding names of oppression and avarice. Oppression is often the consequence, but seldom or never the means of riches; and though avarice will preserve a man from being necessitously poor, it generally makes him too timorous to be wealthy.

But there is another and greater distinction for which no truly natural or religious reason can be assigned, and that is, the distinction of men into KINGS and SUBJECTS. Male and female are the distinctions of nature, good and bad the distinctions of heaven; but how a race of men came into the world so exalted above the rest, and distinguished like some new species, is worth enquiring into, and whether they are the means of happiness or of misery to mankind.

In the early ages of the world, according to the scripture chronology, there were no kings; the consequence of which was there were no wars; it is the pride of kings which throw mankind into confusion. Holland without a king hath enjoyed more peace for this last century than any of the monarchial governments in Europe. Antiquity favors the same remark; for the quiet and rural lives of the first patriarchs hath a happy something in them, which vanishes away when we come to the history of Jewish royalty.

Government by kings was first introduced into the world by the Heathens, from whom the children of Israel copied the custom. It was the most prosperous invention the Devil ever set on foot for the promotion of idolatry. The Heathens paid divine honors to their deceased kings, and the Christian world hath improved on the plan by doing the same to their living ones. How impious is the title of sacred majesty applied to a worm, who in the midst of his splendor is crumbling into dust.

As the exalting one man so greatly above the rest cannot be justified on the equal rights of nature, so neither can it be defended on the authority of scripture; for the will of the Almighty, as declared by Gideon and the prophet Samuel, expressly disapproves of government by kings. All anti-monarchial parts of scripture have been very smoothly glossed over in monarchial governments, but they undoubtedly merit the attention of countries which have their governments yet to form. 'Render unto Caesar the things which are Caesar's' is the scriptural doctrine of courts, yet it is no support of monarchial government, for the Jews at that time were without a king, and in a state of vassalage to the Romans.

Near three thousand years passed away from the Mosaic account of the creation, till the Jews under a national delusion requested a king. Till then their form of government (except in extraordinary cases, where the Almighty interposed) was a kind of republic administered by a judge and the elders of the tribes. Kings they had none, and it was held sinful to acknowledge any being under that title but the Lords of Hosts. And when a man seriously reflects on the idolatrous homage which is paid to the persons of Kings, he need not wonder, that the Almighty, ever jealous of his honor, should disapprove of a form of government which so impiously invades the prerogative of heaven.

Monarchy is ranked in scripture as one of the sins of the Jews, for which a curse in reserve is denounced against them. The history of that transaction is worth attending to. The children of Israel being oppressed by the Midianites, Gideon marched against them with a small army, and victory, thro' the divine interposition, decided in his favor. The Jews elate with success, and attributing it to the generalship of Gideon, proposed making him a king, saying, Rule thou over us, thou and thy son and thy son's son. Here was temptation in its fullest extent; not a kingdom only, but an hereditary one, but Gideon in the piety of his soul replied, I will not rule over you, neither shall my son rule over you, THE LORD SHALL RULE OVER YOU. Words need not be more explicit; Gideon doth not decline the honor but denieth their right to give it; neither doth he compliment them with invented declarations of his thanks, but in the positive stile of a prophet charges them with disaffection to their proper sovereign, the King of Heaven.

About one hundred and thirty years after this, they fell again into the same error. The hankering which the Jews had for the idolatrous customs of the Heathens, is something exceedingly unaccountable; but so it was, that laying hold of the misconduct of Samuel's two sons, who were entrusted with some secular concerns, they came in an abrupt and clamorous manner to Samuel, saying, Behold thou art old and thy sons walk not in thy ways, now make us a king to judge us like all the other nations. And here we cannot but observe that their motives were bad, viz. that they might be like unto other nations, i. e. the Heathens, whereas their true glory laid in being as much unlike them as possible. But the thing displeased Samuel when they said, give us a king to judge us; and Samuel prayed unto the Lord, and the Lord said unto Samuel, Hearken unto the voice of the people in all that they say unto thee, for they have not rejected thee, but they have rejected me, THE I SHOULD NOT REIGN OVER THEM. According to all the works which have done since the day; wherewith they brought them up out of Egypt, even unto this day; wherewith they have forsaken me and served other Gods; so do they also unto thee. Now therefore hearken unto their voice, howbeit, protest solemnly unto them and show them the manner of the king that shall reign over them, i. e. not of any particular king, but the general manner of the kings of the earth, whom Israel was so eagerly copying after. And notwithstanding the great distance of time and difference of manners, the character is still in fashion, And Samuel told all the words of the Lord unto the people, that asked of him a king. And he said, This shall be the manner of the king that shall reign over you; he will take your sons and appoint them for himself for his chariots, and to be his horsemen, and some shall run before his chariots (this description agrees with the present mode of impressing men) and he will appoint him captains over thousands and captains over fifties, and will set them to ear his ground and to read his harvest, and to make his instruments of war, and instruments of his chariots; and he will take your daughters to be confectioneries and to be cooks and to be bakers (this describes the expense and luxury as well as the oppression of kings) and he will take your fields and your olive yards, even the best of them, and give them to his servants; and he will take the tenth of your seed, and of your vineyards, and give them to his officers and to his servants (by which we see that bribery, corruption, and favoritism are the standing vices of kings) and he will take the tenth of your men servants, and your maid servants, and your goodliest young men and your asses, and put them to his work; and he will take the tenth of your sheep, and ye shall be his servants, and ye shall cry out in that day because of your king which ye shall have chosen, AND THE LORD WILL NOT HEAR YOU IN THAT DAY. This accounts for the continuation of monarchy; neither do the characters of the few good kings which have lived since, either sanctify the title, or blot out the sinfulness of the origin; the high encomium given of David takes no notice of him officially as a king, but only as a man after God's own heart. Nevertheless the People refused to obey the voice of Samuel, and they said. Nay, but we will have a king over us, that we may be like all the nations, and that our king may judge us, and go out before us and fight our battles. Samuel continued to reason with them, but to no purpose; he set before them their ingratitude, but all would not avail; and seeing them fully bent on their folly, he cried out, I will call unto the Lord, and he shall sent thunder and rain (which then was a punishment, being the time of wheat harvest) that ye may perceive and see that your wickedness is great which ye have done in the sight of the Lord, IN ASKING YOU A KING. So Samuel called unto the Lord, and the Lord sent thunder and rain that day, and all the people greatly feared the Lord and Samuel And all the people said unto Samuel, Pray for thy servants unto the Lord thy God that we die not, for WE HAVE ADDED UNTO OUR SINS THIS EVIL, TO ASK A KING. These portions of scripture are direct and positive. They admit of no equivocal construction. That the Almighty hath here entered his protest against monarchial government is true, or the scripture is false. And a man hath good reason to believe that there is as much of king-craft, as priest-craft in withholding the scripture from the public in Popish countries. For monarchy in every instance is the Popery of government.

To the evil of monarchy we have added that of hereditary succession; and as the first is a degradation and lessening of ourselves, so the second, claimed as a matter of right, is an insult and an imposition on posterity. For all men being originally equals, no one by birth could have a right to set up his own family in perpetual preference to all others for ever, and though himself might deserve some decent degree of honors of his contemporaries, yet his descendants might be far too unworthy to inherit them. One of the strongest natural proofs of the folly of hereditary right in kings, is, that nature disapproves it, otherwise she would not so frequently turn it into ridicule by giving mankind an ass for a lion.

Secondly, as no man at first could possess any other public honors than were bestowed upon him, so the givers of those honors could have no power to give away the right of posterity, and though they might say 'We choose you for our head,' they could not, without manifest injustice to their children, say 'that your children and your children's children shall reign over ours for ever.' Because such an unwise, unjust, unnatural compact might (perhaps) in the next succession put them under the government of a rogue or a fool. Most wise men, in their private sentiments, have ever treated hereditary right with contempt; yet it is one of those evils, which when once established is not easily removed; many submit from fear, others from superstition, and the more powerful part shares with the king the plunder of the rest.

This is supposing the present race of kings in the world to have had an honorable origin; whereas it is more than probable, that could we take off the dark covering of antiquity, and trace them to their first rise, that we should find the first of them nothing better than the principal ruffian of some restless gang, whose savage manners of preeminence in subtlety obtained him the title of chief among plunderers; and who by increasing in power, and extending his depredations, overawed the quiet and defenseless to purchase their safety by frequent contributions. Yet his electors could have no idea of giving hereditary right to his descendants, because such a perpetual exclusion of themselves was incompatible with the free and unrestrained principles they professed to live by. Wherefore, hereditary succession in the early ages of monarchy could not take place as a matter of claim, but as something casual or complemental; but as few or no records were extant in those days, and traditionary history stuffed with fables, it was very easy, after the lapse of a few generations, to trump up some superstitious tale, conveniently timed, Mahomet like, to cram hereditary right down the throats of the vulgar. Perhaps the disorders which threatened, or seemed to threaten on the decease of a leader and the choice of a new one (for elections among ruffians could not be very orderly) induced many at first to favor hereditary pretensions; by which means it happened, as it hath happened since, that what at first was submitted to as a convenience, was afterwards claimed as a right.

England, since the conquest, hath known some few good monarchs, but groaned beneath a much larger number of bad ones, yet no man in his senses can say that their claim under William the Conqueror is a very honorable one. A French bastard landing with an armed banditti, and establishing himself king of England against the consent of the natives, is in plain terms a very paltry rascally original. It certainly hath no divinity in it. However, it is needless to spend much time in exposing the folly of hereditary right, if there are any so weak as to believe it, let them promiscuously worship the ass and lion, and welcome. I shall neither copy their humility, nor disturb their devotion.

Yet I should be glad to ask how they suppose kings came at first? The question admits but of three answers, viz. either by lot, by election, or by usurpation. If the first king was taken by lot, it establishes a precedent for the next, which excludes hereditary succession. Saul was by lot yet the succession was not hereditary, neither does it appear from that transaction there was any intention it ever should. If the first king of any country was by election, that likewise establishes a precedent for the next; for to say, that the right of all future generations is taken away, by the act of the first electors, in their choice not only of a king, but of a family of kings for ever, hath no parallel in or out of scripture but the doctrine of original sin, which supposes the free will of all men lost in Adam; and from such comparison, and it will admit of no other, hereditary succession can derive no glory. For as in Adam all sinned, and as in the first electors all men obeyed; as in the one all mankind were subjected to Satan, and in the other to Sovereignty; as our innocence was lost in the first, and our authority in the last; and as both disable us from reassuming some former state and privilege, it unanswerably follows that original sin and hereditary succession are parallels. Dishonorable rank! Inglorious connection! Yet the most subtle sophist cannot produce a juster simile.

As to usurpation, no man will be so hardy as to defend it; and that William the Conqueror was an usurper is a fact not to be contradicted. The plain truth is, that the antiquity of English monarchy will not bear looking into.

But it is not so much the absurdity as the evil of hereditary succession which concerns mankind. Did it ensure a race of good and wise men it would have the seal of divine authority, but as it opens a door to the foolish, the wicked; and the improper, it hath in it the nature of oppression. Men who look upon themselves born to reign, and others to obey, soon grow insolent; selected from the rest of mankind their minds are early poisoned by importance; and the world they act in differs so materially from the world at large, that they have but little opportunity of knowing its true interests, and when they succeed to the government are frequently the most ignorant and unfit of any throughout the dominions.

Another evil which attends hereditary succession is, that the throne is subject to be possessed by a minor at any age; all which time the regency, acting under the cover of a king, have every opportunity and inducement to betray their trust. The same national misfortune happens, when a king worn out with age and infirmity, enters the last stage of human weakness. In both these cases the public becomes a prey to every miscreant, who can tamper successfully with the follies either of age or infancy.

The most plausible plea, which hath ever been offered in favor of hereditary succession, is, that it preserves a nation from civil wars; and were this true, it would be weighty; whereas, it is the most barefaced falsity ever imposed upon mankind. The whole history of England disowns the fact. Thirty kings and two minors have reigned in that distracted kingdom since the conquest, in which time there have been (including the Revolution) no less than eight civil wars and nineteen rebellions. Wherefore instead of making for peace, it makes against it, and destroys the very foundation it seems to stand on.

The contest for monarchy and succession, between the houses of York and Lancaster, laid England in a scene of blood for many years. Twelve pitched battles, besides skirmishes and sieges, were fought between Henry and Edward.

Twice was Henry prisoner to Edward, who in his turn was prisoner to Henry. And so uncertain is the fate of war and the temper of a nation, when nothing but personal matters are the ground of a quarrel, that Henry was taken in triumph from a prison to a palace, and Edward obliged to fly from a palace to a foreign land; yet, as sudden transitions of temper are seldom lasting, Henry in his turn was driven from the throne, and Edward recalled to succeed him. The parliament always following the strongest side.

This contest began in the reign of Henry the Sixth, and was not entirely extinguished till Henry the Seventh, in whom the families were united. Including a period of 67 years, viz. from 1422 to 1489.

In short, monarchy and succession have laid (not this or that kingdom only) but the world in blood and ashes. 'Tis a form of government which the word of God bears testimony against, and blood will attend it.

If we inquire into the business of a king, we shall find that in some countries they have none; and after sauntering away their lives without pleasure to themselves or advantage to the nation, withdraw from the scene, and leave their successors to tread the same idle round. In absolute monarchies the whole weight of business civil and military, lies on the king; the children of Israel in their request for a king, urged this plea 'that he may judge us, and go out before us and fight our battles.' But in countries where he is neither a judge nor a general, as in England, a man would be puzzled to know what is his business.

The nearer any government approaches to a republic the less business there is for a king. It is somewhat difficult to find a proper name for the government of England. Sir William Meredith calls it a republic; but in its present state it is unworthy of the name, because the corrupt influence If the crown, by having all the places in its disposal, hath so effectually swallowed up the power, and eaten out the virtue of the house of commons (the republican part in the constitution) that the government of England is nearly as monarchical as that of France or Spain. Men fall out with names without understanding them. For it is the republican and not the monarchical part of the constitution of England which Englishmen glory in, viz. the liberty of choosing an house of commons from out of their own body and it is easy to see that when the republican virtue fails, slavery ensues. My is the constitution of England sickly, but because monarchy hath poisoned the republic, the crown hath engrossed the commons?

In England a king hath little more to do than to make war and give away places; which in plain terms, is to impoverish the nation and set it together by the ears. A pretty business indeed for a man to be allowed eight hundred thousand sterling a year for, and worshipped into the bargain! Of more worth is one honest man to society, and in the sight of God, than all the crowned ruffians that ever lived.

1. *What, according to Paine, are the arguments against a monarchy? How does he use history to support his conclusions?*
2. *Discuss the elements from this excerpt of Common Sense that were most likely to be influential in Jefferson's drafting of the Declaration of Independence.*

5-5 Abigail Adams and John Adams Letters; Abigail Adams Letter to Mercy Otis Warren

These letters are written between Abigail Adams and her husband John, the future president, then a member of the Continental Congress in Pennsylvania. Many women were active in the Revolutionary War-from supporting the war effort by raising money to billeting soldiers-and Abigail Adams's letter is an example of how involvement in the Revolution raised questions about what freedom for all would mean. Abigail Adams's letter to her husband is followed by one to their friend, the historian, poet, and playwright, Mercy Otis Warren.

From *The Adams Family Correspondence*, eds. L. H. Butterfield et al. (Cambridge: Belknap Press of Harvard University Press, 1963), vol. I, 29-31.

[Abigail Adams to John Adams, March 31, 1776]

I long to hear that you have declared an independancy [sic]-and by the way in the new Code of Laws which I suppose it will be necessary for you to make I would desire you would Remember
the Ladies, and be more generous and favourable to them than your ancestors. Do not put such unlimited power into the hands of the Husbands. Remember all men would be tyrants if they could. If
perticuliar care and attention is not paid to the Ladies we are determined to foment a Rebelion, and will not hold ourselves bound by any Laws in which we have no voice, or Representation.

That your Sex are Naturally Tyrannical is a Truth so thoroughly established as to admit of no dispute, but such of you as wish to be happy willingly give up the harsh title of Master for the more tender and endearing one of Friend. Why then, not put it out of the power of the vicious and the Lawless to use us with cruelty and indignity with impunity. Men of Sense in all Ages abhor those customs which treat us only as the vassals of your Sex. Regard us then as Beings placed by providence under your protection and in immitation of the Supreem Being make use of that power only for our happiness.

[John Adams to Abigail Adams, April 14, 1776]

As to Declarations of Independency, be patient. Read our Privateering Laws, and our Commercial Laws. What signifies a Word.

As to your extraordinary Code of Laws, I cannot but laugh. We have been told that our Struggle has loosened the bands of Government every where. That Children and Apprentices were disobedient-that schools and Colledges were grown turbulent -that Indians slighted their Guardians and Negroes grew insolent to their Masters. But your Letter was the first Intimation that another

Tribe more numerous and powerfull than all the rest were grown discontented.-This is rather too coarse a Compliment but you are so saucy, I wont blot it out.

Depend upon it, We know better than to repeal our Masculine systems. Altho they are in full Force, you know they are little more than Theory. We dare not exert our Power in its full Latitude. We are obliged to go fair, and softly, and in Practice you know We are the subjects. We have only the Name of Masters, and rather than give up this, which would compleatly subject Us to the Despotism of the Peticoat, I hope General Washington, and all our brave Heroes would fight....

[Abigail Adams to Mercy Otis Warren]

Braintree April 27 1776
He is very saucy to me in return for a List of Female Grievances which I transmitted to him. I think I will get you to join me in a petition to Congress. I thought it was very probable our wise Statesmen would erect a New Government and form a new code of Laws. I ventured to speak a word on behalf of our Sex, who are rather hardly dealte with by the Laws of England which gives such unlimited power to the Husband to use his wife Ill.

I requested that our Legislators would consider our case and as all Men of Delicacy and Sentiment are adverse to Exercising the power they possess, yet as there is a natural propensity in Human Nature to domination, I thought the most generous plan was to put it out of the power of the Arbitrary and tyranick to injure us with impunity by Establishing some Laws in favour upon just and Liberal principals.

I believe I even threatened fomenting a Rebellion in case we were not considered and assured him we would not hold ourselves bound by any Laws in which we had neither a voice nor representation.

In return he tells me he cannot but Laugh at my extraordinary Code of Laws. That he had heard their Struggle had loosened the bands of Government, that children and apprentices were disobedient,

that Schools and Colleges had grown turbulent, that Indians slighted their Guardians, and Negroes grew insolent to their Masters. But my Letter was the first intimation that another Tribe more numerous and powerful than all the rest were grown discontented. This is rather too coarse a complement, he adds, but that I am so saucy he wont blot it out.

So I have helped the Sex abundantly, but I will tell him I have only been making trial of the Disinterestedness of his Virtue, and when weigh'd in the balance have found it wanting.

It would be bad policy to grant us greater power say they since under all the disadvantages we Labour we have the ascendency over their Hearts.

And charm by accepting, by submitting sway.

[Abigail Adams to John Adams, May 7, 1776]

I can not say that I think you very generous to the Ladies, for whilst you are proclaiming peace and good will to men, Emancipating all Nations, you insist upon retaining an absolute power over Wives. But you must remember that Arbitrary power is like most other things which are very hard, very liable to be broken ≈ and notwithstanding all your wise Laws and Maxims we have it in our power not only to free our selves but to subdue our Masters, and without violence throw both your natural and legal authority at our feet
"Charm by accepting, by submitting sway
Yet have our Humour most when we obey."

1. *What is Abigail Adams' opinion of men in power and what is her request to John Adams as they declare independence?*
2. *How does John Adams respond to her concerns? In light of Abigail Adams' letter to Mercy Otis Warren, does this response seem to satisfy Abigail Adams? What does the second letter to John Adams suggest?*

5-6 Petition of "A Grate Number of Blackes of the Province" to Governor Thomas Gage and the Members of the Massachusetts General Court (1774)

Echoing the natural rights language of the rebellious colonists, this petition sought to extend these rights to the slave population. Using the arguments of natural rights, moral outrage, and Christian principle, the petitioners seek to achieve the same rights as the colonists who are calling for independence. It would, however, be many years before such rights would be extended.

Your Petitioners apprehend we have in common with all other men a naturel right to our freedoms without Being depriv'd of them by our fellow men as we are a freeborn Pepel and have never forfeited this Blessing by aney compact or agreement whatever. But we were unjustly dragged by the cruel hand of power from our dearest friends and sum of us stolen from the bosoms of our tender Parents and from a Populous Pleasant and plentiful country and Brought hither to be made slaves for Life in a Christian land. Thus we are deprived of every thing that hath a tendency to make life even tolerable, the endearing ties of husband and wife we are strangers to. . . . Our children are also taken from us by force and sent maney miles from us. . . . Thus our Lives are imbittered. . . . There is a great number of us sencear. . . . members of the Church of Christ how can the master and the slave be said to fulfil that command Live in love let Brotherly Love contuner and abound Beare yea one nothers Bordenes. How can the master be said to Beare my Borden when he Beares me down which the. . . . chanes of slavery. . . . Nither can we reap an equal benefet from the laws of the Land which doth not justifi but condemns Slavery or if there had bin aney Law to hold us in Bondage. . . . ther never was aney to inslave our children for life when Born in a free Countrey. We therefore Bage your Excellency and Honours will. . . . cause an act of the legislative to be pessed that we may obtain our Natural right our freedoms and our children be set at lebety at the yeare of twenty one. . . .

1. *What is the primary plea of the writers of this petition?*
2. *What is their reasoning for this request?*
3. *What ideals do they appeal to in their plea?*

5-7 Joseph Warren, "Account of the Battle of Lexington" (1775)

An early and vocal American revolutionary, Joseph Warren was a doctor with a promising career when he was politicized by the Stamp Act and other British measures. He became a close friend and ally of Samuel Adams, wrote many articles against British "tyranny", and served on the Committee of Correspondence before being commissioned in the Massachusetts force. Warren was present at Lexington where his example was an inspiration to his men. He was killed early in the war becoming the first colonial officer to die in combat.

Source: Hezekiah Niles, ed., *Principles and Acts of the Revolution* (Baltimore: W.O. Niles, 1822), 434–435.

MASSACHUSETTS.
IN PROVINCIAL CONGRESS
Watertown, April 26, 1775
TO THE INHABITANTS OF GREAT BRITAIN.

Friends and fellow subjects,

Hostilities are at length commenced in this colony, by the troops under command of general Gage; and it being of the greatest importance, that an early, true, and authentic account of this inhuman proceeding should be know to you, the congress of this colony have transmitted the same, and for want of a session of the hon. continental congress, think it proper to address you on this alarming occasion.

By the clearest depositions, relative to this transaction, it will appear, *that,* on the night preceding the 19th of April, instant, a body of the king's troops, under command of colonel Smith, were secretly landed at Cambridge, with an apparent design to take or destroy the military and other stores, provided for the defence of this colony, and deposited at Concord; that some inhabitants of the colony, on the night aforesaid whilst travelling peaceable on the road between Boston and Concord, were seized and greatly abused by armed men, who appeared to be officers of general Gage's army; that the town of Lexington, by these means, was alarmed, and a company of the inhabitants mustered on the occasion; that the regular troops, on their way to Concord, marched into the said town of Lexington, and the said company, on their approach, began to disperse; that notwithstanding this, the regulars rushed on with great violence, and first began hostilities, by firing on the said Lexington company, whereby, they killed eight, and wounded several others; that the regulars continued their fire until those of the said company, who were neither killed nor wounded, had made their escape; that colonel Smith, with the detachment, then marched to Concord, where a number of provincials were again fired on by the troops, two of them killed and several wounded, before any of the provincials fired on them; and that these hostile measures of the troops produced an engagement that lasted through the day, in which many of he provincials, and more of the regular troops, were killed and wounded.

To give a particular account of the ravages of the troops, as they retreated from Concord to Charles Town, would be very difficult, if not impracticable; let it suffice to say, that a great number of the houses on the road were plundered, and rendered unfit for use; several were burnt; women in child-bed were driven by the soldiery naked into the streets; old men, peaceably in their houses, were shot dead, and such scenes exhibited, as would disgrace the annals of he most unciv-ilized nations.

These, brethren, are marks of ministerial vengeance against this colony, for refusing, with her sister colonies, a submission to slavery; but they have not yet detached us from our royal sovereign we profess to be his loyal and dutiful subjects; and so hardly dealt with as we have been, are still ready, with our lives and fortunes, to defend his person, family, crown and dignity; nevertheless, to the persecution and tyranny of his cruel ministry, we will not tamely submit; appealing to Heaven for the justice of our cause, "we determine to die, or be free."

We cannot think that the honor, wisdom, and valor of Britons, will suffer them to be longer inactive spectators of *measures,* in which they themselves are so deeply interested; measures pursued in opposition to the solemn protests of many noble lords, and expressed sense of conspicuous commons, whose knowledge and virtue have long characterized them as some of the greatest men in the nation; *measures,* executing, contrary to the interest, petitions, and resolves of many large, respectable counties, cities, and boroughs, in Great Britain; *measures* highly incompatible with justice, but still pursued with a specious pretence of easing he nation of its burthens; *measures* which, if successful, must end in the ruin and slavery of Britain, as well as the persecuted American colonies.

We sincerely hope, that the Great Sovereign of the Universe, who hath so often appeared for the English nation, will support you in every rational and manly exertion with these colonies, for saving it form ruin, and that, in a constitutional connection with our mother country, we shall soon be altogether a free and happy people.

Signed by order,

JOS. WARREN, president

1. Who are the primary aggressors according to this account? Describe some of the actions detailed in this account as evidence of this aggression.
2. What appeal is made to the people of Britain by the author of this letter? What is the goal of this document?

5-8 Thomas Jefferson, "Original Rough Draught" of the Declaration of Independence (1776)

The "original Rough draught" of the Declaration of Independence, one of the great milestones in American history, shows the evolution of the text from the initial "fair copy" draft by Thomas Jefferson to the final text adopted by Congress on the morning of July 4, 1776.

A Declaration of the Representatives of the United States of America, in General Congress assembled.

When in the course of human events it becomes necessary for a people to advance from that subordination in which they have hitherto remained, & to assume among the powers of the earth the equal & independent station to which the laws of nature & of nature's god entitle them, a decent respect to the opinions of mankind requires that they should declare the causes which impel them to the change.

We hold these truths to be sacred & undeniable that all men are created equal & independant, that from that equal creation they derive rights inherent & inalienable, among which are the preservation of life, & liberty, & the pursuit of happiness; that to secure these ends, governments are instituted among men, deriving their just powers from the consent of the governed; that whenever any form of government shall become destructive of these ends, it is the right of the people to alter or to abolish it, & to institute new government, laying its foundation on such principles & organising it's powers in such form, as to them shall seem most likely to effect their safety & happiness. prudence indeed will dictate that governments long established should not be changed for light & transient causes: and accordingly all experience hath shewn that mankind are more disposed to suffer while evils are sufferable, than to right themselves by abolishing the forms to which they are accustomed. but when a long train of abuses & usurpations, begun at a distinguished period, & pursuing invariably the same object, evinces a design to subject them to arbitrary power, it is their right, it is their duty, to throw off such government & to provide new guards for their future security. such has been the patient sufference of these colonies; & such is now the necessity which contrains them to expunge their former systems of government. the history of his present majesty, is a history of unremitting injuries and usurpations, among which no one fact stands single or solitary to contradict the uniform tenor of the rest, all of which have in direct object the establishment of an absolute tyranny over these states. to prove this, let facts be submitted to a candid world, for the truth of which we pledge a faith yet unsullied by falsehood.

he has refused his assent to laws the most wholesome and necessary for the public good:

he has forbidden his governors to pass laws of immediate & pressing importance, unless suspended in their operation till his assent should be obtained; and when so suspended, he has neglected utterly to attend to them.

he has refused to pass other laws for the accommodation of large districts of people unless those people would relinquish the right of representation, a right inestimable to them, & formidable to tyrants alone.

he has dissolved Representative houses repeatedly & continually, for opposing with manly firmness his invasions on the rights of the people:

he has refused for a long space of time to cause others to be elected, whereby the legislative powers, incapable of annihilation, have returned to the people at large for their exercise, the state remaining in the mean time exposed to all the dangers of invasion from without, & convulsions within:

he has endeavored to prevent the population of these states; for that purpose obstructing the laws for naturalization of foreigners; refusing to pass others to encourge their migrations hither; & raising the conditions of new appropriations of lands:

he has suffered the administration of justice totally to cease in some of these colonies, refusing his assent to laws for establishing judiciary powers:

he has made our judges dependent on his will alone, for the tenure of their offices, and amount of their salaries:

he has erected a multitude of new offices by a self-assumed power, & sent hither swarms of officers to harrass our people & eat out their substance:

he has kept among us in times of peace standing armies & ships of war:

he has affected to render the military, independant of & superior to the civil power:

he has combined with others to subject us to a jurisdiction foreign to our constitutions and unacknowleged by our laws; giving his assent to their pretended acts of legislation, for quartering large bodies of armed troops among us;

for protecting them by a mock-trial from punishment for any murders they should commit on the inhabitants of these states;

for cutting off our trade with all parts of the world;

for imposing taxes on us without our consent;

for depriving us of the benefits of trial by jury; for transporting us beyond seas to be tried for pretended offences:

for taking away our charters, & altering fundamentally the forms of our governments;

for suspending our own legislatures & declaring themselves invested with power to legislate for us in all cases whatsoever:

he has abdicated government here, withdrawing his governors, & declaring us out of his allegiance & protection:

he has plundered our seas, ravaged our coasts, burnt our towns & destroyed the lives of our people:

he is at this time transporting large armies of foreign mercenaries to compleat the works of death, desolation & tyranny, already begun with circumstances of cruelty & perfidy unworthy the head of a civilized nation:

he has endeavored to bring on the inhabitants of our frontiers the merciless Indian savages, whose known rule of warfare is an undistinguished destruction of all ages, sexes, & conditions of existence:

he has incited treasonable insurrections in our fellow-subjects, with the allurements of forefeiture & confiscation of our property:

He has waged cruel war against human nature itself, violating it's most sacred rights of life & liberty in the persons of a distant people who never offended him, captivating & carrying them into slavery in another hemisphere, or to incur miserable death in their transportation thither. this piratical warfare, the opprobrium of *infidel* powers, is the warfare of the CHRISTIAN king of Great Britain. determined to keep open a market where MEN should be bought & sold, he has prostituted his negative for suppressing every legislative attempt to prohibit or to restrain this execrable commerce: and that this assemblage of horrors might want no fact of distinguished die, he is now exciting those very people to rise in arms among us, and to purchase that liberty of which *he* has deprived them, by murdering the people upon whom *he* also obtruded them; thus paying off former crimes committed against the liberties of one people, with crimes which he urges them to commit against the *lives* of another.

in every stage of these oppressions we have petitioned for redress in the most humble terms; our repeated petitions have been answered by repeated injury. a prince whose character is thus marked by every act which may define a tyrant, is unfit to be the ruler of a people who mean to be free. future ages will scarce believe that the hardiness of one man, adventured within the short comnpass of 12 years only, on so many acts of tyranny without a mask, over a people fostered & fixed in principles of liberty.

Nor have we been wanting in attentions to our British brethren. we have warned them from time to time of attempts by their legislature to extend a jurisdiction over these our states. we have reminded them of the circumstances of our emigration & settlement here, no one of which could warrant so strange a pretension: that these were effected at the expence of our own blood & treasure, unassisted by the wealth or the strength of Great Britain: that in constituting indeed our several forms of government, we had adopted one common king, thereby laying a foundation for perpetual league & amity with them: but that submission to their parliament was no part of our constitution, nor ever in idea, if history may be credited: and we appealed to their native justice & magnanimity, as well as to the ties of our common kindred to disavow these usurpations which were likely to interrupt our correspondence & connection. they too have been deaf to the voice of justice & of consanguinity, & when occasions have been given them, by the regular course of their laws, of removing from their councils the disturbers of our harmony, they have by their free election re-established them in power. at this very time too they are permitting their chief magistrate to send over not only soldiers of our common blood, but Scotch & foreign mercenaries to invade & deluge us in blood. these facts have given the last stab to agonizing affection, and manly spirit bids us to renounce for ever these unfeeling brethren. we must endeavor to forget our former love for them, and to hold them as we hold the rest of mankind, enemies in war, in peace friends, we might have been a free & a great people together; but a communication of grandeur & of freedom it seems is below their dignity. be it so, since they will have it: the road to glory & happiness is open to us to; we will climb it in a separate state, and acquiesce in the necessity which pronounces our everlasting Adieu!

We therefore the representatives of the United States of America in General Congress assembled do, in the name & by authority of the good people of these states, reject and renounce all allegiance & subject to the kings of Great Britain & all others who may hereafter claim by, through, or under them; we utterly dissolve & break off all political connection which may have heretofore subsisted between us & the people or parliament of Great Britain; and finally we do assert and declare these colonies to be free and independent states, and that as free & independent states they shall hereafter have power to levy war, conclude peace, contract alliances, establish commerce, & to do all other acts and things which independent states may of right do. And for the support of this declaration we mutually pledge to each other our lives, our fortunes, & our sacred honour.

1. *What truths are undeniable according to Jefferson? Identify the course of action necessitated by the denial of these truths. How do these ideas set the stage for the Revolution against Britain?*
2. *Summarize the facts set forth by Jefferson as evidence of "a history of unremitting injuries".*
3. *What complaints are leveled against the king in regard to slavery?*
4. *According to this document, what steps have been taken by the colonists to address their concerns before this declaration of independence? How have these attempts been answered by Britain? What is the final resolution of this document?*

5-9   Rights of Women in an Independent Republic

Abigail and John Adams had one of the most extraordinary partnerships of their (or any other) time. Two powerful minds are revealed in their correspondence, and the influence of Abigail Adams on her husband is revealed in these letters. Arguably, the most important questions raised by the move for independence was who should share in the newly posited freedoms. These letters illuminate this struggle that continues to this day.

Abigail Adams to John Adams, Braintree, 31 March 1776

I long to hear that you have declared an independancy-and by the way in the new Code of Laws which I suppose it will be necessary for you to make I desire you would Remember the Ladies, and be more generous and favourable to them than your ancestors. Do not put such umlimited power into the hands of the Husbands. Remember all Men would be tyrants if they could. If perticuliar care and attention is not paid to the Laidies we are determined to foment a Rebelion, and will not hold ourselves bound by any Laws in which we have no voice, or Representation.

That your Sex are Naturally Tyrannical is a Truth so thoroughly established as to admit of no dispute, but such of you as wish to be happy willingly give up the harsh title of Master for the more tender and endearing one of Friend. Why then, not put it out of the power of the vicious and the Lawless to use us with cruelty and indignity with impunity. Men of Sense in all Ages abhor those customs which treat us only as the vassals of your Sex. Regard us then as Beings placed by providence under your protection and in immitation of the Supreem Being make use of that power only for our happiness.

John Adams to Abigail Adams, Philadelphia, 14 April 1776

As to Declarations of Independency, be patient. Read our Privateering Laws, and our Commercial Laws. What signifies a Word.

As to your extraordinary Code of Laws, I cannot but laugh. We have been told that our Struggle has loosened the bands of Government every where. That Children and Apprentices were disobedient-that schools and Colledges were grown turbulent-that Indians slighted their Guardians and Negroes grew insolent to their Masters. But your Letter was the first Intimation that another Tribe more numerous and powerful than all the rest were grown discontented.-This is rather too coarse a Compliment but you are so saucy, I wont blot it out.

Depend upon it, We know better than to repeal our Masculine systems. Altho they are in full Force, you know they are little more than Theory. We dare not exert our Power in its full Latitude. We are obliged to go fair, and softly, and in Practice you know We are the subjects. We have only the Name of Masters, and rather than give up this, which would compleatly subject Us to the Despotism of the Peticoat, I hope General Washington, and all our brave Heroes would fight. I am sure every good Politician would plot, as long as he would against Despotism, Empire, Monarchy, Aristocracy, Oligarchy, or Ochlocracy.-A fine Story indeed. I begin to think the Ministry as deep as they are wicked. After stirring up Tories, Landjobbers, Trimmers, Bigots, Canadians, Indians, Negrows, Hanoverians, Hessians, Russians, Irish Roman Catholicks, Scotch Renegadoes, at last they have stimulated the [illegible in original] to demand new Priviledges and threaten to rebell.

John Adams to John Sullivan, Philadelphia, 26 May 1776

It is certain in Theory, that the only moral Foundation of Government is the Consent of the People. But to what an Extent Shall We carry this Principle? Shall We Say, that every Individual of the Community, old and young, male and female, as well as rich and poor, must consent, expressly to every Act of Legislation? No, you will Say. This is impossible. How then does the Right arise in the Majority to govern the Minority, against their Will? Whence arises the Right of the Men to govern Women, without their Consent? Whence the Right of the old to bind the Young, without theirs.

But let us first Suppose, that the whole Community of every Age, Rank, Sex, and Condition, has a Right to vote. This Community, is assembled-a Motion is made and carried by a Majority of one Voice. The Minority will not agree to this. Whence arises the Right of the Majority to govern, and the Obligation of the Minority to obey? from Necessity, you will Say, because there can be no other Rule, But why exclude Women? You will Say, because their Delicacy renders them unfit for Practice and Experience, in the great Business of Life, and the hardy Enterprizes of War, as well as the arduous Cares of State. Besides, their attention is So much engaged with the necessary Nurture of their Children, that Nature has made them fittest for domestic Cares. And Children have not Judgment or Will of their own. True. But will not these Reasons apply to others? Is it not equally true, that Men in general in every Society, who are wholly destitute of Property, and also too little acquainted with public Affairs to form a Right Judgment, and too dependent upon other Men to have a Will of their own? If this is a Fact, if you give to every Man, who has no Property, a Vote, will you not make a fine encouraging Provision for Corruption by your fundamental Law? Such is the Frailty of the human Heart, that very few Men, who have no Property, have any Judgment of their own. They talk and vote as they are directed by Some Man of Property, who has attached their Minds to his Interest.

Upon my Word, sir, I have long thought an Army, a Piece of Clock Work and to be governed only by Principles and Maxims, as fixed as any in Mechanicks, and by all that I have read in the History of Mankind, and in Authors, who have Speculated upon Society and Government, I am much inclined to think, a Government must manage a Society in the Same manner; and that this is Machinery too.

Harrington has Shewn that Power always follows property. This I believe to be as infallible a Maxim, in Politics, as, that Action and Reaction are equal, as in Mechanicks. Nay I believe We may advance one Step farther and affirm that the Ballance of Power in a Society, accompanies the Ballance of Property in Land. The only possible Way then of preserving the Ballance of Power on the side of equal Liberty and public Virtue, is to make the Acquisition of Land easy to every Member of Society: to make a Division of the Land into Small Quantities, So that the Multitude may be possessed of landed Estates. If the Multitude is possessed of the Ballance of real Estate, the Multitude will have the Ballance of Power, and in that Case the Multitude will take Care of the Liberty, Virtue, and Interest of the Multitude in all Acts of Government.

I believe these Principles have been felt, if not understood in the Massachusetts Bay, from the Beginning: And therefore I Should think that Wisdom and Policy would dictate in these Times, to be very cautious of making Alterations. Our people have never been very rigid in Scrutinizing into the Qualifications of Voters, and I presume they will not now begin to be so. But I would not advise them to make any alteration in the Laws, at present, respecting the Qualifications of Voters.

Your Idea, that those Laws, which affect the Lives and personal Liberty of all, or which inflict corporal Punishment, affect those, who are not qualified to vote, as well as those who are, is just. But, So they do Women, as well as Men, Children as well as Adults. What Reason Should there be, for excluding a Man of Twenty years, Eleven Months and twenty-seven days old, from a Vote when you admit one, who is twenty one? The Reason is, you must fix Some Period in Life, when the Understanding and Will of Men in general is fit to be trusted by the Public. Will not the Same Reason justify the State in fixing upon Some certain Quantity of Property, as a Qualification.

The Same Reasoning, which will induce you to admit all Men, who have no Property, to vote, with those who have, for those Laws, which affect the Person will prove that you ought to admit Women and Children: for generally Speaking, Women and Children, have as good Judgment, and as independent Minds as those Men who are wholly destitute of Property: these last being to all Intents and Purposes as much dependent upon others, who will please to feed, cloath, and employ them, as Women are upon their Husbands, or Children on their Parents.

As to your Idea, or proportioning the Votes of Men in Money Matters, to the Property they hold, it is utterly impracticable. There is no possible Way of Ascertaining, at any one Time, how much every Man in a Community, is worth; and if there was, So fluctuating is Trade and Property, that this State of it, would change in half an Hour. The Property of the whole Community, is Shifting every Hour, and no Record can be kept of the Changes.

Society can be governed only by general Rules. Government cannot accommodate itself to every particular Case, as it happens, nor to the Circumstances of particular Persons. It must establish general, comprehensive Regulations for Cases and Persons. The only Question is, which general Rule, will accommodate most Cases and most Persons.

Depend upon it, sir, it is dangerous to open So fruitfull a Source of Controversy and Altercation, as would be opened by attempting to alter the Qualifications of Voters. There will be no End of it. New Claims will arise. Women will demand a Vote. Lads from 12 to 21 will think their Rights not enough attended to, and every Man, who has not a Farthing, will demand an equal Voice with any other in all Acts of State. It tends to confound and destroy all Distinctions, and prostrate all Ranks, to one common Levell. I am &c.

1. *Examine and summarize the reasons given by John Adams for excluding women and men without property from voting?*
2. *Identify and explain John Adams' reasoning and plan for ensuring that the multitude of people possess the balance of power.*
3. *What reasoning does John Adams use to argue against allowing all men, regardless of personal property, to vote? Overall what are his opinions regarding any change in voter qualifications?*

5-10 The Rise of Partisan Warfare in the South (1778)

As British strategy shifted after 1778 toward winning the hearts and minds of the South (as well as its ports), the nature of the war also changed as southern loyalists and patriots fought each other in skirmishes and battles—many of which were never recorded—turning the revolution in the South into a bloody civil war. Depredations, both real and imagined, committed by both sides gave rise to calls for vengeance. The following documents recount two battles, Waxhaws (May 29, 1780) and King's Mountain (October 7, 1780), from the viewpoint of the defeated. Neither account is without bias and embellishment.

> **Source:** William Dobein James, *A Sketch of the Life of Brigadier General Francis Marion* (1821). The letter is found in the appendix.
> ftp://ftp.ibiblio.org/pub/docs/books/gutenberg/etext97/jjmar11.txt
> http://www.patriotresource.com/documents/brownfield.html
> *The Royal Gazette*, (New York), February 24, 1781.
> http://www.royalprovincial.com/history/battles/kingslet.htm

Dear Sir,

In obedience to your request, I send you a detailed account of the defeat and massacre of Col. Buford's regiment, near the borders of North Carolina, on the road leading from Camden to Salisbury. This regiment consisting of three hundred and fifty men, well appointed and equipped, had marched from Virginia for the relief of Charleston, and had advanced to Santee, where they were met by intelligence of the surrender; a retreat then became unavoidable. Between this place and Camden they fell in with Gen. Caswell, at the head of about seven hundred North Carolina militia, whose object had been the same, and whose retreat became equally imperious. At Camden these two corps unfortunately separated; Caswell filed off to Pedee, and Buford pursued the road to Salisbury. This measure was accounted for by the want of correct intelligence of Tarleton's prompt and rapid movements, who was in full pursuit with three hundred cavalry, and each a soldier of infantry behind him. Neglecting Caswell and his militia, the pursuit was continued after Buford to the Waxhaw. Finding he was approximating this corps, he dispatched a flag, saying he was at Barclay's with seven hundred men, and summoned them to surrender on the terms granted to the garrison in Charleston. Buford immediately laid the summons before a council of his officers with three distinct propositions from himself: Shall we comply with Tarleton's summons? Shall we abandon the baggage, and, by a rapid movement, save ourselves? or, shall we fortify ourselves by the waggons, and wait his approach?

The first and second were decidedly rejected by the unanimous voice of the council, declaring it to be incompatible with their honour as soldiers, or the duty they owed their country, either to surrender or abandon the baggage on the bare statement of Tarleton. They had no certainty of the truth of his assertion, and that it might be only a *ruse de guerre* to alarm their fears and obtain a bloodless victory. The third was also negatived on the ground, that although they might by this means defend themselves against Tarleton, but as no succour was near, and as Tarleton could, in a short time, obtain reinforcements from Cornwallis, against which no effectual resistance could be made, this measure would be unavailable.

The discussion soon resulted in a resolution to continue the march, maintaining the best possible order for the reception of the enemy. In a short time Tarleton's bugle was heard, and a furious attack was made on the rear guard, commanded by Lieut. Pearson. Not a man escaped. Poor Pearson was inhumanely mangled on the face as he lay on his back. His nose and lip were bisected obliquely; several of his teeth were broken out in the upper jaw, and the under completely divided on each side. These wounds were inflicted after he had fallen, with several others on his head, shoulders, and arms. As a just tribute to the honour and Job-like patience of poor Pearson, it ought to be mentioned, that he lay for five weeks without uttering a single groan. His only nourishment was milk, drawn from a bottle through a quill. During that period he was totally deprived of speech, nor could he articulate distinctly after his wounds were healed.

This attack gave Buford the first confirmation of Tarleton's declaration by his flag. Unfortunately he was then compelled to prepare for action, on ground which presented no impediment to the full action of cavalry. Tarleton having arranged his infantry in the centre, and his cavalry on the wings, advanced to the charge with the horrid yells of infuriated demons. They were received with firmness, and completely checked, until the cavalry were gaining the rear. Buford now perceiving that further resistance was hopeless, ordered a flag to be hoisted and the arms to be grounded, expecting the usual treatment sanctioned by civilized warfare. This, however, made no part of Tarleton's creed. His ostensible pretext, for the relentless barbarity that ensued, was, that his horse was killed under him just as the flag was raised. He affected to believe that this was done afterwards, and imputed it to treachery on the part of Buford; but, in reality, a safe opportunity was presented to gratify that thirst for blood which marked his character in every conjuncture that promised probable impunity to himself. Ensign Cruit, who advanced with the flag, was instantly cut down. Viewing this as an earnest of what they were to expect, a resumption of their arms was attempted, to sell their lives as dearly as possible; but before this was fully effected, Tarleton with his cruel myrmidons was in the midst of them, when commenced a scene of indiscriminate carnage never surpassed by the ruthless atrocities of the most barbarous savages.

The demand for quarters, seldom refused to a vanquished foe, was at once found to be in vain; not a man was spared and it was the concurrent testimony of all the survivors, that for fifteen minutes after every man was prostrate. They went over the ground plunging their bayonets into every one that exhibited any signs of life, and in some instances, where several had fallen one over the other, these monsters were seen to throw off on the point of the bayonet the uppermost, to come at those beneath. Capt. Carter, who commanded the artillery and who led the van, continued his march without bringing his guns into action; this conduct excited suspicions unfavourable to the character of Carter, and these were strengthened by his being paroled on the ground, and his whole company without insult or injury being made prisoners of war. Whether he was called to account for his conduct, I have never learnt. These excepted, the only survivors of this tragic scene were Capts. Stokes, Lawson and Hoard, Lieuts. Pearson and Jamison, and Ensign Cruit.

To consign to oblivion the memory of these gallant suffering few would be culpable injustice. When men have devoted their lives to the service of their country, and whose fate has been so singularly disastrous; there is an honest anxiety concerning them, springing from the best and warmest feelings of our nature, which certainly should be gratified. This is peculiarly the truth in regard to Capt. John Stokes, although in his military character perhaps not otherwise distinguished from his brother officers, than by the number of his wounds and the preeminence of sufferings. He received twenty-three wounds, and as he never for a moment lost his recollection, he often repeated to me the manner and order in which they were inflicted.

Early in the sanguinary conflict he was attacked by a dragoon, who aimed many deadly blows at his head, all of which by the dexterous use of the small sword he easily parried; when another on the right, by one stroke, cut off his right hand through the metacarpal bones. He was then assailed by both, and instinctively attempted to defend his head with his left arm until the forefinger was cut off, and the arm hacked in eight or ten places from the wrist to the shoulder. His head was then laid open almost the whole length of the crown to the eye brows. After he fell he received several cuts on the face and shoulders. A soldier passing on in the work of death, asked if he expected quarters? Stokes answered I have not, nor do I mean to ask quarters, finish me as soon as possible; he then transfixed him twice with his bayonet. Another asked the same question and received the same answer, and he also thrust his bayonet twice through his body. Stokes had his eye fixed on a wounded British officer, sitting at some distance, when a sergeant came up, who addressed him with apparent humanity, and offered him protection from further injury at the risk of his life. All I ask, said Stokes, is to be laid by that officer that I may die in his presence. While performing this generous office the humane sergeant was twice obliged to lay him down, and stand over him to defend him against the fury of his comrades. Doct. Stapleton, Tarleton's surgeon, whose name ought to be held up to eternal obloquy, was then dressing the wounds of the officer. Stokes, who lay bleeding at every pore, asked him to do something for his wounds, which he scornfully and inhumanely refused, until peremptorily ordered by the more humane officer, and even then only filled the wounds with rough tow, the particles of which could not be separated from the brain for several days.

Capt. Stokes was a native of Pittsylvania county, Virginia. He was early intended for the bar, and having gone through the usual course of classical and other preparatory studies, he commenced the practice with the most flattering indications of future eminence. But the calm pursuits of peace not comporting with the ardour of his mind, he relinquished the fair prospect of professional emolument, and accepted a captaincy in Buford's regiment.

At this catastrophe, he was about twenty-seven years of age. His height was about the common standard; his figure and appearance, even in his mangled situation, inspired respect and veneration; and the fire of genius that sparkled in his dark piercing eye, gave indications of a mind fitted not only for the field, but for all the departments of civil life.

Shortly after the adoption of the constitution of the United States, he was promoted to the bench in the Federal Court—married Miss Pearson—and settled on the Yadkin river, where the county is called Stokes, after his name.

(Signed,)
R. Brownfield.

Charlestown, January 30th, 1781.

I think the last letter I wrote you was from Fort Moultrie, which I left a few days after.

We marched to a place called Ninety Six, which is about two hundred miles from Charleston; we lay there about a fortnight in good quarters, after which we proceeded to the frontiers of South Carolina, and frequently passed the line into North Carolina, and can say with propriety, that there is not a regiment or detachment of his Majesty's service, that ever went through the fatigues, or suffered so much, as our detachment.

That you may have some faint idea of our suffering, I shall mention a few particulars.

In the first place we were separated from all the army, acting with the militia; we never lay two nights in one place, frequently making forced marches of twenty and thirty miles in one night; skirmishing very often; the greatest part of our time without rum or wheat flour-rum is a very essential article, for in marching ten miles we would often be obliged to ford two or three rivers, which wet the men up to their waists.

In this disagreeable situation, we remained till the seventh of October, when we were attacked by two thousand five hundred Rebels, under the command of Gen. Williams. Col. Ferguson had under his command eight hundred militia, and our detachment, which at that time was reduced to an hundred men. The action commenced about two o'clock in the afternoon, and was very severe for upwards of an hour, during which the Rebels were charged and drove back several times, with considerable slaughter.

When our detachment charged, for the first time, it fell to my lot to put a Rebel Captain to death, which I did most effectually, with one blow of my sword; the fellow was at least six feet high, but I had rather the advantage, as I was mounted on an elegant horse, and he on foot. But their numbers enabled them to surround us and the North Carolina regiment, which consisted of about three hundred men.

Seeing this, and numbers being out of ammunition which naturally threw the rest of the militia into confusion, our gallant little detachment, which consisted of only seventy men, exclusive of twenty who acted as dragoons, and ten who drove wagons, etc., when we marched to the field of action, were all killed and wounded but twenty, and those brave fellows were soon crowded into an heap by the militia. Capt. DePeyster, on whom the command devolved, seeing it impossible to form six men together, thought it necessary to surrender, to save the lives of the brave men who were left.

We lost in this action, Maj. Ferguson, of the Seventy-first regiment, a man strongly attached to his King and country, well informed in the art of war, brave, humane, and an agreeable companion-in short, he was universally esteemed in the army, and I have every reason to regret his unhappy fate.

We lost eighteen men killed on the spot—Capt. Ryerson and thirty-two Sergeants and privates wounded, of Maj. Ferguson's detachment. Lieutenant M'Ginnis of Allen's regiment, Skinner's brigade, killed; taken prisoners, two Captains, four Lieutenants, three Ensigns, one Surgeon, and fifty-four Sergeants and privates, including the wounded, wagoners, etc. The militia killed, one hundred, including officers; wounded, ninety; taken prisoners about six hundred; our baggage all taken, of course. The Rebels lost Brig.-Gen. Williams, and one hundred and thirty-five, including officers, killed; wounded nearly equal to ours.

The morning after the action we were marched sixteen miles, previous to which orders were given by the Rebel Col. Campbell (whom the command devolved on) that should they be attacked on their march, they were to fire on, and destroy their prisoners. The party was kept marching two days without any kind of provisions. The officers' baggage, on the third day's march, was all divided among the Rebel officers. Shortly after we were marched to Bickerstaff's settlement, where we arrived on the thirteenth.

On the fourteenth, a court martial, composed of twelve field officers, was held for the trial of the militia prisoners; when, after a short hearing, they condemned thirty of the most principal and respectable characters, whom they considered to be most inimical to them, to be executed; and, at six o'clock in the evening of the same day, executed Col. Mills, Capt. Chitwood, Capt. Wilson, and six privates; obliging every one of their officers to attend at the death of those brave, but unfortunate Loyalists, who all, with their last breath and blood, held the Rebels and their cause as infamous and base, and as they were turning off, extolled their King and the British Government.

On the morning of the fifteenth, Col. Campbell had intelligence that Col. Tarleton was approaching him, when he gave orders to his men, that should Col. Tarleton come up with them, they were immediately to fire on Capt. DePeyster and his officers, who were in the front, and then a second volley on the men.

During this day's march the men were obliged to give thirty-five Continental dollars for a single ear of Indian corn, and forty for a drink of water, they not being allowed to drink when fording a river; in short, the whole of the Rebels' conduct from the surrender of the party into their hands is incredible to relate. Several of the militia that were worn out with fatigue, and not being able to keep up, were cut down, and trodden to death in the mire.

After the party arrived at Moravian Town, in North Carolina, we officers were ordered in different houses. Dr. Johnson (who lived with me) and myself were turned out of our bed at an unseasonable hour of the night, and threatened with immediate death if we did not make room for some of Campbell's officers; Dr. Johnson was, after this, knocked down, and treated in the basest manner, for endeavoring to dress a man whom they had cut on the march.

The Rebel officers would often go in amongst the prisoners, draw their swords, cut down and wound those whom their wicked and savage minds prompted. This is a specimen of Rebel lenity—you may report it without the least equivocation, for upon the word and honor of a gentleman, this description is not equal to their barbarity. This kind of treatment made our time pass away very disagreeably.

After we were in Moravian Town about a fortnight, we were told we could not get paroles to return within the British lines; neither were we to have any till we were moved over the mountains in the back parts of Virginia, where we were to live on hoe cake and milk; in consequence of this, Capt. Taylor, Lieut. Stevenson and myself, chose rather to trust the hand of fate, and agreeable to our inclinations, set out from Moravian Town the fifth of November, and arrived at the British lines the twentieth.

From this town to Ninety Six, which was the first post we arrived at, is three hundred miles; and from Ninety Six to Charlestown, two hundred, so that my route was five hundred miles. The fatigues of this jaunt I shall omit till I see you, although I suffered exceedingly; but thank God am now in Charlestown in good quarters.

1. While Robert Brownfield's account of the battle of the Waxhaws was written after the fact, it nevertheless is an accurate representation of the stories that were circulated in South Carolina following the engagement. What effect do you think stories such as this would have had on the nonaligned inhabitants of the South whose property lay in the path of General Cornwallis's advancing army? What effect would it have had on Loyalist enlistments into the British army?
2. What might be an explanation (not a justification) for the way in which the British prisoners were treated following the Battle of King's Mountain?

PART SIX
FORGING A CONSTITUTION

6-1 Constitution of Pennsylvania (1776)

In the wake of the movement for independence, the colonies now saw themselves as individual sovereign entities. They wrote their own constitutions many of which were quite different in specifics. This example from Pennsylvania reveals several clauses that became a part of the United States Constitution. It also, however, went farther than the eventual national Constitution.

A Declaration of the Rights of the Inhabitants of the Commonwealth, or State of Pennsylvania

I. That all men are born equally free and independent, and have certain natural inherent and inalienable rights, amongst which are the enjoying and defending life and liberty, acquiring, possessing and protecting property, and pursuing and obtaining happiness and safety.

II. That all men have a natural and unalienable right to worship Almighty God according to the dictates of their own consciences and understanding: And that no man ought or of right can be compelled to attend any religious worship, or erect or support any place of worship, or maintain any ministry, contrary to, or against, his own free will and consent: Nor can any man, who acknowledges the being of a God, be justly deprived or abridged of any civil right as a citizen, on account of his religious sentiments or peculiar mode of religious worship: And that no authority can or ought to be vested in, or assumed by any power whatever, that shall in any case interfere with, or in any manner controul, the right of conscience in the free exercise of religious worship.

III. That the people of this State have the sole, exclusive and inherent right of governing and regulating the internal police of the same.

IV. That all power being originally inherent in, and consequently derived from, the people; therefore all officers of government, whether legislative or executive, are their trustees and servants, and at all times accountable to them.

V. That government is, or ought to be, instituted for the common benefit, protection and security of the people, nation or community; and not for the particular emolument or advantage of any single man, family or set of men, who are a part only of that community; And that the community hath an indubitable, unalienable and indefeasible right to reform, alter, or abolish government in such a manner as shall be by that community judged most conducive to the public weal.

VI. That those who are employed in the legislative and executive business of the State, may be restrained from oppression, the people have a right, at such periods as they may think proper, to reduce their public officers to a private station, and supply the vacancies by certain and regular elections.

VII. That all elections ought to be free; and that all free men having a sufficient evident common interest with, and attachment to the community, have a right to elect officers, or to be elected into office.

VIII. That every member of society hath a right to be protected in the enjoyment of life, liberty and property, and therefore is bound to contribute his proportion towards the expence of that protection, and yield his personal service when necessary, or an equivalent thereto: But no part of a man's property can be justly taken from him, or applied to public uses, without his own consent, or that of his legal representatives: Nor can any man who is conscientiously scrupulous of bearing arms, be justly compelled thereto, if he will pay such equivalent, nor are the people bound by any laws, but such as they have in like manner assented to, for their common good.

IX. That in all prosecutions for criminal offences, a man hath a right to be heard by himself and his council, to demand the causes and nature of his accusation, to be confronted with the witnesses, to call for evidence in his favour, and a speedy public trial, by an impartial jury of the country, without the unanimous consent of which jury he cannot be found guilty; nor can he be compelled to give evidence against himself; nor can any man be justly deprived of his liberty except by the laws of the land, or the judgment of his peers.

X. That the people have a right to hold themselves, their houses, papers, and possessions free from search and seizure, and therefore warrants without oaths or affirmations first made, affording a sufficient foundation for them, and whereby any officer or messenger may be commanded or required to search suspected places, or to seize any person or persons, his or their property, not particularly described, are contrary to that right, and ought not to be granted.

XI. That in controversies respecting property, and in suits between man and man, the parties have a right to trial by jury, which ought to be held sacred.

XII. That the people have a right to freedom of speech, and of writing, and publishing their sentiments; therefore the freedom of the press ought not to be restrained.

XIII. That the people have a right to bear arms for the defence of themselves and the state; and as standing armies in the time of peace are dangerous to liberty, they ought not to be kept up; And that the military should be kept under strict subordination to, and governed by, the civil power.

XIV. That a frequent recurrence to fundamental principles, and a firm adherence to justice, moderation, temperance, industry, and frugality are absolutely necessary to preserve the blessings of liberty, and keep a government free: The people ought therefore to pay particular attention to these points in the choice of officers and representatives, and have a right to exact a due and constant regard to them, from their legislatures and magistrates, in the making and executing such laws as are necessary for the good government of the state.

XV. That all men have a natural inherent right to emigrate from one state to another that will receive them, or to form a new state in vacant countries, or in such countries as they can purchase, whenever they think that thereby they may promote their own happiness.

XVI. That the people have a right to assemble together, to consult for their common good, to instruct their representatives, and to apply to the legislature for redress of grievances, by address, petition, or remonstrance.

1. *Identify and summarize the natural rights of all men as described by the first three articles of this constitution.*
2. *What should be the relationship between the government and the people according to this document.*
3. *Identify and describe some of the basic personal freedoms ascribed to all men by this document.*

6-2   A Declaration of the Rights of the Inhabitants of the Commonwealth of Massachusetts (1780)

Written by the great American revolutionary and statesman, John Adams, the Massachussetts Constitution is the oldest continuous and functional constitution in the world. Adams considered the document one of his greatest accomplishments and many of its components were later incorporated into the Bill of Rights of the United States Constitution. These include elements of religious freedom, and, most clearly, provisions against illegal search and seizure. Based in part on Virginia declarations authored by George Mason, the Massachusetts Declaration is a foundational document.

Source: Francis N. Thorpe, ed., *The Federal and State Constitutions,* 7 vols. (Washington, D.C., Government Printing Office, 1909), vol. III, pp. 1888◆1895.

Constitution or Form of Government for the Commonwealth of Massachusetts 1780 Preamble

The end of the institution, maintenance, and administration of government, is to secure the existence of the body politic, to protect it, and to furnish the individuals who compose it with the power of enjoying in safety and tranquillity their natural rights, and the blessings of life: and whenever these great objects are not obtained, the people have a right to alter the government, and to take measures necessary for their safety, prosperity, and happiness.

The body of politic is formed by a voluntary association of individuals: it is a social compact, by which the whole people covenants with each citizen, and each citizen with the whole people, that all shall be governed by certain laws for the common good. It is the duty of the people, therefore, in framing a constitution of government, to provide for an equitable mode of making laws, as well as for an impartial interpretation and a faithful execution of them; that every man may, at all times, find his security in them.

We, therefore, the people of Massachusetts, acknowledging, with grateful hearts, the goodness of the great Legislator of the universe, in affording us, in the course of His providence, an opportunity, deliberately and peaceably, without fraud, violence, or surprise, of entering into an original, explicit, and solemn compact with each other; and of forming a new constitution of civil government, for ourselves and posterity; and devoutly imploring His direction in so interesting a design, do agree upon, ordain, and establish the following *Declaration of Rights, and Frame of Government,* as the CONSTITUTION OF THE COMMONWEALTH OF MASSACHUSETTS.

Part the First
A Declaration of the Rights of the Inhabitants of the Commonwealth of Massachusets

ARTICLE I. All men are born free and equal, and have certain natural, essential, and unalienable rights; among which may be reckoned the right of enjoying and defending their lives and liberties; that of acquiring, possessing, and protecting property; in fine, that of seeking and obtaining their safety and happiness.

ARTICLE II. It is the right as well as the duty of all men in society, publicly, and at stated seasons, to worship the SUPREME BEING, the great Creator and Preserver of the universe. And no subject shall be hurt, molested, or restrained, in his person, liberty, or estate, for worshipping GOD in the manner and season most agreeable to the dictates of his own conscience; or for his religious profession of sentiments; provided he doth not disturb the public peace, or obstruct others in their religious worship.

ARTICLE III. [As the happiness of a people, and the good order and preservation of civil government, essentially depend upon piety, religion, and morality; and as these cannot be generally diffused through a community but by the institution of the public worship of GOD, and of public instructions in piety, religion, and morality: Therefore, to promote their happiness, and to secure the good order and preservation of their government, the people of this commonwealth have a right to invest their legislature with power to authorize and require, and the legislature shall, from time to time, authorize and require the several towns, parishes, precincts, and other bodies politic, or religious societies, to make suitable provision, at their own expense, for the institution of the public worship of GOD, and for the support and maintenance of public Protestant teachers of piety, religion, and morality, in all cases where such provision shall not be made voluntarily.

And the people of this commonwealth have also a right to, and do, invest their legislature with a authority to enjoin upon all the subjects an attendance upon the instructions of the public teachers aforesaid, at stated times and seasons, if there be any on whose instructions they can conscientiously and conveniently attend.

Provided, notwithstanding, that the several towns, parishes, precincts, and other bodies politic, or religious societies, shall, at all times, have the exclusive right of electing their public teachers, and of contracting with them for their support and maintenance.

And all moneys paid by the subject to the support of public worship, and of the public teachers aforesaid, shall, if he require it, be uniformly applied to the support of the public teacher or teachers of his own religious sect or denomination, provided there be any on whose instructions he attends; otherwise it may be paid towards the support of the teacher or teachers of the parish or precinct in which the said moneys are raised.

And every denomination of Christians, demeaning themselves peaceably, and as good subjects of the commonwealth, shall be equally under the protection of the law: and no subordination of any one sect or denomination to another shall ever be established by law.]

ARTICLE IV. The people of this commonwealth have the sole and exclusive right of governing themselves, as a free, sovereign, and independent state; and do, and forever hereafter shall, exercise and enjoy every power, jurisdiction, and right, which is not, or may not hereafter be, by them expressly delegated to the United States of America, in Congress assembled.

ARTICLE V. All power residing originally in the people, and being derived from them, the several magistrates and officers of government, vested with authority, whether legislative, executive, or judicial, are their substitutes and agents, and are at all times accountable to them.

ARTICLE VI. No man, nor corporation, or association of men, have any other title to obtain advantages, or particular and exclusive privileges, distinct from those of the community, than what arises from the consideration of services rendered to the public; and this title being in nature neither hereditary, nor transmissible to children, or descendants, or relations by blood, the idea of a man born a magistrate, lawgiver, or judge, is absurd and unnatural.

ARTICLE VII. Government is instituted for the common good; for the protection, safety, prosperity, and happiness of the people; and not for the profit, honor, or private interest of any one man, family, or class of men: Therefore the people alone have an incontestible unalienable, and indefeasible right to institute government; and to reform, alter, or totally change the same, when their protection, safety, prosperity, and happiness require it.

ARTICLE VIII. In order to prevent those who are vested with authority from becoming oppressors, the people have a right at such periods and in such manner as they shall establish by their frame of government, to cause their public officers to return to private life; and to fill up vacant places by certain and regular elections and appointments.

ARTICLE IX. All elections ought to be free; and all the inhabitants of this commonwealth having such qualifications as they shall establish by their frame of government, have an equal right to elect officers, and to be elected, for public employments.

ARTICLE X. Each individual of the society has a right to be protected by it in the enjoyment of his life, liberty, and property, according to standing laws. He is obliged, consequently, to contribute his share to the expense of this protection; to give his personal service, or an equivalent, when necessary: but no part of the property of any individual can, with justice, be taken from him, or applied to public uses, without his own consent, or that of the representative body of the people. In fine, the people of this commonwealth are not controllable by any other laws than those to which their constitutional representative body have given their consent. And whenever the public exigencies require that the property of any individual should be appropriated to public uses, he shall receive a reasonable compensation therefor.

ARTICLE XI. Every subject of the commonwealth ought to find a certain remedy, by having recourse to the laws, for all injuries or wrongs which he may receive in his person property, or character. He ought to obtain right and justice freely, and without being obliged to purchase it; completely, and without any denial; promptly, and without delay; conformably to the laws.

ARTICLE XII. No subject shall be held to answer for any crimes or offence, until the same is fully and plainly, substantially, and formally, described to him; or be compelled to accuse, or furnish evidence against himself. And every subject shall have a right to produce all proofs that may be favorable to him; to meet the witnesses against him face to face, and to be fully heard in his defence by himself, or his counsel, at his election. And no subject shall be arrested, imprisoned, despoiled, or deprived of his property, immunities, or privileges, put out of the protection of the law, exiled, or deprived of his life, liberty, or estate, but by the judgement of his peers, or the law of the land.

And the legislature shall not make any law that shall subject any person to capital or infamous punishment, excepting for the government of the army and navy, without trial by jury.

ARTICLE XIII. In criminal prosecutions, the verification of facts, in the vicinity where they happen, is one of the greatest securities of the life, liberty, and property of the citizen.

ARTICLE XIV. Every subject has a right to be secure from all unreasonable searches, and seizures, of his person, his houses, his papers, and all his possessions. All warrants, therefore, any contrary to this right, if the cause or foundation of them be not previously supported by oath or affirmation, and if the order in the warrant to a civil officer, to make search in suspected places, or to arrest one or more suspected persons, or to seize their property, be not accompanied with a special designation of he persons or objects of search, arrest, or seizure; and no warrant ought to be issued but in cases, and with the formalities prescribed by the laws.

ARTICLE XV. In all controversies concerning property, and in all suits between two or more persons, except in cases in which it has heretofore been otherways used and practised, the parties have a right to a trial by jury; and this method of procedure shall be held sacred, unless, in causes arising on the high seas, and such as relate to mariners' wages, the legislature shall hereafter find it necessary to alter it.

ARTICLE XVI. The liberty of the press is essential to the security of freedom in a state it ought not, therefore, to be restricted in this commonwealth.

XVII. The people have a right to keep and to bear arms for the common defence. And as, in time of peace, armies are dangerous to liberty, they ought not to be maintained without the consent of the legislature; and the military power shall always be held in an exact subordination to the civil authority, and be governed by it.

ARTICLE XVIII. A frequent recurrence to the fundamental principles of he constitution, and a constant adherence to those of piety, justice, moderation, temperance, industry, and frugality, are absolutely necessary to preserve the advantages of liberty, and to maintain a free government. The people ought, consequently, to have a particular attention to all those principles, in the choice of their officers and representatives; and they have a right to require of their lawgivers and magistrates an exact and constant observance of them, in the formation and execution of the laws necessary for the good administration of he commonwealth.

ARTICLE XIX. The people have a right in an orderly and peaceable manner, to assemble to consult upon the common good; give instructions to their representatives, and to request of the legislative body, by the way of addresses, petitions, or remonstrances, redress of the wrongs done them, and of the grievances they suffer.

ARTICLE XX. The power of suspending the laws, or the execution of the laws, ought never to be exercised but by the legislature, or by authority derived from it, to be exercised in such particular cases only as the legislature shall expressly provide for.

ARTICLE XXI. The freedom of deliberation, speech, and debate, in either house of the legislature, is so essential to the rights of the people, that it cannot be the foundation of any accusation or prosecution, action or complaint, in any other court or place whatsoever.

ARTICLE XXII. The legislature ought frequently to assemble for the redress of grievances, for correcting, strengthening, and confirming the laws, and for making new laws, as the common good may require.

ARTICLE XXIII. No subsidy, charge, tax, impost, or duties ought to be established, fixed, laid, or levied, under any pretext whatsoever, without the consent of the people or their representatives in the legislature.

ARTICLE XXIV. Laws made to punish for actions done before the existence of such laws, and which have not been declared crimes by preceding laws, are unjust, oppressive, and inconsistent with the fundamental principles of a free government.

ARTICLE XXV. No subject ought, in any case, or in any time, to be declared guilty of treason or felony by the legislature. ARTICLE XXVI. No magistrate or court of law shall demand excessive bail or sureties, impose excessive fines, or inflict cruel or unusual punishments.

ARTICLE XXVII. In time of peace, no soldier ought to be quartered in any house without the consent of the owner; and in time of war, such quarters ought not to be made but by the civil magistrate, in a manner ordained by the legislature.

ARTICLE XXVIII. No person can in any case be subject to law-martial, or to any penalties or pains, by virtue of that law, except those employed in the army or navy, and except the militia in actual service, but by authority of the legislature.

ARTICLE XXIX. It is essential to the preservation of the rights of every individual, his life, liberty, property, and character, that there be an impartial interpretation of the laws, and administration of justice. It is the right of every citizen to be tried by judges as free, impartial, and independent as the lot of humanity will admit. It is, therefore, not only the best policy, but for the security of the rights of the people, and of every citizen, that the judges of the supreme judicial court should hold their offices as long as they behave themselves well; and that they should have honorable salaries ascertained and established by standing laws.

ARTICLE XXX. In the government of this commonwealth, the legislative department shall never exercise the executive and judicial powers, or either of them; the executive shall never exercise the legislative and judicial powers, or either of them; the judicial shall never exercise the legislative and executive powers, or either of them; to the end it may be a government of laws and not of men.

Part the Second
The Fame of Government

The people, inhabiting the territory formerly called the Province of Massachusetts Bay, do hereby solemnly and mutually agree with each other, to form themselves into a free, sovereign, and independent body politic, or state, by the name of THE COMMONWEALTH OF MASSACHUSETTS.

CHAPTER I
THE LEGISLATIVE POWERSECTION I. THE GENERAL COURT

ARTICLE I. The department of legislation shall be formed by two branches, a Senate and House of Representatives; each of which shall have a negative on the other.

The legislative body shall assemble every year [on the last Wednesday in May, and at such other times as they shall judge necessary; and shall dissolve and be dissolved on the day next preceding the said last Wednesday in May;] and shall be styled, THE GENERAL COURT OF MASSACHUSETTS.

ARTICLE II. No bill or resolve of the senate or house of representatives shall become a law, and have force as such, until it shall have been laid before the governor for his revisal; and if he, upon such revision, approve thereof, he shall signify his approbation by signing the same. But if he have any objection to the passing of such bill or resolve, he shall return the same, together with his objections thereto, in writing, to the senate or house of representatives, in whichsoever the same shall have originated; who shall enter the objections sent down by the governor, at large, on their records, and proceed to reconsider the said bill or resolve. But if after such reconsideration, two-thirds of the said senate or house of representatives, shall, notwithstanding the said objections, agree to pass the same, it shall, together with the objections, be sent to the other branch of the legislature, where it shall also be reconsidered, and if approved by two-thirds of the members present, shall have the force of law; but in all such cases, the votes of both houses shall be determined by yeas and nays; and the names of the persons voting for, or against, the said bill or resolve, shall be entered upon the public records of the commonwealth.

And in order to prevent unnecessary delays, if any bill or resolve shall not be returned by the governor within five days after it shall have been presented, the same shall have the force of law.

ARTICLE III. The general court shall forever have full power and authority to erect and constitute judicatories and courts of record, or other courts, to be held in the name of the commonwealth, for the hearing, trying, and determining of all manner of crimes, offences, pleas, processes, plaints, actions, matters, causes, and things whatsoever, arising or happening within the commonwealth, or between or concerning persons inhabiting, or residing, or brought within the same; whether the same be criminal or civil, or whether the said crimes be capital or not capital, and whether the said pleas be real, personal, or mixed; and for the awarding and making out of execution thereupon. To which courts and judicatories are hereby given and granted full power and authority, from time to time, to administer oaths or affirmations, for the better discovery of truth in any matter in controversy or depending before them.

ARTICLE IV. And further, full power and authority are hereby given and granted to the said general court, from time to time, to make, ordain, and establish, all manner of wholesome and reasonable orders, laws, statutes, and ordinances, directions and instructions, either with penalties or without; so as the same be not repugnant or contrary to this constitution, as they shall judge to be for the good and welfare of this commonwealth, and for the government and ordering thereof, and of the subjects of the same, and for the necessary support and defence of the government thereof; and to name and settle annually, or provide by fixed laws for the naming and settling, all civil officers within the said commonwealth, the election and constitution of whom are not hereafter in this form of government otherwise provided for; and to set forth the several duties, powers, and limits, of the several civil and military officers of this commonwealth, and the forms of such oaths or affirmations as shall be respectively administered unto them for the execution of their several offices and places, so as the same be not repugnant or contrary to this constitution; and to impose and levy proportional and reasonable assessments, rates, and taxes, upon all the inhabitants of, and persons resident, and estates lying, within the said commonwealth; and also to impose and levy reasonable duties and excises upon any produce, goods, wares, merchandise, and commodities, whatsoever, brought into, produced, manufactured, or being within the same; to be issued and disposed of by warrant, under the hand of the governor of this commonwealth for the time being, with the advice and consent of the council, for the public service, in the necessary defence and support of the government of the said commonwealth, and the protection and preservation of the subjects thereof, according to such acts as are or shall be in force within the same.

And while the public charges of government, or any part thereof, shall be assessed on polls and estates, in the manner that has hitherto been practised, in order that such assessments may be made with equality, there shall be a valuation of estates within the commonwealth, taken anew once in every ten years at least, and as much oftener as the general court shall order.

1. *Summarize the relevance of this document in regard to the practice of religion. What practices are to be protected and encouraged? What religious practices are unprotected by this document?*
2. *What provisions are made to ensure that government serves the people and to protect against corrupt government?*
3. *What legal protections and rights are afforded every citizen under this constitution?*
4. *What basic personal freedoms are granted by this document?*
5. *Summarize the basic organization of the government as stipulated by the second part of this document.*

6-3 George Washington, The Newburgh Address (1783)

While waiting for the formal negotiated peace settlement, several officers in the colonial army wrote a notice threatening to withhold their services for the duration and also to perhaps stay together after the war to gain their demands. Brought on by frustration with the Continental Congress' and its inability to pay the officers and settle on their pensions, this discontent threatened to become a military coup. Washington gave this address in an effort to quell the potential uprising. The address carried the day and the officers revolt never materialized.

To the Officers of the Army

Gentlemen-A fellow soldier, whose interest and affections bind him strongly to you, whose past sufferings have been as great, and whose future fortune may be as desperate as yours-would beg leave to address you.

Age has its claims, and rank is not without its pretensions to advise: but, though unsupported by both, he flatters himself, that the plain language of sincerity and experience will neither be unheard nor unregarded.

Like many of you, he loved private life, and left it with regret. He left it, determined to retire from the field, with the necessity that called him to it, and not till then-not till the enemies of his country, the slaves of power, and the hirelings of injustice, were compelled to abandon their schemes, and acknowledge America as terrible in arms as she had been humble in remonstrance. With this object in view, he has long shared in your toils and mingled in your dangers. He has felt the cold hand of poverty without a murmur, and has seen the insolence of wealth without a sigh. But, too much under the direction of his wishes, and sometimes weak enough to mistake desire for opinion, he has till lately-very lately-believed in the justice of his country. He hoped that, as the clouds of adversity scattered, and as the sunshine of peace and better fortune broke in upon us, the coldness and severity of government would relax, and that, more than justice, that gratitude would blaze forth upon those hands, which had upheld her, in the darkest stages of her passage, from impending servitude to acknowledged independence. But faith has its limits as well as temper, and there are points beyond which neither can be stretched, without sinking into cowardice or plunging into credulity.-This, my friends, I conceive to be your situation.-Hurried to the very verge of both, another step would ruin you forever.-To be tame and unprovoked when injuries press hard upon you, is more than weakness; but to look up for kinder usage, without one manly effort of your own, would fix your character, and shew the world how richly you deserve those chains you broke. To guard against this evil, let us take a review of the ground upon which we now stand, and from thence carry our thoughts forward for a moment, into the unexplored field of expedient.

After a pursuit of seven long years, the object for which we set out is at length brought within our reach. Yes, my friends, that suffering courage of yours was active once-it has conducted the United States of America through a doubtful and a bloody war. It has placed her in the chair of independency, and peace returns again to bless-whom? A country willing to redress your wrongs, cherish your worth and reward your services, a country courting your return to private life, with tears of gratitude and smiles of admiration, longing to divide with you that independency which your gallantry has given, and those riches which your wounds have preserved? Is this the case? Or is it rather a country that tramples upon your rights, disdains your cries and insults your distresses? Have you not, more than once, suggested your wishes, and made known your wants to Congress? Wants and wishes which gratitude and policy should have anticipated, rather than evaded. And have you not lately, in the meek language of entreating memorials, begged from their justice, what you would no longer expect from their favour? How have you been answered? Let the letter which you are called to consider to-morrow make reply.

If this, then, be your treatment, while the swords you wear are necessary for the defence of America, what have you to expect from peace, when your voice shall sink, and your strength dissipate by division? When those very swords, the instruments and companions of your glory, shall be taken from your sides, and no remaining mark of military distinction left but your wants, infirmities and scars? Can you then consent to be the only sufferers by this revolution, and retiring from he field, grow old in poverty, wretchedness and contempt? Can you consent to wade through the vile mire of dependency, and owe the miserable remnant of that life to charity, which has hitherto been spent in honor? If you can-GO-and carry with you the jest of tories and scorn of whigs-the ridicule, and what is worse, the pity of the world. Go, starve, and be forgotten! But, if your spirit should revolt at this; if you have sense enough to discover, and spirit enough to oppose tyranny under whatever garb it may assume; whether it be the plain coat of republicanism, or the splendid robe of royalty; if you have yet learned to discriminate between a people and a cause, between men and principles-awake; attend to your situation and redress yourselves. If the present moment be lost, every future effort is in vain; and your threats then, will be as empty as your entreaties now.

I would advise you, therefore, to come to some final opinion upon what you can bear, and what you will suffer. If your determination be in any proportion to your wrongs, carry your appeal from the justice to the fears of government.

Change the milk-and-water style of your last memorial; assume a bolder tone-decent, but lively, spirited and determined, and suspect the man who would advise to more moderation and longer forbearance. Let two or three men, who can feel as well as write, be appointed to draw up your last remonstrance; for, I would no longer give it the sueing, soft, unsuccessful epithet of memorial. Let it be represented in language that will neither dishonor you by its rudeness, nor betray you by its fears, what has been promised by Congress, and what has been performed, how long and how patiently you have suffered, how little you have asked, and how much of that little has been denied. Tell them that, though you were the first, and would wish to be the last to encounter danger: though despair itself can never drive you into dishonor, it may drive you from the field: that the wound often irritated, and never healed, may at length become incurable; and that the slightest mark of indignity from Congress now, must operate like the grave, and part you forever: that in any political event, the army has its alternative. If peace, that nothing shall separate them from your arms but death: if war, that courting the auspices, and inviting the direction of your illustrious leader, you will retire to some unsettled country, smile in your turn, and "mock when their fear cometh on." But let it represent also, that should they comply with the request of your late memorial, it would make you more happy and them more respectable. That while war should continue, you would follow their standard into the field, and when it came to an end, you would withdraw into the shade of private life, and give the world another subject of wonder and applause; an army victorious over its enemies-victorious over itself.

1. *How does Washington gain the sympathy and support of his readers in the opening paragraphs?*
2. *How did demobilization present a threat to the honor and welfare of the soldiers of the army?*
3. *What actions have Washington's listeners undertaken thus far to right what they consider injustice and ingratitude on the part of Congress? What is Washington's opinion of these efforts? What does Washington encourage his listeners to do in order to win their cause?*
4. *How does Washington urge forceful action without encouraging violent rebellion?*

6-4 Henry Knox, Letter to George Washington (1786)

Henry Knox was a good friend and trusted advisor of General and later President George Washington. As a General in the colonial army, Knox was a specialist in the utilization of artillery and his exploits become well known. He later became the first Secretary of War in Washington's Cabinet. Their relationship is demonstrated by this letter to Washington which gives Knox's view of government in the wake of Shay's Rebellion.

I have lately been far eastward of Boston on private business, and was no sooner returned here than the commotions in Massachusetts [Shay's Rebellion] hurried me back to Boston on a public account.

Our political machine, composed of thirteen independent sovereignties, have been perpetually operating against each other and against the federal head ever since the peace. The powers of Congress are totally inadequate to preserve the balance between the respective States, and oblige them to do those things which are essential for their own welfare or for the general good. The frame of mind in the local legislatures seems to be exerted to prevent the federal constitution from having any good effect. The machine works inversely to the public good in all its parts: not only is State against State, and all against the federal head, but the States within themselves possess the name only without having the essential concomitant of government, the power of preserving the peace, the protection of the liberty and property of the citizens. On the very first impression of faction and licentiousness, the fine theoretic government of Massachusetts has given way, and its laws [are] trampled under foot. Men at a distance, who have admired our systems of government unfounded in nature, are apt to accuse the rulers, and say that taxes have been assessed too high and collected too rigidly. This is a deception equal to any that has been hitherto entertained. That taxes may be the ostensible cause is true, but that they are the true cause is as far remote from truth as light from darkness. The people who are the insurgents have never paid any or but very little taxes. But they see the weakness of government: they feel at once their own poverty compared with the opulent, and their own force, and they are determined to make use of the latter in order to remedy the former.

The creed is, that the property of the United States has been protected from the confiscations of Britain by the joint exertions of all, and therefore ought to be the common property of all; and he that attempts opposition to this creed is an enemy to equality and justice, and ought to be swept from the face of the earth. In a word, they are determined to annihilate all debts public and private, and have agrarian laws, which are easily effected by the means of unfunded paper money, which shall be a tender in all cases whatever. The numbers of these people may amount, in Massachusetts, to one-fifth part of several populous countries; and to them may be added the people of similar sentiments from the States of Rhode Island, Connecticut, and New Hampshire, so as to constitute a body of twelve or fifteen thousand desperate and unprincipled men. They are chiefly of the young and active part of the community, more easily collected than kept together afterwards. But they will probably commit overt acts of treason, which will compel them to embody for their own safety. Once embodied, they will be constrained to submit to discipline for the same reason.

Having proceeded to this length, for which they are now ripe, we shall have a formidable rebellion against reason, the principle of all government, and against the very name of liberty.

This dreadful situation, for which our government have made no adequate provision, has alarmed every man of principle and property in New England. They start as from a dream, and ask what can have been the cause of our delusion? What is to give us security against the violence of lawless men? Our government must be braced, changed, or altered to secure our lives and property. We imagined that the mildness of our government and the wishes of the people were so correspondent that we were not as other nations, requiring brutal force to support the laws.

But we find that we are men,-actual men, possessing all the turbulent passions belonging to that animal, and that we must have a government proper and adequate for him.

The people of Massachusetts, for instance, are far advanced in this doctrine, and the men of property and the men of station and principle there are determined to endeavour to establish and protect them in their lawful pursuits; and, what will be efficient in all cases of internal commotions or foreign invasions, they mean that liberty shall form the basis,-liberty resulting from an equal and firm administration of law.

They wish for a general government of unity, as they see that the local legislatures must naturally and necessarily tend to retard the general government. We have arrived at that point of time in which we are forced to see our own humiliation, as a nation, and that a progression in this line cannot be a productive of happiness, private or public. Something is wanting, and something must be done, or we shall be involved in all the horror of failure, and civil war without a prospect of its termination. Every friend to the liberty of his country is bound to reflect, and step forward to prevent the dreadful consequences which shall result from a government of events. Unless this is done, we shall be liable to be ruled by an arbitrary and capricious armed tyranny, whose word and will must be law.

1. *Explain Knox's concerns regarding the effect of state local legislatures working in opposition to Congress?*
2. *What beliefs (although held by a "desperate and unprincipled" minority) stand as a threat to those that own property in America? What does Knox suggest is necessary to alleviate this threat of rebellion? What does Knox suggest would be the ultimate outcome if this situation is not redressed?*

6-5   Marquis de Chastellux, Travels in North America (1786)

A familiar figure among the French Encylopedists, the Marquis de Chastellux came to the American colonies as a major general under Rochambeau in 1780. During his three years in America he traveled much in between campaigns and upon his return to France he wrote this account of the colonies. It stands in a long line of European examinations of the American people and landscape.

The Virginians differ essentially from the inhabitants to the north and eastward of the Bay [Chesapeake], not only in the nature of their climate, soil, and agriculture, but also in that indelible character which every nation acquires at the moment of its origin, and which by perpetuating itself from generation to generation, justifies this great principle, that *every thing which is partakes of that which has been.* . . .

The government [of Virginia] may become democratic, as it is at the present moment; but the national character, the very spirit of the government, will always be aristocratic. Nor can this be doubted when one considers that another cause is still operating to produce the same result. I am referring to slavery, not because it is a mark of distinction or special privilege to possess Negroes, but because the sway held over them nourishes vanity and sloth, two vices which accord wonderfully with established prejudices. It will doubtless be asked how these prejudices have been reconciled with the present revolution, founded on such different principles. I shall answer that they have perhaps contributed to it; that while New England revolted through reason and calculation, Virginia revolted through pride. . . .

Thus, States, like individuals, are born with a temperament of their own, the bad effects of which may be corrected by the régime of government and by habits, but which can never be entirely changed. Thus, legislators, like doctors, ought never presume to believe that they can bestow, at will, a particular temperament on bodies politic, but should attempt to understand the temper they already have, while striving to combat the disadvantages and increase the advantages resulting from it. A general glance at the different states of America will serve to substantiate this opinion.

The peoples of New England had no other motive for setting in the New World than to escape from the arbitrary power of their monarchs, who were both the sovereigns of the State and the heads of the Church, and who were at that time exercising the double tyranny of despotism and intolerance. They were not adventurers, they were men who wished to live in peace, and who labored to live. Their doctrine taught equality and enjoined work and industry. The soil, naturally barren, affording but scanty resources, they resorted to fishing and navigation; and at this hour, they are still friends to equality and industry; they are fishermen and navigators.

The states of New York and the Jerseys were settled by necessitous Dutchmen who lacked land in their own country, and who concerned themselves much more with domestic economy than with public government. These people have kept this same spirit: their interests and their efforts are, so to speak, individual; their views are centered on their families, and it is only from necessity that these families form a state. . . .

If you go farther to the south, and cross the Delaware, you will find that the government of Pennsylvania, in its origin, was founded on two very opposite principles; it was a government of property, in itself feudal, or if you will, a patriarchal government, but whose spirit was characterized by the greatest tolerance and the most complete liberty. Penn's family at first formed the vain idea of establishing a sort of Utopia, a perfect government, and then of deriving the greatest possible advantage from their immense property by attracting foreigners from all parts. As a result of this the people of Pennsylvania has no identity of its own, it is mixed and confused, and more attached to individual than to public liberty, more inclined to anarchy than to democracy.

Maryland, subjected at first to proprietary government, and considered only as a private domain, long remained in a state of the most absolute dependence. Now for the first time it deserves being regarded as a state; but this state seems to be taking shape under good auspices. It may become important after the present revolution, because it was nothing before.

There remain the two Carolinas and Georgia, but I am not sufficiently acquainted with these three states to subject them to my observations, which may not be as correct as they appear to me, but which are in any case delicate and require more than a superficial examination. I know only that North Carolina, peopled for the most part by Scotsmen, brought thither by poverty rather than by industry, is a prey to brigandage and to internal dissensions; and that South Carolina, whose only commerce is the export trade, owes its existence to its seaports, especially to the city of Charleston, which rapidly increased and became a commercial town, where foreigners have abounded, as at Marseilles and Amsterdam, so that the manners there are polished and easy, that the inhabitants love pleasure, the arts, and society-and that this country is in general more European than the rest of America.

Now if there be any accuracy in this sketch, let my readers compare the spirit of the states of America with their present government. I ask them to make the comparison at the present moment, twenty years hence, fifty years hence, and I am persuaded that although these governments resemble each other in that they are all democratic, there will always be found the traces of their former character, of that spirit which has presided over the formation of peoples and the establishment of nations.

Virginia will retain its distinctive character longer than the other states; either because prejudices are the more durable, the more absurd and frivolous they are, or because those which injure only a part of the human race are more noticeable than those which affect all mankind. In the present revolution the old families have with pain seen new men occupying distinguished situations in the army and in the magistracy. . . .

. . . But if Reason must blush at beholding such prejudices so strongly established among new peoples, Humanity has still more to suffer from the state of poverty in which a great number of white people live in Virginia. It is in this state, for the first time since I crossed the sea, that I have seen poor people. For, among these rich plantations where the Negro alone is wretched, one often finds miserable huts inhabited by whites, whose wane looks and ragged garments bespeak poverty. At first I found it hard to understand how, in a country where there is still so much land to clear, men who do not refuse to work could remain in misery. . . .

Beneath this class of inhabitants we must place the Negroes, whose situation would be even more lamentable than theirs, . . . On seeing them ill lodged, ill clothed, and often overwhelmed with work, I concluded that their treatment was as rigorous as everywhere else. I was assured, however, that it was extremely mild in comparison to what they experience in the sugar colonies. You do not, indeed, generally hear, as in Santo Domingo and in Jamaica, the sound of whips and the cries of the unhappy wretches whose bodies are being lashed. This is because the people of Virginia are in general milder than the inhabitants of the sugar islands, who consist wholly of avid men, eager to make their fortune and return to Europe. Another reason is that the yield of agriculture in Virginia not being of so great a value, labor is not urged on the Negroes with so much severity. . . .

One cannot conceal the fact that the abolition of slavery in America is an extremely delicate question. The Negroes in Virginia amount to two hundred thousand. They at least equal, if they do not exceed, the number of white men. . . . Sufficient attention has not been paid to the difference between slavery, such as we have kept it in our colonies, and slavery as it was generally established among the ancients. A white slave, in ancient times, had not other cause of humiliation than his present lot; if he was freed, he could mix straightway with free men and become their equal. Hence that emulation among the slaves to obtain their liberty, either as a favor or to purchase it with the fruit of their labor. Two advantages resulted from this: the possibility of enfranchising them without danger, and that ambition generally prevalent among them, which turned to the advantage of morals and of industry. But in the present case, it is not only the slave who is beneath his master; it is the Negro who is beneath the white man. No act of enfranchisement can efface this unfortunate distinction; accordingly the Negroes do not seem very anxious to obtain their freedom, nor much pleased when they have obtained it. The free Negroes continue to live with the Negro slaves, and never with the white men, so that only when they have some special work or trade, and want to turn it to their profit, does their interest make them wish to leave the state of bondage.

1. *Examine and discuss why the author is persuaded that the spirit of the government of Virginia will always be aristocratic.*
2. *Summarize the author's beliefs regarding why particular individual states sought independence.*
3. *In what ways is Virginia and its population noted to be different from other states by the author?*
4. *Examine and explain the difference between slavery as it existed in the colonies and slavery "as it was generally established among the ancients"? What effect does the author believe this will have on the institution of slavery in the colonies?*

6-6 Shays's Rebellion: Letters of Generals William Shepard and Benjamin Lincoln to Governor James Bowdoin of Massachusetts (1787)

Shay's Rebellion was a reaction to the poor economic times following the Revolutionary War and before the Constitutional Convention. Led by former Revolutionary Army Captain Daniel Shays, the rebellion protested high property taxes, poll taxes and unstable currency. Shay's Rebellion was put down militarily but its impact was great as it became one of the precipitating causes of the constitutional convention and the creation of a stronger central government.

[General Shepard to Governor Bowdoin]

Springfield
January 26, 1787

The unhappy time is come in which we have been obliged to shed blood. Shays, who was at the head of about twelve hundred men, marched yesterday afternoon about four o'clock, towards the public buildings in battle array. He marched his men in an open column by platoons. I sent several times by one of my aides, and two other gentlemen, Captains Buffington and Woodbridge, to him to know what he was after, or what he wanted. His reply was, he wanted barracks, and barracks he would have and stores. The answer returned was he must purchase them dear, if he had them.

He still proceeded on his march until he approached within two hundred and fifty yards of the arsenal. He then made a halt. I immediately sent Major Lyman, one of my aides, and Capt. Buffington to inform him not to march his troops any nearer the arsenal on his peril, as I was stationed here by order of your Excellency and the Secretary at War, for the defence of the public property; in case he did I should surely fire on him and his men. A Mr. Wheeler, who appeared to be one of Shays' aides, met Mr. Lyman, after he had delivered my orders in the most peremptory manner, and made answer, that was all he wanted. Mr. Lyman returned with his answer.

Shays immediately put his troops in motion, and marched on rapidly near one hundred yards. I then ordered Major Stephens, who commanded the artillery, to fire upon them. He accordingly did. The two first shots he endeavored to overshoot them, in hopes they would have taken warning without firing among them, but it had no effect on them. Major Stephens then directed his shot through the center of his column. The fourth or fifth shot put their whole column into the utmost confusion. Shays made an attempt to display the column, but in vain. We had one howitz which was loaded with grapeshot, which when fired, gave them great uneasiness.

Had I been disposed to destroy them, I might have charged upon their rear and flanks with my infantry and the two field pieces, and could have killed the greater part of his whole army within twenty-five minutes. There was not a single musket fired on either side. I found three men dead on the spot, and one wounded, who is since dead. One of our artillery men by inattention was badly wounded. Three muskets were taken up with the dead, which were all deeply loaded.

I have received no reinforcement yet, and expect to be attacked this day by their whole force combined.

[General Lincoln to Governor Bowdoin]

Head Quarters, Springfield
January 28th, 1787

We arrived here yesterday about noon with one regiment from Suffolk, one from Essex, one from Middlesex, and one from Worcester, with three companies of artillery, a corps of horse, and a volunteer corps under the command of Colonel Baldwin; the other company of artillery with the other regiment from Middlesex and another from Worcester which were as a cover to our stores arrived about eight o'clock in the evening. On my arrival, I found that Shays had taken a post at a little village six miles north of this, with the whole force under his immediate command, and that Day had taken post in West Springfield, and that he had fixed a guard at the ferry house on the west side of the river, and that he had a guard at the bridge over Agawam river. By this disposition all communication from the north and west in the usual paths was cut off.

From a consideration of this insult on Government, that by an early move we should instantly convince the insurgents of its ability and determination speedily to disperse them; that we wanted the houses occupied by these men to cover our own troops; that General Patterson was on his march to join us, which to obstruct was an object with them; that a successful movement would give spirits to the troops; that it would be so was reduced to as great a certainty, as can be had in operations of this kind; from these considerations, Sir, with many others, I was induced to order the troops under arms at three o'clock in the afternoon, although the most of them had been so from one in the morning.

We moved about half after three, and crossed the river upon the ice, with the four regiments; four pieces of artillery; the light horse, and the troops of this division, under General Shepard moved up the river on the ice, with an intention to fall in between Shays who was on the east side of the river, and Day on the west, and to prevent a junction as well as to cut off Day's retreat. We supposed that we should hereby encircle him with a force so superior that he would not dare to fire upon us which would effectually prevent bloodshed, as our troops were enjoined in the most positive manner not to fire without orders. The moment we showed ourselves upon the river the guard at the ferry house turned out and left the pass open to us. They made a little show of force for a minute or two near the meeting house, and then retired in the utmost confusion and disorder. Our horse met them at the west end of the village, but the insurgents found means by crossing the fields and taking to the woods to escape them; some were taken who are aggravatedly guilty, but not the most so.

The next news we had of them, was by an express from Northampton, that part of them arrived in the south end of their town about eleven o'clock. Shays also in a very precipitate manner left his post a[t] Chickabee, and some time in the night passed through South Hadley, on his way to Amherst.

As soon as our men are refreshed this morning, we shall move northward, leaving General Shepard here as a cover to the magazines; perhaps we may overtake Shays and his party, we shall do it, unless they disperse. If they disperse, I shall cover the troops in some convenient place, and carry on our operations in a very different way.

1. What actions does General Shepard seem to have taken to avert and then minimize the loss of life in putting down the rebellion?

2. Analyze the response of the participants in Shay's rebellion to the advances of the armed forces.

6-7 Divergent Reactions to Shays's Rebellion

In 1786, western Massachusetts erupted in violence as disgruntled farmers led by Revolutionary War veteran Daniel Shays sought relief from burdensome taxes and mounting debt. In 1787, the "Shaysites," numbering over 1200, marched on the federal arsenal at Springfield only to be turned back by local militia. General Benjamin Lincoln arrived on the scene with reinforcements and soon put the rebellion to an end. While armed protests such as this raised concerns about the power of the Confederation government and the possibility of anarchy, not all of the leaders of the new republic were in agreement over the seriousness of the situation.

Source: *Archiving Early America, Historic Documents From 18th Century America*
http://www.earlyamerica.com/review/summer/letter.html
The George Washington Papers at the Library of Congress, 1741–1799. *The Writings of George Washington from the Original Manuscript Sources, 1745–1799.* John C. Fitzpatrick, Editor.—vol. 29
http://lcweb2.loc.gov/cgi-bin/query/r?ammem/mgw:@field(DOCID+@lit(gw290127
http://lcweb2.loc.gov/cgi-bin/query/r?ammem/mgw:@field(DOCID+@lit(gw290129

THOMAS JEFFERSON TO JAMES MADISON

Paris, January 30th, 1787

Dear Sir,

My last to you was of the 16th of December; since which, I have received yours of November 25 and December 4, which afforded me, as your letters always do, a treat on matters public, individual, and economical. I am impatient to learn your sentiments on the late troubles in the Eastern states. So far as I have yet seen, they do not appear to threaten serious consequences. Those states have suffered by the stoppage of the channels of their commerce, which have not yet found other issues. This must render money scarce and make the people uneasy. This uneasiness has produced acts absolutely unjustifiable; but I hope they will provoke no severities from their governments. A consciousness of those in power that their administration of the public affairs has been honest may, perhaps, produce too great a degree of indignation; and those characters, wherein fear predominates over hope, may apprehend too much from these instances of irregularity. They may conclude too hastily that nature has formed man insusceptible of any other government than that of force, a conclusion not founded in truth or experience.

Societies exist under three forms, sufficiently distinguishable: (1) without government, as among our Indians; (2) under governments, wherein the will of everyone has a just influence, as is the case in England, in a slight degree, and in our states, in a great one; (3) under governments of force, as is the case in all other monarchies, and in most of the other republics.

To have an idea of the curse of existence under these last, they must be seen. It is a government of wolves over sheep. It is a problem, not clear in my mind, that the first condition is not the best. But I believe it to be inconsistent with any great degree of population. The second state has a great deal of good in it. The mass of mankind under that enjoys a precious degree of liberty and happiness. It has its evils, too, the principal of which is the turbulence to which it is subject. But weigh this against the oppressions of monarchy, and it becomes nothing. Malo periculosam libertatem quam quietam servitutem. Even this evil is productive of good. It prevents the degeneracy of government and nourishes a general attention to the public affairs.

I hold it that a little rebellion now and then is a good thing, and as necessary in the political world as storms in the physical. Unsuccessful rebellions, indeed, generally establish the encroachments on the rights of the people which have produced them. An observation of this truth should render honest republican governors so mild in their punishment of rebellions as not to discourage them too much. It is a medicine necessary for the sound health of government. . . .

Yours affectionately,
Th. Jefferson

GEORGE WASHINGTON TO BENJAMIN LINCOLN, FEBRUARY 24, 1787

Mount Vernon, February 24, 1787.

Sir: I have received your letter of the 24th. Ulto. and receipt for Messrs. Josiah Watson and Co. bill of Exchange which was enclosed. I am much obliged to you for the account of the political situation of your State which you gave me, and am very happy to find by later advices that matters are likely soon to terminate entirely in favour of Government by the total suppression of the insurgents, and it adds much to the satisfaction which these accounts give that it may be effected with so little bloodshed, I hope some good will come out of so much evil, by giving energy and respectability to the Government. General Lincoln's situation must have been very painful to be obliged to march against those men whom he had heretofore looked upon as his fellow Citizens and some of whom had perhaps been his companions in the field, but as they had by their repeated outrages forfeited all right to Citizenship, his duty and patriotism must have got the better of every other consideration and led him with alacrity to support the Government. I am, etc.

GEORGE WASHINGTON TO HENRY KNOX, FEBRUARY 25, 1787

Mount Vernon, February 25, 1787.

Accept, my dear General Knox my affectionate thanks for your obliging favors of the 29th, 30th, and 31st. of Jany. and 1st. 8th. and 12th. of the present month. They were indeed, exceedingly satisfactory, and relieving to my mind which had been filled with great and anxious uneasiness for the issue of General Lincoln's operations, and the dignity of Government. On prospect of the happy termination of this insurrection I sincerely congratulate you; hoping that good may result from the cloud of evils which threatned, not only the hemisphere of Massachusetts but by spreading its baneful influence, the tranquility of the Union. Surely Shays must be either a weak man, the dupe of some characters who are yet behind the curtain, or has been deceived by his followers. Or which may be more likely, he did not conceive that there was energy enough in the Government to bring matters to the crisis to which they have been pushed. It is to be hoped the General Court of that State concurred in the report of the Committee, that a rebellion did actually exist. This would be decisive, and the most likely means of putting the finishing stroke to the business.

We have nothing new in this quarter except the dissentions which prevailed in, and occasioned the adjournment of, the Assembly of Maryland; that an appeal might be made to the people for their sentiments on the conduct of their representative in the Senate and Delegates respecting a paper omission; which was warmly advocated by the latter and opposed by the former, and which may be productive of great, and perhaps dangerous divisions. Our Affairs, generally, seem really, to be approaching to some awful crisis. God only knows what the result will be. It shall be my part to hope for the best; as to see this Country happy whilst I am gliding down the stream of life in tranquil retirement is so much the wish of my Soul, that nothing on this side Elysium can be placed in competition with it. I hope the postponement of your journey to this State does not amount to a relinquishment of it, and that it is unnecessary to assure you of the sincere pleasure I should have at seeing you under this roof. Mrs. Washington unites with me in every good wish for Mrs. Knox yourself and family. With sentiments of the warmest friendship etc.

PS. I had wrote this letter and was on the point of sending it with others to the Post Office when your favor of the 15th. instt. was handed to me. The spirit and decision of the Court is very pleasing and I hope will be attended with happy consequences.

1. *What does Thomas Jefferson mean when he says "a little rebellion now and then is a good thing?" Do you think he was being a little too complacent?*
2. *What do you think explains the divergent opinions of Jefferson and Washington concerning Shays's rebellion?*

6-8 The "Distracting Question" in Philadelphia (1787)

Of the many problems facing the delegates at the Constitutional convention in Philadelphia, none was more challenging than the issue of representation. Thanks to the publication of James Madison's notes, readers have been able to "witness" the debates—including the discussion of the three-fifths compromise. Madison noted in his introduction, however, that "It may be proper to remark, that, with a very few exceptions, the speeches were neither furnished, nor revised, nor sanctioned, by the speakers, but written out from my notes, aided by the freshness of my recollections.

> **Source:** The Avalon Project at the Yale Law School
> http://www.yale.edu/lawweb/avalon/debates/711.htm

Wednesday July 11, 1787
IN CONVENTION

Mr. RANDOLPH's motion requiring the Legislre. to take a periodical census for the purpose of redressing inequalities in the Representation, was resumed.

Mr. SHERMAN was agst. shackling the Legislature too much. We ought to choose wise & good men, and then confide in them.

Mr. MASON. The greater the difficulty we find in fixing a proper rule of Representation, the more unwilling ought we to be, to throw the task from ourselves, on the Genl. Legislre. He did not object to the conjectural ratio which was to prevail in the outset; but considered a Revision from time to time according to some permanent & precise standard as essential to ye. fair representation required in the 1st. branch. According to the present population of America, the Northn. part of it had a right to preponderate, and he could not deny it. But he wished it not to preponderate hereafter when the reason no longer continued. From the nature of man we may be sure, that those who have power in their hands will not give it up while they can retain it. On the contrary we know they will always when they can rather increase it. If the S. States therefore should have 3/4 of the people of America within their limits, the Northern will hold fast the majority of Representatives. 1/4 will govern the 3/4. The S. States will complain: but they may complain from generation to generation without redress. Unless some principle therefore which will do justice to them hereafter shall be inserted in the Constitution, disagreeable as the declaration was to him, he must declare he could neither vote for the system here, nor support it, in his State. Strong objections had been drawn from the danger to the Atlantic interests from new Western States. Ought we to sacrifice what we know to be right in itself, lest it should prove favorable to States which are not yet in existence. If the Western States are to be admitted into the Union, as they arise, they must, he wd. repeat, be treated as equals, and subjected to no degrading discriminations. They will have the same pride & other passions which we have, and will either not unite with or will speedily revolt from the Union, if they are not in all respects placed on an equal footing with their brethren. It has been said they will be poor, and unable to make equal contributions to the general Treasury. He did not know but that in time they would be both more numerous & more wealthy than their Atlantic brethren. The extent & fertility of their soil, made this probable; and though Spain might for a time deprive them of the natural outlet for their productions, yet she will, because she must, finally yield to their demands. He urged that numbers of inhabitants; though not always a precise standard of wealth was sufficiently so for every substantial purpose.

Mr. WILLIAMSON was for making it the duty of the Legislature to do what was right & not leaving it at liberty to do or not do it. He moved that Mr. Randolph's proposition be postpond. in order to consider the following "that in order to ascertain the alterations that may happen in the population & wealth of the several States, a census shall be taken of the free white inhabitants and 3/5 ths. of those of other descriptions on the 1st. year after this Government shall have been adopted and every year thereafter; and that the Representation be regulated accordingly."

Mr. RANDOLPH agreed that Mr. Williamson's proposition should stand in the place of his. He observed that the ratio fixt for the 1st. meeting was a mere conjecture, that it placed the power in the hands of that part of America, which could not always be entitled to it, that this power would not be voluntarily renounced; and that it was consequently the duty of the Convention to secure its renunciation when justice might so require; by some constitutional provisions. If equality between great & small States be inadmissible, because in that case unequal numbers of Constituents wd. be represented by equal number of votes; was it not equally inadmissible that a larger & more populous district of America should hereafter have less representation, than a smaller & less populous district. If a fair representation of the people be not secured, the injustice of the Govt. will shake it to its foundations. What relates to suffrage is justly stated by the celebrated Montesquieu, as a fundamental article in Republican Govts. If the danger suggested by Mr. Govr. Morris be real, of advantage being taken of the Legislature in pressing moments, it was an additional reason, for tying their hands in such a manner that they could not sacrifice their trust to momentary considerations. Congs. have pledged the public faith to New States, that they shall be admitted on equal terms. They never would nor ought to accede on any other. The census must be taken under the direction of the General Legislature. The States will be too much interested to take an impartial one for themselves.

Mr. BUTLER & Genl. PINKNEY insisted that blacks be included in the rule of Representation, equally with the Whites: and for that purpose moved that the words "three fifths" be struck out.

Mr. GERRY thought that 3/5 of them was to say the least the full proportion that could be admitted.

Mr. GHORUM. This ratio was fixed by Congs. as a rule of taxation. Then it was urged by the Delegates representing the States having slaves that the blacks were still more inferior to freemen. At present when the ratio of representation is to be established, we are assured that they are equal to freemen. The arguments on ye. former occasion had convinced him that 3/5 was pretty near the just proportion and he should vote according to the same opinion now.

Mr. BUTLER insisted that the labour of a slave in S. Carola. was as productive & valuable as that of a freeman in Massts., that as wealth was the great means of defence and utility to the Nation they were equally valuable to it with freemen; and that consequently an equal representation ought to be allowed for them in a Government which was instituted principally for the protection of property, and was itself to be supported by property.

Mr. MASON, could not agree to the motion, notwithstand it was favorable to Virga. because he thought it unjust. It was certain that the slaves were valuable, as they raised the value of land, increased the exports & imports, and of course the revenue, would supply the means of feeding & supporting an army, and might in cases of emergency become themselves soldiers. As in these important respects they were useful to the community at large, they ought not to be excluded from the estimate of Representation. He could not however regard them as equal to freemen and could not vote for them as such. He added as worthy of remark, that the Southern States have this peculiar species of property, over & above the other species of property common to all the States.

Mr. WILLIAMSON reminded Mr. Ghorum that if the Southn. States contended for the inferiority of blacks to whites when taxation was in view, the Eastern States on the same occasion contended for their equality. He did not however either then or now, concur in either extreme, but approved of the ratio of 3/5.

On Mr. Butlers motion for considering blacks as equal to Whites in the apportiontnt. of Representation.

Massts. no. Cont. no. [N. Y. not on floor.] N. J. no. Pa. no. Del. ay. Md. no. Va. no N. C. no. S. C. ay. Geo. ay.

Mr. Govr. MORRIS said he had several objections to the proposition of Mr. Williamson. 1. It fettered the Legislature too much. 2. It would exclude some States altogether who would not have a sufficient number to entitle them to a single Representative. 3. It will not consist with the Resolution passed on Saturday last authorising the Legislature to adjust the Representation from time to time on the principles or population & wealth or with the principles of equity. If slaves were to be considered as inhabitants, not as wealth, then the sd.. Resolution would not be pursued. If as wealth, then why is no other wealth but slaves included? These objections may perhaps be removed by amendments. His great objection was that the number of inhabitants was not a proper standard of wealth. The amazing difference between the comparative numbers & wealth of different Countries, rendered all reasoning superfluous on the subject. Numbers might with greater propriety be deemed a measure of stregth, than of wealth, yet the late defence made by G. Britain, agst. her numerous enemies proved in the clearest manner, that it is entirely fallacious even in this respect.

Mr. KING thought there was great force in the objections of Mr. Govr. Morris: he would however accede to the proposition for the sake of doing something.

Mr. RUTLIDGE contended for the admission of wealth in the estimate by which Representation should be regulated. The Western States will not be able to contribute in proportion to their numbers; they shd. not therefore be represented in that proportion. The Atlantic States will not concur in such a plan. He moved that "at the end of years after the 1st. meeting of the Legislature, and of every years thereafter, the Legislature shall proportion the Representation according to the principles of wealth & population"

Mr. SHERMAN thought the number of people alone the best rule for measuring wealth as well as representation; and that if the Legislature were to be governed by wealth, they would be obliged to estimate it by numbers. He was at first for leaving the matter wholly to the discretion of the Legislature; but he had been convinced by the observations of [Randolph & Mr. Mason,] that the periods & the rule, of revising the Representation ought to be fixt by the Constitution

Mr. REID thought the Legislature ought not to be too much shackled. It would make the Constitution like Religious Creeds, embarrassing to those bound to conform to them & more likely to produce dissatisfaction and scism, than harmony and union.

Mr. MASON objected to Mr. Rutlidge motion, as requiring of the Legislature something too indefinite & impracticable, and leaving them a pretext for doing nothing.

Mr. WILSON had himself no objection to leaving the Legislature entirely at liberty. But considered wealth as an impracticable rule.

Mr. GHORUM. If the Convention who are comparatively so little biassed by local views are so much perplexed, How can it be expected that the Legislature hereafter under the full biass of those views, will be able to settle a standard. He was convinced by the arguments of others & his own reflections, that the Convention ought to fix some standard or other.

Mr. Govr. MORRIS. The argts. of others & his own reflections had led him to a very different conclusion. If we can't agree on a rule that will be just at this time, how can we expect to find one that will be just in all times to come. Surely those who come after us will judge better of things present, than we can of things future. He could not persuade himself that numbers would be a just rule at any time. The remarks of [Mr. Mason] relative to the Western Country had not changed his opinion on that head. Among other objections it must be apparent they would not be able to furnish men equally enlightened, to share in the administration of our common interests. The Busy haunts of men not the remote wilderness, was the proper school of political Talents. If the Western people get the power into their hands they will ruin the Atlantic interests. The Back members are always most averse to the best measures. He mentioned the case of Pena. formerly. The lower part of the State had ye. power in the first instance. They kept it in yr. own hands & the Country was ye. better for it. Another objection with him agst. admitting the blacks into the census, was that the people of Pena would revolt at the idea of being put on a footing with slaves. They would reject any plan that was to have such an effect. Two objections had been raised agst. leaving the adjustment of the Representation from time, to time, to the discretion of the Legislature. The l.was they would be unwilling to revise it at all. The 2. that by referring to wealth they would be bound by a rule which if willing, they would be unable to execute. The 1st. objn. distrusts their fidelity. But if their duty, their honor & their oaths will not bind them, let us not put into their hands our liberty, and all our other great interests: let us have no Govt. at all. 2. If these ties will bind them we need not distrust the practicability of the rule. It was followed in part by the Come. in the apportionment of Representatives yesterday reported to the House. The best course that could be taken would be to leave the interests of the people to the Representatives of the people.

Mr. MADISON, was not a little surprised to hear this implicit confidence urged by a member who on all occasions, had inculcated so strongly, the political depravity of men, and the necessity of checking one vice and interest by opposing to them another vice & interest. If the Representatives of the people would be bound by the ties he had mentioned, what need was there of a Senate? What of a Revisionary power? But his reasoning was not only inconsistent with his former reasoning, but with itself. At the same time that he recommended this implicit confidence to the Southern States in the Northern Majority, he was still more zealous in exhorting all to a jealousy of Western Majority. To reconcile the gentln. with himself, it must be imagined that he determined the human character by the points of the compass. The truth was that all men having power ought to be distrusted to a certain degree. The case of Pena. had been mentioned where it was admitted that those who were possessed of the power in the original settlement, never admitted the new settlemts. to a due share of it. England was a still more striking example. The power there had long been in the hands of the boroughs, of the minority; who had opposed & defeated every reform which had been attempted. Virga. was in a lesser degree another example. With regard to the Western States, he was clear & firm in opinion, that no unfavorable distinctions were admissible either in point of justice or policy. He thought also that the hope of contributions to the Treasy. from them had been much underrated. Future contributions it seemed to be understood on all hands would be principally levied on imports & exports. The extent and fertility of the Western Soil would for a long time give to agriculture a preference over manufactures. Trials would be repeated till some articles could be raised from it that would bear a transportation to places where they could be exchanged for imported manufactures. Whenever the Mississpi should be opened to them, which would of necessity be ye. case, as soon as their population would subject them to any considerable share of the public burdin, imposts on their trade could be collected with less expence & greater certainty, than on that of the Atlantic States. In the mean time, as their supplies must pass thro' the Atlantic States, their contributions would be levied in the same manner with those of the Atlantic States. He could not agree that any substantial objection lay agst. fixig numbers for the perpetual standard of Representation. It was said that Representation & taxation were to go together; that taxation and wealth ought to go together, that population & wealth were not measures of each other. He admitted that in different climates, under different forms of Govt. and in different stages of civilization the inference was perfectly just. He would admit that in no situation, numbers of inhabitants were an accurate measure of wealth. He contended however that in the U. States it was sufficiently so for the object in contemplation. Altho' their climate varied considerably, yet as the Govts. the laws, and the manners of all were nearly the same, and the intercourse between different parts perfectly free, population, industry, arts, and the value of labour, would constantly tend to equalize themselves. The value of labour, might be considered as the principal criterion of wealth and ability to support taxes; and this would find its level in different places where the intercourse should be easy & free, with as much certainty as the value of money or any other thing. Wherever labour would yield most, people would resort, till the competition should destroy the inequality. Hence it is that the people are constantly swarming from the more to the less populous places-from Europe to Ama. from the Northn. & Middle parts of the U. S. to the Southern & Western. They go where land is cheaper, because there labour is dearer. If it be true that the same quantity of produce raised on the banks of the Ohio is of less value, than on the Delaware, it is also true that the same labor will raise twice or thrice, the quantity in the former, that it will raise in the latter situation.

Col. MASON. Agreed with Mr. Govr. Morris that we ought to leave the interests of the people to the Representatives of the people: but the objection was that the Legislature would cease to be the Representatives of the people. It would continue so no longer than the States now containing a majority of the people should retain that majority. As soon as the Southern & Western population should predominate, which must happen in a few years, the power wd. be in the hands of the minority, and would never be yielded to the majority, unless provided for by the Constitution

On the Question for postponing Mr. Williamson's motion, in order to consider that of Mr. Rutlidge it passed in the negative.

Massts. ay. Cont. no. N. J. no. Pa. ay. Del. ay. Md. no. Va. no. N. C. no. S. C. ay. Geo. ay.

On the question on the first clause of Mr. Williamson's motion as to taking a census of the free inhabitants; it passed in the affirmative Masts. ay. Cont. ay. N. J. ay. Pa. ay. Del. no. Md. no. Va. ay. N. C. ay. S. C. no. Geo. no. the next clause as to 3/5 of the negroes considered.

Mr. KING. being much opposed to fixing numbers as the rule of representation, was particularly so on account of the blacks. He thought the admission of them along with Whites at all, would excite great discontents among the States having no slaves. He had never said as to any particular point that he would in no event acquiesce in & support it; but he wd. say that if in any case such a declaration was to be made by him, it would be in this. He remarked that in the temporary allotment of Representatives made by the Committee, the Southern States had received more than the number of their white & three fifths of their black inhabitants entitled them to.

Mr. SHERMAN. S. Carola. had not more beyond her proportion than N. York & N. Hampshire, nor either of them more than was necessary in order to avoid fractions or reducing them below their proportion. Georgia had more; but the rapid growth of that State seemed to justify it. In general the allotment might not be just, but considering all circumstances, he was satisfied with it.

Mr. GHORUM. supported the propriety of establishing numbers as the rule. He said that in Massts. estimates had been taken in the different towns, and that persons had been curious enough to compare these estimates with the respective numbers of people; and it had been found even including Boston, that the most exact proportion prevailed between numbers & property. He was aware that there might be some weight in what had fallen from his colleague, as to the umbrage which might be taken by the people of the Eastern States. But he recollected that when the proposition of Congs. for changing the 8th. art: of Confedn. was before the Legislature of Massts. the only difficulty then was to satisfy them that the negroes ought not to have been counted equally with whites instead of being counted in the ratio of three fifths only.

Mr. WILSON did not well see on what principle the admission of blacks in the proportion of three fifths could be explained. Are they admitted as Citizens? then why are they not admitted on an equality with White Citizens? are they admitted as property? then why is not other property admitted into the computation? These were difficulties however which he thought must be overruled by the necessity of compromise. He had some apprehensions also from the tendency of the blending of the blacks with the whites, to give disgust to the people of Pena. as had been intimated by his Colleague [Mr. Govr. Morris]. But he differed from him in thinking numbers of inhabts. so incorrect a measure of wealth. He had seen the Western settlemts. of Pa. and on a comparison of them with the City of Philada. could discover little other difference, than that property was more unequally divided among individuals here than there. Taking the same number in the aggregate in the two situations he believed there would be little difference in their wealth and ability to contribute to the public wants.

Mr. Govr. MORRIS was compelled to declare himself reduced to the dilemma of doing injustice to the Southern States or to human nature, and he must therefore do it to the former. For he could never agree to give such encouragement to the slave trade as would be given by allowing them a representation for their negroes, and he did not believe those States would ever confederate on terms that would deprive them of that trade.

On Question for agreeing to include 3/5 of the blacks Massts. no. Cont. ay. N. J. no. Pa. no. Del. no. Mard. no. Va. ay. N. C. ay. S. C. no. Geo. ay. On the question as to taking census "the first year after meeting of the Legislature"

Masts. ay. Cont. no. N. J. ay. Pa. ay. Del. ay. Md. no. Va. ay. N. C. ay. S. ay. Geo. no

On filling the blank for the periodical census, with 15 years, Agreed to nem. con.

Mr. MADISON moved to add after "15 years," the words "at least" that the Legislature might anticipate when circumstances were likely to render a particular year inconvenient.

On this motion for adding "at least," it passed in the negative the States being equally divided.

Mas. ay. Cont. no. N. J. no. Pa. no. Del. no. Md. no. Va. ay. N. C. ay. S. C. ay. Geo. ay.

A Change of the phraseology of the other clause so as to read; "and the Legislature shall alter or augment the representation accordingly" was agreed to nem. con.

On the question on the whole resolution of Mr. Williamson as amended.

Mas. no. Cont. no. N. J. no. Del. no. Md. no. Va. no. N. C. no. S. C. no. Geo. no.

1. *How did the question of the addition of future western states complicate the already tricky issue of representation? What does Gouverneur Morris mean when he states, "The Back members are always most averse to the best measures?"*
2. *What were some of the alternatives to the three-fifths compromise regarding the representation of blacks?*

6-9   Patrick Henry Speaks Against Ratification of the Constitution (1788)

Patrick Henry, the noted Virginia delegate to the Constitutional Convention, opposed a federal form of government in the United States. Here, at a debate during the convention, Henry discusses his objections to the new form of government.

Source: Jonathan Elliot, ed., *The Debates in the Several State Conventions on the Adoption of the Federal Constitution* 2nd ed., 5 vols. (Philadelphia: J. B. Lippincott Company, 1907).

Mr. Chairman, the public mind, as well as my own, is extremely uneasy at the proposed change of government. Give me leave to form one of the number of those who wish to be thoroughly acquainted with the reasons of this perilous and uneasy situation, and why we are brought hither to decide on this great national question. I consider myself as the servant of the people of this commonwealth, as a sentinel over their rights, liberty, and happiness. I represent their feelings when I say that they are exceedingly uneasy at being brought from that state of full security, which they enjoyed, to the present delusive appearance of things. A year ago, the minds of our citizens were at perfect repose. Before the meeting of the late federal Convention at Philadelphia, a general peace and a universal tranquillity prevailed in this country; but, since that period, they are exceedingly uneasy and disquieted. When I wished for an appointment to this Convention, my mind was extremely agitated for the situation of public affairs. I conceived the republic to be in extreme danger. If our situation be thus uneasy, whence has arisen this fearful jeopardy? It arises from this fatal system; it arises from a proposal to change our government—a proposal that goes to the utter annihilation of the most solemn engagements of the states—a proposal of establishing nine states into a confederacy, to the eventual exclusion of four states. It goes to the annihilation of those solemn treaties we have formed with foreign nations.

The present circumstances of France—the good offices rendered us by that kingdom—require our most faithful and most punctual adherence to our treaty with her. We are in alliance with the Spaniards, the Dutch, the Prussians; those treaties bound us as thirteen states confederated together. Yet here is a proposal to sever that confederacy. Is it possible that we shall abandon all our treaties and national engagements?—and for what? I expected to hear the reasons for an event so unexpected to my mind and many others. Was our civil polity, or public justice, endangered or sapped? Was the real existence of the country threatened, or was this preceded by a mournful progression of events? This proposal of altering our federal government is of a most alarming nature! Make the best of this new government—say it is composed by any thing but inspiration—you ought to be extremely cautious, watchful, jealous of your liberty; for, instead of securing your rights, you may lose them forever. If a wrong step be now made, the republic may be lost forever. If this new government will not come up to the expectation of the people, and they shall be disappointed, their liberty will be lost, and tyranny must and will arise. I repeat it again, and I beg gentlemen to consider, that a wrong step, made now, will plunge us into misery, and our republic will be lost. It will be necessary for this Convention to have a faithful historical detail of the facts that preceded the session of the federal Convention, and the reasons that actuated its members in proposing an entire alteration of government, and to demonstrate the dangers that awaited us. If they were of such awful magnitude as to warrant a proposal so extremely perilous as this, I must assert, that this Convention has an absolute right to a thorough discovery of every circumstance relative to this great event. And here I would make this inquiry of those worthy characters who composed a part of the late federal Convention. I am sure they were fully impressed with the necessity of forming a great consolidated government, instead of a confederation. That this is a consolidated government is demonstrably clear; and the danger of such a government is, to my mind, very striking I have the highest veneration for those gentlemen; but, sir, give me leave to demand, What right had they to say, *We, the people?* My political curiosity, exclusive of my anxious solicitude for the public welfare, leads me to ask, Who authorized them to speak the language of, *We, the people,* instead of, *We, the states?* States are the characteristics and the soul of a confederation. If the states be not the agents of this compact, it must be one great, consolidated, national government, of the people of all the states. . .. It is not mere curiosity that actuates me: I wish to hear the real, actual, existing danger, which should lead us to take those steps, so dangerous in my conception.

Disorders have arisen in other parts of America; but here, sir, no dangers, no insurrection or tumult have happened; every thing has been calm and tranquil. But, notwithstanding this, we are wandering on the great ocean of human affairs. . ... The federal Convention ought to have amended the old system; for this purpose they were solely delegated; the object of their mission extended to no other consideration. You must, therefore, forgive the solicitation of one unworthy member to know what danger could have arisen under the present Confederation, and what are the causes of this proposal to change our government. . ...

. . .Under the same despised government, we commanded the respect of all Europe: wherefore are we now reckoned otherwise? The American spirit has fled from hence: it has gone to regions where it has never been expected; it has gone to the people of France, in search of a splendid government—a strong, energetic government. Shall we imitate the example of those nations who have gone from a simple to a splendid government? Are those nations more worthy of our imitation? What can make an adequate satisfaction to them for the loss they have suffered in attaining such a government—for the loss of their liberty? If we admit this consolidated government, it will be because we like a great, splendid one. Some way or other we must be a great and mighty empire; we must have an army, and a navy, and a number of things. When the American spirit was in its youth, the language of America was different: liberty, sir, was then the primary object. We are descended from a people whose government was founded on liberty: our glorious forefathers of Great Britain made liberty the foundation of every thing. That country is become a great, mighty, and splendid nation; not because their government is strong and energetic, but, sir, because liberty is its direct end and foundation. We drew the spirit of liberty from our British ancestors: by that spirit we have triumphed over every difficulty. But now, sir, the American spirit, assisted by the ropes and chains of consolidation, is about to convert this country into a powerful and mighty empire. If you make the citizens of this country agree to become the subjects of one great consolidated empire of America, your government will not have sufficient energy to keep them together. Such a government is incompatible with the genius of republicanism. There will be no checks, no real balances, in this government. What can avail your specious, imaginary balances, your rope-dancing, chain-rattling, ridiculous ideal checks and contrivances? But, sir, we are not feared by foreigners; we do not make nations tremble. Would this constitute happiness, or secure liberty? I trust, sir, our political hemisphere will ever direct their operations to the security of those objects. . ...

. . .With respect to that part of the proposal which says that every power not granted remains with the people, it must be previous to adoption, or it will involve this country in inevitable destruction. To talk of it as a thing subsequent, not as one of your unalienable rights, is leaving it to the casual opinion of the Congress who shall take up the consideration of that matter. They will not reason with you about the effect of this Constitution. They will not take the opinion of this committee concerning its operation. They will construe it as they please. If you place it subsequently, let me ask the consequences. Among ten thousand implied powers which they may assume, they may, if we be engaged in war, liberate every one of your slaves if they please. And this must and will be done by men, a majority of whom have not a common interest with you. They will, therefore, have no feeling of your interests. It has been repeatedly said here, that the great object of a national government was national defence. That power which is said to be intended for security and safety may be rendered detestable and oppressive. If they give power to the general government to provide for the general defence, the means must be commensurate to the end. All the means in the possession of the people must be given to the government which is intrusted with the public defence. In this state there are two hundred and thirty-six thousand blacks, and there are many in several other states. But there are few or none in the Northern States; and yet, if the Northern States shall be of opinion that our slaves are numberless, they may call forth every national resource. May Congress not say, that every black man must fight? Did we not see a little of this last war? We were not so hard pushed as to make emancipation general; but acts of Assembly passed that every slave who would go to the army should be free. Another thing will contribute to bring this event about. Slavery is detested. We feel its fatal effects—we deplore it with all the pity of humanity. Let all these considerations, at some future period, press with full force on the minds of Congress. Let that urbanity, which I trust will distinguish America, and the necessity of national defence,—let all these things operate on their minds; they will search that paper, and see if they have power of manumission. And have they not, sir? Have they not power to provide for the general defence and welfare? May they not think that these call for the abolition of slavery? May they not pronounce all slaves free, and will they not be warranted by that power? This is no ambiguous implication or logical deduction. The paper speaks to the point: they have the power in clear, unequivocal terms, and will clearly and certainly exercise it. As much as I deplore slavery, I see that prudence forbids its abolition. I deny that the general government ought to set them free, because a decided majority of the states have not the ties of sympathy and fellow-feeling for those whose interest would be affected by their emancipation. The majority of Congress is to the north, and the slaves are to the south.

In this situation, I see a great deal of the property of the people of Virginia in jeopardy, and their peace and tranquillity gone. I repeat it again, that it would rejoice my very soul that every one of my fellow-beings was emancipated. As we ought with gratitude to admire that decree of Heaven which has numbered us among the free, we ought to lament and deplore the necessity of holding our fellowmen in bondage. But is it practicable, by any human means, to liberate them without producing the most dreadful and ruinous consequences? We ought to possess them in the manner we inherited them from our ancestors, as their manumission is incompatible with the felicity of our country. But we ought to soften, as much as possible, the rigor of their unhappy fate. I know that, in a variety of particular instances, the legislature, listening to complaints, have admitted their emancipation. Let me not dwell on this subject. I will only add that this, as well as every other property of the people of Virginia, is in jeopardy, and put in the hands of those who have no similarity of situation with us. This is a local matter, and I can see no propriety in subjecting it to Congress.

1. To what events does Patrick Henry attribute the disruption of peace and tranquility formerly prevalent in the country?
2. How is a consolidated government a threat to the original spirit of America according to Henry?
3. Explain how the issue of slavery plays a part in Henry's reasoning in this piece? What are Patrick Henry's beliefs regarding the right of Congress to emancipate slaves? Identify the conflict between state rights and national authority as it relates to slavery.

6-10   Benjamin Banneker, Letter to Thomas Jefferson (1791)

Benjamin Banneker's almanacs and letters illustrate African Americans' quest to eradicate slavery and racial discrimination. Banneker was a native of Baltimore County, Maryland. He attended grammar school only briefly, but Banneker's keen innate intelligence enabled him to teach himself astronomy and mathematics. He became so accomplished in math and science that by 1791, he traveled with his neighbor Major Andrew Ellicott to Washington, D.C., on a surveying expedition of the area where the U.S. capital would be established. In addition, Banneker compiled data on astronomical matters. Later, he composed and had printed Benjamin Banneker's Pennsylvania, Delaware, Maryland and Virginia Almanac and Ephemeris, for the Year of Our Lord, 1792. He mailed the publication to Thomas Jefferson and included his famous antislavery "Letter to Thomas Jefferson." Jefferson replied in writing, and his response and Banneker's letter were printed in pamphlet form. Banneker died in 1806 in Baltimore, Maryland, known as an abolitionist, astronomer, and successful almanac writer.

From Silvio A. Bedini, *The Life of Benjamin Banneker* (New York: Landmark Enterprises, 1984), 152-159.

Sir, I am fully sensible of the greatness of that freedom which I take with you on the present occasion; a liberty which Seemed to me Scarcely allowable, when I reflected on that distibguished, and dignifying station in which you Stand; and the almost general prejudice and prepossession which is so previlent in the world against those of my complexion....

Sir I freely and Chearfully acknoweldge, that I am of the African race, and, in that colour which is natural to them of the deepest dye: and it is under a Sense of the most profound gratitude to the Supreme Ruler of the universe, that I do now confess to you, that I am not under that State of tyrannical thralldom, and inhuman capivity, to which too many of my bretheren are doomed; but that I have abundantly tasted of the fruition of those bessings which proceed from that free and unequalled liberty with which you are favoured and which I hope you will willingly allow you have received from the immediate Hand of that Being from whom proceedeth every good and perfect gift.

Sir, Suffer me to recall to your mind that time in which the Arms and tyranny of the British Crown were exerted with powerful effort, in order to reduce you to a State of Servitude; look back I entreat you on the variety of dangers to which you were exposed, reflect on that time in which every human aid appeared unavailable, and in which even hope and fortitude wore the greatful Sense of your miraculous and providential preservation; You cannot but acknowledge, that the present freedom and tranquility which you enjoy you have mercifully received, and that it is the peculiar blessing of Heaven.

This, Sir, was a time in whch you clearly saw into the injustice of a State of Slavery, and in which you have Just apprehension of the horrors of its condition, it was now Sir, that you abhorrence thereof was so excited, that you publickly held forth this true and invaluable doctrine, which is worthy to be recorded and remembered in all Succeeding ages. "We hold these truths to be Self evident, that all men are created equal, and that they are endowed by their creator with certain inalienable rights, that amongst them are life, liberty, and the persuit of happiness." . . .

Sir, I suppose that your knowledge of the situation of my brethern is too extensive to need a recital here; neither shall I presume to prescribe methods by which they may be relieved, otherwise than by recommending to you, and all others, to wean yourselves from those narrow prejudices which you have imbibed with respect to them, and as Job proposed to his friends, "Put your Souls in their Souls' stead," thus shall your hearts be enlarged with kindness and benevolence towards them, and thus shall you need neither the direction of myself or others in what manner to proceed herein.

And now, Sir, altho my Sympathy and affection for my brethern hath caused my enlargement thus far, I ardently hope that your candour and generosity will plead with you in my behalf, when I make known to you, that it was not originally my design; but that having taken up my pen in order to direct to you as a present, a copy of an Almanack which I have calculated for the Succeeding year, I was unexpectedly and unavoidably led thereto....

1. *Explain how Banneker creates a connection between himself and Jefferson in the first few paragraphs of this letter.*
2. *Around what basic truth, well known to Jefferson, does Banneker organize his plea? What is his reasoning in this letter?*

6-11   James Wilson, An Introductory Lecture To a Course of Law Lectures (1791)

Born in Scotland, James Wilson emigrated to Pennsylvania where he became a professor and lawyer of great distinction. A dedicated revolutionary, Wilson served in the continental congress and in several other posts where he distinguished himself with his intellect. Very active in the government of Pennsylvania, Wilson was involved in the creation of that state's constitution. He was later appointed to the Supreme Court by President Washington. In this document, he tackles the issue of women and education.

I have been zealous-I hope I have not been altogether unsuccessful-in contributing the best of my endeavours towards forming a system of government; I shall rise in importance, if I can be equally successful-I will not be less zealous-in contributing the best of my endeavours towards forming a system of education likewise, in the United States. I shall rise in importance, because I shall rise in usefulness.

What are laws without manners? How can manners be formed, but by a proper education?

Methinks I hear one of the female part of my audience exclaim-What is all this to us? We have heard much of societies, of states, of governments, of laws, and of a law education. Is every thing made for your sex? Why should not we have a share? Is our sex less honest, or less virtuous, or less wise than yours?

Will any of my brethren be kind enough to furnish me with answers to these questions?-I must answer them, it seems, myself? and I mean to answer them most sincerely.

Your sex is neither less honest, nor less virtuous, nor less wise than ours. With regard to the two first of these qualities, a superiority, on our part, will not be pretended: with regard to the last, a pretension of superiority cannot be supported.

I will name three women; and I will then challenge any of my brethren to name three men superiour to them in vigour and extent of abilities. My female champions are, Semiramis of Nineveh; Zenobia, the queen of the East; and Elizabeth of England. I believe it will readily be owned, that three men of superiour active talents cannot be named.

You will please, however, to take notice, that the issue, upon which I put the characters of these three ladies, is not that they were *accomplished*; it is, that they were *able* women.

This distinction immediately reminds you, that a woman may be an able, without being an accomplished female character.

In this latter view, I did not produce the three female characters I have mentioned. I produced them as women, merely of distinguished abilities-of abilities equal to those displayed by the most able of our sex.

But would you wish to be tried by the qualities of our sex? I will refer you to a more proper standard-that of your own.

All the three able characters, I have mentioned, had, I think, too much of the masculine in them. Perhaps I can conjecture the reason. Might it not be owing, in a great measure-might it not be owing altogether to the masculine employments, to which they devoted themselves?

Two of them were able warriors: all of them were able queens; but in all of them, we feel and we regret the loss of the lovely and accomplished woman: and let me assure you, that, in the estimation of our sex, the loss of the love and accomplished woman is irreparable, even when she is lost in the queen.

For these reasons, I doubt much, whether it would be proper that you should undertake the management of publick affairs. You have, indeed, heard much of publick government and publick law: but these things were not made for themselves: they were made for something better; and of that something better, you form the better part-I mean society-I mean particularly domestick society: there the lovely and accomplished woman shines with superiour lustre.

By some politicians, society has been considered as only the scaffolding of government; very improperly, in my judgment. In the just order of things, government is the scaffolding of society: and if society could be built and kept entire without government, the scaffolding might be thrown down, without the least inconvenience or cause of regret.

Government is, indeed, highly necessary; but it is highly necessary to a fallen state. Had man continued innocent, society, without the aids of government, would have shed its benign influence even over the bowers of Paradise.

For those bowers, how finely was your sex adapted! But let it be observed, that every thing else was finished, before Heaven's "last best gift" was introduced: let it be also observed, that, in the pure and perfect commencement of society, there was a striking difference between the only two persons, who composed it. . . .

Her accomplishments indicated her destination. Female beauty is the expression of female virtue. The purest complexion, the finest features, the most elegant shape are uninteresting and insipid, unless we can discover, by them, the emotions of the mind. How beautiful and engaging, on the other hand, are the features, the looks, and the gestures, while they disclose modesty, sensibility, and every sweet and tender affection! When these appear, there is a "Soul upon the countenance." . . .

How many purposes may be served at once, if things are done in the proper way! I have been giving a recipe for the improvement and preservation of female beauty; but I find that I have, at the same time, been delivering instructions for the culture and refinement of female virtue; and have been pointing at the important purposes, which female virtue is fittedf and intended to accomplish.

If nature evinces her designs by her works; you were destined to embellish, to refine, and to exalt the pleasures and virtues of social life.

To protect and to improve social life, is, as we have seen, the end of government and law. If, therefore, you have no share in the formation, you have a most intimate connexion with the effects, of a good system of law and government.

That plan of education, which will produce, or promote, or preserve such a system, is, consequently, an object to you peculiarly important.

But if you would see such a plan carried into complete effect, you must, my amiable hearers, give it your powerful assistance. The pleasing task of forming your daughters is almost solely yours. In my plan of education for your sons, I must solicit you to cooperate. Their virtues, in a certain proportion-the refinement of their virtues, in a much greater proportion, must be moulded on your example.

In your sex, too, there is a natural, an easy, and, often, a pure flow of diction, which lays the best foundation for that eloquence, which, in a free country, is so important to ours.

The style of some of the finest orators of antiquity was originally formed on that of their mothers, or of other ladies, to whose acquaintance they had the honour of being introduced.

I have already mentioned the two Scevofl among the illustrious Roman characters. One of them was married to Lfllia, a lady, whose virtues and accomplishments rendered her one of the principal ornaments of Rome. She possessed the elegance of language in so eminent a degree, that the first speakers of the age were ambitious of her company. The graces of her unstudied elocution were the purest model, by which they could refine their own.

Cicero was in the number of those, who improved by the privilege of her conversation. In his writing, he speaks in terms of the warmest praise concerning her singular talents. He mentions also the conversation of her daughters and grand daughters, as deserving particular notice.

The province of early education by the female sex, was deemed, in Rome, an employment of so much dignity, that ladies of the first rank did not disdain it. We find the names of Aurelia and Attia, the mothers of Julius Cflsar and of Augustus, enumerated in the list of these honourable patronesses of education.

The example of the highly accomplished Cornelia, the daughter of the great Africanus, and the mother of the Gracchi, deserves uncommon attention. She shone, with singular lustre, in all these endowments and virtues that can dignify the female character.

She was, one day, visited by a lady of Campania, who was extremely fond of dress and ornament. This lady, after having displayed some very rich jewels of her own, expressed a wish to be favoured with the view of those which Cornelia had; expected to see some very superb ones, in the toilet of a lady of such distinguished birth and character. Cornelia diverted the conversation, till her sons came into the room: "These are my jewels," said she, presenting them to the Campanian lady.

Cicero had seen her letters: his expressions concerning them are very remarkable. "I have read," says he, "the letters of Cornelia, the mother of the Gracchi; and it appears, that her sons were not so much nourished by the milk, as formed by the style of their mother."

You see now, my fair and amiable hearers, how deeply and nearly interested you are in a proper plan for law education. By some of you, whom I know to be well qualified for taking in it the share, which I have described, that share will be taken. By the younger part of you, the good effects of such a plan will, I hope, be participated: for those of my pupils, who themselves shall become most estimable, will treat you with the highest degree of estimation.

1. *How does Wilson respond to the question of whether women are considered less honest, or less virtuous, or less wise than men?*
2. *Identify and explain the role for women in education proposed by Wilson.*

6-12 Molly Wallace, Valedictory Oration (1792)

In this fascinating document, Molly Wallace, valedictory speaker at the Young Ladies Academy of Philadelphis, discusses whether women should be allowed to speak in public while, of course, speaking in public. In a time that tended to agree with Samuel Johnson that a woman speaking in public was similar to a trained animal act, Wallace's speech is all the more interesting.

The silent and solemn attention of a respectable audience, has often, at the beginning of discourses intimidated, even veterans, in the art of public elocution. What then must my situation be, when my sex, my youth and inexperience all conspire to make me tremble at the talk which I have undertaken? . . . With some, however, it has been made a question, whether we ought ever to appear in so public a manner. Our natural timidity, the domestic situation to which by nature and custom we seem destined, are, urged as arguments against what I have now undertaken:-Many sarcastical observations have been handed out against female oratory: But to what do they amount? Do they not plainly inform us, that, because we are females, we ought therefore to be deprived of what is perhaps the most effectual means of acquiring a just, natural and graceful delivery? No one will pretend to deny, that we should be taught to read in the best manner. And if to read, why not to speak? . . . But yet it might be asked, what, has a female character to do with declamation? That she should harangue at the head of an Army, in the Senate, or before a popular Assembly, is not pretended, neither is it requested that she ought to be an adept in the stormy and contentious eloquence of the bar, or in the abstract and subtle reasoning of the Senate; -we look not for a female Pitt, Cicero, or Demosthenes.

There are more humble and milder scenes than those which I have mentioned, in which a woman may display her elocution. There are numerous topics, on which she may discourse without impropriety, in the discussion of which, she may instruct and please others, and in which she may exercise and improve her own understanding. After all, we do not expect women should become perfect orators. Why then should they be taught to speak in public? This question may possibly be answered by asking several others.

Why is a boy diligently and carefully taught the Latin, the Greek, or the Hebrew language, in which he will seldom have occasion, either to write or to converse? Why is he taught to demonstrate the propositions of Euclid, when during his whole life, he will not perhaps make use of one of them? Are we taught to dance merely for the sake of becoming dancers? No, certainly. These things are commonly studied, more on account of the habits, which the learning of them establishes, than on account of any important advantages which the mere knowledge of them can afford. So a young lady, from the exercise of speaking before a properly selected audience, may acquire some valuable habits, which, otherwise she can obtain from no examples, and that no precept can give. But, this exercise can with propriety be performed only before a select audience: a promiscuous and indiscriminate one, for obvious reasons, would be absolutely unsuitable, and should always be carefully avoided. . . .

1. Summarize Molly Wallace's defense of her right, and a woman's right, to speak publicly. What caution does she also offer to her audience regarding the propriety of women speaking in public?

PART SEVEN
THE FEDERALIST ERA

7-1   James Madison Defends the Constitution (1788)

The Constitutional debates between Federalists and Anti-Federalists were often heated. Here, James Madison responds to Patrick Henry's concerns about the power of the federal government to directly tax the people.

Source: Jonathan Elliot, ed., *The Debates in the Several State Conventions on the Adoption of the Federal Constitution.* 2nd ed., 5 vols. (Philadelphia: J. B. Lippincott Company, 1907).

Comparisons have been made between the friends of this Constitution and those who oppose it: although I disapprove of such comparisons, I trust that in point of truth, honor, candor, and rectitude of motives, the friends of this system, here and in other states, are not inferior to its opponents. But professions of attachment to the public good, and comparisons of parties, ought not to govern or influence us now. We ought, sir, to examine the Constitution on its own merits solely: we are to inquire whether it will promote the public happiness: its aptitude to produce this desirable object ought to be the exclusive subject of our present researches. In this pursuit, we ought not to address our arguments to the feelings and passions, but to those understandings and judgments which were selected by the people of this country, to decide this great question by a calm and rational investigation. I hope that gentlemen, in displaying their abilities on this occasion, instead of giving opinions and making assertions, will condescend to prove and demonstrate, by a fair and regular discussion. . . .. I must take the liberty to make some observations on what was said by another gentleman (Mr. Henry) He told us that this Constitution ought to be rejected because it endangered the public liberty, in his opinion, in many instances. Give me leave to make one answer to that observation: Let the dangers which this system is supposed to be replete with be clearly pointed out: if any dangerous and unnecessary powers be given to the general legislature, let them be plainly demonstrated, and let us not rest satisfied with general assertions of danger, without examination. If powers be necessary, apparent danger is not a sufficient reason against conceding them. . . ..

. . . I must confess I have not been able to find his usual consistency in the gentleman's argument on this occasion. He informs us that the people of the country are at perfect repose,—that is, every man enjoys the fruits of his labor peaceably and securely, and that every thing is in perfect tranquillity and safety. I wish sincerely, sir, this were true. If this be their happy situation, why has every state acknowledged the contrary? Why were deputies from all the states sent to the general Convention? Why have complaints of national and individual distresses been echoed and reechoed throughout the continent? Why has our general government been so shamefully disgraced, and our Constitution violated? Wherefore have laws been made to authorize a change, and wherefore are we now assembled here? A federal government is formed for the protection of its individual members. Ours has attacked itself with impunity. Its authority has been disobeyed and despised. I think I perceive a glaring inconsistency in another of his arguments. He complains of this Constitution, because it requires the consent of at least three fourths of the states to introduce amendments which shall be necessary for the happiness of the people. The assent of so many he urges as too great an obstacle to the admission of salutary amendments, which, he strongly insists, ought to be at the will of a bare majority. We hear this argument, at the very moment we are called upon to assign reasons for proposing a constitution which puts it in the power of nine states to abolish the present inadequate, unsafe, and pernicious Confederation! In the first case, he asserts that a majority ought to have the power of altering the government, when found to be inadequate to the security of public happiness. In the last case, he affirms that even three fourths of the community have not a right to alter a government which experience has proved to be subversive of national felicity! nay, that the most necessary and urgent alterations cannot be made without the absolute unanimity of all the states! Does not the thirteenth article of the Confederation expressly require that no alteration shall be made without the unanimous consent of all the states? Could any thing in theory be more perniciously improvident and injudicious than this submission of the will of the majority to the most trifling minority? Have not experience and practice actually manifested this theoretical inconvenience to be extremely impolite? Let me mention one fact, which I conceive must carry conviction to the mind of any one: the smallest state in the Union has obstructed every attempt to reform the government; that little member has repeatedly disobeyed and counteracted the general authority; nay, has even supplied the enemies of its country with provisions. Twelve states had agreed to certain improvements which were proposed, being thought absolutely necessary to preserve the existence of the general government; but as these improvements, though really indispensable, could not, by the Confederation, be introduced into it without the consent of every state, the refractory dissent of that little state prevented their adoption. The inconveniences resulting from this requisition, of unanimous concurrence in alterations in the Confederation, must be known to every member in this Convention; it is therefore needless to remind them of them. Is it not self-evident that a trifling minority ought not to bind the majority? Would not foreign influence be exerted with facility over a small minority? Would the honorable gentleman agree to continue the most radical defects in the old system, because the petty state of Rhode Island would not agree to remove them? . . . .

Give me leave to say something of the nature of the government, and to show that it is safe and just to vest it with the power of taxation. There are a number of opinions; but the principal question is, whether it be a federal or consolidated government. In order to judge properly of the question before us, we must consider it minutely in its principal parts. I conceive myself that it is of a mixed nature; it is in a manner unprecedented; we cannot find one express example in the experience of the world. It stands by itself. In some respects it is a government of a federal nature; in others, it is of a consolidated nature. Even if we attend to the manner in which the Constitution is investigated, ratified, and made the act of the people of America, I can say, notwithstanding what the honorable gentleman has alleged, that this government is not completely consolidated, nor is it entirely federal. Who are parties to it? The people—but not the people as composing one great body; but the people as composing thirteen sovereignties. Were it, as the gentleman asserts, a consolidated government, the assent of a majority of the people would be sufficient for its establishment; and, as a majority have adopted it already, the remaining states would be bound by the act of the majority, even if they unanimously reprobated it. Were it such a government as is suggested, it would be now binding on the people of this state, without having had the privilege of deliberating upon it. But, sir, no state is bound by it, as it is, without its own consent. Should all the states adopt it, it will be then a government established by the thirteen states of America, not through the intervention of the legislatures, but by the people at large. In this particular respect, the distinction between the existing and proposed governments is very material. The existing system has been derived from the dependent derivative authority of the legislatures of the states; whereas this is derived from the superior power of the people. If we look at the manner in which alterations are to be made in it, the same idea is, in some degree, attended to. By the new system, a majority of the states cannot introduce amendments; nor are all the states required for that purpose; three fourths of them must concur in alterations; in this there is a departure from the federal idea. The members to the national House of Representatives are to be chosen by the people at large, in proportion to the numbers in the respective districts. When we come to the Senate, its members are elected by the states in their equal and political capacity. But had the government been completely consolidated, the Senate would have been chosen by the people in their individual capacity, in the same manner as the members of the other house. Thus it is of a complicated nature; and this complication, I trust, will be found to exclude the evils of absolute consolidation, as well as of a mere confederacy. If Virginia was separated from all the states, her power and authority would extend to all cases: in like manner, were all powers vested in the general government, it would be a consolidated government; but the powers of the federal government are enumerated; it can only operate in certain cases; it has legislative powers on defined and limited objects, beyond which it cannot extend its jurisdiction.

But the honorable member has satirized, with peculiar acrimony, the powers given to the general government by this Constitution. I conceive that the first question on this subject is, whether these powers be necessary; if they be, we are reduced to the dilemma of either submitting to the inconvenience or losing the Union. Let us consider the most important of these reprobated powers; that of direct taxation is most generally objected to. With respect to the exigencies of government, there is no question but the most easy mode of providing for them will be adopted. When, therefore, direct taxes are not necessary, they will not be recurred to. It can be of little advantage to those in power to raise money in a manner oppressive to the people. To consult the conveniences of the people will cost them nothing, and in many respects will be advantageous to them. Direct taxes will only be recurred to for great purposes. What has brought on other nations those immense debts, under the pressure of which many of them labor? Not the expenses of their governments, but war. If this country should be engaged in war,—and I conceive we ought to provide for the possibility of such a case,Ñhow would it be carried on? By the usual means provided from year to year? As our imports will be necessary for the expenses of government and other common exigencies, how are we to carry on the means of defence? How is it possible a war could be supported without money or credit? And would it be possible for a government to have credit without having the power of raising money? No; it would be impossible for any government, in such a case, to defend itself. Then, I say, sir, that it is necessary to establish funds for extraordinary exigencies, and to give this power to the general government; for the utter inutility of previous requisitions on the states is too well known. . .. This must be obvious to every member here; I think, therefore, that it is necessary, for the preservation of the Union, that this power shall be given to the general government.

But it is urged that its consolidated nature, joined to the power of direct taxation, will give it a tendency to destroy all subordinate authority; that its increasing influence will speedily enable it to absorb the state governments. I cannot think this will be the case. If the general government were wholly independent of the governments of the particular states, then, indeed, usurpation might be expected to the fullest extent. But, sir, on whom does this general government depend? It derives its authority from these governments, and from the same sources from which their authority is derived. The members of the federal government are taken from the same men from whom those of the state legislatures are taken. If we consider the mode in which the federal representatives will be chosen, we shall be convinced that the general will never destroy the individual governments; . . .

1. *What are Madison's disagreements with Patrick Henry regarding the general welfare of America and the laws concerning the number of states' votes needed to make alterations to the Constitution?*
2. *What is Madison's argument for the right of government to tax the people?*

7-2 [William Maclay], "For the Independent Gazetteer" (1790)

William Maclay was one of the first two Senators from Pennsylvania, drawing a two year term. He is best know today for a nearly daily journal that he kept of those first years of the Senate which, because of Senate secrecy rules in place until 1795, is among the only records of that body at that time. A supporter of the Constitution, Maclay became an outspoken opponent of the Federalists (he has been called the first Jeffersonian Republican) as this document demonstrates.

Mr. PRINTER,

I am a poor distressed woman [the United States of America], who for the thirteen or fourteen years since I kept house, have had as great a variety of fortune as ever beset any female. Glorious gleams of sunshine indeed have I had, and happiness ever seemed in my reach; yet by the mismanagement of servants, in brakeing cups and saucers, spoiling provisions, &c. I think I am likely to be ruined. A few days ago I expected to put an end to all my troubles, by sending for a worthy gentleman [George Washington], who had often taken me out of the gutter, when I considered myself as irretrievably fallen. Hearing he was at hand, I requested my neighbour (as good a man I thought as could be) to brush the furniture, and sweep the house, where I used to lodge my best friends. Now could you think it, Sir? Off he runs, and buys such an heap of pots and pans, and dishes and ladles, as run me to ten or twelve pounds of expence. Good Lord! and all this after my being so much in debt already. I determined not to pay him. But what of that? Sawny [Alexander Hamilton] the servant, who had the keeping of the trifle of cash I was possessed of, the moment my back was turned, gave him the money. Was there ever such a trick? People tell me the Grand Jury [Congress] should indict him; but la Sir, the Jury know all about it, and I am afraid will take no notice of him, but lye by, till it suits them too, to get a slap at me.

Mr. Printer, I think I am not deficient in the qualities of my head; my heart I know to be possessed of the principles of rectitude. Is it not dreadful that my concerns should be knocked about at this rate, every body doing what they please with me? After describing my situation, you cannot expect me to tell my name, but pray publish my case, which is a plain one. Perhaps some humane person may direct me how to get out of my difficulties.

1. *Identify the concerns regarding Hamilton's fiscal program as they are described in this letter.*
2. *Interpret the events described in this letter to the actual events to which they relate.*
3. *What truths are undeniable according to Jefferson? Identify the course of action necessitated by the denial of these truths. How do these ideas set the stage for the Revolution against Britain?*

7-3 Alexander Hamilton, Final Version of "An Opinion on the Constitutionality of an Act to Establish a Bank" (1791)

An important document in the history of constitutional interpretation, this document sought to avoid a veto by President Washington of Alexander Hamilton's National Bank. In the early years of the Republic, finances were in great disarray and Hamilton, who had been Washington's aide de camp, a chief writer of the Federalist Papers, and was now the nation's first Secretary of the Treasury, sought to stabilize this condition with a national bank. Madison and others were violently opposed and Washington himself was poised to veto the measure. Hamilton's defense of the Bank became a classic statement of the implied powers of the Constitution.

The Secretary of the Treasury having perused with attention the papers containing the opinions of the Secretary of State and Attorney General [Edmund Randolph and Thomas Jefferson] concerning the constitutionality of the bill for establishing a National Bank proceeds according to the order of the President [George Washington] to submit the reasons which have induced him to entertain a different opinion.

It will naturally have been anticipated that, in performing this task he would feel uncommon solicitude. Personal considerations alone arising from the reflection that the measure originated with him would be sufficient to produce it: The sense which he has manifested of the great importance of such an institution to the successful administration of the department under his particular care; and an expectation of serious ill consequences to result from a failure of the measure, do not permit him to be without anxiety on public accounts. But the chief solicitude arises from a firm persuasion, that principles of construction like those espoused by the Secretary of State and the Attorney General would be fatal to the just & indispensable authority of the United States.

In entering upon the argument it ought to be premised, that the objections of the Secretary of State and Attorney General are founded on a general denial of the authority of the United States to erect corporations. The latter indeed expressly admits, that if there be any thing in the bill which is not warranted by the constitution, it is the clause of incorporation.

Now it appears to the Secretary of the Treasury, that this *general principle* is *inherent* in the very *definition of Government* and *essential* to every step of the progress to be made by that of the United States; namely-that every power vested in a Government is in its nature *sovereign*, and includes by *force* of the *term*, a right to employ all the *means* requisite, and fairly *applicable* to the attainment of the *ends* of such power; and which are not precluded by restrictions & exceptions specified in the constitution; or not immoral, or not contrary to the essential ends of political society.

This principle in its application to Government in general would be admitted as an axiom. And it will be incumbent upon those, who may incline to deny it, to *prove* a distinction; and to shew that a rule which in the general system of things is essential to the preservation of the social order is inapplicable to the United States.

The circumstances that the powers of sovereignty are in this country divided between the National and State Governments, does not afford the distinction required. It does not follow from this, that each of the *portions* of powers delegated to the one or to the other is not sovereign *with regard to its proper objects*. It will only *follow* from it, that each has sovereign power as to *certain things*, and not as to *other things*. To deny that the Government of the United States has sovereign power as to its declared purposes & trusts, because its power does not extend to all cases, would be equally to deny, that the State Governments have sovereign power in any case; because their power does not extend to every case. The tenth section of the first article of the constitution exhibits a long list of very important things which they may not do. And thus the United States would furnish the singular spectacle of a *political society* without *sovereignty*, or of a people *governed* without *government*.

If it would be necessary to bring proof to a proposition so clear as that which affirms that the powers of the federal government, *as to its objects*, are sovereign, there is a clause of its constitution which would be decisive. It is that which declares, that the constitution and the laws of the United States made in pursuance of it, and all treaties made or which shall be made under their authority shall be the supreme law of the land. The power which can create the *Supreme law* of the land, in any case, is doubtless sovereign *as to such case*.

This general & indisputable principle puts at once an end to the *abstract* question-Whether the United States have power to *erect a corporation*? that is to say, to give a *legal* or *artificial capacity* to one or more persons, distinct from the natural. For it is unquestionably incident to *sovereign power* to erect corporations, and consequently to *that* of the United Strates, in *relation to the objects* intrusted to the management of the government. The difference is this-where the authority of the government is general, it can create corporations in *all cases*; where it is confined to certain branches of legislation, it can create corporations only in those cases.

Here then as far as concerns the reasonings of the Secretary of State & the Attorney General, the affirmative of the constitutionality of the bill might be permitted to rest. It will occur to the President that the principle here advanced has been untouched by either of them. . . .

It is not denied, that there are *implied*, as well as *express* powers, and that the former are as effectually delegated as the latter. And for the sake of accuracy it shall be mentioned, that there is another class of powers, which may be properly denominated *resulting* powers. It will not be doubted that if the United States should make a conquest of any of the territories of its neighbours, they would possess sovereign jurisdiction over the conquered territory. This would rather be a result from the whole mass of the powers of the government & from the nature of political society, than a consequence of either of the powers specially enumerated.

But be this as it may, it furnishes a striking illustration of the general doctrine contended for it. It shews an extensive case, in which a power of erecting corporations is either implied in, or would result from some or all of the powers, vested in the National Government. The jurisdiction acquired over such conquered territory would certainly be competent to every species of legislation.

To return-It is conceded, that implied powers are to be considered as delegated equally with express ones.

Then it follows, that as a power of erecting a corporation may as well be *implied* as any other thing; it may as well be employed as an *instrument* or *mean* of carrying into execution any of the specified powers, as any other instrument or mean whatever. The only question must be, in this as in every other case, whether the mean to be employed, or in this instance the corporation to be erected, has a natural relation to any of the acknowledged objects or lawful ends of the government. Thus a corporation may not be erected by congress, for superintending the police of the city of Philadelphia because they are not authorised to *regulate* the *police* of that city; but one may be erected in relation to the collection of the taxes, or to the trade with foreign countries, or to the trade between the States, or with the Indian Tribes, because it is the province of the federal government to regulate those objects & because it is incident to a general *sovereign* or *legislative power* to *regulate* a thing, to employ all the means which relate to its regulation to the *best & greatest advantage.*

A strange fallacy seems to have crept into the manner of thinking & reasoning upon the subject. Imagination appears to have been unusually busy concerning it. An incorporation seems to have been regarded as some great, independent, substantive thing-as a political end of peculiar magnitude & moment; whereas it is truly to be considered as a *quality, capacity,* or *mean* to an end. Thus a mercantile company is formed with a certain capital for the purpose of carrying on a particular branch of business. Here the business to be prosecuted is the *end*; the association in order to form the requisite capital is the primary mean. Suppose that an incorporation were added to this; it would only be to add a new *quality* to that association; to give it an artificial capacity by which it would be enabled to prosecute the business with more safety & convenience.

That the importance of the power of incorporaton has been exaggerated, leading to erroneous conclusions, will further appear from tracing it to its origin. The roman law is the source of it, according to which a *voluntary* association of individuals at *any time* or *for any purpose* was capable of producing it. In England, whence our notions of it are immediately borrowed, it forms a part of the executive authority, & the exercise of it has been often *delegated* by that authority. Whence therefore the ground of the supposition, that it lies beyond the reach of all those very important portions of sovereign power, legislative as well as executive, which belong to the government of the United States?

To this mode of reasoning respecting the right of employing all the means requisite to the execution of the specified powers of the Government, it is objected that none but *necessary* & proper means are to be employed, & the Secretary of State [Jefferson] maintains, that no means are to be considered as *necessary*, but those without which the grant of the power would be *nugatory*. Nay so far does he go in his restrictive interpretation of the word, as even to make the case of *necessity* which shall warrant the constitutional exercise of the power to depend on *casual & temporary* circumstances, an idea which alone refutes the construction. The *expediency* of exercising a particular power, at a particular time, must indeed depend on *circumstance* but the constitutional right of exercising it must be uniform & invariable-the same to day, as to morrow.

All the arguments therefore against the constitutionality of the bill derived from the accidental existence of certain State-banks: institutions which *happen* to exist to day, & for ought that concerns the government of the United States, may disappear to morrow, must not only be rejected as fallacious, but must be viewed as demonstrative, that there is a *radical* source of error in the reasoning.

It is essential to the being of the National government, that so erroneous a conception of the meaning of the word *necessary*, should be exploded.

It is certain, that neither the grammatical, or popular sense of the term requires that construction. According to both, *necessary* often means no more *than needful, requisite, incidental, useful,* or *conducive* to. It is a common mode of expression to say, that it is *necessary* for a government or a person to do this or that thing, when nothing more is intended or understood, than that the interests of the government or person require, or will be promoted, by the doing of this or that thing. The imagination can be at no loss for exemplifications of the use of the word in this sense.

And it is the true one in which it is to be understood as used in the constitution. The whole turn of the clause containing it, indicates that it was the intent of the convention, by that clause to give a liberal latitude to the exercise of the specified powers. The expressions have peculiar comprehensiveness. They are-"to make *all laws*, necessary & proper for *carrying into execution* the foregoing powers & all *other powers* vested by the constituion in the *government* of the United States, or in any *department* or *officer* thereof." To understand the word as the Secretary of State does, would be to depart from its obvious & popular sense, and to give it a *restrictive* operation; an idea never before entertained. It would be to give it the same force as if the word *absolutely* or *indispensibly* had been prefixed to it.

Such a construction would beget endless uncertainty & embarassment. The cases must be palpable & extreme in which it could be pronounced with certainty, that a measure was absolutely necessary, or one without which the exercise of a given power would be nugatory. There are few measures of any government, which would stand so severe a test. To insist upon it, would be to make the criterion of the exercise of any implied power a *case of extreme necessity*; which is rather a rule to justify the overleaping of the bounds of constitutional authority, than to govern the ordinary exercise of it.

It may be truly said of every government, as well as of that of the United States, that it has only a right, to pass such laws as are necessary & proper to accomplish the objects intrusted to it. For no government has a right to do *merely what it pleases*. Hence by a process of reasoning similar to that of the Secretary of State, it might be proved, that neither of the State governments has a right to incorporate a bank. It might be shewn, that all the public business of the State, could be performed without a bank, and inferring thence that it was unnecessary it might be argued that it could not be done, because it is against the rule which has been just mentioned. A like mode of reasoning would prove, that there was no power to incorporate the Inhabitants of a town, with a few to a more perfect police: For it is certain, that an incorporation may be dispensed with, though it is better to have one. It is to be remembered, that there is no *express* power in any State constitution to erect corporations.

The *degree* in which a measure is necessary, can never be a test of the *legal* right to adopt it. That must ever be a matter of opinion; and can only be a test of expediency. The *relation* between the *measure* and the *end*, between the *nature* of *the mean* employed towards the execution of a power and the object of that power, must be the criterion of constitutionality not the more or less of *necessity* or *utility*. . . .

This restrictive interpretation of the word *necessary* is also contrary to this sound maxim of construction namely, that the powers contained in a constitution of government, especially those which concern the general administration of the affairs of a country, its finances, trade, defence & ought to be construed liberally, in advancement of the public good. This rule does not depend on the particular form of a government or on the particular demarkation of the boundaries of its powers, but on the nature and objects of government itself. The means by which national exigencies are to be provided for, national inconveniences obviated, national prosperity promoted, are of such infinite variety, extent and complexity, that there must, of necessity, be great latitude of discretion in the selection & application of those means. Hence consequently, the necessity & propriety of exercising the authorities intrusted to a government on principles of liberal construction. . . .

The truth is that difficulties on this point are inherent in the nature of the federal constitution. They result inevitably from a division of the legislative power. The consequence of this division is, that there will be cases clearly within the power of the National Government; others clearly without its power; and a third class, which will leave room for controversy & difference of opinion, & concerning which a reasonable latitude of judgment must be allowed.

But the doctrine which is contended for is not chargeable with the consequence imputed to it. It does not affirm that the National government is sovereign in all respects, but that it is sovereign to a certain extent: that is, to the extent of the objects of its specified powers.

It leaves therefore a criterion of what is constitutional, and of what is not so. This criterion is the *end* to which the measure relates as a *mean*. If the end be clearly comprehended within any of the specified powers, & if the measure have an obvious relation to that end, and is not forbidden by any particular provision of the constitution-it may safely be deemed to come within the compass of the national authority. There is also this further criterion which may materially assist the decision. Does the proposed measure abridge a preexisting right of any State, or of any individual? If it does not, there is a strong presumption in favour of its constitutionality; & slighter relations to any declared object of the constitution may be permitted to turn the scale. . . .

A hope is entertained, that it has by this time been made to appear, to the satisfaction of the President, that a bank has a natural relation to the power of collecting taxes; to that of borrowing money; to that of regulating trade; to that of providing for the common defence: and that as the bill under consideration contemplates the government in the light of a joint proprietor of the stock of the bank, it brings the case within the provision of the clause of the constitution which immediately respects the property of the United States.

1. Identify and Summarize Hamilton's opinion regarding the establishment of a National Bank
2. How does his consideration of what is "necessary" in government affect his reasoning?

7-4 Questions Concerning the Constitutionality of the National Bank (1791)

On December 14, 1780, Secretary of the Treasury Alexander Hamilton presented to Congress his plan for the establishment of a national bank-an institution necessary he believed, to ensure a stable currency and the proper allocation of capital for development. Unsure of the constitutionality of Hamilton's proposal, President Washington sought the opinion of Thomas Jefferson (as well as Hamilton and Attorney General Edmund Randolph). Jefferson's argument against the bank was based upon his belief in the limited powers and strict construction of the Constitution. Washington, however, ultimately sided with Hamilton's doctrine of implied powers and his assertion of broad federal authority.

> **Source:** The Avalon Project at the Yale Law School
> http://www.yale.edu/lawweb/avalon/jeffop1.htm

OPINION ON THE CONSTITUTIONALITY OF A NATIONAL BANK

February 15, 1791

The bill for establishing a National Bank undertakes among other things:

1. The subscribers into a corporation.

2. To enable them in their corporate capacities to receive grants of land; and so far is against the laws of Mortmain.
3. To make alien subscribers capable of holding lands; and so far is against the laws of Alienage.
4. To transmit these lands, on the death of a proprietor, to a certain line of successors; and so far changes the course of Descents.
5. To put the lands out of the reach of forfeiture or escheat; and so far is against the laws of Forfeiture and Escheat.
6. To transmit personal chattels to successors in a certain line; and so far is against the laws of Distribution.
7. To give them the sole and exclusive right of banking under the national authority; and so far is against the laws of Mono poly.
8. To communicate to them a power to make laws paramount to the laws of the States: for so they must be construed, to protect the institution from the control of the State legislatures; and so, probably, they will be construed.

I consider the foundation of the Constitution as laid on this ground: That "all powers not delegated to the United States, by the Constitution, nor prohibited by it to the States, are reserved to the States or to the people." [Xth amendment.] To take a single step beyond the boundaries thus specially drawn around the powers of Congress, is to take possession of a boundless field of power, no longer susceptible of any definition. The incorporation of a bank, and the powers assumed by this bill, have not, in my opinion, been delegated to the United States, by the Constitution.

I. They are not among the powers specially enumerated: for these are: 1st A power to lay taxes for the purpose of paying the debts of the United States; but no debt is paid by this bill, nor any tax laid. Were it a bill to raise money, its origination in the Senate would condemn it by the Constitution.

2d. "To borrow money." But this bill neither borrows money nor ensures the borrowing it. The proprietors of the bank will be just as free as any other money holders, to lend or not to lend their money to the public. The operation proposed in the bill, first, to lend them two millions, and then to borrow them back again, cannot change the nature of the latter act, which will still be a payment, and not a loan, call it by what name you please.

3. To "regulate commerce with foreign nations, and among the States, and with the Indian tribes." To erect a bank, and to regulate commerce, are very different acts. He who erects a bank, creates a subject of commerce in its bills; so does he who makes a bushel of wheat, or digs a dollar out of the mines; yet neither of these persons regulates commerce thereby. To make a thing which may be bought and sold, is not to prescribe regulations for buying and selling. Besides, if this was an exercise of the power of regulating commerce, it would be void, as extending as much to the internal commerce of every State, as to its external. For the power given to Congress by the Constitution does not extend to the internal regulation of the commerce of a State, (that is to say of the commerce between citizen and citizen,) which remain exclusively with its own legislature; but to its external commerce only, that is to say, its commerce with another State, or with foreign nations, or with the Indian tribes. Accordingly the bill does not propose the measure as a regulation of trade, but as "productive of considerable advantages to trade." Still less are these powers covered by any other of the special enumerations.

II. Nor are they within either of the general phrases, which are the two following: —

1. To lay taxes to provide for the general welfare of the United States, that is to say, "to lay taxes for the purpose of providing for the general welfare." For the laying of taxes is the power, and the general welfare the purpose for which the power is to be exercised. They are not to lay taxes ad libitum for any purpose they please; but only to pay the debts or provide for the welfare of the Union. In like manner, they are not to do anything they please to provide for the general welfare, but only to lay taxes for that purpose. To consider the latter phrase, not as describing the purpose of the first, but as giving a distinct and independent power to do any act they please, which might be for the good of the Union, would render all the preceding and subsequent enumerations of power completely useless.

It would reduce the whole instrument to a single phrase, that of instituting a Congress with power to do whatever would be for the good of the United States; and, as they would be the sole judges of the good or evil, it would be also a power to do whatever evil they please.

It is an established rule of construction where a phrase will bear either of two meanings, to give it that which will allow some meaning to the other parts of the instrument, and not that which would render all the others useless. Certainly no such universal power was meant to be given them. It was intended to lace them up straitly within the enumerated powers, and those without which, as means, these powers could not be carried into effect. It is known that the very power now proposed as a means was rejected as an end by the Convention which formed the Constitution. A proposition was made to them to authorize Congress to open canals, and an amendatory one to empower them to incorporate. But the whole was rejected, and one of the reasons for rejection urged in debate was, that then they would have a power to erect a bank, which would render the great cities, where there were prejudices and jealousies on the subject, adverse to the reception of the Constitution.

2. The second general phrase is, "to make all laws necessary and proper for carrying into execution the enumerated powers." But they can all be carried into execution without a bank. A bank therefore is not necessary, and consequently not authorized by this phrase.

It has been urged that a bank will give great facility or convenience in the collection of taxes. Suppose this were true: yet the Constitution allows only the means which are "necessary," not those which are merely "convenient" for effecting the enumerated powers. If such a latitude of construction be allowed to this phrase as to give any non-enumerated power, it will go to every one, for there is not one which ingenuity may not torture into a convenience in some instance or other, to some one of so long a list of enumerated powers. It would swallow up all the delegated powers, and reduce the whole to one power, as before observed. Therefore it was that the Constitution restrained them to the necessary means, that is to say, to those means without which the grant of power would be nugatory.

But let us examine this convenience and see what it is. The report on this subject, page 3, states the only general convenience to be, the preventing the transportation and re-transportation of money between the States and the treasury, (for I pass over the increase of circulating medium, ascribed to it as a want, and which, according to my ideas of paper money, is clearly a demerit.) Every State will have to pay a sum of tax money into the treasury; and the treasury will have to pay, in every State, a part of the interest on the public debt, and salaries to the officers of government resident in that State. In most of the States there will still be a surplus of tax money to come up to the seat of government for the officers residing there. The payments of interest and salary in each State may be made by treasury orders on the State collector. This will take up the greater part of the money he has collected in his State, and consequently prevent the great mass of it from being drawn out of the State. If there be a balance of commerce in favor of that State against the one in which the government resides, the surplus of taxes will be remitted by the bills of exchange drawn for that commercial balance. And so it must be if there was a bank. But if there be no balance of commerce, either direct or circuitous, all the banks in the world could not bring up the surplus of taxes but in the form of money. Treasury orders then, and bills of exchange may prevent the displacement of the main mass of the money collected, without the aid of any bank; and where these fail, it cannot be prevented even with that aid.

Perhaps, indeed, bank bills may be a more convenient vehicle than treasury orders. But a little difference in the degree of convenience, cannot constitute the necessity which the constitution makes the ground for assuming any non-enumerated power.

Besides; the existing banks will, without a doubt, enter into arrangements for lending their agency, and the more favorable, as there will be a competition among them for it; whereas the bill delivers us up bound to the national bank, who are free to refuse all arrangement, but on their own terms, and the public not free, on such refusal, to employ any other bank. That of Philadelphia, I believe, now does this business, by their post-notes, which, by an arrangement with the treasury, are paid by any State collector to whom they are presented. This expedient alone suffices to prevent the existence of that necessity which may justify the assumption of a non-enumerated power as a means for carrying into effect an enumerated one. The thing may be done, and has been done, and well done, without this assumption; therefore, it does not stand on that degree of necessity which can honestly justify it.

It may be said that a bank whose bills would have a currency all over the States, would be more convenient than one whose currency is limited to a single State. So it would be still more convenient that there should be a bank, whose bills should have a currency all over the world. But it does not follow from this superior conveniency, that there exists anywhere a power to establish such a bank; or that the world may not go on very well without it.

Can it be thought that the Constitution intended that for a shade or two of convenience, more or less, Congress should be authorised to break down the most ancient and fundamental laws of the several States; such as those against Mortmain, the laws of Alienage, the rules of descent, the acts of distribution, the laws of escheat and forfeiture, the laws of monopoly? Nothing but a necessity invincible by any other means, can justify such a prostitution of laws, which constitute the pillars of our whole system of jurisprudence. Will Congress be too straight-laced to carry the constitution into honest effect, unless they may pass over the foundation-laws of the State government for the slightest convenience of theirs?

The negative of the President is the shield provided by the constitution to protect against the invasions of the legislature: 1. The right of the Executive. 2. Of the Judiciary. 3. Of the States and State legislatures. The present is the case of a right remaining exclusively with the States, and consequently one of those intended by the Constitution to be placed under its protection.

It must be added, however, that unless the President's mind on a view of everything which is urged for and against this bill, is tolerably clear that it is unauthorised by the Constitution; if the pro and the con hang so even as to balance his judgment, a just respect for the wisdom of the legislature would naturally decide the balance in favor of their opinion. It is chiefly for cases where they are clearly misled by error, ambition, or interest, that the Constitution has placed a check in the negative of the President.

1. According to Jefferson, how might Hamilton's national bank violate the yet to be ratified Tenth Amendment?

2. It can be argued that Jefferson's objections to Hamilton's plan extend beyond the issue of its constitutionality. Discuss the ways in which the national bank could support Hamilton in building up his own political power?

7-5   Opposing Visions for the New Nation (1791)

As Secretary of the Treasury during the Washington Administration, Alexander Hamilton released on December 5, 1791, what in essence way the capstone of his comprehensive economic program—the "Report on Manufactures." His plan included the establishment of a program of protective tariffs and the use of government revenue to support new industries. The result, he believed, would be the development of an industrial economy in the United States. Secretary of State Thomas Jefferson, on the other hand, espoused the virtues of the yeoman farmer. Twelve years Hamilton's senior, Jefferson wrote in his Notes on Virginia that "Those that labor in the earth are the chosen people of God. . . ." The opposing ideologies of these two men still resonate today.

> **Source:** *The Works of Alexander Hamilton*, ed. H. C. Lodge (New York: G. P. Putnam's Sons, 1904).
> http://www.multied.com/documents/Manufactures.html
> The Avalon Project at the Yale Law School
> http://www.yale.edu/lawweb/avalon/jevifram.htm

REPORT ON MANUFACTURES (1791)

The expediency of encouraging manufactures in the United States . . . appears at this time to be pretty generally admitted. The embarrassments which have obstructed the progress of our external trade, have led to serious reflections on the necessity of enlarging the sphere of our domestic commerce. The restrictive regulations, which, in foreign markets, abridge the vent of the increasing surplus of our agricultural produce . . . beget an earnest desire that a more extensive demand for that surplus may be created at home. . . .

To affirm that the labor of the manufacturer is unproductive, because he consumes as much of the produce of land as he adds value to the raw material which he manufactures, is not better founded than it would be to affirm that the labor of the farmer, which furnishes materials to the manufacturer, is unproductive, because he consumes an equal value of manufactured articles. Each furnishes a certain portion of the produce of his labor to the other, and each destroys a corresponding portion of the produce of the labor of the other. In the meantime, the maintenance of two citizens, instead of one, is going on; the State has two members instead of one; and they, together, consume twice the value of what is produced from the land. . . .

It is now proper to proceed a step further, and to enumerate the principal circumstances from which it may be inferred that manufacturing establishments not only occasion a positive augmentation of the produce and revenue of the society, but that they contribute essentially to rendering them greater than they could possibly be without such establishments. These circumstances are:

1. The division of labor.
2. An extension of the use of machinery.
3. Additional employment to classes of the community not ordinarily engaged in the business.
4. The promoting of emigration from foreign countries.
5. The furnishing greater scope for the diversity of talents and dispositions, which discriminate men from each other.
6. The affording a more ample and various field for enterprise.
7. The creating, in some instances, a new, and securing, in all, a more certain and steady demand for the surplus produce of the soil.

Each of these circumstances has a considerable influence upon the total mass of industrious effort in a community; together, they add to it a degree of energy and effect which is not easily conceived. . .

1. As to the Division of Labor

It has justly been observed, that there is scarcely any thing of greater moment in the economy of a nation than the proper division of labor. The separation of occupations causes each to be carried to a much greater perfection than it could possibly acquire if they were blended. This arises principally from three circumstances:

1st. The greater skill and dexterity naturally resulting from a constant and undivided application to a single object.. . .
2d. The economy of time, by avoiding the loss of it, incident to a frequent transition from one operation to another of a different nature.. . .

3d. An extension of the use of machinery. A man occupied on a single object will have it more in his power, and will be more naturally led to exert his imagination, in devising methods to facilitate and abridge labor, than if he were perplexed by a variety of independent and dissimilar operations.. . .

2. As to an Extension of the Use of Machinery, a Point Which, Though Partly Anticipated, Requires to be Placed in One or Two Additional Lights

The employment of machinery forms an item of great importance in the general mass of national industry. It is an artificial force brought in aid of the natural force of man; and, to all the purposes of labor, is an increase of hands, an accession of strength, unencumbered too by the expense of maintaining the laborer. May it not, therefore, be fairly inferred, that those occupations which give greatest scope to the use of this auxiliary, contribute most to the general stock of industrious effort, and, in consequence, to the general product of industry?. . .

3. As to the Additional Employment of Classes of the Community not Originally Engaged in the Particular Business

This is not among the least valuable of the means by which manufacturing institutions contribute to augment the general stock of industry and production. In places where those institutions prevail, besides the persons regularly engaged in them, they afford occasional and extra employment to industrious individuals and families, who are willing to devote the leisure resulting from the intermissions of their ordinary pursuits to collateral labors, as a resource for multiplying their acquisitions or their enjoyments. The husbandman himself experiences a new source of profit and support from the increased industry of his wife and daughters, invited and stimulated by the demands of the neighboring manufactories.

It is worthy of particular remark that, in general, women and children are rendered more useful, and the latter more early useful, by manufacturing establishments, than they would otherwise be. Of the number of persons employed in the cotton manufactories of Great Britain, it is computed that four sevenths, nearly, are women and children, of whom the greatest proportion are children, and many of them of a very tender age.. . .

4. As to Promoting of Emigration from Foreign Countries

Men reluctantly quit one course of occupation and livelihood for another, unless invited to it by very apparent and proximate advantages. Many who would go from one country to another, if they had a prospect of continuing with more benefit the callings to which they have been educated, will often not be tempted to change their situation by the hope of doing better in some other way. Manufacturers who, listening to the powerful invitations of a better price for their fabrics or their labor, of greater cheapness of provisions and raw materials, of an exemption from the chief part of the taxes, burdens, and restraints which they endure in the Old World, of greater personal independence and consequence, under the operation of a more equal government, and of what is far more precious than mere religious toleration, a perfect equality of religious privileges, would probably flock from Europe to the United States, to pursue their own trades or professions, if they were once made sensible of the advantages they would enjoy, and were inspired with an assurance of encouragement and employment, will, with difficulty, be induced to transplant themselves, with a view to becoming cultivators of land.. . .

5. As to the Furnishing Greater Scope for the Diversity of Talents and Dispositions, Which Discriminate Men from Each Other

If there be any thing in a remark often to be met with, namely, that there is, in the genius of the people of this country, a peculiar aptitude for mechanic improvements, it would operate as a forcible reason for giving opportunities to the exercise of that species of talent, by the propagation of manufactures.

6. As to the Affording a More Ample and Various Field for Enterprise

The spirit of enterprise, useful and prolific as it is, must necessarily be contracted or expanded, in proportion to the simplicity or variety of the occupations and productions which are to be found in a society. It must be less in a nation of mere cultivators, than in a nation of cultivators and merchants; less in a nation of cultivators and merchants, than in a nation of cultivators, artificers, and merchants.

7. As to the Creating, In Some Instances, A New, and Securing, in all, a More Certain and Steady Demand for the Surplus Produce of the Soil

This is among the most important of the circumstances which have been indicated. It is a principal means by which the establishment of manufactures contributes to an augmentation of the produce or revenue of a country, and has an immediate and direct relation to the prosperity of agriculture.

It is evident that the exertions of the husbandman will be steady or fluctuating, vigorous or feeble, in proportion to the steadiness or fluctuation, adequateness or inadequateness, of the markets on which he must depend for the vent of the surplus which may be produced by his labor; and that such surplus, in the ordinary course of things, will be greater or less in the same proportion. . . .

This idea of an extensive domestic market for the surplus produce of the soil, is of the first consequence. It is, of all things, that which most effectually conduces to a flourishing state of agriculture. If the effect of manufactories should be to detach a portion of the hands which would otherwise be engaged in tillage, it might possibly cause a smaller quantity of lands to be under cultivation; but, by their tendency to procure a more certain demand for the surplus produce of the soil, they would, at the same time, cause the lands which were in cultivation to be better improved and more productive. And while, by their influence, the condition of each individual farmer would be meliorated, the total mass of agricultural production would probably be increased. For this must evidently depend as much upon the degree of improvement, if not more, than upon the number of acres under culture. . . .

The foregoing considerations seem sufficient to establish, as general propositions, that it is the interest of nations to diversify, the industrious pursuits of the individuals who compose them; that the establishment of manufactures is calculated not only to increase the general stock of useful and productive labor, but even to improve the state of agriculture in particular,—certainly to advance the interests of those who are engaged in it. . . .

NOTES ON THE STATE OF VIRGINIA (1785)

Query XIX

The present state of manufactures, commerce, interior and exterior trade?

Manufactures

We never had an interior trade of any importance. Our exterior commerce has suffered very much from the beginning of the present contest. During this time we have manufactured within our families the most necessary articles of cloathing. Those of cotton will bear some comparison with the same kinds of manufacture in Europe; but those of wool, flax and hemp are very coarse, unsightly, and unpleasant: and such is our attachment to agriculture, and such our preference for foreign manufactures, that be it wise or unwise, our people will certainly return as soon as they can, to the raising raw materials, and exchanging them for finer manufactures than they are able to execute themselves.

The political economists of Europe have established it as a principle that every state should endeavour to manufacture for itself. and this principle, like many others, we transfer to America, without calculating the difference of circumstance which should often produce a difference of result. In Europe the lands are either cultivated, or locked up against the cultivator. Manufacture must therefore be resorted to of necessity not of choice, to support the surplus of their people. But we have an immensity of land courting the industry of the husbandman. Is it best then that all our citizens should be employed in its improvement, or that one half should be called off from that to exercise manufactures and handicraft arts for the other? Those who labour in the earth are the chosen people of God, if ever he had a chosen people, whose breasts he has made his peculiar deposit for substantial and genuine virtue. It is the focus in which he keeps alive that sacred fire, which otherwise might escape from the face of the earth. Corruption of morals in the mass of cultivators is a phaenomenon of which no age nor nation has furnished an example. It is the mark set on those, who not looking up to heaven, to their own soil and industry, as does the husbandman, for their subsistence, depend for it on the casualties and caprice of customers. Dependance begets subservience and venality, suffocates the germ of virtue, and prepares fit tools for the designs of ambition. This, the natural progress and consequence of the arts, has sometimes perhaps been retarded by accidental circumstances: but, generally speaking, the proportion which the aggregate of the other classes of citizens bears in any state to that of its husbandman, is the proportion of its unsound to its healthy parts, and is a good-enough barometer whereby to measure its degree of corruption. While we have land to labour then, let us never wish to see our citizens occupied at a work-bench, or twirling a distaff. Carpenters, masons, smiths, are wanting in husbandry: but, for the general operations of manufacture, let our work-shops remain in Europe. It is better to carry provisions and materials to workmen there, than bring them to the provisions and materials, and with them their manners and principles. The loss by the transportation of commodities across the Atlantic will be made up in happiness and permanence of government. The mobs of great cities add just so much to the support of pure government, as sores do to the strength of the human body. It is the manners and spirit of a people which preserve a republic in vigour. A degeneracy in these is a canker which soon eats to the heart of its laws and constitution.

1. *According to Hamilton's Report, what should be the relationship between agriculture and industry in the United States? How important is free enterprise and free trade in Hamilton's plan?*
2. *According to Thomas Jefferson, what is the danger inherent in an industrial economy?*

7-6   An African American Calls for an End to Slavery (1791)

In 1752, Benjamin Banneker, an African American farmer, mathematician, surveyor, and astronomer attracted attention by building a clock entirely out of wood that kept precise time for years. Pursuing his self-taught interest in mathematics and astronomy, Banneker accurately predicted a solar eclipse in 1789. The following year he was appointed by President George Washington to work with Andrew Ellicott in surveying the District of Columbia. As an essayist and pamphleteer, Banneker published the Pennsylvania, Delaware, Maryland, and Virginia Almanac and Ephemeris, which listed tides, astronomical information, and eclipses calculated by Banneker himself. He sent a copy of his almanac to Secretary of State Thomas Jefferson along with the following letter asking Jefferson's aid in bringing about an end to slavery and better conditions for African Americans. Jefferson's response is also included.

> **Source:** The History Net: African American History
> http://afroamhistory.about.com/library/blbanneker_letter.htm

Maryland, Baltimore County, August 19, 1791.
SIR,

I AM fully sensible of the greatness of that freedom, which I take with you on the present occasion; a liberty which seemed to me scarcely allowable, when I reflected on that distinguished and dignified station in which you stand, and the almost general prejudice and prepossession, which is so prevalent in the world against those of my complexion.

I suppose it is a truth too well attested to you, to need a proof here, that we are a race of beings, who have long labored under the abuse and censure of the world; that we have long been looked upon with an eye of contempt; and that we have long been considered rather as brutish than human, and scarcely capable of mental endowments.

Sir, I hope I may safely admit, in consequence of that report which hath reached me, that you are a man far less inflexible in sentiments of this nature, than many others; that you are measurably friendly, and well disposed towards us; and that you are willing and ready to lend your aid and assistance to our relief, from those many distresses, and numerous calamities, to which we are reduced. Now Sir, if this is founded in truth, I apprehend you will embrace every opportunity, to eradicate that train of absurd and false ideas and opinions, which so generally prevails with respect to us; and that your sentiments are concurrent with mine, which are, that one universal Father hath given being to us all; and that he hath not only made us all of one flesh, but that he hath also, without partiality, afforded us all the same sensations and endowed us all with the same faculties; and that however variable we may be in society or religion, however diversified in situation or color, we are all of the same family, and stand in the same relation to him.

Sir, if these are sentiments of which you are fully persuaded, I hope you cannot but acknowledge, that it is the indispensable duty of those, who maintain for themselves the rights of human nature, and who possess the obligations of Christianity, to extend their power and influence to the relief of every part of the human race, from whatever burden or oppression they may unjustly labor under; and this, I apprehend, a full conviction of the truth and obligation of these principles should lead all to. Sir, I have long been convinced, that if your love for yourselves, and for those inestimable laws, which preserved to you the rights of human nature, was founded on sincerity, you could not but be solicitous, that every individual, of whatever rank or distinction, might with you equally enjoy the blessings thereof; neither could you rest satisfied short of the most active effusion of your exertions, in order to their promotion from any state of degradation, to which the unjustifiable cruelty and barbarism of men may have reduced them.

Sir, I freely and cheerfully acknowledge, that I am of the African race, and in that color which is natural to them of the deepest dye; and it is under a sense of the most profound gratitude to the Supreme Ruler of the Universe, that I now confess to you, that I am not under that state of tyrannical thralldom and inhuman captivity, to which too many of my brethren are doomed, but that I have abundantly tasted of the fruition of those blessings, which proceed from that free and unequalled liberty with which you are favored; and which, I hope, you will willingly allow you have mercifully received, from the immediate hand of that Being, from whom proceedeth every good and perfect Gift. Sir, suffer me to recall to your mind that time, in which the arms and tyranny of the British crown were exerted, with every powerful effort, in order to reduce you to a state of servitude: look back, I entreat you, on the variety of dangers to which you were exposed; reflect on that time, in which every human aid appeared unavailable, and in which even hope and fortitude wore the aspect of inability to the conflict, and you cannot but be led to a serious and grateful sense of your miraculous and providential preservation; you cannot but acknowledge, that the present freedom and tranquility which you enjoy you have mercifully received, and that it is the peculiar blessing of Heaven.

This, Sir, was a time when you clearly saw into the injustice of a state of slavery, and in which you had just apprehensions of the horrors of its condition. It was now that your abhorrence thereof was so excited, that you publicly held forth this true and invaluable doctrine, which is worthy to be recorded and remembered in all succeeding ages: "We hold these truths to be self-evident, that all men are created equal; that they are endowed by their Creator with certain unalienable rights, and that among these are, life, liberty, and the pursuit of happiness." Here was a time, in which your tender feelings for yourselves had engaged you thus to declare, you were then impressed with proper ideas of the great violation of liberty, and the free possession of those blessings, to which you were entitled by nature; but, Sir, how pitiable is it to reflect, that although you were so fully convinced of the benevolence of the Father of Mankind, and of his equal and impartial distribution of these rights and privileges, which he hath conferred upon them, that you should at the same time counteract his mercies, in detaining by fraud and violence so numerous a part of my brethren, under groaning captivity and cruel oppression, that you should at the same time be found guilty of that most criminal act, which you professedly detested in others, with respect to yourselves.

I suppose that your knowledge of the situation of my brethren, is too extensive to need a recital here; neither shall I presume to prescribe methods by which they may be relieved, otherwise than by recommending to you and all others, to wean yourselves from those narrow prejudices which you have imbibed with respect to them, and as Job proposed to his friends, "put your soul in their souls' stead"; thus shall your hearts be enlarged with kindness and benevolence towards them; and thus shall you need neither the direction of myself or others, in what manner to proceed herein. And now, Sir, although my sympathy and affection for my brethren hath caused my enlargement thus far, I ardently hope, that your candor and generosity will plead with you in my behalf, when I make known to you, that it was not originally my design; but having taken up my pen in order to direct to you, as a present, a copy of an Almanac, which I have calculated for the succeeding year, I was unexpectedly and unavoidably led thereto.

This calculation is the production of my arduous study, in this my advanced stage of life; for having long had unbounded desires to become acquainted with the secrets of nature, I have had to gratify my curiosity herein, through my own assiduous application to Astronomical Study, in which I need not recount to you the many difficulties and disadvantages, which I have had to encounter. And although I had almost declined to make my calculation for the ensuing year, in consequence of that time which I had allotted therefore, being taken up at the Federal Territory, by the request of Mr. Andrew Ellicott, yet finding myself under several engagements to Printers of this state, to whom I had communicated my design, on my return to my place of residence, I industriously applied myself thereto, which I hope I have accomplished with correctness and accuracy; a copy of which I have taken the liberty to direct to you, and which I humbly request you will favorably receive; and although you may have the opportunity of perusing it after its publication, yet I choose to send it to you in manuscript previous thereto, that thereby you might not only have an earlier inspection, but that you might also view it in my own hand writing.

And now, Sir, I shall conclude, and subscribe myself, with the most profound respect, Your most obedient humble servant,

BENJAMIN BANNEKER.

To Mr. BENJAMIN BANNEKER.
Philadelphia, August 30, 1791.

SIR,

I THANK you, sincerely, for your letter of the 19th instant, and for the Almanac it contained. No body wishes more than I do, to see such proofs as you exhibit, that nature has given to our black brethren talents equal to those of the other colors of men; and that the appearance of the want of them, is owing merely to the degraded condition of their existence, both in Africa and America. I can add with truth, that no body wishes more ardently to see a good system commenced, for raising the condition, both of their body and mind, to what it ought to be, as far as the imbecility of their present existence, and other circumstances, which cannot be neglected, will admit.

I have taken the liberty of sending your Almanac to Monsieur de Condozett, Secretary of the Academy of Sciences at Paris, and Member of the Philanthropic Society, because I considered it as a document, to which your whole color had a right for their justification, against the doubts which have been entertained of them.

I am with great esteem, Sir, Your most obedient Humble Servant,

THOMAS JEFFERSON.

1. *Why do you think Benjamin Banneker chose Thomas Jefferson—the secretary of state—as the recipient of his appeal rather than, say, President Washington?*
2. *What arguments did Banneker make for ending slavery and improving the conditions of African Americans? Do you think he had realistic expectations? Why or why not?*

7-7   Backcountry Turmoil Puts the New Government to the Test (1794)

On March 3, 1781, Congress passed an excise tax on whiskey as part of Alexander Hamilton's financial plan. The Pennsylvania and Virginia backcountry, already embroiled in Indian affairs, erupted over what in essence was a new tax on their staple crop—corn. Farmers were in the habit of turning their corn into whiskey because it was the easiest and cheapest way to transport the crop to seaport markets. General disregard for the new tax and sporadic acts of violence led Hamilton to encourage President Washington to use military force to put down the "rebellion."

> **Source:** Claypoole's *Daily Advertiser*, August 11, 1794
> http://www.earlyamerica.com/earlyamerica/milestones/whiskey/text.html

A PROCLAMATION

Whereas, combinations to defeat the execution of the laws laying duties upon spirits distilled within the United States and upon stills have from the time of the commencement of those laws existed in some of the western parts of Pennsylvania.

And whereas, the said combinations, proceeding in a manner subversive equally of the just authority of government and of the rights of individuals, have hitherto effected their dangerous and criminal purpose by the influence of certain irregular meetings whose proceedings have tended to encourage and uphold the spirit of opposition by misrepresentations of the laws calculated to render them odious; by endeavors to deter those who might be so disposed from accepting offices under them through fear of public resentment and of injury to person and property, and to compel those who had accepted such offices by actual violence to surrender or forbear the execution of them; by circulation vindictive menaces against all those who should otherwise, directly or indirectly, aid in the execution of the said laws, or who, yielding to the dictates of conscience and to a sense of obligation, should themselves comply therewith; by actually injuring and destroying the property of persons who were understood to have so complied; by inflicting cruel and humiliating punishments upon private citizens for no other cause than that of appearing to be the friends of the laws; by intercepting the public officers on the highways, abusing, assaulting, and otherwise ill treating them; by going into their houses in the night, gaining admittance by force, taking away their papers, and committing other outrages, employing for these unwarrantable purposes the agency of armed banditti disguised in such manner as for the most part to escape discovery;

And whereas, the endeavors of the legislature to obviate objections to the said laws by lowering the duties and by other alterations conducive to the convenience of those whom they immediately affect (though they have given satisfaction in other quarters), and the endeavors of the executive officers to conciliate a compliance with the laws by explanations, by forbearance, and even by particular accommodations founded on the suggestion of local considerations, have been disappointed of their effect by the machinations of persons whose industry to excite resistance has increased with every appearance of a disposition among the people to relax in their opposition and to acquiesce in the laws, insomuch that many persons in the said western parts of Pennsylvania have at length been hardy enough to perpetrate acts, which I am advised amount to treason, being overt acts of levying war against the United States, the said persons having on the 16th and 17th of July last past proceeded in arms (on the second day amounting to several hundreds) to the house of John Neville, inspector of the revenue for the fourth survey of the district of Pennsylvania; having repeatedly attacked the said house with the persons therein, wounding some of them; having seized David Lenox, marshal of the district of Pennsylvania, who previous thereto had been fired upon while in the execution of his duty by a party of armed men, detaining him for some time prisoner, till, for the preservation of his fife and the obtaining of his liberty, he found it necessary to enter into stipulations to forbear the execution of certain official duties touching processes issuing out of a court of the United States; and having finally obliged the said inspector of the revenue and the said marshal from considerations of personal safety to fly from that part of the country, in order, by a circuitous route, to proceed to the seat of government, avowing as the motives of these outrageous proceedings an intention to prevent by force of arms the execution of the said laws, to oblige the said inspector of the revenue to renounce his said office, to withstand by open violence the lawful authority of the government of the United States, and to compel thereby an alteration in the measures of the legislature and a repeal of the laws aforesaid;

And whereas, by a law of the United States entitled "An act to provide for calling forth the militia to execute the laws of the Union, suppress insurrections, and repel invasions," it is enacted that whenever the laws of the United States shall be opposed or the execution thereof obstructed in any state by combinations too powerful to be suppressed by the ordinary course of judicial proceedings or by the powers vested in the marshals by that act, the same being notified by an associate justice or the district judge, it shall be lawful for the President of the United States to call forth the militia of such state to suppress such combinations and to cause the laws to be duly executed. And if the militia of a state, when such combinations may happen, shall refuse or be insufficient to suppress the same, it shall be lawful for the President, if the legislature of the United States shall not be in session, to call forth and employ such numbers of the militia of any other state or states most convenient thereto as may be necessary; and the use of the militia so to be called forth may be continued, if necessary, until the expiration of thirty days after the commencement of the ensuing session; Provided always, that, whenever it may be necessary in the judgment of the President to use the military force hereby directed to be called forth, the President shall forthwith, and previous thereto, by proclamation, command such insurgents to disperse and retire peaceably to their respective abodes within a limited time;

And whereas, James Wilson, an associate justice, on the 4th instant, by writing under his hand, did from evidence which had been laid before him notify to me that "in the counties of Washington and Allegany, in Pennsylvania, laws of the United States are opposed and the execution thereof obstructed by combinations too powerful to be suppressed by the ordinary course of judicial proceedings or by the powers vested in the marshal of that district";

And whereas, it is in my judgment necessary under the circumstances of the case to take measures for calling forth the militia in order to suppress the combinations aforesaid, and to cause the laws to be duly executed; and I have accordingly determined so to do, feeling the deepest regret for the occasion, but withal the most solemn conviction that the essential interests of the Union demand it, that the very existence of government and the fundamental principles of social order are materially involved in the issue, and that the patriotism and firmness of all good citizens are seriously called upon, as occasions may require, to aid in the effectual suppression of so fatal a spirit;

Therefore, and in pursuance of the proviso above recited, I. George Washington, President of the United States, do hereby command all persons, being insurgents, as aforesaid, and all others whom it may concern, on or before the 1st day of September next to disperse and retire peaceably to their respective abodes. And I do moreover warn all persons whomsoever against aiding, abetting, or comforting the perpetrators of the aforesaid treasonable acts; and do require all officers and other citizens, according to their respective duties and the laws of the land, to exert their utmost endeavors to prevent and suppress such dangerous proceedings.

In testimony whereof I have caused the seal of the United States of America to be affixed to these presents, and signed the same with my hand. Done at the city of Philadelphia the seventh day of August, one thousand seven hundred and ninety-four, and of the independence of the United States of America the nineteenth.

G. WASHINGTON,

By the President, Edm. Randolph

1. *Why did Washington call out the militia rather than use the army to put down the Whiskey Rebellion? Why do you think so many militiamen (12,900) responded to the call?*
2. *What effect did Washington's response to this domestic crisis have on questions regarding the power of the central government? What do you think Jefferson's reaction was to Washington's proclamation?*

7-8   George Washington, Farewell Address (1796)

Washington's Farewell Address was similar to one he had prepared with the help pf James Madison at the end of his first term, when he had contemplated retiring from public office. In May 1796, Washington wrote a first draft of a new address based on Madison's old notes, then presented manuscript to Alexander Hamilton for revisions. Hamilton rewrote the document, careful to preserve Washington's ideas or "sentiments," as he liked to call them. The result, rewritten again by Washington in a final version, was a product of adoption and adaption, but nonetheless representing the thoughts, ideas, and principles of the retiring president. Perhaps the most famous of his speeches, Washington's Farewell Address was never actually delivered orally. It first appeared in Philadelphia's American Daily Advertiser on September 19, 1796, and was later reprinted in other newspapers.

Observe good faith and justice toward all nations. Cultivate peace and harmony with all. Religion and morality enjoin this conduct. And can it be that good policy does not equally enjoin it? It will be worthy of a free, enlightened, and, at no distant period, a great nation to give to mankind the magnanimous and too novel example of a people always guided by an exalted justice and benevolence. . . .

In the execution of such a plan nothing is more essential than that permanent, inveterate antipathies against particular nations and passionate attachments for others should be excluded, and that, in place of them just and amicable feelings toward all should be cultivated. The nation which indulges toward another an habitual hatred or an habitual fondness is in some degree a slave. It is a slave to its animosity or to its affection either of which is sufficient to lead it astray from its duty and its interest. . . .

The nation prompted by ill will and resentment sometimes impels to war the government, contrary to the best calculations of policy. The government sometimes participates in the national propensity, and adopts through passion what reason would reject. . . .

So, likewise, a passionate attachment of one nation for another produces a variety of evils. Sympathy for the favorite nation, facilitating the illusion of an imaginary common interest in cases where no real common interest exists, and infusing into one the enmities of the other, betrays the former into a participation in the quarrels and wars of the latter without adequate inducement or justification. . . .

As avenues to foreign influence in innumerable ways, such attachments are particularly alarming to the truly enlightened and independent patriot. How many opportunities do they afford to tamper with domestic factions to practice the arts of seduction, to mislead public opinion, to influence or awe the public councils! Such an attachment of a small or weak toward a great and powerful nation dooms the former to be the satellite of the latter.

Against the insidious wiles of foreign influence (I conjure you to believe me, fellow citizens) the jealousy of a free people ought to be constantly awake, since history and experience prove that foreign influence is one of the most baneful foes of republican government. . . .

The great rule of conduct for us in regard to foreign nations is, in extending our commercial relation, to have with them as little political connection as possible. So far as we have already formed engagements, let them be fulfilled with perfect good faith. Here let us stop.

Europe has a set of primary interests which to us have no, or a very remote, relation. Hence she must be engaged in frequent controversies, the causes of which are essentially foreign to our concerns. Hence, therefore, it must be unwise in us to implicate ourselves by artificial ties in the ordinary vicissitudes of her politics, or the ordinary combinations and collisions of her friendships or enmities.

Our detached and distant situation invites and enables us to pursue a different course. If we remain one people, under an efficient government, the period is not far off when we may defy material injury from external annoyance; when we may take such an attitude as will cause the neutrality we may at any time resolve upon to be scrupulously respected; when belligerent nations, under the impossibility of making acquisitions upon us, will not lightly hazard the giving us provocation; when we may choose peace or war, as our interest, guided by justice, shall counsel.

Why forego the advantages of so peculiar a situation? Why quit our own to stand upon foreign ground? Why, by interweaving our destiny with that of any part of Europe, entangle our peace and prosperity in the toils of European ambition, rivalship, interest, humor, or caprice?

It is our true policy to steer clear of permanent alliances with any portion of the foreign world, so far, I mean, as we are now at liberty to do it. For let me not be understood as capable of patronizing infidelity to existing engagements. I hold the maxim of less applicable to public than to private affairs that honesty is always the best policy. I repeat, therefore, let those engagements be observed in their genuine sense. But in my opinion it is unnecessary and would be unwise to extend them.

Taking care always to keep ourselves by suitable establishments on a respectable defensive posture, we may safely trust to temporary alliances for extraordinary emergencies.

Harmony, liberal intercourse with all nations, are recommended by policy, humanity, and interest. But even our commercial policy should hold an equal an impartial hand, neither seeking nor granting exclusive favors or preference; . . . constantly keeping in view that it is folly in one nation to look for disinterested favors from another; that it must pay with a portion of its independence for whatever it may accept under that character; that by such acceptance it may place itself in the condition of having given equivalents for nominal favors, and yet of being reproached with ingratitude for not giving more. There can be no greater error than to expect or calculate upon real favors from nation to nation. It is an illusion which experience must cure, which a just pride ought to discard.

1. Explain.why Washington warns against habitual hatred or fondness for other countries?
2. Identify and explain the foreign policy for America proposed by Washington in this address.

7-9 The Alien and Sedition Acts (1798)

Written in response to fears of war with Revolutionary France, The Alien and Sedition Acts also sought to injure the new Jeffersonian Republican party which, it was thought, harbored support of the Revolutionary Government. The high number of recent immigrants active in the party was also seen as evidence of disloyalty. The acts triggered several constitutional disputes and some were imprisoned. The election of Thomas Jefferson to the Presidency ended the enforcement of these infamous laws, though elements of them were utilized years later.

The Alien Act

June 25, 1798. Statute II., Chap. LVIII.-An Act Concerning Aliens

SECTION I. *Be it enacted by the Senate and House of Representatives of the United States of America in Congress assembled,* That it shall be lawful for the President of the United States at any time during the continuance of this act, to *order* all such *aliens* as he shall judge dangerous to the peace and safety of the United States, or shall have reasonable grounds to suspect are concerned in any treasonable or secret machinations against the government thereof, to depart out of the territory of the United States, within such time as shall be expressed in such order, which order shall be served on such alien by delivering him a copy thereof, or leaving the same at his usual abode, and returned to the office of the Secretary of State, by the marshal or other person to whom the same shall be directed. And in case any alien, so ordered to depart, shall be found at large within the United States after the time limited in such order for his departure, and not having obtained a *license* from the President to reside therein, or having obtained such *license* shall not have conformed thereto, every such alien shall, on conviction thereof, be imprisoned for a term not exceeding three years, and shall never after be admitted to become a citizen of the United States. *Provided always and be it further enacted,* that if any alien so ordered to depart shall prove to the satisfaction of the President, by evidence to be taken before such person or persons as the President shall direct who are for that purpose hereby authorized to administer oaths, that no injury or danger to the United States will arise from suffering such alien to reside therein, the President may grant a *license* to such alien to remain within the United States for such time as he shall judge proper, and at such place as he may designate. And the President may also require of such alien to enter into a bond to the United States, in such penal sum as he may direct, with one or more sufficient sureties to the satisfaction of the person authorized by the President to take the same, conditioned for the good behavior of such alien during his residence in the United States, and not violating his license, which license the President may revoke whenever he shall think proper.

SEC. 2. *And be it further enacted,* That is shall be lawful for the President of the United States, whenever he may deem it necessary for the public safety, to order to be removed out of the territory thereof, any alien who may or shall be in prison in pursuance of this act; and to cause to be arrested and sent out of the United States such of those aliens as shall have been ordered to depart therefrom and shall not have obtained a license as aforesaid, in all cases where, in the opinion of the President, the public safety requires a speedy removal. And if any alien so removed or sent out of the United States by the President shall voluntarily return thereto, unless by permission of the President of the United States, such alien on conviction thereof, shall be imprisoned so long as, in the opinion of the President, the public safety may require.

SEC. 3. *And be it further enacted,* That every master or commander of any ship or vessel which shall come into any port of the United States after the first day of July next, shall immediately on his arrival make report in writing to the collector, or other chief officer of the customs of such port, of all aliens, if any, on board his vessel, specifying their names, age, the place of nativity, the country from which they shall have come, the nation to which they belong and owe allegiance, their occupation and a description of their persons, as far as he shall be informed thereof, and on failure, every such master and commander shall forfeit and pay three hundred dollars, for the payment whereof on default of such master or commander, such vessel shall also be holden, and may by such collector or other officer of the customs be detained. And it shall be the duty of such collector, or other officer of the customs, forthwith to transmit to the office of the department of state true copies of all such returns.

SEC. 4. *And be it further enacted,* That the circuit and district courts of the United States, shall respectively have cognizance of all crimes and offences against this act. And all marshals and other officers of the United States are required to execute all precepts and orders of the President of the United States issued in pursuance or by virtue of this act.

SEC. 5. *And be it further enacted*, That it shall be lawful for any alien who may be ordered to be removed from the United States, by virtue of this act, to take with him such part of his goods, chattels, or other property, as he may find convenient; and all property left in the United States by any alien, who may be removed, as aforesaid, shall be, and remain subject to his order and disposal, in the same manner as if this act had not been passed.

SEC. 6. *And be it further enacted*, That this act shall continue and be in force for and during the term of two years from the passing thereof.

APPROVED, June 25, 1798.-*Statutes at Large of the United States*, ed. 1850, Vol. I., pp. 570-572.

The Second Alien Act

July 6, 1798. Statute II., Chap. LXVI.-An Act respecting Alien Enemies

SECTION 1. *Be it enacted by the Senate and House of Representatives of the United States of America in Congress assembled*, That whenever there shall be a declared war between the United States and any foreign nation or government, or any invasion or predatory incursion shall be perpetrated, attempted, or threatened against the territory of the United States, by any foreign nation or government, and the President of the United States shall make public proclamation of the event, all natives, citizens, denizens, or subjects of the hostile nation or government, being males of the age of fourteen years and upwards, who shall be within the United States, and not actually naturalized, shall be liable to be apprehended, restrained, secured and removed, as alien enemies. And the President of the United States shall be, and he is hereby authorized, in any event, as aforesaid, by his proclamation thereof or other public act, to direct the conduct to be observed, on the part of the United States, towards the aliens who shall become liable, as aforesaid; the manner and degree of the restraint to which they shall be subject, and in what cases, and upon what security their residence shall be permitted, and to provide for the removal of those, who, not being permitted to reside within the United States, shall refuse or neglect to depart therefrom; and to establish any other regulations which shall be found necessary in the premises and for the public safety: Provided, that aliens resident within the United States, who shall become liable as enemies, in the manner aforesaid, and who shall not be chargeable with actual hostility, or other crime against the public safety, shall be allowed for the recovery, disposal, and removal of their goods and effects, and for their departure, the full time which is, or shall be stipulated by any treaty, where any shall have been between the United States and the hostile nation or government, of which they shall be natives, citizens, denizens or subjects: and when no such treaty shall have existed, the President of the United States may ascertain and declare such reasonable time as may be consistent with the public safety, and according to the dictates of humanity and national hospitality.

SEC. 2. *And be it further enacted*, That after any proclamation shall be made as aforesaid, it shall be the duty of the several courts of the United States, and of each state, having criminal jurisdiction, and of the several judges and justices of the courts of the United States, and they shall be, and are hereby respectively, authorized upon complaint, against any alien or alien enemies, as aforesaid, who shall be resident and at large within such jurisdiction or district, to the danger of the public peace or safety, and contrary to the tenor or intent of such proclamation, or other regulations which the President of the United States shall and may establish in the premises, to cause such alien or aliens to be duly apprehended and convened before such court, judge or justice; and after a full examination and hearing on such complaint, and sufficient cause therefor appearing, shall and may order such alien or aliens to be removed out of the territory of the United States, or to give such sureties for their good behaviour, or to be otherwise restrained, conformably to the proclamation or regulations which shall or may be established as aforesaid, and may imprison, or otherwise secure such alien or aliens, until the order which shall and may be made, as aforesaid, shall be performed.

SEC. 3. *And be it further enacted*, That it shall be the duty of the marshal of the district in which any alien enemy shall be apprehended, who by condemnment of the United States, or by the order of any court judge or justice, as aforesaid, shall be required to depart, and to be removed, as aforesaid, to provide therefor, and to execute such order, by himself or his deputy, or other discreet person or persons to be employed by him, by causing a removal of such alien out of the territory of the United States; and for such removal the marshal shall have the warrant of the President of the United States, or of the court, judge or justice ordering the same, as the case may be.

APPROVED, July 6, 1798.-*Statutes at Large of the United States,* ed. of 1850, Vol. I., p. 577.

The Sedition Act

July 14, 1798. Chap. LXXIV.-An Act in addition to the act, entitled ''An Act for the punishment of certain crimes against the United States''

SECTION I. *Be it enacted by the Senate and House of Representatives of the United States of America, in Congress assembled,* That if any persons shall unlawfully combine or conspire together, with intent to oppose any measure or measures of the government of the United States, which are or shall be directed by proper authority, or to impede the operation of any law of the United States, or to intimidate or prevent any person holding a place of office in or under the government of the United States, from undertaking, performing or executing, his trust or duty; and if any person or persons, with intent as aforesaid, shall counsel, advise or attempt to procure any insurrection, riot, unlawful assembly, or combination, whether such conspiracy, threatening, counsel, advice, or attempt shall have the proposed effect or not, he or they shall be deemed guilty of a high misdemeanor, and on conviction, before any court of the United States having jurisdiction thereof, shall be punished by a fine not exceeding five thousand dollars, and by imprisonment during a term not less than six months nor exceeding five years; and further, at the discretion of the court may be holden to find sureties for his good behaviour in such sum, and for such time, as the said court may direct.

SEC. 2. *And be it further enacted,* That if any person shall write, print, utter or publish, or shall cause or procure to be written, printed, uttered or published, or shall knowingly and willingly assist or aid in writing, printing, uttering or publishing any false, scandalous and malicious writing or writings against the government of the United States, or the President of the United States, with intent to defame the said government, or either house of the said Congress, or the said President, or to bring them, or either of them, into contempt or disrepute; or to excite against them, or either or any of them, the hatred of the good people of the United States, or to stir up sedition within the United States, or to excite any unlawful combinations therein, for opposing (or resisting any law of the United States,) or any act of the President of the United States, done in pursuance of any such law, or of the powers in him vested by the Constitution of the United States, or to resist, oppose, or defeat any such law or act, or to aid, encourage or abet any hostile designs of any foreign nation against the United States, their people or government, then such person, being thereof convicted before any court of the United States having jurisdiction thereof, shall be punished by a fine not exceeding two thousand dollars, and by imprisonment not exceeding two years.

SEC. 3. *And be it further enacted and declared,* That if any person shall be prosecuted under this act, for the writing or publishing any libel aforesaid, it shall be lawful for the defendant, upon the trial of the cause, to give in evidence in his defence, the truth of the matter contained in the publication charged as a libel. And the jury who shall try the cause, shall have a right to determine the law and the fact, under the direction of the court, as in other cases.

SEC. 4. *And be it further enacted,* That this act shall continue and be in force until the third day of March, one thousand eight hundred and one, and no longer: *Provided,* that the expiration of the act shall not prevent or defeat a prosecution and punishment of any offence against the law, during the time it shall be in force.

APPROVED, July 14, 1798.-*Statutes at Large of the United States,* ed., of 1850, Vol. I., p. 596.

1. *Summarize rights that are given to the President in the First and Second Alien Acts. How are these acts intended to protect the nation?*
2. *Summarize the Sedition Act. What limits are placed on freedom of speech and press by this Act?*

7-10   Questions of Constitutionality and the Roots of Nullification (1798)

The Alien and Sedition Acts of 1798, proposed by Federalists in Congress and sanctioned by President Adams, not only targeted foreigners in the United States, but limited the freedom of speech and the press for all citizens. Republicans saw the four measures as highly partisan (which they were) and chose to challenge their constitutionality. Thomas Jefferson and James Madison, working in union with the state legislatures of Kentucky and Virginia, drafted resolutions denouncing the acts and advanced the theories of nullification and interposition. Neither state, however, actually took steps to nullify the Alien and Sedition Acts, nor did they attempt to interpose their authority against the measures.

Source: The Avalon Project at the Yale Law School
http://www.yale.edu/lawweb/avalon/virres.htm
http://www.yale.edu/lawweb/avalon/kenres.htm

VIRGINIA RESOLUTION: 1798

RESOLVED, That the General Assembly of Virginia, doth unequivocally express a firm resolution to maintain and defend the Constitution of the United States, and the Constitution of this State, against every aggression either foreign or domestic, and that they will support the government of the United States in all measures warranted by the former.

That this assembly most solemnly declares a warm attachment to the Union of the States, to maintain which it pledges all its powers; and that for this end, it is their duty to watch over and oppose every infraction of those principles which constitute the only basis of that Union, because a faithful observance of them, can alone secure its existence and the public happiness.

That this Assembly doth explicitly and peremptorily declare, that it views the powers of the federal government, as resulting from the compact, to which the states are parties; as limited by the plain sense and intention of the instrument constituting the compact; as no further valid that they are authorized by the grants enumerated in that compact; and that in case of a deliberate, palpable, and dangerous exercise of other powers, not granted by the said compact, the states who are parties thereto, have the right, and are in duty bound, to interpose for arresting the progress of the evil, and for maintaining within their respective limits, the authorities, rights and liberties appertaining to them.

That the General Assembly doth also express its deep regret, that a spirit has in sundry instances, been manifested by the federal government, to enlarge its powers by forced constructions of the constitutional charter which defines them; and that implications have appeared of a design to expound certain general phrases (which having been copied from the very limited grant of power, in the former articles of confederation were the less liable to be misconstrued) so as to destroy the meaning and effect, of the particular enumeration which necessarily explains and limits the general phrases; and so as to consolidate the states by degrees, into one sovereignty, the obvious tendency and inevitable consequence of which would be, to transform the present republican system of the United States, into an absolute, or at best a mixed monarchy.

That the General Assembly doth particularly protest against the palpable and alarming infractions of the Constitution, in the two late cases of the "Alien and Sedition Acts" passed at the last session of Congress; the first of which exercises a power no where delegated to the federal government, and which by uniting legislative and judicial powers to those of executive, subverts the general principles of free government; as well as the particular organization, and positive provisions of the federal constitution; and the other of which acts, exercises in like manner, a power not delegated by the constitution, but on the contrary, expressly and positively forbidden by one of the amendments thereto; a power, which more than any other, ought to produce universal alarm, because it is leveled against that right of freely examining public characters and measures, and of free communication among the people thereon, which has ever been justly deemed, the only effectual guardian of every other right.

That this state having by its Convention, which ratified the federal Constitution, expressly declared, that among other essential rights, "the Liberty of Conscience and of the Press cannot be cancelled, abridged, restrained, or modified by any authority of the United States," and from its extreme anxiety to guard these rights from every possible attack of sophistry or ambition, having with other states, recommended an amendment for that purpose, which amendment was, in due time, annexed to the Constitution; it would mark a reproachable inconsistency, and criminal degeneracy, if an indifference were now shown, to the most palpable violation of one of the Rights, thus declared and secured; and to the establishment of a precedent which may be fatal to the other.

That the good people of this commonwealth, having ever felt, and continuing to feel, the most sincere affection for their brethren of the other states; the truest anxiety for establishing and perpetuating the union of all; and the most scrupulous fidelity to that constitution, which is the pledge of mutual friendship, and the instrument of mutual happiness; the General Assembly doth solemnly appeal to the like dispositions of the other states, in confidence that they will concur with this commonwealth in declaring, as it does hereby declare, that the acts aforesaid, are unconstitutional; and that the necessary and proper measures will be taken by each, for co-operating with this state, in maintaining the Authorities, Rights, and Liberties, referred to the States respectively, or to the people.

That the Governor be desired, to transmit a copy of the foregoing Resolutions to the executive authority of each of the other states, with a request that the same may be communicated to the Legislature thereof; and that a copy be furnished to each of the Senators and Representatives representing this state in the Congress of the United States.

Agreed to by the Senate, December 24, 1798.

KENTUCKY RESOLUTION: 1799

Resolutions in General Assembly

THE representatives of the good people of this commonwealth in general assembly convened, having maturely considered the answers of sundry states in the Union, to their resolutions passed at the last session, respecting certain unconstitutional laws of Congress, commonly called the alien and sedition laws, would be faithless indeed to themselves, and to those they represent, were they silently to acquiesce in principles and doctrines attempted to be maintained in all those answers, that of Virginia only excepted. To again enter the field of argument, and attempt more fully or forcibly to expose the unconstitutionality of those obnoxious laws, would, it is apprehended be as unnecessary as unavailing.

We cannot however but lament, that in the discussion of those interesting subjects, by sundry of the legislatures of our sister states, unfounded suggestions, and uncandid insinuations, derogatory of the true character and principles of the good people of this commonwealth, have been substituted in place of fair reasoning and sound argument. Our opinions of those alarming measures of the general government, together with our reasons for those opinions, were detailed with decency and with temper, and submitted to the discussion and judgment of our fellow citizens throughout the Union. Whether the decency and temper have been observed in the answers of most of those states who have denied or attempted to obviate the great truths contained in those resolutions, we have now only to submit to a candid world. Faithful to the true principles of the federal union, unconscious of any designs to disturb the harmony of that Union, and anxious only to escape the fangs of despotism, the good people of this commonwealth are regardless of censure or calumniation.

Least however the silence of this commonwealth should be construed into an acquiescence in the doctrines and principles advanced and attempted to be maintained by the said answers, or least those of our fellow citizens throughout the Union, who so widely differ from us on those important subjects, should be deluded by the expectation, that we shall be deterred from what we conceive our duty; or shrink from the principles contained in those resolutions: therefore.

RESOLVED, That this commonwealth considers the federal union, upon the terms and for the purposes specified in the late compact, as conducive to the liberty and happiness of the several states: That it does now unequivocally declare its attachment to the Union, and to that compact, agreeable to its obvious and real intention, and will be among the last to seek its dissolution: That if those who administer the general government be permitted to transgress the limits fixed by that compact, by a total disregard to the special delegations of power therein contained, annihilation of the state governments, and the erection upon their ruins, of a general consolidated government, will be the inevitable consequence: That the principle and construction contended for by sundry of the state legislatures, that the general government is the exclusive judge of the extent of the powers delegated to it, stop nothing short of despotism; since the discretion of those who administer the government, and not the constitution, would be the measure of their powers: That the several states who formed that instrument, being sovereign and independent, have the unquestionable right to judge of its infraction; and that a nullification, by those sovereignties, of all unauthorized acts done under colour of that instrument, is the rightful remedy: That this commonwealth does upon the most deliberate reconsideration declare, that the said alien and sedition laws, are in their opinion, palpable violations of the said constitution; and however cheerfully it may be disposed to surrender its opinion to a majority of its sister states in matters of ordinary or doubtful policy; yet, in momentous regulations like the present, which so vitally wound the best rights of the citizen, it would consider a silent acquiescence as highly criminal: That although this commonwealth as a party to the federal compact; will bow to the laws of the Union, yet it does at the same time declare, that it will not now, nor ever hereafter, cease to oppose in a constitutional manner, every attempt from what quarter so ever offered, to violate that compact:

AND FINALLY, in order that no pretexts or arguments may be drawn from a supposed acquiescence on the part of this commonwealth in the constitutionality of those laws, and be thereby used as precedents for similar future violations of federal compact; this commonwealth does now enter against them, its SOLEMN PROTEST.

Drafted February 22, 1799.

1. *What was at the heart of the Republican arguments in the Kentucky and Virginia Resolutions against the Alien and Sedition Acts? Looking ahead, what future issues in American history might resurrect a version of these arguments?*
2. *The Kentucky Resolution of 1799 included here is actually the second of two documents issued by the Kentucky legislature. This second version includes responses to objections voiced by northern states to the earlier design. Why do you think northern states might be particularly troubled by these resolutions?*

7-11 Reverend Peter Cartwright on Cane Ridge and the "New Lights" (1801)

In 1801, sixteen-year-old Peter Cartwright witnessed the religious revivals at Cane Ridge in Logan County, Kentucky. Moved to the point of conversion, Cartwright joined the Methodist Episcopal Church where he became a deacon in 1806. Ordained an elder in 1808, Cartwright traveled Methodist circuits through Kentucky and Indiana until 1823, when he moved to Illinois. For most of the next fifty years he was a presiding elder of the Methodist Episcopal Church. A participant in Illinois politics, Cartwright served two terms in the state legislature, but was defeated in a bid for Congress in 1846 by Abraham Lincoln. In 1856 he published his autobiography from which this excerpt was taken.

Source: W. P. Strickland, ed., *Autobiography of Peter Cartwright, The Backwoods Preacher*, (New York: Carlton & Porter, 1856), 30–33.

http://www.mun.ca/rels/restmov/texts/rmeyes/cart.html

Somewhere between 1800 and 1801, in the upper part of Kentucky, at a memorable place called "Cane Ridge," there was appointed a sacramental meeting by some of the Presbyterian ministers, at which meeting, seemingly unexpected by ministers or people, the mighty power of God was displayed in a very extraordinary manner; many were moved to tears, and bitter and loud crying for mercy. The meeting was protracted for weeks. Ministers of almost all denominations flocked in from far and near. The meeting was kept up by night and day. Thousands heard of the mighty work, and came on foot, on horseback, in carriages and wagons. It was supposed that there were in attendance at times during the meeting from twelve to twenty-five thousand people. Hundreds fell prostrate under the mighty power of God, as men slain in battle. Stands were erected in the woods from which preachers of different Churches proclaimed repentance toward God and faith in our Lord Jesus Christ, and it was supposed, by eye and ear witnesses, that between one and two thousand souls were happily and powerfully converted to God during the meeting. It was not unusual for one, two, three, and four to seven preachers to be addressing the listening thousands at the same time from the different stands erected for the purpose. The heavenly fire spread in almost every direction. It was said, by truthful witnesses, that at times more than one thousand persons broke into loud shouting all at once, and that the shouts could be heard for miles around. From this camp-meeting, for so it ought to be called, the news spread through all the Churches, and through all the land, and it excited great wonder and surprise; but it kindled a religious flame that spread all over Kentucky and through many other states. And I may here be permitted to say, that this was the first camp-meeting ever held in the United States, and here our camp-meetings took their rise.

As Presbyterian, Methodist, and Baptist ministers all united in the blessed work at this meeting, when they returned home to their different congregations, and carried the news of this mighty work, the revival spread rapidly throughout the land; but many of the ministers and members of the synod of Kentucky thought it all disorder, and tried to stop the work. They called their preachers who were engaged in the revival to account, and censured and silenced them. These ministers then rose up and unitedly renounced the jurisdiction of the Presbyterian Church, organized a Church of their own, and dubbed it with the name of Christian. Here was the origin of what was called the New Lights. They renounced the Westminster Confession of Faith, and all Church discipline, and professed to take the New Testament for their Church discipline. They established no standard of doctrine; every one was to take the New Testament, read it, and abide his own construction of it. Marshall, M'Namar, Dunlevy, Stone, Huston, and others, were the chief leaders in this trash trap. Soon a diversity of opinion sprang up, and they got into a Babel confusion. Some preached Arian, some Socinian, and some Universalist doctrines; so that in a few years you could not tell what was harped or what was danced. They adopted the mode of immersion, the water-god of all exclusive errorists; and directly there was a mighty controversy about the way to heaven, whether it was by water or by dry land.

In the meantime a remnant of preachers that broke off from the Methodist Episcopal Church in 1792, headed by James O'Kelly, who had formed a party because he could not be a bishop in said Church, which party he called the Republican Methodist Church, came out to Kentucky and formed a union with these New Lights. Then the Methodist Episcopal Church had war, and rumors of war, almost on every side. The dreadful diversity of opinion among these New Lights, their want of any standard of doctrines, or regular Church discipline, made them an easy prey to prowling wolves of any description.

Soon the Shaker priests came along, and off went M'Namar, Dunlevy, and Huston, into that foolish error. Marshall and others retraced their steps. B. W. Stone stuck to his New Lightism, and fought many bloodless battles, till he grew old and feeble, and the mighty Alexander Campbell, the great, arose and poured such floods of regenerating water about the old man's cranium, that he formed a union with this giant errorist, and finally died, not much lamented out of the circle of a few friends. And this is the way with all the New Lights, in the government, morals, and discipline of the Church. This Christian, or New Light Church, is a feeble and scattered people, though there are some good Christians among them. I suppose since the day of Pentecost, there was hardly ever a greater revival of religion than at Cane Ridge; and if there had been steady, Christian ministers, settled in Gospel doctrine and Church discipline, thousands might have been saved to the Church that wandered off in the mazes of vain, speculative divinity, and finally made shipwreck of the faith, fell back, turned infidel, and lost their religion and their souls forever. But evidently a new impetus was given to the work of God, and many, very many, will have cause to bless God forever for this revival of religion throughout the length and breadth of our Zion.

1. As depicted by Peter Cartwright, what were the characteristics of the Cane Ridge camp meetings?
2. What characteristics of life in the backcountry might have contributed to the success of evangelical Protestantism?

7-12 *Marbury v. Madison* (1803)

The Marbury versus Madison case revolved around William Marbury, who had been appointed a justice of the peace by President John Adams two days before Adams ended his term. The new President, Thomas Jefferson, denied Marbury the position by directing the Secretary of State James Madison not to deliver the commission. Marbury filed a lawsuit, asking the Supreme Court to issue a writ of mandamus, forcing Madison to deliver the commission. Chief Justice John Marshall ruled that the court was not authorized to issue writs of mandamus and more importantly, in the following excerpt from the decision, made it clear that the Supreme Court did, however, have the power to declare legislation unconstitutional, thereby maintaining the balance of power in government. This is one of the landmark decisions of the Supreme Court, giving them more authority than they had previously held.

[CHIEF JUSTICE MARSHALL DELIVERED THE OPINION OF THE COURT.]

In the order in which the Court has viewed this subject, the following questions have been considered and decided: 1st. Has the applicant a right to the commission he demands? 2d. If he has a right, and that right has been violated, do the laws of this country afford him a remedy? 3d. If they do afford him a remedy, is it a mandamus issuing from this court? . . .

It is . . . the opinion of the Court: 1st. That by signing the commission of Mr. Marbury, the President of the United States appointed him a justice of the peace for the county of Washington, in the District of Columbia; and that the seal of the United States, affixed thereto by the secretary of state, is conclusive testimony of the verity of the signature, and of the completion of the appointment; and that the appointment conferred on him a legal right to the office for the space of five years. 2d. That, having this legal title to the office, he has a consequent right to the commission; a refusal to deliver which is a plain violation of that right, for which the laws of his country afford him a remedy. 3d. It remains to be inquired whether he is entitled to the remedy for which he applies? . . .

This . . . is a plain case for a mandamus, either to deliver the commission, or a copy of it from the record; and it only remains to be inquired, whether it can issue from this court?

The act to establish the judicial courts of the United States authorizes the Supreme Court, "to issue writs of mandamus, in cases warranted by the principles and usages of law, to any courts appointed or persons holding office, under the authority of the United States." The secretary of state, being a person holding an office under the authority of the United States, is precisely within the letter of this description; and if this court is not authorized to issue a writ of mandamus to such an officer, it must be because the law is unconstitutional . . .

The Constitution vests the whole judicial power of the United States in one Supreme Court, and such inferior courts as Congress shall, from time to time, ordain and establish. . . .

In the distribution of this power, it is declared that "the Supreme Court shall have original jurisdiction in all cases affecting ambassadors, other public ministers and consuls, and those in which a state shall be a party. In all other cases, the Supreme Court shall have appellate jurisdiction." . . .

If it had been intended to leave it in the discretion of the legislature to apportion the judicial power between the supreme and inferior courts according to the will of that body, it would certainly have been useless to have proceeded further than to have defined the judicial power, and the tribunals in which it should be vested. The subsequent part of the section is mere surplusage, is entirely without meaning, . . .

It cannot be presumed that any clause in the Constitution is intended to be without effect . . .

To enable this court, then, to issue a mandamus, it must be shown to be an exercise of appellate jurisdiction . . .

The authority, therefore, given to the Supreme Court, by the Act establishing the judicial courts of the United States, to issue writs of mandamus to public officers, appears not to be warranted by the Constitution . . .

1. Summarize the reasoning and legal decision regarding whether or not withholding Marbury's commission was a violation of his right to appointment.
2. Summarize the relationship that exists among the Constitution, the legislative branch of government, and the Supreme Court as it is discussed in this document? What is the role of the Supreme court in relation to the Constitution?

PART EIGHT
JEFFERSON AND THE REPUBLIC

8-1 "Memoirs of a Monticello Slave, as Dictated to Charles Campbell by Isaac" (1847)

A man of many and diverse interests and accomplishments, Thomas Jefferson is one of the greatest of American figures. An enduring stain on his reputation, however, is the fact that he kept slaves until the end of his life. This document demonstrates his qualities but the very fact that it is written by a man who was his slave points to his shortcomings.

Old Master was never seen to come out before breakfast-about 8 o'clock. If it was warm weather he wouldn't ride out till evening: studied upstairs till bell ring for dinner. When writing he had a copyin' machine. While he was a-writin' he wouldn't suffer nobody to come in his room. Had a dumb-waiter; when he wanted anything he had nothin' to do but turn a crank and the dumb-waiter would bring him water or fruit on a plate or anything he wanted. Old Master had abundance of books; sometimes would have twenty of 'em down on the floor at once-read fust one, then tother. Isaac has often wondered how Old Master came to have such a mighty head; read so many of them books; and when they go to him to ax him anything, he go right straight to the book and tell you all about it. He talked French and Italian. Madzay talked with him; his place was called Colle. General Redhazel (Riedesel) stayed there. He (Mazzei) lived at Monticello with Old Master some time. Didiot, a Frenchman, married his daughter Peggy, a heavy chunky looking woman-mighty handsome. She had a daughter Frances and a son Francis; called the daughter Franky. Mazzei brought to Monticello Antonine, Jovanini, Francis, Modena, and Belligrini, all gardeners. My Old Master's garden was monstrous large: two rows of palings, all 'round ten feet high.

Mr. Jefferson had a clock in his kitchen at Monticello; never went into the kitchen except to wind up the clock. He never would have less than eight covers at dinner if nobody at table but himself. Had from eight to thirty-two covers for dinner. Plenty of wine, best old Antigua rum and cider; very fond of wine and water. Isaac never heard of his being disguised in drink. He kept three fiddles; played in the arternoons and sometimes arter supper. This was in his early time. When he begin to git so old, he didn't play. Kept a spinnet made mostly in shape of a harpsichord; his daughter played on it. Mr. Fauble, a Frenchman that lived at Mr. Walker's, a music man, used to come to Monticello and tune it. There was a *fortepiano* and a guitar there. Never seed anybody play on them but the French people. Isaac never could git acquainted with them; could hardly larn their names. Mr. Jefferson always singing when ridin' or walkin'; hardly see him anywhar outdoors but what he was a-singin'. Had a fine clear voice, sung minnits (minuets) and sich; fiddled in the parlor. Old Master very kind to servants.

The fust year Mr. Jefferson was elected President, he took Isaac on to Philadelphia. He was then about fifteen years old; traveled on horseback in company with a Frenchman named Joseph Rattiff and Jim Hemings, a body servant. Fust day's journey they went from Monticello to old Nat Gordon's, on the Fredericksburg road, next day to Fredericksburg, then to Georgetown, crossed the Potomac there, and so to Philadelphia-eight days a-goin'. Had two ponies and Mr. Jefferson's tother riding horse Odin. Mr. Jefferson went in the phaeton. Bob Hemings drove; changed horses on the road. When they got to Philadelphia, Isaac stayed three days at Mr. Jefferson's house. Then he was bound prentice to one Bringhouse, a tinner; he lived in the direction of the Waterworks. Isaac remembers seeing the image of a woman thar holding a goose in her hand-the water spouting out of the goose's mouth. This was the head of Market Street. Bringhouse was a short, mighty small, neat-made; treated Isaac very well. Went thar to larn the tinner's trade. Fust week larnt to cut out and sodder; make little pepper boxes and graters and sich, out of scraps of tin, so as not to waste any till he had larnt. Then to making cups. Every Sunday Isaac would go to the President's house-large brick house, many windows; same house Ginral Washington lived in before when he was President. Old Master used to talk to me mighty free and ax me, "How you come on Isaac, larning de tin business?" As soon as he could make cups pretty well, he carred three or four to show him. Isaac made four dozen pint cups a day and larnt to tin copper and sheets (sheet iron)-make 'em tin. He lived four years with Old Bringhouse. One time Mr. Jefferson sent to Bringhouse to tin his copper kittles and pans for kitchen use; Bringhouse sent Isaac and another prentice thar-a white boy named Charles; can't think of his other name. Isaac was the only black boy in Bringhouse's shop. When Isaac carred the cups to his Old Master to show him, he was mightily pleased. Said, "Isaac you are larnin mighty fast; I bleeve I must send you back to Vaginny to car on the tin business. You is growin too big; no use for you to stay here no longer."

1. Analyze Isaac's account of the "Old Master's" lifestyle. How would you characterize his leisure? What seems to be his demeanor toward his slaves?

2. What does this first hand account reveal about different aspects of the life of a slave?

8-2   Thomas Jefferson, "First Inaugural Address" (1801)

Years after his presidency, Thomas Jefferson would call the election of 1800 "as real a revolution in the principles of our government as that of 1776 was in its form." His view of an agrarian republic was in sharp contrast to what he saw as the Federalists trend towards increasing national power and the Alien and Sedition Acts were, he thought, threatening civil liberties. His First Inaugural Address advanced many of the notions of what would be called Jefferson Democracy.

Friends and Fellow Citizens:

Called upon to undertake the duties of the first executive office of our country, I avail myself of the presence of that portion of my fellow citizens which is here assembled to express my grateful thanks for the favor with which they have been pleased to look toward me, to declare a sincere consciousness that the task is above my talents, and that I approach it with those anxious and awful presentiments which the greatness of the charge and the weakness of my powers so justly inspire. A rising nation, spread over a wide and fruitful land, traversing all the seas with the rich productions of their industry, engaged in commerce with nations who feel power and forget right, advancing rapidly to destinies beyond the reach of mortal eye-when I contemplate these transcendent objects and see the honor, the happiness, and the hopes of this beloved country committed to the issue and the auspices of this day, I shrink from the contemplation and humble myself before the magnitude of the undertaking. Utterly indeed should I despair did not the presence of many whom I here see remind me that in the other high authorities provided by our Constitution I shall find resources of wisdom, of virtue, and of zeal on which to rely under all difficulties. To you then, gentlemen, who are charged with the sovereign functions of legislation, and to those associated with you, I look with encouragement for that guidance and support which may enable us to steer with safety the vessel in which we are all embarked amidst the conflicting elements of a troubled world.

During the contest of opinion through which we have passed, the animation of discussions and of exertions has sometimes worn an aspect which might impose on strangers unused to think freely and to speak and to write what they think. But this being now decided by the voice of the nation, enounced according to the rules of the Constitution, all will of course arrange themselves under the will of the law and unite in common efforts for the common good. All, too, will bear in mind this sacred principle that, though the will of the majority is in all cases to prevail, that will, to be rightful, must be reasonable; that the minority possess their equal rights, which equal laws must protect and to violate which would be oppression. Let us then, fellow citizens, unite with one heart and one mind; let us restore to social intercourse that harmony and affection without which liberty, and even life itself, are but dreary things. And let us reflect that, having banished from our land that religious intolerance under which mankind so long bled and suffered, we have yet gained little if we countenance a political intolerance as despotic, as wicked, and capable of as bitter and bloody persecutions. During the throes and convulsions of the ancient world, during the agonizing spasms of infuriated man, seeking through blood and slaughter his long-lost liberty, it was not wonderful that the agitation of the billows should reach even this distant and peaceful shore, that this should be more felt and feared by some and less by others, and should divide opinions as to measures of safety.

But every difference of opinion is not a difference of principle. We have called by different names brethren of the same principle. We are all republicans; we are all federalists. If there be any among us who would wish to dissolve this Union or to change its republican form, let them stand undisturbed as monuments of the safety with which error of opinion may be tolerated, where reason is left free to combat it. I know, indeed, that some honest men fear that a republican government cannot be strong; that this government is not strong enough. But would the honest patriot, in the full tide of successful experiment, abandon a government which has so far kept us free and firm, on the theoretic and visionary fear that this government, the world's best hope, may by possibility want energy to preserve itself? I trust not. I believe this, on the contrary, the strongest government on earth. I believe it the only one where every man, at the call of the law, would fly to the standard of the law and would meet invasions of the public order as his own personal concern. Sometimes it is said that man cannot be trusted with the government of himself. Can he then be trusted with the government of others? Or have we found angels, in the form of kings, to govern him? Let history answer this question.

Let us then, with courage and confidence, pursue our own federal and republican principles, our attachment to Union and representative government. Kindly separated by nature and a wide ocean from the exterminating havoc of one quarter of the globe; too high-minded to endure the degradations of the others; possessing a chosen country, with room enough for our descendants to the thousandth and thousandth generation; entertaining a due sense of our equal right to the use of our own faculties, to the acquisitions of our own industry, to honor and confidence from our fellow citizens, resulting not from birth but from our actions and their sense of them; enlightened by a benign religion, professed indeed and practiced in various forms, yet all of them including honesty, truth, temperance, gratitude, and the love of man; acknowledging and adoring an overruling Providence which, by all its dispensations, proves that It delights in the happiness of man here and his greater happiness hereafter; with all these blessings, what more is necessary to make us a happy and a prosperous people? Still one thing more, fellow citizens-a wise and frugal government which shall restrain men from injuring one another, shall leave them otherwise free to regulate their own pursuits of industry and improvement, and shall not take from the mouth of labor the bread it has earned. This is the sum of good government, and this is necessary to close the circle of our felicities.

About to enter, fellow citizens, on the exercise of duties which comprehend everything dear and valuable to you, it is proper you should understand what I deem the essential principles of our government and, consequently, those which ought to shape its administration. I will compress them within the narrowest compass they will bear, stating the general principle but not all its limitations: Equal and exact justice to all men, of whatever state or persuasion, religious or political; peace, commerce, and honest friendship with all nations, entangling alliances with none; the support of the State governments in all their rights, as the most competent administrations for our domestic concerns and the surest bulwarks against anti-republican tendencies; the preservation of the general government in its whole constitutional vigor, as the sheet anchor of our peace at home and safety abroad; a jealous care of the right of election by the people, a mild and safe corrective of abuses which are lopped by the sword of revolution where peaceable remedies are unprovided; absolute acquiescence in the decisions of the majority, the vital principle of republics from which there is no appeal but to force, the vital principle and immediate parent of despotism; a well-disciplined militia, our best reliance in peace and for the first moments of war till regulars may relieve them; the supremacy of the civil over the military authority; economy in the public expense, that labor may be lightly burdened; the honest payment of our debts and sacred preservation of the public faith; encouragement of agriculture, and of commerce as its handmaid; the diffusion of information, and arraignment of all abuses at the bar of the public person, under the protection of the habeas corpus; and trial by juries, impartially selected. These principles form the bright constellation which has gone before us and guided our steps through an age of revolution and reformation. The wisdom of our sages and blood of our heroes have been devoted to their attainment; they should be the creed of our political faith, the text of civic instruction, the touchstone by which to try the services of those we trust; and should we wander from them in moments of error or of alarm, let us hasten to retrace our steps and to regain the road which alone leads to peace, liberty, and safety.

I repair then, fellow citizens, to the post you have assigned me. With experience enough in subordinate offices to have seen the difficulties of this, the greatest of all, I have learned to expect that it will rarely fall to the lot of imperfect man to retire from this station with the reputation and the favor which bring him into it. Without pretensions to that high confidence you reposed in our first and great revolutionary character, whose pre-eminent services had entitled him to the first place in his country's love and destined for him the fairest page in the volume of faithful history, I ask so much confidence only as may give firmness and effect to the legal administration of your affairs. I shall often be thought wrong by those whose positions will not command a view of the whole ground. I ask your indulgence for my own errors, which will never be intentional, and your support against the errors of others who may condemn what they would not if seen in all its parts. The approbation implied by your suffrage is a great consolation to me for the past, and my future solicitude will be to retain the good opinion of those who have bestowed it in advance, to conciliate that of others by doing them all the good in my power, and to be instrumental to the happiness and freedom of all.

Relying then on the patronage of your good will, I advance with obedience to the work, ready to retire from it whenever you become sensible how much better choice it is in your power to make. And may that Infinite Power which rules the destinies of the universe lead our councils to what is best and give them a favorable issue for your peace and prosperity.

1. What encouragement does Jefferson offer regarding unification between people and politicians of divided opinions in his speech?
2. Identify and explain what Jefferson defines as the "sum of good government" and "the essential principles of our government."

8-3 Margaret Bayard Smith Meets Thomas Jefferson (1801)

Margaret Bayard Smith was a now forgotten novelist who married a Jeffersonian newspaperman. Her letters written over the course of 40 years provide a rare personal insight into government and various government figures. In these documents, Smith provides a description of the appearance and virtues of Jefferson and comments on the peaceful transfer of power from the Federalists to the Jeffersonian Republicans.

Margaret Bayard Smith to Miss Susan B. Smith (1801)

Let me write to you my dear Susan, e're that glow of enthusiasm has fled, which now animates my feelings; let me congratulate not only you, but all my fellow citizens, on an event which will have so auspicious an influence on their political welfare. I have this morning witnessed one of the most interesting scenes, a free people can ever witness. The changes of administration, which in every government and in every age have most generally been epochs of confusion, villainy and bloodshed, in this our happy country take place without any species of distraction, or disorder. This day, has one of the most amiable and worthy men taken that seat to which he was called by the voice of his country. I cannot describe the agitation I felt, while I looked around on the various multitude and while I listened to an address, containing principles the most correct, sentiments the most liberal, and wishes the most benevolent, conveyed in the most appropriate and elegant language and in a manner mild as it was firm. If doubts of the integrity and talents of Mr. Jefferson ever existed in the minds of any one, methinks this address must forever eradicate them. The Senate chamber was so crowded that I believe not another creature could enter. On one side of the house the Senate sat, the other was resigned by the representatives to the ladies. The roof is arched, the room half circle, every inch of ground was occupied. It has been conjectured by several gentlemen whom I've asked, that there was near a thousand persons within the walls. The speech was delivered in so low a tone that few heard it. Mr. Jefferson had given your Brother a copy early in the morning, so that on coming out of the house, the paper was distributed immediately. Since then there has been a constant succession of persons coming for the papers.

Margaret Bayard Smith, "Reminiscences" (1800)

"And is this," said I, after my first interview with Mr. Jefferson, "the violent democrat, the vulgar demagogue, the bold atheist and profligate man I have so often heard denounced by the federalists? Can this man so meek and mild, yet dignified in his manners, with a voice so soft and low, with a countenance so benignant and intelligent, can he be that daring leader of a fraction, that disturber of the peace, that enemy of all rank and order?" Mr. Smith, indeed, (himself a democrat) had given me a very different description of this celebrated individual; but his favourable opinion I attributed in a great measure to his political feelings, which led him zealously to support and exalt the party to which he belonged, especially its popular and almost idolized leader. Thus the virulence of party-spirit was somewhat neutralized, nay, I even entertained towards him the most kindly dispositions, knowing him to be not only politically but personally friendly to my husband; yet I did believe that he was an ambitious and violent demagogue, coarse and vulgar in his manners, awkward and rude in his appearance, for such had the public journals and private conversations of the federal party represented him to be.

In December, 1800, a few days after Congress had for the first time met in our new Metropolis, I was one morning sitting alone in the parlour, when the servant opened the door and showed in a gentleman who wished to see my husband. The usual frankness and care with which I met strangers, were somewhat checked by the dignified and reserved air of the present visitor; but the chilled feeling was only momentary, for after taking the chair I offered him in a free and easy manner, and carelessly throwing his arm on the table near which he sat, he turned towards me a countenance beaming with an expression of benevolence and with a manner and voice almost femininely soft and gentle, entered into conversation on the commonplace topics of the day, from which, before I was conscious of it, he had drawn me into observations of a more personal and interesting nature. I know not how it was, but there was something in his manner, his countenance and voice that at once unlocked my heart, and in answer to his casual enquiries concerning our situation in our new home, as he called it, I found myself frankly telling him what I liked or disliked in our present circumstances and abode. I knew now who he was, but the interest with which he listened to my artless details, induced the idea he was some intimate acquaintance or friend of Mr. Smith's and put me perfectly at my ease; in truth so kind and conciliating were his looks and manners that I forgot he was not a friend of my own, until on the opening of the door, Mr. Smith entered and introduced the stranger to me as Mr. Jefferson.

I felt my cheeks burn and my heart throb, and not a word more could I speak while he remained. Nay, such was my embarrassment I could scarcely listen to the conversation carried on between him and my husband. For several years he had been to me an object of peculiar interest. In fact my destiny, for on his success in the pending presidential election, or rather the success of the democratic party, (their interests were identical) my condition in life, my union with the man I loved, depended. In addition to this personal interest, I had long participated in my husband's political sentiments and anxieties, and looked upon Mr. Jefferson as the corner stone on which the edifice of republican liberty was to rest, looked upon him as the champion of human rights, the reformer of abuses, the head of the republican party, which must rise or fall with him, and on the triumph of the republican party I devoutly believed the security and welfare of my country depended. Notwithstanding those exalted views of Mr. Jefferson as a political character; and ardently eager as I was for his success, I retained my previously conceived ideas of the coarseness and vulgarity of his appearance and manners and was therefore equally awed and surprised, on discovering the stranger whose deportment was so dignified and gentlemanly, whose language was so refined, whose voice was so gentle, whose countenance was so benignant, to be no other than Thomas Jefferson. How instantaneously were all these preconceived prejudices dissipated, and in proportion to their strength, was the reaction that took place in my opinions and sentiments. I felt that I had been the victim of prejudice, that I had been unjust. The revolution of feeling was complete and from that moment my heart warmed to him with the most affectionate interest and I implicitly believed all that his friends and my husband believed and which the after experience of many years confirmed. Yes, not only was he great, but a truly good man!

1. *Summarize Margaret Bayard Smith's thoughts and feelings regarding the inauguration of Jefferson.*
2. *Describe the author's opinions of Jefferson after meeting him in contrast to her pre-conceived notions regarding his character. What seem to be Jefferson's dominant characteristics according to Margaret Bayard Smith?*

8-4 Constitutionality of the Louisiana Purchase (1803)

The Louisiana Purchase doubled the size of the nation. The 828,000 square miles were purchased from France for fifteen million dollars or about four cents an acre. The circumstances of the purchase were sudden and the Federalists argued that the Constitution made no provision for the purchase of land. Jefferson, who was usually a strict constructionist, argued for a broad view of the Constitution in this case. These documents discuss the purchase and Jefferson's justification.

Thomas Jefferson to John C. Breckinridge

Monticello, Aug. 12, 1803

DEAR SIR,-The enclosed letter, tho' directed to you, was intended to me also, and was left open with a request, that when perused, I would forward it to you. It gives me occasion to write a word to you on the subject of Louisiana, which being a new one, an interchange of sentiments may produce correct ideas before we are to act on them.

Our information as to the country is very incompleat; we have taken measures to obtain it in full as to the settled part, which I hope to receive in time for Congress. The boundaries, which I deem not admitting question, are the high lands on the western side of the Mississippi enclosing all it's waters, the Missouri of course, and terminating in the line drawn from the northwestern point of the Lake of the Woods to the nearest source of the Missipi, as lately settled between Gr Britain and the U S. We have some claims to extend on the sea coast Westwardly to the Rio Norte or Bravo, and better, to go Eastwardly to the Rio Perdido, between Mobile & Pensacola, the antient boundary of Louisiana. These claims will be a subject of negociation with Spain, and if, as soon as she is at war, we push them strongly with one hand, holding out a price in the other, we shall certainly obtain the Floridas, and all in good time. In the meanwhile, without waiting for permission, we shall enter into the exercise of the natural right we have always insisted on with Spain, to wit, that of a nation holding the upper part of streams, having a right of innocent passage thro' them to the ocean. We shall prepare her to see us practise on this, & she will not oppose it by force.

Objections are raising to the Eastward against the vast extent of our boundaries, and propositions are made to exchange Louisiana, or a part of it, for the Floridas. But, as I have said, we shall get the Floridas without, and I would not give one inch of the waters of the Mississippi to any nation, because I see in a light very important to our peace the exclusive right to it's navigation, & the admission of no nation into it, but as into the Potomak or Delaware, with our consent & under our police. These federalists see in this acquisition the formation of a new confederacy, embracing all the waters of the Missipi, on both sides of it, and a separation of it's Eastern waters from us. These combinations depend on so many circumstances which we cannot foresee, that I place little reliance on them. We have seldom seen neighborhood produce affection among nations. The reverse is almost the universal truth. Besides, if it should become the great interest of those nations to separate from this, if their happiness should depend on it so strongly as to induce them to go through that convulsion, why should the Atlantic States dread it? But especially why should we, their present inhabitants, take side in such a question? When I view the Atlantic States, procuring for those on the Eastern waters of the Missipi friendly instead of hostile neighbors of it's Western waters, I do not view it as an Englishman would the procuring future blessing for the French nation, with whom he has no relations of blood or affection. The future inhabitants of the Atlantic & Missipi States will be our sons. We leave them in distinct but bordering establishments. We think we see their happiness in their union, & we wish it. Events may prove it otherwise; and if they see their interest in separation, why should we take side with our Atlantic rather than our Missipi descendants? It is the elder and the younger son differing. God bless them both, & keep them in union, if it be for their good, but separate them, if it be better. The inhabited part of Louisiana, from Point Coupèe to the sea, will of course be immediately a territorial government, and soon a State. But above that, the best use we can make of the country for some time, will be to give establishments in it to the Indians on the East side of the Missipi, in exchange for their present country, and open land offices in the last, & thus make this acquisition the means of filling up the Eastern side, instead of drawing off it's population. When we shall be full on this side, we may lay off a range of States on the Western bank from the head to the mouth, & so, range after range, advancing compactly as we multiply.

This treaty must of course be laid before both Houses, because both have important functions to exercise respecting it. They, I presume, will see their duty to their country in ratifying & paying for it, so as to secure a good which would otherwise probably be never again in their power. But I suppose they must then appeal to *the nation* for an additional article to the Constitution, approving & confirming an act which the nation had not previously authorized. The constitution has made no provision for our holding foreign territory, still less for incorporating foreign nations into our Union. The Executive in seizing the fugitive occurrence which so much advances the good of their country, have done an act beyond the Constitution. The Legislature in casting behind them metaphysical subtleties, and risking themselves like faithful servants, must ratify & pay for it, and throw themselves on their country for doing for them unauthorized what we know they would have done for themselves had they been in a situation to do it. It is the case of a guardian, investing the money of his ward in purchasing an important adjacent territory; & saying to him when of age, I did this for your good; I pretend to no right to bind you: you may disavow me, and I must get out of the scrape as I can: I thought it my duty to risk myself for you. But we shall not be disavowed by the nation, and their act of indemnity will confirm & not weaken the Constitution, by more strongly marking out its lines.

We have nothing later from Europe than the public papers give. I hope yourself and all the Western members will make a sacred point of being at the first day of the meeting of Congress; for *vestra res agitur*.

Accept my affectionate salutations & assurances of esteem & respect.

Thomas Jefferson to Wilson Cary Nicholas

Monticello, Sep. 7, 1803

DEAR SIR,-Your favor of the 3d was delivered me at court; but we were much disappointed at not seeing you here, Mr. Madison & the Gov. being here at the time. I enclose you a letter from Monroe on the subject of the late treaty. You will observe a hint in it, to do without delay what we are bound to do. There is reason, in the opinion of our ministers, to believe, that if the thing were to do over again, it could not be obtained, & that if we give the least opening, they will declare the treaty void. A warning amounting to that has been given to them, & an unusual kind of letter written by their minister to our Secretary of State, direct. Whatever Congress shall think it necessary to do, should be done with as little debate as possible, & particularly so far as respects the constitutional difficulty. I am aware of the force of the observations you make on the power given by the Constn to Congress, to admit new States into the Union, without restraining the subject to the territory then constituting the U S. But when I consider that the limits of the U S are precisely fixed by the treaty of 1783, that the Constitution expressly declares itself to be made for the U S, I cannot help believing the intention was to permit Congress to admit into the Union new States, which should be formed out of the territory for which, & under whose authority alone, they were then acting. I do not believe it was meant that they might receive England, Ireland, Holland, &c. into it, which would be the case on your construction. When an instrument admits two constructions, the one safe, the other dangerous, the one precise, the other indefinite, I prefer that which is safe & precise. I had rather ask an enlargement of power from the nation, where it is found necessary, than to assume it by a construction which would make our powers boundless. Our peculiar security is in possession of a written Constitution. Let us not make it a blank paper by construction. I say the same as to the opinion of those who consider the grant of the treaty making power as boundless. If it is, then we have no Constitution. If it has bounds, they can be no others than the definitions of the power which that instrument gives. It specifies & delineates the operations permitted to the federal government, and gives all the powers necessary to carry these into execution. Whatever of these enumerated objects is proper for a law, Congress may make the law; whatever is proper to be executed by way of a treaty, the President & Senate may enter into the treaty; whatever is to be done by a judicial sentence, the judges may pass the sentence. Nothing is more likely than that their enumeration of powers is defective. This is the ordinary case of all human works. Let us go on then perfecting it, by adding, by way of amendment to the Constitution, those powers which time & trial show are still wanting. But it has been taken too much for granted, that by this rigorous construction the treaty power would be reduced to nothing. I had occasion once to examine its effect on the French treaty, made by the old Congress, & found that out of thirty odd articles which that contained, there were one, two, or three only which could not now be stipulated under our present Constitution. I confess, then, I think it important, in the present case, to set an example against broad construction, by appealing for new power to the people. If, however, our friends shall think differently, certainly I shall acquiesce with satisfaction; confiding, that the good sense of our country will correct the evil of construction when it shall produce ill effects.

No apologies for writing or speaking to me freely are necessary. On the contrary, nothing my friends can do is so dear to me, & proves to me their friendship so clearly, as the information they give me of their sentiments & those of others on interesting points where I am to act, and where information & warning is so essential to excite in me that due reflection which ought to precede action. I leave this about the 21st, and shall hope the District Court will give me an opportunity of seeing you.

Accept my affectionate salutations, & assurances of cordial esteem & respect.

Thomas Paine to John C. Breckinridge

I know little and can learn but little of the extent and present population of Louisiana. After the cession be completed and the territory annexed to the United States it will, I suppose, be formed into states, one, at least, to begin with. The people, as I have said, are new to us and we to them and a great deal will depend on a right beginning. As they have been transferred backward and forward several times from one European Government to another it is natural to conclude they have no fixed prejudices with respect to foreign attachments, and this puts them in a fit disposition for their new condition. The established religion is roman; but in what state it is as to exterior ceremonies (such as processions and celebrations), I know not. Had the cession to France continued with her, religion I suppose would have been put on the same footing as it is in that country, and there no ceremonial of religion can appear on the streets or highways; and the same regulation is particularly necessary now or there will soon be quarrels and tumults between the old settlers and the new. The Yankees will not move out of the road for a little wooden Jesus stuck on a stick and carried in procession nor kneel in the dirt to a wooden Virgin Mary. As we do not govern the territory as provinces but incorporated as states, religion there must be on the same footing it is here, and Catholics have the same rights as Catholics have with us and no others. As to political condition the Idea proper to be held out is, that we have neither conquered them, nor bought them, but formed a Union with them and they become in consequence of that union a part of the national sovereignty.

The present Inhabitants and their descendants will be a majority for some time, but new emigrations from the old states and from Europe, and intermarriages, will soon change the first face of things, and it is necessary to have this in mind when the first measures shall be taken. Everything done as an expedient grows worse every day, for in proportion as the mind grows up to the full standard of sight it disclaims the expedient. America had nearly been ruined by expedients in the first stages of the revolution, and perhaps would have been so, had not *Common Sense* broken the charm and the Declaration of Independence sent it into banishment.

1. In Jefferson's opinion, of what importance is the Mississippi River to the safety, security, and unity of the American states?
2. What concerns are noted by Thomas Paine in terms of religious differences between the population of the existing Union and the inhabitants of the new territories?

8-5   The United States Navy and the Bombardment of Tripoli (1803)

In September 1803, the U.S.S. Constitution entered the waters off of North Africa and remained there until October 1807. Her mission was to protect American commerce in the Mediterranean from the Barbary pirates. Between August and September 1804, the U.S. Naval squadron attacked the well-defended harbor of Tripoli and engaged Tripolian corsairs five times. The following documents are excerpts from the journal of the captain of the Constitution, Edward Preble, as well as the log book kept by Nathaniel Haraden, the ship's sailing master, detailing the attacks of August 3 and 7.

> **Source:** *Naval Documents Related to the United States Wars with the Barbary Powers* (Washington, D.C.: Government Printing Office, 1942), 4: 338–340, 376–77.
> http://www.history.navy.mil/docs/war1812/const3.htm

Extract from journal kept on board the U. S. Frigate *Constitution* by Captain Edward Preble, U. S. Navy, Saturday, 4 August 1804

Wind E b S. Standing off shore on the Starbord Tack the signal out to come within hail spoke the different Vessels and acquainted their Commanders that it was my Intention to attack the shipping & Batteries,—directed the Gun Boats & Bombs to be prepared for immediate service.—

at 12 1/2 pm Tack'd & stood for the Batteries. Back'd the Main Topsail, at 1/2 1 pm made the general signal to follow the motions of the Commodore. filled the Main topsail & stood in towards the Batteries, at 1/4 past 2 made the signal for the Bombs & Gun Boats to advance & attack the ships & Batteries. 1/2 past 2 general signal for Battle. the whole squadron advanc'd within point Blank shot of the Enemies Batteries & shipping, our Gun Boats in two divisions the 1st consisting of 3 Boats Commanded by Capt Somers the 2d of three Boats by Capt Decatur, at 3/4 past 2 the Action commenced on our side by throwing a shell into the Town, and in an Instant the whole Squadron were engaged.—the Enemies Gun Boats were Anchored with springs on, in three divisions the Eastern or van division consisted of 9 Boats the center of 7 Boats, and the Western or Rear of 5 Boats. As the wind was from the Eastward our Boats were ordered to lead in to Windward and attack the Enemy. the Rear & center division of the Enemies Boats are close under their Batteries, & the

Van division consisting of their largest Boats are within Grape distance of the Bashaws Castle & fort English at 3 observed our Gun Boats engaged in close action with the Enemies Boats, while a tremendous fire was kept up by this ship and the rest of the Squadron. Capt Decatur with *No. 4* Lt Trippe of *No 6* & Lt Bainbridge of *No. 5* & Lt James Decatur of *No. 2* attacked the enemy's Boats within Pistol shot. *No. 1* Capt Somers fell to Leward but fetched up with the Enemy's Rear of 5 Boats which he gallantly attacked disabled & drove in although within pistol shot of the Batteries. *No. 3* Lt Blake did not go into close Action, had he gone down to the assistance of Capt Somers it is probable they would have captured the Rear Boats. Capt Decatur Boarded and after a stout and obstinate resistance took possession of two of the Enemies Gun Boats, Lt Trip Boarded and carried a third. Lt James Decatur in the Act of Boarding to take possession of a fourth Boat was shot through the Head & Mortally wounded the officer next in command (Mn Brown) hauled off. Lt Bainbridge had his Latten Yard shot away early in the Action which prevented him from taking a Boat but he Galled the Enemy by a steady fire within Musket shot, indeed he pursued the Enemy until his Boat touch'd the ground under the Batteries. the Bombs kept their stations which were well chosen, by Lt Dent & Lt Robinson, who commanded them, and threw a number of shells into the town although the spray of the sea occasioned by the enemies shot almost covered them, three different times the Enemies Gun Boats rallied and attempted to surround ours. I as often made the signal to cover them, which was properly attended to by the Brigs & Schooners, and the fire from this ship not only had the desired effect on the enemies flotilla by keeping them in check and disabling them, but silenced one of their principal Batteries for some time, at 1/2 past 4 pm made the signal for the Bombs to retire from action out of Gun shot, and a few minutes after the general signal to Cease firing and Tow out the Prizes & disabled Boats. sent our Barge and Jolly Boat to assist in that duty. Tack'd ship & fired two Broadsides in stays which drove the Tripolines out of the Castle & brought down the Steeple of a Mosque, by this time the wind began to freshen from N E at 4 3/4 PM hauled off to take the Bombs in tow, at 5 pm Brought to, two miles from their Batteries, Recd Lt James Decatur on board from *Gun Boat No. 2*, he was shot through the Head (in Boarding a Tripoline Boat which had struck to him) he expired in a few moments after he was brought into the ship.— We lay to until 10 PM to receive the Prisoners on board captured in the Prizes, then made sail & stood off to the N E the wind Veering to the E S E.—we have all the surgeons of the squadron on board dressing the wounded.—

During the Action we fired 262 Rounds shot besides Grape double head & Canister from this ship and were several times within 3 cables lengths of the Rocks & Batteries where our soundings were from 10 to 16 faths the Officers Seamen & Marines of the Squadron behaved Gallantly throughout the Action. Capt Decatur in Gun Boat No 4 particularly distinguished himself as did Lt Trip of No 6. Our loss in Killed & Wounded has been considerable the damage we recd in this ship is a 24 pound shot nearly through the center of the Mainmast 20 feet from the deck, Main Top Gallant R Yard & sail shot away, one of the Fore shrouds and the sails & running rigging considerably cut one of the 24 pounders on the Quarter deck was struck by a 24 pound shot which damaged the Gun and carriage and shattered the Arm of a Marine to pieces, Gun Boat No. 2 had her latteen yard shot away, & the Rigging & sails of the Brigs and Schooners were considerably cut. We captured 3 Gun Boats two of which carried each a long Brass 24 pounder & two Brass Howitzers and 36 men with a plenty of muskets pistols pikes sabres &c, the other mounted a long Brass 18 pounder & two Howitzers & 24 men 44 Tripolines were killed on board of the 3 boats and 52 made prisoners, 26 of which were wounded, 17 of them very badly 3 of which died soon after they were brought on board, the Enemy must have suffered very much in Killed & wounded among their Shipping and on shore, one of their Boats was sunk in the harbour several of them had their decks nearly cleared of men by our shot, and several shells burst in the Town, which must have done great execution. — We have lost in Killed & Wounded Viz

Killed	Wounded
Lt James Decatur	Capt Decatur slight
	Lt Tripp[e] severely
	10 Seamen & Marines wounded

Total   1 Officer Killed
2 Officers wounded
10 Seamen and Marines Wounded

Extract from log book kept by Sailing Master Nathaniel Haraden, U.S. Navy, on board U.S. Frigate *Constitution*, Saturday, 4 August 1804

Fresh breezes from E b N. We are standing off shore 2 or 3 Miles from Tripoli with a signal out, for the Squadron to come within hail — We spoke them, & directed the Gun Boats & Bombards to be ready for immediate service —

We made a short board off till 12 1/2 Noon when we tacked in for the Batteries, and made signal for the Gun boats & Bombards to cast off — Our Gun boats are in two divisions — The first is commanded by Capt Somers of the *Nautilus*,

Lt Decatur & Lt Blake; The 2d division by Capt Decatur of the *Enterprize*, Lt. Tripp[e] & Lt. Bainbridge The Bombards are commanded by Capt Dent of the *Scourge* & Lt. Robinson of the *Constitution* —

The Enemy's gun boats are the same in number as on Saturday last, and are stationed in three divisions as a line of defense — The two Western divisions are close under the Batteries, and the 3d consisting of their largest boats carrying either long 24 or 32 pounders is to the Eastward, and under cover of Grape from the Batteries — A few minutes after we tacked in towards the batteries we backed the main topsail to make some arrangements in the Squadron —

At 1 1/4 P.M. made the *Nautilus* signal to make more sail, & a few minutes after made signal for the Bombards to take their stations, and for the Gun boats to advance Capt Decatur and Lieuts J. Decatur. Tripp & Bainbridge led in for the Eastern division of the Enemy's Gun boats — At 2 P.M. made signal to advance — We were now within gun shot of all the Enemy's batteries and stood in within a mile of them before a shot was exchanged — At 2 3/4 Bombard No. 1 hove a shell — The enemy's batteries and Gun boats immediately commenced firing which we returned with our Larboard Guns —

Capt Decatur boarded and after a stout resistance took possession of two of the enemy's Gun boats; Lieut Trip boarded & carried a third — Lt. J. Decatur in the Act of boarding a third was mortally wounded and the Officer next in command hauled off—

Lt Bainbridges boat was partly disabled in proceeding to the Attack — however she was in, and in close action Capt Somers was some way astern when the signal to advance was made — He came up with every possible expedition, received the fire of four boats, and pursued them within musket shot of the Bashaws castle The Bombards kept their stations and continued to throw shells, although nearly covered with the spray of the Enemy's shot.—

Gun boat No. 3 was not in close action.

Three different times we made the general signal to cover the Boats —

At 4 P.M. the Enemy's boats attempted to surround Capt Somers — The *Vixen* bore down to his support, and we immediately hove about & gave them our starboard Guns, on which they all retreated under the Batteries. At 4 1/2 P.M. made the Bombards signal to haul off, and a few minutes after, the general signal to cease firing, and tow out the prizes, and disabled boats.

Sent two boats from the *Constitution* to assist in Towing out the Prizes Tacked within half a Gun shot of the Bashaws Castle & round Battery, and gave them a full broadside in stays, which drove them out of the Castle & brought down a steeple in the direction of the Castle.

By this time the wind freshened and began to Veer to N E.

At 4 3/4 P.M. we hauled off & made signal to take the Bombards & gun boats in Tow. At 5 P.M. brought to, two miles from the Batteries —

Rec'd Lt. J. Decatur from *Gun Boat No. 2* — He was wounded in the head and Expired in a few minutes after being brought on board.

Extract from journal kept on board the U.S. Frigate *Constitution*, by Captain Edward Preble, U.S. Navy, Wednesday, 8 August 1804

At Anchor 6 miles N NE from Tripoli becalmed, the Gun boats & Bombs advancing with all their sweeps, at 1/2 past 1 a light Breeze from the N NE, We Immediately weighd & stood in for the Town, but the wind being on shore could not with prudence attack or allow any of the squadron to attack the Batteries, as in case of a mast being shot away the loss of a vessel would probably ensue. at 1/2 past 2 PM Made the signal for the Gun Boats and Bombs to attack the Batteries & Town from the West, when they immediately opened a tremendous fire within half cannon shot of the Town & less than that distance of a Battery of 7 heavy 24 pounders this Battery in less than two hours was silenc'd excepting one Gun I presume the others were dismounted as the Walls were almost totally destroyed, the Bombs were well and effectually employed by Lt. Comdt. Dent & Lt. Robinson of the *Constitution*, Lt. Robinson from a dangerous position he took, threw 28 shells into the Town, but the well directed fire of heavy artillery from the Enemy obliged him to shift his station not however until the cloths of every man in the Boat was wet through with the spray of sea which the Enemies shot threw over them, Lt. Dent threw 20 shells from a position not so favorable as Lt. Robinson's but which a strong Westerly current in shore would not allow him to change, At 1/4 past 3 PM a Frigate in sight in the Offing standing for the town, made the *Argus*'s Signal to speak, ordered her chase the strange sail at 1/4 past 3 PM the magazine of one our Gun boats No. 9 Blew up & she immediately sunk — She had on board thirty Officers seamen & Marines 10 of which were killed & six badly wounded, among the Killed were Lt. R. Caldwell 1st of the *Syren* Mr. Dorsey Midshipman and two good Officers. — Mr. Spence Midshipmen & 13 Men were picked up unhurt —

The Enemies Gun Boats and Galleys 17 in number are all in motion under their Batteries, and appear to meditate an attack on our Bombs & Gun Boats, ordered the *Argus Nautilus Vixen* & *Enterprize* to Windward in reserve to cut them off from the harbour if they should attack, & the *Syren* & *Vixen* to leeward to support and cover any of our Boats that might be disabled, kept to windward with the *Constitution* — ready to bear down & support the Whole, at 1/2 past 5 PM the Wind began to blow fresh from the N NE Made the signal for Bombs and Gun Boats to retire out of Gun shot of the Enemy and be taken in tow by their respective Vessels. at 6 PM *Argus* made the signal that the strange sail was a friend. in the Action of this day No. 6 Commanded by Lt. Wadsworth had her Latten Yard shot away. No. 4 Capt Decatur a shot in the Hull, No. 8 lost 2 Men killed by a cannon shot, some of the other boats received trifling damage. the Gun Boats fired about 50 Rounds each. the Enemy must have lost many men & the buildings in the city must have received considerable damage from our shot and shells. All the officers & men engaged in Action behaved gallantly, at 3/4 past 6 all the Boats were in tow & the squadron in 35 fathoms Water hard bottom.

1. *In a time retrenchment, Jefferson's involvement in the Tripolitan War seemed to go counter to Republican desires. What options might Jefferson have pursued short of military action? Why do you think he chose the option that he did—even though it meant a considerable financial commitment?*
2. *In addition to protecting American commerce in the Mediterranean, what message was the United States sending to Europe and the world through its action against the Barbary states?*

8-6　A Matter of Honor or Vengeance? (1804)

In the election of 1804, Vice President Aaron Burr was not only replaced by George Clinton, but he was also refused a position in Jefferson's second administration. Burr tried to recoup his political fortunes by running for the governorship of New York, but was defeated, largely through the influence of Hamilton who referred to the former vice president as a "dangerous man, and one who ought not to be trusted with the reigns of government." A few months after this defeat, the men meet on the dueling grounds at Weehawken, New Jersey. Each fired a shot from a .56 caliber dueling pistol. Burr, unharmed, mortally wounded Hamilton who died the next day.

> **Source:** William Coleman, ed., *A Collection of the Facts and Documents Relative to the Death of Major-General Alexander Hamilton* (New York, 1804); Matthew L. Davis, ed., *Memoirs of Aaron Burr, with Miscellaneous Selections from His Correspondence*, 2 vols. (New York, Harper 1836–1837).
> http://uhs.tusd.k12.az.us/departments/social/apush/burr_01.htm

Aaron Burr to Alexander Hamilton: the first in a series of letters which led to the duel.

SIR,

I send for your perusal a letter signed Charles D. Cooper, which, though apparently published some time ago, has but very recently come to my knowledge. Mr. Van Ness, who does me the favour to deliver this, will point out to you that clause of the letter to which I particularly request your attention.

You must perceive, Sir, the necessity of a prompt and unqualified acknowledgement or denial of the use of any expression which would warrant the assertions of Dr. Cooper.

I have the honour to be your obedient servant,

A. BURR

Letter from Alexander Hamilton to Aaron Burr

New-York, June 20, 1804.

SIR,

I have maturely reflected on the subject of your letter of the 18th inst., and the more I have reflected the more I have become convinced, that I could not, without manifest impropriety, make the avowal or disavowal which you seem to think necessary. The clause pointed out by Mr. Van Ness is in these terms: "I could detail to you a still more despicable opinion which General Hamilton has expressed of Mr. Burr." To endeavour to discover the meaning of this declaration, I was obliged to seek in the antecedent part of this letter for the opinion to which it referred as having been already disclosed. I found it in these words: "General Hamilton and Judge Kent have declared, in substance, that they looked upon Mr. Burr to be a dangerous man, and one who ought not to be trusted with the reins of government."

The language of Dr. Cooper plainly implies that he considered this opinion of you, which he attributes to me as a despicable one; but he affirms that I have expressed some other, more despicable, without, however, mentioning to whom, when, or where. 'Tis evident that the phrase "still more despicable" admits of infinite shades, from very light to very dark. How am I to judge of the degree intended? or how shall I annex any precise idea to language so indefinite?

Between gentlemen, despicable and more despicable are not worth the pains of distinction; when therefore you do not interrogate me as to the opinion which is specifically ascribed to me, I must conclude, that you view it as within the limits to which the animadversions of political opponents upon each other may justifiably extend, and consequently as not warranting the idea of it which Doctor Cooper appears to entertain. If so, what precise inference could you draw, as a guide for your conduct, were I to acknowledge that I had expressed an opinion of you still more despicable than the one which is particularized? How could you be sure that even this opinion had exceeded the bounds which you would yourself deem admissible between political opponents?

But I forbear further comment on the embarrassment, to which the requisition you have made naturally leads. The occasion forbids a more ample illustration, though nothing could be more easy than to pursue it.

Repeating that I cannot reconcile it with propriety to make the acknowledgement or denial you desire, I will add that I deem it inadmissible on principle, to consent to be interrogated as to the justice of the inferences which may be drawn by others from whatever I may have said of a political opponent, in the course of fifteen years competition. If there were no other objection to it this is sufficient, that it would tend to expose my sincerity and delicacy to injurious imputations from every person who may at any time have conceived the import of my expressions, differently from what I may then have intended or may afterward recollect. I stand ready to avow or disavow promptly and explicitly any precise or definite opinion which I may be charged with having declared of any Gentleman. More than this cannot fitly be expected from me; and especially it cannot be reasonably expected that I shall enter into an explanation upon a basis so vague as that which you have adopted. I trust on more reflection you will see the matter in the same light with me. If not, I can only regret the circumstances and must abide the consequences.

The publication of Doctor Cooper was never seen by me till after the receipt of your letter.

I have the honour to be, &c.,

A. HAMILTON

Aaron Burr to Alexander Hamilton

New-York, 21st June, 1804
SIR,

Your letter of the 20th inst. has been this day received. Having considered it attentively, I regret to find in it nothing of that sincerity and delicacy which you profess to value.

Political opposition can never absolve gentlemen from the necessity of a rigid adherence to the laws of honour, and the rules of decorum. I neither claim such privilege nor indulge it in others.

The common sense of mankind affixes to the epithet adopted by Doctor Cooper, the idea of dishonour. It has been publicly applied to me under the sanction of your name. The question is not, whether he has understood the meaning of the word, or has used it according to syntax, and with grammatical accuracy; but, whether you have authorized this application, either directly or by uttering expressions or opinions derogatory to my honour. The time "when" is in your own knowledge, but no way material to me, as the cal- has now first been disclosed, so as to become the subject of my notice, and as the effect is present and palpable.

Your letter has furnished me with new reasons for requiring a definite reply.

I have the honour to be,
Sir, your obedient

A. BURR

As Hamilton's "second," Nathaniel Pendleton read the following to Burr's friend and "second," William Van Ness:

General Hamilton says he cannot imagine to what Dr. Cooper may have alluded, unless it were to a conversation at Mr. Taylor's in Albany, last winter, (at which he and Gen. Hamilton were present). Gen. Hamilton cannot recollect distinctly the particulars of that conversation so as to undertake to repeat them, without running the risk of varying, or omitting what might be deemed important circumstances. The expressions are entirely forgotten, and the specific ideas imperfectly remembered; but to the best of his recollection it consisted of comments on the political principles and views of Col. Burr, and the results that might be expected from them in the event of his election as Governor, without reference to any particular instance of past conduct, or to private character.

At the request of Van Ness, Pendleton put Hamilton's statement in writing:

In answer to a letter properly adapted to obtain from General Hamilton a declaration whether he had charged Col. Burr with any particular instance of dishonourable conduct, or had impeached his private character, either in the conversation alluded to by Dr. Cooper, or in any other particular instance to be specified; he would be able to answer consistently with his honour, and the truth, in substance, that the conversation to which Dr. Cooper alluded, turned wholly on political topics, and did not attribute to Col. Burr any instance of dishonourable conduct, nor relate to his private character; and in relation to any other language or conversation of General Hamilton which Col. Burr will specify, a prompt and frank avowal or denial will be given.

The statement drawn up by the seconds in the duel, Pendleton and Van Ness:

Col. Burr arrived first on the ground, as had been previously agreed: when Gen. Hamilton arrived the parties exchanged salutations, and the seconds proceeded to make their arrangements. They measured the distance, ten full paces, and cast lots for the choice of position, as also to determine by whom the word should be given, both of which fell to the second of Gen. Hamilton. They then proceeded to load the pistols in each other's presence, after which the parties took their stations. The gentleman who was to give the word, then explained to the parties the rules which were to govern them in firing, which were as follows: "The parties being placed at their stations . . . the second who gives the word shall ask them whether they are ready; being answered in the affirmative, he shall say 'Present!' after this the parties shall present and fire when they please . . . If one fires before the other, the opposite second shall say one, two, three, fire . . . and he shall then fire or lose his fire." He then asked if they were prepared; being answered in the affirmative, he gave the word present, as had been agreed on, and both parties presented and fired in succession—the intervening time is not expressed, as the seconds do not precisely agree on that point. The fire of Colonel Burr took effect, and General Hamilton almost instantly fell. Col. Burr then advanced toward General Hamilton, with a manner and gesture that appeared to General Hamilton's friend to be expressive of regret, but without speaking, turned about and withdrew, being urged from the field by his friend as has been subsequently stated, with a view to prevent his being recognised by the surgeon and bargemen, who were then approaching. No further communication took place between the principals, and the barge that carried Col. Burr immediately returned to the city. We conceive it proper to add that the conduct of the parties in this interview was perfectly proper as suited the occasion.

The following was found among Hamilton's papers:

On my expected interview with Col. Burr, I think it proper to make some remarks explanatory of my conduct motives, and views.

I was certainly desirous of avoiding this interview for the most cogent reasons.

1. My religious and moral principles are strongly opposed to the practice of duelling, and it would ever give me pain to be obliged to shed the blood of a fellow creature in a private combat forbidden by the laws.

2. My wife and children are extremely dear to me, and my life is of the utmost importance to them, in various views.

3. I feel a sense of obligation towards my creditors; who in case of accident to me, by the forced sale of my property, may be in some degree sufferers. I did not think myself at liberty as a man of probity, lightly to expose them to this hazard.

4. I am conscious of no ill will to Col. Burr, distinct from political opposition, which, as I trust, has proceeded from pure and upright motives. Lastly, I shall hazard much, and can possibly gain nothing by the issue of the interview.

But it was, as I conceive, impossible for me to avoid it. There were intrinsic difficulties in the thing, and artificial embarrassments, from the manner of proceeding on the part of Col. Burr.

Intrinsic, because it is not to be denied, that my animadversions on the political principles, character, and views of Col. Burr, have been extremely severe; and on different occasions, I, in common with many others, have made very unfavourable criticisms on particular instances of the private conduct of this gentleman.

In proportion as these impressions were entertained with sincerity, and uttered with motives and for purposes which might appear to me commendable, would be the difficulty (until they could be removed by evidence of their being erroneous) of explanation or apology. The disavowal required of me by Col. Burr, in a general and indefinite form, was out of my power, if it had really been proper for me to submit to be so questioned; but I was sincerely of opinion that this could not be, and in this opinion, I was confirmed by that of a very moderate and judicious friend whom I consulted. Besides that, Col. Burr appeared to me to assume, in the first instance, a tone unnecessarily peremptory and menacing, and in the second, positively offensive. Yet I wished, as far as might be practicable, to leave a door open to accommodation. This, I think, will be inferred from the written communications made by me and by my direction, and would be confirmed by the conversations between Mr. Van Ness and myself, which arose out of the subject.

I am not sure whether, under all the circumstances, I did not go further in the attempt to accommodate, than a punctilious delicacy will justify. If so, I hope the motives I have stated will excuse me.

It is not my design, by what I have said, to affix any odium on the conduct of Col. Burr, in this case. He doubtless has heard of animadversions of mine which bore very hard upon him; and it is probable that as usual they were accompanied with some falsehoods. He may have supposed himself under a necessity of acting as he has done. I hope the grounds of his proceeding have been such as ought to satisfy his own conscience.

I trust, at the same time, that the world will do me the justice to believe, that I have not censured him on light ground, nor from unworthy inducements. I certainly have had strong reasons for what I may have said, though it is possible that in some particulars, I may have been influenced by misconstruction or misinformation. It is also my ardent wish that I may have been more mistaken than I think I have been, and that he, by his future conduct, may show himself worthy of all confidence and esteem, and prove an ornament and blessing to the country.

As well because it is possible that I may have injured Col. Burr, however convinced myself that my opinions and declarations have been well founded, as from my general principles and temper in relation to similar affairs, I have resolved, if our interview is conducted in the usual manner, and it pleases God to give me the opportunity, to reserve and throw away my first fire, and I have thoughts even of reserving my second fire—and thus giving a double opportunity to Col. Burr to pause and to reflect.

It is not, however, my intention to enter into any explanations on the ground—Apology from principle, I hope, rather than pride, is out of the question.

To those who, with me, abhorring the practice of duelling, may think that I ought on no account to have added to the number of bad examples, I answer, that my relative situation, as well in public as private, enforcing all the considerations which constitute what men of the world denominate honour, imposed on me (as I thought) a peculiar necessity not to decline the call. The ability to be in future useful, whether in resisting mischief or effecting good, in those crises of our public affairs which seem likely to happen, would probably be inseparable from a conformity with public prejudice in this particular.

A letter from Aaron Burr to Joseph Alston, his son-in-law

New-York, July 13, 1804.

General Hamilton died yesterday. The malignant federalists or tories, and the embittered Clintonians, unite in endeavouring to excite public sympathy in his favour and indignation against his antagonist. Thousands of absurd falsehoods are circulated with industry. The most illiberal means are practised in order to produce excitement. and, for the moment, with effect.

I propose leaving town for a few days, and meditate also a journey for some weeks, but whither is not resolved. Perhaps to Statesburgh. You will hear from me again in about eight days.

A. BURR

1. What purpose do you think dueling served in the social and political world of the late eighteenth and early nineteenth centuries?
2. Considering that he had already lost his son, Philip, in a duel at Weehawken less than three years earlier, what prevented Alexander Hamilton from ending the quarrel with an apology or an explanation?

8-7 Fisher Ames, "The Republican. No. II" (1804)

After Jefferson's election in 1800, many former opponents moderated their attacks on Republicanism. But Fisher Ames (1758-1808) was not among them. An acerbic Massachusetts lawyer, Ames championed strong central authority and reviled egalitarianism. He claimed that the federal government should be built on an aristocracy of "the wise and good and opulent." Ames served in the House of Representatives for three terms. Illness cut short his political career, and in retirement he wrote stinging blasts against the "Southern Jacobins," his term for Republican leaders who mouthed radical philosophies while holding slaves.

Source:
http://occawlonline.pearsoned.com/bookbind/pubbooks/divine5e/medialib/timeline/docs/divdocs10.html

We justly consider the condition of civil liberty as the most exalted to which any nation can aspire; but high as its rank is, and precious as are its prerogatives, it has not pleased God, in the order of his providence, to confer this preeminent blessing, except upon a very few, and those very small, spots of the universe. The rest sit in darkness, and as little desire the light of liberty, as they are fit to endure it.

We are ready to wonder, that the best gifts are the most sparingly bestowed, and rashly to conclude, that despotism is the decree of heaven, because by far the largest part of the world lies bound in its fetters. But either on tracing the course of events in history, or on examining the character and passions of man, we shall find that the work of slavery is his own, and that he is not condemned to wear chains till he has been his own artificer to forge them. We shall find that society cannot subsist, and that the streets of Boston would be worse than the lion's den, unless the appetites and passions of the violent are made subject to an adequate control. How much control will be adequate to that end, is a problem of no easy solution beforehand, and of no sort of difficulty after some experience. For all who have any thing to defend, and all indeed who have nothing to ask protection for but their lives, will desire that protection; and not only acquiesce, but rejoice in the progress of those slave-making intrigues and tumults, which at length assure to society its repose, though it sleeps in bondage. Thus it will happen, and as it is the course of nature, it cannot be resisted, that there will soon or late be control and government enough.

It is also obvious, that there may be, and probably will be, the least control and the most liberty there, where the turbulent passions are the least excited, and where the old habits and sober reasons of the people are left free to govern them.

Hence it is undeniably plain, that the mock patriots, the opposers of Washington and the Constitution, from 1788 to this day, who, under pretext of being the people's friends, have kept them in a state of continual jealousy, irritation, and discontent, have deceived the people, and perhaps themselves, in regard to the tendency of their principles and conduct; for instead of lessening the pressure of government, and contracting the sphere of its powers, they have removed the field-marks that bounded its exercise, and left it arbitrary and without limits. The passions of the people have been kept in agitation, till the influence of truth, reason, and the excellent habits we derive from our ancestors is lost or greatly impaired; till it is plain, that those, whom manners and morals can no longer govern, must be governed by force; and that force a dominant faction derives from the passions of its adherents; on that alone they rely.

Take one example, which will illustrate the case as well as a hundred; the British treaty [Jay's Treaty 1793] was opposed by a faction, headed by six or eight mob leaders in our cities, and a rabble, whom the arts of these leaders had trained for their purpose. Could a feeble government, could mere truth and calm reason, pointing out the best public interest, have carried that treaty through, and effected its execution in good faith, had not the virtue and firmness of Washington supplied an almost superhuman energy to its powers at the moment? No treaty made by the government has ever proved more signally beneficial. The nature of the treaty, however, is not to the point of the present argument. Suppose a mob opposition had defeated it, and confusion, if not war, had ensued, the confusion that very society is fated to suffer, when, on a trial of strength, a faction in its bosom is found stronger than its government; on this supposition, and that the conquering faction had seized the reins of power, is it to be believed that they would not instantly provide against a like opposition to their own treaties? Did they not so provide, and annex Louisiana, and squander millions in a week? Have we not seen in France, how early and how effectually the conqueror takes care to prevent another rival from playing the same game, by which he himself prevailed against his predecessor?

Let any man, who has any understanding, exercise it to see that the American jacobin party, by rousing the popular passions, inevitably augments the powers of government, and contracts within narrower bounds, and on a less sound foundation, the privileges of the people.

Facts, yes facts, that speak in terror to the soul, confirm this speculative reasoning. What limits are there to the prerogatives of the present administration? and whose business is it, and in whose power does it lie, to keep them within those limits? Surely not in the senate: the small States are now in vassalage, and they obey the nod of Virginia. Not in the judiciary: that fortress, which the Constitution had made too strong for an assault, can now be reduced by famine. The Constitution, alas! that sleeps with Washington, having no mourners but the virtuous, and no monument but history. Louisiana, in open and avowed defiance of the Constitution, is by treaty to be added to the union; the bread of the children of the union is to be taken and given to the dogs.

Judge then, good men and true, judge by the effects, whether the tendency of the intrigues of the party was to extend or contract the measure of popular liberty. Judge whether the little finger of Jefferson is not thicker than the loins of Washington's administration; and, after you have judged, and felt the terror that will be inspired by the result, then reflect how little your efforts can avail to prevent the continuance, nay, the perpetuity of his power. Reflect, and be calm. Patience is the virtue of slaves, and almost the only one that will pass for merit with their masters.

1. What warnings and fears are expressed in this document regarding the powers of government?
2. Identify and explain the specific criticisms leveled against the organization of the American government.

8-8   Sacagawea Interprets for Lewis and Clark (1804)

In November 1804, Meriwether Lewis, William Clark, and the Corps of Discovery arrived at the Hidatsa-Mandan villages near present day Bismarck, North Dakota. There they met and hired Toussaint Charbonneau, a French-Canadian fur trader and Sacagawea ("Canoe Launcher"), one of his two Shoshone "wives." Lewis and Clark believed Sacagawea could be important in trading for horses when the Corps reached the Bitterroot mountains and the Shoshones. While Sacagawea did not speak English, she spoke Shoshone and Hidatsa. Charbonneau spoke Hidatsa and French. It was hoped that when the expedition met the Shoshones, Sacagawea would talk with them, then translate to Hidatsa for Charbonneau, who would translate into French. The Corps' Francois Labiche spoke French and English, and would make the final translation so that Lewis and Clark could understand.

> **Source:** Meriwether Lewis and William Clark, *History of the Expedition of Captains Lewis and Clark*, 2 Vols. (Chicago: A. C. McClurg & Co., 1924), 1: 406–411.

SATURDAY, August 17. Captain Lewis rose very early and despatched Drewyer and the Indian down the river in quest of the boats. Shields was sent out at the same time to hunt, while M'Neal prepared a breakfast out of the remainder of the meat. Drewyer had been gone about two hours, and the Indians were all anxiously waiting for some news, when an Indian who had straggled a short distance down the river returned with a report that he had seen the white men, who were only a short distance below, and were coming on. The Indians were all transported with joy, and the chief in the warmth of his satisfaction renewed his embrace to Captain Lewis, who was quite as much delighted as the Indians themselves. The report proved most agreeably true. On setting out at seven o'clock, Captain Clark, with Charbonneau and his wife, walked on shore; but they had not gone more than a mile before Captain Clark saw Sacagawea, who was with her husband one hundred yards ahead, begin to dance and show every mark of the most extravagant joy, turning round him and pointing to several Indians, whom he now saw advancing on horseback, sucking her fingers at the same time to indicate that they were of her native tribe. As they advanced Captain Clark discovered among them Drewyer dressed like an Indian, from whom he learnt the situation of the party. While the boats were performing the circuit he went towards the forks with the Indians, who, as they went along, sang aloud with the greatest appearance of delight. We soon drew near to the camp, and just as we approached it a woman made her way through the crowd towards Sacagawea, and recognising each other, they embraced with the most tender affection. The meeting of these two young women had in it something peculiarly touching, not only in the ardent manner in which their feelings were expressed, but from the real interest of their situation. They had been companions in childhood; in the war with the Minnetarees they had both been taken prisoners in the same battle, they had shared and softened the rigours of their captivity, till one of them had escaped from the Minnetarees, with scarce a hope of ever seeing her friend relieved from the hands of her enemies. While Sacagawea was renewing among the women the friendships of former days, Captain Clark went on, and was received by Captain Lewis and the chief, who, after the first embraces and salutations were over, conducted him to a sort of circular tent or shade of willows. Here he was seated on a white robe, and the chief immediately tied in his hair six small shells resembling pearls, an ornament highly valued by these people, who procured them in the course of trade from the seacoast. The moccasins of the whole party were then taken off, and after much ceremony the smoking began. After this the conference was to be opened, and glad of an opportunity of being able to converse more intelligibly, Sacagawea was sent for; she came into the tent, sat down, and was beginning to interpret, when in the person of Cameahwait she recognised her brother; she instantly jumped up and ran and embraced him, throwing over him her blanket and weeping profusely; the chief was himself moved, though not in the same degree. After some conversation between them she resumed her seat, and attempted to interpret for us, but her new situation seemed to overpower her, and she was frequently interrupted by her tears. After the council was finished, the unfortunate woman learnt that all her family were dead except two brothers, one of whom was absent, and a son of her eldest sister, a small boy, who was immediately adopted by her. The canoes arriving soon after, we formed a camp in a meadow on the left side, a little below the forks, took out our baggage, and by means of our sails and willow poles formed a canopy for our Indian visitors. About four o'clock the chiefs and warriors were collected, and after the customary ceremony of taking off the moccasins and smoking a pipe, we explained to them in a long harangue the purposes of our visit, making themselves one conspicuous object of the good wishes of our government, on whose strength as well as its friendly disposition we expatiated. We told them of their dependence on the will of our government for all future supplies of whatever was necessary either for their comfort or defence; that as we were sent to discover the best route by which merchandise could be conveyed to them, and no trade would be begun before our return, it was mutually advantageous that we should proceed with as little delay as possible; that we were under the necessity of requesting them to furnish us with horses to transport our baggage across the mountains, and a guide to show us the route, but that they should be amply remunerated for their horses, as well as for every other service they should render us. In the meantime our first wish was, that they should immediately collect as many horses as were necessary to transport our baggage to their village, where, at our leisure, we would trade with them for as many horses as they could spare.

The speech made a favourable impression; the chief in reply thanked us for our expressions of friendship towards himself and his nation, and declared their willingness to render us every service. He lamented that it would be so long before they should be supplied with firearms, but that till then they could subsist as they had heretofore done. He concluded by saying that there were not horses here sufficient to transport our goods, but that he would return to the village tomorrow, and bring all his own horses, and encourage his people to come over with theirs. The conference being ended to our satisfaction, we now inquired of Cameahwait what chiefs were among the party, and he pointed out two of them. We then distributed our presents: to Cameahwait we gave a medal of the small size, with the likeness of President Jefferson, and on the reverse a figure of hands clasped with a pipe and tomahawk; to this was added a uniform coat, a shirt, a pair of scarlet leggings, a carrot of tobacco, and some small articles. Each of the other chiefs received a small medal struck during the presidency of General Washington, a shirt, handkerchief, leggings, a knife, and some tobacco. Medals of the same sort were also presented to two young warriors, who though not chiefs were promising youths and very much respected in the tribe. These honorary gifts were followed by presents of paint, moccasins, awls, knives, beads, and looking-glasses. We also gave them all a plentiful meal of Indian corn, of which the hull is taken off by being boiled in lye; and as this was the first they had ever tasted, they were very much pleased with it. They had indeed abundant sources of surprise in all they saw: the appearance of the men, their arms, their clothing, the canoes, the strange looks of the negro, and the sagacity of our dog, all in turn shared their admiration, which was raised to astonishment by a shot from the airgun; this operation was instantly considered as *a great medicine*, by which they as well as the other Indians mean something emanating directly from the Great Spirit, or produced by his invisible and incomprehensible agency. The display of all these riches had been intermixed with inquiries into the geographical situation of their country, for we had learnt by experience that to keep the savages in good temper their attention should not be wearied with too much business, but that the serious affairs should be enlivened by a mixture of what is new and entertaining. Our hunters brought in very seasonably four deer and an antelope, the last of which we gave to the Indians, who in a very short time devoured it. After the council was over, we consulted as to our future operations. The game does not promise to last here for a number of days, and this circumstance combined with many others to induce our going on as soon as possible. Our Indian information as to the state of the Columbia is of a very alarming kind, and our first object is of course to ascertain the practicability of descending it, of which the Indians discourage our expectations. It was therefore agreed that Captain Clark should set off in the morning with eleven men, furnished, besides their arms, with tools for making canoes; that he should take Charbonneau and his wife to the camp of the Shoshonees, where he was to leave them, in order to hasten the collection of horses; that he was then to lead his men down to the Columbia, and if he found it navigable, and the timber in sufficient quantity, begin to build canoes. As soon as he had decided as to the propriety of proceeding down the Columbia or across the mountains, he was to send back one of the men with information of it to Captain Lewis, who by that time would have brought up the whole party and the rest of the baggage as far as the Shoshonee village.

Preparations were accordingly made this evening for such an arrangement. The sun is excessively hot in the day time, but the nights very cold, and rendered still more unpleasant from the want of any fuel except willow brush. The appearances, too, of game for many days' subsistence are not very favourable.

1. *The Shoshone were known to have horses that the Corps of Discovery would need to cross the western mountains. What do you think the expedition would have done had they not found a Shoshone band or been able to trade for horses?*
2. *What was the relationship between Sacagawea and the Shoshone band encountered by the Corps? Do you think this relationship aided in the trading process and the success of the expedition? Why or why not?*

8-9 An "Uncommon Genius" Advocates Indian Unity (1809)

In the summer of 1809, Shawnee Chief Tecumseh began the first of four diplomatic tours through the American frontier in an effort to unite Indian people against white encroachment. He was, according to Governor William Henry Harrison of the Indiana Territory, "one of those uncommon geniuses, which spring up occasionally to produce revolutions and overturn the order of thing." Tecumseh believed that the land was the common property of all the tribes—consequently, its defense was the responsibility of all. What follows is a description of the Shawnee chief as recorded by Captain John B. Glegg, an aide-de-camp for British General Isaac Brock from whom Tecumseh sought help in turning back the Americans. Also included are two of Tecumseh's speeches—first to the Osages in the winter of 1811–1812 and then to a council of mixed tribes in May 1812.

Source: Galafilms Multimedia Production Company, Canada, *War of 1812*
http:www.galafilm.com/1812/e/people/tecumseh.html

CAPTAIN JOHN B. GLEGG, AN AIDE-DE-CAMP FOR BRITISH GENERAL ISAAC BROCK:

Tecumseh's appearance was very prepossessing; his figure light and finely proportioned; his age I imagined to be about five and thirty; in height, five feet nine or ten inches; his complexion, light copper; countenance, oval, with bright hazel eyes beaming cheerfulness, energy and decision. Three small silver crowns, or coronets, were suspended from the lower cartilage of his aqualine nose; and a large silver medallion of George III. . .was attached to a mixed coloured wampum string, and hung around his neck. His dress consisted of a plain, neat uniform, tanned deerskin jacket, with long trousers of the same material, the seams of both being covered with neatly cut fringe; and he had on his feet leather moccasins, much ornamented with work made from the dyed quills of the porcupine.

TECUMSEH'S SPEECH TO THE OSAGES IN THE WINTER OF 1811–1812:

Brothers we all belong to one family; we are all children of the Great Spirit; we walk in the same path; slake our thirst at the same spring; and now affairs of the greatest concern lead us to smoke the pipe around the same council fire!

Brothers, —We are friends; we must assist each other to bear our burdens. The blood of many of our fathers and brothers has run like water on the ground, to satisfy the avarice of the white men. We, ourselves, are threatened with a great evil; nothing will pacify them but the destruction of all the red men.

Brothers, — When the white men first set foot on our grounds, they were hungry; they had no place on which to spread their blankets, or to kindle their fires. They were feeble; they could do nothing for themselves. Our fathers commiserated their distress, and shared freely with them whatever the Great Spirit had given his red children. They gave them food when hungry, medicine when sick, spread skins for them to sleep on, and gave them grounds, that they might hunt and raise corn.

Brothers, —The white people came among us feeble, and now we have made them strong, they wish to kill us, or drive us back, as they would wolves and panthers.

Brothers, —The white men are not friends to the Indians: at first, they only asked for land sufficient for a wigwam; now, nothing will satisfy them but the whole of our hunting grounds, from the rising to the setting sun.

Brothers, —The white men want more than our hunting grounds; they wish to kill our warriors; they would even kill our old men, women and little ones.

Brothers, —Many winters ago, there was no land; the sun did not rise and set: all was darkness. The Great Spirit made all things. He gave the white people a home beyond the great waters. He supplied these grounds with game, and gave them to his red children; and he gave them strength and courage to defend them.

Brothers — My people wish for peace; the red men all wish for peace; but where the white people are, there is no peace for them, except it be the bosom of our mother.

Brothers, — The white men despise and cheat the Indians; they abuse and insult them; they do not think the red men sufficiently good to live. The red men have borne many and great injuries; they ought to suffer them no longer. My people will not; they are determined on vengeance; they will drink the blood of the white people.

Brothers, — My people are brave and numerous; but the white people are too strong for them alone. I wish you to take up the tomahawk with them. If we all unite, we will cause the rivers to stain the great waters with their blood.

Brothers, — if you do not unite with us, they will first destroy us, and then you will be an easy prey to them. They have destroyed many nations of red men because they were not united, because they were not friends to each other.

Brothers, — The white people send runners amongst us; they wish to make us enemies that they may sweep over and desolate our hunting grounds, like devastating winds, or rushing waters.

Brothers, — Our Great Father, over the great waters, is angry with the white people, our enemies. He will send his brave warriors against them; he will send us rifles, and whatever else we want — he is our friend, and we are his children.

Brothers, — Who are the white people that we should fear them? They cannot run fast, and are good marks to shoot at: they are only men; our fathers have killed many of them; we are not squaws, and we will stain the earth red with blood.

Brothers, — The Great Spirit is angry with our enemies; he speaks in thunder, and the earth swallows up villages, and drinks up the Mississippi. The great waters will cover their lowlands; their corn cannot grow; and the Great Spirit will sweep those who escape to the hills from the earth with his terrible breath.

Brothers, — We must be united; we must smoke the same pipe; we must fight each other's battles; and more than all, we must love the Great Spirit; he is for us; he will destroy our enemies, and make all his red children happy."

Tecumseh's speech to the tribal council in the spring of 1812:

Father, & Brother Hurons!

Brother Hurons, You say you were employed by our Father and Your own Chiefs to come and have some conversation with us, and we are happy to see You and to hear Your and our Father's Speech. We heartily thank You both for having taken the condition of our poor Women and children to Your considerations: We plainly see that You pity us by the concern You shew for our welfare; and we should deem ourselves much to blame if we did not listen to the Counsel of Our Father and our Brothers the Hurons.

Father and Brothers! We have not brought these misfortunes on ourselves; we have done nothing wrong, but we will now point out to You those who have occasioned all the mischief.

Our Younger Brothers the Potawatomies, (pointing to them) in spite of our repeated counsel to them to remain quiet and live in peace with the Big Knives, would not listen to us. When I left home last year to go to the Creek Nation, I passed at Post Vincennes and was stopped by the Big Knives, and did not immediately know the reason, but I was soon informed that the Potawatomies had killed some of their people; I told the Big Knives to remain quiet until my return, when I should make peace and quietness prevail. On my return I found my Village reduced to ashes by the Big Knives. You cannot blame Your Younger Brothers the Shawanoes for what has happened; the Potawatomies occasioned the misfortune. Had I been at home and heard of the advance of the American Troops towards our Village, I should have gone to meet them and shaking them by the hand, have asked them the reason of their appearance in such hostile guise.

Father & Brothers! You tell us to retreat or to turn to one side should the Big Knives come against us; had I been at home in the late unfortunate affair I should have done so, but those I left at home were (I cannot call them men) a poor set of people, and their Scuffle with the Big Knives I compare to a struggle between little children who only scratch each others faces. The Kikapoos and Winibiegoes have since been at Post Vincennes and settled that matter amicably.

Father and brothers, The Potawatomies hearing that our Father and You were on the way here for peaceful purposes, grew very angry all at once and killed twenty-seven of the Big Knives.

Brothers! — We Shawanoes, Kikapoos and Winibiegoes, hope You will not find fault with us for having detained You and Our Father's words; and our eldest Brothers.

Father & Brothers! We will now in a few words declare to You our whole hearts. If we hear of the Big Knives coming towards our villages to speak peace, we will receive them; but if we Hear of any of our people being hurt by them, or if they unprovokedly advance against us in a hostile manner, be assured we will defend ourselves like men. And if we hear of any of our people having being killed, We will immediately send to all the Nations on or towards the Mississippi, and all this Island will rise like one man. Then Father and Brothers it will be impossible for You or either of You to restore peace between us."

1. *What approach and/or arguments did Tecumseh employ in making his case for a pan-Indian alliance? What arguments could be made against such a union?*
2. *Why do you think Tecumseh sought aid from the British? Would he not be exchanging one problem for another?*

8-10   Indian Hostilities (1812)

Stories of the British inciting Native American groups to attack American settlers abounded in the days immediately preceding the War of 1812. Here, in an excerpt from the Pennsylvania Gazette, the British are blamed for "Indian hostilities" in the Indiana and Illinois territories.

Source: *The Pennsylvania Gazette*, 4 March 1812.

The following is an extract of a letter from a gentleman at St. Charles, Louisiana Territory, dated Jan. 10, 1812.

In answer to your enquiry, respecting Indian hostilities in this quarter, I have to inform you, that some of the reports that have found their way into the public prints are much exaggerated, but are generally true. The depredations committed by them have been principally in Indiana and Illinois territories; some horses have been taken in this territory, but I believe no murders have been committed by them for the last ten or twelve months. I had flattered myself that the drubbing given them by the troops under the command of Gov. Harrison would have disposed them to return to order. In this it appears I was mistaken, for this day, by an express from Fort Madison, we are informed of cruel murders committed on some traders, about 100 miles above that Fort, by a party of the Pecant nation. A Mr. Hunt, son of the late Col. Hunt, of the United States' army, and a Mr. Prior, were trading in that quarter—their houses about 3 miles distance from each other. The party of Indians came to Hunt's house, and appeared friendly until they obtained admittance into the house—they then shot down two men that Mr. Hunt had with him, seized him and a boy, who was his interpreter, tied them, and packed up the goods that were in the house, and carried them off. Mr. Hunt discovered that they believed him to be an Englishman, and on that account saved his life. They told him that they had sent another party to kill Prior, and carry off his goods, and that they intended in a short time to take the Fort—after which they would come on and kill every American they could find. They took Mr. Hunt and his boy with them some distance, but night came on, and proved extremely dark, which fortunately gave them an opportunity of escaping, and they arrived safe at Fort Madison on the sixth day.

The hostilities that have taken place, together with the mysterious conduct of the few Indians that are passing amongst us, lead me to believe they are determined for war, and that they are set on by British agents. If we go to war with England, I calculate on some very warm work in this quarter.

1. Summarize the nature of the Indian hostilities noted in this document. What conclusions does the author draw from these events?

8-11 The British Attack Baltimore (1814)

On September 13, 1814, Fort McHenry and its 1,000 defenders under Lieutenant Colonel George Armistead became the object of a British naval attack. After twenty-five hours of continuous bombardment, the British withdrew having failed to destroy the fort and enter Baltimore harbor. Prior to the attack, Washington lawyer Francis Scott Key, accompanied government agent John Skinner on board the British flagship in Chesapeake Bay in an effort to secure the release of Dr. William Beanes, who had been taken prisoner. The British officers agreed to release Dr. Beanes, however, the three men were not permitted to return to Baltimore until after the bombardment of Fort McHenry. The three Americans returned to their ship and waited behind the British fleet while it shelled the fort. Witnessing the unsuccessful British attack, Key wrote down the words to a poem which was soon distributed as a handbill under the title "Defense of Fort McHenry." It was later renamed "The Star-Spangled Banner" and became the lyrics for the national anthem in 1931.

> **Source:** John Brannan, ed. *Official Letters of the Military and Naval Officers of the United States During the War with Great Britain in the Years 1812, 13, 14, & 15 With Some Additional Letters and Documents Elucidating the History of that Period.* (Washington: 1823), p.. 439–441.
> http://www.hillsdale.edu/dept/History/Documents/War/America/1812/East/1814-McHenry-Armistead.htm

Fort McHenry, September 24, 1814

A severe indisposition, the effect of great fatigue and exposure, has prevented me heretofore from presenting you with an account of the attack on this post. On the night of Saturday the 10th instant, the British fleet, consisting of ships of the line, heavy frigates and bomb vessels, amounting in the whole to 30 sail, appeared at the mouth of the river Patapsco, with every indication of an attempt upon the city of Baltimore. My own force consisted of one company of United States' artillery, under captain Evans, and two companies of sea-fencibles, under captains Bunbury and Addison. Of these three companies, 35 men were unfortunately on the sick list, and unfit for duty. I had been furnished with two companies of volunteer artillery from the city of Baltimore under captain Berry and lieutenant commandant Pennington. To these I must add another very fine company of volunteer artillerists, under judge Nicholson, who had proffered their services to aid in the defense of this post whenever an attack might be apprehended; and also a detachment from commodore Barney's flotilla, under lieutenant Redman. Brigadier general Winder had also furnished me with about 600 infantry, under the command of lieutenant colonel Stewart and major Lane, consisting of detachments from the 12th, 14th, 36th, and 38th regiments of United States' troops—the total amounting to about 1000 effective men.

On Monday morning, very early, it was perceived that the enemy was landing troops on the east side of the Patapsco, distance about ten miles. During that day and the ensuing night, he had brought sixteen ships (including five bomb ships) within about two miles and a half of this fort. I had arranged my force as follows:—the regular artillerists under captain Evans, and the volunteers under captain Nicholson, manned the bastions in the Star Fort. Captains Bunbury's, Addison's, Rodman's, Berry's, and lieutenant commandant Pennington's commands were stationed on the lower works, and the infantry, under lieutenant colonel Stewart and major Lane, were in the outer ditch, to meet the enemy at his landing, should he attempt one.

On Tuesday morning, about sun-rise, the enemy commenced the attack from his five bomb vessels, at the distance of about two miles, and kept up an incessant and well directed bombardment. We immediately opened our batteries, and kept up a brisk fire from our guns and mortars, but unfortunately our shot and shells all fell considerably short of him. This was to me a most distressing circumstance; as it left us exposed to a constant and tremendous shower of shells, without the most remote possibility of our doing him the slightest injury. It affords me the highest gratification to state, that though we were left thus exposed, and thus inactive, not a man shrunk from the conflict.

About two o'clock PM one of the 24 pounders of the southwest bastion, under the immediate command of captain Nicholson, was dismounted by a shell, the explosion from which killed his second lieutenant, and wounded several of his men; the bustle necessarily produced in removing the wounded and replacing the gun, probably induced the enemy to suspect we were in a state of confusion, as he brought in three of his bomb ships, to what I believed to be good striking distance. I immediately ordered a fire to be opened, which was obeyed with alacrity through the whole garrison, and in half an hour those intruders again sheltered themselves by withdrawing beyond our reach. We gave three cheers, and again ceased firing—The enemy continued throwing shells, with one or two slight intermissions, till one o'clock in the morning of Wednesday, when it was discovered that he had availed himself of the darkness of the night, and had thrown a considerable force above to our right; they had approached very near to Fort Covington, when they began to throw rockets; intended, I presume, to give them an opportunity of examining the shores—as I have since understood, they had detached 1250 picked men, with scaling ladders, for the purpose of storming this fort. We once more had an opportunity of opening our batteries, and kept up a continued blaze for nearly two hours, which had the effect again to drive them off.

In justice to lieutenant Newcomb, of the United States' navy, who commanded at fort Covington, with a detachment of sailors, and lieutenant Webster, of the flotilla, who commanded the six gun battery near that fort, I ought to state, that during this time they kept up an animated, and I believe, a very destructive fire, to which I am persuaded, we are much indebted in repulsing the enemy. One of his sunken barges has since been found with two dead men in it; others have been seen floating in the river. The only means we had of directing our guns, was by the blaze of their rockets, and the flashes of their guns. Had they ventured to the same situation in the day time, not a man would have escaped.

The bombardment continued on the part of the enemy until 7 o'clock on Wednesday morning, when it ceased; and about 9, their ships got under weigh, and stood down the river. During the bombardment, which lasted 25 hours (with two slight intermissions) from the best calculation I can make, from 15 to 1800 shells were thrown by the enemy. A few of these fell short. A large proportion burst over us, throwing their fragments among us, and threatening destruction. Many passed over, and about 400 fell within the works. Two of the public buildings are materially injured, the others but slightly. I am happy to inform you (wonderful as it may appear) that our loss amounts only to four men killed, and 24 wounded. The latter will all recover. Among the killed, I have to lament the loss of lieutenant Clagget, and sergeant Clemm, both of captain Nicholson's volunteers; two men whose fate is to be deplored, not only for their personal bravery, but for their high standing, amiable demeanor, and spotless integrity in private life. Lieutenant Russel, of the company under lieutenant Pennington, received, early in the attack, a severe contusion in the heal; notwithstanding which he remained at his post during the whole bombardment.

Were I to name any individuals who signalized themselves, it would be doing injustice to others. Suffice it to say, that every officer and soldier under my command did their duty to my entire satisfaction.

1. Do you think the British anticipated the war to be over once they captured and burned much of the nation's capital on August 24th? Why do you think the United States chose to keep fighting?
2. To what do you attribute the British failure in capturing Fort McHenry?

8-12 Report and Resolutions of the Hartford Convention (1814)

The antipathy of New England Federalists toward Republican directives in general and the War of 1812 in particular culminated in the Hartford Convention in December 1814. The convention was attended by delegates from Connecticut, Massachusetts, New Hampshire, Rhode Island, and Vermont. Although some delegates proposed New England's secession from the Union, moderation prevailed. The final report recommends a series of seven amendments to the Constitution to protect New England from perceived attacks on its sovereignty and assets. Word of the convention and its resolutions arrived in Washington, D.C. just after the news of Andrew Jackson's victory at New Orleans and the Treaty of Ghent.

Source: Dwight, Theodore, *History of the Hartford Convention*, (Boston, Russell, Odiorne, & Co., 1833), p. 368.
http://edale1.home.mindspring.com/Report%20and%20Resolutions%20of%20the%20Hartford%20Convention.htm

Nothing more can be attempted in this report than a general allusion to the principal outlines of the policy which has produced this vicissitude. Among these may be numbered:

First. — A deliberate and extensive system for effecting a combination among certain states, by exciting local jealousies and ambitions, so as to secure to popular leaders in one section of the Union, the control of public affairs in perpetual succession. To which primary object most other characteristics of the system may be reconciled.

Secondly. — The political intolerance displayed and avowed in excluding from office men of unexceptional merit, for want of adherence to the executive creed.

Thirdly. — The infraction of the judiciary authority and rights, by depriving judges of their offices in violation of the constitution.

Fourthly. — The abolition of existing taxes, requisite to prepare the country for those changes to which nations are always exposed, with a view to the acquisition of popular favor.

Fifthly. — The influence of patronage in the distribution of offices, which in these states has been almost invariably made among men the least entitled to such distinction, and who have sold themselves as ready instruments for distracting public opinion, and encouraging administration to hold in contempt the wishes and remonstrances of a people thus apparently divided.

Sixthly. — The admission of new states into the Union formed at pleasure in the western region, has destroyed the balance of power which existed among the original States, and deeply affected their interest.

Seventhly. — The easy admission of naturalized foreigners, to places of trust, honor or profit, operating as an inducement to the malcontent subjects of the old world to come to these States, in quest of executive patronage, and to repay it by an abject devotion to executive measures.

Eighthly. — Hostility to Great Britain, and partiality to the late government of France, adopted as coincident with popular prejudice, and subservient to the main object, party power. Connected with these must be ranked erroneous and distorted estimates of the power and resources of those nations, of the probable results of their controversies, and of our political relations to them respectively.

Lastly and principally. — A visionary and superficial theory in regard to commerce, accompanied by a real hatred but feigned regard to its interests, and a ruinous perseverance in efforts to render it an instrument of coercion and war.

But it is not conceivable that the obliquity of any administration could, in so short a period, have so nearly consummated the work of national ruin, unless favored by defects in the constitution.

To enumerate all the improvements of which that instrument is susceptible, and to propose such amendments as might render it in all respects perfect, would be a task which this convention has not thought proper to assume. They have confined their attention to such as experience has demonstrated to be essential, and even among these, some are considered entitled to a more serious attention than others. They are suggested without any intentional disrespect to other states, and are meant to be such as all shall find an interest in promoting. Their object is to strengthen, and if possible to perpetuate, the union of the states, by removing the grounds of existing jealousies, and providing for a fair and equal representation, and a limitation of powers, which have been misused.

THEREFORE RESOLVED,

That it be and hereby is recommended to the legislatures of the several states represented at this Convention, to adopt all such measures as may be necessary effectually to protect the citizens of said states from the operation and effects of all acts which have been or may be passed by the Congress of the United States, which shall contain provisions, subjecting the militia or other citizens to forcible drafts, conscriptions, or impressments, not authorized by the Constitution of the United States.

Resolved, That it be and hereby is recommended to the said Legislatures, to authorize an immediate and earnest application to be made to the government of the United States, requesting their consent to some arrangement, whereby the said states may, separately or in concert, be empowered to assume upon themselves the defense of their territory against the enemy; and a reasonable portion of the taxes, collected within said States, may be paid into the respective treasuries thereof, and appropriated to the payment of the balance due such states, and to the future defense of the same. The amount so paid into the treasuries to be credited, and the disbursements made as aforesaid to be charged to the United States.

Resolved, That it be, and hereby is, recommended to the legislatures of the aforesaid states to pass laws (where it has not already been done) authorizing the governors or commanders-in-chief of their militia to make detachments from the same, or to form voluntary corps, as shall be most convenient and conformable to their constitutions, and to cause the same to be well armed, equipped, and disciplined, and held in readiness for service; and upon the request of the governor of either of the other states to employ the whole of such detachment or corps, as well as the regular forces of the state, or such part thereof as may be required and can be spared consistently with the safety of the state, in assisting the state, making such request to repel any invasion thereof which shall be made or attempted by the public enemy.

Resolved, That the following amendments of the constitution of the United States be recommended to the states represented as aforesaid, to be proposed by them for adoption by the state legislatures, and in such cases as may be deemed expedient by a convention chosen by the people of each state.

And it is further recommended, that the said states shall persevere in their efforts to obtain such amendments, until the same shall be effected.

First, Representatives and direct taxes shall be apportioned among the several states which may be included in within this Union, according to their respective numbers of free persons, including those bound to serve for a term of years, and excluding Indians not taxed, and all other persons.

Second, No new state shall be admitted into the Union by Congress, in virtue of the power granted by the constitution, without the concurrence of two thirds of both houses.

Third, Congress shall not have the power to lay any embargo on the ships or vessels of the citizens of the United States, in the ports or harbors thereof, for more than sixty days.

Fourth, Congress shall not have the power, without the concurrence of two thirds of both houses, to interdict the commercial intercourse between the United States and any foreign nation, or the dependencies thereof.

Fifth, Congress shall not make or declare war, or authorize acts of hostility against any foreign nation, without the concurrence of two thirds of both houses, except such acts of hostility be in defense of the territories of the United States when actually invaded.

Sixth, No person who shall hereafter be naturalized, shall be eligible as a member of the senate or the house of representatives of the United States, nor capable of holding any civil office under the authority of the United States.

Seventh, The same person shall not be elected president of the United States a second time; nor shall the president be elected from the same state two terms in succession.

Resolved, That if the application of these states to the government of the United States, recommended in a foregoing resolution, should be unsuccessful and peace should not be concluded, and the defense of these states should be neglected, as it has since the commencement of the war, it will, in the opinion of this convention, be expedient for the legislatures of the several states to appoint delegates to another convention, to meet at Boston . . . with such powers and instructions as the exigency of a crisis so momentous may require.

1. Not all Federalists lived in New England. How do you think those Federalists who were not represented in Hartford (especially those in the South) felt about the convention's resolutions?
2. How do you think these resolutions and the Federalist Party might have been viewed by the American people in the wake of their perceived victory in the War of 1812?

8-13   Davy Crockett, Advice to Politicians (1833)

A figure today belonging as much to myth as reality, Davy Crockett had a long a varied career. A frontiersman and soldier, Crockett became a Democratic Congressman but was defeated after several disagreements with Andrew Jackson. He was later elected again as a Whig. It is reported that when he was later defeated again he said, "You can all go to hell and I'm going to Texas" He did so and was later killed in the Alamo.

"Attend all public meetings," says I, "and get some friend to move that you take the chair. If you fail in this attempt, make a push to be appointed secretary. The proceeding of course will be published, and your name is introduced to the public. But should you fail in both undertakings, get two or three acquaintances, over a bottle of whisky, to pass some resolutions, no matter on what subject. Publish them, even if you pay the printer. It will answer the purpose of breaking the ice, which is the main point in these matters.

"Intrigue until you are elected an officer of the militia. This is the second step toward promotion, and can be accomplished with ease, as I know an instance of an election being advertised, and no one attending, the innkeeper at whose house it was to be held, having a military turn, elected himself colonel of his regiment." Says I, "You may not accomplish your ends with as little difficulty, but do not be discouraged-Rome wasn't built in a day.

"If your ambition or circumstances compel you to serve your country and earn three dollars a day, by becoming a member of the legislature, you must first publicly avow that the constitution of the state is a shackle upon free and liberal legislation, and is, therefore, of as little use in the present enlightened age as an old almanac of the year in which the instrument was framed. There is policy in this measure, for by making the constitution a mere dead letter, your headlong proceedings will be attributed to a bold and unshackled mind; whereas, it might otherwise be thought they arose from sheer mulish ignorance. 'The Government' has set the example in his [Jackson's] attack upon the Constitution of the United States, and who should fear to follow where 'the Government' leads?

"When the day of election approaches, visit your constituents far and wide. Treat liberally, and drink freely, in order to rise in their estimation, though you fall in your own. True, you may be called a drunken dog by some of the clean-shirt and silk-stocking gentry, but the real roughnecks will style you a jovial fellow. Their votes are certain, and frequently count double.

"Do all you can to appear to advantage in the eyes of the women. That's easily done. You have but to kiss and slabber [slobber over] their children, wipe their noses, and pat them on the head. This cannot fail to please their mothers, and you may rely on your business being done in that quarter.

"Promise all that is asked," said I, "and more if you can think of anything. Offer to build a bridge or a church, to divide a county, create a batch of new offices, make a turnpike, or anything they like. Promises cost nothing; therefore, deny nobody who has a vote or sufficient influence to obtain one.

"Get up on all occasions, and sometimes on no occasion at all, and make long-winded speeches, though composed of nothing else than wind. Talk of your devotion to your country, your modesty and disinterestedness, or on any such fanciful subject. Rail against taxes of all kinds, officeholders, and bad harvest weather; and wind up with a flourish abut the heroes who fought and bled for our liberties in the times that tried men's souls. To be sure, you run the risk of being considered a bladder of wind, or an empty barrel. But never mind that; you will find enough of the same fraternity to keep you in countenance.

"If any charity be going forward, be at the top of it, provided it is to be advertised publicly. If not, it isn't worth your while. None but a fool would place his candle under a bushel on such an occasion.

"These few directions." said I, "if properly attended to, will do your business. And when once elected-why, a fig for the dirty children, the promises, the bridges, the churches, the taxes, the offices, and the subscriptions. For it is absolutely necessary to forget all these before you can become a thoroughgoing politician, and a patriot of the first water."

1. *Identify and summarize the main thrust of Crockett's satirical piece.*
2. *What common stereotypes of politicians does Crockett target?*

PART NINE
ECONOMIC AND SOCIAL CHANGE

9-1 "The Western Country," Extracts from Letters Published in Niles' Weekly Register (1816)

Niles' Register — also known as The Weekly Register, Niles' Weekly Register, and Niles' National Register — was a newsweekly founded by Hezekiah Niles in 1811. It was published by Niles or his successors until 1849. It covered both the United States and the world. The Register was famous in its own day for its comprehensiveness and reliability — it was routinely cited as an authoritative source of information in courtrooms and legislatures — and it has since become a standard source of information for historians and genealogists.

The western country continues to rise in population and importance with unabated rapidity. This town has been, since the war, full to overflowing; many being obliged to leave it after coming from the Eastern states, not being able to get a *room* to dwell in. More houses will be built this summer than during the last three years together. Manufactories of several important kinds are establishing, among which is a steam grist and saw mill. The surveyor general is making arrangements for laying out, agreeably to late acts of Congress, towns at the Lower Rapids of Sandusky, and at the Rapids of the Miami of the Lakes. The local situation of the latter cannot but render it a most important place. It will be situated at some point within the reservation of twelve miles square, to which vessels of a small tonnage can ascend, and as near the foot of the rapids as may be. I believe the time not very distant when the wealth and resources of the western country will be brought almost to your doors, by means of an extensive inland navigation through the lakes and the grand canal proposed to be made in New York. It will be an easy matter to connect the Miami of the Lakes and the Miami of the Ohio by a canal, the face of the country between the head of the navigation of each of those rivers being quite level. What an extensive inland navigation would then be opened!-from New Orleans to the Hudson!

The whole of that fine tract in Indiana territory, generally called Harrison's purchase, is now surveyed, and will be offered for sale. That part in Jeffesonville district to commence on the first Monday in September next; and that part in Vincennes district on the second Monday in the same month. This tract contains near *three millions of acres* of excellent land; and is, perhaps, the greatest body of good land in the western country. Indiana will be settled as fast as Ohio.

To the foregoing it is pleasant to add the following abstract of an account of the town of Mount Pleasant in Ohio, from the Western Herald.

The town of Mount Pleasant, in Jefferson country, in 1806, containing only seven families, living mostly in cabins-*last summer* it had between 80 and 90 families and about 500 souls, besides journeymen and laborers, transient persons, and its private buildings were mostly of brick.

There were 7 stores; 3 taverns; 3 saddler's, 3 hatter's, 4 blacksmith's, 4 weaver's, 6 boot and shoe maker's, 8 carpenter's, 3 tailor's, 3 cabinet maker's, 1 baker's, 1 apothecary's, and 2 waggon maker's shops-2 tanneries; 1 shop for making wool carding machines; 1 with a machine for spinning wool; 1 manufactory for spinning thread from *flax*; 1 nail factory; 2 wool carding machines. The public buildings were-1 meeting house belonging to the society of Friends, or Quakers, built of brick, two-stories high, with galleries, 92 feet by 60; 1 brick school house, 46 by 22 feet; and 1 brick markethouse, 32 by 16.

Within the distance of six miles from the town were-9 merchant mills; 1 grist mills; 12 saw mills; 1 paper mill, with 2 vats; 1 woolen factory, with 4 looms, and 2 fulling mills.

1. Analyze and summarize the progress of westward expansion as it is detailed in this account. What are the author's hopes and expectations concerning this Western Country?

9-2 The Cherokee Treaty of 1817

In the interest of promoting orderly white expansion in the years immediately following the War of 1812, the United States government sought to open up lands adjacent to existing settlement and discourage widespread dispersal into the more distant west. Between 1816 and 1828, seventeen treaties relating to land cessions or boundary adjustments were signed between the United States Government and the five major Indian nations in the South. In a treaty signed on July 8, 1817, the Cherokee Nation agreed to give up two large tracts of land in North Carolina and Georgia in exchange for one of equal size west of the Mississippi River. Although signed by a substantial number of chiefs, the treaty spawned factions within the Cherokee Nation that would intensify in the decades to come.

Source: The Treaty of Cherokee Agency, in *American State Papers, Indian Affairs* (Washington: GPO, 1934), 2:129–31.
http://members.nbci.com/histroll/treaties/treaty2.html

Articles of a treaty concluded, at the Cherokee Agency, within the Cherokee nation, between major general Andrew Jackson, Joseph M'Minn, governor of the state of Tennessee, and general David Meriwether, commissioners plenipotentiary of the United States of America, of the one part, and the chiefs, head men, and warriors, of the Cherokee nation, east of the Mississippi river, and the chiefs, head men, and warriors, of the Cherokees on the Arkansas river, and their deputies, John D. Chisholm and James Rogers, duly authorized by the chiefs of the Cherokees on the Arkansas river, in open council, by written power of attorney, duly signed and executed, in presence of Joseph Sevier and William Ware.

WHEREAS in the autumn of the year one thousand eight hundred and eight, a deputation from the Upper and Lower Cherokee towns, duly authorized by their nation, went on to the city of Washington, the first named to declare to the President of the United States their anxious desire to engage in the pursuits of agriculture and civilized life, in the country they then occupied, and to make known to the President of the United States the impracticability of inducing the nation at large to do this, and to request the establishment of a division line between the upper and lower towns, so as to include all the waters of the Hiwassee river to the upper town, that, by thus contracting their society within narrow limits, they proposed to begin the establishment of fixed laws and a regular government: The deputies from the lower towns to make known their desire to continue the hunter life, and also the scarcity of game where they then lived, and, under those circumstances, their wish to remove across the Mississippi river, on some vacant lands of the United States. And whereas the President of the United States, after maturely considering the petitions of both parties, on the ninth day of January, A.D. one thousand eight hundred and nine, including other subjects, answered those petitions as follows:

"The United States, my children, are the friends of both parties, and, as far as can be reasonably asked, they are willing to satisfy the wishes of both. Those who remain may be assured of our patronage, our aid, and good neighborhood. Those who wish to remove, are permitted to send an exploring party to reconnoiter the country on the waters of the Arkansas and White rivers, and the higher up the better, as they will be the longer unapproached by our settlements, which will begin at the mouths of those rivers. The regular districts of the government of St. Louis are already laid off to the St. Francis.

"When this party shall have found a tract of country suiting the emigrants, and not claimed by other Indians, we will arrange with them and you the exchange of that for a just portion of the country they leave, and to a part of which, proportioned to their numbers, they have a right. Every aid towards their removal, and what will be necessary for them there, will then be freely administered to them; and when established in their new settlements, we shall still consider them as our children, give them the benefit of exchanging their peltries for what they will want at our factories, and always hold them firmly by the hand."

And whereas the Cherokees, relying on the promises of the President of the United States, as above recited, did explore the country on the west side of the Mississippi, and made choice of the country on the Arkansas and White rivers, and settled themselves down upon United States' lands, to which no other tribe of Indians have any just claim, and have duly notified the President of the United States thereof, and of their anxious desire for the full and complete ratification of his promise, and, to that end, as notified by the President of the United States, have sent on their agents, with full powers to execute a treaty, relinquishing to the United States all the right, title, and interest, to all lands of right to them belonging, as part of the Cherokee nation, which they have left, and which they are about to leave, proportioned to their numbers, including, with those now on the Arkansas, those who are about to remove thither, and to a portion of which they have an equal right agreeably to their numbers.

Now, know ye, that the contracting parties, to carry into full effect the before recited promises with good faith, and to promote a continuation of friendship with their brothers on the Arkansas river, and for that purpose to make an equal distribution of the annuities secured to be paid by the United States to the whole Cherokee nation, have agreed and concluded on the following articles, viz:

ARTICLE 1

The chiefs, head men, and warriors, of the whole Cherokee nation, cede to the United States all the lands lying north and east of the following boundaries, viz: Beginning at the high shoals of the Appalachy river, and running thence, along the boundary line between the Creek and Cherokee nations, westwardly to the Chatahouchy river; thence, up the Chatahouchy river, to the mouth of Souque creek; thence, continuing with the general course of the river until it reaches the Indian boundary line, and, should it strike the Turrurar river, thence, with its meanders, down said river to its mouth, in part of the proportion of land in the Cherokee nation east of the Mississippi, to which those now on the Arkansas and those about to remove there are justly entitled.

ARTICLE 2

The chiefs, head men, and warriors, of the whole Cherokee nation, do also cede to the United States all the lands lying north and west of the following boundary lines, viz: Beginning at the Indian boundry line that runs from the north bank of the Tennessee river, opposite to the mouth of Hywassee river, at a point on the top of Walden's ridge, where it divides the waters of the Tennessee river from those of the Sequatchie river; thence, along the said ridge, southwardly, to the bank of the Tennessee river, at a point near to a place called the Negro Sugar Camp, opposite to the upper end of the first island above Running Water Town; thence, westwardly, a straight line to the mouth of Little Sequatchie river; thence, up said river, to its main fork; thence, up its northernmost fork, to its source; and thence, due west, to the Indian boundary line.

ARTICLE 3

It is also stipulated by the contracting parties, that a census shall be taken of the whole Cherokee nation, during the month of June, in the year of our Lord one thousand eight hundred and eighteen, in the following manner, viz: That the census of those on the east side of the Mississippi river, who declare their intention of remaining, shall be taken by a commissioner appointed by the President of the United States, and a commissioner appointed by the Cherokees on the Arkansas river; and the census of the Cherokees on the Arkansas river, and those removing there, and who, at that time, declare their intention of removing there, shall be taken by a commissioner appointed by the President of the United States, and one appointed by the Cherokees east of the Mississippi river.

ARTICLE 4

The contracting parties do also stipulate that the annuity due from the United States to the whole Cherokee nation for the year one thousand eight hundred and eighteen, is to be divided between the two parts of the nation in proportion to their numbers, agreeably to the stipulations contained in the third article of this treaty; and to be continued to be divided thereafter in proportion to their numbers; and the lands to be apportioned and surrendered to the United States agreeably to the aforesaid enumeration, as the proportionate part, agreeably to their numbers, to which those who have removed, and who declare their intention to remove, have a just right, including these with the lands ceded in the first and second articles of this treaty.

ARTICLE 5

The United States bind themselves, in exchange for the lands ceded in the first and second articles hereof, to give to that part of the Cherokee nation on the Arkansas as much land on said river and White river as they have or may hereafter receive from the Cherokee nation east of the Mississippi, acre for acre, as the just proportion due that part of the nation on the Arkansas agreeably to their numbers; which is to commence on the north side of the Arkansas river, at the mouth of Point Remove or Budwell's Old Place; thence, by a straight line, northwardly, to strike Chataunga mountain, or the hill first above Shield's Ferry on White river, running up and between said rivers for complement, the banks of which rivers to be the lines; and to have the above line, from the point of beginning to the point on White river, run and marked, which shall be done soon after the ratification of this treaty; and all citizens of the United States, except Mrs. P. Lovely, who is to remain where she lives during life, removed from within the bounds as above named. And it is further stipulated, that the treaties heretofore between the Cherokee nation and the United States are to continue in full force with both parts of the nation, and both parts thereof entitled to all the immunities and privilege which the old nation enjoyed under the aforesaid treaties; the United States reserving the right of establishing factories, a military post, and roads, within the boundaries above defined.

ARTICLE 6

The United States do also bind themselves to give to all the poor warriors who may remove to the western side of the Mississippi river, one rifle gun and ammunition, one blanket, and one brass kettle, or, in lieu of the brass kettle, a beaver trap, which is to be considered as a full compensation for the improvements which they may leave; which articles are to be delivered at such point as the President of the United States may direct: and to aid in the removal of the emigrants, they further agree to furnish flat bottomed boats and provisions sufficient for that purpose: and to those emigrants whose improvements add real value to their lands, the United States agree to pay a full valuation for the same, which is to be ascertained by a commissioner appointed by the President of the United States for that purpose, and paid for as soon after the ratification of this treaty as practicable. The boats and provisions promised to the emigrants are to be furnished by the agent on the Tennessee river, at such time and place as the emigrants may notify him of; and it shall be his duty to furnish the same.

ARTICLE 7

And for all improvements which add real value to the lands lying within the boundaries ceded to the United States, by the first and second articles of this treaty, the United States do agree to pay for at the time, and to be valued in the same manner, as stipulated in the sixth article of this treaty; or, in lieu thereof, to give in exchange improvements of equal value which the emigrants may leave, and for which they are to receive pay. And it is further stipulated, that all these improvements, left by the emigrants within the bounds of the Cherokee nation east of the Mississippi river, which add real value to the lands, and for which the United States shall give a consideration, and not so exchanged, shall be rented to the Indians by the agent, year after year, for the benefit of the poor and decrepit of that part of the nation east of the Mississippi river, until surrendered by the nation, or to the nation. And it is further agreed, that the said Cherokee nation shall not be called upon for any part of the consideration paid for said improvements at any future period.

ARTICLE 8

And to each and every head of any Indian family residing on the east side of the Mississippi river, on the lands that are now, or may hereafter be, surrendered to the United States, who may wish to become citizens of the United States, the United States do agree to give a reservation of six hundred and forty acres of land, in a square, to include their improvements, which are to be as near the centre thereof as practicable, in which they will have a life estate, with a reversion in fee simple to their children, reserving to the widow her dower, the register of whose names is to be filed in the office of the Cherokee agent, which shall be kept open until the census is taken as stipulated in the third article of this treaty. Provided, That if any of the heads of families, for whom reservations may be made, should remove therefrom, then, in that case, the right to revert to the United States. And provided further, That the land which may be reserved under this article, be deducted from the amount which has been ceded under the first and second articles of this treaty.

ARTICLE 9

It is also provided by the contracting parties, that nothing in the foregoing articles shall be construed so as to prevent any of the parties so contracting from the free navigation of all the waters mentioned therein.

ARTICLE 10

The whole of the Cherokee nation do hereby cede to the United States all right, title, and claim, to all reservations made to Doublehead and others, which were reserved to them by a treaty made and entered into at the city of Washington, bearing date the seventh of January, one thousand eight hundred and six.

ARTICLE 11

It is further agreed that the boundary lines of the lands ceded to the United States by the first and second articles of this treaty, and the boundary line of the lands ceded by the United States in the fifth article of this treaty, is to be run and marked by a commissioner or commissioners appointed by the President of the United States, who shall be accompanied by such commissioners as the Cherokees may appoint; due notice thereof to be given to the nation.

ARTICLE 12

The United States do also bind themselves to prevent the intrusion of any of its citizens within the lands ceded by the first and second articles of this treaty, until the same shall be ratified by the President and Senate of the United States, and duly promulgated.

ARTICLE 13

The contracting parties do also stipulate that this treaty shall take effect and be obligatory on the contracting parties so soon as the same shall be ratified by the President of the United States, by and with the advice and consent of the Senate of the United States.

In witness of all and every thing herein determined, by and between the before recited contracting parties, we have, in full and open council, at the Cherokee Agency, this eighth day of July, A.D. one thousand eight hundred and seventeen, set our hands and seals.

1. *What conditions of this treaty might have been appealing to some Cherokee leaders? Why do you think a significant number of chiefs signed it?*
2. *In its quest for orderly white settlement, what other options might the United States Government have pursued short of displacing native peoples in the South?*

9-3   The Case for the Erie Canal

In 1807, Jesse Hawley was imprisoned for debt in Canandaigua, New York, largely as result of his business expenditures in transporting flour from the mills in Geneva. Hoping to render himself "useful to society," Hawley wrote a series of essays published in the Genesee Messenger under the name "Hercules," on the wisdom and reality of building an overland canal across New York State. His essays materially contributed to enlighten public opinion with regard to a projected canal. In a letter written to Hawley in 1822, De Witt Clinton wrote "I have no hesitation in stating, that the first suggestion of a canal from Lake Erie to the Hudson River, which came to my knowledge, was communicated in essays under the signature of 'Hercules'."

> **Source:** David Hosack, *Memoir of De Witt Clinton* (New York: J. Seymour, 1829)
> http://www.history.rochester.edu/canal/bib/hosack/APPOT.html

In consequence of the difference and conflict of political sentiments which pervade the United States, respecting the administration of the government, and the appropriation of their resources, it is probable that it will be left to the future politician to duly appreciate and justly admire the ingenuity and patriotism of Mr. Jefferson, which devised and promulgated the idea of appropriating the surplus revenue of the United States, after the payment of the national debt, to the improvement of canals, roads, &c. which he threw out in his second inaugural speech.

It appears by the president's last message, that there is a greater surplus of revenue than was anticipated at the time the terms for the discharge of the national debt were stipulated; so as to leave a sum of money in the treasury without any appropriation; for the use of which he has suggested its application to the improvement of some great national object, the undertaking of which is to be immediately commenced.

I will presume to assert, that the president himself will agree that, if not even before, at least, next to the utility of a National Institute, is the improvement of the navigation of our fresh waters.

This admitted, the next inquiry is—where and what waters can be improved, to afford the most extensive and immediate benefits to the agricultural and commercial interests of the United States?

With due deference to the president of the United States, and the committees appointed by the national legislature, who now have the subject under consideration, I will presume to suggest to them, that improvement which would afford the most immediate, and consequently the most extensive advantages which any other in the United States can possibly do. It is the connecting the waters of Lake Erie and those of the Mohawk and Hudson rivers by means of a canal.

As this project is probably not more than twelve months old in human conception, but imperfect data can be furnished on the subject at present—such as I am possessed of, I will add.

It ought to commence at the foot of Lake Erie, as soon as a suitable place can be found to afford a draft on its waters—to gain and preserve a moderate descent of ground it will have to pursue a north-eastern course for some miles, it then may pursue an east course and cross the Genesee River, somewhere above its Falls, thence near to, and probably in the channel of, Mud Creek, an outlet of Canandaigua Lake, and follow them into Seneca River; but leaving that, up stream to Jack's Rifts, for the purpose of preserving the head of water—thence meandering along between the high and low grounds of Onondaga and Oneida counties, going south of their lakes, and let it fall into the Mohawk and mingle with its waters somewhere above Utica.

The distance from Buffalo village, at the foot of Lake Erie, to Canandaigua, is ninety miles according to the present road—from thence, on the Seneca turnpike to Utica, is one hundred and twelve miles—making two hundred and two miles from Lake Erie to Utica. It is possible that the angles of the roads are equal to the necessary meanderings of the canal through so extensive and level a country. By Ellicott's map of the Holland company's tract, the level of the waters of Lake Erie are four hundred and fifty feet above that of Ontario. The level of the Mohawk above that of Ontario is not correctly known, but we can approximate the fact from the following comparative statement. From the canal at Rome or Fort Stanwix, down Wood Creek to Oneida Lake, is twenty miles through a tract of very level land, say ten feet fall. Oneida Lake thirty miles in length, say three feet fall—from thence to Three River Point, eighteen miles, say twelve feet fall—thence to Oswego Falls, twelve miles, say ten feet fall. The Falls a quarter of a mile, say fifteen feet fall—thence to Lake Ontario twenty-four miles, say fifteen feet fall, makes the elevation of Rome sixty-five feet above the waters of Ontario. From Rome to Utica, sixteen miles by land, and twenty-eight by water with good current, say twenty-five feet fall, which deduct from sixty-five leaves forty feet, the elevation of the Mohawk at Utica above the Ontario. As the whole of this calculation is conjectured without ever seeing any part of the ground except the villages of Utica and Rome, it cannot be pretended that it is correct; yet it is presumed to be sufficiently large. Deduct the difference between Utica and Ontario (forty feet) from the difference between Erie and Ontario (four hundred and fifty feet) and it leaves four hundred and ten feet fall, between the waters of Erie and the Mohawk at Utica, which will average two feet a mile on the whole distance.

The result of this crude calculation is sufficient, and merely intended to demonstrate the possibility, and even practicability, of the undertaking. When we consider the Herculean task performed on sundry canals in Europe, the crossing Genesee river and other streams which intersect the course of the route, cannot be admitted as insuperable obstacles to the undertaking.

Pretending to no knowledge in the science of canalling, consequently no calculation on the probable expenses will be hazarded—but the level country through which it would take its course, is such, that more than half the distance would require no further digging than to sink the ditch sufficient for the depth of water and its necessary banks; and it is obvious that it would require but few stone. The western part of the Genesee county and Onondaga county afford a sufficient supply. Other tracts no doubt would furnish at least partial supplies by occasional beds and quarried. The principal use of stone contemplated here is to wall the banks of the ditch. Where stone was scarce, timber could be substituted in the first essay, and stone could be boated to supply its place when decayed.

The magnitude of this improvement is far beyond the reach of individual capital in America, for the present age, and probably for a century to come. The present governor of the state of New-York has indeed suggested the idea of calling into its aid British capitalists; but as their object, by vesting their capital in foreign stock, would be the double consideration of having that stock permanent, and to receive from it a rate of interest above that which they can obtain for their capital in their own market; consequently both the immense agricultural and commercial interests of America, flowing through this channel, must for ever, by an inexhaustible load of taxes, be tributary to foreign capitalists.

America already suffers by foreign capitalists drawing from her resources large sums, in premiums, from her stocks and new lands; from which she can have no possible reciprocity of interest, except merely in the contemplation of redressing at some future day, the wrongs of foreign nations, in spoliations on her commerce, by a sequestration of this foreign capital. And unless the government holds the idea of sequestration in reserve, as the dernier resort for the redress of foreign aggressions, there can scarcely be a palliative argument offered by them for their toleration to foreigners, of foreign residence, by their superior wealth drawing a private revenue from our best resources. We, therefore, can alone, with confidence, turn our attention and our best hopes to a patriotic government, whose treasury must in a few years, be amply competent to the undertaking; which, when finished, may be given to us for an insignificant tax.

When completed, this would afford a course of navigation from New-York, by sloop navigation to Albany, 160 miles—from Albany to Buffalo, by boat navigation, 300 miles—from Buffalo to Chicago by sloop navigation, 1200 miles; making a distance of 1600 miles of inland navigation up stream, where the cargo has to be shifted but three times.

The probable charges of freight would be—from New-York to Albany (the present price on small packages of merchandise up freight is about) five dollars per ton, from thence to Buffalo (full large enough, including no charge for lockage) fifty dollars a ton, from thence to Chicago, say large fifty dollars per ton—is equal to 105 dollars per ton, or five cents per pound nearly. From Chicago harbour it might be continued up its river, by portage, into and down the Illinois, and up the Mississippi; and into, as yet, almost unknown regions.

The navigation of the four largest lakes in the known world, together with all their tributary streams—the agricultural products and the commerce of all the surrounding country, would pass through this canal—and even the fifth (Ontario) would become its tributary.—The additional duty on the Canadian trade alone would defray the annual repairs of the canal.

The vast extension of and facility to commerce, together with the additional spur to industry which this canal would give, would in twenty years redeem the principal and interest of their expenditure, at the rate of their present imposts, by its additional increase.

Its invitation to the culture of the fertile soil surrounding these extensive navigable waters, would be such, that in a few generations the exhibition of their improvements and the display of their wealth, would even scarcely be equaled by the old world.

—HERCULES

1. According to Hawley, how should a canal of this magnitude be funded? What does he think of the prospect of using foreign investors?
2. What benefits would this canal bring to the state of New York—other than lowering the cost of transportation?

9-4 John Marshall Affirms the Power of the Federal Government

In the case of McCulloch v. Maryland, Chief Justice John Marshall delivered arguably his most important interpretation of the Constitution—endorsing the doctrine of broad construction and implied powers. The case focused on the right of the state of Maryland to levy a tax on the Baltimore branch of the Bank of the United States and thereby assert its sovereignty over the federal institution. The Supreme Court's decision was unanimous—upholding the power of Congress to charter the bank and stating that the state's (Maryland) right to tax it was contrary to the supreme law of the land.

Source: *The American Revolution—an HTML Project*
http://odur.let.rug.nl/~usa/D/1801-1825/marshallcases/mar02.htm
also in Henry Steele Commanger, ed., *Documents of American History* (New York: Appleton-Century-Crofts, 1949), 213–220.

In the case now to be determined, the defendant, a sovereign State, denies the obligation of a law enacted by the legislature of the Union, and the plaintiff, on his part, contests the validity of an act which has been passed by the legislature of that State. The Constitution of our country, in its most interesting and vital parts, is to be considered; the conflicting powers of the government of the Union and of its members, as marked in that constitution, are to be discussed; and an opinion given, which may essentially influence the great operations of the government. No tribunal can approach such a question without a deep sense of its importance, and of the awful responsibility involved in its decision. But it must be decided peacefully, or remain a source of hostile legislation, perhaps of hostility of a still more serious nature; and if it is to be so decided, by this tribunal alone can the decision be made. On the Supreme Court of the United States has the constitution of our country devolved this important duty.

The first question made in the cause is, has Congress power to incorporate a bank?

It has been truly said that this can scarcely be considered as an open question, entirely unprejudiced by the former proceedings of the nation respecting it. The principle now contested was introduced at a very early period of our history, has been recognized by many successive legislatures, and has been acted upon by the judicial department, in cases of peculiar delicacy, as a law of undoubted obligation. . . .

The power now contested was exercised by the first Congress elected under the present constitution. The bill for incorporating the bank of the United States did not steal upon an unsuspecting legislature, and pass unobserved. Its principle was completely understood, and was opposed with equal zeal and ability. After being resisted, first in the fair and open field of debate, and afterwards in the executive cabinet, with as much persevering talent as any measure has ever experienced, and being supported by arguments which convinced minds as pure and as intelligent as this country can boast, it became a law. The original act was permitted to expire; but a short experience of the embarrassments to which the refusal to revive it exposed the government, convinced those who were most prejudiced against the measure of its necessity, and induced the passage of the present law. It would require no ordinary share of intrepidity to assert that a measure adopted under these circumstances was a bold and plain usurpation, to which the constitution gave no countenance.

These observations belong to the cause; but they are not made under the impression that, were the question entirely new, the law would be found irreconcilable with the constitution.

In discussing this question, the counsel for the State of Maryland have deemed it of some importance, in the construction of the constitution, to consider that instrument not as emanating from the people, but as the act of sovereign and independent States. The powers of the general government, it has been said, are delegated by the States, who alone are truly sovereign; and must be exercised in subordination to the States, who alone possess supreme dominion.

It would be difficult to sustain this proposition. The Convention which framed the constitution was indeed elected by the State legislatures. But the instrument, when it came from their hands, was a mere proposal, without obligation, or pretensions to it. It was reported to the then existing Congress of the United States, with a request that it might "be submitted to a convention of delegates, chosen in each State by the people thereof, under the recommendation of its legislature, for their assent and ratification." This mode of proceeding was adopted; and by the convention, by Congress, and by the State legislatures, the instrument was submitted to the people. They acted upon it in the only manner in which they can act safely, effectively, and wisely, on such a subject, by assembling in convention. It is true, they assembled in their several States—and where else should they have assembled? No political dreamer was ever wild enough to think of breaking down the lines which separate the States, and of compounding the American people into one common mass. Of consequence, when they act, they act in their States. But the measures they adopt do not, on that account, cease to be the measures of the people themselves, or become the measures of the State governments.

From these conventions the constitution derives its whole authority. The government proceeds directly from the people; is "ordained and established" in the name of the people; and is declared to be ordained, "in order to form a more perfect union, establish justice, ensure domestic tranquility, and secure the blessings of liberty to themselves and to their posterity." The assent of the States, in their sovereign capacity, is implied in calling a convention, and thus submitting that instrument to the people. But the people were at perfect liberty to accept or reject it; and their act was final. It required not the affirmance, and could not be negatived, by the State governments. The constitution, when thus adopted, was of complete obligation, and bound the State sovereignties. . . . of this fact on the case), is, emphatically, and truly, a government of the people. In form and in substance it emanates from them. Its powers are granted by them, and are to be exercised directly on them, and for their benefit.

This government is acknowledged by all to be one of enumerated powers. The principle, that it can exercise only the powers granted to it, [is] now universally admitted. But the question respecting the extent of the powers actually granted, is perpetually arising, and will probably continue to arise, as long as our system shall exist. . . .

Among the enumerated powers, we do not find that of establishing a bank or creating a corporation. But there is no phrase in the instrument which, like the articles of confederation, excludes incidental or implied powers; and which requires that everything granted shall be expressly and minutely described. Even the 10th amendment, which was framed for the purpose of quieting the excessive jealousies which had been excited, omits the word "expressly," and declares only that the powers "not delegated to the United States, nor prohibited to the States, are reserved to the States or to the people"; thus leaving the question, whether the particular power which may become the subject of contest has been delegated to the one government, or prohibited to the other, to depend on a fair construction of the whole instrument. The men who drew and adopted this amendment had experienced the embarrassments resulting from the insertion of this word in the articles of confederation, and probably omitted it to avoid those embarrassments. A constitution, to contain an accurate detail of all the subdivisions of which its great powers will admit, and of all the means by which they may be carried into execution, would partake of the prolixity of a legal code, and could scarcely be embraced by the human mind. It would probably never be understood by the public. Its nature, therefore, requires, that only its great outlines should be marked, its important objects designated, and the minor ingredients which compose those objects be deduced from the nature of the objects themselves. That this idea was entertained by the framers of the American constitution, is not only to be inferred from the nature of the instrument, but from the language. Why else were some of the limitations, found in the ninth section of the 1st article, introduced? It is also, in some degree, warranted by their having omitted to use any restrictive term which might prevent its receiving a fair and just interpretation. In considering this question, then, we must never forget that it is a constitution we are expounding.

Although, among the enumerated powers of government, we do not find the word "bank," or "incorporation," we find the great powers to lay and collect taxes; to borrow money; to regulate commerce; to declare and conduct a war; and to raise and support armies and navies. The sword and the purse, all the external relations, and no inconsiderable portion of the industry of the nation, are entrusted to its government. It can never be pretended that these vast powers draw after them others of inferior importance, merely because they are inferior. Such an idea can never be advanced. But it may with great reason be contended, that a government, entrusted with such ample powers, on the due execution of which the happiness and prosperity of the nation so vitally depends, must also be entrusted with ample means for their execution. The power being given, it is the interest of the nation to facilitate its execution. It can never be their interest, and cannot be presumed to have been their intention, to clog and embarrass its execution by withholding the most appropriate means . . . require it) which would impute to the framers of that instrument, when granting these powers for the public good, the intention of impeding their exercise by withholding a choice of means? If, indeed, such be the mandate of the constitution, we have only to obey; but that instrument does not profess to enumerate the means by which the powers it confers may be executed; nor does it prohibit the creation of a corporation, if the existence of such a being be essential to the beneficial exercise of those powers. It is, then, the subject of fair inquiry, how far such means may be employed.

It is not denied, that the powers given to the government imply the ordinary means of execution. That, for example, of raising revenue, and applying it to national purposes, is admitted to imply the power of conveying money from place to place, as the exigencies of the nation may require, and of employing the usual means of conveyance. But it is denied that the government has its choice of means; or, that it may employ the most convenient means, if, to employ them, it be necessary to erect a corporation. . . .

The government which has a right to do an act, and has imposed on it the duty of performing that act, must, according to the dictates of reason, be allowed to select the means; and those who contend that it may not select any appropriate means, that one particular mode of effecting the object is excepted, take upon themselves the burden of establishing that exception. . . . The power of creating a corporation, though appertaining to sovereignty, is not like the power of making war, or levying taxes, or of regulating commerce, a great substantive and independent power, which cannot be implied as incidental to other powers, or used as a means of executing them. It is never the end for which other powers are exercised, but a means by which other objects are accomplished. . . . The power of creating a corporation is never used for its own sake, but for the purpose of effecting something else. No sufficient reason is, therefore, perceived, why it may not pass as incidental to those powers which are expressly given, if it be a direct mode of executing them.

But the constitution of the United States has not left the right of Congress to employ the necessary means, for the execution of the powers conferred on the government, to general reasoning. To its enumeration of powers is added that of making "all laws which shall be necessary and proper for carrying into execution the foregoing powers, and all other powers vested by this constitution, in the government of the United States, or in any department thereof."

The counsel for the State of Maryland have urged various arguments, to prove that this clause, though in terms a grant of power, is not so in effect; but is really restrictive of the general right, which might otherwise be implied, of selecting means for executing the enumerated powers. . . .

Almost all compositions contain words, which, taken in their rigorous sense, would convey a meaning different from that which is obviously intended. It is essential to just construction, that many words which import something excessive should be understood in a more mitigated sense—in that sense which common usage justifies. The word "necessary" is of this description. It has not a fixed character peculiar to itself. It admits of all degrees of comparison; and is often connected with other words, which increase or diminish the impression the mind receives of the urgency it imports. A thing may be necessary, very necessary, absolutely or indispensably necessary. To no mind would the same idea be conveyed by these several phrases. This comment on the word is well illustrated by the passage cited at the bar, from the 20th section of the 1st article of the constitution. It is, we think, impossible to compare the sentence which prohibits a State from laying "imposts, or duties on imports or exports, except what may be absolutely necessary for executing its inspection laws," with that which authorizes Congress "to make all laws which shall be necessary and proper for carrying into execution" the powers of the general government, without feeling a conviction that the convention understood itself to change materially the meaning of the word "necessary," by prefixing the word "absolutely." This word, then, like others, is used in various senses; and, in its construction, the subject, the context, the intention of the person using them, are all to be taken into view.

Let this be done in the case under consideration. The subject is the execution of those great powers on which the welfare of a nation essentially depends. It must have been the intention of those who gave these powers, to insure, as far as human prudence could insure, their beneficial execution. This could not be done by confiding the choice of means to such narrow limits as not to leave it in the power of Congress to adopt any which might be appropriate, and which were conducive to the end. This provision is made in a constitution intended to endure for ages to come, and, consequently, to be adapted to the various crises of human affairs. To have prescribed the means by which government should, in all future time, execute its powers, would have been to change, entirely, the character of the instrument, and give it the properties of a legal code. It would have been an unwise attempt to provide, by immutable rules, for exigencies which, if foreseen at all, must have been seen dimly, and which can be best provided for as they occur. To have declared that the best means shall not be used, but those alone without which the power given would be nugatory, would have been to deprive the legislature of the capacity to avail itself of experience, to exercise its reason, and to accommodate its legislation to circumstances. If we apply this principle of construction to any of the powers of the government, we shall find it so pernicious in its operation that we shall be compelled to discard it. . . .

The result of the most careful and attentive consideration bestowed upon this clause is, that if it does not enlarge, it cannot be construed to restrain the powers of Congress, or to impair the rights of the legislature to exercise its best judgment in the selection of measures to carry into execution the constitutional powers of the government. If no other motive for its insertion can be suggested, a sufficient one is found in the desire to remove all doubts respecting the right to legislate on that vast mass of incidental powers which must be involved in the constitution, if that instrument be not a splendid bauble.

We admit, as all must admit, that the powers of the government are limited, and that its limits are not to be transcended. But we think the sound construction of the constitution must allow to the national legislature that discretion, with respect to the means by which the powers it confers are to be carried into execution, which will enable that body to perform the high duties assigned to it, in the manner most beneficial to the people. Let the end be legitimate, let it be within the scope of the constitution, and all means which are appropriate, which are plainly adapted to that end, which are not prohibited, but consist with the letter and spirit of the constitution, are constitutional. . . .

Should Congress, in the execution of its powers, adopt measures which are prohibited by the constitution; or should Congress, under the pretext of executing its powers, pass laws for the accomplishment of objects not entrusted to the government; it would become the painful duty of this tribunal, should a case requiring such a decision come before it, to say that such an act was not the law of the land. But where the law is not prohibited, and is really calculated to effect any of the objects entrusted to the government, to undertake here to inquire into the degree of its necessity, would be to pass the line which circumscribes the judicial department, and to tread on legislative ground. This court disclaims all pretensions to such a power.

After this declaration, it can scarcely be necessary to say that the existence of State banks can have no possible influence on the question. No trace is to be found in the constitution of an intention to create a dependence of the government of the Union on those of the States, for the execution of the great powers assigned to it. Its means are adequate to its ends; and on those means alone was it expected to rely for the accomplishment of its ends. To impose on it the necessity of resorting to means which it cannot control, which another government may furnish or withhold, would render its course precarious, the result of its measures uncertain, and create a dependence on other governments, which might disappoint its most important designs, and is incompatible with the language of the constitution. But were it otherwise, the choice of means implies a right to choose a national bank in preference to State banks, and Congress alone can make the election.

After the most deliberate consideration, it is the unanimous and decided opinion of this Court, that the act to incorporate the Bank of the United States is a law made in pursuance of the constitution, and is a part of the supreme law of the land. . . .

It being the opinion of the Court, that the act incorporating the bank is constitutional; and that the power of establishing a branch in the State of Maryland might be properly exercised by the bank itself, we proceed to inquire—

2. Whether the State of Maryland may, without violating the constitution, tax that branch?

That the power of taxation is one of vital importance; that it is retained by the States; that it is not abridged by the grant of a similar power to the government of the Union; that it is to be concurrently exercised by the two governments: are truths which have never been denied. But, such is the paramount character of the constitution, that its capacity to withdraw any subject from the action of even this power, is admitted. The States are expressly forbidden to lay any duties on imports or exports, except what may be absolutely necessary for executing their inspection laws. If the obligation of this prohibition must be conceded, the same paramount character would seem to restrain, as it certainly may restrain, a State from such other exercise of this power; as is in its nature incompatible with, and repugnant to, the constitutional laws of the Union. . . .

On this ground the counsel for the bank place its claim to be exempted from the power of a State to tax its operations. There is no express provision for the case, but the claim has been sustained on a principle which so entirely pervades the constitution, is so intermixed with the materials which compose it, so interwoven with its web, so blended with its texture, as to be incapable of being separated from it, without rending it into shreds.

This great principle is, that the constitution and the laws made in pursuance thereof are supreme; that they control the constitution and laws of the respective States, and cannot be controlled by them. From this, which may be almost termed an axiom, other propositions are deduced as corollaries, on the truth or error of which, and on their application to this case, the cause has been supposed to depend. These are, 1st. that a power to create implies a power to preserve. 2nd. That a power to destroy, if wielded by a different hand, is hostile to, and incompatible with these powers to create and to preserve. 3d. That where this repugnancy exists, that authority which is supreme must control, not yield to that over which it is supreme. . . .

That the power of taxing by the States may be exercised so as to destroy it, is too obvious to be denied. But taxation is said to be an absolute power, which acknowledges no other limits than those expressly prescribed in the constitution, and like sovereign power of every other description, is trusted to the discretion of those who use it. But the very terms of this argument admit that the sovereignty of the State, in the article of taxation itself, is subordinate to, and may be controlled by, the constitution of the United States. How far it has been controlled by that instrument must be a question of construction. In making this construction, no principle not declared, can be admissible, which would defeat the legitimate operations of a supreme government. It is of the very essence of supremacy to remove all obstacles to its action within its own sphere, and so to modify every power vested in subordinate governments, as to exempt its own operations from their own influence. This effect need not be stated in terms. It is so involved in the declaration of supremacy, so necessarily implied in it, that the expression of it could not make it more certain. We must, therefore, keep it in view while construing the constitution.

The argument on the part of the State of Maryland is, not that the States may directly resist a law of Congress, but that they may exercise their acknowledged powers upon it, and that the constitution leaves them this right in the confidence that they will not abuse it.

Before we proceed to examine this argument, and to subject it to the test of the constitution, we must be permitted to bestow a few considerations on the nature and extent of this original right of taxation, which is acknowledged to remain with the States. It is admitted that the power of taxing the people and their property is essential to the very existence of government, and may be legitimately exercised on the objects to which it is applicable, to the utmost extent to which the government may choose to carry it. The only security against the abuse of this power, is found in the structure of the government itself. In imposing a tax the legislature acts upon its constituents. . . .

The sovereignty of a State extends to everything which exists by its own authority, or is so introduced by its permission; but does it extend to those means which are employed by Congress to carry into execution powers conferred on that body by the people of the United States? We think it demonstrable that it does not. Those powers are not given by the people of a single State. They are given by the people of the United States, to a government whose laws, made in pursuance of the constitution, are declared to be supreme. Consequently, the people of a single State cannot confer a sovereignty which will extend over them.

If we measure the power of taxation residing in a State, by the extent of sovereignty which the people of a single State possess, and can confer on its government, we have an intelligible standard, applicable to every case to which the power may be applied. We have a principle which leaves the power of taxing the people and property of a State unimpaired; which leaves to a State the command of all its resources, and which places beyond its reach, all those powers which are conferred by the people of the United States on the government of the Union, and all those means which are given for the purpose of carrying those powers into execution. We have a principle which is safe for the States, and safe for the Union. We are relieved, as we ought to be, from clashing sovereignty; from interfering powers; from a repugnancy between a right in one government to pull down what there is an acknowledged right in another to build up; from the incompatibility of a right in one government to destroy what there is a right in another to preserve. We are not driven to the perplexing inquiry, so unfit for the judicial department, what degree of taxation is the legitimate use, and what degree may amount to the abuse of the power. The attempt to use it on the means employed by the government of the Union, in pursuance of the constitution, is itself an abuse, because it is the usurpation of a power which the people of a single State cannot give.

We find, then, on just theory, a total failure of this original right to tax the means employed by the government of the Union, for the execution of its powers. The right never existed, and the question whether it has been surrendered, cannot arise.

But, waiving this theory for the present, let us resume the inquiry, whether this power can be exercised by the respective States, consistently with a fair construction of the constitution?

That the power to tax involves the power to destroy; that the power to destroy may defeat and render useless the power to create; that there is a plain repugnance, in conferring on one government a power to control the constitutional measures of another, which other, with respect to those very measures, is declared to be supreme over that which exerts the control, are propositions not to be denied. But all inconsistencies are to be reconciled by the magic of the word CONFI-DENCE. Taxation, it is said, does not necessarily and unavoidably destroy. To carry it to the excess of destruction would be an abuse, to presume which, would banish that confidence which is essential to all government.

But is this a case of confidence? Would the people of any one State trust those of another with a power to control the most insignificant operations of their State government? We know they would not. Why, then, should we suppose that the people of any one State should be willing to trust those of another with a power to control the operations of a government to which they have confided their most important and most valuable interests? In the legislature of the Union alone, are all represented. The legislature of the Union alone, therefore, can be trusted by the people with the power of controlling measures which concern all, in the confidence that it will not be abused. This, then, is not a case of confidence, and we must consider it as it really is.

If we apply the principle for which the State of Maryland contends, to the constitution generally, we shall find it capable of changing totally the character of that instrument. We shall find it capable of arresting all the measures of the government, and of prostrating it at the foot of the States. The American people have declared their constitution, and the laws made in pursuance thereof, to be supreme; but this principle would transfer the supremacy, in fact, to the States.

If the States may tax one instrument, employed by the government in the execution of its powers, they may tax any and every other instrument. They may tax the mail; they may tax the mint; they may tax patent rights; they may tax the papers of the custom-house; they may tax judicial process; they may tax all the means employed by the government, to an excess which would defeat all the ends of government. This was not intended by the American people. They did not design to make their government dependent on the States. . . .

The Court has bestowed on this subject its most deliberate consideration. The result is a conviction that the States have no power, by taxation or otherwise, to retard, impede, burden, or in any manner control, the operations of the constitutional laws enacted by Congress to carry into execution the powers vested in the general government. This is, we think, the unavoidable consequence of that supremacy which the constitution has declared.

We are unanimously of opinion, that the law passed by the legislature of Maryland, imposing a tax on the Bank of the United States, is unconstitutional and void.

This opinion does not deprive the States of any resources which they originally possessed. It does not extend to a tax paid by the real property of the bank, in common with the other real property within the State, nor to a tax imposed on the interest which the citizens of Maryland may hold in this institution, in common with other property of the same description throughout the State. But this is a tax on the operations of the bank, and is, consequently, a tax on the operation of an instrument employed by the government of the Union to carry its powers into execution. Such a tax must be unconstitutional.

1. *How can it be argued that the case of McCulloch v. Maryland is perhaps the best representation of judicial nationalism?*
2. *What might be the long-term consequences of the Marshall Court's decision? What future issues or concerns could be affected by this ruling?*

9-5 Thomas Jefferson Reacts to the "Missouri Question" (1820)

In this letter, seventy-seven-year-old Thomas Jefferson wrote to John Holmes, a Congressman from Maine, criticizing the Missouri Compromise. Jefferson believed that the debate over the compromise was an example of unnecessary federal interference in a Southern institution. Jefferson expressed the fear of many Americans that conflicting views over the expansion of slavery and the power of the federal government had brought the United States to the verge of disunion.

Source: Library of Congress, *Thomas Jefferson Papers*, Series 1. General Correspondence. 1651–1827, *Thomas Jefferson to John Holmes, April 22, 1820*
http://memory.loc.gov

Monticello, April 22, 1820

I thank you, Dear Sir, for the copy you have been so kind as to send me of the letter to your constituents on the Missouri question. It is a perfect justification to them. I had for a long time ceased to read newspapers, or pay any attention to public affairs, confident they were in good hands, and content to be a passenger in our bark to the shore from which I am not distant. But this momentous question, like a firebell in the night, awakened and filled me with terror. I considered it at once as the knell of the Union. It is hushed, indeed, for the moment. But this is a reprieve only, not a final sentence. A geographical line, coinciding with a marked principle, moral and political, once conceived and held up to the angry passions of men, will never be obliterated; and every new irritation will mark it deeper and deeper. I can say, with conscious truth, that there is not a man on earth who would sacrifice more than I would to relieve us from this heavy reproach, in any *practicable* way.

The cession of that kind of property, for so it is misnamed, is a bagatelle which would not cost me a second thought, if, in that way, a general emancipation and *expatriation* could be effected; and gradually, and with due sacrifices, I think it might be. But as it is, we have the wolf by the ears, and we can neither hold him, nor safely let him go. Justice is in one scale, and self-preservation in the other. Of one thing I am certain, that as the passage of slaves from one state to another would not make a slave of a single human being who would not be so without it, so their diffusion over a greater surface would make them individually happier, and proportionally facilitate the accomplishment of their emancipation, by dividing the burden on a greater number of coadjutors. An abstinence too, from this act of power, would remove the jealousy excited by the undertaking of Congress to regulate the condition of the different descriptions of men composing a state. This certainly is the exclusive right of every state, which nothing in the Constitution has taken from them and given to the general government. Could Congress, for example, say that the non-freemen of Connecticut shall be freemen, or that they shall not emigrate into any other state?

I regret that I am now to die in the belief, that the useless sacrifice of themselves by the generation of '76, to acquire self-government and happiness to their country, is to be thrown away by the unwise and unworthy passions of their sons, and that my only consolation is to be, that I live not to weep over it. If they would but dispassionately weigh the blessings they will throw away against an abstract principle more likely to be effected by union than by scission, they would pause before they would perpetrate this act of suicide on themselves, and of treason against the hopes of the world. To yourself, as the faithful advocate of the Union, I tender the offering of my high esteem and respect.

1. *Describe Jefferson's mood as he wrote this letter. What must have been going through his mind as he reviewed the debates over statehood for Missouri?*
2. *Discuss the metaphor Jefferson used to describe the institution of slavery? How appropriate is it? What does it reveal about Jefferson's thoughts over the future of the institution?*

9-6   The Monroe Doctrine and a Reaction (1823)

One of the most important foreign policy statements in American History, The Monroe Doctrine declared the Americas off limits to future European colonization. Most immediately proclaimed in reaction to Russian statements and Spanish and British activities in Central and South America, the Doctrine was a foreign policy declaration of independence and became a cornerstone of American Policy for many years.

In the discussion to which this interest [Russia's on the northwest coast] has given rise, the occasion has been judged proper for asserting, as a principle in which the rights and interests of the United States are involved, that the American continents, by the free and independent condition which they have assumed and maintain, are henceforth not to be considered as subjects for the future colonization by any European powers. . . .

The political system of the Allied Powers [Holy Alliance] is essentially different . . . from that of America. This difference proceeds from that which exists in their prospective [monarchical] governments; and to the defence of our own . . . this whole nation is devoted. We owe it, therefore, to candor and to the amicable relations existing between the United States and those powers to declare that we should consider any attempt on their part to extend their system to any portion of this hemisphere as dangerous to our peace and safety.

With the existing colonies or dependencies of any European power, we have not interfered and shall not interfere. But with the governments [of Spanish America] who have declared their independence and maintained it, and whose independence we have, on great consideration and on just principles, acknowledged, we could not view any interposition for the purpose of oppressing them, or controlling in any other light than as the manifestation of an unfriendly disposition toward the United States. . . .

Our policy in regard to Europe, which was adopted at an early stage of the wars which have so long agitated that quarter of the globe, nevertheless remains the same, which is, not to interfere in the internal concerns of any of its powers; to consider the government *de facto* as the legitimate government for us; to cultivate friendly relations with it, and to preserve those relations by a frank, firm, and manly policy, meeting in all instances the just claims of every power, submitting to injuries from none.

But in regard to those [American] continents, circumstances are eminently and conspicuously different. It is impossible that the Allied Powers should extend their political system to a portion of either continent without endangering our peace and happiness. Nor can anyone believe that our southern brethren, if left to themselves, would adopt it of their own accord. It is equally impossible, therefore, that we should behold such interposition in any form with indifference.

[Baltimore *Chronicle*, Editorial]

We can tell . . . further that this high-toned, independent, and dignified message will not be read by the crowned heads of Europe without a revolting stare of astonishment. The conquerors of Bonaparte, with their laurels still green and blooming on their brows, and their disciplined animal machines, called armies, at their backs, could not have anticipated that their united force would so soon be defied by a young republic, whose existence, as yet, cannot be measured with the ordinary life of man.

This message itself constitutes an era in American history, worthy of commemoration. . . . We are confident that, on this occasion, we speak the great body of American sentiment, such as exulting millions are ready to re-echo. . . . We are very far from being confident that, if Congress occupy the high and elevated ground taken in the Message, it may not, under the smiles of Divine Providence, be the means of breaking up the Holy Alliance.

Of this we are positively sure: that all timidity, wavering imbecility, an backwardness on our part will confirm these detested tyrants in their confederacy; paralyze the exertions of freedom in every country; accelerate the fall of those young sister republics whom we have recently recognized; and, perhaps, eventually destroy our own at the feet of absolute monarchy.

1. In general, what does the Monroe Doctrine prescribe in regard to American foreign policy? What is the rationale for this policy?
2. Summarize the tone and message of the response to this doctrine published in the Baltimore Chronicle.

9-7 Henry Clay, "Defense of the American System" (1832)

Henry Clay was an American statesman for over 40 years, serving as Secretary of State, Speaker of the House and Senate Leader. He ran, unsuccessfully, for President five times. The focus of Clay's efforts was the so called "American System" which is the subject of this document. The system was designed to reduce dependence and develop American resources and included tariffs, a national bank and federal subsidies for transportation. With these measures Clay sought economic development and a more unified America.

I have now to perform the more pleasing task of exhibiting an imperfect sketch of the existing state of the unparalleled prosperity of the country. On a general survey, we behold cultivation extended, the arts flourishing, the face of the country improved; our people fully and profitably employed, and the public countenance exhibiting tranquility, contentment and happiness. And if we descend into particulars, we have the agreeable contemplation of a people out of debt, land rising slowly in value, but in a secure and salutary degree; a ready though not extravagant market for all the surplus productions of our industry; innumerable flocks and herds browsing and gamboling on ten thousand hills and plains, covered with rich and verdant grasses; our cities expanded, and whole villages springing up, as it were, by enchantment; our exports and imports increased and increasing; our tonnage, foreign and coastwise, swelling and fully occupied; the rivers of our interior animated by the perpetual thunder and lightning of countless steam-boats; the currency sound and abundant; the public debt of two wars nearly redeemed; and, to crown all, the public treasury overflowing, embarrassing Congress, not to find subjects of taxation, but to select the objects which shall be liberated from the impost. If the term of seven years were to be selected, of the greatest prosperity which this people have enjoyed since the establishment of their present constitution, it would be exactly that period of seven years which immediately followed the passage of the tariff of 1824.

This transformation of the condition of the country from gloom and distress to brightness and prosperity, has been mainly the work of American legislation, fostering American industry, instead of allowing it to be controlled by foreign legislation, cherishing foreign industry. The foes of the American System, in 1824, with great boldness and confidence, predicted, 1st. The ruin of the public revenue, and the creation of a necessity to resort to direct taxation. The gentleman from South Carolina, (General Hayne,) I believe, thought that the tariff of 1824 would operate a reduction of revenue to the large amount of eight millions of dollars. 2d. The destruction of our navigation. 3d. The desolation of commercial cities. And 4th. The augmentation of the price of objects of consumption, and further decline in that of the articles of our exports. Every prediction which they made has failed-utterly failed. Instead of the ruin of the public revenue, with which they then sought to deter us from the adoption of the American System, we are now threatened with its subversion, by the vast amount of the public revenue produced by that system. . . .

If the system of protection be founded on principles erroneous in theory, pernicious in practice-above all if it be unconstitutional, as is alledged, it ought to be forthwith abolished, and not a vestage of it suffered to remain. But, before we sanction this sweeping denunciation, let us look a little at this system, its magnitude, its ramifications, its duration, and the high authorities which have sustained it. We shall see that its foes will have accomplished comparatively nothing, after having achieved their present aim of breaking down our iron-founderies, our woollen, cotton, and hemp manufactories, and our sugar plantations. The destruction of these would, undoubtedly, lead to the sacrifice of immense capital, the ruin of many thousands of our fellow citizens, and incalculable loss to the whole community. But their prostration would not disfigure, nor produce greater effect upon the *whole* system of protection, in all its branches, than the destruction of the beautiful domes upon the capitol would occasion to the magnificent edifice which they surmount. Why, sir, there is scarcely an interest, scarcely a vocation in society, which is not embraced by the beneficence of this system.

It comprehends our coasting tonnage and trade, from which all foreign tonnage is absolutely excluded.

It includes all our foreign tonnage, with the inconsiderable exception made by the treaties of reciprocity with a few foreign powers.

It embraces our fisheries, and all our hardy and enterprising fishermen.

It extends to almost every mechanic and: to tanners, cordwainers, tailors, cabinet-makers, hatters, tinners, brass-workers, clock-makers, coach-makers, tallow-chandlers, trace-makers, rope-makers, cork-cutters, tobacconists, whip-makers, paper-makers, umbrella-makers, glass-blowers, stocking-weavers, butter-makers, saddle and harness-makers, cutlers, brush-makers, book-binders, dairy-men, milk-farmers, black-smiths, type-founders, musical instrument-makers, basket-makers, milliners, potters, chocolate-makers, floor-cloth-makers, bonnet-makers, hair-cloth-makers, copper-smiths, pencil-makers, bellows-makers, pocket book-makers, card-makers, glue-makers, mustard-makers, lumber-sawyers, saw-makers, scale-beam-makers, scythe-makers, wood-saw-makers, and many others. The mechanics enumerated, enjoy a measure of protection adapted to their several conditions, varying from twenty to fifty per cent. The extent and importance of some of these artizans may be estimated by a few particulars. The tanners, curriers, boot and shoe-makers, and other workers in hides, skins and leather, produce an ultimate value per annum of forty millions of dollars; the manufacturers of hats and caps produce an annual value of fifteen millions; the cabinet-makers twelve millions; the manufacturers of bonnets and hats for the female sex, lace, artificial flowers, combs, &c. seven millions; and the manufacturers of glass, five millions.

It extends to all lower Louisiana, the Delta of which might as well be submerged again in the Gulf of Mexico, from which it has been a gradual conquest, as now to be deprived of the protecting duty upon is great staple.

It effects the cotton planter himself, and the tobacco planter, both of whom enjoy protection.

The total amount of the capital vested in sheep, the land to sustain them, wool, woollen manufacturers, and woollen fabrics, and the subsistence of the various persons directly or indirectly employed in the growth and manufacture of the article of wool, is estimated at one hundred and sixty-seven millions of dollars, and the number of persons at one hundred and fifty thousand.

The value of iron, considered as a raw material, and of its manufacturers, is estimated at twenty-six millions of dollars per annum. Cotton goods, exclusive of the capital vested in the manufacture, and of the cost of the raw material, are believed to amount annually, to about twenty millions of dollars.

These estimates have been carefully made, by practical men of undoubted character, who have brought together and embodied their information. Anxious to avoid the charge of exaggeration, they have sometimes placed their estimates below what was believed to be the actual amount of these interests. With regard to the quantity of bar and other iron annually produced, it is derived from the known works themselves; and I know some in western States which they have omitted in their calculations. . . .

When gentlemen have succeeded in their design of an immediate or gradual destruction of the American System, what is their substitute? Free trade? Free trade! The call for free trade is as unavailing as the cry of a spoiled child, in its nurse's arms, for the moon, or the stars that glitter in the firmament of heaven. It never has existed, it never will exist. Trade implies, at least two parties. To be free, it should be fair, equal and reciprocal. But if we throw our ports wide open to the admission of foreign productions, free of all duty, what ports of any other foreign nation shall we find open to the free admission of our surplus produce? We may break down all barriers to free trade on our part, but the work will not be complete until foreign powers shall have removed theirs. There would be freedom on one side, and restrictions, prohibitions and exclusions on the other. The bolts, and the bars, and the chains of all other nations will remain undisturbed. It is, indeed, possible, that our industry and commerce would accommodate themselves to this unequal and unjust, state of things; for, such is the flexibility of our nature, that it bends itself to all circumstances. The wretched prisoner incarcerated in a jail, after a long time becomes reconciled to his solitude, and regularly notches down the passing days of his confinement.

Gentlemen deceive themselves. It is not free trade that they are recommending to our acceptance. It is in effect, the British colonial system that we are invited to adopt; and, if their policy prevail, it will lead substantially to the re-colonization of these States, under the commercial dominion of Great Britain. . . .

Gentlemen are greatly deceived as to the hold which this system has in the affections of the people of the United States. They represent that it is the policy of New England, and that she is most benefitted by it. If there be any part of this Union which has been most steady, most unanimous, and most determined in its support, it is Pennsylvania. Why is not that powerful State attacked? Why pass her over, and aim the blow at New England? New England came reluctantly into the policy. In 1824 a majority of her delegation was opposed to it. From the largest State of New England there was but a solitary vote in favor of the bill. That enterprising people can readily accommodate their industry to any policy, provided it be *settled.* They supposed this was fixed, and they submitted to the decrees of government. And the progress of public opinion has kept pace with the developments of the benefits of the system. Now, all New England, at least in this house (with the exception of one small still voice) is in favor of the system. In 1824 all Maryland was against it; now the majority is for it. Then, Louisiana, with one exception, was opposed to it; now, without any exception, she is in favor of it. The march of public sentiment is to the South. Virginia will be the next convert; and in less than seven years, if there be no obstacles from political causes, or prejudices industriously instilled, the majority of eastern Virginia will be, as the majority of western Virginia now is, in favor of the American System. North Carolina will follow later, but not less certainly. Eastern Tennessee is now in favor of the system. And finally, its doctrines will pervade the whole Union, and the wonder will be, that they ever should have been opposed.

1. What is the state of the "American System" as it is described in this document?
2. Explain the opinion expressed in this document regarding "Free Trade."

9-8 Imminent Dangers to the Free Institutions of the United States through Foreign Immigration (1835)

In the early 1830s, Samuel Morse (who would later invent the telegraph), began attacking in print the Leopoldine Society to Aid the Missions, which was making contributions to the bishop of Cincinnati in order to advance Catholicism in Ohio. Morse wrote a series of articles calling this a foreign conspiracy, urging Protestants to put aside their sectarian differences and unite against the lenient immigration laws, which he contended were endangering the foundations of the American state.

Source: Samuel F. B. Morse, *Imminent Dangers to the Free Institutions of the United States through Foreign Immigration* (New York: E. B. Clayton, 1835).

. . .Our country, in the position it has given to foreigners who have made it their home, has pursued a course in relation to them, totally different from that of any other country in the world. This course, while it is liberal without example, subjects our institutions to peculiar dangers. In all other countries the foreigner, to whatever privileges he may be entitled by becoming a subject, can never be placed in a situation to be politically dangerous, for he has no share in the government of the country; . . .

. . .The writer believes, that since the time of the American Revolution, which gave the principles of Democratic liberty a home, those principles have never been in greater jeopardy than at the present moment. To his reasons for thus believing, he invites the unimpassioned investigation of every American citizen. If there is danger, let it arouse to defence. If it is a false alarm, let such explanations be given of most suspicious appearances as shall safely allay it. It is no party question, and the attempt to make it one, should be at once suspected. It concerns all of every party.

There is danger of reaction from Europe; and it is the part of common prudence to look for it, and to provide against it. The great political truth has recently been promulged at the capital of one of the principal courts of Europe, at Vienna, and by one of the profoundest scholars of Germany, (Frederick Schlegel, a devoted Roman Catholic, and one of the Austrian Cabinet,) the great truth, clearly and unanswerably proved, that the political revolutions to which European governments have been so long subjected, from the popular desires for liberty, are the natural effects of the Protestant Reformation. That Protestantism favours Republicanism, while Popery as naturally supports Monarchical power. In these lectures, . . .there is a most important allusion to this country; and as it demonstrates one of the principal connecting points between European and American politics, and is the key to many of the mysterious doings that are in operation against American institutions under our own eyes, let Americans treasure it well in their memories. This is the passage:—"THE GREAT NURSERY of these destructive principles, (the principles of Democracy,) the GREAT REVOLUTIONARY SCHOOL for FRANCE and THE REST OF EUROPE, is NORTH AMERICA!" Yes, (I address Democratic Americans,) the influence of this Republican government, of your democratic system, is vitally felt by Austria. She confesses it. It is proscribed by the Austrian Cabinet. This country is designated directly to all her people, and to her allied despots, as the great plague spot of the world, the poisoned fountain whence flow all the deadly evils which threaten their own existence. . ... Is it wonderful after such an avowal in regard to America, that she should do something to rid herself and the world of such a tremendous evil? . . .

But how shall she attack us? She cannot send her armies, they would be useless. She has told us by the mouth of her Counsellor of Legation, that Popery, while it is the natural antagonist to Protestantism, is opposed in its whole character to Republican liberty, and is the promoter and supporter of arbitrary power. How fitted then is Popery for her purpose! This she can send without alarming our fears, or, at least, only the fears of those "miserable," "intolerant fanatics," and "pious bigots," who affect to see danger to the liberties of the country in the mere introduction of a religious system opposed to their own, and whose cry of danger, be it ever so loud, will only be regarded as the result of "sectarian fear," and the plot ridiculed as a "quixotic dream." But is there any thing so irrational in such a scheme? Is it not the most natural and obvious act for Austria to do, with her views of the influence of Popery upon the form of government, its influence to pull down Republicanism, and build up monarchy; I say, is it not her most obvious act to send Popery to this country if it is not here, or give it a fresh and vigorous impulse if it is already here? At any rate she is doing it. She has set herself to work with all her activity to disseminate throughout the country the Popish religion. Immediately after the delivery of Schlegel's lectures, which was in the year 1828, a great society was formed in the Austrian capital, in Vienna, in 1829. The late Emperor, and Prince Metternich, and the Crown Prince, (now Emperor,) and all the civil and ecclesiastical officers of the empire, with the princes of Savoy and Piedmont, uniting in it, and calling it after the name of a canonized King, St. Leopold. This society is formed for a great and express purpose. . ."of promoting the greater activity of Catholic missions in America;" these are the words of their own reports. Yes; these Foreign despots are suddenly stirred up to combine and promote the greater activity of Popery in this country; and this, too, just after they had been convinced of the truth, or, more properly speaking, had their memories quickened with it, that Popery is utterly opposed to Republican liberty. These are the facts in the case. Americans, explain them in your own way. If any choose to stretch their charity so far as to believe that these crowned gentlemen have combined in this Society solely for religious purposes; that they have organized a Society to collect moneys to be spent in this country, and have sent Jesuits as their almoners, and shiploads of Roman Catholic emigrants, and for the sole purpose of converting us to the religion of Popery, and without any political design, credat Judaeus Apella, non ego.

Let us examine the operations of this Austrian Society, for it is hard at work all around us; yes, here in this country, from one end to the other, at our very doors, in this city. Its emissaries are here. And who are these emissaries? They are JESUITS. This society of men, after exerting their tyranny for upwards of 200 years, at length became so formidable to the world, threatening the entire subversion of all social order, that even the Pope, whose devoted subjects they are, and must be, by the vow of their society, was compelled to dissolve them. They had not been suppressed, however, for 50 years, before the waning influence of Popery and Despotism required their useful labours, to resist the spreading light of Democratic liberty, and the Pope, (Pius VII,) simultaneously with the formation of the Holy Alliance, revived the order of the Jesuits. . ... And do Americans need to be told what Jesuits are? If any are ignorant, let them inform themselves of their history without delay; no time is to be lost: their workings are before you in every day's events: they are a secret society, a sort of Masonic order, with superadded features of most revolting odiousness, and a thousand times more dangerous. They are not confined to one class in society; they are not merely priests, or priests of one religious creed, they are merchants, and lawyers, and editors, and men of any profession, and no profession, having no outward badge, (in this country,) by which to be recognised; they are about in all your society. They can assume any character, that of angels of light, or ministers of darkness, to accomplish their one great end, the service upon which they are sent, whatever that service may be. "They are all educated men, prepared, and sworn to start at any moment, in any direction, and for any service, commanded by the general of their order, bound to no family, community, or country, by the ordinary ties which bind men; and sold for life to the cause of the Roman Pontiff."

Is there no danger to the Democracy of the country from such formidable foes arrayed against it? Is Metternich its friend? Is the Pope its friend? Are his official documents, now daily put forth, Democratic in their character?

O there is no danger to the Democracy; for those most devoted to the Pope, the Roman Catholics, especially the Irish Catholics, are all on the side of Democracy. Yes; to be sure they are on the side of Democracy. They are just where I should look for them. Judas Iscariot joined with the true disciples. Jesuits are not fools. They would not startle our slumbering fears, by bolting out their monarchical designs directly in our teeth, and by joining the opposing ranks, except so far as to cover their designs. This is a Democratic country, and the Democratic party is and ever must be the strongest party, unless ruined by traitors and Jesuits in the camp. Yes; it is in the ranks of Democracy I should expect to find them, and for no good purpose be assured. Every measure of Democratic policy in the least exciting will be pushed to ultraism, so soon as it is introduced for discussion. Let every real Democrat guard against this common Jesuitical artifice of tyrants, an artifice which there is much evidence to believe is practicing against them at this moment, an artifice which if not heeded will surely be the ruin of Democracy: it is founded on the well-known principle that "extremes meet." The writer has seen it pass under his own eyes in Europe, in more than one instance. When in despotic governments popular discontent, arising from the intolerable oppressions of the tyrants of the people, has manifested itself by popular outbreakings, to such a degree as to endanger the throne, and the people seemed prepared to shove their masters from their horses, and are likely to mount, and seize the reins themselves; then, the popular movement, unmanageable any longer by resistance, is pushed to the extreme. The passions of the ignorant and vicious are excited to outrage by pretended friends of the people. Anarchy ensues; and then the mass of the people, who are always lovers of order and quiet, unite at once in support of the strong arm of force for protection; and despotism, perhaps, in another, but preconcerted shape, resumes its iron reign. Italy and Germany are furnishing examples every day. If an illustration is wanted on a larger scale, look at France in her late Republican revolution, and in her present relapse into despotism. . ..

. . .It is in the Roman Catholic ranks that we are principally to look for the materials to be employed by the Jesuits, and in what condition do we find this sect at present in our country? We find it spreading itself into every nook and corner of the land; churches, chapels, colleges, nunneries and convents, are springing up as if by magic every where; an activity hitherto unknown among the Roman Catholics pervades all their ranks, and yet whence the means for all these efforts? Except here and there funds or favours collected from an inconsistent Protestant, (so called probably because born in a Protestant country, who is flattered or wheedled by some Jesuit artifice to give his aid to their cause,) the greatest part of the pecuniary means for all these works are from abroad. They are the contributions of his Majesty the Emperor of Austria, of Prince Metternich, of the late Charles X., and the other Despots combined in the Leopold Society. And who are the members of the Roman Catholic communion? What proportion are natives of this land, nurtured under our own institutions, and well versed in the nature of American liberty? Is it not notorious that the greater part are Foreigners from the various Catholic countries of Europe. Emigration has of late years been specially promoted among this class of Foreigners, and they have been in the proportion of three to one of all other emigrants arriving on our shores; they are from Ireland, Germany, Poland, and Belgium. From about the period of the formation of the Leopold Society, Catholic emigration increased in an amazing degree. Colonies of Emigrants, selected, perhaps, with a view to occupy particular places, (for, be it remembered, every portion of this country is as perfectly known at Vienna and Rome as in any part of our own country), have been constantly arriving. The principal emigrants are from Ireland and Germany. We have lately been told by the captain of a lately arrived Austrian vessel, which, by the by, brought 70 emigrants from Antwerp! that a desire is suddenly manifested among the poorer class of the Belgian population, to emigrate to America. They are mostly, if not all, Roman Catholics, be it remarked, for Belgium is a Catholic country, and Austrian vessels are bringing them here. Whatever the cause of all this movement abroad to send to this country their poorer classes, the fact is certain, the class of emigrants is known, and the instrument, Austria, is seen in it—the same power that directs the Leopold Foundation. . . .

. . .I have shown what are the Foreign materials imported into the country, with which the Jesuits can work to accomplish their designs. Let us examine this point a little more minutely. These materials are the varieties of Foreigners of the same Creed, the Roman Catholic, over all of whom the Bishops or Vicars General hold, as a matter of course, ecclesiastical rule; and we well know what is the nature of Roman Catholic ecclesiastical rule,—it is the double refined spirit of despotism, which, after arrogating to itself the prerogatives of Deity, and so claiming to bind or loose the soul eternally, makes it, in the comparison, but a mere trifle to exercise absolute sway in all that relates to the body. The notorious ignorance in which the great mass of these emigrants have been all their lives sunk, until their minds are dead, makes them but senseless machines; they obey orders mechanically, for it is the habit of their education, in the despotic countries of their birth. And can it be for a moment supposed by any one that by the act of coming to this country, and being naturalized, their darkened intellects can suddenly be illuminated to discern the nice boundary where their ecclesiastical obedience to their priests ends, and their civil independence of them begins? The very supposition is absurd. They obey their priests as demigods, from the habit of their whole lives; they have been taught from infancy that their priests are infallible in the greatest matters, and can they, by mere importation to this country, be suddenly imbued with the knowledge that in civil matters their priests may err, and that they are not in these also their infallible guides? Who will teach them this? Will their priests? Let common sense answer this question. Must not the priests, as a matter almost of certainty, control the opinions of their ignorant flock in civil as well as religious matters? and do they not do it?

Mr. Jefferson, . . .foresaw, predicted, and issued his warning, on the great danger to the country of this introduction of foreigners. He doubted its policy, even when the advantages seemed to be greatest. He says, "The present desire of America, (in 1781,) is to produce rapid population by as great importations of foreigners as possible. But is this founded in policy? . . .Are there no inconveniences to be thrown into the scale against the advantage expected from a multiplication of numbers by the importation of foreigners? It is for the happiness of those united in society to harmonize as much as possible in matters which they must of necessity transact together."

What was dimly seen by the prophetic eye of Jefferson, is actually passing under our own eyes. Already have foreigners increased in the country to such a degree, that they justly give us alarm. They feel themselves so strong, as to organize themselves even as foreigners into foreign bands, and this for the purpose of influencing our elections. That they are men who having professed to become Americans, by accepting our terms of naturalization, do yet, in direct contradiction to their professions, clan together as a separate interest, and retain their foreign appellation; that it is with such a separate foreign interest, organizing in the midst of us, that Jesuits in the pay of foreign powers are tampering; that it is this foreign corps of religionists that Americans of both parties have been for years in the habit of basely and traitorously encouraging to erect into an umpire of our political divisions, thus virtually surrendering the government into the hands of Despotic powers. In view of these facts, which every day's experience proves to be facts, is it not time, high time, that a true American spirit were roused to resist this alarming inroad of foreign influence upon our institutions, to avert dangers to which we have hitherto shut our eyes, and which if not remedied, and that immediately, will inevitably change the whole character of our government. I repeat what I first said, this is no party question, it concerns native Americans of all parties.

1. *Explain why America is feared by some of the governments of Europe, namely Austria. What connection is drawn between Protestantism and Republicanism?*
2. *What charges does Morse level against the Austrian Society? How are these charges supported?*
3. *How do Morse's concerns relate to immigration? What are Morse's attitudes regarding foreigners in America?*

9-9 *The Harbinger,* Female Workers of Lowell (1836)

The famous Lowell system of factory management attracted young farm girls to work in the fully mechanized factories of Lowell. The system was paternalistic and included, at first, good wages, clean places to live and close supervision. The response was great but as economic times declined, so did wages and working conditions. This document explores the life of Lowell factory workers during this time.

We have lately visited the cities of Lowell [Mass.] and Manchester [N.H.] and have had an opportunity of examining the factory system more closely than before. We had distrusted the accounts which we had heard from persons engaged in the labor reform now beginning to agitate New England. We could scarcely credit the statements made in relation to the exhausting nature of the labor in the mills, and to the manner in which the young women-the operatives-lived in their boardinghouses, six sleeping in a room, poorly ventilated.

We went through many of the mills, talked particularly to a large number of the operatives, and ate at their boardinghouses, on purpose to ascertain by personal inspection the facts of the case. We assure our readers that very little information is possessed, and no correct judgments formed, by the public at large, of our factory system, which is the first germ of the industrial or commercial feudalism that is to spread over our land. . . .

In Lowell live between seven and eight thousand young women, who are generally daughters of farmers of the different states of New England. Some of them are members of families that were rich in the generation before. . . .

The operatives work thirteen hours a day in the summer time, and from daylight to dark in the winter. At half past four in the morning the factory bell rings, and at five the girls must be in the mills. A clerk, placed as a watch, observes those who are a few minutes behind the time, and effectual means are taken to stimulate to punctuality. This is the morning commencement of the industrial discipline (should we not rather say industrial tyranny?) which is established in these associations of this moral and Christian community.

At seven the girls are allowed thirty minutes for breakfast, and at noon thirty minutes more for dinner, except during the first quarter of the year, when the time is extended to forty-five minutes. But within this time they must hurry to their boardinghouses and return to the factory, and that through the hot sun or the rain or the cold. A meal eaten under such circumstances must be quite unfavorable to digestion and health, as any medical man will inform us. After seven o'clock in the evening the factory bell sounds the close of the day's work.

Thus thirteen hours per day of close attention and monotonous labor are extracted from the young women in these manufactories. . . . So fatigued-we should say, exhausted and worn out, but we wish to speak of the system in the simplest language-are numbers of girls that they go to bed soon after their evening meal, and endeavor by a comparatively long sleep to resuscitate their weakened frames for the toil of the coming day.

When capital has got thirteen hours of labor daily out of a being, it can get nothing more. It would be a poor speculation in an industrial point of view to own the operative; for the trouble and expense of providing for times of sickness and old age would more than counterbalance the difference between the price of wages and the expenses of board and clothing. The far greater number of fortunes accumulated by the North in comparison with the South shows that hireling labor is more profitable for capital than slave labor.

Now let us examine the nature of the labor itself, and the conditions under which it is performed. Enter with us into the large rooms, when the looms are at work. The largest that we saw is in the Amoskeag Mills at Manchester. . . . The din and clatter of these five hundred looms, under full operation, struck us on first entering as something frightful and infernal, for it seemed such an atrocious violation of one of the faculties of the human soul, the sense of hearing. After a while we became somewhat used to it, and by speaking quite close to the ear of an operative and quite loud, we could hold a conversation and make the inquiries we wished.

The girls attended upon an average three looms; many attended four, but this requires a very active person, and the most unremitting care. However, a great many do it. Attention to two is as much as should be demanded of an operative. This gives us some idea of the application required during the thirteen hours of daily labor. The atmosphere of such a room cannot of course be pure; on the contrary, it is charged with cotton filaments and dust, which, we are told, are very injurious to the lungs.

On entering the room, although the day was warm, we remarked that the windows were down. We asked the reason, and a young woman answered very naively, and without seeming to be in the least aware that this privation of fresh air was anything else than perfectly natural, that "when the wind blew, the threads did not work well." After we had been in the room for fifteen or twenty minutes, we found ourselves, as did the persons who accompanied us, in quite a perspiration, produced by a certain moisture which we observed in the air, as well as by the heat. . . .

The young women sleep upon an average six in a room, three beds to a room. There is no privacy, no retirement, here. It is almost impossible to read or write alone, as the parlor is full and so many sleep in the same chamber. A young woman remarked to us that if she had a letter to write, she did it on the head of a bandbox, sitting on a trunk, as there was no space for a table.

So live and toil the young women of our country in the boardinghouses and manufactories which the rich an influential of our land have built for them.

1. *Summarize this accounts description of living conditions in Lowell. What is the daily life of a Lowell worker like?*
2. *Describe the working conditions presented in this account? What hazards and unhealthful conditions are observed?*

9-10   James F. Cooper, Notions of the Americans (1840)

Best known for his Leatherstocking series of novels including "The Deerslayer"," The Last of the Mohicans" and three others, James Fennimore Cooper become known as our "national novelist". He was, however, an excellent naval historian and a commentator on politics and social concerns. Cooper saw himself as an educator of the population in democracy and his works reflect that concern. Notions of the Americans was written during a stay in Europe of several years and represents his observations of America.

Five-and-twenty years ago engineers from Europe began to make their appearance in America. They brought with them the rules of science, and a competent knowledge of the estimates of force, and the adaptation of principles to results; but they brought them, all calculated to meet the contingencies of the European man. Experience showed that they neither knew how to allow for the difficulties of a novel situation, nor for the excess of intellect they were enabled to use. Their estimates were always wild, uncertain, and fatal, in a country that was still experimenting. But five-and-twenty years ago was too soon for canals in America. It was wise to wait for a political symptom in a country where a natural impulse will always indicate the hour for action. Though five-and-twenty, or twenty, or even fifteen years, were too soon, still ten were not. Ten years ago, demonstrations had been made which enabled keen observers to detect that the time for extraordinary exertion had come. The great western canal of New-York was conceived and planned. But instead of seeking for European engineers, a few of the common surveyors of the country were called to the aid of those who were intrusted with the duty of making the estimates; and men of practical knowledge, who understood the people with whom they had to deal, and who had tutored their faculties in the thousand collisions of active life, were brought to the task as counsellors. The result is worthy of grave attention. The work, in its fruits and in its positive extent, exceeded any thing of a similar nature ever attempted in Christendom. The authority to whom responsibility was due, was more exacting than any of our hemisphere. Economy was inculcated to a degree little known in other nations; and, in short, greater accuracy than usual was required under circumstances apparently the least favourable to attain it. Now, this canal was made (with such means) at a materially less cost, in infinitely less time, and with a boldness in the estimates, and an accuracy in the results, that were next to marvellous.

There was not a man of any reputation for science employed in the work. But the utmost practical knowledge of men and of things was manifested in the whole of the affair. The beginning of each year brought its estimate of the expense, and of the profits, and the close its returns, in wonderful conformity. The labour is completed, and the benefit is exceeding the hopes of the most sanguine.

In this sketch of the circumstances under which the New-York canal has been made, we may trace the cause of the prodigious advance of this nation. Some such work as this was necessary to demonstrate to the world, that the qualities which are so exclusively the fruits of liberty and of a diffused intelligence, have an existence elsewhere than in the desires of the good. Without it, it might have been said the advance of America is deceptive; she is doing no more than our own population could do under circumstances that admitted of so much display, but she will find the difference between felling trees, and burning forests, and giving the finish which denotes the material progress of society. The mouths of such critics are now silenced. The American can point to his ploughs, to his ships, to his canals, to his bridges, and, in short, to every thing that is useful in his particular state of society, and demand, where a better or cheaper has been produced, under any thing like circumstances of equality?

It is vain to deny the causes of the effects of the American system. . . . since they rest on principles that favour the happiness and prosperity of the human race. We should not cavil about names, nor minor distinctions, in governments, if the great and moving principles are such as contemplate the improvement of the species in the masa and not in exclusive and selfish exceptions. . . .

The construction of canals, on a practical scale, the mining for coal, the exportation of cotton goods, and numberless other improvements, which argue an advancing state of society, have all sprung into existence within the last dozen years. It is a knowledge of these facts, with a clear and sagacious understanding of their immense results, coupled with the exciting moral causes, that render the American sanguine, aspiring, and confident in his anticipations. He sees that his nation lives centuries in an age, and he feels no disposition to consider himself a child, because other people, in their dotage, choose to remember the hour of his birth.

How pitiful do the paltry criticisms on an inn, or the idle, and, half the time, vulgar comments on the vulgarity of a *parvenu*, become, when objects and facts like these are pressing themselves on the mind! I have heard it said, that there are European authors who feel a diffidence of contracting acquaintances with American gentlemen, because they feel a consciousness of having turned the United States into ridicule! I can tell these unfortunate subjects of a precipitate opinion, that they may lay aside their scruples. No American of any character, or knowledge of his own country, can feel any thing but commiseration for the man who has attempted to throw ridicule on a nation like this. The contest is too unequal to admit of any doubt as to the result, and the wiser way will be for these Quixotes in literature to say and think as little as possible about their American tilting match, in order that the world may not liken their lances to that used by the hero of La Mancha, and their helmets to barbers' basins.

1. Summarize Cooper's attitude toward the birth and maturation of American ingenuity and technology. How does the construction of the Erie Canal capture this process of technological and mechanical advancement?
2. According to Cooper, what is the significance of the Erie Canal and similar structures and accomplishments in relation to European attitudes toward America and Americans?

9-11 Resolutions of the Boston Carpenters' Strike (1845)

The Boston Carpenters' strike was one of the earliest in which the ten-hour day was a principal issue. Work hours (in addition to pay) were a prominent issue in later factory strikes in Lowell and elsewhere in New England. The journeymen in the Boston strike also expected a "family wage." Unlike the girls at Lowell, men needed to support families on their salaries. The master carpenters, however, suggest that the strike may not be the work of native Bostonians but some "foreign growth" — perhaps some of the newly arrived Irish and German immigrants.

Resolutions of Journeymen Carpenters

Notice to house carpenters and housewrights in the country. An advertisement having appeared in the papers of this city, giving information that there is at this time a great demand for workmen in this branch of mechanical business in this city, it is considered a duty to state for the benefit of our brethren of the trade that we are not aware of any considerable demand for labor in this business, as there is, at this time, a very considerable number of journeymen carpenters who are out of employ, and the probable inducement which led to the communication refereed to arises from a disposition manifested on the part of the builders in this city to make their own terms as to the price of labor and the number of hours labor which shall hereafter constitute a day's work. It being a well-known fact that the most unreasonable requirements have been hith-erto extracted with regard to the terms of labor of journeymen mechanics in this city; and it is further well known that in the cities of New York, Philadelphia, Baltimore, and most of the other cities of much more liberal and equitable course of policy has been adopted by the master-builders, on this subject, giving to their journeymen that fair and liberal support to which they are unquestionably entitled. It is an undoubted fact that, on the present system, it is impossible for a jour-neyman housewright and house carpenter to maintain a family at the present time with the wages which are now usually given to the journeymen house carpenters in this city.

Resolutions of Master Carpenters

Resolved, That we learn with surprise and regret that a large number of those who are employed as journeymen in this city have entered into a combination for the purpose of altering the time of commencing and terminating their daily labor from that which has been customary from time immemorial, thereby lessening the amount of labor each day in a very consid-erable degree.

Resolved, That we consider such a combination as unworthy of that useful and industrious class of the commu-nity who are engaged in it; that it is fraught with numerous and pernicious evils, not only as respect their employers but the public at large, and especially themselves; for all journeymen of good character and of skill may expect very soon to become masters and, like us, the employers of others; and by the measure which they are now inclined to adopt they will entail upon themselves the inconvenience to which they seem desirous that we should not be exposed?

Resolved, That we consider the measure proposed, as calculated to exert a very unhappy influence on our appren-tices-by seducing them from that course of industry and economy of time to which we are anxious to inure them. That it will expose the journeymen themselves to many temptations and improvident practices from which they are happily secure; while they attend to that wise and salutary maxim of mechanics, "Mind your business." That we consider idleness as the most deadly bane to usefulness and honorable living; and knowing (such is human nature that, where there is no necessity, there is no exertion, we fear and dread the consequences of such a measure upon the morals and well-being of society).

Resolved, That we cannot believe this project to have originated with many of the faithful and industrious sons of New England but are compelled to consider it an evil of foreign growth, and one which, we hope and trust, will not take root in the favored soil of Massachusetts. And especially that our city, the early rising and industry of whose inhabitants are universally proverbial, may not be infested with the unnatural production.

Resolved, That if such a measure were ever to be proper and necessary, the time has not yet arrived when it is so; if it would ever be just, it cannot be at a time like the present, when builders have generally made their engagements and contracts for the season, having predicated their estimates and prices upon the original state of things in reference to jour-neymen. And we appeal therefore to the good sense, the honesty, and justice of all who are engaged in this combination, and ask them to review their doings, contemplate their consequences, and then act as becomes men of sober sense and of prudence.

Resolved, finally, That we will make no alteration in the manner of employing journeymen as respects the time of commencing and leaving work and that we will employ no man who persists in adhering to the project of which we com-plain.

1. What is employment situation in Boston compared to that of other major cities according to the Journeymen Carpenters? What is the intent of the Journeymen Carpenters in describing the situation in this way?

2. How does the situation described by the Journey Carpenters compare with the scenario presented by the Master Carpenters?

3. Summarize the logic of the Resolutions of the Master Carpenters. On what do they base their plea for the Journeymen Carpenters to return to work under the existing conditions?

9-12 The Trials of a Slave Girl

Harriet Jacobs was born into slavery in Edenton, North Carolina, in 1813. After suffering years of phys-ical and sexual abuse from her owner, Dr. James Norcom ("Dr. Flint"), Jacobs became involved with a white neighbor, Samuel Sawyer, simply so she could stay away from Norcom. Sawyer and Jacobs had two children together, Joseph and Louisa. In 1842, Jacobs escaped to the North where she became active in the antislavery movement. At the urging of several female abolitionists, she wrote Incidents in the Life of a Slave Girl, which was published in Boston in 1861 under the pseudonym, Linda Brent. The book is significant for its description of the sexual abuse of female slaves, avoided by most nineteenth-century critics of the institution.

Source: Jacobs, Harriet Ann, 1813–1897, *Incidents in the Life of a Slave Girl: Written by Herself,* Electronic Edition.
http:docsouth.unc.edu/jacobs/jacobs.html#jac44

DURING the first years of my service in Dr. Flint's family, I was accustomed to share some indulgences with the children of my mistress. Though this seemed to me no more than right, I was grateful for it, and tried to merit the kindness by the faithful discharge of my duties. But I now entered on my fifteenth year—a sad epoch in the life of a slave girl. My master began to whisper foul words in my ear. Young as I was, I could not remain ignorant of their import. I tried to treat them with indifference or contempt. The master's age, my extreme youth, and the fear that his conduct would be reported to my grandmother, made him bear this treatment for many months. He was a crafty man, and resorted to many means to accomplish his purposes. Sometimes he had stormy, terrific ways, that made his victims tremble; sometimes he assumed a gentleness that he thought must surely subdue. Of the two, I preferred his stormy moods, although they left me trembling. He tried his utmost to corrupt the pure principles my grandmother had instilled. He peopled my young mind with unclean images, such as only a vile monster could think of. I turned from him with disgust and hatred. But he was my master. I was compelled to live under the same roof with him—where I saw a man forty years my senior daily violating the most sacred commandments of nature. He told me I was his property; that I must be subject to his will in all things. My soul revolted against the mean tyranny. But where could I turn for protection? No matter whether the slave girl be as black as ebony or as fair as her mistress. In either case, there is no shadow of law to protect her from insult, from violence, or even from death; all these are inflicted by fiends who bear the shape of men. The mistress, who ought to protect the helpless victim, has no other feelings towards her but those of jealousy and rage. The degradation, the wrongs, the vices, that grow out of slavery, are more than I can describe. They are greater than you would willingly believe. Surely, if you credited one half the truths that are told you concerning the helpless millions suffering in this cruel bondage, you at the north would not help to tighten the yoke. You surely would refuse to do for the master, on your own soil, the mean and cruel work which trained bloodhounds and the lowest class of whites do for him at the south.

Every where the years bring to all enough of sin and sorrow; but in slavery the very dawn of life is darkened by these shadows. Even the little child, who is accustomed to wait on her mistress and her children, will learn, before she is twelve years old, why it is that her mistress hates such and such a one among the slaves. Perhaps the child's own mother is among those hated ones. She listens to violent outbreaks of jealous passion, and cannot help understanding what is the cause. She will become prematurely knowing in evil things. Soon she will learn to tremble when she hears her master's footfall. She will be compelled to realize that she is no longer a child. If God has bestowed beauty upon her, it will prove her greatest curse. That which commands admiration in the white woman only hastens the degradation of the female slave. I know that some are too much brutalized by slavery to feel the humiliation of their position; but many slaves feel it most acutely, and shrink from the memory of it. I cannot tell how much I suffered in the presence of these wrongs, nor how I am still pained by the retrospect. My master met me at every turn, reminding me that I belonged to him, and swearing by heaven and earth that he would compel me to submit to him. If I went out for a breath of fresh air, after a day of unwearied toil, his footsteps dogged me. If I knelt by my mother's grave, his dark shadow fell on me even there. The light heart which nature had given me became heavy with sad forebodings. The other slaves in my master's house noticed the change. Many of them pitied me; but none dared to ask the cause. They had no need to inquire. They knew too well the guilty practices under that roof; and they were aware that to speak of them was an offence that never went unpunished.

I longed for some one to confide in. I would have given the world to have laid my head on my grandmother's faithful bosom, and told her all my troubles. But Dr. Flint swore he would kill me, if I was not as silent as the grave. Then, although my grandmother was all in all to me, I feared her as well as loved her. I had been accustomed to look up to her with a respect bordering upon awe. I was very young, and felt shamefaced about telling her such impure things, especially as I knew her to be very strict on such subjects. Moreover, she was a woman of a high spirit. She was usually very quiet in her demeanor; but if her indignation was once roused, it was not very easily quelled. I had been told that she once chased a white gentleman with a loaded pistol, because he insulted one of her daughters. I dreaded the consequences of a violent outbreak; and both pride and fear kept me silent. But though I did not confide in my grandmother, and even evaded her vigilant watchfulness and inquiry, her presence in the neighborhood was some protection to me. Though she had been a slave, Dr. Flint was afraid of her. He dreaded her scorching rebukes. Moreover, she was known and patronized by many people; and he did not wish to have his villany made public. It was lucky for me that I did not live on a distant plantation, but in a town not so large that the inhabitants were ignorant of each other's affairs. Bad as are the laws and customs in a slaveholding community, the doctor, as a professional man, deemed it prudent to keep up some outward show of decency.

O, what days and nights of fear and sorrow that man caused me! Reader, it is not to awaken sympathy for myself that I am telling you truthfully what I suffered in slavery. I do it to kindle a flame of compassion in your hearts for my sisters who are still in bondage, suffering as I once suffered.

I once saw two beautiful children playing together. One was a fair white child; the other was her slave, and also her sister. When I saw them embracing each other, and heard their joyous laughter, I turned sadly away from the lovely sight. I foresaw the inevitable blight that would fall on the little slave's heart. I knew how soon her laughter would be changed to sighs. The fair child grew up to be a still fairer woman. From childhood to womanhood her pathway was blooming with flowers, and overarched by a sunny sky. Scarcely one day of her life had been clouded when the sun rose on her happy bridal morning.

How had those years dealt with her slave sister, the little playmate of her childhood? She, also, was very beautiful; but the flowers and sunshine of love were not for her. She drank the cup of sin, and shame, and misery, whereof her persecuted race are compelled to drink.

In view of these things, why are ye silent, ye free men and women of the north? Why do your tongues falter in maintenance of the right? Would that I had more ability! But my heart is so full, and my pen is so weak! There are noble men and women who plead for us, striving to help those who cannot help themselves. God bless them! God give them strength and courage to go on! God bless those, every where, who are laboring to advance the cause of humanity! . . .

Dr. Flint contrived a new plan. He seemed to have an idea that my fear of my mistress was his greatest obstacle. In the blandest tones, he told me that he was going to build a small house for me, in a secluded place, four miles away from the town. I shuddered; but I was constrained to listen, while he talked of his intention to give me a home of my own, and to make a lady of me. Hitherto, I had escaped my dreaded fate, by being in the midst of people. My grandmother had already had high words with my master about me. She had told him pretty plainly what she thought of his character, and there was considerable gossip in the neighborhood about our affairs, to which the open-mouthed jealousy of Mrs. Flint contributed not a little. When my master said he was going to build a house for me, and that he could do it with little trouble and expense, I was in hopes something would happen to frustrate his scheme; but I soon heard that the house was actually begun. I vowed before my Maker that I would never enter it. I had rather toil on the plantation from dawn till dark; I had rather live and die in jail, than drag on, from day to day, through such a living death. I was determined that the master, whom I so hated and loathed, who had blighted the prospects of my youth, and made my life a desert, should not, after my long struggle with him, succeed at last in trampling his victim under his feet. I would do any thing, every thing, for the sake of defeating him. What could I do? I thought and thought, till I became desperate, and made a plunge into the abyss.

And now, reader, I come to a period in my unhappy life, which I would gladly forget if I could. The remembrance fills me with sorrow and shame. It pains me to tell you of it; but I have promised to tell you the truth, and I will do it honestly, let it cost me what it may. I will not try to screen myself behind the plea of compulsion from a master; for it was not so. Neither can I plead ignorance or thoughtlessness. For years, my master had done his utmost to pollute my mind with foul images, and to destroy the pure principles inculcated by my grandmother, and the good mistress of my childhood. The influences of slavery had had the same effect on me that they had on other young girls; they had made me prematurely knowing, concerning the evil ways of the world. I know what I did, and I did it with deliberate calculation.

But, O, ye happy women, whose purity has been sheltered from childhood, who have been free to choose the objects of your affection, whose homes are protected by law, do not judge the poor desolate slave girl too severely! If slavery had been abolished, I, also, could have married the man of my choice; I could have had a home shielded by the laws; and I should have been spared the painful task of confessing what I am now about to relate; but all my prospects had been blighted by slavery. I wanted to keep myself pure; and, under the most adverse circumstances, I tried hard to preserve my self-respect; but I was struggling alone in the powerful grasp of the demon Slavery; and the monster proved too strong for me. I felt as if I was forsaken by God and man; as if all my efforts must be frustrated; and I became reckless in my despair.

I have told you that Dr. Flint's persecutions and his wife's jealousy had given rise to some gossip in the neighborhood. Among others, it chanced that a white unmarried gentleman had obtained some knowledge of the circumstances in which I was placed. He knew my grandmother, and often spoke to me in the street. He became interested for me, and asked questions about my master, which I answered in part. He expressed a great deal of sympathy, and a wish to aid me. He constantly sought opportunities to see me, and wrote to me frequently. I was a poor slave girl, only fifteen years old.

So much attention from a superior person was, of course, flattering; for human nature is the same in all. I also felt grateful for his sympathy, and encouraged by his kind words. It seemed to me a great thing to have such a friend. By degrees, a more tender feeling crept into my heart. He was an educated and eloquent gentleman; too eloquent, alas, for the poor slave girl who trusted in him. Of course I saw whither all this was tending. I knew the impassable gulf between us; but to be an object of interest to a man who is not married, and who is not her master, is agreeable to the pride and feelings of a slave, if her miserable situation has left her any pride or sentiment. It seems less degrading to give one's self, than to submit to compulsion. There is something akin to freedom in having a lover who has no control over you, except that which he gains by kindness and attachment. A master may treat you as rudely as he pleases, and you dare not speak; moreover, the wrong does not seem so great with an unmarried man, as with one who has a wife to be made unhappy. There may be sophistry in all this; but the condition of a slave confuses all principles of morality, and, in fact, renders the practice of them impossible.

When I found that my master had actually begun to build the lonely cottage, other feelings mixed with those I have described. Revenge, and calculations of interest, were added to flattered vanity and sincere gratitude for kindness. I knew nothing would enrage Dr. Flint so much as to know that I favored another; and it was something to triumph over my tyrant even in that small way. I thought he would revenge himself by selling me, and I was sure my friend, Mr. Sands, would buy me. He was a man of more generosity and feeling than my master, and I thought my freedom could be easily obtained from him. The crisis of my fate now came so near that I was desperate. I shuttered to think of being the mother of children that should be owned by my old tyrant. I knew that as soon as a new fancy took him, his victims were sold far off to get rid of them; especially if they had children. I had seen several women sold, with his babies at the breast. He never allowed his offspring by slaves to remain long in sight of himself and his wife. Of a man who was not my master I could ask to have my children well supported; and in this case, I felt confident I should obtain the boon. I also felt quite sure that they would be made free. With all these thoughts revolving in my mind, and seeing no other way of escaping the doom I so much dreaded, I made a headlong plunge. Pity me, and pardon me, O virtuous reader! You never knew what it is to be a slave; to be entirely unprotected by law or custom; to have the laws reduce you to the condition of a chattel, entirely subject to the will of another. You never exhausted your ingenuity in avoiding the snares, and eluding the power of a hated tyrant; you never shuddered at the sound of his footsteps, and trembled within hearing of his voice. I know I did wrong. No one can feel it more sensibly than I do. The painful and humiliating memory will haunt me to my dying day. Still, in looking back, calmly, on the events of my life, I feel that the slave woman ought not to be judged by the same standard as others.

The months passed on. I had many unhappy hours. I secretly mourned over the sorrow I was bringing on my grandmother, who had so tried to shield me from harm. I knew that I was the greatest comfort of her old age, and that it was a source of pride to her that I had not degraded myself, like most of the slaves. I wanted to confess to her that I was no longer worthy of her love; but I could not utter the dreaded words.

As for Dr. Flint, I had a feeling of satisfaction and triumph in the thought of telling him. From time to time he told me of his intended arrangements, and I was silent. At last, he came and told me the cottage was completed, and ordered me to go to it. I told him I would never enter it. He said, "I have heard enough of such talk as that. You shall go, if you are carried by force; and you shall remain there." I replied, "I will never go there. In a few months I shall be a mother."

He stood and looked at me in dumb amazement, and left the house without a word. I thought I should be happy in my triumph over him. But now that the truth was out, and my relatives would hear of it, I felt wretched. Humble as were their circumstances, they had pride in my good character. Now, how could I look them in the face? My self-respect was gone! I had resolved that I would be virtuous, though I was a slave. I had said, "Let the storm beat! I will brave it till I die." And now, how humiliated I felt!

I went to my grandmother. My lips moved to make confession, but the words stuck in my throat. I sat down in the shade of a tree at her door and began to sew. I think she saw something unusual was the matter with me. The mother of slaves is very watchful. She knows there is no security for her children. After they have entered their teens she lives in daily expectation of trouble. This leads to many questions. If the girl is of a sensitive nature, timidity keeps her from answering truthfully, and this well-meant course has a tendency to drive her from maternal counsels. Presently, in came my mistress, like a mad woman, and accused me concerning her husband. My grandmother, whose suspicions had been previously awakened, believed what she said. She exclaimed, "O Linda! has it come to this? I had rather see you dead than to see you as you now are. You are a disgrace to your dead mother." She tore from my fingers my mother's wedding ring and her silver thimble. "Go away!" she exclaimed, "and never come to my house, again." Her reproaches fell so hot and heavy, that they left me no chance to answer. Bitter tears, such as the eyes never shed but once, were my only answer. I rose from my seat, but fell back again, sobbing. She did not speak to me; but the tears were running down her furrowed cheeks, and they scorched me like fire. She had always been so kind to me! So kind! How I longed to throw myself at her feet, and tell her all the truth! But she had ordered me to go, and never to come there again. After a few minutes, I mustered strength, and started to obey her. With what feelings did I now close that little gate, which I used to open with such an eager hand in my childhood! It closed upon me with a sound I never heard before.

Where could I go? I was afraid to return to my master's. I walked on recklessly, not caring where I went, or what would become of me. When I had gone four or five miles, fatigue compelled me to stop. I sat down on the stump of an old tree. The stars were shining through the boughs above me. How they mocked me, with their bright, calm light! The hours passed by, and as I sat there alone a chilliness and deadly sickness came over me. I sank on the ground. My mind was full of horrid thoughts. I prayed to die; but the prayer was not answered. At last, with great effort I roused myself, and walked some distance further, to the house of a woman who had been a friend of my mother. When I told her why I was there, she spoke soothingly to me; but I could not be comforted. I thought I could bear my shame if I could only be reconciled to my grandmother. I longed to open my heart to her. I thought if she could know the real state of the case, and all I had been bearing for years, she would perhaps judge me less harshly. My friend advised me to send for her. I did so; but days of agonizing suspense passed before she came. Had she utterly forsaken me? No. She came at last. I knelt before her, and told her the things that had poisoned my life; how long I had been persecuted; that I saw no way of escape; and in an hour of extremity I had become desperate. She listened in silence. I told her I would bear any thing and do any thing, if in time I had hopes of obtaining her forgiveness. I begged of her to pity me, for my dead mother's sake. And she did pity me. She did not say, "I forgive you;" but she looked at me lovingly, with her eyes full of tears. She laid her old hand gently on my head, and murmured, "Poor child! Poor child!"

1. Based upon your reading of this excerpt from Harriet Jacobs's narrative, what power and influence did the matriarchs of the slave family have in both the slave community and among white owners? Why do you think this was so?
2. Why do you think the wives and mothers of slave owners did not do more to stop the physical and sexual abuse of female slaves?

PART TEN
JACKSONIAN DEMOCRACY

10-1 Joseph Smith and the Beginnings of Mormonism (1823)

Affected by the great religious ferment occurring around his Manchester, New York, home in 1820, four-teen-year-old Joseph Smith sought to discover which religion he should join. In 1823, Smith said he was visited by an angel named Moroni, who told him of an ancient record containing God's interactions with the early inhabitants of the American continent. In 1827, Smith found this record, inscribed on golden plates, and began translating its words by the "gift of God." The resulting manuscript, the Book of Mormon, was published in March 1830. The following month, Smith organized The Church of Jesus Christ of Latter-Day Saints and became its first president.

Source: "The Testimony of the Prophet Joseph Smith," The Church of Jesus Christ of Latter-Day Saints
http://www.lds.org/library/display/0,4945,104-1-3-1,FF.html

During this time of great excitement my mind was called up to serious reflection and great uneasiness. . . . I often said to myself: What is to be done? Who of all these parties are right; or, are they all wrong together? If any one of them be right, which is it, and how shall I know it?

While I was laboring under the extreme difficulties caused by the contests of these parties of religionists, I was one day reading the Epistle of James, first chapter and fifth verse, which reads: "If any of you lack wisdom, let him ask of God, that giveth to all men liberally, and upbraideth not; and it shall be given him."

Never did any passage of scripture come with more power to the heart of man than this did at this time to mine. It seemed to enter with great force into every feeling of my heart. I reflected on it again and again, knowing that if any person needed wisdom from God, I did; for how to act I did not know, and unless I could get more wisdom than I then had, I would never know; for the teachers of religion of the different sects understood the same passages of scripture so differently as to destroy all confidence in settling the question by an appeal to the Bible.

At length I came to the conclusion that I must either remain in darkness and confusion, or else I must do as James directs, that is, ask of God. I at length came to the determination to "ask of God," concluding that if he gave wisdom to them that lacked wisdom, and would give liberally, and not upbraid, I might venture.

In accordance with this, my determination to ask of God, I retired to the woods to make the attempt. It was on the morning of a beautiful, clear day, early in the spring of eighteen hundred and twenty. It was the first time in my life that I had made such an attempt, for amidst all my anxieties I had never as yet made the attempt to pray vocally.

After I had retired to the place where I had previously designed to go, having looked around me, and finding myself alone, I kneeled down and began to offer up the desires of my heart to God. I had scarcely done so, when immediately I was seized upon by some power which entirely overcame me, and had such an astonishing influence over me as to bind my tongue so that I could not speak. Thick darkness gathered around me, and it seemed to me for a time as if I were doomed to sudden destruction.

But, exerting all my powers to call upon God to deliver me out of the power of this enemy which had seized upon me, and at the very moment when I was ready to sink into despair and abandon myself to destruction—not to an imaginary ruin, but to the power of some actual being from the unseen world, who had such marvelous power as I had never before felt in any being—just at this moment of great alarm, I saw a pillar of light exactly over my head, above the brightness of the sun, which descended gradually until it fell upon me.

It no sooner appeared than I found myself delivered from the enemy which held me bound. When the light rested upon me I saw two Personages, whose brightness and glory defy all description, standing above me in the air. One of them spake unto me, calling me by name and said, pointing to the other—"This is My Beloved Son. Hear Him!"

My object in going to inquire of the Lord was to know which of all the sects was right, that I might know which to join. No sooner, therefore, did I get possession of myself, so as to be able to speak, than I asked the Personages who stood above me in the light, which of all the sects was right (for at this time it had never entered into my heart that all were wrong)—and which I should join.

I was answered that I must join none of them, for they were all wrong; and the Personage who addressed me said that all their creeds were an abomination in his sight; that those professors were all corrupt; that: "they draw near to me with their lips, but their hearts are far from me, they teach for doctrines the commandments of men, having a form of godliness, but they deny the power thereof."

He again forbade me to join with any of them; and many other things did he say unto me, which I cannot write at this time. When I came to myself again, I found myself lying on my back, looking up into heaven. When the light had departed, I had no strength; but soon recovering in some degree, I went home.

I soon found . . . that my telling the story had excited a great deal of prejudice against me among professors of religion, and was the cause of great persecution, which continued to increase; and though I was an obscure boy, only between fourteen and fifteen years of age, and my circumstances in life such as to make a boy of no consequence in the world, yet men of high standing would take notice sufficient to excite the public mind against me, and create a bitter persecution; and this was common among all the sects—all united to persecute me.

It caused me serious reflection then, and often has since, how very strange it was that an obscure boy, of a little over fourteen years of age, and one, too, who was doomed to the necessity of obtaining a scanty maintenance by his daily labor, should be thought a character of sufficient importance to attract the attention of the great ones of the most popular sects of the day, and in a manner to create in them a spirit of the most bitter persecution and reviling. But strange or not, so it was, and it was often the cause of great sorrow to myself.

However, it was nevertheless a fact that I had beheld a vision. I have thought since, that I felt much like Paul, when he made his defense before King Agrippa, and related the account of the vision he had when he saw a light, and heard a voice; but still there were but few who believed him; some said he was dishonest, others said he was mad; and he was ridiculed and reviled. But all this did not destroy the reality of his vision. He had seen a vision, he knew he had, and all the persecution under heaven could not make it otherwise; and though they should persecute him unto death, yet he knew, and would know to his latest breath, that he had both seen a light and heard a voice speaking unto him, and all the world could not make him think or believe otherwise.

So it was with me. I had actually seen a light, and in the midst of that light I saw two Personages, and they did in reality speak to me; and though I was hated and persecuted for saying that I had seen a vision, yet it was true; and while they were persecuting me, reviling me, and speaking all manner of evil against me falsely for so saying, I was led to say in my heart: Why persecute me for telling the truth? I have actually seen a vision; and who am I that I can withstand God, or why does the world think to make me deny what I have actually seen? For I had seen a vision; I knew it, and I knew that God knew it, and I could not deny it, neither dared I do it; at least I knew that by so doing I would offend God, and come under condemnation.

I had now got my mind satisfied so far as the sectarian world was concerned—that it was not my duty to join with any of them, but to continue as I was until further directed. I had found the testimony of James to be true—that a man who lacked wisdom might ask of God, and obtain, and not be upbraided.

I continued to pursue my common vocations in life until the twenty-first of September, one thousand eight hundred and twenty-three, all the time suffering severe persecution at the hands of all classes of men, both religious and irreligious, because I continued to affirm that I had seen a vision.

During the space of time which intervened between the time I had the vision and the year eighteen hundred and twenty-three—having been forbidden to join any of the religious sects of the day, and being of very tender years, and persecuted by those who ought to have been my friends and to have treated me kindly, and if they supposed me to be deluded to have endeavored in a proper and affectionate manner to have reclaimed me—I was left to all kinds of temptations; and, mingling with all kinds of society, I frequently fell into many foolish errors, and displayed the weakness of youth, and the foibles of human nature; which, I am sorry to say, led me into divers temptations, offensive in the sight of God. In making this confession, no one need suppose me guilty of any great or malignant sins. A disposition to commit such was never in my nature.

On the evening of the above-mentioned twenty-first of September, after I had retired to my bed for the night, I betook myself to prayer and supplication to Almighty God for forgiveness of all my sins and follies, and also for a manifestation to me, that I might know of my state and standing before him; for I had full confidence in obtaining a divine manifestation, as I previously had one.

While I was thus in the act of calling upon God, I discovered a light appearing in my room, which continued to increase until the room was lighter than at noonday, when immediately a personage appeared at my bedside, standing in the air, for his feet did not touch the floor.

He had on a loose robe of most exquisite whiteness. It was a whiteness beyond anything earthly I had ever seen; nor do I believe that any earthly thing could be made to appear so exceedingly white and brilliant. His hands were naked, and his arms also, a little above the wrist; so, also, were his feet naked, as were his legs, a little above the ankles. His head and neck were also bare. I could discover that he had no other clothing on but this robe, as it was open, so that I could see into his bosom.

Not only was his robe exceedingly white, but his whole person was glorious beyond description, and his countenance truly like lightning. The room was exceedingly light, but not so very bright as immediately around his person. When I first looked upon him, I was afraid; but the fear soon left me.

He called me by name, and said unto me that he was a messenger sent from the presence of God to me, and that his name was Moroni; that God had a work for me to do; and that my name should be had for good and evil among all nations, kindreds, and tongues, or that it should be both good and evil spoken of among all people.

He said there was a book deposited, written upon gold plates, giving an account of the former inhabitants of this continent, and the source from whence they sprang. He also said that the fulness of the everlasting Gospel was contained in it, as delivered by the Savior to the ancient inhabitants;

Also, that there were two stones in silver bows—and these stones, fastened to a breastplate, constituted what is called the Urim and Thummim—deposited with the plates; and the possession and use of these stones were what constituted "seers" in ancient or former times; and that God had prepared them for the purpose of translating the book.

After telling me these things, he commenced quoting the prophecies of the Old Testament. He first quoted part of the third chapter of Malachi; and he quoted also the fourth or last chapter of the same prophecy, though with a little variation from the way it reads in our Bibles. Instead of quoting the first verse as it reads in our books, he quoted it thus:

"For behold, the day cometh that shall burn as an oven, and all the proud, yea, and all that do wickedly shall burn as stubble; for they that come shall burn them, saith the Lord of Hosts, that it shall leave them neither root nor branch."

And again, he quoted the fifth verse thus: "Behold, I will reveal unto you the Priesthood, by the hand of Elijah the prophet, before the coming of the great and dreadful day of the Lord."

He also quoted the next verse differently: "And he shall plant in the hearts of the children the promises made to the fathers, and the hearts of the children shall turn to their fathers. If it were not so, the whole earth would be utterly wasted at his coming."

In addition to these, he quoted the eleventh chapter of Isaiah, saying that it was about to be fulfilled. He quoted also the third chapter of Acts, twenty-second and twenty-third verses, precisely as they stand in our New Testament. He said that that prophet was Christ; but the day had not yet come when "they who would not hear his voice should be cut off from among the people," but soon would come.

He also quoted the second chapter of Joel, from the twenty-eighth verse to the last. He also said that this was not yet fulfilled, but was soon to be. And he further stated that the fulness of the Gentiles was soon to come in. He quoted many other passages of scripture, and offered many explanations which cannot be mentioned here.

Again, he told me, that when I got those plates of which he had spoken—for the time that they should be obtained was not yet fulfilled—I should not show them to any person; neither the breastplate with the Urim and Thummim; only to those to whom I should be commanded to show them; if I did I should be destroyed. While he was conversing with me about the plates, the vision was opened to my mind that I could see the place where the plates were deposited, and that so clearly and distinctly that I knew the place again when I visited it.

After this communication, I saw the light in the room begin to gather immediately around the person of him who had been speaking to me, and it continued to do so until the room was again left dark, except just around him; when, instantly I saw, as it were, a conduit open right up into heaven, and he ascended till he entirely disappeared, and the room was left as it had been before this heavenly light had made its appearance.

I lay musing on the singularity of the scene, and marveling greatly at what had been told to me by this extraordinary messenger; when, in the midst of my meditation, I suddenly discovered that my room was again beginning to get lighted, and in an instant, as it were, the same heavenly messenger was again by my bedside.

He commenced, and again related the very same things which he had done at his first visit, without the least variation; which having done, he informed me of great judgments which were coming upon the earth, with great desolations by famine, sword, and pestilence; and that these grievous judgments would come on the earth in this generation. Having related these things, he again ascended as he had done before.

By this time, so deep were the impressions made on my mind, that sleep had fled from my eyes, and I lay overwhelmed in astonishment at what I had both seen and heard. But what was my surprise when again I beheld the same messenger at my bedside, and heard him rehearse or repeat over again to me the same things as before; and added a caution to me, telling me that Satan would try to tempt me (in consequence of the indigent circumstances of my father's family), to get the plates for the purpose of getting rich. This he forbade me, saying that I must have no other object in view in getting the plates but to glorify God, and must not be influenced by any other motive than that of building his kingdom; otherwise I could not get them.

After this third visit, he again ascended into heaven as before, and I was again left to ponder on the strangeness of what I had just experienced; when almost immediately after the heavenly messenger had ascended from me for the third time, the cock crowed, and I found that day was approaching, so that our interviews must have occupied the whole of that night.

I shortly after arose from my bed, and, as usual, went to the necessary labors of the day; but, in attempting to work as at other times, I found my strength so exhausted as to render me entirely unable. My father, who was laboring along with me, discovered something to be wrong with me, and told me to go home. I started with the intention of going to the house; but, in attempting to cross the fence out of the field where we were, my strength entirely failed me, and I fell helpless on the ground, and for a time was quite unconscious of anything.

The first thing that I can recollect was a voice speaking unto me, calling me by name. I looked up, and beheld the same messenger standing over my head, surrounded by light as before. He then again related unto me all that he had related to me the previous night, and commanded me to go to my father and tell him of the vision and commandments which I had received.

I obeyed; I returned to my father in the field, and rehearsed the whole matter to him. He replied to me that it was of God, and told me to go and do as commanded by the messenger. I left the field, and went to the place where the messenger had told me the plates were deposited; and owing to the distinctness of the vision which I had had concerning it, I knew the place the instant that I arrived there.

Convenient to the village of Manchester, Ontario county, New York, stands a hill of considerable size, and the most elevated of any in the neighborhood. On the west side of this hill, not far from the top, under a stone of considerable size, lay the plates, deposited in a stone box. This stone was thick and rounding in the middle on the upper side, and thinner towards the edges, so that the middle part of it was visible above the ground, but the edge all around was covered with earth.

Having removed the earth, I obtained a lever, which I got fixed under the edge of the stone, and with a little exertion raised it up. I looked in, and there indeed did I behold the plates, the Urim and Thummim, and the breastplate, as stated by the messenger. The box in which they lay was formed by laying stones together in some kind of cement. In the bottom of the box were laid two stones crossways of the box, and on these stones lay the plates and the other things with them.

I made an attempt to take them out, but was forbidden by the messenger, and was again informed that the time for bringing them forth had not yet arrived, neither would it, until four years from that time; but he told me that I should come to that place precisely in one year from that time, and that he would there meet with me, and that I should continue to do so until the time should come for obtaining the plates.

Accordingly, as I had been commanded, I went at the end of each year, and at each time I found the same messenger there, and received instruction and intelligence from him at each of our interviews, respecting what the Lord was going to do, and how and in what manner his kingdom was to be conducted in the last days.

As my father's worldly circumstances were very limited, we were under the necessity of laboring with our hands, hiring out by day's work and otherwise, as we could get opportunity. Sometimes we were at home, and sometimes abroad, and by continuous labor were enabled to get a comfortable maintenance.

At length the time arrived for obtaining the plates, the Urim and Thummim, and the breastplate. On the twenty-second day of September, one thousand eight hundred and twenty-seven, having gone as usual at the end of another year to the place where they were deposited, the same heavenly messenger delivered them up to me with this charge: that I should be responsible for them; that if I should let them go carelessly, or through any neglect of mine, I should be cut off; but that if I would use all my endeavors to preserve them, until he, the messenger, should call for them, they should be protected.

I soon found out the reason why I had received such strict charges to keep them safe, and why it was that the messenger had said that when I had done what was required at my hand, he would call for them. For no sooner was it known that I had them, than the most strenuous exertions were used to get them from me. Every stratagem that could be invented was resorted to for that purpose. The persecution became more bitter and severe than before, and multitudes were on the alert continually to get them from me if possible. But by the wisdom of God, they remained safe in my hands, until I had accomplished by them what was required at my hand. When, according to arrangements, the messenger called for them, I delivered them up to him; and he has them in his charge until this day, being the second day of May, one thousand eight hundred and thirty-eight. . . .

On the 5th day of April, 1829, Oliver Cowdery came to my house, until which time I had never seen him. He stated to me that having been teaching school in the neighborhood where my father resided, and my father being one of those who sent to the school, he went to board for a season at his house, and while there the family related to him the circumstances of my having received the plates, and accordingly he had come to make inquiries of me.

Two days after the arrival of Mr. Cowdery (being the 7th of April) I commenced to translate the Book of Mormon, and he began to write for me.

1. Why do you think Joseph Smith and his followers became objects of persecution in his home state of New York?
2. What social factors might influence an individual to join the early Mormon Church?

10-2   A "Corrupt Bargain" or Politics as Usual? (1824)

The immediate outcome of the election of 1824 was inconclusive—both in the electoral college and in the popular vote—yet it was clearly a defeat for Henry Clay and his American System. With the election thrown into the House of Representatives, Speaker Clay's influence was nevertheless decisive. Clay's support for John Quincy Adams carried the New Englander to victory. Soon, Adams appointed Clay to the office of secretary of state, the proving ground for three successive presidents, triggering accusations of political maneuvering. The following excerpt is from Adams's diary during the months following the election when his future was uncertain.

> **Source:** Charles Francis Adams, ed. *Memoirs of John Quincy Adams*, 12 Volumes (Philadelphia: J. B. Lippincott & Co., 1875).

17th. At the office. Visits from W. Kelly, Senator from Louisiana, Letcher, member of H. R. from Kentucky, and G. B. English. Letcher came ostensibly with a claim of an assistant to the Marshal of Kentucky for additional compensation for his service in taking the census of 1820. But his apparent main object was to talk about the Presidential election. The account was yesterday received of the choice of electors in Louisiana by the Legislature, from which it is rendered almost certain that three of the votes have been for General Jackson, probably four, and perhaps all five—but certainly none for Mr. Clay. This leaves Mr. Crawford with forty-one, and Mr. Clay with thirty-seven, electoral votes. Mr. Crawford, therefore, will, and Mr. Clay will not, be one of the three persons from whom the House of Representatives, voting by States, will be called to choose a President. Mr. Letcher is an intimate friend of Mr. Clay's, and lodges at the same house with him. He expects that after the result is known, that Mr. Clay cannot be voted for in the House, there will be meetings of the people in the several counties instructing their members to vote for Jackson, and perhaps that similar instructions will be sent on by their Legislature. These, he supposes, will be gotten up by what they call the *Relief* party in the politics of the State, and by men like Rowan, Barry, and Bibb, secondary leaders of the State, not daring to oppose Clay openly, on account of his own popularity in the State, but seizing upon the first opportunity afforded them indirectly to put him down. Letcher is evidently alarmed at this, and, in the midst of strong professions of indepdnence, and of indifference about retaining his seat, is plainly not prepared to act definitively in opposition to the will of his constituents. He intimated that the Relief party were in fact hostile to Mr. Clay; that of the Kentucky delegation here, a large portion were warmly attached to him; that lately, speaking of what might ensue here, he had expressed the wish to go in harmony with his friends—which Letcher said he interpreted as a wish that his friends would go in harmony with him. Colonel R. M. Johnson, Letcher thinks, is warmly of the Relief party, and as to the Presidency, determined to be at all events on the strongest side. I observed to Letcher that Colonel R. M. had candidly told me so himself.

Letcher wished to know what my sentiments toward Clay were, and I told him without disguise that I harbored no hostility against him; that whatever of difference there had been between us had arisen altogether from him, and not from me. I adverted to Jonathan Russell's attack upon me, which, I said, I believed Mr. Clay had been privy to and countenanced. But, having completely repelled that attack, I felt no animosity against any person concerned in it.

Letcher said Clay's friends thought he had been wrong in his letter against me concerning that affair. It was written in a moment of excitement. He was sure Clay felt now no hostility to me. He had spoken respectfully of me, and was a man of sincerity. Of the fourteen electors of Kentucky, seven voted for Calhoun as Vice-President; and this vote I thought, and Letcher fully concurred in the opinion, was more hostile to Clay than any vote for Jackson as President could be. It held up Calhoun as a future competitor against Clay, and thereby postponed all his prospects indefinitely. The drift of all Letcher's discourse was much the same as Wyer had told me, that Clay would willingly support me if he could thereby serve himself, and the substance of his *meaning* was, that if Clay's friends could *know* that he would have a prominent share in the Administration, that might induce them to vote for me, even in the face of instructions. But Letcher did not profess to have any authority from Clay for what he said, and he made no definite propositions. He spoke of his interview with me as altogether confidential, and in my answers to him I spoke in mere general terms.

* * *

23d . . . R. P. Letcher had a long conversation with me upon the subject which he had broached the other day. The object appeared to me to be to convince me of the importance of obtaining an election in the House of Representatives at the first ballot, and that it would be obtainable by securing the votes of the States of Kentucky, Ohio, Indiana, Illinois, Missouri, and Louisiana. I told him candidly that, however desirable this might be, it would be utterly impracticable, and that I had no expectation of receiving the vote of his own State of Kentucky. He seemed anxious to convince me that I *might* receive it, and enumerated the whole delegation, stating how each of them was now disposed—a majority of them being *uncommitted*. I consider Letcher as moving for Mr. Clay; and this anxiety of a friend of Clay's, that I should obtain the election at the first ballot in the House, is among the whimsical results of political combination at this time—"Incedo super ignes."

* * *

. . . At noon I went to the President's drawing-room, which was much crowded. Mrs. Adams, being quite unwell, did not go. I presented to the President, with Mr. Rebello, the Brazilian Chargé d'Affaires, Mr. Oliveira, Secretary of Legation, whom he had yesterday introduced to me at the Department of State. Robert P. Letcher, a member of the House of Representatives from Kentucky, asked me if I should go to the Department after the drawing-room. I said I should. He said he would call there, and did. He told me he had received from home many letters lately, and several this morning; that the members of the Kentucky Legislature would, in their private capacities, and not by Legislative Act, recommend to the members from the State in the House to vote for General Jackson as President, and popular meetings to pass similar resolutions had been, and would be, got up. But I might rely upon it they would have no effect. The vote of Kentucky in the House was fixable and unalterable. He spoke of the difference between Mr. Clay and me as giving concern to some of the members of the delegation, and intimated a wish that I should have some conversation with Mr. Clay upon the subject. I told him I would very readily, and whenever it might suit the convenience of Mr. Clay. . . .

I attended the dinner given by the members of both Houses of Congress to General La Fayette, at Williamson's Hotel. It was attended also by the President. About one hundred and fifty members of the two Houses were present, and about thirty officers of the Government—civil and military. . . . Mr. Clay made a speech about Bolivar and the cause of South America, and seemed very desirous of eliciting speeches from me and Mr. Calhoun. He told me that he should be glad to have with me soon some confidential conversation upon public affairs. I said I should be happy to have it whenever it might suit his convenience.

9th. . . . Mr. Clay came at six, and spent the evening with me in a long conversation explanatory of the past and prospective of the future. He said that the time was drawing near when the choice must be made in the House of Representatives of a President from the three candidates presented by the electoral colleges; that he had been much urged and solicited with regard to the part in that transaction that he should take, and had not been five minutes landed at his lodgings before he had been applied to by a friend of Mr. Crawford's, in a manner so gross that it had disgusted him; that some of my friends also, disclaiming, indeed, to have any authority from me, had repeatedly applied to him, directly or indirectly, urging considerations personal to himself as motives to his cause. He had thought it best to reserve for sometime his determination to himself: first, to give a decent time for his own funeral solemnities as a candidate; and, secondly, to prepare and predispose all his friends to a state of neutrality between the three candidates who would be before the House, so that they might be free ultimately to take that course which might be most conducive to the public interest. The time had now come at which he might be explicit in his communication with me, and he had for that purpose asked this confidential interview. He wished me, as far as I might think proper, to satisfy him with regard to some principles of great public importance, but without any personal considerations for himself. In the question to come before the House between General Jackson, Mr. Crawford, and myself, he had no hesitation in saying that his preference would be for me.

* * *

15th. Horatio Seymour, S. U. S. from Vermont, in great concern about the instructions, from the Kentucky House of Representatives to the members of that delegation here, to vote for General Jackson as President. He is alarmed for its probable effect on the votes of all the Western States. I advised him to see and converse with Mr. Clay.

Colonel R. M. Johnson, S. U. S. from Kentucky, who told me there was an article in the Lexington Reporter stating that it was said the instructions had been given by the advice of one of the Senators of the State at Washington; and, as it was known Talbot took no part in the election, the imputation was upon him (Johnson). But he solemnly protested that he had not written any such letter, and intimated that the instructions were given in consequence of Mr. Clay's own partisans having taken so much pains to make me unpopular in the State, for which he believed they were now very sorry. Johnson professed neutrality between General Jackson and me, and said he should be well satisfied if either of us should be elected.

* * *

17th. W. C. Bradley, member from Vermont, was here, and afterwards W. Plumer, Jr., of New Hampshire, much concerned about these instructions from the Legislature of Kentucky. Bradley said he had seen Clay this morning, who told him the resolutions would confirm the majority of the delegation in their determination to vote otherwise, but who spoke of the event of the election as exceedingly uncertain—of Missouri and Illinois particularly, the votes of both the States being in single persons. Bradley said he had urged Clay to see me, but Clay had told him it was altogether unnecessary—that his course was fixed, and he should consider the elevation of the Hero as the greatest calamity which could befall the country.

* * *

18th. Dr. Thornton called this morning to give me some information respecting the prospects of the election. It respected the Kentucky and Ohio delegations, and concurred with what I had heard before.

Mr. S. L. Southard came, to ask for the papers he had left with me yesterday, of which Mr. Kirkpatrick wishes to take copies. I gave them to him. He then asked me some questions respecting the election, upon which I spoke to him with entire confidence. I asked him if he wished me so to speak to him, and he said he did. I told him of the present state of things, so far as it is known to myself; of the present prospect, that a majority of the friends of Mr. Clay and Mr. Crawford would finally vote for me, but that the whole of the aspect may be changed from day to day.

* * *

20th. Morning visits at my house from A. H. Everett, J. Sloane, member from Ohio, with a Mr. Bissell, from that State, D. P. Cook, member from Illinois, and W. Plumer, Jr., from New Hampshire. J. Reed, member from Massachusetts, came, but, finding company with me, promised to call again. Cook told me that some time since he had been informed by three persons of weight in the Western delegations that they would all vote for General Jackson. He had received also letters from some of his warmest friends in Illinois, and of those who had been my warmest friends, advising him, in that event, to vote with the other Western members, as by standing out alone

Scott then proceeded to speak of the approaching election, and said that he had made up his mind to vote with the other Western delegates, but intimated that he should incur great opposition for it in his own State. He spoke of himself as being entirely devoted to Mr. Clay, and of his hope that he would be a member of the next Administration.

I told him that he would not expect me to enter upon details with regard to the formation of an Administration, but that if I should be elected by the suffrages of the West I should naturally look to the West for much of the support that I should need.

He parted from me apparently satisfied.

Reed came to speak about Webster, Louis McLane, and the federalists. His own disposition is favorable to me; but Webster is specially apprehensive that the federalists will be excluded from office by me.

I told Reed that I should exclude no person for political opinions, or for personal opposition to me; that my great object would be to break up the remnant of old party distinctions, and bring the whole people together in sentiment as much as possible.

Bradley told me that General Jackson had yesterday, or the day before, paid a visit to Mr. Crawford, and they had been reconciled together, with mutual assurances that there had never been any *personal* hostility towards each other. I have expected this movement ever since the development of the Western phalanx, and if, as is highly probable, it brings all the Crawford force in the House to bear in favor of Jackson, it will be decisive of the election.

* * *

29th. . . . I dined with Mr. George Sullivan. The party consisted of Mr. Clay, the Speaker, Mr. Salazar, the Colombian Minister, J. S. Johnston, Senator, and E. Livingston, member from Louisiana, T. Newton, W. Archer, and J. Taliaferro, members from Virginia, James Hamilton, member from South Carolina, A. H. Everett, and Miss Stockton, who is residing with Mrs. Sullivan. The party, though variously selected, was exceedingly good-humored and jovial, and it was past nine in the evening when we broke up.

On my return home, Mr. Clay came in, and sat with me a couple of hours, discussing all the prospects and probabilities of the Presidential election. He spoke to me with the utmost freedom of men and things; intimated doubts and pre-possessions concerning individual friends of mine, to all which I listened with due consideration. He was anxious for the conciliation of Webster and Louis McLane, and expressed some jealousy as from Webster of the persons by whom he supposed me to be surrounded.

I told him the sources of Webster's anxieties, and my own earnest desire to conciliate him; the manner in which my overtures had been received by him, and my own high opinion of his talents and capacities for service.

* * *

31st. . . . I called at the President's, and found Messrs. Calhoun and Southard with him, but they immediately withdrew. I delivered to him two or three dispatches received from R. Rush, and the letter last received from S. Mullowny. I also read to him the note received from S. Rebello, Chargé d'Affaires from Brazil, proposing an alliance offensive and defensive; which, he said, must be declined. He soon began to speak, however, of the nominations, and said he believed he should send them in immediately.

I observed that I should be perfectly satisfied if he would determine upon his selection of the persons now, and prepare the nominations; but I was convinced it would much increase the excitement, already great and every day inflaming, if he should send in the nominations *now* or before the election. I asked him if he had been advised to this measure by Mr. Calhoun.

He said he had, and by Mr. Southard, by Mr. Elliott, Senator from Georgia, and by Mr. Taliaferro, member from Virginia.

I said that the motives of all these gentlemen, or of those by whom they were instigated, were suspicions of me—suspicions that I was using these vacant missions as lures to promote my own election in the House. They wished to take this weapon out of my hands. They were mistaken. The only person whom I wished to recommend to him was one of those whom he proposed to nominate. I was willing he should fix all his nominations *now*. It would disconcert no arrangements of mine, and I had no suspicion that General Jackson would use the suspension of them to promote *his* election.

* * *

Feb. 2nd. . . . I called at the president's with dispatches from H. Allen, in Chili, and from R. Rush, at London. The last answers to letters from me of 27th November last—the sixty-eighth day. Referring to the conversation that I had with the President yesterday, I asked if I had understood him correctly that he had determined not to make the nominations to the vacant offices at all.

He said I had.

I said I had understood the alternative was, that he should make them before or after the election. So far as I was personally concerned, I should prefer that even now he would make the nominations before the election, rather than that he should omit to make them altogether. I had wished him to determine upon his choice now, without making it known, but not leave the nominations as prizes to be held out by, or to, any one to purchase votes. Among the candidates whom he had mentioned to me were two members of Congress, one holding, the other supposed to influence, votes. It would be difficult for the successor to nominate either of them, especially if the votes in question should be for him. The nominations belonged properly to his Administration, and my wish was that it should be really his Administration to the last moment of its existence. If the election should fall upon me, I should therefore entreat of him, as a favor, that he would make the nominations as his own, and as he would have made them at any other period of his Administration. If, as was more probable, General Jackson should be chosen, I should of course have nothing further to say; but, having no suspicion that he would anticipate his power of nomination by pledges, I presumed he would equally acquiesce in Mr. Monroe's making the nominations. . . .

* * *

3d. The flood of visitors is unceasing. Mr. Webster called and spent the evening with me. The excitement of electioneering is kindling into fury. George Kremer's "Another Card," in answer to that of H. Clay on Monday, appeared in the Intelligencer this morning. Mr. Clay called upon the House to institute an investigation. Kremer did the same, and a debate ensued upon it in the House, which is postponed till to-morrow.

* * *

Webster's talk was about the election. He read to me a letter from Warfield, of Maryland, to him, concerning the election, and asking advice of him with regard to his vote; and the draft of an answer which he had prepared; and said he would send it or not, as I should think proper. He said that J. Lee, also of Maryland, had consulted him too, and was under impressions similar to those of Warfield. Their concern was lest, in the event of my election, the federalists should be treated as a proscribed party. Webster's answer to Warfield expressed entire confidence that I should be governed by no such considerations, and said that he should show this confidence by his vote. It intimated a hope that the object of the Administration would be to promote harmony among the people, and that the disposition would be marked by conferring some one prominent appointment upon a person of that party.

I observed that if that referred to the formation of an Administration, it would imply more than I could confirm.

He said it did not—but to an appointment perhaps of a Judge.

I said I approved altogether of the general spirit of his answer, and should consider it as one of the objects nearest to my heart to bring the whole people of the Union to harmonize together. I must, however, candidly tell him that I believed either General Jackson or Mr. Crawford would pursue precisely the same principle, and that no Administration could possibly succeed upon any other.

* * *

Feb. 4. . . . I delivered to the President the letter I had written him yesterday upon the subject of the nominations to the foreign missions, and told him that I wished to put it as a deposit in his hands, for a testimonial that I had not used those missions to promote any purpose of my own.

He took the paper, and said he would not communicate it to any one; that he was aware of the extreme circumspection with which it was necessary for me at this moment to act; that his own situation was also one of great difficulty; that his impression at the beginning of the present session of Congress had been to leave these appointments to be made by his successor, whose confidential officers the persons receiving them would be. He had been afterwards urged to make the nominations, but had yielded to the consideration presented by me, in which he had thought there was great weight, that these nominations could scarcely have been made at this crisis without having some improper effect on the pending election. But, in determining upon the postponement, he had thought best to put it on the other ground, of leaving the appointments to his successor, because that, operating equally upon both, could not be attributed to the influence of either. He said he had no doubt of my kind and friendly disposition to himself, and not the most distant suspicion that I had used, or would use, those appointments for any electioneering purpose.

* * *

5th. D. P. Cook called this morning, as he had promised. I reminded him of what he had told me of Ingham's conversations with him respecting the Government of Arkansas, and of McDuffie's talk with him in Ingham's chamber; and I asked him to put in writing the substance of all those conversations. I said I did not ask him to do this for me, but for himself. I told him that all this would be history hereafter, and that those conversations would be an important part of history. He said he regretted not having written them down at the time. I said it would have been better then, but, the time being still very recent, little would now be lost of the substance, and the longer it should be delayed, the less full and correct would the statement be.

He said he would write it. The substance was, that Ingham, knowing Cook to be a candidate for the appointment of Governor of Arkansas, urged him to declare openly that he would vote for Jackson, and intimated that he should then have the appointment. Cook says he offended Ingham by his answer to this proffer, and Ingham has said nothing of it since. McDuffie's argument was to the same purpose; that General Jackson's election would depend upon his (Cook's) vote; that there was a moral obligation to vote for Jackson, who had the greatest number of electoral votes; that if I should be elected, it would only be by Clay's corrupt coalition with me, and that the people would be so disgusted with this that there would be a systematic and determined opposition from the beginning, so that the Administration could not get along. It would be overthrown, and he would be involved in its ruin.

* * *

Tracy and Crowninshield were here this morning, and gave accounts of the attempt at accommodation. An apology was drawn up disclaiming any intention of imputing corruption to Clay, and declaring that he knew no fact ascertaining that any bargain had been made, which Kremer professed himself ready to sign, and which Clay declared would be satisfactory to him.

* * *

9th. May the blessing of God rest upon the event of this day!—the second Wednesday in February, when the election of a President of the United States for the term of four years, from the 4th of March next, was consummated. Of the votes in the electoral colleges, there were ninety-nine for Andrew Jackson, of Tennessee; eighty-four for John Quincy Adams, of Massachusetts; forty-one for William Harris Crawford, of Georgia; and thirty-seven for Henry Clay, of Kentucky: in all, two hundred and sixty-one. This result having been announced, on opening and counting the votes in joint meeting of the two Houses, the House of Representatives immediately proceeded to the vote by ballot from the three highest candidates, when John Quincy Adams received the votes of thirteen, Andrew Jackson of seven, and William H. Crawford of four States. The election was thus completed, very unexpectedly, by a single ballot. Alexander H. Everett gave me the first notice, both of the issue of the votes of the electoral colleges as announced in the joint meeting, and of the final vote as declared.

* * *

10th. Mr. Southard called, as I had requested, at ten. I invited him to remain at the head of the Navy Department; to which he consented. I told him that I should offer the Department of State to Mr. Clay, and should invite Mr. Crawford to remain in the Department of the Treasury.

* * *

Feb. 11. . . . I was at the President's, and again repeated the request that he would make the nominations which had been postponed till after the election. He said he would take it into consideration. I told the President I had invited Mr. Crawford to remain at the head of the Treasury Department, and showed him the letter I had received from him this morning, in very friendly terms declining the offer. I then said that I should offer the Department of State to Mr. Clay, considering it due to his talents and services, to the Western section of the Union, whence he comes, and to the confidence in me manifested by their delegations; that for the Treasury and War Departments I should be glad to take his advice, and to consult him with reference to other objects of public interest, if it would be agreeable to him.

Feb. 12. . . . General Brown entered this morning into an argument to convince me that it would not be expedient that Mr. Clay should be Secretary of State. He had a high opinion of Mr. Clay, but if I should offer him the Department he hoped he would not accept it, and he believed it would be better if I should not offer it to him. General Brown wished that De Witt Clinton should be the Secretary of State. I listened to what he said, and then told him I had already made the offer to Mr. Clay. Brown's next wish is that Clinton should be Secretary of the Treasury. The members of Congress all advise variously for the formation of a Cabinet, and many are anxious to be treated confidentially.

1. *Is there any evidence in Adams's writings that he bargained with Henry Clay to win the presidency? What dangers are there in using memoirs as sources?*
2. *Whether true or not, how do you think accusations of a "corrupt bargain" would affect Adams's presidency? How might his family background make the matter worse?*

10-3   A Disaffected Mason Speaks Out Against the Order (1826)

In 1826, William Morgan, an erstwhile member of the New York Masons, authored Illustrations of Masonry, a purported revelation of Masonic secret rituals. Morgan disappeared mysteriously—reported drowned at Niagara Falls by members of the order. Although never proven, Masonry's involvement in Morgan's disappearance led to public disaffection and refusal to support Masons for public office. The Antimason Party, organized in 1827 was the ultimate manifestation of this antipathy. What follows is the publisher's introduction to Morgan's exposé, written following the authors disappearance.

Source: William Morgan, *Illustrations of Masonry*, (New York: David C. Miller, 1827)
http://www.utlm.org/onlinebooks/captmorgansfreemasonry1.htm#2

In the absence of the author, or rather compiler of the following work, who was kidnapped and carried away from the village of Batavia, on the 11th day of September, 1826, by a number of Freemasons, it devolves upon the publisher to attempt to set forth some of the leading views that governed those who embarked in the undertaking.

To contend with prejudice, and to struggle against customs and opinions, which superstition, time, and ignorance have hallowed, requires time, patience, and magnanimity. When we begin to pull down the strongholds of error, the batteries we level against them, though strong, and powerful; and victorious at last, are at first received with violence; and when in our conquering career we meet with scoffs and revilings from the beseiged partisans of untenable positions, it the more forcibly impresses us we are but men; and that in every work of reformation and renovation we must encounter various difficulties. For a full confirmation of our statement we might refer to the history of the world. It is not our intention, however, to give a full detail of the whims and caprices of man to bring forth the historic records of other years as proof of the windings and shiftings of the various characters who have "Strutted their brief hour on life's stage" in order to convince that customs, associations, and institutions are like the lives of the authors and abettors, fleeting and fragile. Many of them rise up as bubbles on the ocean, and die away. Circumstances give them existence, and when these causes cease to exist, they go into the same gulf of oblivion as countless exploded opinions and tenets have gone before them. The mind that formed and planned them, goes on in its dazzling flight, bounding over barrier after barrier, till it has arrived at the ultimate goal of consummation.

The daily occurrences before us bring forth the full conviction that the emanation from the God of light is gradually ascending to regions of greater intellectual brilliancy.

When we view man, in the infancy of society, as in the childhood of his existence, he is weak, powerless and defenceless; but in his manhood and riper years, he has grown to his full stature, and stands forth in commanding attitude, the favored and acknowledged lord of the world. For his comfort and well-being as a member of society, rules and regulations are necessary. In the various stages of his progress, these systematic improvements undergo various changes, according to circumstances and situations. What is proper and necessary in one grade of society, is wholly useless, and may be alarming in another. Opinions and usages that go down in tradition, and interfere not with our improvements in social concerns, adhere to us more closely and become entwined in all our feelings. It is to this we owe our bigoted attachment to antiquity—it is this that demands from us a superstitious reverence for the opinions and practices of men of former times, and closes the ear against truth, and blinds the eyes to the glare of new lights and new accessions of knowledge through which medium only can they break in upon the mind.

We have within ourselves the knowledge; and everywhere around us the proofs that we are beings destined not to stand still. In our present state of advancement, we look with pity on the small progress of our fathers in arts and sciences, and social institutions; and when compared with our elevated rank, we have just cause of pride and of grateful feelings. They did well for the times in which they lived, but to the ultimatum of perfectability we are nearer, and in the monuments we have before us of the skill and genius of our times and age, we have only fulfilled these destinies for which we were created; and we object to every obstacle that opposes or attempts to oppose the will of heaven.

In the present enlightened state to which society has advanced, we contend that the opinions and tenets and pretended secrecies of "olden times," handed down to us, should be fully, fairly and freely canvassed; that from the mist and darkness which have hung over them, they should come out before the open light of day, and be subject to the rigid test of candid investigation. These, preliminary remarks lead as to the main object of our introduction.

We come to lay before the world the claims of an institution which has been sanctioned by ages, venerated for wisdom, exalted for "light;" but, an institution whose benefits have always been overrated, and whose continuance is not in the slightest degree, necessary. We meet it with its high requirements, its "time honored customs," its swelling titles, and shall show it in its nakedness and simplicity. Strip it of its "borrowed trappings" and it is a mere nothing, a toy not now worthy the notice of a child to sport with. We look back to it as, at one period, a "cement of society and bond of union"— we view it as, at one time, a venerable fort—but now in ruins—which contained within its walls many things that dignified and adorned human nature. We give it due credit for the services it has done; but at present when light has gone abroad into the utmost recesses and comers of the world—when information is scattered wide around us, and knowledge is not closeted in cloisters and cells but "stalks abroad with her beams of light, and her honors and rewards," we may now, when our minority has expired, act up to our character and look no longer to Masonry as our guide and conductor; it has nothing in it now valuable that is not known to every inquiring mind. It contains, wrapped up in its supposed mysteries, no useful truth, no necessary knowledge that has not gone forth to the world through other channels and by other means. If we would have a knowledge of sacred history—of the religion and practices of the Jews, and the terms and technicalities of the Mosaic institutions, we can have recourse to the Bible. If we wish further communications from heaven, we have open to our view the pages of the New Testament. If we would "climb the high ascent of human science, and trace the mighty progress of human genius in every gigantic effort of mind in logic, geometry, mathematics, chemistry, and every other branch of knowledge," we ridicule the idea that Masonry, in her retirements, contains the arts and sciences. The sturdiest Mason in the whole fraternity is not bold enough to uphold or maintain the opinion for one moment in sober reality. The origin of the institution is easily traced to the rude ages of the world—to a body of mechanics, or a corporation of operative workmen, who formed signs and regulations, the more easily to carry on their work, and to protect their order. [The very obligations solemnly tendered to every member, carry the strongest internal evidence of the semi-barbarity that prevailed at the time of the institution of the order,] In the course of time, as society increased, and knowledge became more general, it spread, and embracing in its grasp other objects than at first, it enrolled in its ranks men of the first respectability in wealth, talents and worth. But that there is anything intrinsically valuable in the signs, symbols, or words of Masonry, no man of sense will contend. That there is not any hidden secret which operates as a talismanic charm on its possessors, every man of intelligence, Mason or no Mason, must candidly acknowledge. It is worse than idleness for the defenders of the order, at the present day to entrench themselves behind their outward show—the semblance before the world—and to say they are in possession of superior knowledge.

We pretend not to act under a cover. We shall "tell the truth, the whole truth, and nothing but the truth." Masonry, it is true, has long been eulogized in song—it has formed the burthen of the poet's theme, and been the subject of the orator's best performances. Fancy has been almost exhausted in bringing out "new flowers to deck the fairy queen;" but when we come behind the scenes, what is the picture we behold? Are we to rest satisfied with the ipse dixit of others, or to examine the truth for ourselves? The touchstone is before our readers in the present publication.

Masonry is of itself naked and worthless. It consists of gleanings from the Holy Scriptures, and from the arts and sciences, which have shone in the world. Linking itself with philosophy and science and religion, on this it rests all its claims to veneration and respect. Take away this borrowed aid, and it falls into ruins.

Much weight is still attached to the argument, that as a tie uniting men—that, as a significant speech, symbolically speaking every language, and at the same time embodying in its constitution everything that is valuable, it should command respect. We meet this argument with facts that cannot be controverted. We put it on a basis that will fling into the back ground every quibble and artifice on the subject; and, in the language of a polemic writer, we challenge opposition to our position.

The religion inculcated by the Son of Man does all this; and in no possible situation can man be placed, that the benign influence of Christianity does not completely supersede the use of a mere human institution. Place a brother in a desert, unfriended and unknown,—leave him in a wilderness where human footsteps never printed the ground, the Divine Benefactor is at his side, and watches over him with parental guidance. Let him be driven on a barbarous coast, in the midst of savage men, and there it is that the breathings of the divine influence spreads around him its shield, brings him into civilized society—in the busy walks of men and are we to be told, as members of community, sojourners on earth, and candidates for heaven, we must be taught our duty at a Mason's lodge? Wherever Masonry exercises its influence with success, there Christianity can have, or should have a more powerful effect. Whenever Masonry claims "kindred with the skies," and exalts herself above every living sublunary thing, then, with an unhallowed step, it obtrudes on the sacred borders of religion, and decks itself in borrowed garments.

Entrenched within these strong walls—decked with all the glitter of high sounding professions, claiming what does not belong to it,—it dazzles "but to bewilder and destroy." In its train, in these United States, are enrolled many periodical works devoted to Masonry; and under the guise of patronizing mechanics—the arts and sciences—lend their aid to carry on the imposing delusion. They take up the specious title of throwing a little illumination on this benighted country, from their secret depositories. Arrogating to itself what should deck other's brows—assuming to be the parton, the life and soul of all that is great and valuable—it deceives many of its votaries, and from its gaudy premises the most untenable and onerous conclusions are drawn.

Are we astonished at the wild and heedless manner in which many of the votaries of Masonry rush into every excess, putting at defiance the laws of our civil institutions, which suffer no one to put in jeopardy, but by due forms, and disregarding the command of the Most High, which says, "Thou shalt not kill?" —we can readily trace the cause to the impressions and practices obtained from its false tenets and descriptive arrogance. Masonry is to the modern world what the whore of Babylon was to the ancient; and is the beast with seven heads and ten horns, ready to tear out our bowels, and *scatter them to the four winds of heaven.*

Masonry gives rogues and evil-minded characters an opportunity of visiting upon their devoted victim, all the ills attending combined power, when exerted to accomplish destruction. It works unseen, at all silent hours, and secret times and places; and, like death when summoning his diseases, pounces upon its devoted subject, and lays him prostrate in the dust. Like the great enemy of man, it has shown its cloven foot, and put the public upon its guard against its secret machinations.

This part of the subject requires no further discussion either by way of ridicule or downright sincerity, but the remark which cannot be too often reiterated, that the world, in its present advanced state, requires no such order for our social intercourse; and when the Masonic mania prevails as it now does in this country, we are exalting a mere human ordinance, with its useless trumpery and laughable accompaniments, for the sublime and unadorned lessons of Heaven.

To some men it is galling and mortifying in the extreme to give up their darling systems. With the increase of years their fondness becomes so great that they cling to them with wild and bewildered attachment. But we would ask them, where now are the Knights of Malta and Jerusalem, and the objects that called forth their perils and journeyings? Where are the crusades and excursions on which our Grand Commanders, Generalissimos and Sir Knights are to be engaged. . . . . .In no other excursions than Cervantes describes of his redoubtable hero *Don Quixote.* The days and occasions that called forth these deeds of chivalry and valor have passed like those before the flood; and the *mock* dignitaries and *puppet show* actions of Masons in their imitation call forth pity and indignation. When we now see the gaudy show in a lodge-room, and a train of nominal officers with their distinction and badges, it may give us some faint idea of scenes that are past, and may gratify an idle curiosity, but produces no substantial good under heaven. When monasteries and cloisters, and inquisitor's cells and prisons have been broken up before the sweeping march of the moral mind, why this unnecessary mummery should be so much countenanced in this country, above all other countries in the world, is a matter of astonishment.

The day we trust will never arrive here, when ranks in Masonry will be stepping-stones to places of dignity and power—when this institution will be a machine to press down the free born spirit of men. We have now no tyrant to rule over us—no kingly potentate to move over our heads the rod of authority; but high in our elevation, and invincible in our strongholds, we put at defiance secret cabals and associations. The public opinion is like a mighty river, and gigantic in its course it will sweep every interposing obstacle before it.

In the work which we submit to the public we have given false coloring to nothing; nor in these remarks have we set down aught in malice. In the firm discharge of our undertaking we have been stem and unbending as the rugged mountain oak; and persecutions, pains and perils have not deterred us from our purpose. We have triumphed over tumult, and clamor, and evil speaking.

When our book goes out to the world, it will meet with attacks of a violent nature from one source, and men of mock titles and order will endeavor to heap upon it every calumny. Men more tenacious of absolute forms and practice than they are attentive to truth and honor, will deny our expositions, and call us liars and impostors.

Such is the treatment, however ungenerous and unjust, which we expect to meet, and for which we are prepared. Truth, we know, is majestic and will finally prevail. The little petty effusions of malice that will be thrown out, will die with their authors, whom this work will survive.

We now aver, in defiance of whatever may be said to the contrary—no matter by whom, how exalted his rank—that this book is what it pretends to be; that it is a master key to the secrets of Masonry; that in the pages before him, the man of candor and inquiry can judge for himself, and then a proper judgment will be formed of our intention.

1. What, in essence, is the author's main concern about the practices of the Masonic Order? What argument(s) does he give against such practices?
2. Why do you think that certain individuals living in the United States during the 1820s and 1830s might be particularly sensitive about organizations such as the Masons?

10-4 The "Commoner" Takes Office (1828)

The inauguration of Andrew Jackson in 1829 marked a new era in American politics and economic opportunity as the new president's supporters sought to democratize both during what some historians have called "the age of the common man." Although the sixty-one-year-old Jackson, suffering from a severe headache and chronic cough, could barely be heard by those in attendance, Jackson's inaugural was the first in which the "people" played an important role and which they attended en masse. Although vague on particulars, the new president outlined his agenda for the country, emphasizing the need for reform.

Source: *American Treasures of the Library of Congress*
http://lcweb.loc.gov/exhibits/treasures/trr075a.html

Fellow-Citizens:

About to undertake the arduous duties that I have been appointed to perform by the choice of a free people, I avail myself of this customary and solemn occasion to express the gratitude which their confidence inspires and to acknowledge the accountability which my situation enjoins. While the magnitude of their interests convinces me that no thanks can be adequate to the honor they have conferred, it admonishes me that the best return I can make is the zealous dedication of my humble abilities to their service and their good.

As the instrument of the Federal Constitution it will devolve on me for a stated period to execute the laws of the United States, to superintend their foreign and their confederate relations, to manage their revenue, to command their forces, and, by communications to the Legislature, to watch over and to promote their interests generally. And the principles of action by which I shall endeavor to accomplish this circle of duties it is now proper for me briefly to explain.

In administering the laws of Congress I shall keep steadily in view the limitations as well as the extent of the Executive power trusting thereby to discharge the functions of my office without transcending its authority. With foreign nations it will be my study to preserve peace and to cultivate friendship on fair and honorable terms, and in the adjustment of any differences that may exist or arise to exhibit the forbearance becoming a powerful nation rather than the sensibility belonging to a gallant people.

In such measures as I may be called on to pursue in regard to the rights of the separate States I hope to be animated by a proper respect for those sovereign members of our Union, taking care not to confound the powers they have reserved to themselves with those they have granted to the Confederacy.

The management of the public revenue—that searching operation in all governments—is among the most delicate and important trusts in ours, and it will, of course, demand no inconsiderable share of my official solicitude. Under every aspect in which it can be considered it would appear that advantage must result from the observance of a strict and faithful economy. This I shall aim at the more anxiously both because it will facilitate the extinguishment of the national debt, the unnecessary duration of which is incompatible with real independence, and because it will counteract that tendency to public and private profligacy which a profuse expenditure of money by the Government is but too apt to engender. Powerful auxiliaries to the attainment of this desirable end are to be found in the regulations provided by the wisdom of Congress for the specific appropriation of public money and the prompt accountability of public officers.

With regard to a proper selection of the subjects of impost with a view to revenue, it would seem to me that the spirit of equity, caution and compromise in which the Constitution was formed requires that the great interests of agriculture, commerce, and manufactures should be equally favored, and that perhaps the only exception to this rule should consist in the peculiar encouragement of any products of either of them that may be found essential to our national independence.

Internal improvement and the diffusion of knowledge, so far as they can be promoted by the constitutional acts of the Federal Government, are of high importance.

Considering standing armies as dangerous to free governments in time of peace, I shall not seek to enlarge our present establishment, nor disregard that salutary lesson of political experience which teaches that the military should be held subordinate to the civil power. The gradual increase of our Navy, whose flag has displayed in distant climes our skill in navigation and our fame in arms; the preservation of our forts, arsenals, and dockyards, and the introduction of progressive improvements in the discipline and science of both branches of our military service are so plainly prescribed by prudence that I should be excused for omitting their mention sooner than for enlarging on their importance. But the bulwark of our defense is the national militia, which in the present state of our intelligence and population must render us invincible.

As long as our Government is administered for the good of the people, and is regulated by their will; as long as it secures to us the rights of person and of property, liberty of conscience and of the press, it will be worth defending; and so long as it is worth defending a patriotic militia will cover it with an impenetrable aegis. Partial injuries and occasional mortifications we may be subjected to, but a million of armed freemen, possessed of the means of war, can never be conquered by a foreign foe. To any just system, therefore, calculated to strengthen this natural safeguard of the country I shall cheerfully lend all the aid in my power.

It will be my sincere and constant desire to observe toward the Indian tribes within our limits a just and liberal policy, and to give that humane and considerate attention to their rights and their wants which is consistent with the habits of our Government and the feelings of our people.

The recent demonstration of public sentiment inscribes on the list of Executive duties, in characters too legible to be overlooked, the task of reform, which will require particularly the correction of those abuses that have brought the patronage of the Federal Government into conflict with the freedom of elections, and the counteraction of those causes which have disturbed the rightful course of appointment and have placed or continued power in unfaithful or incompetent hands.

In the performance of a task thus generally delineated I shall endeavor to select men whose diligence and talents will insure in their respective stations able and faithful cooperation, depending for the advancement of the public service more on the integrity and zeal of the public officers than on their numbers.

A diffidence, perhaps too just, in my own qualifications will teach me to look with reverence to the examples of public virtue left by my illustrious predecessors, and with veneration to the lights that flow from the mind that founded and the mind that reformed our system. The same diffidence induces me to hope for instruction and aid from the coordinate branches of the Government, and for the indulgence and support of my fellow-citizens generally. And a firm reliance on the goodness of that Power whose providence mercifully protected our national infancy, and has since upheld our liberties in various vicissitudes, encourages me to offer up my ardent supplications that He will continue to make our beloved country the object of His divine care and gracious benediction.

1. *What does Jackson say about the relationship between the Federal government and the various states? What does he imply about his administration's future relations with Indian nations/tribes?*
2. *What does Jackson identify as the catalyst for his "task of reform"? To whom might he directing his comments? Why?*

10-5 Andrew Jackson, First Annual Message to Congress (1829)

In the early nineteenth century, the lands occupied by southeastern and northwestern Native American groups, including the Cherokee, Chickasaw, Choctaw, Seminole, Fox, and Creek, were closed in upon by an expanding frontier of white settlement. In this address, President Jackson, a former frontiersman and Indian fighter, cloaked his argument for the relocation of Native Americans in the language of concern and honor. Indian removal helped bring about economic expansion for the new republic, but at tremendous cost to both the Native Americans who fought displacement and who moved west.

From *Messages and Papers of the Presidents*, ed. J. D. Richardson, National Archives and Records Administration, (1896), II, 456–459 (Dec. 8, 1829).

The condition and ulterior destiny of the Indian tribes within the limits of some of our states have become objects of much interest and importance. It has long been the policy of government to introduce among them the arts of civilization, in the hope of gradually reclaiming them from a wandering life. This policy has, however, been coupled with another wholly incompatible with its success. Professing a desire to civilize and settle them, we have at the same time lost no opportunity to purchase their lands and thrust them farther into the wilderness. By this means they have not only been kept in a wandering state, but been led to look upon us as unjust and indifferent to their fate....

Our conduct toward these people is deeply interesting to our national character. Their present condition, contrasted with what they once were, makes a most powerful appeal to our sympathies. Our ancestors found them the uncontrolled possessors of these vast regions. By persuasion and force they have been made to retire from river to river and from mountain to mountain, until some of the tribes have become extinct and others have left but remnants to preserve for awhile their once terrible names. Surrounded by the whites with their arts of civilization, which, by destroying the resources of the savage, doom him to weakness and decay, the fate of the Mohegan, the Narragansett, and the

Delaware is fast overtaking the Choctaw, the Cherokee, and the Creek. That this fate surely awaits them if they remain within the limits of the states does not admit of a doubt. Humanity and national honor demand that every effort should be made to avert so great a calamity....

As a means of effecting this end, I suggest for our consideration the propriety of setting apart an ample district west of the Mississippi, and without [outside] the limits of any state or territory now formed, to be guaranteed to the Indian tribes as long as they shall occupy it, each tribe having a distinct control over the portion designated for its use. There they may be secured in the enjoyment of governments of their own choice, subject to no other control from the United States than such as may be necessary to preserve peace on the frontier and between the several tribes. There the benevolent may endeavor to teach them the arts of civilization, and, by promoting union and harmony among them, to raise up an interesting commonwealth, destined to perpetuate the race and to attest the humanity and justice of this government.

This emigration should be voluntary, for it would be as cruel as unjust to compel the aborigines to abandon the graves of their fathers and seek a home in a distant land. But they should be distinctly informed that if they remain within the limits of the states they must be subject to their laws.

1. According the Andrew Jackson, what had been the impact of white settlement on Native Americans?

2. How had the government addressed the issue of Native Americans and what did he propose to do?

10-6 "Memorial of the Cherokee Nation" (1830)

The Washington administration had established a policy designed to "civilize" the Indians, and the Cherokee, more than any other Native American group, had done so-by codifying their own legal system, printing their own newspapers, and even owning slaves. However, no amount of assimilation helped the Cherokee when the state of Georgia demanded their land. During the "trail of tears," when the Cherokee were forced to march to Oklahoma, more than 4,000 Cherokee died. The "Memorial of the Cherokee Nation" appeared in Nile's Weekly Register in 1830.

We are aware that some persons suppose it will be for our advantage to remove beyond the Mississippi. We think otherwise. Our people universally think otherwise. Thinking that it would be fatal to their interests, they have almost to a man sent their memorial to Congress, deprecating the necessity of a removal. . . . It is incredible that Georgia should ever have enacted the oppressive laws to which reference is here made, unless she had supposed that something extremely terrific in its character was necessary in order to make the Cherokees willing to remove. We are not willing to remove; and if we could be brought to this extremity, it would be not by argument, nor because our judgment was satisfied, not because our condition will be improved; but only because we cannot endure to be deprived of our national and individual rights and subjected to a process of intolerable oppression.

We wish to remain on the land of our fathers. We have a perfect and original right to remain without interruption or molestation. The treaties with us, and laws of the United States made in pursuance of treaties, guaranty our residence and our privileges, and secure us against intruders. Our only request is, that these treaties may be fulfilled, and these laws executed.

But if we are compelled to leave our country, we see nothing but ruin before us. The country west of the Arkansas territory is unknown to us. From what we can learn of it, we have no prepossessions in its favor. All the inviting parts of it, as we believe, are preoccupied by various Indian nations, to which it has been assigned. They would regard us as intruders. . . . The far greater part of that region is, beyond all controversy, badly supplied with wood and water; and no Indian tribe can live as agriculturists without these articles. All our neighbors . . . would speak a language totally different from ours, and practice different customs. The original possessors of that region are now wandering savages lurking for prey in the neighborhood. . . . Were the country to which we are urged much better than it is represented to be, . . . still it is not the land of our birth, nor of our affections. It contains neither the scenes of our childhood, nor the graves of our fathers.

. . . We have been called a poor, ignorant, and degraded people. We certainly are not rich; nor have we ever boasted of our knowledge, or our moral or intellectual elevation. But there is not a man within our limits so ignorant as not to know that he has a right to live on the land of his fathers, in the possession of his immemorial privileges, and that this right has been acknowledged by the United States; nor is there a man so degraded as not to feel a keen sense of injury, on being deprived of his right and driven into exile. . . .

1. Identify and summarize the Cherokee Tribe's objections to moving west beyond the Arkansas Territory. How is American expansion westward impacting the lives of the Cherokee?

2. What rights are claimed in this Memorial?

10-7 Andrew Jackson, Veto of the Bank Bill (1832)

Few presidents have had such ardent admirers and staunch critics. Jackson had a varied political career before becoming a hero in the War of 1812. His reputation as an Indian Fighter made him a popular favorite. He built on this reputation, returned to the Senate and eventually was elected President as a champion of the "common man". His fight against the Second Bank was a very important element of this "Jacksonian Democracy". Jackson's violent opposition to the bank is reflected in this veto message.

To the Senate:

The bill "to modify and continue" the act entitled "An act to incorporate the subscribers to the Bank of the United States" was presented to me on the 4th July instant. Having considered it with that solemn regard to the principles of the Constitution which the day was calculated to inspire, and come to the conclusion that it ought not to become a law, I herewith return it to the Senate, in which it originated, with my objections.

A bank of the United States is in many respects convenient for the Government and useful to the people. Entertaining this opinion, and deeply impressed with the belief that some of the powers and privileges possessed by the existing bank are unauthorized by the Constitution, subversive of the rights of the States, and dangerous to the liberties of the people, I felt it my duty at an early period of my Administration to call the attention of Congress to the practicability of organizing an institution combining all its advantages and obviating these objections. I sincerely regret that in the act before me I can perceive none of those modifications of the bank charter which are necessary, in my opinion, to make it compatible with justice, with sound policy, or with the Constitution of our country.

The present corporate body, denominated the president, directors, and company of the Bank of the United States, will have existed at the time this act is intended to take effect twenty years. It enjoys an exclusive privilege of banking under the authority of the General Government, a monopoly of its favor and support, and, as a necessary consequence, almost a monopoly of the foreign and domestic exchange. The powers, privileges, and favors bestowed upon it in the original character, by increasing the value of the stock far above its par value, operated as a gratuity of many millions to the stockholders. . . .

It is not our own citizens only who are to receive the bounty of our Government. More than eight millions of the stock of this bank are held by foreigners. By this act the American Republic proposes virtually to make them a present of some millions of dollars. For these gratuities to foreigners and to some of our own opulent citizens the act secures no equivalent whatever. . . .

It is not conceivable how the present stockholders can have any claim to the special favor of the Government. The present corporation has enjoyed its monopoly during the period stipulated in the original contract. If we must have such a corporation, why should not the Government sell out the whole stock and thus secure to the people the full market value of the privileges granted? Why should not Congress create and sell twenty-eight millions of stock, incorporating the purchasers with all the powers and privileges secured in this act and putting the premium upon the sales into the Treasury?

But this act does not permit competition in the purchase of this monopoly. It seems to be predicated on the erroneous idea that the present stockholders have a prescriptive right not only to the favor but to the bounty of Government. It appears that more than a fourth part of the stock is held by foreigners and the residue is held by a few hundred of our own citizens, chiefly of the richest class. For their benefit does this act exclude the whole American people from competition in the purchase of this monopoly and dispose of it for many millions less than it is worth. This seems the less excusable because some of our citizens not now stockholders petitioned that the door of competition might be opened, and offered to take a charter on terms much more favorable to the Government and country. . . .

It is to be regretted that the rich and powerful too often bend the acts of government to their selfish purposes. Distinctions in society will always exist under every just government. Equality of talents, of education, or of wealth can not be produced by human institutions. In the full enjoyment of the gifts of Heaven and the fruits of superior industry, economy, and virtue, every man is equally entitled to protection by law; but when the laws undertake to add to these natural and just advantages artificial distinctions, to grant titles, gratuities, and exclusive privileges, to make the rich richer and the potent more powerful, the humble members of society-the farmers, mechanics, and laborers-who have neither the time nor the means of securing like favors to themselves, have a right to complain of the injustice of their Government. There are no necessary evils in government. Its evils exist only in its abuses. If it would confine itself to equal protection, and, as Heaven does its rains, shower its favors alike on the high and the low, the rich and the poor, it would be an unqualified blessing. In the act before me there seems to be a wide and unnecessary departure from these just principles.

Nor is our Government to be maintained or our Union preserved by invasions of the rights and powers of the several States. In thus attempting to make our General Government strong we make it weak. Its true strength consists in leaving individuals and States as much as possible to themselves-in making itself felt, not in its power, but in its beneficence; not in its control, but in its protection; not in binding the States more closely to the center, but leaving each to move unobstructed in its proper orbit.

Experience should teach us wisdom. Most of the difficulties our Government now encounters and most of the dangers which impend over our Union have sprung from an abandonment of the legitimate objects of Government by our national legislation, and the adoption of such principles as are embodied in this act. Many of our rich men have not been content with equal protection and equal benefits, but have besought us to make them richer by act of Congress. By attempting to gratify their desires we have in the results of our legislation arrayed section against section, interest against interest, and man against man, in a fearful commotion which threatens to shake the foundations of our Union. It is time to pause in our career to review our principles, and if possible revive that devoted patriotism and spirit of compromise which distinguished the sages of the Revolution and the fathers of our Union. If we can not at once, in justice to interests vested under improvident legislation, make our Government what it ought to be, we can at least take a stand against all new grants of monopolies and exclusive privileges, against any prostitution of our Government to the advancement of the few at the expense of the many, and in favor of compromise and gradual reform in our code laws and system of political economy.

1. Summarize and explain Jackson's reasoning for vetoing the Bank Bill.

10-8 President Andrew Jackson's Proclamation Regarding Nullification (1832)

Andrew Jackson squared off against the formidable Senator from South Carolina John C. Calhoun in this struggle which sought to take states rights to their fullest extension. Coming in a long line of efforts to limit federal power and define sovereignty, Nullification posited that a state convention could declare any act of the national congress null and void. The immediate reason for the desire for nullification was to repeal that federal tariffs that South Carolina saw as crippling their economy. Nullification would later become another cause of southern discontent that exploded in the Civil War. Jackson's position is made clear in this document.

> **Source**: Paul Leicester Ford, *The Federalist : A commentary on the Constitution of the United States by Alexander Hamilton, James Madison and John Jay edited with notes, illustrative documents and a copious index by Paul Leicester Ford* (New York: Henry Holt and Company, 1898).

Whereas a convention, assembled in the State of South Carolina, have passed an ordinance, by which they declare that the several acts and parts of acts of the Congress of the United States, purporting to be laws for the imposing of duties and imposts on the importation of foreign commodities, and now having actual operation and effect within the United States, and more especially "two acts for the same purposes, passed on the 29th of May, 1828, and on the 14th of July, 1832, are unauthorized by the Constitution of the United States, and violate the true meaning and intent thereof, and are null and void, and no law," nor binding on the citizens of that State or its officers, and by the said ordinance it is further declared to he unlawful for any of the constituted authorities of the State, or of the United States, to enforce the payment of the duties imposed by the said acts within the same State, and that it is the duty of the legislature to pass such laws as may be necessary to give full effect to the said ordinances:

And whereas, by the said ordinance it is further ordained, that, in no case of law or equity, decided in the courts of said State, wherein shall be drawn in question the validity of the said ordinance, or of the acts of the legislature that may be passed to give it effect, or of the said laws of the United States, no appeal shall be allowed to the Supreme Court of the United States, nor shall any copy of the record be permitted or allowed for that purpose; and that any person attempting to take such appeal, shall be punished as for a contempt of court:

And, finally, the said ordinance declares that the people of South Carolina will maintain the said ordinance at every hazard, and that they will consider the passage of any act by Congress abolishing or closing the ports of the said State, or otherwise obstructing the free ingress or egress of vessels to and from the said ports, or any other act of the Federal Government to coerce the State, shut up her ports, destroy or harass her commerce, or to enforce the said acts otherwise than through the civil tribunals of the country, as inconsistent with the longer continuance of South Carolina in the Union; and that the people of the said State will thenceforth hold themselves absolved from all further obligation to maintain or preserve their political connection with the people of the other States, and will forthwith proceed to organize a separate government, and do all other acts and things which sovereign and independent States may of right do.

And whereas the said ordinance prescribes to the people of South Carolina a course of conduct in direct violation of their duty as citizens of the United States, contrary to the laws of their country, subversive of its Constitution, and having for its object the instruction of the Union—that Union, which, coeval with our political existence, led our fathers, without any other ties to unite them than those of patriotism and common cause, through the sanguinary struggle to a glorious independence—that sacred Union, hitherto inviolate, which, perfected by our happy Constitution, has brought us, by the favor of Heaven, to a state of prosperity at home, and high consideration abroad, rarely, if ever, equaled in the history of nations; to preserve this bond of our political existence from destruction, to maintain inviolate this state of national honor and prosperity, and to justify the confidence my fellow-citizens have reposed in me, I, Andrew Jackson, President of the United States, have thought proper to issue this my PROCLAMATION, stating my views of the Constitution and laws applicable to the measures adopted by the Convention of South Carolina, and to the reasons they have put forth to sustain them, declaring the course which duty will require me to pursue, and, appealing to the understanding and patriotism of the people, warn them of the consequences that must inevitably result from an observance of the dictates of the Convention.

Strict duty would require of me nothing more than the exercise of those powers with which I am now, or may hereafter be, invested, for preserving the Union, and for the execution of the laws. But the imposing aspect which opposition has assumed in this case, by clothing itself with State authority, and the deep interest which the people of the United States must all feel in preventing a resort to stronger measures, while there is a hope that anything will be yielded to reasoning and remonstrances, perhaps demand, and will certainly justify, a full exposition to South Carolina and the nation of the views I entertain of this important question, as well as a distinct enunciation of the course which my sense of duty will require me to pursue.

The ordinance is founded, not on the indefeasible right of resisting acts which are plainly unconstitutional, and too oppressive to be endured, but on the strange position that any one State may not only declare an act of Congress void, but prohibit its execution—that they may do this consistently with the Constitution—that the true construction of that instrument permits a State to retain its place in the Union, and yet be bound by no other of its laws than those it may choose to consider as constitutional. It is true they add, that to justify this abrogation of a law, it must be palpably contrary to the Constitution, but it is evident, that to give the right of resisting laws of that description, coupled with the uncontrolled right to decide what laws deserve that character, is to give the power of resisting all laws. For, as by the theory, there is no appeal, the reasons alleged by the State, good or bad, must prevail. If it should be said that public opinion is a sufficient check against the abuse of this power, it may be asked why it is not deemed a sufficient guard against the passage of an unconstitutional act by Congress. There is, however, a restraint in this last case, which makes the assumed power of a State more indefensible, and which does not exist in the other. There are two appeals from an unconstitutional act passed by Congress—one to the judiciary, the other to the people and the States. There is no appeal from the State decision in theory; and the practical illustration shows that the courts are closed against an application to review it, both judges and jurors being sworn to decide in its favor. But reasoning on this subject is superfluous, when our social compact in express terms declares, that the laws of the United States, its Constitution, and treaties made under it, are the supreme law of the land; and for greater caution adds, "that the judges in every State shall be bound thereby, anything in the Constitution or laws of any State to the contrary notwithstanding." And it may be asserted, without fear of refutation, that no federative government could exist without a similar provision. Look, for a moment, to the consequence. If South Carolina considers the revenue laws unconstitutional, and has a right to prevent their execution in the port of Charleston, there would be a clear constitutional objection to their collection in every other port, and no revenue could be collected anywhere; for all imposts must be equal. It is no answer to repeat that an unconstitutional law is no law, so long as the question of its legality is to be decided by the State itself, for every law operating injuriously upon any local interest will be perhaps thought, and certainly represented, as unconstitutional, and, as has been shown, there is no appeal.

If this doctrine had been established at an earlier day, the Union would have been dissolved in its infancy. The excise law in Pennsylvania, the embargo and non-intercourse law in the Eastern States, the carriage tax in Virginia, were all deemed unconstitutional, and were more unequal in their operation than any of the laws now complained of; but, fortunately, none of those States discovered that they had the right now claimed by South Carolina. The war into which we were forced, to support the dignity of the nation and the rights of our citizens, might have ended in defeat and disgrace instead of victory and honor, if the States, who supposed it a ruinous and unconstitutional measure, had thought they possessed the right of nullifying the act by which it was declared, and denying supplies for its prosecution. Hardly and unequally as those measures bore upon several members of the Union, to the legislatures of none did this efficient and peaceable remedy, as it is called, suggest itself. The discovery of this important feature in our Constitution was reserved to the present day. To the statesmen of South Carolina belongs the invention, and upon the citizens of that State will, unfortunately, fall the evils of reducing it to practice.

If the doctrine of a State veto upon the laws of the Union carries with it internal evidence of its impracticable absurdity, our constitutional history will also afford abundant proof that it would have been repudiated with indignation had it been proposed to form a feature in our Government.

In our colonial state, although dependent on another power, we very early considered ourselves as connected by common interest with each other. Leagues were formed for common defense, and before the Declaration of Independence, we were known in our aggregate character as the United Colonies of America. That decisive and important step was taken jointly. We declared ourselves a nation by a joint, not by several acts; and when the terms of our confederation were reduced to form, it was in that of a solemn league of several States, by which they agreed that they would, collectively, form one nation, for the purpose of conducting some certain domestic concerns, and all foreign relations. In the instrument forming that Union, is found an article which declares that "every State shall abide by the determinations of Congress on all questions which by that Confederation should be submitted to them."

Under the Confederation, then, no State could legally annul a decision of the Congress, or refuse to submit to its execution, but no provision was made to enforce these decisions. Congress made requisitions, but they were not complied with. The Government could not operate on individuals. They had no judiciary, no means of collecting revenue.

But the defects of the Confederation need not be detailed. Under its operation we could scarcely be called a nation. We had neither prosperity at home nor consideration abroad. This state of things could not be endured, and our present happy Constitution was formed, but formed in vain, if this fatal doctrine prevails. It was formed for important objects that are announced in the preamble made in the name and by the authority of the people of the United States, whose delegates framed, and whose conventions approved it.

The most important among these objects, that which is placed first in rank, on which all the others rest, is "to form a more perfect Union." Now, is it possible that, even if there were no express provision giving supremacy to the Constitution and laws of the United States over those of the States, it can be conceived that an Instrument made for the purpose of "forming; a more perfect Union" than that of the confederation, could be so constructed by the assembled wisdom of our country as to substitute for that confederation a form of government, dependent for its existence on the local interest, the party spirit of a State, or of a prevailing faction in a State? Every man, of plain, unsophisticated understanding, who hears the question, will give such an answer as will preserve the Union. Metaphysical subtlety, in pursuit of an impracticable theory, could alone have devised one that is calculated to destroy it.

I consider, then, the power to annul a law of the United States, assumed by one State, incompatible with the existence of the Union, contradicted expressly by the letter of the Constitution, unauthorized by its spirit, inconsistent with every principle on which It was founded, and destructive of the great object for which it was formed.

After this general view of the leading principle, we must examine the particular application of it which is made in the ordinance.

The preamble rests its justification on these grounds: It assumes as a fact, that the obnoxious laws, although they purport to be laws for raising revenue, were in reality intended for the protection of manufactures, which purpose it asserts to be unconstitutional; that the operation of these laws is unequal, that the amount raised by them is greater than is required by the wants of the Government; and, finally, that the proceeds are to be applied to objects unauthorized by the Constitution. These are the only causes alleged to justify an open opposition to the laws of the country, and a threat of seceding from the Union, if any attempt should be made to enforce them. The first virtually acknowledges that the law in question was passed under a power expressly given by the Constitution, to lay and collect imposts, but its constitutionality is drawn in question from the motives of those who passed it. However apparent this purpose may be in the present case, nothing can be more dangerous than to admit the position that an unconstitutional purpose, entertained by the members who assent to a law enacted under a constitutional power, shall make that law void; for how is that purpose to be ascertained? Who is to make the scrutiny? How often may bad purposes be falsely imputed ? In how many cases are they concealed by false professions? In how many is no declaration of motive made? Admit this doctrine and you give to the States an uncontrolled right to decide, and every law may be annulled under this pretext. If, therefore, the absurd and dangerous doctrine should be admitted, that a State may annul an unconstitutional law, or one that it deems such, it will not apply to the present case.

The next objection is, that the laws in question operate unequally. This objection may be made with truth to every law that has been or can be passed. The wisdom of man never yet contrived a system of taxation that would operate with perfect equality. If the unequal operation of a law makes it unconstitutional and if all laws of that description may be abrogated by any State for that cause, then, indeed, is the federal Constitution unworthy of the slightest effort for its preservation. We have hitherto relied on it as the perpetual bond of our Union. We have received it as the work of the assembled wisdom of the nation We have trusted to it as to the sheet-anchor of our safety, in the stormy times of conflict with a foreign or domestic foe. We have looked to it with sacred awe as the palladium of our liberties, and with all the solemnities of religion have pledged to each other our lives and fortunes here, and our hopes of happiness hereafter, in its defense and support. Were we mistaken, my countrymen, in attaching this importance to the Constitution of our country? Was our devotion paid to the wretched, inefficient, clumsy contrivance, which this new doctrine would make it? Did we pledge ourselves to the support of an airy nothing—a bubble that must be blown away by the first breath of disaffection? Was this self-destroying, visionary theory the work of the profound statesmen, the exalted patriots, to whom the task of constitutional reform was intrusted? Did the name of Washington sanction, did the States deliberately ratify, such an anomaly in the history of fundamental legislation? No. We were not mistaken. The letter of this great instrument is free from this radical fault; its language directly contradicts the imputation, its spirit, its evident intent, contradicts it. No, we did not err. Our Constitution does not contain the absurdity of giving power to make laws, and another power to resist them. The sages, whose memory will always be reverenced, have given us a practical, and, as they hoped, a permanent constitutional compact. The Father of his Country did not affix his revered name to so palpable an absurdity. Nor did the States, when they severally ratified it, do so under the impression that a veto on the laws of the United States was reserved to them, or that they could exercise it by application. Search the debates in all their conventions—examine the speeches of the most zealous opposers of federal authority—look at the amendments that were proposed. They are all silent—not a syllable uttered, not a vote given, not a motion made, to correct the explicit supremacy given to the laws of the Union over those of the States, or to show that implication, as is now contended, could defeat it. No, we have not erred! The Constitution is still the object of our reverence, the bond of our Union, our defense in danger, the source of our prosperity in peace. It shall descend, as we have received it, uncorrupted by sophistical construction to our posterity; and the sacrifices of local interest, of State prejudices, of personal animosities, that were made to bring it into existence, will again be patriotically offered for its support.

The two remaining objections made by the ordinance to these laws are, that the sums intended to be raised by them are greater than are required, and that the proceeds will be unconstitutionally employed. The Constitution has given expressly to Congress the right of raising revenue, and of determining the sum the public exigencies will require. The States have no control over the exercise of this right other than that which results from the power of changing the representatives who abuse it, and thus procure redress. Congress may undoubtedly abuse this discretionary power, but the same may be said of others with which they are vested. Yet the discretion must exist somewhere. The Constitution has given it to the representatives of all the people, checked by the representatives of the States, and by the executive power. The South Carolina construction gives it to the legislature, or the convention of a single State, where neither the people of the different States, nor the States in their separate capacity, nor the chief magistrate elected by the people, have any representation. Which is the most discreet disposition of the power? I do not ask you, fellow-citizens, which is the constitutional disposition—that instrument speaks a language not to be misunderstood. But if you were assembled in general convention, which would you think the safest depository of this discretionary power in the last resort? Would you add a clause giving it to each of the States, or would you sanction the wise provisions already made by your Constitution? If this should be the result of your deliberations when providing for the future, are you—can you—be ready to risk all that we hold dear, to establish, for a temporary and a local purpose, that which you must acknowledge to be destructive, and even absurd, as a general provision? Carry out the consequences of this right vested in the different States, and you must perceive that the crisis your conduct presents at this day would recur whenever any law of the United States displeased any of the States, and that we should soon cease to be a nation.

The ordinance with the same knowledge of the future that characterizes a former objection, tells you that the proceeds of the tax will be unconstitutionally applied. If this could be ascertained with certainty, the objection would, with more propriety, be reserved for the law so applying the proceeds, but surely cannot be urged against the laws levying the duty.

These are the allegations contained in the ordinance. Examine them seriously, my fellow-citizens—judge for yourselves. I appeal to you to determine whether they are so clear, so convincing, as to leave no doubt of their correctness, and even if you should come to this conclusion, how far they justify the reckless, destructive course which you are directed to pursue. Review these objections and the conclusions drawn from them once more. What are they! Every law, then, for raising revenue, according to the South Carolina ordinance, may be rightfully annulled, unless it be so framed as no law ever will or can be framed. Congress have a right to pass laws for raising revenue, and each State has a right to oppose their execution—two rights directly opposed to each other; and yet is this absurdity supposed to be contained in an instrument drawn for the express purpose of avoiding collisions between the States and the general government, by an assembly of the most enlightened statesmen and purest patriots ever embodied for a similar purpose.

In vain have these sages declared that Congress shall have power to lay and collect taxes, duties, imposts, and excises—in vain have they provided that they shall have power to pass laws which shall be necessary and proper to carry those powers into execution, that those laws and that Constitution shall be the "supreme law of the land; that the judges in every State shall be bound thereby, anything in the constitution or laws of any State to the contrary notwithstanding." In vain have the people of the several States solemnly sanctioned these provisions, made them their paramount law, and individually sworn to support them whenever they were called on to execute any office.

Vain provisions! Ineffectual restrictions! Vile profanation of oaths! Miserable mockery of legislation! If a bare majority of the voters in any one State may, on a real or supposed knowledge of the intent with which a law has been passed, declare themselves free from its operation—say here it gives too little, there too much, and operates unequally—here it suffers articles to be free that ought to be taxed, there it taxes those that ought to be free—in this case the proceeds are intended to be applied to purposes which we do not approve, in that the amount raised is more than is wanted. Congress, it is true, are invested by the Constitution with the right of deciding these questions according to their sound discretion. Congress is composed of the representatives of all the States, and of all the people of all the states; but WE, part of the people of one State, to whom the Constitution has given no power on the subject from whom it has expressly taken it away—we, who have solemnly agreed that this Constitution shall be our law—we, most of whom have sworn to support it—we now abrogate this law, and swear, and force others to swear, that it shall not be obeyed—and we do this, not because Congress have no right to pass such laws; this we do not allege; but because they have passed them with improper views. They are unconstitutional from the motives of those who passed them, which we can never with certainty know, from their unequal operation; although it is impossible from the nature of things that they should be equal—and from the disposition which we presume may be made of their proceeds, although that disposition has not been declared. This is the plain meaning of the ordinance in relation to laws which it abrogates for alleged unconstitutionality. But it does not stop here. It repeals, in express terms, an important part of the Constitution itself, and of laws passed to give it effect, which have never been alleged to be unconstitutional. The Constitution declares that the judicial powers of the United States extend to cases arising under the laws of the United States, and that such laws, the Constitution and treaties, shall be paramount to the State constitutions and laws. The judiciary act prescribes the mode by which the case may be brought before a court of the United States, by appeal, when a State tribunal shall decide against this provision of the Constitution. The ordinance declares there shall be no appeal; makes the State law paramount to the Constitution and laws of the United States; forces judges and jurors to swear that they will disregard their provisions; and even makes it penal in a suitor to attempt relief by appeal. It further declares that it shall not be lawful for the authorities of the United States, or of that State, to enforce the payment of duties imposed by the revenue laws within its limits.

Here is a law of the United States, not even pretended to be unconstitutional, repealed by the authority of a small majority of the voters of a single State. Here is a provision of the Constitution which is solemnly abrogated by the same authority.

On such expositions and reasonings, the ordinance grounds not only an assertion of the right to annul the laws of which it complains, but to enforce it by a threat of seceding from the Union if any attempt is made to execute them.

This right to secede is deduced from the nature of the Constitution, which they say is a compact between sovereign States who have preserved their whole sovereignty, and therefore are subject to no superior; that because they made the compact, they can break it when in their opinion it has been departed from by the other States. Fallacious as this course of reasoning is, it enlists State pride, and finds advocates in the honest prejudices of those who have not studied the nature of our government sufficiently to see the radical error on which it rests.

The people of the United States formed the Constitution, acting through the State legislatures, in making the compact, to meet and discuss its provisions, and acting in separate conventions when they ratified those provisions; but the terms used in its construction show it to be a government in which the people of all the States collectively are represented. We are ONE PEOPLE in the choice of the President and Vice President. Here the States have no other agency than to direct the mode in which the vote shall be given. The candidates having the majority of all the votes are chosen. The electors of a majority of States may have given their votes for one candidate, and yet another may be chosen. The people, then, and not the States, are represented in the executive branch.

In the House of Representatives there is this difference, that the people of one State do not, as in the case of President and Vice President, all vote for all the members, each State electing only its own representatives. But this creates no material distinction. When chosen, they are all representatives of the United States, not representatives of the particular State from which they come. They are paid by the United States, not by the State; nor are they accountable to it for any act done in performance of their legislative functions; and however they may in practice, as it is their duty to do, consult and prefer the interests of their particular constituents when they come in conflict with any other partial or local interest, yet it is their first and highest duty, as representatives of the United States, to promote the general good.

The Constitution of the United States, then, forms a government, not a league, and whether it be formed by compact between the States, or in any other manner, its character is the same. It is a government in which ale the people are represented, which operates directly on the people individually, not upon the States; they retained all the power they did not grant. But each State having expressly parted with so many powers as to constitute jointly with the other States a single nation, cannot from that period possess any right to secede, because such secession does not break a league, but destroys the unity of a nation, and any injury to that unity is not only a breach which would result from the contravention of a compact, but it is an offense against the whole Union. To say that any State may at pleasure secede from the Union, is to say that the United States are not a nation because it would be a solecism to contend that any part of a nation might dissolve its connection with the other parts, to their injury or ruin, without committing any offense. Secession, like any other revolutionary act, may be morally justified by the extremity of oppression; but to call it a constitutional right, is confounding the meaning of terms, and can only be done through gross error, or to deceive those who are willing to assert a right, but would pause before they made a revolution, or incur the penalties consequent upon a failure.

Because the Union was formed by compact, it is said the parties to that compact may, when they feel themselves aggrieved, depart from it; but it is precisely because it is a compact that they cannot. A compact is an agreement or binding obligation. It may by its terms have a sanction or penalty for its breach, or it may not. If it contains no sanction, it may be broken with no other consequence than moral guilt; if it have a sanction, then the breach incurs the designated or implied penalty. A league between independent nations, generally, has no sanction other than a moral one; or if it should contain a penalty, as there is no common superior, it cannot be enforced. A government, on the contrary, always has a sanction, express or implied; and, in our case, it is both necessarily implied and expressly given. An attempt by force of arms to destroy a government is an offense, by whatever means the constitutional compact may have been formed; and such government has the right, by the law of self-defense, to pass acts for punishing the offender, unless that right is modified, restrained, or resumed by the constitutional act. In our system, although it is modified in the case of treason, yet authority is expressly given to pass all laws necessary to carry its powers into effect, and under this grant provision has been made for punishing acts which obstruct the due administration of the laws.

It would seem superfluous to add anything to show the nature of that union which connects us; but as erroneous opinions on this subject are the foundation of doctrines the most destructive to our peace, I must give some further development to my views on this subject. No one, fellow-citizens, has a higher reverence for the reserved rights of the States than the magistrate who now addresses you. No one would make greater personal sacrifices, or official exertions, to defend them from violation; but equal care must be taken to prevent, on their part, an improper interference with, or resumption of, the rights they have vested in the nation.

The line has not been so distinctly drawn as to avoid doubts in some cases of the exercise of power. Men of the best intentions and soundest views may differ in their construction of some parts of the Constitution, but there are others on which dispassionate reflection can leave no doubt. Of this nature appears to be the assumed right of secession. It rests, as we have seen, on the alleged undivided sovereignty of the States, and on their having formed in this sovereign capacity a compact which is called the Constitution, from which, because they made it, they have the right to secede. Both of these positions are erroneous, and some of the arguments to prove them so have been anticipated.

The States severally have not retained their entire sovereignty. It has been shown that in becoming parts of a nation, not members of a league, they surrendered many of their essential parts of sovereignty. The right to make treaties, declare war, levy taxes, exercise exclusive judicial and legislative powers, were all functions of sovereign power. The States, then, for all these important purposes, were no longer sovereign. The allegiance of their citizens was transferred in the first instance to the government of the United States; they became American citizens, and owed obedience to the Constitution of the United States, and to laws made in conformity with the powers vested in Congress. This last position has not been, and cannot be, denied. How then, can that State be said to be sovereign and independent whose citizens owe obedience to laws not made by it, and whose magistrates are sworn to disregard those laws, when they come in conflict with those passed by another? What shows conclusively that the States cannot be said to have reserved an undivided sovereignty, is that they expressly ceded the right to punish treason—not treason against their separate power, but treason against the United States. Treason is an offense against sovereignty, and sovereignty must reside with the power to punish it. But the reserved rights of the States are not less sacred because they have for their common interest made the general government the depository of these powers. The unity of our political character (as has been shown for another purpose) commenced with its very existence. Under the royal government we had no separate character; our opposition to its oppression began as UNITED COLONIES. We were the UNITED STATES under the Confederation, and the name was perpetuated and the Union rendered more perfect by the federal Constitution. In none of these stages did we consider ourselves in any other light than as forming one nation. Treaties and alliances were made in the name of all. Troops were raised for the joint defense. How, then, with all these proofs, that under all changes of our position we had, for designated purposes and with defined powers, created national governments—how is it that the most perfect of these several modes of union should now be considered as a mere league that may be dissolved at pleasure? It is from an abuse of terms. Compact is used as synonymous with league, although the true term is not employed, because it would at once show the fallacy of the reasoning. It would not do to say that our Constitution was only a league, but it is labored to prove it a compact (which, in one sense, it is), and then to argue that as a league is a compact, every compact between nations must, of course, be a league, and that from such an engagement every sovereign power has a right to recede. But it has been shown that in this sense the States are not sovereign, and that even if they were, and the national Constitution had been formed by compact, there would be no right in any one State to exonerate itself from the obligation.

So obvious are the reasons which forbid this secession, that it is necessary only to allude to them. The Union was formed for the benefit of all. It was produced by mutual sacrifice of interest and opinions. Can those sacrifices be recalled? Can the States, who magnanimously surrendered their title to the territories of the West, recall the grant? Will the inhabitants of the inland States agree to pay the duties that may be imposed without their assent by those on the Atlantic or the Gulf, for their own benefit? Shall there be a free port in one State, and enormous duties in another? No one believes that any right exists in a single State to involve all the others in these and countless other evils, contrary to engagements solemnly made. Everyone must see that the other States, in self-defense, must oppose it at all hazards.

These are the alternatives that are presented by the convention: A repeal of all the acts for raising revenue, leaving the government without the means of support; or an acquiescence in the dissolution of our Union by the secession of one of its members. When the first was proposed, it was known that it could not be listened to for a moment. It was known if force was applied to oppose the execution of the laws, that it must be repelled by force—that Congress could not, without involving itself in disgrace and the country in ruin, accede to the proposition; and yet if this is not done in a given day, or if any attempt is made to execute the laws, the State is, by the ordinance, declared to be out of the Union. The majority of a convention assembled for the purpose have dictated these terms, or rather this rejection of all terms, in the name of the people of South Carolina. It is true that the governor of the State speaks of the submission of their grievances to a convention of all the States; which, he says, they ''sincerely and anxiously seek and desire.'' Yet this obvious and constitutional mode of obtaining the sense of the other States on the construction of the federal compact, and amending it, if necessary, has never been attempted by those who have urged the State on to this destructive measure. The State might have proposed a call for a general convention to the other States, and Congress, if a sufficient number of them concurred, must have called it. But the first magistrate of South Carolina, when he expressed a hope that "on a review by Congress and the functionaries of the general government of the merits of the controversy," such a convention will be accorded to them, must have known that neither Congress, nor any functionary in the general government, has authority to call such a convention, unless it be demanded by two-thirds of the States. This suggestion, then, is another instance of the reckless inattention to the provisions of the Constitution with which this crisis has been madly hurried on; or of the attempt to persuade the people that a constitutional remedy has been sought and refused. If the legislature of South Carolina "anxiously desire" a general convention to consider their complaints, why have they not made application for it in the way the Constitution points out? The assertion that they "earnestly seek" is completely negatived by the omission.

This, then, is the position in which we stand. A small majority of the citizens of one State in the Union have elected delegates to a State convention; that convention has ordained that all the revenue laws of the United States must be repealed, or that they are no longer a member of the Union. The governor of that State has recommended to the legislature the raising of an army to carry the secession into effect, and that he may be empowered to give clearances to vessels in the name of the State. No act of violent opposition to the laws has yet been committed, but such a state of things is hourly apprehended, and it is the intent of this instrument to PROCLAIM, not only that the duty imposed on me by the Constitution, "to take care that the laws be faithfully executed," shall be performed to the extent of the powers already vested in me by law or of such others as the wisdom of Congress shall devise and Entrust to me for that purpose; but to warn the citizens of South Carolina, who have been deluded into an opposition to the laws, of the danger they will incur by obedience to the illegal and disorganizing ordinance of the convention—to exhort those who have refused to support it to persevere in their determination to uphold the Constitution and laws of their country, and to point out to all the perilous situation into which the good people of that State have been led, and that the course they are urged to pursue is one of ruin and disgrace to the very State whose rights they affect to support.

Fellow-citizens of my native State! let me not only admonish you, as the first magistrate of our common country, not to incur the penalty of its laws, but use the influence that a father would over his children whom he saw rushing to a certain ruin. In that paternal language, with that paternal feeling, let me tell you, my countrymen, that you are deluded by men who are either deceived themselves or wish to deceive you. Mark under what pretenses you have been led on to the brink of insurrection and treason on which you stand! First a diminution of the value of our staple commodity, lowered by over-production in other quarters and the consequent diminution in the value of your lands, were the sole effect of the tariff laws. The effect of those laws was confessedly injurious, but the evil was greatly exaggerated by the unfounded theory you were taught to believe, that its burdens were in proportion to your exports, not to your consumption of imported articles. Your pride was aroused by the assertions that a submission to these laws was a state of vassalage, and that resistance to them was equal, in patriotic merit, to the opposition our fathers offered to the oppressive laws of Great Britain. You were told that this opposition might be peaceably—might be constitutionally made—that you might enjoy all the advantages of the Union and bear none of its burdens. Eloquent appeals to your passions, to your State pride, to your native courage, to your sense of real injury, were used to prepare you for the period when the mask which concealed the hideous features of DISUNION should be taken off. It fell, and you were made to look with complacency on objects which not long since you would have regarded with horror. Look back to the arts which have brought you to this state—look forward to the consequences to which it must inevitably lead! Look back to what was first told you as an inducement to enter into this dangerous course. The great political truth was repeated to you that you had the revolutionary right of resisting all laws that were palpably unconstitutional and intolerably oppressive—it was added that the right to nullify a law rested on the same principle, but that it was a peaceable remedy! This character which was given to it, made you receive with too much confidence the assertions that were made of the unconstitutionality of the law and its oppressive effects. Mark, my fellow-citizens, that by the admission of your leaders the unconstitutionality must be palpable, or it will not justify either resistance or nullification! What is the meaning of the word palpable in the sense in which it is here used? that which is apparent to everyone, that which no man of ordinary intellect will fail to perceive. Is the unconstitutionality of these laws of that description? Let those among your leaders who once approved and advocated the principles of protective duties, answer the question; and let them choose whether they will be considered as incapable, then, of perceiving that which must have been apparent to every man of common understanding, or as imposing upon your confidence and endeavoring to mislead you now. In either case, they are unsafe guides in the perilous path they urge you to tread. Ponder well on this circumstance, and you will know how to appreciate the exaggerated language they address to you. They are not champions of liberty emulating the fame of our Revolutionary fathers, nor are you an oppressed people, contending, as they repeat to you, against worse than colonial vassalage. You are free members of a flourishing and happy Union. There is no settled design to oppress you. You have, indeed, felt the unequal operation of laws which may have been unwisely, not unconstitutionally passed; but that inequality must necessarily be removed. At the very moment when you were madly urged on to the unfortunate course you have begun, a change in public opinion has commenced. The nearly approaching payment of the public debt, and the consequent necessity of a diminution of duties, had already caused a considerable reduction, and that, too, on some articles of general consumption in your State. The importance of this change was underrated, and you were authoritatively told that no further alleviation of your burdens was to be expected, at the very time when the condition of the country imperiously demanded such a modification of the duties as should reduce them to a just and equitable scale. But as apprehensive of the effect of this change in allaying your discontents, you were precipitated into the fearful state in which you now find yourselves.

I have urged you to look back to the means that were used to burly you on to the position you have now assumed, and forward to the consequences they will produce. Something more is necessary. Contemplate the condition of that country of which you still form an important part; consider its government uniting in one bond of common interest and general protection so many different States—giving to all their inhabitants the proud title of AMERICAN CITIZEN—protecting their commerce—securing their literature and arts—facilitating their intercommunication—defending their frontiers—and making their name respected in the remotest parts of the earth! Consider the extent of its territory its increasing and happy population, its advance in arts, which render life agreeable, and the sciences which elevate the mind! See education spreading the lights of religion, morality, and general information into every cottage in this wide extent of our Territories and States! Behold it as the asylum where the wretched and the oppressed find a refuge and support! Look on this picture of happiness and honor, and say, WE TOO, ARE CITIZENS OF AMERICA—Carolina is one of these proud States her arms have defended—her best blood has cemented this happy Union! And then add, if you can, without horror and remorse this happy Union we will dissolve—this picture of peace and prosperity we will deface—this free intercourse we will interrupt—these fertile fields we will deluge with blood—the protection of that glorious flag we renounce—the very name of Americans we discard. And for what, mistaken men! For what do you throw away these inestimable blessings—for what would you exchange your share in the advantages and honor of the Union? For the dream of a separate independence—a dream interrupted by bloody conflicts with your neighbors, and a vile dependence on a foreign power. If your leaders could succeed in establishing a separation, what would be your situation? Are you united at home— are you free from the apprehension of civil discord, with all its fearful consequences? Do our neighboring republics, every day suffering some new revolution or contending with some new insurrection—do they excite your envy? But the dictates of a high duty oblige me solemnly to announce that you cannot succeed. The laws of the United States must be executed. I have no discretionary power on the subject—my duty is emphatically pronounced in the Constitution. Those who told you that you might peaceably prevent their execution, deceived you—they could not have been deceived themselves. They know that a forcible opposition could alone prevent the execution of the laws, and they know that such opposition must be repelled. Their object is disunion, hut be not deceived by names; disunion, by armed force, is TREASON. Are you really ready to incur its guilt? If you are, on the head of the instigators of the act be the dreadful consequences—on their heads be the dishonor, but on yours may fall the punishment—on your unhappy State will inevitably fall all the evils of the conflict you force upon the government of your country. It cannot accede to the mad project of disunion, of which you would be the first victims—its first magistrate cannot, if he would, avoid the performance of his duty—the consequence must be fearful for you, distressing to your fellow-citizens here, and to the friends of good government throughout the world. Its enemies have beheld our prosperity with a vexation they could not conceal—it was a standing refutation of their slavish doctrines, and they will point to our discord with the triumph of malignant joy. It is yet in your power to disappoint them. There is yet time to show that the descendants of the Pinckneys, the Sumpters, the Rutledges, and of the thousand other names which adorn the pages of your Revolutionary history, will not abandon that Union to support which so many of them fought and bled and died. I adjure you, as you honor their memory—as you love the cause of freedom, to which they dedicated their lives—as you prize the peace of your country, the lives of its best citizens, and your own fair fame, to retrace your steps. Snatch from the archives of your State the disorganizing edict of its convention—hid its members to re-assemble and promulgate the decided expressions of your will to remain in the path which alone can conduct you to safety, prosperity, and honor—tell them that compared to disunion, all other evils are light, because that brings with it an accumulation of all—declare that you will never take the field unless the star-spangled banner of your country shall float over you—that you will not be stigmatized when dead, and dishonored and scorned while you live, as the authors of the first attack on the Constitution of your country!—its destroyers you cannot be. You may disturb its peace—you may interrupt the course of its prosperity—you may cloud its reputation for stability—but its tranquillity will be restored, its prosperity will return, and the stain upon its national character will be transferred and remain an eternal blot on the memory of those who caused the disorder.

Fellow-citizens of the United States! the threat of unhallowed disunion—the names of those, once respected, by whom it is uttered—the array of military force to support it—denote the approach of a crisis in our affairs on which the continuance of our unexampled prosperity, our political existence, and perhaps that of all free governments, may depend. The conjuncture demanded a free, a full, and explicit enunciation, not only of my intentions, but of my principles of action, and as the claim was asserted of a right by a State to annul the laws of the Union, and even to secede from it at pleasure, a frank exposition of my opinions in relation to the origin and form of our government, and the construction I give to the instrument by which it was created, seemed to be proper. Having the fullest confidence in the justness of the legal and constitutional opinion of my duties which has been expressed, I rely with equal confidence on your undivided support in my determination to execute the laws—to preserve the Union by all constitutional means—to arrest, if possible, by moderate but firm measures, the necessity of a recourse to force; and, if it be the will of Heaven that the recurrence of its primeval curse on man for the shedding of a brother's blood should fall upon our land, that it be not called down by any offensive act on the part of the United States.

Fellow-citizens! the momentous case is before you. On your undivided support of your government depends the decision of the great question it involves, whether your sacred Union will be preserved, and the blessing it secures to us as one people shall be perpetuated. No one can doubt that the unanimity with which that decision will be expressed, will he such as to inspire new confidence in republican institutions, and that the prudence, the wisdom, and the courage which it will bring to their defense, will transmit them unimpaired and invigorated to our children.

May the Great Ruler of nations grant that the signal blessings with which he has favored ours may not, by the madness of party or personal ambition, be disregarded and lost, and may His wise providence bring those who have produced this crisis to see the folly, before they feel the misery, of civil strife, and inspire a returning veneration for that Union which, if we may dare to penetrate his designs, he has chosen, as the only means of attaining the high destinies to which we may reasonably aspire.

In testimony whereof, I have caused the seal of the United States to be hereunto affixed, having signed the same with my hand.

Done at the City of Washington, this 10th day of December, in the year of our Lord one thousand eight hundred and thirty-two, and of the independence of the United States the fifty-seventh.

ANDREW JACKSON.

By the President

EDW. LIVINGSTON, Secretary of State.

1. Identify and explain the dangers of a state's possession of the right to nullify an act as unconstitutional?
2. Why does Jackson declare that the Constitution is void if the doctrine of nullification prevails? In what ways is it incompatible with the existence of the
3. Explain the dangers inherent in questioning the constitutionality of an act based on the motives of those who passed it.
4. Summarize Jackson's defense of the Constitution against those who would claim it has errors.
5. Summarize and explain Jackson's opinion regarding the right of a state to secede from the Union. What is Jackson's tone in arguing this point?

10-9 The Force Bill (1833)

A key issue in the fight over nullification, Andrew Jackson desired this clause to assert the right of the national government to force compliance and payment of taxes by force of arms if necessary, over a possible nullification. Passed with a compromise tariff bill, which sought to head off sectional trouble, it was later "nullified" by the state of South Carolina.

An Act further to provide for the collection of duties on imports.

Be it enacted by the Senate and House of Representatives of the United States of America, in Congress assembled, That whenever, by reason of unlawful obstructions, combinations, or assemblages of persons, it shall become impracticable, in the judgment of the President, to execute the revenue laws, and collect the duties on imports in the ordinary way, in any collection district, it shall and may be lawful for the President to direct that the custom-house for such district be established and kept in any secure place within some port or harbour of such district, either upon land or on board any vessel; and, in that case, it shall be the duty of the collector to reside at such place, and there to detain all vessels and cargoes arriving within the said district until the duties imposed on said cargoes, by law, be paid in cash, deducting interest according to existing laws; and in such cases it shall be unlawful to take the vessel or cargo from the custody of the proper officer of the customs, unless by process from some court of the United States; and in case of any attempt otherwise to take such vessel or cargo by any force, or combination, or assemblage of persons too great to be overcome by the officers of the customs, it shall and may be lawful for the President of the United States, or such person or persons as he shall have empowered for that purpose, to employ such part of the land or naval forces, or militia of the United States, as may be deemed necessary for the purpose of preventing the removal of such vessel or cargo, and protecting the officers of the customs in retaining the custody thereof.

SEC. 2. *And be it further enacted,* That the jurisdiction of the circuit courts of the United States shall extend to all cases, in law or equity, arising under the revenue laws of the United States, for which other provisions are not already made by law; and if any person shall receive any injury to his person or property for or on account of any act by him done, under any law of the United States, for the protection of the revenue or the collection of duties on imports, he shall be entitled to maintain suit for damage therefor in the circuit court of the United States in the district wherein the party doing the injury may reside, or shall be found. And all property taken or detained by any officer or other person under authority of any revenue law of the United States, shall be irrepleviable, and shall be deemed to be in the custody of the law, and subject only to the orders and decrees of the courts of the United States having jurisdiction thereof. And if any person shall dispossess or rescue, or attempt to dispossess or rescue, any property so taken or detained as aforesaid, or shall aid or assist therein, such person shall be deemed guilty of a misdemeanour . . .

SEC. 5. *And be it further enacted,* That whenever the President of the United States shall be officially informed, by the authorities of any state, or by a judge of any circuit or district court of the United States, in the state, that, within the limits of such state, any law or laws of the United States, or the execution thereof, or of any process from the courts of the United States, is obstructed by the employment of military force, or by any other unlawful means, too great to be overcome by the ordinary course of judicial proceeding, or by the powers vested in the marshal by existing laws, it shall be lawful for him, the President of the United States, forthwith to issue his proclamation, declaring such fact or information, and requiring all such military and other force forthwith to disperse; and if at any time after issuing such proclamation, any such opposition or obstruction shall be made, in the manner or by the means aforesaid, the President shall be, and hereby is, authorized, promptly to employ such means to suppress the same, and to cause the said laws or process to be duly executed . . .

SEC. 6. *And be it further enacted,* That in any state where the jails are not allowed to be used for the imprisonment of persons arrested or committed under the laws of the United States, or where houses are not allowed to be so used, it shall and may be lawful for any marshal, under the direction of the judge of the United States for the proper district, to use other convenient places, within the limits of said state, and to make such other provision as he may deem expedient and necessary for that purpose.

SEC. 8. *And be it further enacted,* That the several provisions contained in the first and fifth sections of this act, shall be in force until the end of the next session of Congress, and no longer.

APPROVED, March 2, 1833.

1. What provisions are made under this bill to assist in the collection of duties and imports and to overcome "unlawful obstructions, combinations, or assemblages of persons" in the pursuit of these collections?

10-10 Black Hawk, "Life of Black Hawk" (1833)

A leader of the Sauk Tribe in Illinois, Black Hawk was a noted war leader until Zebulon Pike's expedition put an end to resistance in the area. He sought to work with Tecumseh in forging a confederacy of tribes and aided the British in the War of 1812. Forced off his land by the 1820's Black Hawk led an expedition to take back the land that culminated with Black Hawk's War. He was defeated in Wisconsin, escaped, but was later turned in. After his death, his bones were dug up and put on display in a museum. This document is an selection from his autobiography.

We generally paid a visit to St. Louis every summer; but, in consequence of the protracted war in which we had been engaged, I had not been there for some years. Our difficulties having all been settled, I concluded to take a small party, that summer, and go down to see our Spanish father. We went-and on our arrival, put up our lodges where the market-house now stands. After painting and dressing, we called to see our Spanish father, and were well received. He gave us a variety of presents, and plenty of provisions. We danced through the town as usual, and its inhabitants all seemed to be well pleased. They appeared to us like brothers-and always gave us good advice.

On my next, and *last*, visit to my Spanish father, I discovered, on landing, that all was not right: every countenance seemed sad and gloomy! I inquired the cause, and was informed that the Americans were coming to take possession of the town and country!-and that we should then lose our Spanish father! This news made myself and band sad-because we had always heard bad accounts of the Americans from Indians who had lived near them!-and we were sorry to lose our Spanish father, who had always treated us with great friendship.

A few days afterwards, the Americans arrived. I took my band, and went to take leave, for the last time, of our father. The Americans came to see him also. Seeing them approach, we passed out at one door, as they entered another-and immediately started, in canoes, for our village on Rock river-not liking the change any more than our friends appeared to, at St. Louis.

On arriving at our village, we gave the news, that strange people had taken St. Louis-and that we should never see our Spanish father again! This information made all our people sorry!

Some time afterwards, a boat came up the river, with a young American chief, and a small party of soldiers. We heard of them, (by runners,) soon after he had passed Salt river. Some of our young braves watched him every day, to see what sort of people he had on board! The boat, at length, arrived at Rock river, and the young chief came on shore with his interpreter-made a speech, and gave us some presents! We, in return, presented him with meat, and such provisions as we could spare.

We were all well pleased with the speech of the young chief. He gave us good advice; said our American father would treat us well. He presented us an American flag, which was hoisted. He then requested us to pull down our *British flags*-and give him our *British medals*-promising to send us others on his return to St. Louis. This we declined, as we wished to have *two Fathers*!

When the young chief started, we sent runners to the Fox village, some miles distant, to direct them to treat him well as he passed-which they did. He went to the head of the Mississippi, and then returned to St. Louis. We did not see any Americans again for some time,-being supplied with goods by British traders.

We were fortunate in not giving up our medals-for we learned afterwards, from our traders, that the chiefs high up on the Mississippi, who gave theirs, never received any in exchange for them. But the fault was not with the young American chief. He was a good man, and a great brave-and died in his country's service.

Some moons after this young chief descended the Mississippi, one of our people killed an American-and was confined, in the prison at St. Louis, for the offence. We held a council at our village to see what could be done for him,-which determined that Quˆsh-quˆ-me, Pˆ-she-pa-ho, Oœ-che-quˆ-ka, and Hˆ-she-quar-hi-qua, should go down to St. Louis, see our American father, and do all they could to have our friend released: by paying for the person killed-thus covering the blood, and satisfying the relations of the man murdered! This being the only means with us of saving a person who had killed another-and we *then* thought it was the same way with the whites!

The party started with the good wishes of the whole nation-hoping they would accomplish the object of their mission. The relatives of the prisoner blacked their faces, and fasted-hoping the Great Spirit would take pity on them, and return the husband and father to his wife and children.

Quˆsh-quˆ-me and party remained a long time absent. They at length returned, and encamped a short distance below the village-but did not come up that day-nor did any person approach their camp! They appeared to be dressed in *fine coats*, and had *medals*! From these circumstances, we were in hopes that they had brought good news. Early the next morning, the Council Lodge was crowded-Quˆsh-quˆ-me and party came up, and gave us the following account of their mission:

"On their arrival at St. Louis, they met their American father, and explained to him their business, and urged the release of their friend. The American chief told them he wanted land-and they had agreed to give him some on the west side of the Mississippi, and some on the Illinois side opposite the Jeffreon. When the business was all arranged, they expected to have their friend released to come home with them. But about the time they were ready to start, their friend was let out of prison, who ran a short distance, and was *shot dead*! This is all they could recollect of what was said and done. They had been drunk the greater part of the time they were in St. Louis."

This is all myself or nation knew of the treaty of 1804. It has been explained to me since. I find, by that treaty, all our country, east of the Mississippi, and south of the Jeffreon, was ceded to the United States for *one thousand dollars* a year! I will leave it to the people of the United States to say, whether our nation was properly represented in this treaty? or whether we received a fair compensation for the extent of country ceded by those *four* individuals? I could say much about this treaty, but I will not, at this time. It has been the origin of all our difficulties.

1. *Summarize the attitude with which the author considers the arrival of expansionist Americans? How do his opinions change at first after meeting the American "chief"?*
2. *Characterize American treatment of the Indians as it is described in this document. Give evidence from the text to support your conclusions.*

10-11 A French Traveler Reports on American Society (1835)

Alexis de Tocqueville was a young aristocratic Frenchman who in 1831 accompanied French publicist Gustave Auguste de Beaumont de la Bonninière to the United States in order to study the penal system there. After returning to France in 1832, Tocqueville wrote Democracy in America, a two-volume study of the American people and their political institutions. Published in 1835, the book is one of the earliest and most insightful studies of American life.

Source: Alexis de Tocqueville, *Democracy in America*, Volume 2 (American Studies at the University of Virginia, Hypertexts)
http://xroads.virginia.edu/~HYPER/DETOC/ch2_05.htm

I DO not propose to speak of those political associations by the aid of which men endeavor to defend themselves against the despotic action of a majority or against the aggressions of regal power. That subject I have already treated. If each citizen did not learn, in proportion as he individually becomes more feeble and consequently more incapable of preserving his freedom single-handed, to combine with his fellow citizens for the purpose of defending it, it is clear that tyranny would unavoidably increase together with equality.

Only those associations that are formed in civil life without reference to political objects are here referred to. The political associations that exist in the United States are only a single feature in the midst of the immense assemblage of associations in that country. Americans of all ages, all conditions, and all dispositions constantly form associations. They have not only commercial and manufacturing companies, in which all take part, but associations of a thousand other kinds, religious, moral, serious, futile, general or restricted, enormous or diminutive. The Americans make associations to give entertainments, to found seminaries, to build inns, to construct churches, to diffuse books, to send missionaries to the antipodes; in this manner they found hospitals, prisons, and schools. If it is proposed to inculcate some truth or to foster some feeling by the encouragement of a great example, they form a society. Wherever at the head of some new undertaking you see the government in France, or a man of rank in England, in the United States you will be sure to find an association.

I met with several kinds of associations in America of which I confess I had no previous notion; and I have often admired the extreme skill with which the inhabitants of the United States succeed in proposing a common object for the exertions of a great many men and in inducing them voluntarily to pursue it.

I have since traveled over England, from which the Americans have taken some of their laws and many of their customs; and it seemed to me that the principle of association was by no means so constantly or adroitly used in that country. The English often perform great things singly, whereas the Americans form associations for the smallest undertakings. It is evident that the former people consider association as a powerful means of action, but the latter seem to regard it as the only means they have of acting.

Thus the most democratic country on the face of the earth is that in which men have, in our time, carried to the highest perfection the art of pursuing in common the object of their common desires and have applied this new science to the greatest number of purposes. Is this the result of accident, or is there in reality any necessary connection between the principle of association and that of equality?

Aristocratic communities always contain, among a multitude of persons who by themselves are powerless, a small number of powerful and wealthy citizens, each of whom can achieve great undertakings single-handed. In aristocratic societies men do not need to combine in order to act, because they are strongly held together. Every wealthy and powerful citizen constitutes the head of a permanent and compulsory association, composed of all those who are dependent upon him or whom he makes subservient to the execution of his designs.

Among democratic nations, on the contrary, all the citizens are independent and feeble; they can do hardly anything by themselves, and none of them can oblige his fellow men to lend him their assistance. They all, therefore, become powerless if they do not learn voluntarily to help one another. If men living in democratic countries had no right and no inclination to associate for political purposes, their independence would be in great jeopardy, but they might long preserve their wealth and their cultivation: whereas if they never acquired the habit of forming associations in ordinary life, civilization itself would be endangered. A people among whom individuals lost the power of achieving great things single-handed, without acquiring the means of producing them by united exertions, would soon relapse into barbarism.

Unhappily, the same social condition that renders associations so necessary to democratic nations renders their formation more difficult among those nations than among all others. When several members of an aristocracy agree to combine, they easily succeed in doing so; as each of them brings great strength to the partnership, the number of its members may be very limited; and when the members of an association are limited in number, they may easily become mutually acquainted, understand each other, and establish fixed regulations. The same opportunities do not occur among democratic nations, where the associated members must always be very numerous for their association to have any power.

I am aware that many of my countrymen are not in the least embarrassed by this difficulty. They contend that the more enfeebled and incompetent the citizens become, the more able and active the government ought to be rendered in order that society at large may execute what individuals can no longer accomplish. They believe this answers the whole difficulty, but I think they are mistaken.

A government might perform the part of some of the largest American companies, and several states, members of the Union, have already attempted it; but what political power could ever carry on the vast multitude of lesser undertakings which the American citizens perform every day, with the assistance of the principle of association? It is easy to foresee that the time is drawing near when man will be less and less able to produce, by himself alone, the commonest necessaries of life. The task of the governing power will therefore perpetually increase, and its very efforts will extend it every day. The more it stands in the place of associations, the more will individuals, losing the notion of combining together, require its assistance: these are causes and effects that unceasingly create each other. Will the administration of the country ultimately assume the management of all the manufactures which no single citizen is able to carry on? And if a time at length arrives when, in consequence of the extreme subdivision of landed property, the soil is split into an infinite number of parcels, so that it can be cultivated only by companies of tillers will it be necessary that the head of the government should leave the helm of state to follow the plow? The morals and the intelligence of a democratic people would be as much endangered as its business and manufactures if the government ever wholly usurped the place of private companies. Feelings and opinions are recruited, the heart is enlarged, and the human mind is developed only by the reciprocal influence of men upon one another. I have shown that these influences are almost null in democratic countries; they must therefore be artificially created, and this can only be accomplished by associations.

When the members of an aristocratic community adopt a new opinion or conceive a new sentiment, they give it a station, as it were, beside themselves, upon the lofty platform where they stand; and opinions or sentiments so conspicuous to the eyes of the multitude are easily introduced into the minds or hearts of all around. In democratic countries the governing power alone is naturally in a condition to act in this manner, but it is easy to see that its action is always inadequate, and often dangerous. A government can no more be competent to keep alive and to renew the circulation of opinions and feelings among a great people than to manage all the speculations of productive industry. No sooner does a government attempt to go beyond its political sphere and to enter upon this new track than it exercises, even unintentionally, an insupportable tyranny; for a government can only dictate strict rules, the opinions which it favors are rigidly enforced, and it is never easy to discriminate between its advice and its commands. Worse still will be the case if the government really believes itself interested in preventing all circulation of ideas; it will then stand motionless and oppressed by the heaviness of voluntary torpor. Governments, therefore, should not be the only active powers; associations ought, in democratic nations, to stand in lieu of those powerful private individuals whom the equality of conditions has swept away.

As soon as several of the inhabitants of the United States have taken up an opinion or a feeling which they wish to promote in the world, they look out for mutual assistance; and as soon as they have found one another out, they combine. From that moment they are no longer isolated men, but a power seen from afar, whose actions serve for an example and whose language is listened to. The first time I heard in the United States that a hundred thousand men had bound themselves publicly to abstain from spirituous liquors, it appeared to me more like a joke than a serious engagement, and I did not at once perceive why these temperate citizens could not content themselves with drinking water by their own firesides. I at last understood that these hundred thousand Americans, alarmed by the progress of drunkenness around them, had made up their minds to patronize temperance.

They acted in just the same way as a man of high rank who should dress very plainly in order to inspire the humbler orders with a contempt of luxury. It is probable that if these hundred thousand men had lived in France, each of them would singly have memorialized the government to watch the public houses all over the kingdom.

Nothing, in my opinion, is more deserving of our attention than the intellectual and moral associations of America. The political and industrial associations of that country strike us forcibly; but the others elude our observation, or if we discover them, we understand them imperfectly because we have hardly ever seen anything of the kind. It must be acknowledged, however, that they are as necessary to the American people as the former, and perhaps more so. In democratic countries the science of association is the mother of science; the progress of all the rest depends upon the progress it has made.

Among the laws that rule human societies there is one which seems to be more precise and clear than all others. If men are to remain civilized or to become so, the art of associating together must grow and improve in the same ratio in which the equality of conditions is increased.

1. According to de Tocqueville, what social conditions render "associations" necessary in a democracy? Do you think his conclusions are applicable today?
2. How do the social reforms of the early nineteenth century serve to demonstrate de Tocqueville's point?

10-12   Female Industry Association, from the New York Herald (1845)

The wide variety of industrial trades in which women worked is demonstrated in this document along with the appalling conditions under which they worked and the terrible wage they received. This early meeting was an effort to band together to improve wages and conditions. The condescending tone of the newspaper demonstrates that difficulty of their efforts.

Seldom or never did the Superior Court of the City Hall contain such an array of beauty under suffering, together with common sense and good order, as it did yesterday, on the occasion of the meeting of the female industrial classes, in their endeavors to remedy the wrongs and oppressions under which they labor, and, for some time past, have labored. At the hour appointed for the adjourned meeting, four o'clock, about 700 females, generally of the most interesting age and appearance, were assembled; and, after a trifling delay, a young lady stepped forward, and in rather a low, diffident tone, moved that Miss Gray take the Chair, which, having been put and carried in the usual business-like way-

Miss Gray (a young woman, neatly dressed, of some 22 or 24 years of age, fair complexion, interesting, thoughtful and intelligent cast of countenance) came forward from the back part of the room. She proceeded to make a few observations on the nature and objects of their movements and intentions, and stated that, finding the class she belonged to were unable to support themselves, honestly and respectably, by their industry, under the present prices they received for their work, had, therefore, come to the determination of endeavoring to obtain something better, by appealing to the public at large, and showing the amount of sufferings under which they at present labored. She then went on to give instances of what wages they were in the habit of receiving in different branches of the business in which she was engaged, and mentioned several employers by name who only paid them from $.10 to $.18 per day; others, who were proficient in the business, after 12 or 14 hours hard labor, could only get about $.25 per day; one employer offered them $.20 per day, and said that if they did not take it, he would obtain girls from Connecticut who would work for less even than what he offered. The only employer who had done them justice was Mr. Beck, of Fourteenth street, who only allowed his girls to be out about two hours, when he complied with their reasonable demands. He was a man who was worthy of the thanks of every girl present, and they wished him health, wealth, and happiness. How was it possible that on such an income they could support themselves decently and honestly, let alone supporting widowed mothers, and some two, three, or four helpless brothers and sisters, which many of them had. Pieces of work for which they last year got seven shillings, this year they could only get three shillings.

A female stepped forward . . . and enquired if the association was confined to any one branch of business, or was it open to all who were suffering under like privations and injustice?

The Chairwoman observed that it was opened to all who were alike oppressed, and it was only by a firm cooperation they could accomplish what they were laboring for.

Another female of equally interesting appearance (Mrs. Storms) then came forward and said that it was necessary the nature and objects of the party should be distinctly understood, particularly by those who were immediately interested; their own position should be fully known. If the supply of labor in the market was greater than the demand, it followed as a matter of course that they could not control the prices; and, therefore, it would be well for those present to look around them and see into what other channels they could turn their industry with advantage. There were many branches of business in which men were employed that they could as well fill. Let them memorialize the merchants in the dry goods department, for instance, and show them this also. That there were hundreds of females in this city who were able to keep the books as well as any man in it. There were various other branches of business in which men were employed for which females alone were suitable and intended. Let these men go to the fields and seek their livelihood as men ought to do, and leave the females their legitimate employment. There were the drapers also, and a number of other branches of trade in which females could be as well if not better and more properly employed. By these means, some thousands would be afforded employment in branches much more valuable to themselves and the community generally. She then proceeded to recommend those present to be moderate in their demands, and not to ask for more than the circumstances of trade would warrant, for if they acted otherwise, it would tend to their more ultimate ruin. Under present circumstances, a very few years broke down their constitutions, and they had no other resource but the alms-house, and what could bring this about sooner than the bread and water diet and rough shelter, which many of them at present were obliged to put up with.

The proceedings of the previous meeting were then read and approved of.

A number of delegates from the following trades entered their names to act as a Committee to regulate future proceedings: tailoresses, plain and coarse sewing, shirt makers, book-folders and stitchers, cap makers, straw workers, dress makers, crimpers, fringe and lace makers, &c.

The following preamble and resolutions were agreed to:

Whereas, the young women attached to the different trades in the city of New York, having toiled a long time for a remuneration totally inadequate for the maintenance of life, and feeling the truth of the Gospel assertion, that "the laborer is worthy of his hire," have determined to take upon themselves the task of asserting their rights against unjust and mercenary employers. It must be remembered by those to whom we address ourselves, that our object is not extortion; our desire, not to reap advantages which will be denied to our employers. The boon we ask is founded upon right, alone! The high prices demanded by tradesmen for their goods renders them amply able to advance wages to a standard, which, while it obviates the present cause of complaint, will render laborers only the more cheerful at their work, and still more earnest and willing to serve their employers. The scarcity of employment, and the low rates of pay which have so long prevailed, have, undoubtedly driven many virtuous females to courses which might, otherwise, have been avoided. Many of the female operatives of this city have families dependent upon their exertions; aged fathers and mothers-young brothers-helpless sisters, who, but for their exertions, must inevitably starve, or betake themselves to that scarcely less horrible alternative-the poor house! Such a picture is enough to bestir the most inert to active exertion; the love of life is a passion inherent in us all, and we feel persuaded that we need no better excuse for the movement to which the glaring injustice of our employers has driven us! . . .

1. *What gender inequalities and difficulties are noted in these minutes? What solutions are proposed and discussed?*
2. *Summarize the resolutions that are finally made.*

PART ELEVEN
REFORMING THE NATION

11-1 Joshua and Sally Wilson Letters to George Wilson (1823)

These letters, from George Wilson's father, Joshua, and his sister Sally, offer advice on courtship and illuminate the expectations placed on young men during this period-to act as breadwinners and be the heads of their families, while young women were expected to stay in their separate sphere-the home-and take care of domestic affairs. In earlier periods, the work of an entire family contributed to a family's economic survival, but in an industrializing society men worked outside the home, for money, and women's home-work became less economically significant.

> From Donald M. Scott and Bernard Wishy, Americas Families, A Documentary History (Chicago: Dorsey Press, 1988).

November 23, 1823

We presume you are already informed that your letter of the 28th was duly received. The delicate and important subject suggested for our consideration form a sufficient reason for some delay that we might not give advice in a matter of such moment without meditation, prayer, and serious conference. It would be very unreasonable for us to attempt to restrain the lawful and laudable desires of our children, all we ought to do is to endeavor to direct and regulate their innocent wishes and curb and conquer those which are vicious. Nor are we ignorant of the great advantages which frequently result from virtuous love and honorable wedlock. But there is a time for all things, and such are the fixed laws of nature that things are only beautiful and useful when they occupy their own time and place. Premature love and marriage are often blighted by the frosts of adversity and satiety leaving hasty lovers to droop in the meridian of life and drag out a miserable existence under the withering influence of disappointment and disgust.... We do not say you have been hasty but we wish you to reflect seriously upon this question. Is not the whole affair premature? We know from experience and observation that schemes which appear reasonable and desirable at the age of twenty wear a very different aspect at twenty five. We think it probable that greater maturity, more experience in business and a larger acquaintance with the world might change your views and feelings. Besides we are not sure that you have sufficiently considered the weighty responsibility. We feel no disposition to place any insuperable barrier in your way. Our advice is that you give the subject that consideration which its importance demands, that you unite with us in praying for divine direction, that every thing be done deliberately, decently, orderly, honorably, and devoutly.

[Joshua Wilson]
December 9, 1823

Your letter of Nov 18 has been duly received. On its contents we have meditated with deep solicitude.... You seem confident that your decision is not premature nor hasty. Here we feel compelled to demur and beg you to weigh the matter again. You express a hope that before great length of time we shall have an opportunity of receiving Miss B much to our satisfaction. Dear George, it will not be any satisfaction to us to see you place a lady in a more precarious condition than you found her and this we are sure would be the case if marriage with this young lady should take place shortly. We must remind you of a pledge given in your former letter and insist upon its obligation, that you marry no woman without the prospect of supporting her in a suitable manner. Think of the circumstances in which she has been educated, of the circle of society in which she has been accustomed to move, of her delicate constitution and refined sensibility and then imagine to yourself her disappointment upon entering into a poor dependent family occupying an indifferent tenement without the means of affording a comfortable lodging or decently accommodating her friends. She has been accustomed to see you in the agreeable aspect of the scholar and a gentleman and she

has seen your father also in flattering circumstances.... We do not say things to discourage you but to show you the necessity of prudence in your plans, diligence in your studies and such application to business as will afford a reasonable prospect of success before you become the head of a family.

Sally Wilson

1. *Summarize the advice given to the young man considering marriage? What should be the young man's primary concern?*
2. *What social expectations are revealed in these letters?*

11-2 Lyman Beecher, Six Sermons on Intemperance (1828)

The patriarch of what would become a very influential American family, Lyman Beecher was educated at Yale and become a minister in several churches before coming to Boston in 1826. He started preaching revivals with intemperance a major theme. He saw drunkenness as the primary sin of America and became a noted speaker for temerence. He later become the President of Lane Seminary in Cincinnati where his "new school" Calvinism came into conflict with the old school. Beecher was a leading figure in the Second Great Awakening.

But of all the ways to hell, which the feet of deluded mortals tread, that of the intemperate is the most dreary and terrific. The demand for artificial stimulus to supply the deficiencies of healthful aliment, is like the rage of thirst, and the ravenous demand of famine. It is famine: for the artificial excitement has become as essential now to strength and cheerfulness, as simple nutrition once was. But nature, taught by habit to require what once she did not need, demands gratification now with a decision inexorable as death, and to most men as irresistible. The denial is a living death. The stomach, the head, the heart, and arteries, and veins, and every muscle, and every nerve, feel the exhaustion, and the restless, unutterable wretchedness which puts out the light of life, and curtains the heavens, and carpets the earth with sackcloth. All these varieties of sinking nature, call upon the wretched man with trumpet tongue, to dispel this darkness, and raise the ebbing tide of life, by the application of the cause which produced these woes, and after a momentary alleviation will produce them again with deeper terrors, and more urgent importunity; for the repetition, at each time renders the darkness deeper, and the torments of self-denial more irresistible and intolerable.

At length, the excitability of nature flags, and stimulants of higher power, and in greater quantities, are required to rouse the impaired energies of life, until at length the whole process of dilatory murder, and worse than purgatorial suffering, having been passed over, the silver cord is loosed, the golden bowl is broken, the wheel at the cistern stops, and the dust returns to the earth as it was, and the spirit to God who gave it.

These sufferings, however, of animal nature, are not to be compared with the moral agonies which convulse the soul. It is an immortal being who sins, and suffers; and as his earthly house dissolves, he is approaching the judgment seat, in anticipation of a miserable eternity. He feels his captivity, and in anguish of spirit clanks his chains and cries for help. Conscience thunders, remorse goads, and as the gulf opens before him, he recoils, and trembles, and weeps, and prays, and resolves, and promises, and reforms, and "seeks it yet again,"-again resolves, and weeps, and prays, and "seeks it yet again!" Wretched man, he has placed himself in the hands of a giant, who never pities, and never relaxes his iron gripe. He may struggle, but he is in chains. He may cry for release, but it comes not; and lost! lost! may be inscribed upon the door posts of his dwelling.

In the mean time these paroxysms of his dying moral nature decline, and a fearful apathy, the harbinger of spiritual death, comes on. His resolution fails, and his mental energy, and his vigorous enterprise; and nervous irritation and depression ensue. The social affections lose their fulness and tenderness, and conscience loses its power, and the heart its sensibility, until all that was once lovely and of good report, retires and leaves the wretch abandoned to the appetites of a ruined animal. In this deplorable condition, reputation expires, business falters and becomes perplexed, and temptations to drink multiply as inclination to do so increases, and the power of resistance declines. And now the vortex roars, and the struggling victim buffets the fiery wave with feebler stroke, and warning supplication, until despair flashes upon his soul, and with an outcry that pierces the heavens, he ceases to strive, and disappears. . . .

Upon national industry the effects of intemperance are manifest and mischievous.

The results of national industry depend on the amount of well-directed intellectual and physical power. But intemperance paralyses and prevents both these springs of human action.

In the inventory of national loss by intemperance, may be set down-the labor prevented by indolence, by debility, by sickness, by quarrels and litigation, by gambling and idleness, by mistakes and misdirected effort, by improvidence and wastefulness, and by the shortened date of human life and activity. Little wastes in great establishments constantly occurring may defeat the energies of a mighty capital. But where the intellectual and muscular energies are raised to the working point daily by ardent spirits, until the agriculture, and commerce, and arts of a nation move on by the power of artificial stimulus, that moral power cannot be maintained, which will guaranty fidelity, and that physical power cannot be preserved and well directed, which will ensure national prosperity. The nation whose immense enterprise is thrust forward by the stimulus of ardent spirits, cannot ultimately escape debility and bankruptcy. . . .

The prospect of a destitute old age, or of a suffering family, no longer troubles the vicious portion of our community. They drink up their daily earnings, and bless God for the poor-house, and begin to look upon it as, of right, the drunkard's home, and contrive to arrive thither as early as idleness and excess will give them a passport to this sinecure of vice. Thus is the insatiable destroyer of industry marching through the land, rearing poor-houses, and augmenting taxation: night and day, with sleepless activity, squandering property, cutting the sinews of industry, undermining vigor, engendering disease, paralysing intellect, impairing moral principle, cutting short the date of life, and rolling up a national debt, invisible, but real and terrific as the debt of England: continually transferring larger and larger bodies of men, from the class of contributors to the national income, to the class of worthless consumers. . . .

The effects of intemperance upon civil liberty may not be lightly passed over.

It is admitted that intelligence and virtue are the pillars of republican institutions, and that the illumination of schools, and the moral power of religious institutions, are indispensable to produce this intelligence and virtue.

But who are found so uniformly in the ranks of irreligion as the intemperate? Who like these violate the Sabbath, and set their mouth against the heavens-neglecting the education of their families-and corrupting their morals? Almost the entire amount of national ignorance and crime is the offspring of intemperance. Throughout the land, the intemperate are hewing down the pillars, and undermining the foundations of our national edifice. Legions have besieged it, and upon every gate the battle-axe rings; and still the sentinels sleep.

Should the evil advance as it has done, the day is not far distant when the great body of the laboring classes of the community, the bones and sinews of the nation, will be contaminated; and when this is accomplished, the right of suffrage becomes the engine of self-destruction. For the laboring classes constitute an immense majority, and when these are perverted by intemperance, ambition needs no better implements with which to dig the grave of our liberties, and entomb our glory.

Such is the influence of interest, ambition, fear, and indolence, that one violent partisan, with a handful of disciplined troops, may overrule the influence of five hundred temperate men, who act without concert. Already is the disposition to temporize, to tolerate, and even to court the intemperate, too apparent, on account of the apprehended retribution of their perverted suffrage. The whole power of law, through the nation, sleeps in the statute book, and until public sentiment is roused and concentrated, it may be doubted whether its execution is possible.

Where is the city, town, or village, in which the laws are not openly violated, and where is the magistracy that dares to carry into effect the laws against the vending or drinking of ardent spirits? Here then an aristocracy of bad influence has already risen up, which bids defiance to law, and threatens the extirpation of civil liberty. As intemperance increases, the power of taxation will come more and more into the hands of men of intemperate habits and desperate fortunes; of course the laws gradually will become subservient to the debtor, and less efficacious in protecting the rights of property. This will be a vital stab to liberty-to the security of which property is indispensable. For money is the sinew of war-and when those who hold the property of a nation cannot be protected in their rights, they will change the form of government, peaceably if they may, by violence if they must.

1. *Identify the physical effects of intemperance discussed in this sermon. What is the ultimate end of a lack of temperance? Compare these effects to the "moral agonies" that are alleged to be the results of intemperance. How does intemperance affect man's spirit?*
2. *What affect does intemperance have on industry, society, and civil Liberty? In what way is this sermon a plea for personal improvement as well as an attempt at wide social reform for the common good?*

11-3 "Early Habits of Industry," The Mother's Magazine (1834)

This document reveals the importance of business, industry and the reforming impulse of the mid 19th century. It calls on mothers to instill early habits of industry that will create successful children and adults.

If, as a distinguished writer has observed, "Man is a bundle of habits," there is perhaps scarcely a subject to which maternal influence should be more unceasingly directed, than the early formation of right habits. And probably there is no one habit more important in a character formed for usefulness, than that of industry and regular application to business.

This habit should be commenced at a very early period; long before the little ones can be very profitable from the fruits of their industry. I know it is often alleged that the labour and care of teaching young children various useful employments, is greater than all the benefits which may be expected to result. But this, I believe, is a fact only in regard to a few of their first lessons.

I have a friend, who is both a gentleman and a scholar. For the sake of employment, his father required his little son, from the early age of eight years, to copy all his letters. I have often heard this friend ascribe his business talent, which, in regard to despatch, punctuality, and order, is seldom equalled, to his father's unremitting efforts, to keep him, at stated intervals, regularly employed.

In the formation of character, I had almost said, habits are every thing. Could the whole amount of knowledge, which a young man has acquired, just entering professional life, after nine years laborious preparatory study, have been at once imparted to his mind, without any effort on his part, the value to him would be immeasurably less than the slow process by which it was acquired. The *mental discipline,* the *intellectual habits,* are worth even more to him than the knowledge gained.

But the importance of a habit may perhaps be best ascertained by its practical result. We refer mothers to the annals of great and good men, in all ages of the world, who have been the benefactors of mankind. By attention to their early history, it will be found, that their learning and talents are not merely the effects of genius, as many suppose, but are the precious fruits of which industry and persevering application were the early bud. The Bible furnishes impressive examples on this subject. Adam in a state of innocence, was required to "dress the garden, and to keep it."

The glorified beings in heaven rest not day nor night. It is said of the great exemplar of the Christian, that "he went about doing good." We are both instructed and warned by such scripture passages as the following: Ex. xx. 9. Eccl. ix. 10: v. 12. Prov. xxiv. 30-34: xx. 4. Ezekiel x. 49. Rom. xii. 11. 2 Thess. v. 10-12. Rev. vii. 15.

When habits of industry and personal effort have been faithfully cherished, it will not be difficult to cultivate those of benevolence and self-denial. Children should be early encouraged and induced to contribute to the various institutions of benevolence in our country; but let it never be done without an effort, and a sacrifice, on their part. They should be made to feel, with David, that "they will not offer to the Lord a sacrifice which costs them nothing."

It is a principle which they may easily apprehend, and one that will be of great value in forming their future characters. At a very early age they can be made to understand something of the wants and woes of the heathen world; and when their sympathies are excited, instruct them in what manner they may begin to aid in sending abroad the blessings of salvation.

Mothers may encourage their little ones to resolve how much they will endeavour to earn in this way, and for such purposes in a year. Let a little book of accounts be prepared for them, in which all their little earnings shall regularly be entered, and as soon as they are able, let them keep these accounts themselves. In this way, several useful habits may be associated,-children may be thus early taught that money is valuable, rather as enabling them to do good, than as a means of selfish or sensual gratification.

The want of suitable regular employment for children, particularly for boys, is an evil extensively felt and deplored, especially by men in professional life, and the inhabitants of large cities and populous villages. Perhaps there is no one class of persons in our country, so highly favored in this particular as *farmers*; and it is one of the peculiar blessings of their condition, of which I fear they are not sufficiently aware, to be suitably grateful.

But in respect to others, a remedy must be supplied, or their children will be ruined. If all other resources fail, it is better to consider a regular portion of each day as "a time to cast away stones, and a time to gather stones together," to be again dispersed for the same object, rather than indulge or connive at habits of idleness.

At one of the most respectable colleges in New-England, the President and Professors have had the wisdom and precaution for a number of years, regularly to send their sons, during a considerable portion of each year, among their friends in the country, to labor on farms. The boys themselves are delighted with the plan, and all the judicious commend it, as affording the most healthful, improving, and pleasant employment. And probably even greater attainments are made in their studies, than if constantly confined in school the whole year. And perhaps not the least advantage which will result, will be found in giving to them an athletic frame, and a sound and vigorous constitution.

But in respect to daughters, the evil cannot be so great. The *domestic duties* of every family furnish sufficient employment to give a habit of industry to our daughters. And with these duties, it is disgraceful for any young lady to be wholly unacquainted; not less disgraceful, certainly, than to be ignorant of her alphabet; if the value of knowledge is to be estimated by its practical utility.

Whenever a young lady becomes herself the mistress of a family, no matter how elevated her station may be, "looking well to the ways of her household" is her *profession.*

What would be thought of the physician, or the pastor, who should enter upon his profession, ignorant of the duties it involved, because he was rich enough to employ a substitute? A knowledge of domestic duties in its various branches and operations, are indispensable for females, and mothers are held responsible, that their daughters acquire it, by a systematic and thorough course of training.

1. *What habits are said to be most useful? How is the encouragement of this habit beneficial to the growth of urban America and the rise of industry and commerce?*
2. *What professional skills should be learned by boys? How do these skills compare or contrast with the professional skills recommended for girls?*

11-4 Charles Finney, "What a Revival of Religion Is" (1835)

Trained as a lawyer, Charles Grandison Finney became one of the most influential and controversial leaders of the Second Great Awakening. He was based at first in New York where urbanization was taking place. Finney welcomed the changes and preached a gospel of personal responsibility that rejected the Calvinism of his denomination. Instead, Finney argued for progress and ambition and the power of the individual, all of which made him a very popular figure among his followers and very dangerous one to the orthodox Presbyterians who saw him as a heretic. His revivals, however, remained immensely popular and he became one of the most successful revivalists of his generation.

It is altogether improbable that religion will ever make progress among *heathen* nations except through the influence of revivals. The attempt is now making to do it by education, and other cautious and gradual improvements. But so long as the laws of mind remain what they are, it cannot be done in this way. There must be excitement sufficient to wake up the dormant moral powers, and roll back the tide of degradation and sin. And precisely so far as our own land approximately to heathenism, it is impossible for God or man to promote religion is such a state of things but by powerful excitements.- This is evident from the fact that this has always been the way in which God has done it. God does not create these excitements, and choose this method to promote religion for nothing, or without reason. Where mankind are so reluctant to obey God, they will not obey until they are excited. For instance, how many there are who know that they ought to be religious, but they are afraid if they become pious they will be laughed at by their companions. Many are wedded to idols, others are procrastinating repentance, until they are settled in life, or until they have secured some favorite worldly interest. Such persons never will give up their false shame, or relinquish their ambitious schemes, till they are so excited that they cannot contain themselves any longer. . . .

It is presupposed that the church is sunk down in a backslidden state, and a revival consists in the return of the church from her backsliding, and in the conversion of sinners.

1. A revival always includes conviction of sin on the part of the church. Backslidden professors cannot wake up and begin right away in the service of God, without deep searching of heart. The fountains of sin need to be broken up. In a true revival, Christians are always brought under such convictions; they see their sins in such a light, that often they find it impossible to maintain a hope of their acceptance with God. It does not always go to that extent; but there are always, in a genuine revival, deep convictions of sin, and often cases of abandoning all hope.

2. Backslidden Christians will be brought to repentance. A revival is nothing else than a new beginning of obedience to God. Just as the case of a converted sinner, the first step is a deep repentance, a breaking down of heart, a getting down into the dust before God, with deep humility, and forsaking of sin.

3. Christians will have their fair renewed. While they are in their backslidden state they are blind to the state of sinners. Their hearts are as hard as marble. The truths of the Bible only appear like a dream. They admit it to be all true; their conscience and their judgment assent to it; but their faith does not see it standing out in bold relief, in all the burning realities of eternity. But when they enter into a revival, they no longer see men as trees walking, but they see things in that strong light which will renew the love of God in their hearts. This will lead them to labor zealously to bring others to him. They will feel grieved that others do not love God, when they love him so much. And they will set themselves feelingly to persuade their neighbors to give him their heart. So their love to men will be renewed. They will be filled with a tender and burning love for souls. They will have a longing desire for the salvation of the whole world. They will be in agony for individuals whom they want to have saves; their friends, relations, enemies. They will not only be urging them to give their hearts to God, but they will carry them to God in the arms of faith, and with strong crying and tears beseech God to have mercy on them, and save their souls from endless burning.

4. A revival breaks the power of the world and sin over Christians. It bring them to such vantage ground that they get a fresh I pulse towards heaven. They have a new foretaste of heaven, and new desires after union to God; and the charm of the world is broken, and the power of sin overcome.

5. When the churches are thus awakened and reformed, the reformation and salvation of sinners will follow, going through the same stages of conviction, repentance, and reformation. Their hearts will be broken down and changed. Very often the most abandoned profligates are among the subjects. Harlots, and drunkards, infidels, and all sorts of abandoned characters, are awakened and converted.

The worst part of human society are softened, and reclaimed, and made to appear as lovely specimens of the beauty of holiness. . . .

You see the error of those who are beginning to think that religion can be better promoted in the world without revivals, and who are disposed to give up all efforts to produce religious excitements. Because there are evils arising in some instances out of great excitements on the subject of religion, they are of opinion that it is best to dispense with them altogether. This cannot, and must not be. True, there is danger of abuses. In cases of great *religious* as well as all other excitements, more for less incidental evils may be expected of course. . . . So in revivals of religion, it is found by experience, that in the present state of the world, religion cannot be promoted to any considerable extent without them.

1. What is Finney's reasoning to support his statement that religion only makes progress through revivals?
2. Summarize the several effects of a revival as proposed by Finney.

11-5   Temperance and the Washingtonians (1836)

At the 1836 spring convention of the American Temperance Union, the society's leadership decided the organization should promote total abstinence from all alcoholic beverages. This step required an entirely new orientation for many of the union's members who had chosen moderation over complete denial. It is not surprising that many individuals were not ready to go along with this new policy, including wealthy contributors who were unwilling to forgo wine. As a result, the temperance movement fell upon lean years. By 1840, many reformers were wondering what could be done to restore the momentum of the years preceding 1836. The stage was set for the emergence of the Washingtonian movement.

Source: History of Alcoholics Anonymous; Text and Articles on the Washingtonian Temperance Society: *The Foundation, Progress and Principles of the Washington Temperance Society of Baltimore, 1842.* http://www.historyofaa.com/Washingtonians/wash1.html

CHAPTER I

Foundation of the Society

The 5th of April, 1840, was an eventful day. Influences were set at work then, which have been developing and extending ever since, and which promise to accomplish much for the good of mankind. On the evening of that day, half a dozen men met in the bar-room of a tavern in Baltimore. They had often met there before, spent their hours in friendly converse, and mingled in the mutual drowning of care in the bowl. It was a place of usual resort to them. And now they had met there as before, to drink together from the poisonous cup, to which they were all too much addicted. Without having become outcasts or sots, they had all confessedly suffered severely from the frequent and intemperate use of intoxicating drinks,—suffered in their health, suffered in their estates, suffered in their families, their habits, their feelings and their reputation.

But though these were plain men, they were men of unusual energy. It is true that alcohol had made its ravages on their characters, their minds, and their hearts. But the energy of manhood still survived. They were the victims, rather than merely the votaries of the pleasures of the bowl. They were in business, and five of them had families. They cared for their business and loved their families. They had all started out in life when young, with the hopes which usually beat high in the hearts of youth in every branch of business, or situation in life, when first entering upon the world. For a time they ran well. Business was fair. Friends were not few. They had married, and were happy.

Had any man told either of them at eighteen, nineteen, or twenty years of age, that twenty-five or thirty would find them drunkards,—that, like thousands around them, they would suffer from the poison of the serpent, and the sting of the adder in the cup, they would have laughed the insinuation to scorn, and honestly too. They never dreamed then of being drunkards. They drank moderately, and freely too. The habits of society at that time,—of all classes of society, even religious, sanctioned the free use of alcoholic drinks; and they went with the multitude never for a moment thinking of evil. But the love of drink particularly of the "social glass," grew upon them gradually and insensibly, until habit was fixed and appetite strong; and ere they had suspected it, they found themselves in the power of a monster, bound hand and foot in chains,—the slaves of their own appetites. And now they frequented the public taverns; and oft at night, or during the day, and even on the Sabbath, instead of being at their business, or with their families, or at church, they were to be found at the Hotel or Grogshop. They knew it was wrong. They saw the evil; they felt it; they lamented it; and times without number did they promise wife and friend and self, that they would drink no more. They were sincere. They meant to be sober. But at some fatal hour they would take one glass again, "just one glass;" and they found themselves as powerless and debased as ever.

It was on the evening of the day on which we have introduced them to the reader, that these six men were once more together at the tavern. Their families were forsaken at home. Their business for the day was done. But neither was entirely forgotten. The bar with its temptations was near them. Their habits were to contend with. And the cravings of an unnatural appetite within were against all good resolves. But these men had not lost all their principle, their energy, or their feeling. They looked to their homes, and they saw that much of domestic bliss, which should gather round the fireside, was banished by the inebriating cup. They looked to their business, and they knew they had suffered there. They counted the cost, and they were astonished at the amount of money they threw away in visiting the dram-shop. They looked back to the days of their youth, when with free hearts and bounding hopes, they had leaped into life, and had looked forward into the future never dreaming of such a slavery. They looked to their reputation, their influence, their health, their feelings, and their energy of character; and they felt that they would lose all these, if they prosecuted much longer the way in which they were hurrying down to death. They looked into the future, and all was clouds and darkness. They deliberately weighed the movement about to be made; and then rising in the energy of their still surviving manhood, they resolved that hour they would drink no more of the poisonous draught forever; and that to carry out their resolutions, they would form a society with a pledge to that effect, and bind themselves under it to each other for life.

This is no fancy sketch. The circumstances have often been stated by the founders of the society, just as we have detailed them. We do not pretend to say, that the feelings and reflections above stated were matters of grave deliberation and discussion among them. The movement had more of a spontaneous character, and was at once and rather impulsively approved as soon as suggested. But these were the silent meditations and reflections, which were working in each individual breast, so that it needed but that the proper chord should be touched, under the circumstances, and their hearts all vibrated together: the matter needed but a proposal to meet the approbation of all. It should also be remarked that the idea of reformation had been suggested among them at a former meeting, but no conclusion had been arrived at, as to either the certainty or the manner of the accomplishment of their purpose.

And now the deed was done. A constitution was agreed upon; and as the movement was a great and important one, a great name was proposed to be affixed as the title of the society. It was adopted. And this was the foundation of the Washington Temperance Society of Baltimore.

From the character of the deed itself, and the extraordinary results, which have proceeded and are yet proceeding from it, justice requires that the names of the founders of this association should be recorded, that they may be handed down in all the future annals of the Temperance cause. William K. Mitchell, John F. Loss, David Anderson, George Stears, Archibald Campbell and James McCurley were the "original six," who founded the Washington Temperance Society of Baltimore, and of course the originators of that new system of Temperance operations, which has of late attracted the attention of the country.

Previous to the evening on which the society was formed, we have intimated that the subject of reformation had been in contemplation among them for several days. When the adoption of a society and pledge was proposed, several difficulties were in the way of their successful organization. These difficulties were mainly the apprehensions of evil influences being introduced into the action of the society, to divert them from their simple purpose, if, as might be, the society should ever become efficient and numerous. Upon suggestion therefore it was resolved among themselves, that they would place the temperance cause, so far as they were concerned, in the position of a unit: that the society, as such, was to recognize no creed of religion, nor party in politics; and that neither political nor religious action of any kind, should ever be introduced into the society's operations. Personal abstinence from all intoxicating drinks was to be the basis, and only requisite of membership. Moral suasion was to be the only means by which they, as a body, were to induce others to adopt their principles. As a society, their whole business was to induce others not to drink intoxicating liquors. They would thus be less likely to excite the suspicions or prejudices of any class of men, and have free access to all; this would render Temperance a simple principle of personal abstinence. It would be, in the language of Father Matthew, "a green spot in the desert of life, where all could meet in peace and harmony."

Moreover they determined that the regular meetings of the society should be meetings for the detail of personal experience, and not for debates, lectures and speeches; that even on matters of necessary business, as few remarks as possible only would be tolerated. Thus all temperance addresses were to be in the form of the individual experience of the several members. The spirit of this rule and common sense were to guide them how far any should be allowed to go in his remarks. The society was thus based on facts, and not on an abstraction, and the principle of common honesty was to direct them in all their movements.

These difficulties being out of the way—the society being now organized, and the constitution and pledge adopted and signed, the founders resolved to hold weekly experience meetings for their own encouragement and benefit, and for the good of others who might be induced to attend.

CHAPTER II

Progress and Influence of the Society

Immediately after the organization of the society, the several members went privately to their friends, especially their former drinking associates, and persuaded them in the spirit of kindness, to abandon strong drink, and join the society. To every excuse and plea that they could not reform, they would reply by referring to their own experience. And they generally clung to a man until they had persuaded him to give up the bottle forever, or at least to go with them to the next meeting of their society. When such was the condition or promise, true to his man, each member on the evening of meeting, instead of going alone and waiting for his friend, would go to his house, or to the Grogshop, and, if necessary, lead him by the arm away from the bar, and conduct him in person to the meeting. This has often been done. When the individual was once within their hall, they regarded him as a easy convert. The experience of others who had been like him, and the good influences set to work upon him, soon led him to feel, think and act aright. Such exertions, judiciously made in the spirit of kindness, have rarely failed of entire success.

In the course of some months, the society gradually increased in numbers and interest.

The aggressive principle, or missionary spirit, once at work, grew and spread with the growth and extension of the society. In the meantime, the members had the benefit of several months' experience in the use of cold water. They began to feel better, to look better, and in every respect to be satisfied with the change in their habits. As some of them expressed it: "They were just waking up from a long sleep of many years, and now only beginning to live." The "experiences" of the members were now more and more interesting, and began to attract somewhat the attention of the public; and through their influence many of the most desperate and hopeless subjects of intemperance were redeemed. By the truly Samaritan conduct of these sacrificing men, many a poor inebriate, whose friends had long given him over as beyond the reach of hope, was rescued from his chains, and elevated from the depths of degradation, to which strong drink had reduced him. Each of these was not only a new experience man, but virtually another missionary.

In six months after its formation, the society numbered eighty or ninety, many of whom were reformed drunkards. And no man could attend their meetings, as the author then first did without seeing that there was a spirit among them which would not die—a principle which would diffuse itself abroad in the community, and pour the richest blessings on the heads of many a family in Baltimore;—and even spread to the farthest borders of the land. As yet, however, their meetings were held in their own private hall, which they had rented for the purpose. The citizens did not generally know of the movement; and such as did, hardly had confidence in the permanency of the reformations.

In November, 1840, their first public meeting was held in the Masonic Hall, which was crowded on the occasion. As this was their first public effort however, and as the object was rather intended to be an introduction to the public, very little experience was given. In addition to these remarks made by gentlemen invited to address the meeting, the President simply stated the principles of the society, that they might be understood by the community. Not long after this another public meeting was called in one of the churches of the city, on which occasion several of the members of the society publicly told their tale of woe and warning, counsel and advice, and with thrilling effect. Numbers were induced to sign the pledge; many of them victims of intemperance. And in the bosom of the society they found a home, and friends to counsel and defend them.

Frequent public experience meetings now followed, and were continued week after week during the entire winter. Public attention was now fully arrested. The meetings, though held in the largest churches of the city, were crowded to excess. Every family that had a poor miserable inebriate connected with it, hailed with joy and hope the influence which this society was exerting in reforming the intemperate, and used every exertion to induce such persons to attend the meetings of the Washington Society, and sign the pledge. And many a good-hearted, yea, noble-hearted man, who had long found the chains of appetite galling to him, and had often wished and tried in vain to shake them off, now went to this society, signed the pledge, and found him-self a free man. Many reformed, whose friends and the community had long since given them over as irrecoverable,—many even from the lowest depths of disgrace and reproach. Some were almost literally dug up out of the earth,—who had not only been abandoned as beyond hope, but who had been forgotten by their early friends, or reckoned among the dead. Many such were brought out of their hiding-places, and to the surprise of their friends, soon after their reformation, they were found "clothed and in their right mind," and prepared to occupy that position in society, which they had forfeited only by dissipation. Insomuch that the society was familiarly known by the expressive title of the "Resurrection Society."

The society was now increasing in numbers so fast, that their regular place of meeting was becoming too small to accommodate them all. A division was contemplated. But it was at length resolved, the branches should be formed in the various sections of the city; this was accordingly done. In the meantime other societies began to spring up in the city, on the same general principles with the Washington; some auxiliary, and others independent. All of these societies under their present organization, (with two or three exceptions,) owe their origin directly or indirectly to the influence of the parent Washington Society, and have borrowed most of their features, as well as obtained most of their life from it. Many of these associations have been very prosperous, and have done incalculable good in reclaiming the intemperate, confirming the temperate, and advancing the common cause. If our assigned limits would allow, it would afford us pleasure to make honourable mention of some of these societies; but as it is, we can not go into any detail respecting them. We hail them as fellow-labourers in a common cause, take them by the hand, and bid them "God speed." We call upon them to rival us in good works, and in adhering to first principles,—and then our motto is: "We be brethren; let us not fall out by the way."

It should be observed that most of the Temperance societies, in existence in this city previous to the formation of the Washington, have either been remodeled or discontinued, and their places filled up by more energetic ones. Many of the societies admit only of grown men as members; but there are others connected with the various churches, or composed entirely of female or youth, where such may join as choose to do so. . . .

CONCLUSION

From the preceding pages we learn that the principal causes of the extraordinary influence of the Washington Temperance Society, are as follow:

1. The drunkard is now regarded in a new light by the Washingtonians. Instead of being considered a cruel monster—a loathsome brute—an object of ridicule, contempt and indignation, as formerly, we are now taught to look upon him as a brother—as more weak perhaps than wicked—as a slave to appetite, and debased by passion—yet still as a man, our own brother. Thus all the sympathies of the public are excited in his behalf.

2. The substitution of personal experience for addresses and lectures, has had the same effect of exciting the sympathy of the community in behalf of the intemperate. A reformed drunkard's experience touches a chord, that vibrates in every human breast. Moreover the drunkard when reformed best knows how to reach the drunkard's heart; for he best understands his feelings.

3. Another cause lies in the simplicity and unity of the pledge, requiring but one thing—personal abstinence. To this add the neutrality of the society, as we have explained it in the preceding pages, and the whole matter is explained on the common principles of human nature.

1. *How would you describe the original membership of the Washingtonian Society? Did their overall goal differ from that of the American Temperance Union?*
2. *What methods and techniques did the members of the Washingtonian Society employ to attract new members? How do you account for their success?*

11-6 A Lowell Mill Girl Tells her Story (1836)

Harriet Hanson Robinson worked in the textile mills of Lowell, Massachusetts from the age of ten in 1834 until 1848. Later, as the wife of a newspaper editor, Robinson wrote an account of her earlier life as female factory worker and a description of the strike of 1836. Deeply involved in the political culture of her time, Robinson explained some of the family dynamics involved, and portrayed women as active participants in their own lives.

Source: *Internet Modern History Sourcebook* http://www.fordham.edu/halsall/mod/robinson-lowell.html

In what follows, I shall confine myself to a description of factory life in Lowell, Massachusetts, from 1832 to 1848, since, with that phase of Early Factory Labor in New England, I am the most familiar—because I was a part of it.

In 1832, Lowell was little more than a factory village. Five "corporations" were started, and the cotton mills belonging to them were building. Help was in great demand and stories were told all over the country of the new factory place, and the high wages that were offered to all classes of workpeople; stories that reached the ears of mechanics' and farmers' sons and gave new life to lonely and dependent women in distant towns and farmhouses. . . . Troops of young girls came from different parts of New England, and from Canada, and men were employed to collect them at so much a head, and deliver them at the factories.

* * *

At the time the Lowell cotton mills were started the caste of the factory girl was the lowest among the employments of women. In England and in France, particularly, great injustice had been done to her real character. She was represented as subjected to influences that must destroy her purity and self-respect. In the eyes of her overseer she was but a brute, a slave, to be beaten, pinched and pushed about. It was to overcome this prejudice that such high wages had been offered to women that they might be induced to become mill girls, in spite of the opprobrium that still clung to this degrading occupation. . . .

The early mill girls were of different ages. Some were not over ten years old; a few were in middle life, but the majority were between the ages of sixteen and twenty-five. The very young girls were called "doffers." They "doffed," or took off, the full bobbins from the spinning frames, and replaced them with empty ones. These mites worked about fifteen minutes every hour and the rest of the time was their own. When the overseer was kind they were allowed to read, knit, or go outside the mill yard to play. They were paid two dollars a week. The working hours of all the girls extended from five o'clock in the morning until seven in the evening, with one half hour each, for breakfast and dinner. Even the doffers were forced to be on duty nearly fourteen hours a day. This was the greatest hardship in the lives of these children. Several years later a ten hour law was passed, but not until long after some of these little doffers were old enough to appear before the legislative committee on the subject, and plead, by their presence, for a reduction of the hours of labor.

Those of the mill girls who had homes generally worked from eight to ten months in the year; the rest of the time was spent with parents or friends. A few taught school during the summer months. Their life in the factory was made pleasant to them. In those days there was no need of advocating the doctrine of the proper relation between employer and employed. Help was too valuable to be ill-treated. . . .

* * *

The most prevailing incentive to labor was to secure the means of education for some male member of the family. To make a gentleman of a brother or a son, to give him a college education, was the dominant thought in the minds of a great many of the better class of mill girls. I have known more than one to give every cent of her wages, month after month, to her brother, that he might get the education necessary to enter some profession. I have known a mother to work years in this way for her boy. I have known women to educate young men by their earnings, who were not sons or relatives. There are many men now living who were helped to an education by the wages of the early mill girls.

It is well to digress here a little, and speak of the influence the possession of money had on the characters of some of these women. We can hardly realize what a change the cotton factory made in the status of the working women. Hitherto woman had always been a money saving rather than a money earning, member of the community. Her labor could command but small return. If she worked out as servant, or "help," her wages were from 50 cents to $1.00 a week; or, if she went from house to house by the day to spin and weave, or do tailoress work, she could get but 75 cents a week and her meals. As teacher, her services were not in demand, and the arts, the professions, and even the trades and industries, were nearly all closed to her.

As late as 1840 there were only seven vocations outside the home into which the women of New England had entered. At this time woman had no property rights. A widow could be left without her share of her husband's (or the family) property, an " encumbrance" to his estate. A father could make his will without reference to his daughter's share of the inheritance. He usually left her a home on the farm as long as she remained single. A woman was not supposed to be capable of spending her own, or of using other people's money. In Massachusetts, before 1840, a woman could not, legally, be treasurer of her own sewing society, unless some man were responsible for her. The law took no cognizance of woman as a money spender. She was a ward, an appendage, a relict. Thus it happened that if a woman did not choose to marry, or, when left a widow, to remarry, she had no choice but to enter one of the few employments open to her, or to become a burden on the charity of some relative.

* * *

One of the first strikes that ever took place in this country was in Lowell in 1836. When it was announced that the wages were to be cut down, great indignation was felt, and it was decided to strike or "turn out" en masse. This was done. The mills were shut down, and the girls went from their several corporations in procession to the grove on Chapel Hill, and listened to incendiary speeches from some early labor reformers.

One of the girls stood on a pump and gave vent to the feelings of her companions in a neat speech, declaring that it was their duty to resist all attempts at cutting down the wages. This was the first time a woman had spoken in public in Lowell, and the event caused surprise and consternation among her audience.

It is hardly necessary to say that, so far as practical results are concerned, this strike did no good. The corporation would not come to terms. The girls were soon tired of holding out, and they went back to their work at the reduced rate of wages. The ill-success of this early attempt at resistance on the part of the wage element seems to have made a precedent for the issue of many succeeding strikes.

1. *According to Harriet Hanson Robinson, what was one of the primary reasons why women worked in the mills?*
2. *Describe the life of a mill girl as depicted by Robinson. What is her assessment of the efficacy of the strike in 1836?*

11-7 "Petition of the Catholics of New York" (1840)

This document was a petition by a group of Catholics for New York's aldermen to provide funds for church sponsored schools to relieve the apprehension many of them had about a so-called Protestant Education, which they felt would undermine Catholic teachings and indoctrinate many young Catholics with a Protestant worldview.

The Petition of the Catholics of New York, Respectfully represents:

That your Petitioners yield to no class in their performance of, and disposition to perform all the duties of citizens.-They bear, and are willing to bear, their portion of every common burden; and feel themselves entitled to a participation in every common benefit.

This participation, they regret to say, has been denied them for years back, in reference to Common School Education in the city of New York, except on conditions with which their conscience, and, as they believe their duty to God, did not, and do not leave them at liberty to comply. . . .

Your Petitioners only claim the benefit of this principle in regard to the public education of their children. They regard the public education which the State has provided as a common benefit, in which they are most desirous and feel that they are entitled to participate; and therefore they pray your Honorable Body that they may be permitted to do so, without violating their conscience.

But your Petitioners do not ask that this prayer be granted without assigning their reasons for preferring it.

In ordinary cases men are not required to assign the motives of conscientious scruples in matters of this kind. But your petitioners are aware that a large, wealthy and concentrated influence is directed against their claim by the Corporation called the Public School Society. . . .

This Society, however, is composed of gentlemen of various sects, including even one or two Catholics. But they profess to exclude all sectarianism from their schools. If they do not exclude sectarianism, they are avowedly no more entitled to the school funds than your petitioners, or any other denomination of professing Christians. If they do, as they profess, exclude sectarianism, then your petitioners contend that they exclude Christianity-and leave to the advantage of infidelity the tendencies which are given to the minds of youth by the influence of this feature and pretension of their system.

If they could accomplish what they profess, other denominations would join your petitioners in remonstrating against their schools. But they do not accomplish it. Your petitioners will show your Honorable Body that they do admit what Catholics call sectarianism, (although others may call it only religion), in a great variety of ways. . . .

The Public School Society, in their report for the year 1832, page 10, describe the effect of these "early religious instructions," without, perhaps, intending to do so; but yet precisely as your petitioners have witnessed it, in such of their children as attended those schools. *"The age at which children are usually sent to school affords a much better opportunity to mould their minds to peculiar and exclusive forms of faith than any subsequent period of life."* In page 11, of the same report, they protest against the injustice of supporting "religion in any shape" by public money; as if the "early religious instruction" which they had themselves authorized in their schools, five years before, was not "religion in some shape," and was not supported by public taxation. They tell us again, in more guarded language, "The Trustees are deeply impressed with the importance of imbuing the youthful mind with religious impressions, and they have endeavored to attain this object, as far as the nature of the institution will admit." Report of 1837. . .

Even the reading of the Scriptures in those schools your petitioners cannot regard otherwise than as sectarian; because Protestants would certainly consider as such the introduction of the Catholic Scriptures, which are different from theirs, and the Catholics have the same ground of objection when the Protestant version is made use of.

Your petitioners have to state further, as grounds of their conscientious objections to those schools, that many of the selections in their elementary reading lessons contain matter prejudicial to the Catholic name and character. The term "POPERY" is repeatedly found in them. This term is known and employed as one of insult and contempt towards the Catholic religion, and it passes into the minds of children with the feeling of which it is the outward expression. Both the historical and religious portions of the reading lessons are selected from Protestant writers, whose prejudices against the Catholic religion render them unworthy of confidence in the mind of your petitioners, at least so far as their own children are concerned. . . .

For these reasons, and others of the same kind, your petitioners cannot, in conscience, and consistently with their sense of duty to God, and to their offspring, intrust the Public School Society with the office of giving "a right direction to the minds of their children." And yet this Society claims that office, and claims for the discharge of it the Common School Funds, to which your petitioners, in common with other citizens, are contributors. In so far as they are contributors, they are not only deprived to the damage and detriment of their religion, in the minds of their own children, and of the rising generation of the community at large. The contest is between the *guaranteed* rights, civil and religious, of the citizen on the one hand, and the pretensions of the Public School Society on the other; and whilst it has been silently going on for years, your petitioners would call the attention of your Honorable Body to its consequences on that class for whom the benefits of public education are most essential-the children of the poor.

This class (your petitioners speak only so far as relates to their own denomination), after a brief experience of the schools of the Public School Society, naturally and deservedly withdrew all confidence from it. Hence the establishment by your petitioners of schools for the education of the poor. The expense necessary for this, was a second taxation, required not by the laws of the land, but by the no less imperious demands of their conscience.

They were reduced to the alternative of seeing their children growing up in entire ignorance, or else taxing themselves anew for private schools, whilst the funds provided for education, and contributed in part by themselves, were given over to the Public School Society, and by them employed as has been stated above. . . .

Your petitioners have to deplore, as a consequence of this state of things, the ignorance and vice to which hundreds, nay thousands of their children are exposed. They have to regret, also, that the education which they can provide, under the disadvantages to which they have been subjected, is not as efficient as it should be. But should your Honorable Body be pleased to designate their schools as entitled to receive a just proportion of the public funds which belong to your petitioners in common with other citizens, their schools could be improved for those who attend, others now growing up in ignorance could be received, and the ends of the Legislature could be accomplished-a result which is manifestly hopeless under the present system.

1. *Examine and Identify the reasoning and evidence used by the petitioners to show that public schools do not in fact exclude sectarianism.*
2. *Identify and explain the goals of this petition.*

11-8 Ralph Waldo Emerson, "Self-Reliance" (1841)

Ralph Waldo Emerson was one of America's greatest philosophers. His rejection of organized religion if favor of "self reliance" Was embraced by many who became transcendentalists. Born into a long line of ministers, Emerson resigned from the pulpit because he could no longer give communion in good conscience. He became an essayist and a lecturer on the Lyceum circuit and his revolutionary addresses including The Divinity School Address, and The American Scholar sought to liberate Americans from European and orthodox influence. He was, however, best known as the "apostle of self-reliance" and his influence on rising generations can hardly be underestimated.

Whoso would be a man, must be a nonconformist. He who would gather immortal palms must not be hindered by the name of goodness, but must explore if it be goodness. Nothing is at last sacred but the integrity of your own mind. Absolve you to yourself, and you shall have the suffrage of the world. I remember an answer which when quite young I was prompted to make to a valued adviser who was wont to importune me with the dear old doctrines of the church. On my saying, "What have I to do with the sacredness of traditions, if I live wholly from within?" my friend suggested,-"But these impulses may be from below, not from above." I replied, "They do not seem to me to be such; but if I am the Devil's child, I will live then from the Devil." No law can be sacred to me but that of my nature. Good and bad are but names very readily transferable to that or this; the only right is what is after my constitution; the only wrong what is against it. A man is to carry himself in the presence of all opposition as if every thing were titular and ephemeral but he. I am ashamed to think how easily we capitulate to badges and names, to large societies and dead institutions. Every decent and well-spoken individual affects and sways me more than is right. I ought to go upright and vital, and speak the rude truth in all ways. If malice and vanity wear the coat of philanthropy, shall that pass? If an angry bigot assumes this bountiful cause of Abolition, and comes to me with his last news from Barbadoes, why should I not say to him, 'Go love thy infant; love thy wood-chopper; be good-natured and modest; have that grace; and never varnish your hard, uncharitable ambition with this incredible tenderness for black folk a thousand miles off. Thy love afar is spite at home.' Rough and graceless would be such greeting, but truth is handsomer than the affection of love. Your goodness must have some edge to it,-else it is none. The doctrine of hatred must be preached, as the counteraction of the doctrine of love, when that pules and whines. I shun father and mother and wife and brother when my genius calls me. I would write on the lintels of the door-post, *Whim*. I hope it is somewhat better than whim at last, but we cannot spend the day in explanation. Expect me not to show cause why I seek or why I exclude company. Then again, do not tell me, as a good man did to-day, of my obligation to put all poor men in good situations. Are they my poor? I tell thee, thou foolish philanthropist, that I grudge the dollar, the dime, the cent I give to such men as do not belong to me and to whom I do not belong. There is a class of persons to whom by all spiritual affinity I am bought and sold; for them I will go to prison if need be; but your miscellaneous popular charities; the education at college of fools; the building of meeting-houses to the vain end to which many now stand; alms to sots, and the thousand-fold Relief Societies;-though I confess with shame I sometimes succumb and give the dollar, it is a wicked dollar, which by and by I shall have the manhood to withhold. . . .

What I must do is all that concerns me, not what the people think. This rule, equally arduous in actual and in intellectual life, may serve for the whole distinction between greatness and meanness. It is the harder because you will always find those who think they know what is your duty better than you know it. It is easy in the world to live after the world's opinion; it is easy in solitude to live after our own; but the great man is he who in the midst of the crowd keeps with perfect sweetness the independence of solitude. . . .

A foolish consistency is the hobgoblin of little minds, adored by little statesmen and philosophers and divines. With consistency a great soul has simply nothing to do. He may as well concern himself with his shadow on the wall. Speak what you think now in hard words and to-morrow speak what to-morrow thinks in hard words again, though it contradict every thing you said to-day.-'Ah, so you shall be sure to be misunderstood.'-Is it so bad then to be misunderstood? Pythagoras was misunderstood, and Socrates, and Jesus, and Luther, and Copernicus, and Galileo, and Newton, and every pure and wise spirit that ever took flesh. To be great is to be misunderstood.

1. What does this excerpt suggest regarding the importance and sovereignty of the individual?
2. In what ways does this document propose modes of living quite different than what would be considered proper social behavior?

11-9 Ja Norcom, Letter to Mary Matilda Norcom (1846)

This letter from Mary Matilda Norcom's father urges her to settle on a man who could "support a family." As mentioned in the introduction to this chapter, Mary did not. Along with an increase in the responsibility placed on a man, who had to provide for his family in the antebellum period by working outside of the home, there was a new emphasis in the nineteenth century on the "affectionate" family-a husband and wife who married for love.

From Donald M. Scott and Bernard Wishy, *Americas Families, A Documentary History* (Chicago: Dorsey Press, 1988).

Edenton, N. C., 19 August 1846

My dear Daughter,

...You must remember, my daughter, what I have said to you, *on a certain subject*. I would not *acknowledge* myself to be *engaged*, affianced, to any man not in a condition to give me a comfortable & respectable support-to place me beyond the chance of want or poverty. I, my dear, could *never never* ratify such an engagement were you to make it. Everything, therefore, in relation to this matter must be *conditional*. It cannot be positive, for, however meritorious a man may be, & how high he might be in my opinion or esteem, I could not sanction his connexion with a daughter of mine, in the "Holy Estate" with the prospect of poverty & wretchedness before her.

Treat the man who honors you with his partiality & preference with candor, politeness-nay, with kindness, *but let him not hope,* if he is inconsiderate enough to wish it, to draw you into a situation in which you would be less comfortable than you are in your father's dwelling, or less comfortable than you could be among your friends, in your present condition. W-is a meritorious and respectable young man, an honour to his family, & worthy of general esteem; and had I a fortune, my daughter, to give you, or the means of making you independent, I see nothing in his character to object to. But his inability to support a family, *as long as it lasts,* is an insurmountable objection, & of the probability of its removal no correct opinion can *now* be formed. Time alone can instruct us on the subject. Pray be prudent, my daughter, and do nothing in your absence from us, that *you would not do in the presence of* your father,

Ja Norcom

1. Summarize and analyze the advice given from mother to daughter on the primary criterion to consider in making decisions regarding marriage.
2. What does this letter reveal about social and economic realities in the mid-nineteenth century?

11-10   Declaration of Sentiments and Resolutions, Woman's Rights Convention, Seneca Falls, New York (1848)

Organized by Lucretia Mott and Elizabeth Cady Stanton, the Seneca Falls Convention was the first national women's rights convention in the United States. This document, obviously modeled on the Declaration of Independence listed the ways in which women had been denied the basic rights inherent in the American idea. Though 40 men attended (including Fredrick Douglass) the convention blamed men for the unjust treatment of women and stated that women must earn independence for themselves. The meeting become the first of many and provided impetus for the burgeoning women' movement.

Source: E. C. Stanton, S. B. Anthony, and Matilda Joslyn Gage, eds., *History of Woman Suffrage*, vol. 1 (Rochester, NY: Charles Mann, 1881), pp. 70–72.

We hold these truths to be self-evident: that all men and women are created equal; that they are endowed by their Creator with certain inalienable rights; that among these are life, liberty, and the pursuit of happiness; that to secure these rights governments are instituted, deriving their just powers from the consent of the governed. . ... But when a long train of abuses and usurpations, pursuing invariably the same object evinces a design to reduce them under absolute despotism, it is their duty to throw off such government, and to provide new guards for their future security. Such has been the patient sufferance of the women under this government, and such is now the necessity which constrains them to demand the equal station to which they are entitled.

The history of mankind is a history of repeated injuries and usurpations on the part of man toward woman, having in direct object the establishment of an absolute tyranny over her. To prove this, let facts be submitted to a candid world.

He has never permitted her to exercise her inalienable right to the elective franchise.

He has compelled her to submit to laws, in the formation of which she had no voice.

He has withheld from her rights which are given to the most ignorant and degraded men—both natives and foreigners.

Having deprived her of this first right of a citizen, the elective franchise, thereby leaving her without representation in the halls of legislation, he has oppressed her on all sides.

He has made her, if married, in the eye of the law, civilly dead.

He has taken from her all right in property, even to the wages she earns.

He has made her, morally, an irresponsible being, as she can commit many crimes with impunity, provided they be done in the presence of her husband. In the covenant of marriage, she is compelled to promise obedience to her husband, he becoming, to all intents and purposes, her master—the law giving him power to deprive her of her liberty, and to administer chastisement.

He has so framed the laws of divorce, as to what shall be the proper causes, and in case of separation, to whom the guardianship of the children shall be given, as to be wholly regardless of the happiness of women—the law, in all cases, going upon a false supposition of the supremacy of man, and giving all power into his hands.

After depriving her of all rights as a married woman, if single, and the owner of property, he has taxed her to support a government which recognizes her only when her property can be made profitable to it.

He has monopolized nearly all the profitable employments, and from those she is permitted to follow, she receives but a scanty remuneration. He closes against her all the avenues to wealth and distinction which he considers most honorable to himself. As a teacher of theology, medicine, or law, she is not known.

He has denied her the facilities for obtaining a thorough education, all colleges being closed against her.

He allows her in Church, as well as State, but a subordinate position, claiming Apostolic authority for her exclusion from the ministry, and, with some exceptions, from any public participation in the affairs of the Church.

He has created a false public sentiment by giving to the world a different code of morals for men and women, by which moral delinquencies which exclude women from society, are not only tolerated, but deemed of little account in man.

He has usurped the prerogative of Jehovah himself, claiming it as his right to assign for her a sphere of action, when that belongs to her conscience and to her God.

He has endeavored, in every way that he could, to destroy her confidence in her own powers, to lessen her self-respect, and to make her willing to lead a dependent and abject life.

Now, in view of this entire disfranchisement of one-half the people of this country, their social and religious degradation—in view of the unjust laws above mentioned, and because women do feel themselves aggrieved, oppressed, and fraudulently deprived of their most sacred rights, we insist that they have immediate admission to all the rights and privileges which belong to them as citizens of the United States.

In entering upon the great work before us, we anticipate no small amount of misconception, misrepresentation, and ridicule; but we shall use every instrumentality within our power to effect our object. We shall employ agents, circulate tracts, petition the State and National legislatures, and endeavor to enlist the pulpit and the press in our behalf. We hope this Convention will be followed by a series of Conventions embracing every part of the country.

The following resolutions were adopted:

Resolved, That such laws as conflict, in any way, with the true and substantial happiness of woman, are contrary to the great precept of nature and of no validity, for this is "superior in obligation to any other."

Resolved, That all laws which prevent woman from occupying such a station in society as her conscience shall dictate, or which place her in a position inferior to that of man, are contrary to the great precept of nature, and therefore of no force or authority.

Resolved, That woman is man's equal—was intended to be so by the Creator, and the highest good of the race demands that she should be recognized as such.

Resolved, That the women of this country ought to be enlightened in regard to the laws under which they live, that they may no longer publish their degradation by declaring themselves satisfied with their present position, nor their ignorance, by asserting that they have all the rights they want.

Resolved, That inasmuch as man, while claiming for himself intellectual superiority, does accord to woman moral superiority, it is pre-eminently his duty to encourage her to speak and teach, as she has an opportunity, in all religious assemblies.

Resolved, That the same amount of virtue, delicacy, and refinement of behavior that is required of woman in the social state, should also be required of man, and the same transgressions should be visited with equal severity on both man and woman.

Resolved, That the objection of indelicacy and impropriety, which is so often brought against woman when she addresses a public audience, comes with a very ill-grace from those who encourage, by their attendance, her appearance on the stage, in the concert, or in feats of the circus.

Resolved, That woman has too long rested satisfied in the circumscribed limits which corrupt customs and a perverted application of the Scriptures have marked out for her, and that it is time she should move in the enlarged sphere which her great Creator has assigned her.

Resolved, That it is the duty of the women of this country to secure to themselves their sacred right to the elective franchise.

Resolved, That the equality of human rights results necessarily from the fact of the identity of the race in capabilities and responsibilities.

Resolved, therefore, That, being invested by the Creator with the same capabilities, and the same consciousness of responsibility for their exercise, it is demonstrably the right and duty of woman, equally with man, to promote every righteous cause by every righteous means; and especially in regard to the great subjects of morals and religion, it is self-evidently her right to participate with her brother in teaching them, both in private and in public, by writing and by speaking, by any instrumentalities proper to be used, and in any assemblies proper to be held; and this being a self-evident truth growing out of the divinely implanted principles of human nature, any custom or authority adverse to it, whether modern or wearing the hoary sanction of antiquity, is to be regarded as a self-evident falsehood, and at war with mankind.

Resolved, That the speedy success of our cause depends upon the zealous and untiring efforts of both men and women, for the overthrow of the monopoly of the pulpit, and for the securing to woman an equal participation with men in the various trades, professions, and commerce.

1. In the "Resolutions" at the end of the document, how does Lucretia Mott attempt to persuade men to agree to equal rights for women?

2. 2. Even though the women's rights movement followed closely on the heels of abolitionism, slaves gained emancipation over fifty years before women won the right to vote in national elections. Why do you think this was the case?

11-11 Horace Mann on Education and National Welfare

In 1837, Horace Mann accepted the position of First Secretary of the State Board of Education in Massachusetts, the first of its kind in the nation, and inaugurated a new era in the history of American education. Over a period of twelve years, Mann transformed the state's assortment of common schools into a system of free public schools, organized on sound educational principles. He also sponsored the first state-supported "normal school" for the training of teachers, a state teachers' association, and a minimum school year of six months. In his twelve annual reports to the board, Mann discussed the larger implications of education in a democracy. His Twelfth Annual Report, included here, expounds a rationale for the support of public education through taxation.

Source: United States Department of State, International Information Programs
http://usinfo.state.gov/usa/infousa/facts/democrac/16.htm

Under the Providence of God, our means of education are the grand machinery by which the "raw material" of human nature can be worked up into inventors and discoverers, into skilled artisans and scientific farmers, into scholars and jurists, into the founders of benevolent institutions, and the great expounders of ethical and theological science. By means of early education, these embryos of talent may be quickened, which will solve the difficult problems of political and economical law; and by them, too, the genius may be kindled which will blaze forth in the Poets of Humanity. Our schools, far more than they have done, may supply the Presidents and Professors of Colleges, and Superintendents of Public Instruction, all over the land; and send, not only into our sister states, but across the Atlantic, the men of practical science, to superintend the construction of the great works of art. Here, too, may those judicial powers be developed and invigorated, which will make legal principles so clear and convincing as to prevent appeals to force; and, should the clouds of war ever lower over our country, some hero may be found,—the nursling of our schools, and ready to become the leader of our armies,—that best of all heroes, who will secure the glories of a peace, unstained by the magnificent murders of the battle-field. . . .

Without undervaluing any other human agency, it may be safely affirmed that the Common School, improved and energized, as it can easily be, may become the most effective and benignant of all the forces of civilization. Two reasons sustain this position. In the first place, there is a universality in its operation, which can be affirmed of no other institution whatever. If administered in the spirit of justice and conciliation, all the rising generation may be brought within the circle of its reformatory and elevating influences. And, in the second place, the materials upon which it operates are so pliant and ductile as to be susceptible of assuming a greater variety of forms than any other earthly work of the Creator. The inflexibility and ruggedness of the oak, when compared with the lithe sapling or the tender germ, are but feeble emblems to typify the docility of childhood, when contrasted with the obduracy and intractableness of man. It is these inherent advantages of the Common School, which, in our own State, have produced results so striking, from a system so imperfect, and an administration so feeble. In teaching the blind, and the deaf and dumb, in kindling the latent spark of intelligence that lurks in an idiot's mind, and in the more holy work of reforming abandoned and outcast children, education has proved what it can do, by glorious experiments. These wonders, it has done in its infancy, and with the lights of a limited experience; but, when its faculties shall be fully developed, when it shall be trained to wield its mighty energies for the protection of society against the giant vices which now invade and torment it;—against intemperance, avarice, war, slavery, bigotry, the woes of want and the wickedness of waste,—then, there will not be a height to which these enemies of the race can escape, which it will not scale, nor a Titan among them all, whom it will not slay.

Now I proceed, then, in endeavoring to show how the true business of the schoolroom connects itself, and becomes identical, with the great interests of society. The former is the infant, immature state of those interests; the latter, their developed, adult state. As "the child is father to the man," so may the training of the schoolroom expand into the institutions and fortunes of the State. . . .

INTELLECTUAL EDUCATION, AS A MEANS OF REMOVING POVERTY, AND SECURING ABUNDANCE

Another cardinal object which the government of Massachusetts, and all the influential men in the State should propose to themselves, is the physical well-being of all the people,—the sufficiency, comfort, competence, of every individual, in regard to food, raiment, and shelter. And these necessaries and conveniences of life should be obtained by each individual for himself, or by each family for themselves, rather than accepted from the hand of charity, or extorted by poor-laws. It is not averred that this most desirable result can, in all instances, be obtained; but it is, nevertheless, the end to be aimed at. True statesmanship and true political economy, not less than true philanthropy, present this perfect theory as the goal, to be more and more closely approximated by our imperfect practice. The desire to achieve such a result cannot be regarded as an unreasonable ambition; for, though all mankind were well-fed, well-clothed, and well-housed, they might still be but half-civilized. . . .

According to the European theory, men are divided into classes,—some to toil and earn, others to seize and enjoy. According to the Massachusetts theory, all are to have an equal chance for earning, and equal security in the enjoyment of what they earn. The latter tends to equality of condition; the former to the grossest inequalities. Tried by any Christian standard of morals, or even by any of the better sort of heathen standards, can any one hesitate, for a moment, in declaring which of the two will produce the greater amount of human welfare; and which, therefore, is the more conformable to the Divine will? The European theory is blind to what constitutes the highest glory, as well as the highest duty, of a State. . . .

I suppose it to be the universal sentiment of all those who mingle any ingredient of benevolence with their notions on Political Economy, that vast and overshadowing private fortunes are among the greatest dangers to which the happiness of the people in a republic can be subjected. Such fortunes would create a feudalism of a new kind; but one more oppressive and unrelenting than that of the Middle Ages. The feudal lords in England, and on the continent, never held their retainers in a more abject condition of servitude, than the great majority of foreign manufacturers and capitalists hold their operatives and laborers at the present day. The means employed are different, but the similarity in results is striking. What force did then, money does now. The villein of the Middle Ages had no spot of earth on which he could live, unless one were granted to him by his lord. The operative or laborer of the present day has no employment, and therefore no bread, unless the capitalist will accept his services. The vassal had no shelter but such as his master provided for him. Not one in five thousand of English operatives, or farm laborers, is able to build or own even a hovel; and therefore they must accept such shelter as Capital offers them. The baron prescribed his own terms to his retainers; those terms were peremptory, and the serf must submit or perish. The British manufacturer or farmer prescribes the rate of wages he will give to his work-people; he reduces these wages under whatever pretext he pleases; and they too have no alternative but submission or starvation. In some respects, indeed, the condition of the modern dependant is more forlorn than that of the corresponding serf class in former times. Some attributes of the patriarchal relation did spring up between the lord and his lieges, to soften the harsh relations subsisting between them. Hence came some oversight of the condition of children, some relief in sickness, some protection and support in the decrepitude of age. But only in instances comparatively few, have kindly offices smoothed the rugged relation between British Capital and British Labor. The children of the work-people are abandoned to their fate; and, notwithstanding the privations they suffer, and the dangers they threaten, no power in the realm has yet been able to secure them an education; and when the adult laborer is prostrated by sickness, or eventually worn out by toil and age, the poor-house, which has all along been his destination, becomes his destiny.

Now two or three things will doubtless be admitted to be true, beyond all controversy, in regard to Massachusetts. By its industrial condition, and its business operations, it is exposed, far beyond any other state in the Union, to the fatal extremes of overgrown wealth and desperate poverty. Its population is more dense than that of any other state. It is four or five times more dense than the average of all the other states, taken together; and density of population has always been one of the proximate causes of social inequality. According to population and territorial extent, there is far more capital in Massachusetts,—capital which is movable, and instantaneously available,—than in any other state in the Union; and probably both these qualifications respecting population and territory could be omitted without endangering the truth of the assertion. It has been recently stated, in a very respectable public journal, on the authority of a writer conversant with the subject, that, from the last of June, 1846, to the 1st of August, 1848, the amount of money invested, by the citizens of Massachusetts, "in manufacturing cities, railroads, and other improvements," is "fifty-seven millions of dollars, of which more than fifty has been paid in and expended." The dividends to be received by the citizens of Massachusetts from June, 1848, to April, 1849, are estimated, by the same writer, at ten millions, and the annual increase of capital at "little short of twenty-two millions." If this be so, are we not in danger of naturalizing and domesticating among ourselves those hideous evils which are always engendered between Capital and Labor, when all the capital is in the hands of one class, and all the labor is thrown upon another?

Now, surely, nothing but Universal Education can counter-work this tendency to the domination of capital and the servility of labor. If one class possesses all the wealth and the education, while the residue of society is ignorant and poor, it matters not by what name the relation between them may be called; the latter, in fact and in truth, will be the servile dependents and subjects of the former. But if education be equally diffused, it will draw property after it, by the strongest of all attractions; for such a thing never did happen, and never can happen, as that an intelligent and practical body of men should be permanently poor. Property and labor, in different classes, are essentially antagonistic; but property and labor, in the same class, are essentially fraternal. The people of Massachusetts have, in some degree, appreciated the truth, that the unexampled prosperity of the State,—its comfort, its competence, its general intelligence and virtue,—is attributable to the education, more or less perfect, which all its people have received; but are they sensible of a fact equally important?—namely, that it is to this same education that two thirds of the people are indebted for not being, to-day, the vassals of as severe a tyranny, in the form of capital, as the lower classes of Europe are bound to in the form of brute force.

Education, then, beyond all other devices of human origin, is the great equalizer of the conditions of men—the balance-wheel of the social machinery. I do not here mean that it so elevates the moral nature as to make men disdain and abhor the oppression of their fellow-men. This idea pertains to another of its attributes. But I mean that it gives each man the independence and the means, by which he can resist the selfishness of other men. It does better than to disarm the poor of their hostility towards the rich; it prevents being poor. Agrarianism is the revenge of poverty against wealth. The wanton destruction of the property of others,—the burning of hay-ricks and corn-ricks, the demolition of machinery, because it supersedes hand-labor, the sprinkling of vitriol on rich dresses,—is only agrarianism run mad. Education prevents both the revenge and the madness. On the other hand, a fellow-feeling for one's class or caste is the common instinct of hearts not wholly sunk in selfish regards for person, or for family. The spread of education, by enlarging the cultivated class or caste, will open a wider area over which the social feelings will expand; and, if this education should be universal and complete, it would do more than all things else to obliterate factitious distinctions in society.

The main idea set forth in the creeds of some political reformers, or revolutionizers, is that some people are poor because others are rich. This idea supposes a fixed amount of property in the community, which, by fraud or force, or arbitrary law, is unequally divided among men; and the problem presented for solution is, how to transfer a portion of this property from those who are supposed to have too much, to those who feel and know that they have too little. At this point, both their theory and their expectation of reform stop. But the beneficent power of education would not be exhausted, even though it should peaceably abolish all the miseries that spring from the coexistence, side by side, of enormous wealth and squalid want. It has a higher function. Beyond the power of diffusing old wealth, it has the prerogative of creating new. It is a thousand times more lucrative than fraud; and adds a thousandfold more to a nation's resources than the most successful conquests. Knaves and robbers can obtain only what was before possessed by others. But education creates or develops new treasures,—treasures not before possessed or dreamed of by any one. . . .

If a savage will learn how to swim, he can fasten a dozen pounds' weight to his back, and transport it across a narrow river, or other body of water of moderate width. If he will invent an axe, or other instrument, by which to cut down a tree, he can use the tree for a float, and one of its limbs for a paddle, and can thus transport many times the former weight, many times the former distance. Hollowing out his log, he will increase, what may be called, its tonnage,—or, rather, its poundage,—and, by sharpening its ends, it will cleave the water both more easily and more swiftly. Fastening several trees together, he makes a raft, and thus increases the buoyant power of his embryo water-craft. Turning up the ends of small poles, or using knees of timber instead of straight pieces, and grooving them together, or filling up the interstices between them, in some other way, so as to make them water-tight, he brings his rude raft literally into ship-shape. Improving upon hull below and rigging above, he makes a proud merchantman, to be wafted by the winds from continent to continent. But, even this does not content the adventurous naval architect. He frames iron arms for his ship; and, for oars, affixes iron wheels, capable of swift revolution, and stronger than the strong sea. Into iron-walled cavities in her bosom, he puts iron organs of massive structure and strength, and of cohesion insoluble by fire. Within these, he kindles a small volcano; and then, like a sentient and rational existence, this wonderful creation of his hands cleaves oceans, breasts tides, defies tempests, and bears its living and jubilant freight around the globe. Now, take away intelligence from the ship-builder, and the steamship,—that miracle of human art,—falls back into a floating log; the log itself is lost; and the savage swimmer, bearing his dozen pounds on his back, alone remains.

And so it is, not in one department only, but in the whole circle of human labors. The annihilation of the sun would no more certainly be followed by darkness, than the extinction of human intelligence would plunge the race at once into the weakness and helplessness of barbarism. To have created such beings as we are, and to have placed them in this world, without the light of the sun, would be no more cruel than for a government to suffer its laboring classes to grow up without knowledge. . .

For the creation of wealth, then,—for the existence of a wealthy people and a wealthy nation,—intelligence is the grand condition. The number of improvers will increase, as the intellectual constituency, if I may so call it, increases. In former times, and in most parts of the world even at the present day, not one man in a million has ever had such a development of mind, as made it possible for him to become a contributor to art or science. Let this development precede, and contributions, numberless, and of inestimable value, will be sure to follow. That Political Economy, therefore, which busies itself about capital and labor, supply and demand, interest and rents, favorable and unfavorable balances of trade; but leaves out of account the element of a wide-spread mental development, is nought but stupendous folly. The greatest of all the arts in political economy is, to change a consumer into a producer; and the next greatest is to increase the producer's producing power;—an end to be directly attained, by increasing his intelligence. . .

POLITICAL EDUCATION

The necessity of general intelligence,—that is, of education, (for I use the terms as substantially synonymous; because general intelligence can never exist without general education, and general education will be sure to produce general intelligence,)—the necessity of general intelligence, under a republican form of government, like most other very important truths, has become a very trite one. It is so trite, indeed, as to have lost much of its force by its familiarity. Almost all the champions of education seize upon this argument, first of all; because it is so simple as to be understood by the ignorant, and so strong as to convince the skeptical. Nothing would be easier than to follow in the train of so many writers, and to demonstrate, by logic, by history, and by the nature of the case, that a republican form of government, without intelligence in the people, must be, on a vast scale, what a mad-house, without superintendent or keepers, would be, on a small one;—the despotism of a few succeeded by universal anarchy, and anarchy by despotism, with no change but from bad to worse. Want of space and time alike forbid me to attempt any full development of the merits of this theme; but yet, in the closing one of a series of reports, partaking somewhat of the nature of a summary of former arguments, an omission of this topic would suggest to the comprehensive mind the idea of incompleteness.

That the affairs of a great nation or state are exceedingly complicated and momentous, no one will dispute. Nor will it be questioned that the degree of intelligence that superintends, should be proportioned to the magnitude of the interests superintended. He who scoops out a wooden dish needs less skill than the maker of a steam-engine or a telescope. The dealer in small wares requires less knowledge than the merchant who exports and imports to and from all quarters of the globe. An ambassador cannot execute his functions with the stock of attainments or of talents sufficient for a parish clerk. Indeed, it is clear, that the want of adequate intelligence,—of intelligence commensurate with the nature of the duties to be performed,—will bring ruin or disaster upon any department. A merchant loses his intelligence, and he becomes a bankrupt. A lawyer loses his intelligence, and he forfeits all the interests of his clients. Intelligence abandons a physician, and his patients die, with more than the pains of natural dissolution. Should judges upon the bench be bereft of this guide, what havoc would be made of the property and the innocence of men! Let this counsellor be taken from executive officers, and the penalties due to the wicked would be visited upon the righteous, while the rewards and immunities of the righteous would be bestowed upon the guilty. And so, should intelligence desert the halls of legislation, weakness, rashness, contradiction, and error would glare out from every page of the statute book. Now, as a republican government represents almost all interests, whether social, civil or military, the necessity of a degree of intelligence adequate to the due administration of them all, is so self-evident, that a bare statement is the best argument.

But in the possession of this attribute of intelligence, elective legislators will never far surpass their electors. By a natural law, like that which regulates the equilibrium of fluids, elector and elected, appointer and appointee, tend to the same level. It is not more certain that a wise and enlightened constituency will refuse to invest a reckless and profligate man with office, or discard him if accidentally chosen, than it is that a foolish or immoral constituency will discard or eject a wise man. This law of assimilation, between the choosers and the chosen, results, not only from the fact that the voter originally selects his representative according to the affinities of good or of ill, of wisdom or of folly, which exist between them; but if the legislator enacts or favors a law which is too wise for the constituent to understand, or too just for him to approve, the next election will set him aside as certainly as if he had made open merchandise of the dearest interests of the people, by perjury and for a bribe. And if the infinitely Just and Good, in giving laws to the Jews, recognized the "hardness of their hearts," how much more will an earthly ruler recognize the baseness or wickedness of the people, when his heart is as hard as theirs! In a republican government, legislators are a mirror reflecting the moral countenance of their constituents. And hence it is, that the establishment of a republican government, without well-appointed and efficient means for the universal education of the people, is the most rash and fool-hardy experiment ever tried by man. Its fatal results may not be immediately developed,—they may not follow as the thunder follows the lightning,—for time is an element in maturing them, and the calamity is too great to be prepared in a day; but, like the slow-accumulating avalanche, they will grow more terrific by delay, and, at length, though it may be at a late hour, will overwhelm with ruin whatever lies athwart their path. It may be an easy thing to make a Republic; but it is a very laborious thing to make Republicans; and woe to the republic that rests upon no better foundations than ignorance, selfishness, and passion. Such a Republic may grow in numbers and in wealth. As an avaricious man adds acres to his lands, so its rapacious government may increase its own darkness by annexing provinces and states to its ignorant domain. Its armies may be invincible, and its fleets may strike terror into nations on the opposite sides of the globe, at the same hour. Vast in its extent, and enriched with all the prodigality of nature, it may possess every capacity and opportunity of being great, and of doing good. But if such a Republic be devoid of intelligence, it will only the more closely resemble an obscene giant who has waxed strong in his youth, and grown wanton in his strength; whose brain has been developed only in the region of the appetites and passions, and not in the organs of reason and conscience; and who, therefore, is boastful of his bulk alone, and glories in the weight of his heel and in the destruction of his arm. Such a Republic, with all its noble capacities for beneficence, will rush with the speed of a whirlwind to an ignominious end; and all good men of after-times would be fain to weep over its downfall, did not their scorn and contempt at its folly and its wickedness, repress all sorrow for its fate. . . .

However elevated the moral character of a constituency may be; however well informed in matters of general science or history, yet they must, if citizens of a Republic, understand something of the true nature and functions of the government under which they live. That any one who is to participate in the government of a country, when he becomes a man, should receive no instruction respecting the nature and functions of the government he is afterwards to administer, is a political solecism. In all nations, hardly excepting the most rude and barbarous, the future sovereign receives some training which is supposed to fit him for the exercise of the powers and duties of his anticipated station. Where, by force of law, the government devolves upon the heir, while yet in a state of legal infancy, some regency, or other substitute, is appointed, to act in his stead, until his arrival at mature age; and, in the meantime, he is subjected to such a course of study and discipline, as will tend to prepare him, according to the political theory of the time and the place, to assume the reins of authority at the appointed age. If, in England, or in the most enlightened European monarchies, it would be a proof of restored barbarism, to permit the future sovereign to grow up without any knowledge of his duties,—and who can doubt that it would be such a proof,—then, surely, it would be not less a proof of restored, or of never-removed barbarism, amongst us, to empower any individual to use the elective franchise, without preparing him for so momentous a trust. Hence, the constitution of the United States, and of our own State, should be made a study in our Public Schools. The partition of the powers of government into the three co-ordinate branches,—legislative, judicial, and executive,—with the duties appropriately devolving upon each; the mode of electing or of appointing all officers, with the reason on which it was founded; and, especially, the duty of every citizen, in a government of laws, to appeal to the courts for redress, in all cases of alleged wrong, instead of undertaking to vindicate his own rights by his own arm; and, in a government where the people are the acknowledged sources of power, the duty of changing laws and rulers by an appeal to the ballot, and not by rebellion, should be taught to all the children until they are fully understood.

Had the obligations of the future citizen been sedulously inculcated upon all the children of this Republic, would the patriot have had to mourn over so many instances, where the voter, not being able to accomplish his purpose by voting, has proceeded to accomplish it by violence; where, agreeing with his fellow-citizens, to use the machinery of the ballot, he makes a tacit reservation, that, if that machinery does not move according to his pleasure, he will wrest or break it? If the responsibleness and value of the elective franchise were duly appreciated, the day of our State and National elections would be among the most solemn and religious days in the calendar. Men would approach them, not only with preparation and solicitude, but with the sobriety and solemnity, with which discreet and religious-minded men meet the great crises of life. No man would throw away his vote, through caprice or wantonness, any more than he would throw away his estate, or sell his family into bondage. No man would cast his vote through malice or revenge, any more than a good surgeon would amputate a limb, or a good navigator sail through perilous straits, under the same criminal passions.

But, perhaps, it will be objected, that the constitution is subject to different readings, or that the policy of different administrations has become the subject of party strife; and, therefore, if any thing of constitutional or political law is introduced into our schools, there is danger that teachers will be chosen on account of their affinities to this or that political party; or that teachers will feign affinities which they do not feel, in order that they may be chosen; and so each school-room will at length become a miniature political club-room, exploding with political resolves, or flaming out with political addresses, prepared, by beardless boys, in scarcely legible hand-writing, and in worse grammar.

With the most limited exercise of discretion, all apprehensions of this kind are wholly groundless. There are different readings of the constitution, it is true; and there are partisan topics which agitate the country from side to side; but the controverted points, compared with those about which there is no dispute, do not bear the proportion of one to a hundred. And what is more, no man is qualified, or can be qualified, to discuss the disputable questions, unless previously and thoroughly versed in those questions, about which there is no dispute. In the terms and principles common to all, and recognized by all, is to be found the only common medium of language and of idea, by which the parties can become intelligible to each other; and there, too, is the only common ground, whence the arguments of the disputants can be drawn.

It is obvious, on the other hand, that if the tempest of political strife were to be let loose upon our Common Schools, they would be overwhelmed with sudden ruin. Let it be once understood, that the schoolroom is a legitimate theatre for party politics, and with what violence will hostile partisans struggle to gain possession of the stage, and to play their parts upon it! Nor will the stage be the only scene of gladiatorial contests. These will rage in all the avenues that lead to it. A preliminary advantage, indispensable to ultimate success, will be the appointment of a teacher of the true faith. As the great majority of the schools in the State are now organized, this can be done only by electing a prudential committee, who will make what he calls political soundness paramount to all other considerations of fitness. Thus, after petty skirmishings among neighbors, the fierce encounter will begin in the district's primary assembly,—in the schoolroom itself. This contest being over, the election of the superintending, or town's committee, must be determined in the same way, and this will bring together the combustibles of each district, to burn with an intenser and a more devouring flame, in the town meeting. It is very possible, nay, not at all improbable, that the town may be of one political complexion, while a majority of the districts are of the opposite. Who shall moderate the fury of these conflicting elements, when they rage against each other; and who shall save the dearest interests of the children from being consumed in the fierce combustion? If parents find that their children are indoctrinated into what they call political heresies, will they not withdraw them from the school; and, if they withdraw them from the school, will they not resist all appropriations to support a school from which they derive no benefit?

But, could the schools, themselves, survive these dangers for a single year, it would be only to encounter others still more perilous. Why should not the same infection that poisons all the relations of the schoolroom, spread itself abroad, and mingle with all questions of external organization and arrangement? Why should not political hostility cause the dismemberment of districts, already too small; or, what would work equal injury, prevent the union of districts, whose power of usefulness would be doubled by a combination of their resources? What better could be expected, than that one set of school books should be expelled, and another introduced, as they might be supposed, however remotely, to favor one party or the other; or, as the authors of the books might belong to one party or the other? And who could rely upon the reports, or even the statistics of a committee, chosen by partisan votes, goaded on by partisan impulses, and responsible to partisan domination; and this, too, without any opportunity of control or check from the minority? Nay, if the schools could survive long enough to meet the crisis, why should not any and every measure be taken, either to maintain an existing political ascendancy, or to recover a lost one, in a school district, or in a town, which has even been taken by unscrupulous politicians, to maintain or to recover an ascendancy at the polls? Into a district, or into a town, voters may be introduced from abroad, to turn the scale. An employer may dismiss the employed, for their refusal to submit to his dictation; or make the bread that is given to the poor man's children, perform the double office of payment for labor to be performed, and of a bribe for principle to be surrendered. And, beyond all this, if the imagination can conceive any thing more deplorable than this, what kind of political doctrines would be administered to the children, amid the vicissitudes of party domination,—their alternations of triumph and defeat? This year, under the ascendancy of one side, the constitution declares one thing: and commentaries, glosses, and the authority of distinguished names, all ratify and confirm its decisions. But victory is a fickle goddess. Next year, the vanquished triumph; and constitution, gloss, and authority, make that sound doctrine, which was pestilent error before, and that false, which was true. Right and wrong have changed sides. The children must now join in chorus to denounce what they had been taught to reverence before, and to reverence what they had been taught to denounce. In the mean time, those great principles, which, according to Cicero, are the same at Rome and at Athens, the same now and forever;—and which, according to Hooker, have their seat in the bosom of God, become the fittest emblems of chance and change.

Long, however, before this series of calamities would exhaust itself upon our schools, these schools themselves would cease to be. The plough-share would have turned up their foundations. Their history would have been brought to a close,—a glorious and ascending history, until struck down by the hand of political parricide; then, suddenly falling with a double ruin,—with death, and with ignominy. But to avoid such a catastrophe, shall all teaching, relative to the nature of our government, be banished from our schools; and shall our children be permitted to grow up in entire ignorance of the political history of their country? In the schools of a republic, shall the children be left without any distinct knowledge of the nature of a republican government; or only with such knowledge as they may pick up from angry political discussions, or from party newspapers; from caucus speeches, or Fourth of July orations,—the Apocrypha of Apocrypha?

Surely, between these extremes, there must be a medium not difficult to be found. And is not this the middle course, which all sensible and judicious men, all patriots, and all genuine republicans, must approve?—namely, that those articles in the creed of republicanism, which are accepted by all, believed in by all, and which form the common basis of our political faith, shall be taught to all. But when the teacher, in the course of his lessons or lectures on the fundamental law, arrives at a controverted text, he is either to read it without comment or remark; or, at most, he is only to say that the passage is the subject of disputation, and that the schoolroom is neither the tribunal to adjudicate, nor the forum to discuss it.

Such being the rule established by common consent, and such the practice, observed with fidelity under it, it will come to be universally understood, that political proselytism is no function of the school; but that all indoctrination into matters of controversy between hostile political parties is to be elsewhere sought for, and elsewhere imparted. Thus, may all the children of the Commonwealth receive instruction in the great essentials of political knowledge,—in those elementary ideas without which they will never be able to investigate more recondite and debatable questions;—thus, will the only practicable method be adopted for discovering new truths, and for discarding,—instead of perpetuating,—old errors; and thus, too, will that pernicious race of intolerant zealots, whose whole faith may be summed up in two articles,—that they, themselves, are always infallibly right, and that all dissenters are certainly wrong,—be extinguished,—extinguished, not by violence, nor by proscription, but by the more copious inflowing of the light of truth.

1. *What does Horace Mann mean when he states that education is the "great equalizer of the conditions of men"?*
2. *According to Mann, what role does education play in the overall health of the Republic?*

11-12 John Humphrey Noyes and Bible Communism (1845 and 1849)

The most extreme examples of religious and reform movements were the planned "utopian" communities that emerged during this period. Shakers and transcendentalists and many others sought religious, social or political perfection in planned communities. John Humphrey Noyes, millenialist and believer in the perfection of the Christian upon conversion started, among others, the Putney Community where his particular ideas of mutual criticism, complex marriage and male continence were practiced. In 1848 after much criticism, he moved his community to Oneida, New York. Seen as a new Moses by his followers, Noyes believed that the second coming of Christ had occurred in 70 ad and that exclusive marriage was idolatrous. In this document Noyes compares his ideas to the theology of Finney and Beecher and advances his own ideas of millennialism and perfectionism.

John Humphrey Noyes, Speech to the Convention of Perfectionists (1845)

Dear Brethren:

As I am prevented from meeting with you in person I will place at your disposal a contribution to the deliberations of the convention in writing.

My attention has been turned of late to the symptoms of advancing conviction on the subject of holiness which are manifesting themselves in the churches, and I see much occasion for rejoicing and hope. . . . Charles G. Finney, the center of the revival spirit, was first affected and compelled to take an advanced position. He drew after him a large body of influential followers and a theological seminary. Now Dr. Beecher, the leader that stands next after Finney in spiritual power, has submitted partially to the truth; and he too draws after him a large body of influential followers and a theological seminary.

I am well aware that Finney and Beecher have not come in line with us and with the Primitive Church on the high grounds of the new covenant. Their advance is but half way; but no hope and expectation are that the work of conviction will forward to conversion.

Let us now ask ourselves, brethren, what line of conduct is marked out for us. I will briefly give my judgment on the question. In the first place I think we ought to feel that the post assigned to us is that of the body-guard of the gospel. We must stand firm for perfect freedom from sin, for security, and for confession. These are the essentials of the new covenant. If we steadfastly abide by the gospel which proclaims these victories of faith, the masses that have begun to move will sure come to it at last.

In the next place we must purge our own ranks of semi-Perfectionism. I have seen many indications within the last year, that there is a class bearing the name of Perfectionist claiming fellowship among us and even assuming to be inspired leaders and teachers, who exert their influence more or less openly and directly against justification, security and confession of salvation from sin. Such men have no right to a place among us. They are not with us in spirit, but with the half converted masses that are moving toward us. Let us draw the line between them and us, that we may fully discharge our responsibilities as God's banner-guard in the coming conflict.

Finally it behooves us to take away all stumbling-blocks from the path of those who are approaching the gospel; to put away childish things; to frown on disorder, fanaticism and licentiousness; to give place among us as fast as possible to the order and discipline of the Primitive Church.

In the Kingdom of God, marriage does not exist. On the other hand there is no proof in the Bible nor in reason that the distinction of sex will ever be abolished. Matt. 22:29-30.

John Humphrey Noyes, "Bible Communism" (1849)

In the Kingdom of God the intimate union that in the world is limited to the married pair extends through the whole body of communicants; without however excluding special companionships founded on special adaptability. John 17:21.

The situation on the day of Pentecost shows the practical tendency of heavenly influences. "All that believed were together, and had all things common; and sold their possessions and goods, and parted them to all, as every man had need."

Communism on the day of Pentecost extended only to goods, it is true. But the same spirit that abolished property in goods would, if allowed full scope, abolish property in persons. Paul expressly places property in goods and property in persons in the same category, and speaks of them together as ready to be abolished by the Kingdom of God.

The Communism of the day of Pentecost is not to be regarded as temporary and circumstantial. The seed of heavenly unity fell into the earth and was buried for a time, but in the harvest at the second coming of Christ it was reproduced and became the universal, eternal principle of the invisible church.

The abolishment of appropriation is involved in the very nature of a true relation to Christ. Appropriation is a branch of egotism. But the grand mystery of the gospel is vital union with Christ, which is the extinguishment of egotism at the center.

The abolishment of worldly restrictions on sexual union is involved in the anti-legality of the gospel. It is incompatible with the perfected freedom, toward which Paul's gospel of "grace without law" leads, that a person should be allowed to love in all directions, and yet be forbidden to express love except in one direction.

The abolishment of marriage is involved in Paul's doctrine of the end of ordinances. Marriage is a worldly ordinance. Christians are dead to the world by the death of Christ. The same reasoning which authorized the abolishment of the Jewish ordinances makes also an end of marriage. . . .

The plea that marriage is founded in nature will not bear investigation. Experience testifies that the human heart is capable of loving more than one at the same time. It is not the loving heart but the green-eyed claimant of the loving heart that sets up the one-love theory.

A system of Complex Marriage will open the prison doors to the victims both of marriage and celibacy: to the married who are oppressed by lust, tied to uncongenial nature separated from their natural mates; to the unmarried who are withered by neglect, diseased by unnatural abstinence, plunged into prostitution by desires that find no lawful outlet. . . .

The chain of evils which holds humanity in ruin has four links: first, a breach with God; second, a disruption of the sexes, involving a special curse on woman; third, oppressive labor, bearing specially on man; fourth, death. The chain of redemption begins with reconciliation with God, proceeds to a restoration of true relations between the sexes, then to a reform of the industrial system, and ends with victory over death.

It was the special function of the Apostolic Church to break up the worldly ecclesiastical system and reopen full communication with God. It is the special function of the present church, availing itself first of the work of the Apostolic Church by union with it and a re-development of its theology, to break up the worldly social system and establish true sexual and industrial relations.

From what precedes it is evident that no one should attempt to revolutionize sexual morality before settlement with God. Holiness, communism of love, association in labor, and immortality must come in their true order. . . .

Sexual shame is factitious and irrational. The more reform that arises from the sentiment of shame attempts hopeless war with nature. Its policy is to prevent pruriency keeping the mind in ignorance of sexual subjects, while nature is constantly thrusting those subjects upon the mind. The only way to elevate love is to clear away the false, debasing associations that usually crowd around it, and substitute true, beautiful ones.

The foregoing principles furnish motives for Association. They develop in a larger partnership the same attraction that draw and bind together a marriage partnership. A Community home, where love is honored and cultivated, will be much more attractive than an ordinary home as the Community outnumbers a pair. . . .

The men and women are called to usher in the Kingdom of God will be guided not merely by theoretical truth but by direct communication with the heavens, as were Abraham, Moses, David, Paul. This will be called a fanatical principle. But it is clearly a Bible principle, and we must place it on high above all others as the palladium of conservatism in the introduction of the new social order.

1. Summarize and explain Noyes' views regarding love and marriage?
2. How would Noyes' redefinition of human relations revolutionize society and industry in his opinion?

11-13   Sojourner Truth, Address to the Woman's Rights Convention, Akron, Ohio (1851)

Frances D. Gage, a pioneer in the Women's Rights Movement during the early nineteenth century, recorded her impressions of Sojourner Truth's speech at the Woman's Rights Convention in Akron, Ohio in 1851. Gage wrote this reminiscence some twelve years after the fact, and tried to capture Truth's speech as she remembered it, complete with what Gage perceived to be Truth's manner of speech and actions before the audience.

Source: E. C. Stanton, S. B. Anthony, and Matilda Joslyn Gage, eds., *History of Woman Suffrage,* vol. 1 (Rochester, NY: Charles Mann, 1881), pp. 115–117.

Reminiscences by Frances D. Gage

The leaders of the movement trembled upon seeing a tall, gaunt black woman in a gray dress and white turban, surmounted with an uncouth sun-bonnet, march deliberately into the church, walk with the air of a queen up the aisle, and take her seat upon the pulpit steps. A buzz of disapprobation was heard all over the house and there fell on the listening ear, "An abolition affair!" "Woman's rights and niggers!" "I told you so! 'Go it, darkey!" . . .When, slowly from her seat in the corner rose Sojourner Truth, who, till now, had scarcely lifted her head. "Don't let her speak!" gasped half a dozen in my ear. She moved slowly and solemnly to the front, laid her old bonnet at her feet, and turned her great speaking eyes to me. There was a hissing sound of disapprobation above and below. I rose and announced "Sojourner Truth," and begged the audience to keep silence for a few moments. . . .

"Wall, chilern, whar dar is so much racket dar must be somethin' out o' kilter. I tink dat 'twixt de niggers of de Souf and de womin at de Norf, all talkin' 'bout rights, de white men will be in a fix pretty soon. But what's all dis here talkin' 'bout?

"Dat man ober dar say dat womin needs to be helped into carriages, and lifted ober ditches, and to hab de best place everywhar. Nobody eber helps me into carriages, or ober mud-puddles, or gibs me any best place!" . . ."And a'n't I a woman? Look at me! Look at my arm! (and she bared her right arm to the shoulder, showing her tremendous muscular power). "I have ploughed, and planted, and gathered into barns, and no man could head me! And a'n't I a woman? I could work as much and eat as much as a man—when I could get it—and bear de lash as well! And a'n't I a woman? I have borne thirteen chilern, and seen 'em mos' all sold off to slavery, and when I cried out with my mother's grief, none but Jesus heard me! And a'n't I a woman?

"Den dey talks 'bout dis ting in de head; what dis dey call it?" ("Intellect," whispered some one near.) "Dat's it, honey. What's dat got to do wid womin's rights or nigger's rights? If my cup won't hold but a pint, and yourn holds a quart, wouldn't ye be mean not to let me have my little half-measure full?" And she pointed her significant finger, and sent a keen glance at the minister who had made the argument. The cheering was long and loud.

"Den dat little man in black dar, he say women can't have as much rights as men, 'cause Christ wan't a woman! Whar did your Christ come from?" Rolling thunder couldn't have stilled that crowd, as did those deep, wonderful tones, as she stood there with outstretched arms and eyes of fire. Raising her voice still louder, she repeated, "Whar did your Christ come from? From God and a woman! Man had nothin' to do wid Him." Oh, what a rebuke that was to that little man.

Turning again to another objector, she took up the defense of Mother Eve. I can not follow her through it all. It was pointed, and witty, and solemn; eliciting at almost every sentence deafening applause; and she ended by asserting: "If de fust woman God ever made was strong enough to turn de world upside down all alone, dese women togedder (and she glanced her eye over the platform) ought to be able to turn it back, and get it right side up again! And now dey is asking to do it, de men better let 'em." Long-continued cheering greeted this. "'Bleeged to ye for hearin' on me, and now ole Sojourner han't got nothin' more to say."

Amid roars of applause, she returned to her corner, leaving more than one of us with streaming eyes, and hearts beating with gratitude. She had taken us up in her arms and carried us safely over the slough of difficulty turning the whole tide in our favor. I have never in my life seen anything like the magical influence that subdued the mobbish spirit of the day, and turned the sneers and jeers of an excited crowd into notes of respect and admiration. Hundreds rushed up to shake hands with her, and congratulate the glorious old mother, and bid her God-speed on her mission of "testifyin' agin concerning the wickedness of this 'ere people."

1. *Describe Gage's impression of the audience's different responses to Sojourner Truth's manner and message. What does Gage's impression seem to be?*
2. *Summarize Sojourner Truth's message to the Woman's Rights Convention. How is this message similar to and different from the message the reader and the crowd might expect from her?*

PART TWELVE
MANIFEST DESTINY

12-1 The Treaties of Velasco (May 14, 1836)

In the wake of his defeat at the battle of San Jacinto, Mexican General and President Antonio Lopez de Santa Anna signed two treaties in the town of Velasco, at the mouth of the Brazos River. The "public" treaty was to be published immediately, and the second, "secret," agreement was to be carried out when the public treaty had been fulfilled. Together, the two treaties roughly established Texas' southern border at the Rio Grande, but this issue would not be fully resolved until 1848 with the Treaty of Guadalupe Hidalgo and the end of the Mexican War.

Source: Texas State Historical Association, Texas History Links, *Links to Some Texas History Primary Resource Documents on the Internet,* compiled by Roger A. Griffin, Ph.D, Professor of History Emeritus, Austin Community College, Austin, Texas.
http://home.austin.rr.com/rgriffin/texhisdocs.html

ARTICLES OF AGREEMENT AT SAN JACINTO

Whereas, The President Santa Anna, with divers officers of his late army, is a prisoner of war in charge of the army of Texas, and is desirous of terminating the contest now existing between the Government of Texas and that of Mexico, in which desire the Generals above named do fully concur, and Whereas, The President of the Republic of Texas, and the Cabinet, are also willing to stay the further effusion of blood, and to see the two neighboring Republics placed in relations of friendship, on terms of reciprocal advantage;

Therefore, it is agreed by the President Santa Anna, and the Generals Don Vicente Filisola, Don Jose Urea, Don Joaquin Ramires y Sesma, and Don Antonio Gaona,

1st. That the armies of Mexico shall with all practicable expedition evacuate the territory of Texas, and retire to Monterey, beyond the Rio Grande.

2d. That the armies, in their retreat, shall abstain from all pillage and devastation, and shall not molest any of the citizens of Texas, and shall not carry with them any cattle or other stock, more than may be absolutely necessary for their subsistence, for which a just price shall be paid. That all private property that may have been captured by either detachment of the army, shall be deposited at the first convenient point of their march, and left under a sufficient guard, until the proper authorities of Texas shall take possession thereof.

3d. That the army of Texas are to march westwardly, and to occupy such posts as the commanding General may think proper, on the east side of the Rio Grande, or Rio Bravo del Norte.

4th. That the President Santa Anna, in his official character as chief of the Mexican nation, and the Generals Don Vicente Filisola, Don Jose Urea, Don Joaquin Ramires y Sesma, and Don Antonio Gaona, as Chiefs of Armies, do solemnly acknowledge, sanction, and ratify, the full, entire, and perfect Independence of the Republic of Texas, with such boundaries as are hereafter set forth and agreed upon for the same. And they do solemnly and respectively pledge themselves, with all their personal and official attributes, to procure without delay, the final and complete ratification and confirmation of this agreement, and all the parts thereof, by the proper and legitimate Government of Mexico, by the incorporation of the same into a solemn and perpetual Treaty of amity and commerce to be negotiated with that Government, at the city of Mexico, by Ministers Plenipotentiary to be deputed by the Government of Texas for this high purpose.

5th. That the following be, and the same are hereby established and made the lines of demarcation between the two Republics of Mexico and of Texas, to wit: The line shall commence at the estuary or mouth of the Rio Grande, on the western bank thereof, and shall pursue the same bank up the said river, to the point where the river assumes the name of the Rio Bravo del Norte, from which point it shall proceed on the said western bank to the head waters, or source of said river, it being understood that the terms Rio Grande and Rio Bravo del Norte, apply to and designate one and the same stream. From the source of said river, the principal head branch being taken to ascertain that source, a due north line shall be run until it shall intersect the boundary line established and described in the Treaty negotiated by and between the Government of Spain and the Government of the United States of the North; which line was subsequently transferred to, and adopted in the Treaty of limits made between the Government of Mexico and that of the United States; and from this point of intersection the line shall be the same as was made and established in and by the several Treaties above mentioned, to continue to the mouth or outlet of the Sabine river, and from thence to the Gulf of Mexico.

6th. That all prisoners taken by the forces of Mexico be forthwith released, and be furnished with free passports to return to their homes; their clothing and small arms to be restored to them.

7th. That all the fortresses of Texas be forthwith restored without dilapidation, and with all the artillery and munitions of war belonging to, them respectively.

8th. The President and Cabinet of the Republic of Texas, exercising the high powers confided to them by the people of Texas, do, for and in consideration of the foregoing stipulations, solemnly engage to refrain from taking the life of the President Santa Anna, and of the several officers of his late army, whom the events of war have made prisoners in their hands, and to liberate the President, Santa Anna, with his private Secretary, and cause him to be conveyed in one of the national vessels of Texas, to Vera Cruz, in order that he may more promptly and effectually obtain the ratification of this compact, and the negotiation of the definitive Treaty herein contemplated by the Government of Mexico with the Government of Texas.

9th. The release of the President Santa Anna shall be made immediately, on receiving the signatures of the Generals, Don Vicente Filasola, Don Jose Urea, Don Joaquin Ramires y Sesma, and Don Antonio Gaona, to this agreement, and his conveyance to Vera Cruz as soon afterwards as may be convenient.

10th. The President Santa Anna, and the Generals Don Vicente Filasola, Don Jose Urea, Don Joaquin Ramires y Sesma, and Don Antonio Gaona, do, by this act of subscribing this instrument, severally and solemnly pledge themselves on their inviolable parole of honour, that in the event the Mexican Government shall refuse or omit to execute, ratify, confirm and perfect this agreement, they will not, on any occasion whatever, take up arms against the people of Texas, or any portion of them, but will consider themselves bound, by every sacred obligation, to abstain from all hostility towards Texas or its citizens.

11th. That the other Mexican officers, prisoners with the Government of Texas, shall remain in custody, as hostages, for the faithful performance of this agreement, and shall be treated with humanity, and the respect due their rank and condition, until the final disposition of the Mexican Government be ascertained, and a Treaty to be predicated upon the above stipulations, shall be made or rejected by that Government. In the event of a refusal to enter into and ratify such Treaty, on the part of the Mexican Government, the Government of Texas reserves to itself the right to dispose of them as they may think proper and equitable, relative to the conduct of the Mexican forces towards the Volunteers and soldiers of Texas, who have heretofore fallen into their hands.

12th. The high contracting parties mutually agree to refer the Treaty intended to be executed and solemnized by the two Governments of Texas and of Mexico, on the basis established in this compact, to the Government of the United States of the North, and to solicit the guarantee of that Government for the fulfilment, by the contracting parties respectively, of their several engagements: the said parties pledging themselves, in case of any disagreement or defalcation, to submit all matters in controversy to the final decision and adjustment of that Government. For this purpose, the contracting parties shall, as soon as practicable after the ratification of said Treaty, depute one or more Commissioners to the Court of Washington, invested with plenary powers to perfect the object of this stipulation.

13th. Any act of hostility on the part of the retreating Mexican troops, or any depredation upon public or private property committed by those troops, or any impediment presented to the occupation of any part of the territory of Texas, by the forces thereof, on the part of the Mexican troops, shall be considered a violation of this agreement.

PUBLIC TREATY OF VELASCO

ARTICLES OF AN AGREEMENT entered into, between his Excellency David G. Burnet, President of the Republic of Texas, of the one part, and General Antonio Lopez de Santa Anna, President, General-in-Chief of the Mexican army, of the other part.

ARTICLE 1.—General Antonio Lopez de Santa Anna agrees that he will not take up arms, nor will he exercise his influence to cause them to be taken up, against the people of Texas during the present war of Independence.

ARTICLE 2.—All hostilities between the Mexican and Texian troops will cease immediately, both on land and water.

ARTICLE 3.—The Mexican troops will evacuate the Territory of Texas, passing to the other side of the Rio Grande del Norte.

ARTICLE 4.—The Mexican army in its retreat shall not take the property of any person without his consent and just indemnification, using only such articles as may be necessary for its subsistence in cases where the owner may not be present, and remitting to the Commander of the Army of Texas, or to the Commissioners to be appointed for the adjustment of such matters, an account of the value of the property consumed, the place where taken, and the name of the owner, if it can be ascertained.

ARTICLE 5.—That all private property, including cattle, horses, negro slaves, or indentured persons, of whatever denomination, that may have been captured by any portion of the Mexican army, or may have taken refuge in the said army since the commencement of the late invasion, shall be restored to the Commander of the Texian army, or to such other persons as may be appointed by the Government of Texas to receive them.

ARTICLE 6.—The troops of both armies will refrain from coming into contact with each other, and to this end the Commander of the army of Texas will be careful riot to approach within a shorter distance of the Mexican army than five leagues.

ARTICLE 7.—The Mexican army shall not make any other delay on its march than that which is necessary to take up their hospitals, baggage, etc., and to cross the rivers: any delay not necessary to these purposes to be considered an infraction of this agreement.

ARTICLE 8.—By express, to be immediately dispatched, this agreement shall be sent to General Vincent Filisola and to General T. J. Rusk, Commander of the Texian army, its order that they may be apprised of its stipulations, and to this end they will exchange engagements to comply with the same.

ARTICLE 9.—That all Texian prisoners now in possession of the Mexican army or its authorities be forthwith released and furnished with free passports to return to their homes, in consideration of which a corresponding number of Mexican prisoners, rank and file, now in possession of the Government of Texas, shall be immediately released. The remainder of the Mexican prisoners that continue in possession of the Government of Texas to be treated with due humanity; any extraordinary comforts that may be furnished them to be at the charge of the Government of Mexico.

ARTICLE 10.—General Antonio Lopez of Santa Anna will be sent to Vera Cruz as soon as it shall be deemed proper.

The contracting parties sign this instrument for the above-mentioned purposes, by duplicate, at the Port of Velasco, this 14th day of May, 1836. David G. Burnet. Antonio Lopez de Santa Anna. James Collingsworth, Secretary of State Bailey Hardeman, Secretary of the Treasury. P. W. Grayson, Attorney-General.

SECRET TREATY OF VELASCO

Port of Velasco, May 14th, 1836. Antonio Lopez de Santa Anna, General-in-Chief of the Army of Operations, and President of the Republic of Mexico, before the Government established in Texas, solemnly pledges himself to fulfill the stipulations contained in the following articles, so far as concerns himself:

ARTICLE 1.—He will not take up arms, nor cause them to be taken up, against the people of Texas, during the present war for Independence.

ARTICLE 2.—He will give his orders that in the shortest time the Mexican troops may leave the Territory of Texas.

ARTICLE 3.—He will so prepare matters in the Cabinet of Mexico, that the mission that may be sent thither by the Government of Texas may be well received, and that by means of negotiations all differences may be settled, and the Independence that has been declared by the Convention may be acknowledged.

ARTICLE 4.—A treaty of comity, amity, acid limits, will be established between Mexico and Texas, the territory of the latter not to extend beyond the Rio Bravo del Norte.

ARTICLE 5.—The present return of General Santa Anna to Vera Cruz being indispensable for the purpose of effecting his solemn engagements, the Government of Texas will provide for his immediate embarkation for said port.

ARTICLE 6.—This instrument being obligatory off one part, as well as off the other, will be signed in duplicate, remaining folded and sealed until the negotiations shall have been concluded, when it will be restored to His Excellency General Santa Anna, no use of it to be made before that time, unless there should be an infraction by either of the contracting parties. Antonio Lopez de Santa Anna. David G. Burnet James Collingsworth, Secretary of State. Bailey Hardeman, Secretary of the Treasury. P. W. Grayson, Attorney-General.

1. In what ways do the public and secret treaties of Velasco differ? Why do you think the participants felt there was a need for a secret treaty?
2. How explicit in the treaties is the line of demarcation between Mexico and the Republic of Texas?

12-2   The Aroostook War (1839)

The Aroostook War was an undeclared, bloodless, "war" that began in the disputed northeastern corner of the United States in 1839. The Peace of Paris in 1783 did not clearly define the boundary between the Canadian province of New Brunswick and what is now Maine. The contested area, called the Madawaska territory (through which ran the Aroostook River), was heavily forested and a valuable source of lumber for whoever controlled it. Joshua Crooker of Minot, Maine, a volunteer in one of the first companies organized to defend the Maine frontier, related his experiences to a reporter from the local newspaper some sixty years after the clash. Crooker was eighty-three years old.

Source: Joshua Crooker, "An Aroostook War Soldier," newspaper clipping dated February 28, 1901. Courtesy of the Androscoggin Historical Society, Auburn, Maine.
http://ftp.rootsweb.com/pub/usgenweb/me/aroostook/war/ljfile1.txt

In the winter of 1841, my brother-in-law, Salomon Cole, being on a visit to Buckfield strongly urged me to return with him to his home in Parkman, which I did. I had been there but a short time when rumors floated freely of British invasion of the Aroostook country for the purpose of cutting ship timber, on the banks of the winding Aroostook, whence it was floated down the river when the ice broke up in the spring. I was at a religious meeting on Sunday when an officer appeared at the church soliciting the enlistment of a company of soldiers, to go immediately to the scene of the depredations in the northern wilderness. This stirring and unusual event awoke in me the war like spirit that lies inherent; in every true American breast. Often had I listened to my grandfather's recital of the scenes he had witnessed in the revolutionary war. The picture of Arnold's valor at Saratoga, the midnight charge at Stony Point, Washington, turning the retreating troops at Monmouth forward to a victory, until, in the imagination, and enthusiasm of youth I feared no opportunity would present itself, in my life time for military service for my Country against England, which by hereditary instinct had always been regarded as our natural enemy.

An enlisting Officer appeared at the church meeting and when the services were over began recruiting. I was the first man to put my name on the roll. Others rapidly followed and by night a company was formed. We had orders to be at Sangerville the next morning for immediate marching. We reached there at 2 o'clock by team and stayed at the tavern, where we went through the process of being mustered. We formed in front of the door and passed singly into the house where each man was examined. The most prominent qualification was that each man should be warmly clothed. We took dinner at this Inn and started over the snowy road for Lincoln, which we reached that night, cold, hungry and tired.

The next morning we received our guns of which there was a great stack in a large building and then we resumed our march on foot. We passed along the Penobscot, through Winn to the junction of the Mattawamkeag with the Penobscot. From the town of Mattawamkeag we turned north, where the townships were designated by the numerals, 1, 2, 3, 4, 5, etc. On, arriving at the 8th township we struck the head waters of P. branch of the Aroostook river. Here was our outpost camp. The soldiers who were stationed or had arrived there came out to receive us. We found quite warm and convenient quarters in rude buildings which had been constructed. I think that it was on Friday that we reached the camp and on the next Monday morning we mustered on the ice and started down river.

The picture presented has never left my memory. The new land agent Jarvis was the commanding officer and mounted on black charger he addressed the troops in a fiery spirit of war. He gave command that every bayonet be fixed and finished by saying if there was a soldier among us who would hesitate to run his bayonet through a British invader he did not want him, and called upon such to lay his arms and return home, while the others were ordered to "forward march." Three soldiers gave up their guns and left the ranks. The drums beat; the fifes piped strains of war. With colors flying the first war began under the fall of silent, slow-descending flakes upon them. My company was about middle way of the command and before and behind were companies following each other, interspersed with horse-teams hauling 36 cannon and military stores and ordnance required for soldiers entering a wilderness in the depth of winter. Fully a mile was taken up in the line of march and the distance to be traveled over by the winding Aroostook was estimated at 72 miles. We halted at noon only long enough to eat our rations of hard-tack and boiled pork. Our tea was the uncooked water of the river drawn through a hole in the ice. By night-fall we reached the half-way place, where some preparation had been made for us. The next day was clear and cold and we had to beat ourselves and rub our faces and ears to keep them from freezing.

It was growing dark when we halted at a place where the river made a bend and the top was covered with hewn timber. Here was the cause of the war. These innocent "Sticks of timber" that lay cold and half-covered with snow had stirred the counsels of nations. Here was the "bone" over which the dogs of war were contending. Here was the scene where Macintosh, our land agent, was seized and carried away into the British Dominion, bound on a horse. Our company was stationed as the picket guard that night to watch for any advance of the foe, as they might come out of the blackness of the forest shade. But the cold winds only came up the river chilling the very marrow of our bones to disturb our cheerless vigil. Never have I passed so severe a trial from wind and weather in the 83 years of my existence as in that first night in the wilderness of the Aroostook. Once in a while through that long night the sounds in the tree tops blowing in the winds were chorused by the dismal hoot of the owls, and the fierce snarls or shrieks of the wild denizens of that vast wilderness, their protest no doubt, to our invasion.

The next morning the plans of the campaign had been formed and were being executed. A fort was to be constructed on the left bank of the river and with Yankee availability, we used in its construction the ship timber that the British had got out on the river. And how rapidly the fort grew into shape. Horses drew the ship timber upon the bank and skillful hands adjusted it readily into a redoubt and the angry-mouthed cannon boldly looked out toward approach.

Seventy-five acres of forest were to be cleared and our guns were exchanged for axes. The snow was four feet deep in the woods but the cutting up of the fallen trees and burning them melted the snow and soon there appeared from our hands a campground snowless and treeless and stumpless and almost as level as a garden plot. Streets were laid out, barracks, officers' quarters, hospital and all the paraphernalia of the camp appeared. In honor of the Governor of the State the place was named Fort Fairfield, which name it has ever since retained.

Besides the general hard work and military drill there was little remarkable to relate. Once in a while a man found in the wood cautiously looking at our camp was brought in blindfolded. The officers examined him and invariably sent him away in the same manner as he came. One day it was announced that the State land agent, who had been carried off, bound on a horse sled into "Bluenose-dom," was to be released and allowed to come back. Several officers with a file of men went down the river to meet him and escort him into camp. When the detachment containing the heroic agent, appeared in sight the cannon mounted in the fort belched forth fiery flames and the whole camp shook as in an earthquake's throe. Thus he received military honors of a returning hero. The first-troops went up as volunteers under command of Land Agent Jarvis, who was appointed in Macintosh's place after his capture, but now soldiers drafted from the militia of the State began to arrive under command of Gen. Houlton, if I remember correctly. There was a little friction between the land agent and Gen. Moulton, the volunteers maintaining that they owed command only to the land agent. We were discharged after having served there forty days. The volunteers had done their work, and it remained for the drafted men to "hold the fort."

1. *How does the Aroostook "war" exemplify the nature of controversies waged between Britain and the United States in North America in the decades immediately following the end of the War of 1812?*
2. *Do you think Crooker was satisfied with his relatively brief service as a volunteer? What had he accomplished?*

12-3 Across the Plains With Catherine Sager Pringle in 1844

As a child, Catherine Sager Pringle emigrated with her family from Ohio to Missouri and soon participated in the long overland journey to Oregon. She preserved her experiences in her diary in 1860. In this excerpt from her first chapter, Pringle relates incidents on the trail and the emotional story of the death of her parents.

Source: The Oregon Trail Web Site
http://www.isu.edu/~trinmich/00.ar.sager1.html

ON THE PLAINS IN 1844

My father was one of the restless ones who are not content to remain in one place long at a time. Late in the fall of 1838 we emigrated from Ohio to Missouri. Our first halting place was on Green River, but the next year we took a farm in Platte County. He engaged in farming and blacksmithing, and had a wide reputation for ingenuity. Anything they needed, made or mended, sought his shop. In 1843, Dr. Whitman came to Missouri. The healthful climate induced my mother to favor moving to Oregon. Immigration was the theme all winter, and we decided to start for Oregon. Late in 1843 father sold his property and moved near St. Joseph, and in April, 1844, we started across the plains. The first encampments were a great pleasure to us children. We were five girls and two boys, ranging from the girl baby to be born on the way to the oldest boy, hardly old enough to be any help.

Starting on the Plains

We waited several days at the Missouri River. Many friends came that far to see the emigrants start on their long journey, and there was much sadness at the parting, and a sorrowful company crossed the Missouri that bright spring morning. The motion of the wagon made us all sick, and it was weeks before we got used to the seasick motion. Rain came down and required us to tie down the wagon covers, and so increased our sickness by confining the air we breathed.

Our cattle recrossed in the night and went back to their winter quarters. This caused delay in recovering them and a weary, forced march to rejoin the train. This was divided into companies, and we were in that commanded by William Shaw. Soon after starting Indians raided our camp one night and drove off a number of cattle. They were pursued, but never recovered.

Soon everything went smooth and our train made steady headway. The weather was fine and we enjoyed the journey pleasantly. There were several musical instruments among the emigrants, and these sounded clearly on the evening air when camp was made and merry talk and laughter resounded from almost every camp-fire.

Incidents of Travel

We had one wagon, two steady yoke of old cattle, and several of young and not well-broken ones. Father was no ox driver, and had trouble with these until one day he called on Captain Shaw for assistance. It was furnished by the good captain pelting the refractory steers with stones until they were glad to come to terms.

Reaching the buffalo country, our father would get some one to drive his team and start on the hunt, for he was enthusiastic in his love of such sport. He not only killed the great bison, but often brought home on his shoulder the timid antelope that had fallen at his unerring aim, and that are not often shot by ordinary marksmen. Soon after crossing South Platte the unwieldy oxen ran on a bank and overturned the wagon, greatly injuring our mother. She lay long insensible in the tent put up for the occasion.

August 1st we nooned in a beautiful grove on the north side of the Platte. We had by this time got used to climbing in and out of the wagon when in motion. When performing this feat that afternoon my dress caught on an axle helve and I was thrown under the wagon wheel, which passed over and badly crushed my limb before father could stop the team. He picked me up and saw the extent of the injury when the injured limb hung dangling in the air.

The Father Dying on the Plains

In a broken voice he exclaimed: "My dear child, your leg is broken all to pieces!" The news soon spread along the train and a halt was called. A surgeon was found and the limb set; then we pushed on the same night to Laramie, where we arrived soon after dark. This accident confined me to the wagon the remainder of the long journey.

After Laramie we entered the great American desert, which was hard on the teams. Sickness became common. Father and the boys were all sick, and we were dependent for a driver on the Dutch doctor who set my leg. He offered his services and was employed, but though an excellent surgeon, he knew little about driving oxen. Some of them often had to rise from their sick beds to wade streams and get the oxen safely across. One day four buffalo ran between our wagon and the one behind. Though feeble, father seized his gun and gave chase to them. This imprudent act prostrated him again, and it soon became apparent that his days were numbered. He was fully conscious of the fact, but could not be reconciled to the thought of leaving his large and helpless family in such precarious circumstances. The evening before his death we crossed Green River and camped on the bank. Looking where I lay helpless, he said: "Poor child! What will become of you?" Captain Shaw found him weeping bitterly. He said his last hour had come, and his heart was filled with anguish for his family. His wife was ill, the children small, and one likely to be a cripple. They had no relatives near, and a long journey lay before them. In piteous tones he begged the Captain to take charge of them and see them through. This he stoutly promised. Father was buried the next day on the banks of Green River. His coffin was made of two troughs dug out of the body of a tree, but next year emigrants found his bleaching bones, as the Indians had disinterred the remains.

We hired a young man to drive, as mother was afraid to trust the doctor, but the kindhearted German would not leave her, and declared his intention to see her safe in the Willamette. At Fort Bridger the stream was full of fish, and we made nets of wagon sheets to catch them. That evening the new driver told mother he would hunt for game if she would let him use the gun. He took it, and we never saw him again. He made for the train in advance, where he had a sweetheart. We found the gun waiting our arrival at Whitman's. Then we got along as best we could with the doctor's help.

Mother planned to get to Whitman's and winter there, but she was rapidly failing under her sorrows. The nights and mornings were very cold, and she took cold from the exposure unavoidably. With camp fever and a sore mouth, she fought bravely against fate for the sake of her children, but she was taken delirious soon after reaching Fort Bridger, and was bed-fast. Travelling in this condition over a road clouded with dust, she suffered intensely. She talked of her husband, addressing him as though present, beseeching him in piteous tones to relieve her sufferings, until at last she became unconscious. Her babe was cared for by the women of the train. Those kind-hearted women would also come in at night and wash the dust from the mother's face and otherwise make her comfortable. We travelled a rough road the day she died, and she moaned fearfully all the time. At night one of the women came in as usual, but she made no reply to questions, so she thought her asleep, and washed her face, then took her hand and discovered the pulse was nearly gone. She lived but a few moments, and her last words were,"Oh, Henry! If you only knew how we have suffered." The tent was set up, the corpse laid out, and next morning we took the last look at our mother's face. The grave was near the road; willow brush was laid in the bottom and covered the body, the earth filled in—then the train moved on.

Her name was cut on a headboard, and that was all that could be done. So in twenty-six days we became orphans. Seven children of us, the oldest fourteen and the youngest a babe. A few days before her death, finding herself in possession of her faculties and fully aware of the coming end, she had taken an affectionate farewell of her children and charged the doctor to take care of us. She made the same request of Captain Shaw. The baby was taken by a woman in the train, and all were literally adopted by the company. No one there but was ready to do us any possible favor. This was especially true of Captain Shaw and his wife. Their kindness will ever be cherished in grateful remembrance by us all. Our parents could not have been more solicitous or careful. When our flour gave out they gave us bread as long as they had any, actually dividing their last loaf. To this day Uncle Billy and Aunt Sally, as we call them, regard us with the affection of parents. Blessings on his hoary head!

At Snake River they lay by to make our wagon into a cart, as our team was wearing out. Into this was loaded what was necessary. Some things were sold and some left on the plains. The last of September we arrived at Grande Ronde, where one of my sister's clothes caught fire, and she would have burned to death only that the German doctor, at the cost of burning his hands, saved her. One night the captain heard a child crying, and found my little sister had got out of the wagon and was perishing in the freezing air, for the nights were very cold. We had been out of flour and living on meat alone, so a few were sent in advance to get supplies from Dr. Whitman and return to us. Having so light a load we could travel faster than the other teams, and went on with Captain Shaw and the advance. Through the Blue Mountains cattle were giving out and left lying in the road. We made but a few miles a day. We were in the country of "Dr. Whitman's Indians," as they called themselves. They were returning from buffalo hunting and frequented our camps. They were loud in praise of the missionaries and anxious to assist us. Often they would drive up some beast that had been left behind as given out and return it to its owner.

One day when we were making a fire of wet wood Francis thought to help the matter by holding his powder-horn over a small blaze. Of course the powder-horn exploded, and the wonder was he was left alive. He ran to a creek near by and bathed his hands and face, and came back destitute of winkers and eyebrows, and his face was blackened beyond recognition. Such were the incidents and dangerous and humorous features of the journey.

We reached Umatilla October 15th, and lay by while Captain Shaw went on to Whitman's station to see if the doctor would take care of us, if only until he could become located in the Willamette. We purchased of the Indians the first potatoes we had eaten since we started on our long and sad journey. October 17th we started for our destination, leaving the baby very sick, with doubts of its recovery. Mrs. Shaw took an affectionate leave of us all, and stood looking after us as long as we were in sight. Speaking of it in later years, she said she never saw a more pitiful sight than that cartful of orphans going to find a home among strangers.

We reached the station in the forenoon. For weeks this place had been a subject for our talk by day and formed our dreams at night. We expected to see log houses, occupied by Indians and such people as we had seen about the forts. Instead we saw a large white house surrounded with palisades. A short distance from the doctor's dwelling was another large adobe house, built by Mr. Gray, but now used by immigrants in the winter, and for a granary in the summer. It was situated near the mill pond, and the grist mill was not far from it.

Between the two houses were the blacksmith shop and the corral, enclosed with slabs set up endways. The garden lay between the mill and the house, and a large field was on the opposite side. A good-sized ditch passed in front of the house, connecting with the mill pond, intersecting other ditches all around the farm, for the purpose of irrigating the land.

We drove up and halted near this ditch. Captain Shaw was in the house conversing with Mrs. Whitman. Glancing through the window, he saw us, and turning to her said: "Your children have come; will you go out and see them?" He then came out and told the boys to "Help the girls out and get their bonnets." Alas! it was easy to talk of bonnets, but not to find them! But one or two were finally discovered by the time Mrs. Whitman had come out. Here was a scene for an artist to describe! Foremost stood the little cart, with the tired oxen that had been unyoked lying near it. Sitting in the front end of the cart was John, weeping bitterly; on the opposite side stood Francis, his arms on the wheel and his head resting on his arms, sobbing aloud; on the near side the little girls were huddled together, bareheaded and barefooted, looking at the boys and then at the house, dreading we knew not what. By the oxen stood the good German doctor, with his whip in his hand, regarding the scene with suppressed emotion.

Thus Mrs. Whitman found us. She was a large, well-formed woman, fair complexioned, with beautiful auburn hair, nose rather large, and large gray eyes. She had on a dark calico dress and gingham sunbonnet. We thought as we shyly looked at her that she was the prettiest woman we had ever seen. She spoke kindly to us as she came up, but like frightened things we ran behind the cart, peeping shyly around at her. She then addressed the boys, asking why they wept, adding: "Poor boys, no wonder you weep!" She then began to arrange things as we threw them out, at the same time conversing with an Indian woman sitting on the ground near by.

A little girl about seven years old soon came and stood regarding us with a timid look. This was little Helen Mar Meed, and though a half-breed, she looked very pretty to us in her green dress and white apron and neat sunbonnet.

Having arranged everything in compact form Mrs. Whitman directed the doctor and the boys where to carry them, and told Helen to show the little girls the way to the house. Seeing my lameness, she kindly took me by the hand and my little sister by the other hand, and thus led us in. As we reached the steps, Captain Shaw asked if she had children of her own. Pointing to a grave at the foot of the hill not far off, she said: "All the child I ever had sleeps yonder." She added that it was a great pleasure to her that she could see the grave from the door. The doctor and boys having deposited the things as directed, went over to the mansion. As we entered the house we saw a girl about nine years old washing dishes. Mrs. Whitman spoke cheerfully to her and said: "Well, Mary Ann, how do you think you will like all these sisters?" Seated in her arm-chair, she placed the youngest on her lap, and calling us round her, asked our names, about our parents, and the baby, often exclaiming as we told our artless story, "Poor children!"

Dr. Whitman came in from the mill and stood in the door, looking as though surprised at the large addition so suddenly made to the family. We were a sight calculated to excite surprise, dirty and sunburned until we looked more like Indians than white children. Added to this, John had cropped our hair so that it hung in uneven locks and added to our uncouth appearance. Seeing her husband standing there, Mrs. Whitman said, with a laugh: "Come in, doctor, and see your children." He sat down and tried to take little Louisa in his arms, but she ran screaming to me, much to the discomfiture of the doctor and amusement of his wife. She then related to him what we had told her in reference to the baby, and expressed her fears lest it should die, saying it was the baby she wanted most of all.

Our mother had asked that we might not be separated, so Captain Shaw now urged the doctor to take charge of us all. He feared the Board might object, as he was sent as a missionary to the Indians. The captain argued that a missionary's duty was to do good, and we certainly were objects worthy of missionary charity. He was finally persuaded to keep us all until spring. His wife did not readily consent, but he told her he wanted boys as well as the girls. Finding the boys willing to stay, he made a written agreement with Captain Shaw that he would take charge of them. Before Captain Shaw reached the valley, Dr. Whitman overtook him and told him he was pleased with the children and he need give himself no further care concerning them. The baby was brought over in few days. It was very sick, but under Mrs. Whitman's judicious care was soon restored to health.

Our faithful friend, the German doctor, left us at last, safe in the motherly care of Mrs. Whitman. Well had he kept his promise to our dying mother.

1. *What were some of the more unfortunate accidents witnessed or experienced by Catherine Sager Pringle along the trail? How many of these mishaps might have been anticipated by the immigrants?*
2. *What do you think Catherine Sager Pringle learned about herself during her trip across the plains in 1844?*

12-4 John L. O'Sullivan, "The Great Nation of Futurity" (1845)

The journalist John L. O'Sullivan (1813-1895), an enthusiastic Jacksonian Democrat, first coined the phrase "manifest destiny" in this article supporting the Annexation of Texas, printed in the Democratic Review for July 1845. O'Sullivan was later involved in other movements to annex additional territories, such as the Spanish colony of Cuba in the Caribbean.

The American people having derived their origin from many other nations, and the Declaration of National Independence being entirely based on the great principle of human equality, these facts demonstrate at once our disconnected position as regards any other nation; that we have, in reality, but little connection with the past history of any of them and still less with all antiquity, its glories, or its crimes. On the contrary, our national birth was the beginning of a new history, the formation and progress of an untried political system, which separates us from the past and connects us with the future only; and so far as regards the entire development of the natural rights of man, in moral, political, and national life, we may confidently assume that our country is destined to be the great nation of futurity.

It is so destined, because the principle upon which a nation is organized fixes its destiny, and that of equality is perfect, is universal. It presides in all the operations of the physical world, and it is also the conscious law of the soul-the self-evident dictate of morality, which accurately defines the duty of man to man, and consequently man's rights as man. Besides, the truthful annals of any nation furnish abundant evidence that its happiness, its greatness, its duration, were always proportionate to the democratic equality in its system of government.

How many nations have had their decline and fall because the equal rights of the minority were trampled on by the despotism of the majority; or the interests of the many sacrificed to the aristocracy of the few; or the rights and interests of all given up to the monarchy of one? These three kinds of government have figured so frequently and so largely in the ages that have passed away that their history, through all time to come, can only furnish a resemblance. Like causes produce like effects, and the true philosopher of history will easily discern the principle of equality, or of privilege, working out its inevitable result. The first is regenerative, because it is natural and right; and the latter is destructive to society, because it is unnatural and wrong.

What friend of human liberty, civilization, and refinement can cast his view over the past history of the monarchies and aristocracies of antiquity, and not deplore that they ever existed? What philanthropist can contemplate the oppressions, the cruelties, and injustice inflicted by them on the masses of mankind and not turn with moral horror from the retrospect?

America is destined for better deeds. It is our unparalleled glory that we have no reminiscences of battlefields, but in defense of humanity, of the oppressed of all nations, of the rights of conscience, the rights of personal enfranchisement. Our annals describe no scenes of horrid carnage, where men were led on by hundreds of thousands to slay one another, dupes and victims to emperors, kings, nobles, demons in the human form called heroes. We have had patriots to defend our homes, our liberties, but no aspirants to crowns or thrones; nor have the American people ever suffered themselves to be led on by wicked ambition to depopulate the land, to spread desolation far and wide, that a human being might be placed on a seat of supremacy.

We have no interest in the scenes of antiquity, only as lessons of avoidance of nearly all their examples. The expansive future is our arena and for our history. We are entering on its untrodden space with the truths of God in our minds, beneficent objects in our hearts, and with a clear conscience unsullied by the past. We are the nation of human progress, and who will, what can, set limits to our onward march? Providence is with us, and no earthly power can. We point to the everlasting truth on the first page of our national declaration, and we proclaim to the millions of other lands that "the gates of hell"-the powers of aristocracy and monarchy-"shall not prevail against it."

The far-reaching, the boundless future, will be the era of American greatness. In its magnificent domain of space and time, the nation of many nations is destined to manifest to mankind the excellence of divine principles; to establish on earth the noblest temple ever dedicated to the worship of the Most High, the Sacred, and the True. Its floor shall be a hemisphere, roof the firmament of the star-studded heavens, and its congregation of Union of many Republics, comprising hundreds of happy millions, calling owning no man master, but governed by God's natural and moral law of equality, the law of brotherhood-of "peace and good will amongst men."

Yes, we are the nation of progress, of individual freedom, of universal enfranchisement. Equality of rights is the cynosure of our union of states, the grand exemplar of the correlative equality of individuals; and, while truth sheds its effulgence, we cannot retrograde without dissolving the one and subverting the other. We must onward to the fulfillment of our mission-to the entire development of the principle of our organization-freedom of conscience, freedom of person, freedom of trade and business pursuits, universality of freedom and equality. This is our high destiny, and in nature's eternal, inevitable decree of cause and effect we must accomplish it. All this will be our future history, to establish on earth the moral dignity and salvation of man-the immutable truth and beneficence of God. For this blessed mission to the nations of the world, which are shut out from the lifegiving light of truth, has America been chosen; and her high example shall smite unto death the tyranny of kings, hierarchs, and oligarchs and carry the glad tidings of peace and good will where myriads now endure in existence scarcely more enviable than that of beasts of the field. Who, then, can doubt that our country is destined to be the great nation of futurity?

1. *What reasoning does O'Sullivan use to support his claim that America "is destined to be the great nation of futurity"?*
2. *Explain the author's attitude toward history.*

12-5   Thomas Corwin, Against the Mexican War (1847)

The Mexican-American war began in early 1846 and ended abruptly — after Americans had marched all the way to Mexico City — less than a year later. The question of who would win the war was never really seriously debated. What was in debate was the character of the American expansion and the question of slavery. Corwin, a Whig senator from Ohio, questioned expansionism and feared that the South would carry slavery wherever it went.

> From *The American Reader: Words That Moved a Nation*, ed. Diane Ravitch
> (New York: HarperCollins, 1991), 77-79.

What is the territory, Mr. President, which you propose to wrest from Mexico? It is consecrated to the heart of the Mexican by many a well-fought battle with his old Castilian master. His Bunker Hills, and Saratogas, and Yorktowns are there! The Mexican can say, "There I bled for liberty! and shall I surrender that consecrated home of my affections to the Anglo-Saxon invaders? What do they want with it? They have Texas already. They have possessed themselves of the territory between the Nueces and the Rio Grande. What else do they want? To what shall I point my children as memorials of that independence which I bequeath to them, when those battlefields shall have passed from my possession?"

Sir, had one come and demanded Bunker Hill of the people of Massachusetts, had England's lion ever showed himself there, is there a man over thirteen and under ninety who would not have been ready to meet him? Is there a river on this continent that would not have run red with blood? Is there a field but would have been piled high with the unburied bones of slaughtered Americans before these consecrated battlefields of liberty should have been wrested from us? But this same American goes into a sister republic, and says to poor, weak Mexico, "Give up your territory, you are unworthy to possess it; I have got one half already, and all I ask of you is to give up the other!" ....

Sir, look at this pretense of want of room. With twenty millions of people, you have about one thousand millions of acres of land, inviting settlement by every conceivable argument, bringing them down to a quarter of a dollar an acre, and allowing every man to squat where the pleases....

There is one topic connected with this subject which I tremble when I approach, and yet I cannot forbear to notice it. It meets you in every step you take; it threatens you which way soever you go in the prosecution of this war. I allude to the question of slavery. Opposition to its further extension, it must be obvious to everyone, is a deeply rooted determination with men of all parties in what we call the nonslaveholding states. New York, Pennsylvania, and Ohio, three of the most powerful, have already sent their legislative instructions here. So it will be, I doubt not, in all the rest. It is vain now to speculate about the reasons for this. Gentlemen of the South may call it prejudice, passion, hypocrisy, fanaticism. I shall not dispute with them now on that point. You and I cannot alter or change this opinion, if we would. These people only say we will not, cannot consent that you shall carry slavery where it does not already exist. They do not seek to disturb you in that institution as it exists in your states. Enjoy it if you will and as you will. This is their language; this their determination. How is it in the South? Can it be expected that they should expend in common their blood and their treasure in the acquisition of immense territory, and then willingly forgo the right to carry thither their slaves, and inhabit the conquered country if they please to do so? Sir, I know the feelings and opinions of the South too well to calculate on this. Nay, I believe they would even contend to any extremity for the mere right, had they no wish to exert it. I believe (and I confess I tremble when the conviction presses upon me) that there is equal obstinacy on both sides of this fearful question.

If, then, we persist in war, which, if it terminates in anything short of a mere wanton waste of blood as well as money, must end (as this bill proposes) in the acquisition of territory, to which at once this controversy must attach-this bill would seem to be nothing less than a bill to produce internal commotion. Should we prosecute this war another moment, or expend one dollar in the purchase or conquest of a single acre of Mexican land, the North and the South are brought into collision on a point where neither will yield. Who can foresee or foretell the result! Who so bold or reckless as to look such a conflict in the face unmoved! I do not envy the heart of him who can realize the possibility of such a conflict without emotions too painful to be endured. Why, then, shall we, the representatives of the sovereign states of the Union-the chosen guardians of this confederated Republic, why should we precipitate this fearful struggle, by continuing a war the result of which must be to force us at once upon a civil conflict? Sir, rightly considered, this is treason, treason to the Union, treason to the dearest interests, the loftiest aspirations, the most cherished hopes of our constituents. It is a crime to risk the possibility of such a contest. It is a crime of such infernal hue that every other in the catalogue of iniquity, when compared with it, whitens into virtue.... Let us abandon all idea of acquiring further territory and by consequence cease at once to prosecute this war. Let us call home our armies, and bring them at once within our own acknowledged limits. Show Mexico that you are sincere when you say you desire nothing by conquest. She has learned that she cannot encounter you in war, and if she had not, she is too weak to disturb you here. Tender her peace, and, my life on it, she will then accept it. But whether she shall or not, you will have peace without her consent. It is your invasion that has made war; your retreat will restore peace. Let us then close forever the approaches of internal feud, and so return to the ancient concord and the old ways of national prosperity and permanent glory. Let us here, in this temple consecrated to the Union, perform a solemn lustration; let us wash Mexican blood from our hands, and on these altars, and in the presence of that image of the Father of his Country that looks down upon us, swear to preserve honorable peace with all the world and eternal brotherhood with each other.

1. *What is the author's reasoning as he argues in favor of Mexican freedom and against further American seizure of Mexican territory?*
2. *Summarize the author's argument that continuing the war effort against Mexico would be tantamount to treason. How does public opinion regarding slavery relate to this point?*

12-6   Chief Seattle, Oration (1854)

Chief Seattle made this speech upon the forced sale of a significant portion of land to the United States. A leader of the Suquamish tribe, the speech was recorded and years later became very important to the environmental movement who saw it as prophetic. The actual text of the speech has been very controversial and competing versions exist. A version written for a movie and never intended to be read as fact was, for a time seen as authentic. The controversy goes on but the values of the speech remain.

. . . Yonder sky that has wept tears of compassion upon my people for centuries untold, and which to us appears changeless and eternal, may change. Today is fair. Tomorrow it may be overcast with clouds. My words are like the stars that never change. Whatever Seattle says the great chief at Washington can rely upon with as much certainty as he can upon the return of the sun or the seasons. The White Chief says that Big Chief at Washington sends us greetings of friendship and goodwill. This is kind of him for we know he has little need of our friendship in return. His people are many. They are like the grass that covers vast prairies. My people are few. They resemble the scattering trees of a storm-swept plain. The great, and-I presume-good White Chief sends us word that he wishes to buy our lands but is willing to allow us enough to live comfortably. This indeed appears just, even generous, for the Red Man no longer has rights that he need respect, and the offer may be wise also, as we are no longer in need of an extensive country.

There was a time when our people covered the land as the waves of a wind-ruffled sea cover its shell-paved floor, but that time long since passed away with the greatness of tribes that are now but a mournful memory. I will not dwell on nor mourn over, our untimely decay, nor reproach my paleface brothers with hastening it as we too may have been some-what to blame.

Youth is impulsive. When our young men grow angry at some real or imaginary wrong, and disfigure their faces with black paint, it denotes that their hearts are black, and that they are often cruel and relentless, and our old men and old women are unable to restrain them. Thus has ever been. Thus it was when the White Men first began to push our forefa-thers further westward. But let us hope that the hostilities between us may never return. We would have everything to lose and nothing to gain. Revenge by young men is considered gain, even at the cost of their own lives, but old men who stay at home in times of war, and mothers who have sons to lose, know better.

Our good father at Washington-for I presume he is now our father as well as yours . . . sends us word that if we do as he desires he will protect us. His brave warriors will be to us a bristling wall of strength, and his wonderful ships of war will fill our harbors so that our ancient enemies far to the northward-the Hydas and Tsimpsians,-will cease to frighten our women, children, and old men. Then in reality will he be our father and we his children. But can that ever be? Your God is not our God! Your God loves your people and hates mine. He folds his strong protecting arms lovingly about the paleface and leads him by the hand as a father leads his infant son-but He has forsaken His red children-if they really are his. Our God, the Great Spirit, seems also to have forsaken us. Your God makes your people wax strong every day. Soon they will fill all the land. Our people are ebbing away like a rapidly receding tide that will never return. The White Man's God cannot love our people or He would protect them. They seem to be orphans who can look nowhere for help. How then can we be brothers? How can your God become our God and renew our prosperity and awaken in us dreams of returning greatness? If we have a common heavenly father He must be partial-for He came to His paleface children. We never saw Him. He gave you laws but had no word for His red children whose teeming multitudes once filled this vast continent as stars fill the firmament. No; we are two distinct races with separate origins and separate destinies. There is little in common between us.

To us the ashes of our ancestors are sacred and their resting place is hallowed ground. You wander far from the graves of your ancestors and seemingly without regret. Your religion was written upon tables of stone by the iron finger of your God so that you could not forget. The Red Man could never comprehend nor remember it. Our religion is the tradi-tions of our ancestors-the dreams of our old men, given them in solemn hours of night by the Great Spirit; and the visions of our sachems, and is written in the hearts of our people.

Your dead cease to love you and the land of their nativity as soon as they pass the portals of the tomb and wander away beyond the stars. They are soon forgotten and never return. Our dead never forget the beautiful world that gave them being. They still love its verdant valleys, its murmuring rivers, its magnificent mountains, sequestered vales and verdant lined lakes and bays, and even yearn in tender, fond affection over the lonely heartened living, and often return from the Happy Hunting Ground to visit, guide, console and comfort them.

Day and night cannot dwell together. The Red Man has ever fled the approach of the White Man, as the morning mist flees before the morning sun.

However, your proposition seems fair and I think that my people will accept it and will retire to the reservation you offer them. Then we will dwell apart in peace. . . .

It matters little where we pass the remnant of our days. They will not be many. The Indians' night promises to be dark. Not a single star of hope hovers above his horizon. Sad-voiced winds moan in the distance. Grim fate seems to be on the Red Man's trail, and wherever he goes he will hear the approaching footsteps of his fell destroyer and prepare stolidly to meet his doom, as does the wounded doe that hears the approaching footsteps of the hunter.

. . . But why would I mourn at the untimely fate of my people? Tribe follows tribe, and nation follows nation, like the waves of the sea. It is the order of nature, and regret is useless. Your time of decay may be distant, but it will surely come, for even the White Man whose God walked and talked with him as friend with friend, cannot be exempt from the common destiny. We may be brothers after all. We will see.

We will ponder your proposition and when we decide we will let you know. But should we accept it, I here and now make this condition that we will not be denied the privilege without molestation of visiting at any time the tombs of our ancestors, friends, and children. . . .

And when the last Red Man shall have perished, and the memory of my tribe shall have become a myth among the White Men, these shores will swarm with the invisible dead of my tribe, and when your children's children think themselves alone in the field, the store, the ship, upon the highway, or in the silence of the pathless woods, they will not be alone. In all the earth there is no place dedicated to solitude. At night when the streets of your cities and villages are silent and you think them deserted, they will throng with the returning hosts that once filled them and still love this beautiful land. The White Man will never be alone.

Let him be just and deal kindly with my people, for the dead are not powerless. Dead, did I say? There is no death, only a change of worlds.

1. what are Chief Seattle's views of America's continued westward expansion? What does he think will be the fate of his people under the pressure of expansion?
2. Describe the tone of this passage. What seems to be Chief Seattle's underlying message? How does he make it clear that America should not assume that its dominance or God's favor is permanent?

PART THIRTEEN
ANTEBELLUM SOUTH

13-1 *State v. Boon* (1801)

Early North Carolina statutes treated the murder of a slave differently than other murders. According to laws in 1741 and 1774, people who murdered slaves were required to compensate their owners (unless they killed in the supression of an insurrection) and they risked jail time if they failed to do so. In 1791 an act of the legislature noted that the distinction of criminality between the murder of a white person and of one who is equally a human creature, but merely of a different complexion, is disgraceful to humanity and degrading in the highest degree to the laws and principles of a free, Christian and enlightened country. The law then provided that the murderer would suffer the same punishment as he would if he killed a free man, but provided exceptions for slaves killed in insurrections and slaves dying under moderate correction. This is an excerpt from the North Carolina Supreme Court decision in the first case brought under the new law, concerning a man, Boon, indicted, convicted, and sentenced to death for killing a slave that belonged to another man.

HALL, J. The prisoner has been found guilty of the offence charged in the indictment [Boon was indicted and convicted under the third section of the act of 1791 for killing a slave belonging to another]; whether any, or what punishment, can be inflicted upon him in consequence
thereof, is not to be decided....

We must consider the words of the enacting clause, without regard to the preamble.... If any person hereafter shall be guilty of killing a slave &c. such offender shall be adjudged guilty of murder &c. and shall suffer the same punishment, as if he had killed a free man. In case the person had killed a free man what punishment would the law have inflicted upon him? Before this question can be solved another must be asked; because upon that, the solution of the first depends. What sort of a killing was it? or what circumstances of aggravation or mitigation attended it? ...That to which the Legislature referred us for the purpose of ascertaining the punishment, proper to be inflicted is, in itself, so doubtful and uncertain that I think no punishment whatever can be inflicted; without using a discretion and indulging a latitude, which in criminal cases, ought never to be allowed a Judge.

...Much latitude of construction ought not to be permitted to operate against life; if it operate at all, it should be in favor of it. Punishments ought to be plainly defined and easy to be understood; they ought not to depend upon construction or arbitrary discretion....

But it has been also contended, on behalf of the state, that the offense with which the prisoner is charged, is a felony at common law, and that having been found guilty by the jury, he ought to be punished, independently of any Act of Assembly on the subject....

Slaves in this country possess no such rights; their condition is ...abject; ...they are not parties to our constitution; it was not made for them.

...it is doubtful whether the offense with which he is charged is a felony at common law or not. It is doubtful whether he ought to be punished or not, that, certainly, is a sufficient reason for discharging him...I cannot hesitate to say, that he ought to be discharged.

JOHNSTON, J. The murder of a slave, appears to me, a crime of the most atrocious and barbarous nature; much more so than killing a person who is free, and on an equal footing. It is an evidence of a most depraved and cruel disposition, to murder one, so much in your power, that he is incapable of making resistance, even in his own defence ...and had there been nothing in our acts of Assembly, I should not hesitate on this occasion to have pronounced sentence of death on the prisoner.

...From the context, and taking every part of the section [of the act of 1791] under consideration, there remains no doubt in my mind respecting the intention of the Legislature; but the judges in this country ...have laid down, and invariably adhered to, very strict rules in the
construction of penal statutes in favor of life . . .
...judgment in this case should be arrested.

TAYLOR, JR....But when the court is called upon, under an act of Assembly, to pronounce
the highest punishment known to the law, they must be satisfied that the language used is clear and explicit to the object intended ...I think no judgment can be pronounced.

1. What attitudes regarding the status of slaves are revealed in these decisions?
2. Compare and contrast the lines of reasoning used in these arguments.

13-2   A Black Abolitionist Speaks Out (1829)

David Walker was born in Wilmington, North Carolina, in 1796 or 1797, to a slave father and a free black mother. Upon reaching adulthood, Walker moved to Boston where he nonetheless faced discrimination. He opened a used clothing store in the city in the 1820s and began interacting with prominent black anti-slavery activists. Soon, Walker himself became involved in antislavery associations and wrote articles for the African American newspaper, the Freedom's Journal. The following excerpts are from Walker's Appeal to the Colored Citizens of the World, his most notable and radical written contribution to abolitionism published in September 1829. Walker died before he could see the effect of his Appeal. Allegations have been made that he was poisoned, but there is no evidence to support this conclusion. Rather, it is believed that Walker died of tuberculosis.

Source: PBS Online, *Africans in America.*
http://cgi.pbs.org/wgbh/aia/part4/4h2931t.html

My dearly beloved Brethren and Fellow Citizens:

Having travelled over a considerable portion of these United States, and having, in the course of my travels, taken the most accurate observations of things as they exist—the result of my observations has warranted the full and unshaken conviction, that we, (coloured people of these United States,) are the most degraded, wretched, and abject set of beings that ever lived since the world began; and I pray God that none like us ever may live again until time shall be no more. They tell us of the Israelites in Egypt, the Helots in Sparta, and of the Roman Slaves, which last were made up from almost every nation under heaven, whose sufferings under those ancient and heathen nations, were, in comparison with ours, under this enlightened and Christian nation, no more than a cypher—or, in other words, those heathen nations of antiquity, had but little more among them than the name and form of slavery; while wretchedness and endless miseries were reserved, apparently in a phial, to be poured out upon, our fathers ourselves and our children, by *Christian* Americans! . . .

. . . I call upon the professing Christians, I call upon the philanthropist, I call upon the very tyrant himself, to show me a page of history, either sacred or profane, on which a verse can be found, which maintains, that the Egyptians heaped the *insupportable insult* upon the children of Israel, by telling them that they were not of the *human family.* Can the whites deny this charge? Have they not, after having reduced us to the deplorable condition of slaves under their feet, held us up as descending originally from the tribes of *Monkeys* or *Orang-Outangs*? O! my God! I appeal to every man of feeling—is not this insupportable? Is it not heaping the most gross insult upon our miseries, because they have got us under their feet and we cannot help ourselves? Oh! pity us we pray thee, Lord Jesus, Master.—Has Mr. Jefferson declared to the world, that we are inferior to the whites, both in the endowments of our bodies and our minds? It is indeed surprising, that a man of such great learning, combined with such excellent natural parts, should speak so of a set of men in chains. I do not know what to compare it to, unless, like putting one wild deer in an iron cage, where it will be secured, and hold another by the side of the same, then let it go, and expect the one in the cage to run as fast as the one at liberty. So far, my brethren, were the Egyptians from heaping these insults upon their slaves, that Pharaoh's daughter took Moses, a son of Israel for her own, as will appear by the following. . . .

The world knows, that slavery as it existed was, mans, (which was the primary cause of their destruction) was, comparatively speaking, no more than a *cypher,* when compared with ours under the Americans. Indeed I should not have noticed the Roman slaves, had not the very learned and penetrating Mr. Jefferson said, "when a master was murdered, all his slaves in the same house, or within hearing, were condemned to death."—Here let me ask Mr. Jefferson, (but he is gone to answer at the bar of God, for the deeds done in his body while living,) I therefore ask the whole American people, had I not rather die, or be put to death, than to be a slave to any tyrant, who takes not only my own, but my wife and children's lives by the inches? Yea, would I meet death with avidity far! far!! in preference to such *servile submission* to the murderous hands of tyrants. Mr. Jefferson's very severe remarks on us have been so extensively argued upon by men whose attainments in literature, I shall never be able to reach, that I would not have meddled with it, were it not to solicit each of my brethren, who has the spirit of a man, to buy a copy of Mr. Jefferson's "Notes on Virginia," and put it in the hand of his son. . . .

But let us review Mr. Jefferson's remarks respecting us some further. Comparing our miserable fathers, with the learned philosophers of Greece, he says: "Yet notwithstanding these and other discouraging circumstances among the Romans, their slaves were often their rarest artists. They excelled too, in science, insomuch as to be usually employed as tutors to their master's children; Epictetus, Terence and Phaedrus, were slaves,—but they were of the race of whites. It is not their *condition* then, but *nature,* which has produced the distinction." See this, my brethren! ! Do you believe that this assertion is swallowed by millions of the whites? Do you know that Mr. Jefferson was one of as great characters as ever lived among the whites? See his writings for the world, and public labours for the United States of America. Do you believe that the assertions of such a man, will pass away into oblivion unobserved by this people and the world? If you do you are much mistaken—See how the American people treat us—have we souls in our bodies? Are we men who have any spirits at all? I know that there are many *swell-bellied* fellows among us, whose greatest object is to fill their stomachs. Such I do not mean—I am after those who know and feel, that we are MEN, as well as other people; to them, I say, that unless we try to refute Mr. Jefferson's arguments respecting us, we will only establish them. . . .

. . . I must observe to my brethren that at the close of the first Revolution in this country, with Great Britain, there were but thirteen States in the Union, now there are twenty-four, most of which are slave-holding States, and the whites are dragging us around in chains and in handcuffs, to their new States and Territories to work their mines and farms, to enrich them and their children—and millions of them believing firmly that we being a little darker than they, were made by our Creator to be an inheritance to them and their children for ever—the same as a parcel of *brutes.*

Are we MEN! !—I ask you, my brethren, are we MEN? Did our Creator make us to be slaves to dust and ashes like ourselves? Are they not dying worms as well as we? Have they not to make their appearance before the tribunal of Heaven, to answer for the deeds done in the body, as well as we? Have we any other Master but Jesus Christ alone? Is he not their Master as well as ours?—What right then, have we to obey and call any other Master, but Himself? How we could be so *submissive* to a gang of men, whom we cannot tell whether they are as good as ourselves or not, I never could conceive. However, this is shut up with the Lord, and we cannot precisely tell—but I declare, we judge men by their works.

The whites have always been an unjust, jealous, unmerciful, avaricious and blood-thirsty set of beings, always seeking after power and authority. . . .

. . . to my no ordinary astonishment, [a] Reverend gentleman got up and told us (coloured people) that slaves must be obedient to their masters—must do their duty to their masters or be whipped—the whip was made for the backs of fools, &c. Here I pause for a moment, to give the world time to consider what was my surprise, to hear such preaching from a minister of my Master, whose very gospel is that of peace and not of blood and whips, as this pretended preacher tried to make us believe. What the American preachers can think of us, I aver this day before my God, I have never been able to define. They have newspapers and monthly periodicals, which they receive in continual succession, but on the pages of which, you will scarcely ever find a paragraph respecting slavery, which is ten thousand times more injurious to this country than all the other evils put together; and which will be the final overthrow of its government, unless something is very speedily done; for their cup is nearly full. Perhaps they will laugh at or make light of this; but I tell you Americans! that unless you speedily alter your course, *you* and your *Country are gone! ! ! ! !* . . .

If any of us see fit to go away, go to those who have been for many years, and are now our greatest earthly friends and benefactors—the English. If not so, go to our brethren, the Haytians, who, according to their word, are bound to protect and comfort us. The Americans say, that we are ungrateful—but I ask them for heaven's sake, what should we be grateful to them for—for murdering our fathers and mothers?—Or do they wish us to return thanks to them for chaining and handcuffing us, branding us, cramming fire down our throats, or for keeping us in slavery, and beating us nearly or quite to death to make us work in ignorance and miseries, to support them and their families. They certainly think that we are a gang of fools. Those among them, who have volunteered their services for our redemption, though we are unable to compensate them for their labours, we nevertheless thank them from the bottom of our hearts, and have our eyes steadfastly fixed upon them, and their labours of love for God and man.—But do slave-holders think that we thank them for keeping us in miseries, and taking our lives by the inches? . . .

Let no man of us budge one step, and let slave-holders come to beat us from our country. America is more our country, than it is the whites—we have enriched it with our *blood and tears.* The greatest riches in all America have arisen from our blood and tears:—and will they drive us from our property and homes, which we have earned with our *blood*? They must look sharp or this very thing will bring swift destruction upon them. The Americans have got so fat on our blood and groans, that they have almost forgotten the God of armies. But let them go on. . . .

Do the colonizationists think to send us off without first being reconciled to us? Do they think to bundle us up like brutes and send us off, as they did our brethren of the State of Ohio? Have they not to be reconciled to us, or reconcile us to them, for the cruelties with which they have afflicted our fathers and us? Methinks colonizationists think they have a set of brutes to deal with, sure enough. Do they think to drive us from our country and homes, after having enriched it with our blood and tears, and keep back millions of our dear brethren, sunk in the most barbarous wretchedness, to dig up gold and silver for them and their children? Surely, the Americans must think that we are brutes, as some of them have represented us to be. They think that we do not feel for our brethren, whom they are murdering by the inches, but they are dreadfully deceived. . . .

What nation under heaven, will be able to do any thing with us, unless God gives us up into its hand? But Americans, I declare to you, while you keep us and our children in bondage, and treat us like brutes, to make us support you and your families, we cannot be your friends. You do not look for it do you? Treat us then like men, and we will be your friends. And there is not a doubt in my mind, but that the whole of the past will be sunk into oblivion, and we yet, under God, will become a united and happy people. The whites may say it is impossible, but remember that nothing is impossible with God. . . .

I count my life not dear unto me, but I am ready to be offered at any moment, For what is the use of living, when in fact I am dead. But remember, Americans, that as miserable, wretched, degraded and abject as you have made us in preceding, and in this generation, to support you and your families, that some of you, (whites) on the continent of America, will yet curse the day that you ever were born. You want slaves, and want us for your slaves ! ! ! My colour will yet, root some of you out of the very face of the earth ! ! ! ! ! ! You may doubt it if you please. I know that thousands will doubt—they think they have us so well secured in wretchedness, to them and their children, that it is impossible for such things to occur. . . .

See your Declaration Americans! ! ! Do you understand your own language? Hear your languages, proclaimed to the world, July 4th, 1776—"We hold these truths to be self evident—that ALL MEN ARE CREATED EQUAL! ! that they *are endowed by their Creator with certain unalienable rights;* that among these are life, *liberty,* and the pursuit of happiness! !" Compare your own language above, extracted from your Declaration of Independence, with your cruelties and murders inflicted by your cruel and unmerciful fathers and yourselves on our fathers and on us—men who have never given your fathers or you the least provocation! ! ! ! ! !

1. What, in essence, is David Walker's approach to abolitionism? What does Walker have to say about Christianity in the advance of slavery?

2. If Walker's Appeal is directed toward slaves, how do you think he expected to get his message to them?

13-3 Nat Turner, Confession (1831)

This is a selection from Nat Turner's confessions, collected by his white lawyer after he had been apprehended for leading a revolt that culminated in the murder of fifty-five whites and the death of at least that many African Americans from white retaliation. The revolt, intended, in Turner◊s words, to "carry terror and devastation," was spurred by his divine vision. This selection describes the origins of Turner◊s sense of his own uniqueness and his divine revelation.

> From Thomas R. Gray, *The Confessions of Nat Turner, The Leader of the Late Insurrection in Southamton Virginia* (Baltimore, 1831).

...To a mind like mine, restless, inquisitive and observant of every thing that was passing, it is easy to suppose that religion was the subject to which it would be directed, and although this subject principally occupied my thoughts-there was nothing that I saw or heard of to which my attention was not directed-The manner in which I learned to read and write, not only had great influence on my own mind, as I acquired it with the most perfect ease, so much so, that I have no recollection whatever of learning the alphabet-but to the astonishment of the family, one day, when a book was shewn to me to keep me from crying, I began spelling the names of different objects-this was a source of wonder to all in the neighborhood, particularly the blacks-and this learning was constantly improved at all opportunities-when I got large enough to go to work, while employed, I was reflecting on many things that would present themselves to my imagination, and whenever an opportunity occurred of looking at a book, when the school children were getting their lessons, I would find many things that the fertility of my own imagination had depicted to me before....

All my time, not devoted to my master's service, was spent either in prayer, or in making experiments in casting different things in moulds made of earth, in attempting to make paper, gun-powder, and many other experiments, that although I could not perfect, yet convinced me of its practicability if I had the means.

I was not addicted to stealing in my youth, nor have ever been-Yet such was the confidence of the negroes in the neighborhood, even at this early period of my life, in my superior judgment, that they would often carry me with them when they were going on any roguery, to plan for them. Growing up among them, with this confidence in my superior judgment, and when this, in their opinions, was perfected by Divine inspiration, from the circumstances already alluded to in my infancy, and which belief was ever afterwards zealously inculcated by the austerity of my life and manners, which became the subject of remark by white and black.

-Having soon discovered to be great, I must appear so, and therefore studiously avoided mixing in society, and wrapped myself in mystery, devoting my time to fasting and prayer-by this time, having arrived to man's estate, and hearing the scriptures commented on at meetings, I was struck with that particular passage which says: "Seek ye the kingdom of Heaven and all things shall be added unto you." I reflected much on this passage, and prayed daily for light on this subject-As I was praying one day at my plough, the spirit spoke to me, saying "Seek ye the kingdom of Heaven and all things shall be added unto you."

Question-what do you mean by the Spirit? Ans.-The Spirit that spoke to the prophets in former days-and I was greatly astonished, and for two years prayed continually, whenever my duty would permit-and then again I had the same revelation, which fully confirmed me in the impression that I was ordained for some great purpose in the hands of the Almighty.

Several years rolled round, in which many events occurred to strengthen me in this my belief. At this time I reverted in my mind to the remarks made of me in my childhood, and the things that had been shewn me-and as it had been said of me in my childhood by those by whom I had been taught to pray, both white and black, and in whom I had the greatest confidence, that I had too much sense to be raised, and if I was, I would never be of any use to any one as a slave. Now finding I had arrived to man's estate, and was a slave, and these revelations being made known to me, I began to direct my attention to this great object, to fulfill the purpose for which, by this time, I felt

assured I was intended.

Knowing the influence I had obtained over the minds of my fellow servants (not by the means of conjuring and such like tricks-for to them I always spoke of such things with contempt) but by the communion of the Spirit whose revelations I often communicated to them, and they believed and said my wisdom came from God. I now began to prepare them for my purpose, by telling them something was about to happen that would terminate in fulfilling the great promise that had been made to me- ....

1. Summarize the evidence provided of Nat Turner's natural genius. How do others react to his intellectual abilities?
2. What are Turner's beliefs regarding his intellect? Describe the process whereby he determines the future course of his life.

13-4 An Abolitionist Defends the *Amistad* Mutineers (1839)

The Amistad case brought international attention to the issue of slavery in America. A group of American abolitionists formed the Amistad Committee to defend the ship's captives and their right to return to Africa. The following passage is a letter written by Lewis Tappan, a leading abolitionist and organizer of the committee, who recounts an interview with the leader of the captured Mendi tribesman, Joseph Cinque. Tappan soon became actively involved in the case by planning the strategy for the court trials, raising money for the defense, writing letters to the New York Journal of Commerce presenting the captive's side of the mutiny, and helping to argue their case before the U. S. Supreme Court. In the year following the release of the Africans, Tappan devoted his energy to arranging for their return home to Sierra Leone.

Source: Exploring *Amistad* at Mystic Seaport
http://amistad.mysticseaport.org/library/news/journal.of.commerce.html

To the Committee on Behalf of the African Prisoners and To the Marshal of the District of Connecticut. *New York Journal of Commerce* 10 Sept., 1839: 2.

Communicated for the Journal of Commerce
New Haven, Sept. 9, 1839.
To the Committee on behalf of the African prisoners:

I arrived here last Friday evening, with three men who are natives of Africa, and who were joined the next day by two others, to act as interpreters in conversing with Joseph Cinquez and his comrades. On going to the jail, the next morning, we found to our great disappointment, that only one of the men, J. F. was able to converse with the prisoners. He is about 30 years of age, a native of Geshee or Gishe, which is about 100 or 150 miles from the mouth of the river Gallinas, in the interior, which is about a day's journey south of Sierra Leone. He was kidnapped when about 12 years of age, and was liberated in Colombia, by Bolivar. He is able to converse a little in the Mandingo dialect, but understands better that of Gallinao, which some of the prisoners can speak. Most of the prisoners can understand him, although none of them can speak his Geshee dialect. You may imagine the joy manifested by these poor Africans, when they heard one of their own color address them in a friendly manner, and in a language they could comprehend!

The prisoners are in comfortable rooms.—They are well clothed in dark striped cotton trowsers, called by some of the manufacturers "hard times," and in striped cotton shirts. The girls are in calico frocks, and have made the little shawls that were given them into turbans. The prisoners eyed the clothes some time, and laughed a good deal among themselves before they put them on. Their food is brought to them in separate tin pans, and they eat it in an orderly manner. In general, they are in good health. One of their number, however, died on Tuesday last, and two or three more are on the sick list and considered dangerous. They probably suffer for want of exercise in the open air. The four children are apparently from 10 to 12 years of age. The boy and two of the girls (who appeared to be sisters) are Mandingos, and the other girl is from Congo. They are robust, are full of hilarity, especially the Mandingos. The sheriff of the county took them to ride in a wagon on Friday. At first their eyes were filled with tears, and they seemed to be afraid, but soon they enjoyed themselves very well, and appeared to be greatly delighted. The children speak only their native dialects. Neither Cinquez nor any of his comrades have been manacled since they have been here. Their demeanor is altogether quiet, kind, and orderly.

Most of the prisoners told the interpreter that they are from Mandingo. The district of Mandingo, in the Senegambia country, is bounded by the Atlantic Ocean, and is directly north of Liberia. Two or three of the men, besides one of the little girls, are natives of Congo, which is on the coast just south of the equator. The man with some of his teeth like tusks, is from Gahula in Congo. The teeth are said to be sharpened and made thus prominent by artificial means. One of the men from Mandingo, named Dama, talks Mandingo, and is a good looking and intelligent man. Cinquez is about 5 feet 8 inches high, of fine proportions, with a noble air. Indeed, the whole company, although thin in flesh, and generally of slight forms, and limbs, especially, are as good looking and intelligent a body of men as we usually meet with. All are young, and several are quite striplings. The Mandingos are described in books as being a very gentle race, cheerful in their dispositions, inquisitive, credulous, simple hearted, and much given to trading propensities. The Mandingo dialects are spoken extensively, and it is said to be the commercial language of nearly the whole coast of West Africa. We found that the following words are nearly the same in the Gallinas of the interpreter, in the Mandingo of the prisoners, in the Mandingo of Mungo Park, and in Jallowka of the German author Adeburg, viz:—Sun, moon, woman, child, father, head, hand, and foot. The numerals do not agree so well. If any person, who reads this statement, can furnish the Committee information concerning the Mandingo language, and its different dialects, particularly for vocabularies, they may render important service in the future examination of these unfortunate Africans. Professor Gibbs, of Yale College, has Adeburg's Mithridates, Park's Travels, and Mollien's Travels in Africa, and Professor Silliman has Prichard's Physical History of Mankind, which are at the service of the Committee.

Senegambia extends 800 miles in length, and where widest is about 700 miles. It is inhabited by different tribes, all negroes, living under petty sovereigns. Among these nations, the Foulahs, Jalcops, and Mandingoes, are the most numerous. Others less prominent are the Feloops, Naloes, Pagoes, Susoos, Timmancis, &c. The Foulahs are Mahomedans. The Mandingoes are the most numerous people of this region. These are partly Mahomedans and partly Pagans. Their original country is Manding, of which the government is said to be a species of republicanism. Nearly all the prisoners appear to be people of this description. The physician says they have nearly all been circumcised. No person will be able to converse with them well until he can speak the dialect of Manding. Persons, however, born on the Gallinas river may be able to converse with some of them. Although there are many native Africans in New York, and some of them came probably from places not remote from the native places of most of these prisoners, yet it is difficult to find an interpreter who can converse with them readily and intelligently. The tribes in Africa are very numerous, almost every tribe has a distinct language, and it often varies, it is said, from village to village.

After conversing awhile, through the interpreter with the men, who are in three different rooms, and with the four children, who are in a room by themselves, we went to the door of the room where Joseph Cinquez is confined: He is with several savage looking fellows, black and white, who are in jail on various charges. Visitors are not allowed to enter this strong hold of the jail, and the inmates can only be seen and conversed with through the aperture of the door. The jailer is fearful that some of them would escape if the door was opened in frequently. Even the other African prisoners are not permitted to hold converse with their Chief. Before they and he were deprived of this privilege, and when he occasionally came among them, they gathered around him, all talking at once, and shaking hands, as if they rejoiced to see him among them. They appeared to look up to him, I am told, with great respect. We found Cinquez stretched upon his bedding on the floor, wholly unclothed, with a single blanket partly wrapped around him. He arose at the call of the jailer, rather reluctantly, and came towards us with a good degree of gracefulness and native dignity. Afterwards we saw him well clothed; but he does not seem to like the tight dress of this country. At first he seemed adverse to answering the questions of the interpreter, and made the impression that he could not speak the Mandingo dialect. But after the interpreter had told him that he had conversed freely with his comrades, he conversed very freely, and with much energy of expression and action. R. S. Baldwin, Esq., of counsel for the prisoners, and Professor Gibbs having accompanied the interpreter.

Joseph Cinquez, as the Spaniards have named him, but who pronounces his name in his own language, Shinquau, says he is a native of the Mandingo country. His father is neither a king nor a chief, but one of the principal men. Shinquau was kidnapped and sent down to the town of Gendema or Geduma, in the Gallina country. The interpreter knows the place, says it is from ten to fifteen miles from the ocean. It is a small town on an inconsiderable river. Here he was put into the hands of King Sharka, and after staying a while was delivered by this king "to a great man" named Fulekower, belonging to Manu, near the mouth of the river Gambia, who disposed of him to the Spaniards. By them he was sent on board a ship, where he met, for the first time, the persons who are now with him in prison. From Shinquau and his comrades we gathered the following statements, nearly in their very words, as translated by the interpreter:—They demanded of the slavers where they were going to take them, but got no satisfactory answer. In one and a half moons, they said, we arrived at Havana. Here they were put ashore, and confined one moon in a house very close. Then they were put on board the schooner which brought them to this country, and continued on board of her about one moon or a month. After being on board the schooner some time, they agreed to take the schooner and go back to their own country. Previous to this the Captain was very cruel and beat them severely. They would not take it, to use their own expression, and therefore turned to and fought for it. After this they did not know which way to go. But at length they told the Spaniards to take them to Sierra Leone. "They made fools of us," said Shinquau, "and did not go to Sierra Leone." In the day time, they said they could tell very well which way to go by the sun, but at night the Spaniards deceived them, and put the vessel the other way. After this said they, we got here, and did not know where we were.

Captain Green, of Sag Harbor, who was one of the first men the prisoner met ashore, before their capture by Lieut. Gedney, of the U.S. brig Washington, and who has given me a circumstantial account, differing in many respects from what has been published, of all that took place, says that the Africans asked him, by one of their number who speaks a little broken English, "What country is this?" He replied, this is America. They immediately asked, "Is it a slave country?" Captain Green answered, it is free here, and safe, and there are no Spanish laws here. Shinquau then gave a sort of whistle, when they all sprang upon their feet and shouted. Captain Green and his associates sprang to their wagon for their guns, supposing the Africans were about to attack them. But Shinquau came up, delivered his cutlass and gun, and even offered his hat, &c, and the rest did the same, indicating that they would give all up, that Capt. G. might take charge of the schooner and everything on board. They however begged of him to take them to Sierre Leone. Shinquau positively assured Capt. G. at the time, and he repeats it now, that they threw nothing overboard. The stories about his loosening his girdle, and letting three or four hundred doubloons drop into the sea, and of diving and keeping under water forty minutes, are considered fabulous. The Africans assert that there was a quantity of doubloons in the trunks that were carried on shore on Long Island, and Captain Green says he heard the money rattle as the trunks were returned to the schooner by order of Lieut. Gedney. On examining the contents of the trunks afterwards no gold was found! Some person, or persons, are supposed to have the money, but who, is a secret. While on shore, at Long Island, Shinquau and his companions, although hungry, and with arms in their hands, would not kill a single animal, or take an article even to satisfy their hunger, without paying generously for it. They appeared, it is true, to know very little about the value of money, and gave a doubloon for a dog, and a small gold piece for some victuals.

The African prisoners are orderly and peaceable among themselves. Some of them sing well, and appear to be in good spirits and grateful for the kindness shown them. Col. Stanton Pendleton, at whose house I stop, is the jailer, and is kind and attentive to the prisoners. He provides them wholesome food in sufficient quantities, and gives every reasonable indulgence to the numerous visitors, from the neighboring towns and elsewhere, who throng the prison continually to see these interesting strangers from a distant land. Col. P. has allowed me to take copies of the warrants of commitment. The little girls, and the negro boy, Antonio, are committed as witnesses, "for neglecting to become recognized to the United States with surety," and Shinquau and his comrades are bound over "for murder on the high seas."

I have read an ingenious and well written article in the Evening Post signed Veto, in which the learned writer presents a pretty full examination of the case of the schooner Amistad. He says that it seems but too probable that the slave holders, Messrs. Ruez and Montez, conscious of the invalidity of their claim in the Civil Courts, have drawn this criminal prosecution (the charge of murder) to give time to their government to make a demand: and he rather singularly says "this raises a far more difficult question." If Veto will turn to Niles' Register for 1823, he will find an elegantly written and very able opinion of Chief Justice Tilghman, of Pa., on this subject, in which that eminent jurist, in giving his own judgment against the claim of a foreign government in the case of a fugitive charged with treason or murder, where there exists no treaty stipulation, as there does not at present between the United States and Spain, refers also to the corroborative opinions of all the preceding Presidents of the United States, (with the exception of the elder Adams, who had not given an opinion) very clearly and satisfactorily shows that the government of this country ought not to surrender persons situated as are Joseph Shinquau and his unfortunate countrymen, who are, by the act of God, thrown upon these shores to find, I trust, that protection and relief of which they had been, probably, forever deprived had it not been for this remarkable and providential interposition.

I remain, very truly, yours,
LEWIS TAPPAN.

P. S. Sabbath evening. The Rev. H. G. Ludlow prayed for the poor Africans this forenoon, very feelingly, at the service in his church. The outer door of the jail was closed today, and visitors generally were not admitted. I distributed some religious tracts, in the morning, to the convicts, and attempted to instruct the African prisoners, especially the children. They pronounce words in English very distinctly, and have already nearly the numerals. In showing them some books containing pictures of tropical animals, birds, &c., they seemed much pleased to recognize those with whose appearance they were acquainted, endeavoring to imitate their voices and actions. With suitable instruction these intelligent and docile Africans would soon learn to read and speak our language, and I cannot but hope that some of the benevolent inhabitants of this city will diligently continue to improve the opportunity to impart instruction to these pagans, brought by the providence of God to their very doors. Towards evening we made a visit to Shinquau, and conversed with him a considerable time. He drew his hand across his throat, as his room mates said he had done frequently before, and asked whether the people here intended to kill him. He was assured that probably no harm would happen to him—that we were his friends—and that he would be sent across the ocean towards the rising sun, home to his friends. His countenance immediately lost the anxious and distressed expression it had before, and beamed with joy. He says he was born about two days travelling from the ocean; that he purchased some goods, and being unable to pay for only two thirds of the amount, he was seized by the traders, his own countrymen, and sold to king Sharka for the remaining third. "I don't tell a bit of a lie about it," he said. He says he left in Africa both his parents, a wife and three children. Two of the children, he remarked, are a little larger than the African girls who are prisoners, and the other about as large. We endeavored to ascertain what his ideas were about a Supreme Being, if he had any. He said, "God is good." His countrymen, he says, know nothing about reading or writing. Tomorrow we expect to have him taken out of his cell, and examined, through the interpreter, by Messrs. Staples and Baldwin.

L. T.

1. *From the text of the letter, what can you infer were the arguments under consideration to return the Mendis to slavery?*
2. *Why do you think prominent individuals such as United States senators and a former president rallied to the defense of the Mendis? What defense do you think would be made for the Amistad captives today?*

13-5 De Bow's Review, "The Stability of the Union," (1850)

The economic and social differences between the north and south are illuminated in this document and the relative well being of slaves in relation to those differences explored. Many in the south saw the industrial north as a different planet with different values. They also saw, in the north, a hypocritical view of slavery, which the south justified as a way of elevating the slave from his condition in Africa.

The South is now with its institutions and capabilities, possessed of that on which half the manufacturing and commercial interests of the world depends. It is the source whence the only means of employing and feeding at least 5,000,000 whites can be drawn, and without which, nearly $1,000,000,000 of active capital in ships and factory would be valued less. A country and institutions so important to the welfare of humanity at large, are not to be trifled with. This country forms one-half of our glorious Union, on terms agreed upon by those immortal men who separated from England, because they would no longer suffer the continuance of the African slave-trade; but, in its independent position, the South holds the welfare of other nations almost entirely within its keeping. The capital and laboring abilities of England are such as to afford the South an outlet for its staple, should it exclude all other customers. The result of such a movement, would be to force other countries to draw their goods from England only. On the other hand, the manufacturing progress of the North is such, that in a few years she may absorb the whole of the southern staple, and place herself at the head of the manufacturing interest for the supply of the world. To the South, it is comparatively of small importance, whether England or the North obtains this mastery. Between the North and England, it is a mortal duel; and yet, in the crisis of this struggle, there are to be found persons at the North so destitute of all moral sense and political acuteness as to attack, in violation of the sacred pledge of the constitution, those institutions which it guarantees, and which are so necessary to the interests of humanity.

The continued harmony of the United States, permitting the industry of each section to furnish materials for the enterprise of the others, the reciprocity of benefits and uninterrupted interchange of mutual productions, facilitated by continually increasing means of intercourse and accumulation of capital, are laying the foundation for an empire of which the world's history not only affords no example, but the magnitude of which the wildest dream of the most imaginative of the world's statesmen has failed to conceive. In this undisturbed progress, the condition of the black race is being elevated on the swelling tide of white progress. Inasmuch as that the first slaves imported were, under their new masters, vastly superior in condition to the nude cannibals by whom they were sold, only because avarice triumphed over appetite so is the condition of the slave of the present day far above that of his progenitor a few generations back. The black race, in its servitude to the whites, has undergone an improvement, which the same race, in its state of African freedom, has failed to manifest.

By whatever degree, physically and morally, the blacks of the United States are superior to the nude cannibals of Africa, are they indebted to the white race for its active, though not disinterested agency. That process of improvement has not ceased, but is ever progressive in the train of white advancement. The huge lumber-car has no vitality of itself, but, attached to the resistless locomotive, moves forward with a vigor not its own. To cast off that race, in dependence on its own resources, is a singular manifestation of desire for its progress. As an indication of the progress in respect of freedom, which that race makes as it is trained to endure it, we may take the numbers classified upon the continent, for three periods, according to the United States census:

Slave States	Free States	Slaves	Free Blacks
1800,	857,095	61,441	73,100
1830,	2,005,475	182,070	137,525
1840,	2,486,226	215,568	172,509

In 1800 there were 36,946 slaves in what are now free States. The emancipation of these increased the free blacks in the free States; but the multiplication of the free blacks in the slave States is much more rapid, and is increasing on the proportion of slaves. Thus, the free blacks in those States, in forty years, reached 25 per cent of the original number of slaves-the emancipation being always 10 per cent of the increase. This has been greatly retarded by the abolition excitement. It is observable that the free blacks do not emigrate from the southern States. Their social position there is less onerous than the nominal freedom of the North. The increase of free blacks at the South, in forty years, was 250 per cent, and, at the North, 140 per cent. It is, undoubtedly, true, that the unconquerable repugnance of the North to permit the presence of blacks, if they can possibly be excluded, has, to a very great extent, checked emancipation. Thus, the constitution passed by Ohio on its organization as a State, with the black laws, passed by its Legislature, by preventing the ingress of slaves, greatly retarded emancipation. To suppose that the ordinance of 1787 stopped slave migration is a great mistake. It was the opposition of the white settlers to the presence of negroes that alone prevented it. Had any number of slaves been settled in Ohio, they would, ultimately, as in New York, have been emancipated, and would, by so much, have reduced the existing number of slaves. Thus, notwithstanding all the false sympathies of the North, the progress of emancipation at the South is quite as rapid as it should be, to avoid convulsions. It is more than probable, that, when the body of free blacks shall have become more considerable, they will supplant slaves as domestic servants, until slavery becomes, in those States, almost entirely predial. There is no comparison between the well-trained free black, subject to dismissal for misconduct as a domestic servant, and the slothful slave who has no fear of loss of place before his eyes. The free blacks must, necessarily, crowd out the slaves by a gradual and regular process, as the latter become more fitted for freedom. It is an inevitable law of political economy, that slavery must cease where trade is free and the population of freemen becomes more dense. This process is gradually and surely elevating the black race; and, to disturb it by any means, is at once to plunge this incapable race into hopeless barbarism, as complete as that which pervades Africa. An earnest desire for progress, political and social, for both races, as well on this continent as upon that of Europe, will find, in a firm adherence to the compromises of the constitution, the only sure mode of accomplishing that double end. To preserve the harmony of the several sections, by refraining from an attack upon that state of things which we may wish did not exist, but which we cannot remedy, is the only mode of ameliorating them. Those political schemers who seek for their own advancement amid the ruins of an empire, the desolation of a continent and the barbarizing of a race of men, will find, in the awakening intelligence of the people, the fiat of their own destruction.

1. *Describe the kind of reciprocal and interdependent relationship between the North and the South that is described in this document.*
2. *What, according to this document, is the best way to secure the stability of the Union, and to ensure the improvement of the black race?*

13-6 Benjamin Drew, Narratives of Escaped Slaves (1855)

Benjamin Drew was a Boston abolitionist who interviewed scores of ex-slaves who had escaped into Canada. These interviews were compiled and published as "The Refugee; Narratives of Fugitive Slaves in Canada Related by Themselves". Along with hundreds of other narratives, these testimonies form a dramatic answer to the southern position that slaves were well treated and much happier than northern laborers. These narratives were powerful tools for abolitionists who used them to stir a northern population often content to accept a positive view of slavery.

[Mrs. James Steward]

The slaves want to get away bad enough. They are not contented with their situation.

I am from the eastern shore of Maryland. I never belonged but to one master; he was very bad indeed. I was never sent to school, nor allowed to go to church. They were afraid we would have more sense than they. I have a father there, three sisters, and a brother. My father is quite an old man, and he is used very badly. Many a time he has been kept at work a whole long summer day without sufficient food. A sister of mine has been punished by his taking away her clothes and locking them up, because she used to run when master whipped her. He kept her at work with only what she could pick up to tie on her for decency. He took away her child which had just begun to walk, and gave it to another woman-but she went and got it afterward. He had a large farm eight miles from home. Four servants were kept at the house. My master could not manage to whip my sister when she was strong. He waited until she was confined, and the second week after her confinement he said, "Now I can handle you, now you are weak." She ran from him, however, and had to go through water, and was sick in consequence.

I was beaten at one time over the head by my master, until the blood ran from my mouth and nose: then he tied me up in the garret, with my hands over my head-then he brought me down and put me in a little cupboard, where I had to sit cramped up, part of the evening, all night, and until between four and five o'clock, next day, without any food. The cupboard was near a fire, and I thought I should suffocate.

My brother was whipped on one occasion until his back was as raw as a piece of beef, and before it got well, master whipped him again. His back was an awful sight.

We were all afraid of master: when I saw him coming, my heart would jump up into my mouth, as if I had seen a serpent.

I have been wanting to come away for eight years back. I waited for Jim Seward to get ready. Jim had promised to take me away and marry me. Our master would allow no marriages on the farm. When Jim had got ready, he let me know-he brought to me two suits of clothes-men's clothes-which he had bought on purpose for me. I put on both suits to keep me warm. We eluded pursuit and reached Canada in safety.

[Mrs. Nancy Howard]

I was born in Anne Arundel County, Maryland-was brought up in Baltimore. After my escape, I lived in Lynn, Mass., seven years, but I left there through fear of being carried back, owing to the fugitive slave law. I have lived in St. Catherines [Ontario, Canada] less than a year.

The way I got away was-my mistress was sick, and went into the country for her health. I went to stay with her cousin. After a month, my mistress was sent back to the city to her cousin's, and I waited on her. My daughter had been off three years. A friend said to me-"Now is your chance to get off." At last I concluded to go-the friend supplying me with money. I was asked no questions on the way north.

My idea of slavery is, that it is one of the blackest, the wickedest things everywhere in the world. When you tell them the truth, they whip you to make you lie. I have taken more lashes for this, than for any other thing, because I would not lie.

One day I set the table, and forgot to put on the carving-fork-the knife was there. I went to the table to put it on a plate. My master said,-"Where is the fork?" I told him "I forgot it." He says,-"You d—d black b—, I'll forget you!"-at the same time hitting me on the head with the carving knife. The blood spurted out-you can see. (Here the woman removed her turban and showed a circular cicatrices denuded of hair, about an inch in diameter, on the top of her head.) My mistress took me into the kitchen and put on camphor, but she could not stop the bleeding. A doctor was sent for. He came but asked no questions. I was frequently punished with raw hides-was hit with tongs and poker and anything. I used when I went out, to look up at the sky, and say, "Blessed Lord, oh, do take me out of this!" It seemed to me I could not bear another lick. I can't forget it. I sometimes dream that I am pursued, and when I wake, I am scared almost to death.

1. *Characterize the treatment of slaves observed and experienced by Mrs. James Steward.*
2. *How has the treatment Mrs. Nancy Howard received as a slave affected her physically and emotionally? What seems to be the common thread in these narratives of escaped slaves?*
3. *How might narratives like these, if publicized, fuel growing disharmony in a nation already experiencing political crisis?*

13-7   George Fitzhugh, "The Blessings of Slavery" (1857)

The descendent of an old southern family that had suffered hard times, Fitzhugh became a lawyer and planter. He became famous for his books "Sociology for the South" and "Cannibals All" which sought to elevate slavery to a higher plane. His call for an end to world capitalism and a society based on servile labor made him an infamous figure. In this document, Fitzhugh explores the idea that slaves are happier than competing "free" laborers and that a society that has embraced slavery is a stable and happy one.

The negro slaves of the South are the happiest, and in some sense, the freest people in the world. The children and the aged and infirm work not at all, and yet have all the comforts and necessaries of life provided for them. They enjoy liberty, because they are oppressed neither by care or labor. The women do little hard work, and are protected from the despotism of their husbands by their masters. The negro men and stout boys work, on the average, in good weather, no more than nine hours a day. The balance of their time is spent in perfect abandon. Besides, they have their Sabbaths and holidays. White men, with som muh of license and abandon, would die of ennui; but negroes luxuriate in corporeal and mental repose. With their faces upturned to the sun, they can sleep at any hour; and quiet sleep is the gretest of human enjoyments. "Blessed be the man who invented sleep." 'Tis happiness in itself-and results from contentment in the present, and confident assurance of the future. We do not know whether free laborers ever sleep. They are fools to do so; for, whilst they sleep, the wily and watchful capitalist is devising means to ensnare and exploit them. The free laborer must work or starve. He is more of a slave than the negro, because he works longer and harder for less allowance than the slave, and has no holiday, because the cares of life with him begin when its labors end. He has no liberty and not a single right. . . .

Until the lands of America are appropriated by a few, population becomes dense, competition among laborers active, employment uncertain, and wages low, the personal liberty of all the whites will continue to be a blessing. We have vast unsettled territories; population may cease to increase slowly, as in most countries, and many centuries may elapse before the question will be practically suggested, whether slavery to capital be preferable to slavery to human masters. But the negro has neither energy nor enterprise, and, even in our sparser populations, finds with his improvident habits, that his liberty is a curse to himself, and a greater curse to the society around him. These considerations, and others equally obvious, have induced the South to attempt to defend negro slavery as an exceptional institution, admitting, nay asserting, that slavery, in the general or in the abstract, is morally wrong, and against common right. With singular inconsistency, after making this admission, which admits away the authority of the Bible, of profane history, and of the almost universal practice of mankind-they turn around and attempt to bolster up the cause of negro slavery by these very exploded authorities. If we mean not to repudiate all divine, and almost all human authority in favor of slavery, we must vindicate that institution in the abstract.

To insist that a status of society, which has been almost universal, and which is expressly and continually justified by Holy Writ, is its natural, normal, and necessary status, under the ordinary circumstances, is on its face a plausible and probable proposition. To insist on less, is to yield our cause, and to give up our religion; for if white slavery be morally wrong, be a violation of natural rights, the Bible cannot be true. Human and divine authority do seem in the general to concur, in establishing the expediency of having masters and slaves of different races. In very many nations of antiquity, and in some of modern times, the law has permitted the native citizens to become slaves to each other. But few take advantage of such laws; and the infrequency of the practice establishes the general truth that master and slave should be of different national descent. In some respects the wider the difference the better, as the slave will feel less mortified by his position. In other respects, it may be that too wide a difference hardens the hearts and brutalizes the feeling of both master and slave. The civilized man hates the savage, and the savage returns the hatred with interest. Hence West India slavery of newly caught negroes is not a very humane, affectionate, or civilizing institution. Virginia negroes have become moral and intelligent. They love their master and his family, and the attachment is reciprocated. Still, we like the idle, but intelligent house-servants, better than the hard-used, but stupid outhands; and we like the mulatto better than the negro; yet the negro is generally more affectionate, contented, and faithful.

The world at large looks on negro slavery as much the worst form of slavery; because it is only acquainted with West India slavery. But our Southern slavery has become a benign and protective institution, and our negroes are confessedly better off than any free laboring population in the world. How can we contend that white slavery is wrong, whilst all the great body of free laborers are starving; and slaves, white or black, throughout the world, are enjoying comfort? . . .

The aversion to negroes, the antipathy of race, is much greater at the North than at the South; and it is very probable that this antipathy to the person of the negro, is confounded with or generates hatred of the institution with which he is usually connected. Hatred to slavery is very generally little more than hatred of negroes.

There is one strong argument in favor of negro slavery over all other slavery; that he, being unfitted for the mechanic arts, for trade, and all skillful pursuits, leaves those pursuits to be carried on by the whites; and does not bring all industry into disrepute, as in Greece and Rome, where the slaves were not only the artists and mechanics, but also the merchants.

Whilst, as a general and abstract question, negro slavery has no other claims over other forms of slavery, except that from inferiority, or rather peculiarity, of race, almost all negroes require masters, whilst only the children, the women, and the very weak, poor, and ignorant, &c., among the whites, need some protective and governing relation of this kind; yet as a subject of temporary, but worldwide importance, negro slavery has become the most necessary of all human institutions.

The African slave trade to America commenced three centuries and a half since. By the time of the American Revolution, the supply of slaves had exceeded the demand for slave labor, and the slaveholders, to get rid of a burden, and to prevent the increase of a nuisance, became violent opponents of the slave trade, and many of them abolitionists. New England, Bristol, and Liverpool, who reaped the profits of the trade, without suffering from the nuisance, stood out for a long time against its abolition. Finally, laws and treaties were made, and fleets fitted out to abolish it; and after a while, the slaves of most of South America, of the West Indies, and of Mexico were liberated. In the meantime, cotton, rice, sugar, coffee, tobacco, and other products of slave labor, came into universal use as necessaries of life. The population of Western Europe, sustained and stimulated by those products, was trebled, and that of the North increased tenfold. The products

of slave labor became scarce and dear, and famines frequent. Now, it is obvious, that to emancipate all the negroes would be to starve Western Europe and our North. Not to extend and increase negro slavery, *pari passu*, with the extension and multiplication of free society, will produce much suffering. If all South America, Mexico, the West Indies, and our Union south of Mason and Dixon's line, of the Ohio and Missouri, were slaveholding, slave products would be abundant and cheap in free society; and their market for their merchandise, manufactures, commerce, &c., illimitable. Free white laborers might live in comfort and luxury on light work, but for the exacting and greedy landlords, bosses, and other capitalists.

We must confess, that overstock the world as you will with comforts and with luxuries, we do not see how to make capital relax its monopoly-how to do aught but tantalize the hireling. Capital, irresponsible capital, begets, and ever will beget, the *immedicabile vulnus* of so-called Free Society. It invades every recess of domestic life, infects its food, its clothing, its drink, its very atmosphere, and pursues the hireling, from the hovel to the poor-house, the prison and the grave. Do what he will, go where he will, capital pursues and persecutes him. "*Haeret lateri lethalis arundo!*"

Capital supports and protects the domestic slave; taxes, oppresses, and persecutes the free laborer.

1. How does Fitzhugh support his claim that, "The negro slaves of the South are the happiest, and in some sense, the freest people in the world"?
2. Identify and explain the author's arguments in favor of the institution of slavery.

PART FOURTEEN
THE SECTIONAL CRISIS

14-1   William Lloyd Garrison, from The Liberator (1831)

William Lloyd Garrison was among the most prominent abolitionists and his long running paper "The Liberator" was a bastion of abolitionist thought and agitation. An opponent of gradual emancipation of slaves, Garrison spoke for immediate abolition. Often threatened, harassed, and abused, Garrison continued his fiery rhetoric even to the point of burning copies of the Constitution at public meetings. This document reveals the general apathy an even hostility of most northerners on the issue of slavery.

During my recent tour for the purpose of exciting the minds of the people by a series of discourses on the subject of slavery, every place that I visited gave fresh evidence of the fact that a great revolution in public sentiment was to be effected in the free states-and particularly in New England-than at the South. I find contempt more bitter, opposition more active, detraction more relentless, prejudice more stubborn, and apathy more frozen, than among slaveowners themselves. Of course, there were individual exceptions to the contrary.

This state of things afflicted but did not dishearten me. I determined, at every hazard, to lift up the standard of emancipation in the eyes of the nation, within sight of Bunker Hill and in the birthplace of liberty. That standard is now unfurled; and long may it float, unhurt by the spoliations of time or the missiles of a desperate foe-yea, till every chain be broken, and every bondman set free! Let Southern oppressors tremble-let all the enemies of the persecuted blacks tremble.
. . .

Assenting to the "self-evident truth" maintained in the American Declaration of Independence "that all men are created equal, and endowed by their Creator with certain inalienable rights-among which are life, liberty, and the pursuit of happiness," I shall strenuously contend for the immediate enfranchisement of our slave population. . . . In Park Street Church, on the Fourth of July, 1829, in an address on slavery, I unreflectingly assented to the popular but pernicious doctrine of gradual abolition. I seize this opportunity to make a full and unequivocal recantation, and thus publicly to ask pardon of my God, of my country, and of my brethren the poor slaves, for having uttered a sentiment so full of timidity, injustice, and absurdity. . . .

I am aware that many object to the severity of my language; but is there not cause for severity? I will be as harsh as truth, and as uncompromising as justice. On this subject I do not wish to think, or speak, or write, with moderation. No! No! Tell a man whose house is on fire to give a moderate alarm; tell him to moderately rescue his wife from the hands of the ravisher; tell the mother to gradually extricate her babe from the fire into which it has fallen-but urge me not to use moderation in a cause like the present. I am in earnest-will not equivocate-I will not excuse-I will not retreat in a single inch-and I will be heard. The apathy of the people is enough to make every statue leap from its pedestal, and to hasten the resurrection of the dead.

It is pretended that I am retarding the cause of emancipation by the coarseness of my invective and the precipitancy of my measures. The charge is not true. On this question my influence-humble as it is-is felt at this moment to a considerable extent, and shall be felt in coming years-not perniciously, but beneficially-not as a curse, but as a blessing. And posterity will bear testimony that I was right.

1. What are Garrison's observations regarding public sentiment about slavery in America?
2. How does Garrison justify his bold stand on slavery and his proposal for immediate abolition?

14-2   Harriet Beecher Stowe, from Uncle Tom's Cabin (1852)

Although she authored several books on New England, Harriet Beacher Stowe was best known for her portrayal of slavery in Uncle Tom's Cabin. The daughter of the most important Puritan preacher of her day, Stowe had a long concern with humanitarian causes. The death of one of Stowe's children prompted her to become involved with the abolitionist movement. Uncle Tom's Cabin outraged the south and solidified the anti-slavery movement in the north. Some even feel the book was one of the factors that brought on the Civil war. The following section finds Uncle Tom, recently purchased by the cruel Simon Legree, on his way to Legree's plantation.

"And now," said Legree, "come here, you Tom. You see, I told ye I didn't buy ye jest for the common work. I mean to promote ye, and make a driver of ye; and tonight ye may jest as well begin to get ye hand in. Now, ye jest take this yer gal and flog her; ye've seen enough on't [of it] to know how." "I beg Mas'r' pardon," said Tom; "hopes Mas'r won't set me at that. It's what I an't used to-never did-and can't do, no way possible."

"Ye'll larn a pretty smart chance of things ye never did know, before I've done with ye!" said Legree, taking up a cowhide and striking Tom a heavy blow across the cheek, and following up the infliction by a shower of blows.

"There!" he said, as he stopped to rest; "now, will ye tell me ye can't do it?"

"Yes, Mas'r," said Tom, putting up his hand, to wipe the blood that trickled down his face. "I'm willin' to work, night and day, and work while there's life and breath in me. But this yer thing I can't feel it right to do; and, Mas'r, I never shall do it-never!"

Tom had a remarkably smooth, soft voice, and a habitually respectful manner that had given Legree an idea that he would be cowardly and easily subdued. When he spoke these last words, a thrill of amazement went through everyone. The poor woman clasped her hands and said, "O Lord!" and everyone involuntarily looked at each other and drew in their breath, as if to prepare for the storm that was about to burst.

Legree looked stupefied and confounded; but at last burst forth: "What! Ye blasted black beast! Tell me ye don't think it right to do what I tell ye! What have any of you cussed cattle to do with thinking what's right? I'll put a stop to it! Why, what do ye think ye are? May be ye think ye're a gentleman, master Tom, to be a telling your master what's right, and what an't! So you pretend it's wrong to flog the gal!"

"I think so, Mas'r," said Tom; "the poor crittur's sick and feeble; 'twould be downright cruel, and it's what I never will do, nor begin to. Mas'r, if you mean to kill me, kill me; but, as to my raising my hand again any one here, I never shall-I'll die first!"

Tom spoke in a mild voice, but with a decision that could not be mistaken. Legree shook with anger; his greenish eyes glared fiercely, and his very whiskers seemed to curl with passion. But, like some ferocious beast, that plays with its victim before he devours it, he kept back his strong impulse to proceed to immediate violence, and broke out into bitterly raillery.

"Well, here's a pious dog, at last, let down among us sinners-a saint, a gentleman, and no less, to talk to us sinners about our sins! Powerful holy crittur, he must be! Here, you rascal, you make believe to be so pious-didn't you never hear, out of yer Bible, 'Servants, obey yer masters'? An't I yer master? Didn't I pay down twelve hundred dollars, cash, for all there is inside yer old cussed black shell? An't yer mine, now, body and soul?" he said, giving Tom a violent kick with his heavy boot; "tell me!"

In the very depth of physical suffering, bowed by brutal oppression, this question shot a gleam of joy an triumph through Tom's soul. He suddenly stretched himself up, and, looking earnestly to heaven, while the tears and blood that flowed down his face mingled, he exclaimed, " No! no! no! my soul an't yours, Mas'r! You haven't bought it-ye can't buy it! It's been bought and paid for by One that is able to keep it. No matter, no matter, you can't harm me!"

"I can't!" said Legree, with a sneer; "we'll see-we'll see! Here Sambo, Quimbo, give this dog such a breakin' in as he won't get over this month!"

The two gigantic Negroes that now laid hold of Tom, with fiendish exultation in their faces, might have formed no unapt personification of powers of darkness. The poor woman screamed with apprehension, and all rose, as by a general impulse, while they dragged him unresisting from the place.

1. *Describe the view of slavery portrayed in this selection from Uncle Tom's Cabin.*
2. *What characteristics does Legree possess and what actions does he do that are symbolic of the practice of slavery?*
3. *How is Tom a symbol of the moral strength and spirit of slaves?*

14-3 *National Convention of Colored People, Report on Abolition (1847)*

During the 1830's a movement of Free African Americans emerged calling on their population to take the lead in abolition arguing that they could not rely on the white population to achieve the end of slavery. In this document, the pervasive nature of slavery is described to counter the common northern view that slavery was restricted to a few plantation owners in the South. Free speech, truth and unity are urged as methods of achieving abolition of slavery.

The Committee appointed to draft a Report respecting the best means of abolishing Slavery and destroying Caste in the United States, beg leave most respectfully to Report: That they have had the important subjects referred to them, under consideration, and have carefully endeavored to examine all their points and bearings to the best of their ability; and from every view they have been able to take they have arrived at the conclusion that the best means of abolishing slavery is proclamation of truth, and that the best means of destroying caste is the mental, moral and industrial improvement of our people.

First, as respects Slavery, Your Committee find this monstrous crime, this stupendous iniquity, closely interwoven with all the great interests, institutions and organizations of the country; pervading and influencing every class and grade of society, securing their support, obtaining their approbation, and commanding their homage. Availing itself of the advantage which age gives to crime, it has perverted the judgment, blunted the moral sense, blasted the sympathies, and created in the great mass,-the overwhelming majority of the people-a moral sentiment altogether favorable to its own character, and its own continuance. Press and pulpit are alike prostituted and made to serve the end of this infernal institution. The power of the government, and the sanctity of religion, church and state, are joined with the guilty oppressor against the oppressed-and the voice of this great nation is thundering in the ear of our enslaved fellow countrymen the terrible fiat, *you shall be slaves or die!* The slave is in the minority, a small minority. The oppressors are an overwhelming majority. The oppressed are three millions, their oppressors are seventeen millions. The one is weak, the other is strong; the one is without arms, without means of concert, and without government; the other possess every advantage in these respects; and the deadly aim of their million of musketry, and loud-mouthed cannon tells the down-trodden slave in unmistakable language, *he must be a slave or die.* In these circumstances, your committee are called upon to report as to the best means of abolishing slavery. And without pretending parties and factions, though did time permit, they would gladly do so, they beg at once to state their entire disapprobation of any plan of emancipation involving a resort to bloodshed. With the facts of our condition before us, it is impossible for us to contemplate any appeal to the slave to take vengence on his guilty master, but with the utmost reprobation. Your Committee regard any counsel of this sort as the perfection of folly, suicidal in the extreme, and abominably wicked. We should utterly frown down and wholly discountenance any attempt to lead our people to confide in brute force as a reformatory instrumentality. All argument put forth in favor of insurrection and bloodshed, however well intended, is either the result of an unpardonable impatience or an atheistic want of faith in the power of truth as a means of regenerating and reforming the world. Again we repeat, let us set our faces against all such absurd, unavailing, dangerous and mischievous ravings, emanating from what source they may. The voice of God and of common sense, equally point out a more excellent way, and that way is a faithful, earnest, and persevering enforcement of the great principles of justice and morality, religion and humanity. These are the only invincible and infallible means within our reach with which to overthrow this foul system of blood and ruin. Your Committee deem it susceptible of the clearest demonstration, that slavery exists in this country, because the people of this country WILL its existence. And they deem it equally clear, that no system or institution can exist for an hour against the earnestly-expressed WILL of the people. It were quite easy to bring to the support of the foregoing proposition powerful and conclusive illustrations from the history of reform in all ages, and especially in our own. But the palpable truths of the propositions, as well as the familiarity of the facts illustrating them, entirely obviate such a necessity.

Our age is an age of great discoveries; and one of the greatest is that which revealed that this world is to be ruled, shaped and guided by the *marvelous might of mind.* The human voice must supersede the roar of cannon. Truth alone is the legitimate antidote of falsehood. Liberty is always sufficient to grapple with tyranny. Free speech-free discussion-peaceful agitation,-the foolishness of preaching these, under God, will subvert this giant crime, and send it reeling to its grave, as if smitten by a voice from the throne of God. Slavery exists because it is popular. It will cease to exist when it is made unpopular. Whatever therefore tends to make Slavery unpopular tends to its destruction. This every Slaveholder knows full well, and hence his opposition to all discussion of the subject. It is an evidence of intense feeling of alarm, when John C. Calhoun calls upon the North to put down what he is pleased to term "this plundering agitation." Let us give the Slaveholder what he most dislikes. Let us expose his crimes and his foul abominations. He is reputable and must be made disreputable. He must be regarded as a moral lepor-slummed as a loathsome wretch-outlawed from Christian communion, and from social respectability-an enemy of God and man, to be execrated by the community till he shall repent of his foul crimes, and give proof of his sincerity by breaking every chain and letting the oppressed go free. Let us invoke the Press and appeal to the pulpit to deal out the righteous denunciations of heaven against oppression, fraud and wrong, and the desire of our hearts will soon be given us in the triumph of Liberty throughout all the land. . . .

1. According to this report, what are the causes and effects of the institution of slavery?
2. Identify and explain the views proposed in this report regarding the best method of abolishing slavery? Why is this method preferred over other alternatives?

14-4 A Dying Statesman Speaks Out Against the Compromise of 1850

At age sixty-eight, John C. Calhoun made his last address to the Senate during the great debate over the Compromise of 1850. Although in a sickly and frail condition, Calhoun prepared his speech with great care and dictated it to his secretary, Joseph Alfred Scoville. Too weak to deliver the speech himself, the senator had James Mason of Virginia read it from a printed version. Calhoun, draped in a black cloak, was assisted to his desk on the Senate floor a few minutes past noon on March 4, 1850, and scanned the crowded galleries as Mason read. He returned to the Senate on March 7 to listen to the speech given by Daniel Webster in favor of the compromise. Calhoun died on March 31, 1850.

Source: The Library of Congress, *American Memory: Historical Collections for the National Digital Library* http://lcweb2.loc.gov/cgi-bin/query/r?ammem/mcc:@field(DOCID+@lit(mcc/009))

March 4, 1850

I have, Senators, believed from the first that the agitation of the subject of slavery would, if not prevented by some timely and effective measure, end in disunion. Entertaining this opinion, I have, on all proper occasions, endeavored to call the attention of each of the two great parties which divide the country to adopt some measure to prevent so great a disaster, but without success. The agitation has been permitted to proceed, with almost no attempt to resist it, until it has reached a period when it can no longer be disguised or denied that the Union is in danger. You have thus had forced upon you the greatest and the gravest question that can ever come under your consideration: How can the Union be preserved?

To give a satisfactory answer to this mighty question, it is indispensable to have an accurate and thorough knowledge of the nature and the character of the cause by which the Union is endangered. Without such knowledge, it is impossible to pronounce, with any certainty, by what measure it can be saved. . . .

The first question, then . . . is: What is it that has endangered the Union? . . .

One of the causes is, undoubtedly, to be traced to the long continued agitation of the slave question on the part of the North and the many aggressions which they have made on the rights of the South during the time. . . .

There is another lying back of it, with which this is intimately connected, that may be regarded as the great and primary cause. That is to be found in the fact that the equilibrium between the two sections in the government, as it stood when the Constitution was ratified and the government put into action, has been destroyed. At that time there was nearly a perfect equilibrium between the two which afforded ample means to each to protect itself against the aggression of the other; but, as it now stands, one section has the exclusive power of controlling the government, which leaves the other without any adequate means of protecting itself against its encroachment and oppression. . . .

The result of the whole is to give the Northern section a predominance in every part of the government and thereby concentrate in it the two elements which constitute the federal government—a majority of states and a majority of their population, estimated in federal numbers. Whatever section concentrates the two in itself possesses the control of the entire government.

But we are just at the close of the sixth decade and the commencement of the seventh. The census is to be taken this year, which must add greatly to the decided preponderance of the North in the House of Representatives and in the electoral college. The prospect is also that a great increase will be added to its present preponderance in the Senate during the period of the decade by the addition of new states. Two territories, Oregon and Minnesota, are already in progress, and strenuous efforts are being made to bring in three additional states from the territory recently conquered from Mexico; which, if successful, will add three other states in a short time to the Northern section, making five states and increasing the present number of its states from fifteen to twenty, and of its senators from thirty to forty. On the contrary, there is not a single territory in progress in the Southern section and no certainty that any additional state will be added to it during the decade.

The prospect, then, is that the two sections in the Senate, should the efforts now made to exclude the South from the newly acquired territories succeed, will stand before the end of the decade twenty Northern states to twelve Southern (considering Delaware as neutral), and forty Northern senators to twenty-eight Southern. This great increase of senators, added to the great increase of members of the House of Representatives and electoral college on the part of the North, which must take place over the next decade, will effectually and irretrievably destroy the equilibrium which existed when the government commenced.

Had this destruction been the operation of time, without the interference of government, the South would have had no reason to complain; but such was not the fact. It was caused by the legislation of this government, which was appointed as the common agent of all and charged with the protection of the interests and security of all.

The legislation by which it has been effected may be classed under three heads. The first is that series of acts by which the South has been excluded from the common territory belonging to all of the states as the members of the federal Union, and which had the effect of extending vastly the portion allotted to the Northern section, and restricting within narrow limits the portion left the South. And the next consists in adopting a system of revenue and disbursements by which an undue proportion of the burden of taxation has been imposed upon the South and an undue proportion of its proceeds appropriated to the North. And the last is a system of political measures by which the original character of the government has been radically changed.

I propose to bestow upon each of these . . . a few remarks with the view of showing that it is owing to the action of this government that the equilibrium between the two sections has been destroyed and the whole powers of the system centered in a sectional majority.

The first of the series of acts by which the South was deprived of its due share of the territories originated with the Confederacy which preceded the existence of this government. It is to be found in the provision of the Ordinance of 1787. Its effect was to exclude the South entirely from that vast and fertile region which lies between the Ohio and the Mississippi rivers now embracing five states and one territory. The next of the series is the Missouri Compromise, which excluded the South from that large portion of Louisiana which lies north of 36°30', excepting what is included in the state of Missouri.

The last of the series excluded the South from the whole of the Oregon Territory. All these, in the slang of the day, were what are called slave territories and not free soil; that is, territories belonging to slaveholding powers and open to the emigration of masters with their slaves. By these several acts, the South was excluded from 1,238,025 square miles, an extent of country considerably exceeding the entire valley of the Mississippi.

To the South was left the portion of the territory of Louisiana lying south of 36°30', and the portion north of it included in the state of Missouri; the portion lying south of 36°30' including the states of Louisiana and Arkansas, and the territory lying west of the latter and south of 36°30', called the Indian Country. These, with the territory of Florida, now the state, make, in the whole, 283,503 square miles. To this must be added the territory acquired with Texas. If the whole should be added to the Southern section, it would make an increase of 325,520, which would make the whole left to the South, 609,023. But a large part of Texas is still in contest between the two sections, which leaves it uncertain what will be the real extent of the portion of her territory that may be left to the South.

I have not included the territory recently acquired by the treaty with Mexico. The North is making the most strenuous efforts to appropriate the whole to herself by excluding the South from every foot of it. If she should succeed, it will add to that from which the South has already been excluded 526,078 square miles, and would increase the whole which the North has appropriated to herself to 1,764,023, not including the portion that she may succeed in excluding us from in Texas.

To sum up the whole, the United States, since they declared their independence, have acquired 2,373,046 square miles of territory, from which the North will have excluded the South if she should succeed in monopolizing the newly acquired territories, from about three-fourths of the whole, leaving to the South but about one-fourth.

Such is the first and great cause that has destroyed the equilibrium between the two sections in the government.

The next is the system of revenue and disbursements which his been adopted by the government. It is well known that the government has derived its revenue mainly from duties on imports. I shall not undertake to show that such duties must necessarily fall mainly on the exporting states, and that the South, as the great exporting portion of the Union, has in reality paid vastly more than her due proportion of the revenue because . . . the subject has on so many occasions been fully discussed. Nor shall I, for the same reason, undertake to show that a far greater portion of the revenue has been disbursed at the North than its due share, and that the joint effect of these causes has been to transfer a vast amount from South to North, which, under an equal system of revenue and disbursement, would not have been lost to her.

If to this be added that many of the duties were imposed, not for revenue but for protection; that is, intended to put money, not in the Treasury but directly into the pocket of the manufacturers, some conception may be formed of the immense amount which, in the long course of sixty years, has been transferred from South to North. There are no data by which it can be estimated with any certainty, but it is safe to say that it amounts to hundreds of millions of dollars. Under the most moderate estimate, it would be sufficient to add greatly to the wealth of the North, and thus greatly increase her population by attracting emigration from all quarters to that section. . . .

That the government claims, and practically maintains, the right to decide in the last resort as to the extent of its powers will scarcely be denied by anyone conversant with the political history of the country. That it also claims the right to resort to force to maintain whatever power she claims, against all opposition, is equally certain. Indeed, it is apparent, from what we daily hear, that this has become the prevailing and fixed opinion of a great majority of the community. Now, I ask, what limitation can possibly be placed upon the powers of a government claiming and exercising such rights? And, if none can be, how can the separate governments of the states maintain and protect the powers reserved to them by the Constitution, or the people of the several states maintain those which are reserved to them, and among others the sovereign powers by which they ordained and established, not only their separate state constitutions and governments but also the Constitution and government of the United States?

But, if they have no constitutional means of maintaining them against the right claimed by this government, it necessarily follows that they hold them at its pleasure and discretion, and that all the powers of the system are in reality concentrated in it. It also follows that the character of the government has been changed, in consequence, from a federal republic, as it originally came from the hands of its framers, and that it has been changed into a great national, consolidated democracy. It has, indeed, at present, all the characteristics of the latter and not one of the former, although it still retains its outward form.

The result of the whole of these causes combined is that the North has acquired a decided ascendancy over every department of this government, and through it a control over all the powers of the system. A single section, governed by the will of the numerical majority, has now in fact the control of the government and the entire powers of the system. What was once a constitutional federal republic is now converted, in reality, into one as absolute as that of the Autocrat of Russia, and as despotic in its tendency as any absolute government that ever existed.

As, then, the North has the absolute control over the government, it is manifest that on all questions between it and the South, where there is a diversity of interests, the interests of the latter will be sacrificed to the former, however oppressive the effects may be, as the South possesses no means by which it can resist through the action of the government. But if there was no question of vital importance to the South, in reference to which there was a diversity of views between the two sections, this state of things might be endured without the hazard of destruction to the South. There is a question of vital importance to the Southern section, in reference to which the views and feelings of the two sections are as opposite and hostile as they can possibly be.

I refer to the relation between the two races in the Southern section, which constitutes a vital portion of her social organization. Every portion of the North entertains views and feelings more or less hostile to it. Those most opposed and hostile regard it a sin, and consider themselves under most sacred obligation to use every effort to destroy it. Indeed, to the extent that they conceive they have power, they regard themselves as implicated in the sin and responsible for suppressing it by the use of all and every means. Those less opposed and hostile regard it as a crime—an offense against humanity, as they call it—and, although not so fanatical, feel themselves bound to use all efforts to effect the same object; while those who are least opposed and hostile regard it as a blot and a stain on the character of what they call the nation, and feel themselves accordingly bound to give it no countenance or support. On the contrary, the Southern section regards the relation as one which cannot be destroyed without subjecting the two races to the greatest calamity and the section to poverty, desolation, and wretchedness; and accordingly they feel bound by every consideration of interest and safety to defend it.

This hostile feeling on the part of the North toward the social organization of the South long lay dormant, but it only required some cause to act on those who felt most intensely that they were responsible for its continuance to call it into action. The increasing power of this government and of the control of the Northern section over all its departments furnished the cause. It was this which made an impression on the minds of many that there was little or no restraint to prevent the government from doing whatever it might choose to do. This was sufficient of itself to put the most fanatical portion of the North in action for the purpose of destroying the existing relation between the two races in the South.

The first organized movement toward it commenced in 1835. Then, for the first time, societies were organized, presses established, lecturers sent forth to excite the people of the North, and incendiary publications scattered over the whole South through the mail. The South was thoroughly aroused. Meetings were held everywhere and resolutions adopted calling upon the North to apply a remedy to arrest the threatened evil, and pledging themselves to adopt measures for their own protection if it was not arrested. At the meeting of Congress, petitions poured in from the North calling upon Congress to abolish slavery in the District of Columbia and to prohibit what they called the internal slave trade between the states, announcing at the same time that their ultimate object was to abolish slavery, not only in the District but in the states and throughout the whole Union.

At this period, the number engaged in the agitation was small and possessed little or no personal influence. Neither party in Congress had, at that time, any sympathy with them or their cause. The members of each party presented their petitions with great reluctance. Nevertheless, as small and as contemptible as the party then was, both of the great parties of the North dreaded them. They felt that, though small, they were organized in reference to a subject which had a great and commanding influence over the Northern mind. Each party on that account, feared to oppose their petitions lest the opposite party should take advantage of the one who might do so by favoring their petitions. The effect was that both united in insisting that the petitions should be received and that Congress should take jurisdiction over the subject for which they prayed. To justify their course they took the extraordinary ground that Congress was bound to receive petitions on every subject, however objectionable it might be, and whether they had or had not jurisdiction over the subject.

These views prevailed in the House oft Representatives, and partially in the Senate; and thus the party succeeded, in their first movements, in gaining what they proposed—a position in Congress from which agitation could be extended over the whole Union. This was the commencement of the agitation, which has ever since continued, and which, as is now acknowledged, has endangered the Union itself.

As for myself, I believed, at that early period, if the party who got up the petitions should succeed in getting Congress to take jurisdiction, that agitation would follow and that it would, in the end, if not arrested, destroy the Union. I then so expressed myself in debate and called upon both parties to take grounds against assuming jurisdiction; but in vain. Had my voice been heeded and had Congress refused to take jurisdiction, by the united votes of all parties the agitation which followed would have been prevented, and the fanatical zeal that gives impulse to the agitation, and which has brought us to our present perilous condition, would have become extinguished from the want of something to feed the flame. That was the time for the North to have shown her devotion to the Union; but, unfortunately, both of the great parties of that section were so intent on obtaining or retaining party ascendancy that all other considerations were overlooked or forgotten.

What has since followed are but the natural consequences. With the success of their first movement, this small, fanatical party began to acquire strength; and, with that, to become an object of courtship to both the great parties. The necessary consequence was a further increase of power and a gradual tainting of the opinions of both of the other parties with their doctrines, until the infection has extended over both, and the great mass of the population of the North who, whatever may be their opinion of the original Abolition Party which still preserves its distinctive organization, hardly ever fail, when it comes to acting, to cooperate in carrying out their measures. . . .

Unless something decisive is done, I again ask what is to stop this agitation before the great and final object at which it aims—the abolition of slavery in the South—is consummated? Is it, then, not certain that if something decisive is not now done to arrest it, the South will be forced to choose between abolition and secession? Indeed, as events are now moving, it will not require the South to secede to dissolve the Union. Agitation will of itself effect it. . . .

It is a great mistake to suppose that disunion can be effected by a single blow. The cords which bind these states together in one common Union are far too numerous and powerful for that. Disunion must be the work of time. It is only through a long process, and successively, that the cords can be snapped, until the whole fabric falls asunder. Already the agitation of the slavery question has snapped some of the most important and has greatly weakened all the others. . . .

If the agitation goes on, the same force, acting with increased intensity . . . will snap every cord, when nothing will be left to hold the states together except force. But surely that can, with no propriety of language, be called a union, when the only means by which the weaker is held connected with the stronger portion is force. It may, indeed, keep them connected; but the connection will partake much more of the character of subjugation on the part of the weaker to the stronger than the union of free, independent, and sovereign states in one confederation, as they stood in the early stages of the government, and which only is worthy of the sacred name of Union.

Having now, senators, explained what it is that endangers the Union, and traced it to its cause, and explained its nature and character, the question again recurs: How can the Union be saved? To this I answer there is but one way by which it can be; and that is by adopting such measures as will satisfy the states belonging to the Southern section that they can remain in the Union consistently with their honor and their safety. There is, again, only one way by which this can be effected, and that is, by removing the causes by which this belief has been produced. Do that and discontent will cease, harmony and kind feelings between the sections be restored, and every apprehension of danger to the Union removed. The question, then, is, By what can this be done? But, before I undertake to answer this question, I propose to show by what the Union cannot be saved.

It cannot, then be saved by eulogies on the Union, however splendid or numerous. The cry of "Union, union, the glorious Union!" can no more prevent disunion than the cry of "Health, health, glorious health!" on the part of the physician can save a patient lying dangerously ill. So long as the Union, instead of being regarded as a protector, is regarded in the opposite character, by not much more than a majority of the States, it will be in vain to attempt to conciliate them by pronouncing eulogies upon it.

Beside, this cry of Union comes commonly from those whom we cannot believe to be sincere. It usually comes from our assailants. But we cannot believe them to be sincere; for, if they loved the Union, they would necessarily be devoted to the Constitution. It made the Union, and to destroy the Constitution would be to destroy the Union. But the only reliable and certain evidence of devotion to the Constitution is, to abstain, on the one hand, from violating it, and to repel, on the other, all attempts to violate it. It is only by faithfully performing these high duties that the Constitution can be preserved, and with it the Union. . . .

The plan of the administration cannot save the Union, because it can have no effect whatever toward satisfying the states composing the Southern section of the Union that they can, consistently with safety and honor, remain in the Union. It is, in fact, but a modification of the Wilmot Proviso. It proposes to effect the same object: to exclude the South from all territory acquired by the Mexican treaty. It is well known that the South is united against the Wilmot Proviso and has committed itself, by solemn resolutions, to resist should it be adopted. Its opposition is not to the name but that which it proposes to effect; that the Southern states hold to be unconstitutional, unjust, inconsistent with their equality as members of the common Union and calculated to destroy irretrievably the equilibrium between the two sections.

These objections equally apply to what, for brevity, I will call the Executive Proviso. There is no difference between it and the Wilmot, except in the mode of effecting the object; and, in that respect, I must say that the latter is much the least objectionable. It goes to its object openly, boldly, and distinctly. It claims for Congress unlimited power over the territories, and proposes to assert it over the territories acquired from Mexico, by a positive prohibition of slavery. Not so the Executive Proviso. It takes an indirect course, and in order to elude the Wilmot Proviso, and thereby avoid encountering the united and determined resistance of the South, it denies, by implication, the authority of Congress to legislate for the territories, and claims the right as belonging exclusively to the inhabitants of the territories.

But to effect the object of excluding the South, it takes care, in the meantime, to let in emigrants freely from the Northern states and all other quarters except from the South, which it takes special care to exclude by holding up to them the danger of having their slaves liberated under the Mexican laws. The necessary consequence is to exclude the South from the territory just as effectually as would the Wilmot Proviso. The only difference in this respect is that what one proposes to effect directly and openly, the other proposes to effect indirectly and covertly.

But the Executive Proviso is more objectionable than the Wilmot in another and more important particular. The latter, to effect its object, inflicts a dangerous wound upon the Constitution by depriving the Southern states, as joint partners and owners of the territories, of their rights in them; but it inflicts no greater wound than is absolutely necessary to effect its object. The former, on the contrary, while it inflicts the same wound, inflicts others equally great and, if possible, greater. . . .

In claiming the right for the inhabitant instead of Congress, to legislate over the territories, in the Executive Proviso it assumes that the sovereignty over the territories is vested in the former; or to express it in the language used in a resolution offered by one of the senators from Texas (General Houston, now absent), they have "the same inherent right of self-government as the people in the states." The assumption is utterly unfounded, unconstitutional, without example, and contrary to the entire practice of the government from its commencement to the present time.

The recent movement of individuals in California to form a constitution and a state government, and to appoint senators and representatives, is the first fruit of this monstrous assumption. If the individuals who made this movement had gone into California as adventurers, and if, as such, they had conquered the territory and established their independence, the sovereignty of the country would have been vested in them as a separate and independent community. In that case they would have had the right to form a constitution and to establish a government for themselves; and if, afterward, they thought proper to apply to Congress for admission into the Union as a sovereign and independent state, all this would have been regular and according to established principles. But such is not the case. It was the United States who conquered California and finally acquired it by treaty. The sovereignty, of course, is vested in them and not in the individuals who have attempted to form a constitution and a state without their consent. All this is clear beyond controversy, unless it can be shown that they have since lost or been divested of their sovereignty.

Nor is it less clear that the power of legislating over the acquired territory is vested in Congress and not, as is assumed, in the inhabitants of the territories. None can deny that the government of the United States has the power to acquire territories, either by war or by treaty; but if the power to acquire exists, it belongs to Congress to carry it into execution. On this point there can be no doubt, for the Constitution expressly provides that Congress shall have power "to make all laws which shall be necessary and proper to carry into execution the foregoing powers" (those vested in Congress) "and all other powers vested by this Constitution in the government of the United States or in any department or officer thereof."

It matters not, then, where the power is vested; for, if vested at all in the government of the United States, or any of its departments or officers, the power of carrying it into execution is clearly vested in Congress. But this important provision, while it gives to Congress the power of legislating over territories, imposes important restrictions on its exercise by restricting Congress to passing laws necessary and proper for carrying the power into execution. The prohibition extends not only to all laws not suitable or appropriate to the object of the power but also to all that are unjust, unequal, or unfair; for all such laws would be unnecessary and improper and therefore unconstitutional.

Having now established beyond controversy that the sovereignty over the territories is vested in the United States—that is, in the several states composing the Union—and that the power of legislating over them is expressly vested in Congress, it follows that the individuals in California who have undertaken to form a constitution and a state, and to exercise the power of legislating without the consent of Congress, have usurped the sovereignty of the state and the authority of Congress, and have acted in open defiance of them both. In other words, what they have done is revolutionary and rebellious in its character, anarchical in its tendency, and calculated to lead to the most dangerous consequences. Had they acted from premeditation and design, it would have been in fact actual rebellion; but such is not the case. The blame lies much less upon them than upon those who have induced them to take a course so unconstitutional and dangerous. They have been led into it by language held here and the course pursued by the executive branch of the government. . . .

Having now shown what cannot save the Union, I return to the question with which I commenced: How can the Union be saved? There is but one way by which it can with any certainty, and that is by a full and final settlement on the principle of justice of all the questions at issue between the two sections. The South asks for justice, simple justice, and less she ought not to take. She has no compromise to offer but the Constitution, and no concession or surrender to make. She has already surrendered so much that she has little left to surrender. Such a settlement would go to the root of the evil and remove all cause of discontent by satisfying the South that she could remain honorably and safely in the Union; and thereby restore the harmony and fraternal feelings between the sections which existed anterior to the Missouri agitation. Nothing else can, with any certainty, finally and forever settle the questions at issue, terminate agitation, and save the Union.

But can this be done? Yes, easily; not by the weaker party, for it can of itself do nothing—not even protect itself—but by the stronger. The North has only to will it to accomplish it; to do justice by conceding to the South an equal right in the acquired territory, and to do her duty by causing the stipulations relative to fugitive slaves to be faithfully fulfilled—to cease the agitation of the slave question; and to provide for the insertion of a provision in the Constitution, by an amendment, which will restore to the South in substance the power she possessed of protecting herself before the equilibrium between the sections was destroyed by the action of this government. There will be no difficulty in devising such a provision—one that will protect the South and which, at the same time, will improve and strengthen the government instead of impairing and weakening it.

But will the North agree to do this? It's for her to answer this question. But I will say she cannot refuse if she has half the love of the Union which she professes to have, or without justly exposing herself to the charge that her love of power and aggrandizement is far greater than her love of the Union. At all events, the responsibility of saving the Union rests on the North and not the South. The South cannot save it by any act of hers, and the North may save it without any sacrifice whatever, unless to do justice and to perform her duties under the Constitution should be regarded by her as a sacrifice.

It is time, Senators, that there should be an open and manly avowal on all sides, as to what is intended to be done. If the question is not now settled, it is uncertain whether it ever can hereafter be; and we, as the representatives of the States of this Union, regarded as governments, should come to a distinct understanding as to our respective views, in order to ascertain whether the great questions at issue can be settled or not. If you, who represent the stronger portion, cannot agree to settle them on the broad principle of justice and duty, say so; and let the States we both represent agree to separate and part in peace. If you are unwilling we should part in peace, tell us so; and we shall know what to do, when you reduce the question to submission or resistance. If you remain silent, you will compel us to infer by your acts what you intend. In that case, California will become the test question. If you admit her, under all the difficulties that oppose her admission, you compel us to infer that you intend to exclude us from the whole of the acquired territories, with the intention of destroying, irretrievably, the equilibrium between the two sections. We would be blind not to perceive, in that case, that your real objects are power and aggrandizement, and infatuated not to act accordingly.

I have now, Senators, done my duty in expressing my opinions fully, freely, and candidly, on this solemn occasion. In doing so, I have been governed by the motives which have governed me in all the stages of the agitation of the slavery question since its commencement. I have exerted myself, during the whole period, to arrest it, with the intention of saving the Union, if it could be done, and if it could not, to save the section where it has pleased Providence to cast my lot, and which I sincerely believe has justice and the Constitution on its side. Having faithfully done my duty to the best of my ability, both to the Union and my section, throughout this agitation, I shall have the consolation, let what will come, that I am free from all responsibility.

1. What does Calhoun say about the status of the equilibrium between the North and the South as represented in the federal government? How does he support his conclusion? What relevance does Clay's compromise have to Calhoun's concerns?
2. According to Calhoun, how can the Union be saved?

14-5 Frederick Douglass, Independence Day Speech (1852)

The most important African American leader of his time, Fredrick Douglass had a profound impact on American notions of slavery. Born in slavery, Douglass escaped at the age of 20 and began writing and speaking against slavery. His volumes of autobiography including "Narrative of the Life of Fredrick Douglass, an American Slave" (1845) were among the greatest of the slave narratives and are now considered classic examples of American autobiography. As a speaker, newspaper editor and writer, Douglass' influence was great. He knew and aided John Brown in his efforts, welcomed the Civil War and until his death in 1895, spoke against Jim Crow laws and lynching. This famous speech is a masterful example of Douglass' use of irony in illuminating the hypocrisy of the celebration of Independene day.

Fellow citizens above your national, tumultuous joy, I hear the mournful wail of millions! whose chains, heave and grievous yesterday, are, today, rendered more intolerable by the jubilee shouts that reach them. If I do forget, it I do not faithfully remember those bleeding children of sorrow this day, "may my right hand forger her cunning, and may ny tongue cleave to the roof of my mouth"! To forget them, to pass lightly over their wrongs, and to chime in with the popular theme would be treason most scandalous and shocking, and would make me a reproach before God and the world. My subject, them, fellow citizens, is *American Slavery*. I shall see this day and its popular characteristics from the slav;s point of view. Standing there identified with the American bondman, making his wrongs mine. I do not hesitate to declare with all my soul that the character and conduct of this nation never looked blacker to me than on this Fourth of July! Whether we turn to the declarations of the past or to the professions of the present, the conduct of the nation seems equally hideous and revolting. America is false to the past, false to the present, and solemnly binds herself to be false to the future. Standing with God and the crushed and bleeding slave on this occasion, I will,in the name of humanity which is outraged, in the name of liberty which is fettered, in the name of the Constitution and the Bible which are disregarded and trampled upon, All the emphasis I can command, everything that serves to perpetuate slavery the great sin and shame of America! "I will not equivocate, I will not excuse"; I will use the severest of language I can command; and yet not one word shall escape that any man, whose judgment is not blinded by prejudice, or who is not at heart a slaveholder, shall not confess to be right and just.

But I fancy I hear someone of my audience say, "It is just in this circumstance that your and your brother abolitionists fail to make a favorable impression on the public mind. Would you argue more and denounce less, would you persuade more and rebuke less, your cause would be much more likely to succeed." But, I submit, where all is plain, there is nothing to be argued. What point in the antislavery creed would you have me argue? On what branch of the subject do the people of this country need light? Must I undertake to prove that the slave is a man? That point is conceded already. Nobody doubts it. The slaveholders themselves acknowledge it the enactment of laws for their government. They acknowledge it when they punish disobedience on the part of the slave. There are seventy-two crimes in the state of Virginia which, if committed by a black man (no matter how ignorant he be), subject him to the punishment of death, while only two of the same crimes will subject a white man to the like punishment. What is this but the acknowledgment that the slave is a moral, intellectual, and responsible being? The manhood of the slave is conceded. It is admitted in the fact that the Southern statute books are covered with enactments forbidding, under severe fines and penalties, the teaching of the slave to read or to write. When you can point to any such laws in reference to the beasts of the field, then I may consent to argue the manhood of the slave. When the dogs in your streets, when the fowls of the air, when the cattle on your hills, when the fish of the sea and the reptiles that crawl shall be unable to distinguish the slave from a brute, then will I argue with you that the slave is a man!

For the present, it is enough to affirm the equal manhood of the Negro race. It is not stonishing that, while we are plowing, planting, and reaping, using all kinds of mechanical tools erecting houses, constructing bridges, building ships, working in metals of brass, iron, copper and silver, and gold; that, while we are reading, writing, and ciphering, acting as clerks, merchants and secretaries, having among us lawyers, doctors, ministers, poets, authors, editors, orators, and teachers; that, while we are engaged in all manner of enterprises common to other men, digging gold in California, capturing the whale in the Pacific, feeding sheep and cattle on the hillside, living, moving, acting, thinking, planning, living in families as husbands, wives, and children, and, above all, confessing and worshipping the Christian's God, and looking hopefully for life and immortality beyond the grave, we are called upon to prove that we are men!

Would you have me argue that man is entitled to liberty? That he is the rightful owner of his own body? You have already declared it. Must I argue the wrongfulness of slavery? Is that a question for republicans? Is it to be settled by the rules of logic and argumentation, as a matter beset with great difficulty, involving a doubtful application of the principle of justice, hart to be understood? How should I look today, in the presence of Americans, dividing and subdividing a discourse, to show that men have a natural right to freedom? speaking of it relatively and positively, negatively and affirmatively? To do so would be to make myself ridiculous and to offer an insult to your understanding. There is not a man beneath the canopy of heaven that does not know that slaver is wrong for him.

What, am I to argue that is wrong to make men brutes, to rob them of their liberty, to work them without wages, to keep them ignorant of their relations to their fellow men, to beat them with sticks, to flay their flesh with the last, to load their limbs with irons, to hunt them with dogs, to sell them at auction, to sunder their families, to knock out their teeth, to burn their flesh, to starve them into obedience and submission to their masters? Must I argue that a system them marked with blood, and stained with pollution, is wrong? No! I will not. I have better employment for my time and strength than such arguments would imply.

What, then remains to be argued? Is it that slavery is not divine; that God did not establish it; that our doctors of divinity are mistaken? There is blasphemy in the thought. That which is inhuman cannot be divine? Who can reason on such a proposition? They that can may; I cannot. The time for such argument is past.

At a time like this, scorching iron, not convincing argument, is needed. O! had I the ability, and could I reach the nation's ear, I would today pour out a fiery stream of biting ridicule, blasting reproach, withering sarcasm, and stern rebuke. For it is not light that is needed, but fire; it is not the gentle shower, but thunder. We need the storm, the whirlwind, and the earthquake. The feeling of the nation must be quickened, the conscience of the nation must be startled; the hypocrisy of the nation must be exposed; and its crimes against God and man must be proclaimed and denounced.

What, to the American slave is your Fourth of July? I answer: a day that reveals to him, more than all other days in the year, the gross injustice and cruelty to which he s the constant victim. To him, your celebration is a sham; your boasted liberty an unholy license; your national greatness, swelling vanity; your sound of rejoicing are empty and heartless; your denunciation of tyrants, brass-fronted impudence; your shouts of liberty and equality, hollow mockery; your prayers and hymns, your sermons and thanksgivings with all your religious parade and solemnity, are, to Him, mere bombast, fraud, deception, impiety, and hypocrisy a thin veil to cover up crimes which would disgrace a nation of savages. There is not a nation of savages. There is not a nation on earth guilty of practices more shocking and bloody than are the people of the United States at this very hour.

Go where you may, search where you will, roam through all the monarchies and despotisms of the Old World, travel through South America, search out every abuse, and when you have found the last, lay your facts by the side of the everyday practices of this nation, and you will say with that, for revolting barbarity and shameless hypocrisy, America reigns without a rival.

1. *How does Douglass use the celebration of the Fourth of July as a foundation for his argument against slavery? Describe his tone in this piece.*
2. *What are the contradictions and injustices of slavery that Douglass brings to light in this speech?*

14-6   Kansas Begins to Bleed (1856)

As proslavery and Free State factions struggled for political control over the Territory of Kansas, tensions increased between devotees of the two opposing points of view until they erupted into outright violence. Individuals on both sides were tarred and feathered, kidnapped, and occasionally killed. On May 21, 1856, the violence escalated dramatically as a group of proslavery men entered Lawrence, a Free State stronghold, and wreaked havoc. This "sack of Lawrence" was followed three days later by a brutal attack led by John Brown upon proslavery settlers at Pottawatomie Creek. In September, a new territorial governor, John W. Geary, arrived and began to restore order to "Bleeding Kansas." Geary's strong antislavery views, however, forced his resignation six months later. Many of the details of this violent period in the history of Kansas can be found in a book written in 1857 by Dr. John Gihon, the governor's private secretary. The excerpt that follows relates the events surrounding the attack on Lawrence.

> **Source:** John H. Gihon, *Geary and Kansas: Governor Geary's Administration in Kansas With a Complete History of the Territory Until July 1857* (Philadelphia: Chas. C. Rhodes, 1857). The Kansas Collection Website, Lynn Nelson, Professor of History at the University of Kansas.
> http://www.ukans.edu/carrie/kancoll/books/gihon/g_intro.htm

On the 5th of May, Judge Lecompte delivered a charge, highly partisan in its character, to the grand jury of Douglas county, of which, the following extract is in his own words:

This territory was organized by an act of Congress, and so far its authority is from the United States. It has a Legislature elected in pursuance of that organic act. This Legislature, being an instrument of Congress, by which it governs the territory, has passed laws; these laws, therefore, are of United States authority and making, and all that resist these laws, resist the power and authority of the United States, and are, therefore, guilty of high treason. Now, gentlemen, if you find that any persons have resisted these laws, then must you, under your oaths, find bills against such persons for high treason. If you find that no such resistance has been made, but that combinations have been formed for the purpose of resisting them, and individuals of influence and notoriety have been aiding and abetting in such combinations, then must you still find bills for constructive treason, as the courts have decided that to constitute treason the blow need not be struck, but only the intention be made evident.

The grand jury accordingly made a presentment, as follows:

The grand jury, sitting for the adjourned term of the First District Court in and for the county of Douglas, in the Territory of Kansas, beg leave to report to the honorable court that, from evidence laid before them, showing that the newspaper known as *The Herald of Freedom*, published at the town of Lawrence, has from time to time issued publications of the most inflammatory and seditious character, denying the legality of the territorial authorities, addressing and commanding forcible resistance to the same, demoralizing the popular mind, and rendering life and property unsafe, even to the extent of advising assassination as a last resort; Also, that the paper known as *The Kansas Free State* has been similarly engaged, and has recently reported the resolutions of a public meeting in Johnson county, in this territory, in which resistance to the territorial laws even unto blood has been agreed upon; and that we respectfully recommend their abatement as a nuisance. Also, that we are satisfied that the building known as the 'Free-State Hotel' in Lawrence has been constructed with the view to military occupation and defence, regularly parapeted and port-holed for the use of cannon and small arms, and could only have been designed as a stronghold of resistance to law, thereby endangering the public safety, and encouraging rebellion and sedition in this country; and respectfully recommend that steps be taken whereby this nuisance may be removed.

OWEN C. STEWART, Foreman.

In order to accomplish the objects of this presentment, which was simply a declaration of war against Lawrence, a number of writs were made out and placed in the hands of the marshal for the arrest of prominent citizens of that place. Although it is asserted that no attempts were made to resist the marshal's deputies in serving these writs, the marshal, on the 11th of May, issued the following proclamation:

TO THE PEOPLE OF KANSAS TERRITORY:

Whereas, certain judicial writs of arrest have been directed to me by the First District Court of the United States, etc., to be executed within the county of Douglas, and whereas an attempt to execute them by the United States Deputy Marshal was evidently resisted by a large number of the citizens of Lawrence, and as there is every reason to believe that any attempt to execute these writs will be resisted by a large body of armed men; now, therefore, the law-abiding citizens of the territory are commanded to be and appear at Lecompton, as soon as practicable, and in numbers sufficient for the execution of the law. Given under my hand, this 11th day of May, 1856.

I. B. DONALSON, United States Marshal for Kansas Territory.

Previous to the publication of this proclamation, Buford's regiment, and other armed bands, had taken up positions in the vicinity of Lawrence, who were not only committing depredations upon the property of the settlers, but were intercepting, robbing, and imprisoning travellers on the public thoroughfares, and threatening to attack the town, in consequence of which a meeting was held, and a committee appointed to address Governor Shannon, stating the facts in gentle terms, and asking his protection against such bands by the United States troops at his disposal.

To this respectful application the committee received the following reply:

Executive Office, May 12, 1856,
Lecompton, K. T.
Gentlemen: Your note of the eleventh inst. is received, and, in reply, I have to state that there is no force around or approaching Lawrence, except the legally constituted posse of the United States Marshal and Sheriff of Douglas county, each of whom, I am informed, have a number of writs in their hands for execution against persons now in Lawrence. I shall in no way interfere with either of these officers in the discharge of their official duties.

If the citizens of Lawrence submit themselves to the territorial laws, and aid and assist the marshal and sheriff in the execution of processes in their hands, as all good citizens are bound to do when called on, they, or all such will entitle themselves to the protection of the law. But so long as they keep up a military or armed organization to resist the territorial laws and the officers charged with their execution, I shall not interpose to save them from the legitimate consequences of their illegal acts.

I have the honor to be yours, with great respect,

WILSON SHANNON.
Messrs. C. W. Toplief, John Hutchinson, W. Y. Roberts

Still desirous of averting the impending difficulties, the citizens of Lawrence held another meeting on the 13th, when the following preamble and resolution were adopted, copies of which were immediately forwarded to Marshal Donalson and Governor Shannon:

Whereas by a proclamation to the people of Kansas Territory, by I. B. Donalson, United States Marshal for said territory, issued on the 11th day of May, 1856, it is alleged that Certain judicial writs of arrest have been directed to him by the First District Court of the United States, etc., to be executed within the county of Douglas, and that an attempt to execute them by the United States Deputy Marshal was violently resisted by a large number of the citizens of Lawrence, and that there is every reason to believe that any attempt to execute said writs will be resisted by a large body of armed men; therefore,

Resolved, By this public meeting of the citizens of Lawrence, held this thirteenth day of May, 1856, that the allegations and charges against us, contained in the aforesaid proclamation, are wholly untrue in fact, and the conclusion which is drawn from them. The aforesaid deputy marshal was resisted in no manner whatever, nor by any person whatever, in the execution of said writs, except by him whose arrest the said deputy marshal was seeking to make. And that we now, as we have done heretofore, declare our willingness and determination, without resistance, to acquiesce in the service upon us of any judicial writs against us by the United States Deputy Marshal for Kansas Territory, and will furnish him with a posse for that purpose, if so requested; but that we are ready to resist, if need be, unto death, the ravages and desolations of an invading mob.

J. A. WAKEFIELD, President.

On the 14th, still another meeting was held at Lawrence, and a letter, signed by a large and respectable committee appointed for the purpose, was sent to the marshal, in which it was affirmed "that no opposition will now, or at any future time, be offered to the execution of any legal process by yourself, or any person acting for you. We also pledge ourselves to assist you, if called upon, in the execution of any legal process.

We declare ourselves to be order-loving and law-abiding citizens; and only await an opportunity to testify our fidelity to the laws of the country, the constitution, and the Union.

We are informed, also, that those men collecting about Lawrence openly declare that it is their attention to destroy the town and drive off the citizens. Of course we do not believe you give any countenance to such threats; but, in view of the excited state of the public mind, we ask protection of the constituted authorities of the government, declaring ourselves in readiness to co-operate with them for the maintenance of the peace, order, and quiet, of the community in which we live.

In reply to this the marshal sends a lengthy communication, intended to be bitterly sarcastic, which he closes with these words:

You say you call upon the constituted authorities of the government for protection. This, indeed, sounds strange from a large body of men armed with Sharpe's rifles, and other implements of war, bound together by oaths and pledges, to resist the laws of the government they call on for protection. All persons in Kansas Territory, without regard to location, who honestly submit to the constituted authorities, will ever find me ready to aid in protecting them; and all who seek to resist the laws of the land, and turn traitors to their country, will find me aiding and enforcing the laws, if not as an officer as a citizen.

Whilst these documents were passing, the roads were blockaded by the marshal's posse of southern volunteers, upon which no man without a passport could safely venture. Captain Samuel Walker, who had carried one of the above-mentioned letters to Lecompton, was fired upon on his return to Lawrence. Mr. Miller, who with two others had gone up to negotiate with the governor for an amicable adjustment of the pending troubles, was taken prisoner by a detachment of Buford's South Carolinians near Lecompton, who knowing him to have been from their own state, tried him for treason and sentenced him to be hung. He contrived, somehow, to get away with the loss of his horse and purse. Mr. Weaver, a sergeant-at-arms of the Congressional Committee, was arrested while in the discharge of his duty, and carried across the Kansas River, to the South Carolinian camp, where after a critical examination of his papers, he was discovered to be in the service of the United States, and released, the officer in command giving him a pass, and kindly advising him to answer promptly, if challenged, otherwise he might be shot. Outrages of this kind became so frequent that all travel was at last suspended.

On the 17th of May the citizens of Lawrence, through a committee, again addressed the United States Marshal, in the words of the following letter:

Lawrence, K. T., May 17, 1866
I. B. DONALSON, U. S. MARSHAL OF K. T.

Dear Sir: We desire to call your attention, as citizens of Kansas, to the fact that a large force of armed men have collected in the vicinity of Lawrence, and are engaged in committing depredations upon our citizens; stopping wagons, arresting, threatening and robbing unoffending travellers upon the highway, breaking open boxes of merchandise, and appropriating their contents; have slaughtered cattle, and terrified many of the women and children.

We have also learned from Governor Shannon, 'that there are no armed forces in the vicinity of this place but the regularly constituted militia of the territory—this is to ask if you recognise them as your posse, and feel responsible for their acts. If you do not, we hope and trust you will prevent a repetition of such acts, and give peace to the settlers.

On behalf of the citizens,

C. W. BABCOCK,
LYMAN ALLEN,
J. A. PERRY

To this communication no reply was given. In the mean time, preparations were going forward, and vigorously prosecuted, for the sacking of Lawrence. The pro-slavery people were to "wipe out" this ill-fated town under authority of law. They had received the countenance of the president—the approbation of the chief justice—the favorable presentment of the grand jury—the concurrence of the governor—the orders of the marshal,—and were prepared to consummate their purpose with the arms of the government, in the hands of a militia force gathered from the remotest sections of the Union.

They concentrated their troops in large numbers around the doomed city, stealing, or, as they termed it, "pressing into the service," all the horses they could find belonging to free-state men, whose cattle were also slaughtered, without remuneration, to feed the marshal's forces; and their stores and dwellings broken open and robbed of arms, provisions, blankets and clothing. And all this under the pretence of "law and order," and in the name and under the sanction of the government of the United States.

The marshal's army had a gallant host of commanders. There was General Atchison, with the Missouri Platte County Rifles, and two pieces of artillery; Captain Dunn, with the Kickapoo Rangers; General Stringfellow, and Colonel Abel, his law-partner, aided by Doctor John H. Stringfellow and Robert S. Kelly, editors of the Squatter Sovereign, with the forces from Doniphan, Atchison and Leavenworth; Colonel Boone, with sundry aids, at the head of companies from Westport, Liberty and Independence; Colonels Wilkes and Buford, with the Carolinians, Georgians and Mississippians; Colonel H. T. Titus, in command of the Douglas County Militia; and many others, too numerous to mention.

The heart of the marshal must have swelled with triumphant pride when he looked upon this posse comitatus, comprising in all not less than eight hundred warlike men. The governor must have reviewed them with that satisfaction which governors only can feel when about to accomplish a mighty undertaking, with the certainty of success. This patriotic host was about to engage in an enterprise that was to redound to their everlasting glory—of the most noble actions that ever called warriors to the field of battle. But where, all this time, was Sheriff Jones, the life and spirit and power of all this chivalric host? Why had he not made his appearance, to encourage with his presence, and cheer with his voice and smiles, these patriotic forces? By some it was still supposed that he was either dead or dying of the wound in his back. Jones was still behind the scenes. The time for his appearance upon the stage had not arrived, and he patiently awaited his proper cue.

On the 19th of May, while these forces were collecting for the destruction of Lawrence, a young man from Illinois, named Jones, had been to a store near Blanton's Bridge, to purchase flour, when he was attacked by two of the marshal's party, who were out as scouts. To escape these men, Jones dismounted and entered the store, into which they followed, and there abused him. He again mounted his horse and left for home, the others following, and swearing that the d---d abolitionist should not escape. When near the bridge, they levelled their guns (United States muskets), and fired. Jones fell mortally wounded, and soon expired.

On the following morning, the 20th, several young men, hearing of this transaction, left Lawrence to visit the scene of the tragedy. One of these was named Stewart, who had but recently arrived from the State of New York. They had gone about a mile and a half, when they met two men, armed with Sharpe's rifles. Some words passed between them, when the two strangers raised their rifles, and, taking deliberate aim at Stewart, fired. One of the balls entered his temple. The work of death was instantly accomplished, and another accusing spirit stood before the bar of God.

Soon after sunrise, on the morning of the 21st, an advanced guard of the marshal's army, consisting of about two hundred horsemen, appeared on the top of Mount Oread, on the outskirts of the town of Lawrence, where their cannon had been stationed late on the preceding night. The town was quiet, and the citizens had resolved to submit without resistance to any outrage that might be perpetrated. About seven o'clock, Doctor Robinson's house, which stood on the side of the hill, was taken possession of, and used as the headquarters of the invaders. At eight o'clock, the main body of the army posted themselves on the outer edge of the town. Deputy Marshal Fain, with ten men, entered Lawrence, and, without molestation, served the writs in his possession, and arrested Judge G. W. Smith and G. W. Deitzler. Fain and his companions dined at the free-state hotel, and afterwards returned to the army on Mount Oread. The marshal then dismissed his monster posse, telling them he had no further use for them.

It was nearly three o'clock in the afternoon, when suddenly another actor appeared upon the stage. The "dead" and "dying,"—immortal Sheriff Jones,—rode rapidly into Lawrence, at the head of twenty-five mounted men; and as he passed along the line of the troops, he was received with deafening shouts of applause. His presence was the signal for action, and a sanction for the outrages that ensued.

Atchison then addressed his forces, in language not sufficiently well selected for ears polite, and then marched the whole column to within a short distance of the hotel, where they halted. Jones now informed Col. Eldridge, the proprietor, that the hotel must be destroyed; he was acting under orders; he had writs issued by the First District Court of the United States to destroy the Free-State Hotel, and the offices of the *Herald of Freedom* and Free Press. The grand jury at Lecompton had indicted them as nuisances, and the court had ordered them to be destroyed. He gave Col. Eldridge an hour and a half to remove his family and furniture, after which time the demolition commenced, and was prosecuted with an earnestness that would have done credit to a better cause.

In the mean time the newspaper offices had been assailed, the presses broken to pieces, and these, with the type and other material, thrown into the Kansas River. The following extract from the report of these transactions, given in the columns of the Lecompton Union, the most rabid pro-slavery paper in Kansas, the Squatter Sovereign excepted, is too significant not to be read with interest:

During this time appeals were made to Sheriff Jones to save the Aid Society's Hotel. This news reached the company's ears, and was received with one universal cry of 'No! no! Blow it up! blow it up!'

About this time a banner was seen fluttering in the breeze over the office of *The Herald of Freedom*. Its color was a blood-red, with a lone star in the centre, and South Carolina above. This banner was placed there by the Carolinians—Messrs. Wrights and a Mr. Cross. The effect was prodigious. One tremendous and long-continued shout burst from the ranks. Thus floated in triumph the banner of South Carolina,—that single white star, so emblematic of her course in the early history of our sectional disturbances. When every southern state stood almost upon the verge of ceding their dearest rights to the north, Carolina stood boldly out, the firm and unwavering advocate of southern institutions.

Thus floated victoriously the first banner of southern rights over the abolition town of Lawrence, unfurled by the noble sons of Carolina, and every whip of its folds seemed a death-stroke to Beecher propagandism and the fanatics of the east. O! that its red folds could have been seen by every southern eye!

Mr. Jones listened to the many entreaties, and finally replied that it was beyond his power to do anything, and gave the occupants so long to remove all private property from it. He ordered two companies into each printing office to destroy the press. Both presses were broken up and thrown into the street, the type thrown in the river, and all the material belonging to each office destroyed. After this was accomplished, and the private property removed from the hotel by the different companies, the cannon were brought in front of the house and directed their destructive blows upon the walls. The building caught on fire, and soon its walls came with a crash to the ground. Thus fell the abolition fortress; and we hope this will teach the Aid Society a good lesson for the future.

Whilst the work of destruction was going on at the printing-offices, the bombardment of the hotel, a strongly constructed three-story stone building, commenced. Kegs of gunpowder had been placed inside and the house fired in numerous places; and whilst the flames were doing their destructive work within, heavy cannon were battering against the walls without; and amid the crackling of the conflagration, the noise of falling walls and timbers, and the roar of the artillery, were mingled the almost frantic yells of satisfaction that constantly burst from the "law and order" lovers of Kansas Territory. Jones himself was in ecstasies. He sat upon his horse, contemplating the havoc he was making, and rubbing his hands with wild delight, exclaimed: "This is the happiest day of my life. I determined to make the fanatics bow before me in the dust, and kiss the territorial laws; and I have done it--by G--d, I have done it!"

And then followed scenes of reckless pillage and wanton destruction in all parts of that ill-fated town. Stores were broken into and plundered of their contents. Bolts and bars were no obstacles to the entrance of drunken and infuriated men into private dwellings, from which most of the inhabitants had fled in terror. From these everything of value was stolen, and much that was useless to the marauders was destroyed.

The closing act of this frightful drama was the burning of the house of Dr. Robinson on the brow of Mount Oread. This was set on fire after the sun had gone down, and the bright light which its flames shed over the country illuminated the paths of the retreating army, as they proceeded toward their homes, pillaging houses, stealing horses, and violating the persons of defenceless women. All these dreadful deeds were done by human authority. There is yet an account to render to a Higher Power!

During the perpetration of these atrocities, one of the pro-slavery intruders accidentally shot himself on Mount Oread, another was killed by the falling of a brick from the free-state hotel, and a third had his leg crushed and broken by falling from his horse when gallopping in pursuit of an unoffending man, whom he had mistaken for Governor Reeder.

1. *Based upon John Gihon's account, and its supporting documents, of the legal and martial proceedings prior to the attack on Lawrence on May 21st, do you think the devastation to the town was preventable?*
2. *How can it be argued that the events in Kansas during 1856 represent the American Civil War in microcosm?*

14-7   A White Southerner Speaks Out Against Slavery (1857)

In 1857, Hinton Rowan Helper, a yeoman farmer from Davie County, North Carolina, published The Impending Crisis of the South. Helper condemned slavery not on humanitarian or moral grounds, but because it was antagonistic to economic progress. Using figures from the 1850 census, Helper asserted that the North was growing faster than the South and that the entire political economy of slavery was responsible for the South's economic stagnation. He concluded with an appeal to non-slaveholders to overthrow the South's planter elite. During the 1860 presidential campaign, the Republican Party widely distributed a condensed version of the book, considering it one of the most effective pieces of propaganda against slavery ever written. Southerners, however, fearful that it would encourage dissension and violence, burned it.

Source: Hinton R. Helper, *The Impending Crisis of the South: How to Meet it* (New York: A. B. Burdick, 1860). Scanned and proofed by T. Lloyd Benson, Department of History, Furman University. http://history.furman.edu/~benson/docs/helper1860.htm

WHY THE NORTH HAS SURPASSED THE SOUTH.

. . .And now that we have come to the very heart and soul of our subject, we feel no disposition to mince matters, but mean to speak plainly, and to the point, without any equivocation, mental reservation, or secret evasion whatever. The son of a venerated parent, who, while he lived, was a considerate and merciful slaveholder, a native of the South, born and bred in North Carolina, of a family whose home has been in the valley of the Yadkin for nearly a century and a half, a Southerner by instinct and by all the influences of thought, habits, and kindred, and with the desire and fixed purpose to reside permanently within the limits of the South, and with the expectation of dying there also—we feel that we have the right to express our opinion, however humble or unimportant it may be, on any and every question that affects the public good; and, so help us God, "sink or swim, live or die, survive or perish," we are determined to exercise that right with manly firmness, and without fear, favor or affection.

And now to the point. In our opinion, an opinion which has been formed from data obtained by assiduous researches, and comparisons, from laborious investigation, logical reasoning, and earnest reflection, the causes which have impeded the progress and prosperity of the South, which have dwindled our commerce, and other similar pursuits, into the most contemptible insignificance; sunk a large majority of our people in galling poverty and ignorance, rendered a small minority conceited and tyrannical, and driven the rest away from their homes; entailed upon us a humiliating dependence on the Free States; disgraced us in the recesses of our own souls, and brought us under reproach in the eyes of all civilized and enlightened nations—may all be traced to one common source, and there find solution in the most hateful and horrible word, that was ever incorporated into the vocabulary of human economy—Slavery!

Reared amidst the institution of slavery, believing it to be wrong both in principle and in practice, and having seen and felt its evil influences upon individuals, communities and states, we deem it a duty, no less than a privilege, to enter bur protest against it, and to use our most strenuous efforts to overturn and abolish it! Then we are an abolitionist? Yes! not merely a freesoiler, but an abolitionist, in the fullest sense of the term. We are not only in favor of keeping slavery out of the territories, but, carrying our opposition to the institution a step further, we here unhesitatingly declare ourselves in favor of its immediate and unconditional abolition, in every state in this confederacy, where it now exists! Patriotism makes us a freesoiler; state pride makes us an emancipationist; a profound sense of duty to the South makes us an abolitionist; a reasonable degree of fellow feeling for the negro, makes us a colonizationist. With the free state men in Kansas and Nebraska, we sympathize with all our heart. We love the whole country, the great family of states and territories, one and inseparable, and would have the word Liberty engraved as an appropriate and truthful motto, on the escutcheon of every member of the confederacy. We love freedom, we hate slavery, and rather than give up the one or submit to the other, we will forfeit the pound of flesh nearest our heart. Is this sufficiently explicit and categorical? If not, we hold ourself in readiness at all times, to return a prompt reply to any proper question that may be propounded.

Our repugnance to the institution of slavery, springs from no one-sided idea, or sickly sentimentality. We have not been hasty in making up our mind on the subject; we have jumped at no conclusions; we have acted with perfect calmness and deliberation; we have carefully considered, and examined the reasons for and against the institution, and have also taken into account the probable consequences of our decision. The more we investigate the matter, the deeper becomes the conviction that we are right; and with this to impel and sustain us, we pursue our labor with love, with hope, and with constantly renewing vigor.

That we shall encounter opposition we consider as certain; perhaps we may even be subjected to insult and violence. From the conceited and cruel oligarchy of the South, we could look for nothing less. But we shall shrink from no responsibility, and do nothing unbecoming a man; we know how to repel indignity, and if assaulted, shall not fail to make the blow recoil upon the aggressor's head. The road we have to travel may be a rough one, but no impediment shall cause us to falter in our course. The line of our duty is clearly defined, and it is our intention to follow it faithfully, or die in the attempt.

But, thanks to heaven, we have no ominous forebodings of the result of the contest now pending between Liberty and Slavery in this confederacy. Though neither a prophet nor the son of a prophet, our vision is sufficiently penetrative to divine the future so far as to be able to see that the "peculiar institution" has but a short, and, as heretofore, inglorious existence before it. Time, the righter of every wrong, is ripening events for the desired consummation of our labors and the fulfillment of our cherished hopes. Each revolving year brings nearer the inevitable crisis. The sooner it comes the better; may heaven, through our humble efforts, hasten its advent.

The first and most sacred duty of every Southerner, who has the honor and the interest of his country at heart, is to declare himself an unqualified and uncompromising abolitionist. No conditional or half-way declaration will avail; no mere threatening demonstration will succeed. With those who desire to be instrumental in bringing about the triumph of liberty over slavery, there should be neither evasion vacillation, nor equivocation. We should listen to no modifying terms or compromises that may be proposed by the proprietors of the unprofitable and ungodly institution. Nothing short of the complete abolition of slavery can save the South from falling into the vortex of utter ruin. Too long have we yielded a submissive obedience to the tyrannical domination of an inflated oligarchy; too long have we tolerated their arrogance and self-conceit; too long have we submitted to their unjust and savage exactions. Let us now wrest from them the sceptre of power, establish liberty and equal rights throughout the land, and henceforth and forever guard our legislative halls from the pollutions and usurpations of pro-slavery demagogues.

It is against slavery on the whole, and against slave-holders as a body, that we wage an exterminating war. Those persons who, under the infamous slave-laws of the South—laws which have been correctly spoken of as a "disgrace to civilization," and which must be annulled simultaneously with the abolition of slavery—have had the vile institution entailed on them contrary to their wills, are virtually on our side; we may, therefore, very properly strike them off from the black list of three hundred and forty-seven thousand slaveholders, who, as a body, have shocked the civilized world with their barbarous conduct, and from whose conceited and presumptuous ranks are selected the officers who do all the legislation, town, county, state and national, for (against) five millions of poor outraged whites, and three millions of enslaved negroes.

Non-slaveholders of the South! farmers, mechanics and workingmen, we take this occasion to assure you that the slaveholders, the arrogant demagogues whom you have elected to offices of honor and profit, have hoodwinked you, trifled with you, and used you as mere tools for the consummation of their wicked designs. They have purposely kept you in ignorance, and have, by moulding your passions and prejudices to suit themselves, induced you to act in direct opposition to your dearest rights and interests. By a system of the grossest subterfuge and misrepresentation, and in order to avert, for a season, the vengeance that will most assuredly overtake them ere long, they have taught you to hate the abolitionists, who are your best and only true friends. Now, as one of your own number, we appeal to you to join us in our patriotic endeavors to rescue the generous soil of the South from the usurped and desolating control of these political vampires. Once and forever, at least so far as this country is concerned the infernal question of slavery must be disposed of; a speedy and perfect abolishment of the whole institution is the true policy of the South—and this is the policy which we propose to pursue. Will you aid us, will you assist us, will you be freemen, or will you be slaves? These are questions of vital importance; weigh them well in your minds, come to a prudent and firm decision, and hold yourselves in readiness to act in accordance therewith. You must either be for us or against us—anti- slavery or pro-slavery; it is impossible for you to occupy a neutral ground; it is as certain as fate itself, that if you do not voluntarily oppose the usurpations and outrages of the slavocrats, they will force you into involuntary compliance with their infamous measures. Consider well the aggressive, fraudulent and despotic power which they have exercised in the affairs of Kansas; and remember that, if, by adhering to erroneous principles of neutrality or non-resistance, you allow them to force the curse of slavery on that vast and fertile field, the broad area of all the surrounding States and Territories—the whole nation, in fact—will soon fall a prey to their diabolical intrigues and machinations. Thus, if you are not vigilant, will they take advantage of your neutrality, and make you and others the victims of their inhuman despotism. Do not reserve the strength of your arms until you shall have been rendered powerless to strike; the present is the proper time for action; under all the circumstances, apathy or indifference is a crime. First ascertain, as nearly as you can, the precise nature and extent of your duty, and then, without a moment's delay, perform it in good faith. To facilitate you in determining what considerations of right, justice and humanity require at your hands, is one of the primary objects of this work; and we shall certainly fail in our desire if we do not accomplish our task in a manner acceptable to God and advantageous to man. . .

HOW SLAVERY CAN BE ABOLISHED.

PRELIMINARY to our elucidation of what we conceive to be the most discreet, fair and feasible plan for the abolition of slavery, we propose to offer a few additional reasons why it should be abolished Among the thousand and one arguments that present themselves in support of our position—which, before we part with the reader, we shall endeavor to define so clearly, that it shall be regarded as ultra only by those who imperfectly understand it—is the influence which slavery invariably exercises in depressing the value of real estate ; and as this is a matter in which the non-slaveholders of the South, of the West, and of the Southwest, are most deeply interested, we shall discuss it in a sort of preamble of some length.

The oligarchs say we cannot abolish slavery without infringing on the right of property. Again we tell them we do not recognize property in man; but even if we did, and if we were to inventory the negroes at quadruple, the value of their last assessment, still, impelled by a sense of duty to others, and as a matter of simple justice to ourselves, we, the non-slaveholders of the South, would be fully warranted in emancipating all the slaves at once, and that, too, without any compensation whatever to those who claim to be their absolute masters and owners We will explain. In 1850, the average value per acre, of land in the Northern States was $28,07; in the Northwestern $11,39; in the Southern $5,34; and in the Southwestern $6,36. Now, in consequence of numerous natural advantages, among which maybe enumerated the greater mildness of climate, richness of soil, deposits of precious metals, abundance and spaciousness of harbors, and super excellence of water-power, we contend that, had it not been for slavery, the average value of land in all the Southern and Southwestern States, would have been at least equal to the average value of the same in the Northern States. We conclude, therefore, and we think the conclusion is founded on principles of equity, that you, the slaveholders, are indebted to us, the non-slaveholders, in the sum of $22,13, which is the difference between $28,07 and $5,34, on every acre of Southern soil in our possession. This claim we bring against you, because slavery, which has inured exclusively to your own benefit, if, indeed, it has been beneficial at all, has shed a blighting influence over our lands, thereby keeping them out of market, and damaging every acre to the amount specified, Sirs! are you ready to settle the account? Let us see how much it is. There are in the fifteen slave States, 346,048 slaveholders, and 544,926,720 acres of land. Now the object is to ascertain how many acres are owned by slaveholders, and now many by non-slaveholders. Suppose we estimate five hundred acres as the average landed property of each slaveholder; will that be fair? We think it will, taking into consideration the fact that 174,503 of the whole number of slaveholders hold less than five slaves each—68,820 holding only one each. According to this hypothesis, the slaveholders own 173,021,000 acres, and the non-slaveholders the balance, with the exception of about 40,000,000 of acres, which belong to the General Government. The case may be stated thus:

Area of the Slave States	644,926,720 acres.
Estimates:	
Acres owned by slaveholders	173,021,000
Acres owned by the government,	40,000,000
	213,024,000
Acres owned by non-slaveholders	331,902,720

Now, chevaliers of the lash, and worshippers of slavery, the total value of three hundred and thirty-one million nine hundred and two thousand seven hundred and twenty acres, at twenty-two dollars and seventy-three cents per acre, is seven billion five hundred and forty-four million one hundred and forty-eight thousand eight hundred and twenty-five dollars; and this is our account against you on a single score. Considering how your villainous institution has retarded the development of our commercial and manufacturing interests, how it has stifled the aspirations of inventive genius; and, above all, how it has barred from us the heaven-born sweets of literature and religion—concernments too sacred to be estimated in a pecuniary point of view—might we not, with perfect justice and propriety, duplicate the amount, and still be accounted modest in our demands? Fully advised, however, of your indigent circumstances, we feel it would be utterly useless to call on you for the whole amount that is due us; we shall, therefore, in your behalf, make another draft on the fund of non-slaveholding generosity, and let the account, meagre as it is, stand as above. Though we have given you all the offices, and you have given us none of the benefits of legislation; though we have fought the battles of the South, while you were either lolling in your piazzas, or playing the tory, and endeavoring to filch from us our birthright of freedom; though you have absorbed the wealth of our communities in sending your own children to Northern seminaries and colleges, or in employing Yankee teachers to officiate exclusively in your own families, and have refused to us the limited privilege of common schools; though you have scorned to patronize our mechanics and industrial enterprises, and have passed to the North for every article of apparel, utility, and adornment; and though you have maltreated, outraged and defrauded us in every relation of life, civil, social, and political, yet we are willing to forgive and forget you, if you will but do us justice on a single count. Of you, the introducers, aiders and abettors of slavery, we demand indemnification for the damage our lands have sustained on account thereof; the amount of that damage is $7,544,148,825; and now, Sirs, we are ready to receive the money, and if it is perfectly convenient to you, we would be glad to have you pay it in specie! It will not avail you, Sirs, to parley or prevaricate. We must have a settlement. Our claim is just and overdue. We have already indulged you too long. Your criminal extravagance has almost ruined us. We are determined that you shall no longer play the profligate, and fair sumptuously every day at our expense. How do you propose to settle? Do you offer us your negroes in part payment? We do not want your negroes. We would not have all of them, nor any number of them, even as a gift. We hold ourselves above the disreputable and iniquitous practices of buying, selling, and owning slaves. What we demand is damages in money, or other absolute property, as an equivalent for the pecuniary losses we have suffered at your hands. You value your negroes at sixteen hundred millions of dollars, and propose to sell them to us for that sum; we should consider ourselves badly cheated, and disgraced for all time, here and hereafter, if we were to take them off your hands at sixteen farthings! We tell you emphatically, we are firmly resolved never to degrade ourselves by becoming the mercenary purchasers or proprietors of human beings. Except for the purpose of liberating them, we would not give a handkerchief or a toothpick for all the slaves in the world. But, in order to show how brazenly absurd are the howls and groans which you invariably set up for compensation, whenever we speak of the abolition of slavery, we will suppose your negroes are worth all you ask for them, and that we are bound to secure to you every cent of the sum before they can become free—in which case, our accounts would stand thus:

Non-slaveholder's account against Slaveholders	$7,544,148,825

Slaveholder's account against	
Non-slaveholders	1,600,000,000
Balance due Non-slaveholders	$5,944,148,825

Now, Sirs, we ask you in all seriousness, Is it not true that you have filched from us nearly five times the amount of the assessed value of your slaves? Why, then, do you still clamor for more? Is it your purpose to make the game perpetual? Think you that we will ever continue to bow at the wave of your wand, that we will bring humanity into everlasting disgrace by licking the hand that smites us, and that with us there is no point beyond which forbearance ceases to be a virtue? Sirs, if these be your thoughts, you are laboring under a most fatal delusion. You can goad us no further; you shall oppress us no longer; heretofore, earnestly but submissively, we have asked you to redress the more atrocious outrages which you have perpetrated against us; but what has been the invariable fate of our petitions? With scarcely a perusal, with a degree of contempt that added insult to injury, you have laid them on the table, and from thence they have been swept into the furnace of oblivion. Henceforth, Sirs, we are demandants, not suppliants. We demand our rights, nothing more, nothing less. It is for you to decide whether we are to have justice peaceably or by violence, for whatever consequences may follow, we are determined to have it one way or the other. Do you aspire to become the victims of white non-slaveholding vengeance by day, and of barbarous massacre by the negroes at night? Would you be instrumental in bringing upon yourselves, your wives, and your children, a fate too horrible to contemplate? shall history cease to cite, as an instance of unexampled cruelty, the Massacre of St. Bartholomew, because the world—the South—shall have furnished, a more direful scene of atrocity and carnage? Sirs, we would not wantonly pluck a single hair from your heads; but we have endured long, we have endured much; slaves only of the most despicable class would endure more. An enumeration or classification of all the abuses, insults, wrongs, injuries, usurpations, and oppressions, to which you have subjected us, would fill a larger volume than this; it is our purpose, therefore, to speak only of those that affect us most deeply. Out of our effects you have long since overpaid yourselves for your negroes; and now, Sirs, you must emancipate them—speedily emancipate them, or we will emancipate them for you!

1. *In this excerpt from The Impending Crisis, what does Hinton Rowan Helper suggest is the duty of "every Southerner who has the honor and interest of his country at heart"? What does he forecast as the course of events for those who follow his counsel?*
2. *What do you think the Republicans saw in Helper's rhetoric that could prove useful to their party's propaganda? Could not Helper be easily dismissed by his detractors as a disenchanted crank?*

14-8   Dred Scott v. Sanford (1857)

The Dred Scott case had a dramatic impact on the sectional divide over slavery and inflamed the passions of abolitionists. The decision by Chief Justice Taney, who became a figure of hatred for many, declared that ex-slave Dred Scott, who was suing for Missouri citizenship, was not a recognized citizen under the Constitution of the United States. The case had direct impact on the several of the compromises put in place to avoid sectional conflict and the new Republican Party viewed it as an attempt to eliminate them.

The Question is simply this: Can a negro, whose ancestors were imported into this country, and sold as slaves, become a member of the political community formed and brought into existence by the Constitution of the United States, and as such become entitled to all the rights, and privileges, and immunities, guarantied [*sic*] by that instrument to the citizen? One of which rights is the privilege of suing in a court of the United States in the cases specified in the constitution.

. . . The only matter in issue before the Court, therefore, is, whether the descendants of such slaves, when they shall be emancipated, or who are born of parents who had become free before their birth, are citizens of a State, in the sense which the word citizen is used in the Constitution. . . .

The words "people of the United States" and "citizens" are synonymous terms. . . . They both describe the political body who, according to our republican institutions, form the sovereignty, and who hold the power and conduct the government through their representatives. . . . The question before us is, whether the class of persons described in the plea in abatement compose a portion of this people, and are constituent members of this sovereignty? We think they are not, under the word "citizens" in the Constitution, and can therefore claim none of the rights and privileges which

that instrument provides for and secures to citizens of the United States. On the contrary, they were at that time considered as a subordinate and inferior class of beings, who had been subjugated

by the dominant race, and whether emancipated or not, yet remained subject to their authority, and had no rights or privileges but such as those who held the power and the government might choose to grant them. . . .

In discussing the question, we must not confound the rights of citizenship which a State may confer within its own limits, and the rights of citizenship as a member of the Union. It does not by any means follow, because he has all the rights and privileges of a citizen of a State, that he must be a citizen of the United States. . . .

In the opinion of the court, the legislation and histories of the times, and the language used in the Declaration of Independence, show, that neither the class of persons who had been imported as slaves, nor their descendants, whether they had become free or not, were then acknowledged as a part of the people, nor intended to be included in the general words used in that memorable instrument. . . .

They had for more than a century before been regarded as beings of an inferior order, and altogether unfit to associate with the white race, either in social or political relations, and so far inferior, that they had no rights which the white man was bound to respect; and that the negro might justly and lawfully be reduced to slavery for his benefit. . . .

. . . there are two clauses in the constitution which point directly and specifically to the negro race as a separate class of persons, and show clearly that they were not regarded as a portion of the people or citizens of the government then formed.

. . . upon full and careful consideration of the subject, the court is of opinion, that, upon the facts stated. . . , Dred Scott was not a citizen of Missouri within the meaning of the constitution of the United States and not entitled as such to sue in its courts. . . .

1. Summarize the reasoning behind the argument that former slaves are not "constituent members of this sovereignty."
2. Identify and characterize the view of the court regarding "the class of persons who had been imported as slaves" and their descendants?

14-9   Abraham Lincoln, "A House Divided" (1858)

Considered America's greatest president, Lincoln was a little know politician and lawyer from Illinois when he entered into his famous debates with Stephen Douglas. He was the first of the new Republicans to be elected President which event precipitated the Southern secession movement. A moderate on the slavery question, Lincoln argued against western expansion of slavery but sought to leave it alone where it already existed. He insisted that the Civil War was a war to preserve the union but his Emancipation Proclamation changed that for many into a moral war against slavery. A master at political oratory, Lincoln is famous for many speeches and phrases which defined the issues so dramatically. One is reproduced here in "A house Divided"

If we could first know where we are, and whither we are tending, we could better judge what to do and how to do it. We are now far into the fifth year since a policy was initiated with the avowed object, and confident promise, of putting an end to slavery agitation. Under the operation of that policy, that agitation has not only not ceased but has constantly augmented. In my opinion, it will not cease until a crisis shall have been reached and passed. "A house divided against itself cannot stand." I believe this government cannot endure permanently half-slave and half-free. I do not expect the Union to be dissolved-I do not expect the house to fall-but I do expect it will cease to be divided. It will become all one thing or all the other. Either the opponents of slavery will arrest the further spread of it and place it where the public mind shall rest in the belief that it is in the course of ultimate extinction or its advocates will push it forward, till it shall become alike lawful in all the states, old as well as new-North as well as South.

1. What is Lincoln's view of America's options as it deals with slavery? Compare/Contrast his perspective with the secession of the South.
2. How do Lincoln's attitudes and actions just before and just after his inaugeration compare or contrast with his resolve that America could not exist as "a house divided" and with his desire to keep the Union together?

PART FIFTEEN
THE CIVIL WAR

15-1 Jefferson Davis, Address to the Provisional Congress of the Confederate States of America (1861)

Jefferson Davis had a long and varied career before reluctantly becoming the first and only President of the Confederacy. A West Point graduate, he was a congressman before becoming a hero in the Mexican War. That success led to his appointment as United States Senator from Mississippi. Davis later became a very able Secretary of War in the administration of Franklin Pierce. He later returned to the Senate where he was a supporter of the extension of slavery. Though he sought to avoid secession, when it happened he resigned from the Senate and was made the President of the Confederate States of America. In this document Davis justifies the Confederacy on historical and constitutional grounds.

The declaration of war made against this Confederacy by Abraham Lincoln, the President of the United States, in his proclamation issued on the 15th day of the present month, rendered it necessary, in my judgment, that you should convene at the earliest practicable moment to devise the measures necessary for the defense of the country. The occasion is indeed an extraordinary one. It justifies me in a brief review of the relations heretofore existing between us and the States which now unite in warfare against us and in a succinct statement of the events which have resulted in this warfare, to the end that mankind may pass intelligent and impartial judgment on its motives and objects. During the war waged against Great Britain by her colonies on this continent a common danger impelled them to a close alliance and to the formation of a Confederation, by the terms of which the colonies, styling themselves States, entered "*severally* into a firm league of friendship with each other for their common defense, the security of their liberties, and their mutual and general welfare, binding themselves to assist each other against all force offered to or attacks made upon them, or any of them, on account of religion, sovereignty, trade, or any other pretense whatever." In order to guard against any misconstruction of their compact, the several States made explicit declaration in a distinct article-that "*each* State *retains its* sovereignty, freedom, and independence, and every power, jurisdiction, and right which is not by this Confederation *expressly delegated* to the United States in Congress assembled." . . .

Strange, indeed, must it appear to the impartial observer, but it is none the less true that all these carefully worded clauses proved unavailing to prevent the rise and growth in the Northern States of a political school which has persistently claimed that the government thus formed was not a compact *between* States, but was in effect a national government, set up *above* and *over* the States. An organization created by the States to secure the blessings of liberty and independence against *foreign* aggression, has been gradually perverted into a machine for their control in their *domestic* affairs. The *creature* has been exalted above its *creators*; the *principles* have been made subordinate to the *agent* appointed by themselves. The people of the Southern States, whose almost exclusive occupation was agriculture, early perceived a tendency in the Northern States to render the common government subservient to their own purposes by imposing burdens on commerce as a protection to their manufacturing and shipping interests. Long and angry controversies grew out of these attempts, often successful, to benefit one section of the country at the expense of the other. And the danger of disruption arising from this cause was enhanced by the fact that the Northern population was increasing, by immigration and other causes, in a greater ratio than the population of the South. By degrees, as the Northern States gained preponderance in the National Congress, self-interest taught their people to yield ready assent to any plausible advocacy of their right as a majority to govern the minority without control. They learned to listen with impatience of their will, and so utterly have the principles of the Constitution been corrupted in the Northern mind that, in the inaugural address delivered by President Lincoln in March last, he asserts as an axiom, which he plainly deems to be undeniable, that the theory of the Constitution requires that in all cases the majority shall govern; and in another memorable instance the same Chief Magistrate did not hesitate to liken the relations between a State and the United States to those which exist between a county and the State in which it is situated and by which it was created. This is the lamentable and fundamental error on which rests the policy that has culminated in his declaration of war against these Confederate States. In addition to the long-continued and deep-seated resentment felt by the Southern States at the persistent abuse of the powers they had delegated to the Congress, for the purpose of enriching the manufacturing and shipping classes of the North at the expense of the South, there has existed for nearly half a century another subject of discord, involving interests of such transcendent magnitude as at all times to create the apprehension in the minds of many devoted lovers of the Union that its permanence was impossible. When the several States delegated certain powers to the United States Congress, a large portion of the laboring population consisted of African slaves imported into the colonies by the mother country. In twelve out of the thirteen States negro slavery existed, and the right of property in slaves was protected by law. This property was recognized in the Constitution, and provision was made against its loss by the escape of the slave. The increase in the number of slaves by further importation from

Africa was also secured by a clause forbidding Congress to prohibit the slave trade anterior to a certain date, and in no clause can there be found any delegation of power to the Congress authorizing it in any manner to legislate to the prejudice, detriment, or discouragement of the owners of that species of property, or excluding it from the protection of the Government.

The climate and soil of the Northern States soon proved unpropitious to the continuance of slave labor, whilst the converse was the case at the South. Under the unrestricted free intercourse between two sections, the Northern States consulted their own interests by selling their slaves to the South and prohibiting slavery within their limits. The South were willing purchasers of a property suitable to their wants, and paid the price of the acquisition without harboring a suspicion that their quiet possession was to be disturbed by those who were inhibited not only by want of constitutional authority, but by good faith as vendors, from disquieting a title emanating from themselves. As soon, however, as the Northern States that prohibited African slavery within their limits had reached a number sufficient to give their representation a controlling voice in the Congress, a persistent and organized system of hostile measures against the rights of the owners of slaves in the Southern States was inaugurated and gradually extended. A continuous series of measures was devised and prosecuted for the purpose of rendering insecure the tenure of property in slaves. Fanatical organizations, supplied with money by voluntary subscriptions, were assiduously engaged in exciting amongst the slaves a spirit of discontent and revolt; means were furnished for their escape from their owners, and agents secretly employed to entice them to abscond; the constitutional provision for their rendition to their owners was first evaded, then openly denounced as a violation of conscientious obligation and religious duty; men were taught that it was a merit to elude, disobey, and violently oppose the execution of the laws enacted to secure the performance of the promise contained in the constitutional compact; owners of slaves were mobbed and even murdered in open day solely for applying to a magistrate for the arrest of a fugitive slave; the dogmas of these voluntary organizations soon obtained control of the Legislatures of many of the Northern States, and laws were passed providing for the punishment, by ruinous fines and long-continued imprisonment in jails and penitentiaries, of citizens of the Southern States who should dare to ask aid of the officers of the law for the recovery of their property. Emboldened by success, the theater of agitation and aggression against the clearly expressed constitutional rights of the Southern States was transferred to the Congress; Senators and Representatives were sent to the common councils of the nation, whose chief title to this distinction consisted in the display of a spirit of ultra fanaticism, and whose business was not "to promote the general welfare or insure domestic tranquility," but to awaken the bitterest hatred against the citizens of sister States by violent denunciation of their institutions; the transaction of public affairs was impeded by repeated efforts to usurp powers not delegated by the Constitution, for the purpose of impairing the security of property in slaves, and reducing those States which held slaves to a condition of inferiority. Finally a great party was organized for the purpose of obtaining the administration of the Government, with the avowed object of using its power for the total exclusion of the slave States from all participation in the benefits of the public domain acquired by all the States in common, whether by conquest or purchase; of surrounding them entirely by States in which slavery should be prohibited; of thus rendering the property in slaves so insecure as to be comparatively worthless, and thereby annihilating in effect property worth thousands of millions of dollars. This party, thus organized, succeeded in the month of November last in the election of its candidate for the Presidency of the United States.

1. Summarize Davis' argument regarding the rights of states and the rights of the United States as they pertain to the declaration of war by the North. Explain the "fundamental error" that has resulted in the war Davis is now confronted with.
2. What actions have been taken by the North to undermine and destroy the successful existence of the southern states according to Davis?
3. Summarize Davis' point of view on the causes of the civil war? What factors are largely responsible for the South's need to defend itself?

15-2   The "Cornerstone Speech" (1861)

On March 21, 1861, Alexander Hamilton Stephens, vice president of the newly established Confederate States of America, stood before an overflowing crowd at the Athenaeum in Savannah, Georgia, and delivered a speech outlining what he believed was the great principle upon which the new government was created. Stephens, an erstwhile lawyer and congressman from Crawfordville, was originally opposed to secession, but chose to remain with his state when it left the Union in January 1861. Elected vice-president of the Confederacy in February, Stephens remained estranged from President Jefferson Davis through much of the war—partly as a result of the following speech. After the war he returned to political service in his native Georgia and in the U. S. House of Representatives. He was elected governor of Georgia in 1882 and died in office. The "Cornerstone Speech" was delivered extemporaneously and no official printed version exists. The text below was taken from a newspaper article in the Savannah Republican.

Source: Henry Cleveland, *Alexander H. Stephens, in Public and Private: With Letters and Speeches, Before, During, and Since the War*, Philadelphia, 1886, pp. 717–729.
http://www.geocities.com/CollegePark/Quad/6460/doct/861crnrstn.html

Savannah, Georgia
March 21, 1861

I was remarking, that we are passing through one of the greatest revolutions in the annals of the world. Seven States have within the last three months thrown off an old government and formed a new. This revolution has been signally marked, up to this time, by the fact of its having been accomplished without the loss of a single drop of blood. [Applause.]

. . . . But not to be tedious in enumerating the numerous changes for the better, allow me to allude to one other—though last, not least. The new constitution has put at rest, forever, all the agitating questions relating to our peculiar institution—African slavery as it exists amongst us—the proper status of the negro in our form of civilization. This was the immediate cause of the late rupture and present revolution. Jefferson in his forecast, had anticipated this, as the "rock upon which the old Union would split." He was right. What was conjecture with him, is now a realized fact. But whether he fully comprehended the great truth upon which that rock stood and stands, may be doubted. The prevailing ideas entertained by him and most of the leading statesmen at the time of the formation of the old constitution, were that the enslavement of the African was in violation of the laws of nature; that it was wrong in principle, socially, morally, and politically. It was an evil they knew not well how to deal with, but the general opinion of the men of that day was that, somehow or other in the order of Providence, the institution would be evanescent and pass away. This idea, though not incorporated in the constitution, was the prevailing idea at that time. The constitution, it is true, secured every essential guarantee to the institution while it should last, and hence no argument can be justly urged against the constitutional guarantees thus secured, because of the common sentiment of the day. Those ideas, however, were fundamentally wrong. They rested upon the assumption of the equality of races. This was an error. It was a sandy foundation, and the government built upon it fell when the "storm came and the wind blew."

Our new government is founded upon exactly the opposite idea; its foundations are laid, its corner-stone rests upon the great truth, that the negro is not equal to the white man; that slavery—subordination to the superior race—is his natural and normal condition. [Applause.] This, our new government, is the first, in the history of the world, based upon this great physical, philosophical, and moral truth. This truth has been slow in the process of its development, like all other truths in the various departments of science. It has been so even amongst us. Many who hear me, perhaps, can recollect well, that this truth was not generally admitted, even within their day. The errors of the past generation still clung to many as late as twenty years ago. Those at the North, who still cling to these errors, with a zeal above knowledge, we justly denominate fanatics. All fanaticism springs from an aberration of the mind—from a defect in reasoning. It is a species of insanity. One of the most striking characteristics of insanity, in many instances, is forming correct conclusions from fancied or erroneous premises; so with the anti-slavery fanatics; their conclusions are right if their premises were. They assume that the negro is equal, and hence conclude that he is entitled to equal privileges and rights with the white man. If their premises were correct, their conclusions would be logical and just—but their premise being wrong, their whole argument fails. I recollect once of having heard a gentleman from one of the northern States, of great power and ability, announce in the House of Representatives, with imposing effect, that we of the South would be compelled, ultimately, to yield upon this subject of slavery, that it was as impossible to war successfully against a principle in politics, as it was in physics or mechanics. That the principle would ultimately prevail. That we, in maintaining slavery as it exists with us, were warring against a principle, a principle founded in nature, the principle of the equality of men. The reply I made to him was, that upon his own grounds, we should, ultimately, succeed, and that he and his associates, in this crusade against our institutions, would ultimately fail. The truth announced, that it was as impossible to war successfully against a principle in politics as it was in physics and mechanics, I admitted; but told him that it was he, and those acting with him, who were warring against a principle. They were attempting to make things equal which the Creator had made unequal.

In the conflict thus far, success has been on our side, complete throughout the length and breadth of the Confederate States. It is upon this, as I have stated, our social fabric is firmly planted; and I cannot permit myself to doubt the ultimate success of a full recognition of this principle throughout the civilized and enlightened world.

As I have stated, the truth of this principle may be slow in development, as all truths are and ever have been, in the various branches of science. It was so with the principles announced by Galileo—it was so with Adam Smith and his principles of political economy. It was so with Harvey, and his theory of the circulation of the blood. It is stated that not a single one of the medical profession, living at the time of the announcement of the truths made by him, admitted them. Now, they are universally acknowledged. May we not, therefore, look with confidence to the ultimate universal acknowledgment of the truths upon which our system rests? It is the first government ever instituted upon the principles in strict conformity to nature, and the ordination of Providence, in furnishing the materials of human society. Many governments have been founded upon the principle of the subordination and serfdom of certain classes of the same race; such were and are in violation of the laws of nature. Our system commits no such violation of nature's laws. With us, all of the white race, however high or low, rich or poor, are equal in the eye of the law. Not so with the negro. Subordination is his place. He, by nature, or by the curse against Canaan, is fitted for that condition which he occupies in our system. The architect, in the construction of buildings, lays the foundation with the proper material—the granite; then comes the brick or the marble. The substratum of our society is made of the material fitted by nature for it, and by experience we know that it is best, not only for the superior, but for the inferior race, that it should be so. It is, indeed, in conformity with the ordinance of the Creator. It is not for us to inquire into the wisdom of his ordinances, or to question them. For his own purposes, he has made one race to differ from another, as he has made "one star to differ from another star in glory."

The great objects of humanity are best attained when there is conformity to his laws and decrees, in the formation of governments as well as in all things else. Our confederacy is founded upon principles in strict conformity with these laws. This stone which was rejected by the first builders "is become the chief of the corner"—the real "corner-stone"—in our new edifice. [Applause.]

I have been asked, what of the future? It has been apprehended by some that we would have arrayed against us the civilized world. I care not who or how many they may be against us, when we stand upon the eternal principles of truth, if we are true to ourselves and the principles for which we contend, we are obliged to, and must triumph. [Immense applause.]

Thousands of people who begin to understand these truths are not yet completely out of the shell; they do not see them in their length and breadth. We hear much of the civilization and christianization of the barbarous tribes of Africa. In my judgment, those ends will never be attained, but by first teaching them the lesson taught to Adam, that "in the sweat of his brow he should eat his bread," [applause,] and teaching them to work, and feed, and clothe themselves.

. . . . Thus far we have seen none of those incidents which usually attend revolutions. No such material as such convulsions usually throw up has been seen. Wisdom, prudence, and patriotism, have marked every step of our progress thus far. This augurs well for the future, and it is a matter of sincere gratification to me, that I am enabled to make the declaration. Of the men I met in the Congress at Montgomery, I may be pardoned for saying this, an abler, wiser, a more conservative, deliberate, determined, resolute, and patriotic body of men, I never met in my life. [Great applause.] Their works speak for them; the provisional government speaks for them; the constitution of the permanent government will be a lasting monument of their worth, merit, and statesmanship. [Applause.]

. . . . Our growth, by accessions from other States, will depend greatly upon whether we present to the world, as I trust we shall, a better government than that to which neighboring States belong. If we do this, North Carolina, Tennessee, and Arkansas cannot hesitate long; neither can Virginia, Kentucky, and Missouri. They will necessarily gravitate to us by an imperious law. We made ample provision in our constitution for the admission of other States; it is more guarded, and wisely so, I think, than the old constitution on the same subject, but not too guarded to receive them as fast as it may be proper. Looking to the distant future, and, perhaps, not very far distant either, it is not beyond the range of possibility, and even probability, that all the great States of the north-west will gravitate this way, as well as Tennessee, Kentucky, Missouri, Arkansas, etc. Should they do so, our doors are wide enough to receive them, but not until they are ready to assimilate with us in principle.

The process of disintegration in the old Union may be expected to go on with almost absolute certainty if we pursue the right course. We are now the nucleus of a growing power which, if we are true to ourselves, our destiny, and high mission, will become the controlling power on this continent. To what extent accessions will go on in the process of time, or where it will end, the future will determine. So far as it concerns States of the old Union, this process will be upon no such principles of reconstruction as now spoken of, but upon reorganization and new assimilation. [Loud applause.] Such are some of the glimpses of the future as I catch them.

. . . . As to whether we shall have war with our late confederates, or whether all matters of differences between us shall be amicably settled, I can only say that the prospect for a peaceful adjustment is better, so far as I am informed, than it has been.

The prospect of war is, at least, not so threatening as it has been. The idea of coercion, shadowed forth in President Lincoln's inaugural, seems not to be followed up thus far so vigorously as was expected. Fort Sumter, it is believed, will soon be evacuated. What course will be pursued toward Fort Pickens, and the other forts on the gulf, is not so well understood. It is to be greatly desired that all of them should be surrendered. Our object is peace, not only with the North, but with the world. All matters relating to the public property, public liabilities of the Union when we were members of it, we are ready and willing to adjust and settle upon the principles of right, equity, and good faith. War can be of no more benefit to the North than to us. Whether the intention of evacuating Fort Sumter is to be received as an evidence of a desire for a peaceful solution of our difficulties with the United States, or the result of necessity, I will not undertake to say. I would fain hope the former. Rumors are afloat, however, that it is the result of necessity. All I can say to you, therefore, on that point is, keep your armor bright and your powder dry. [Enthusiastic cheering.]

The surest way to secure peace, is to show your ability to maintain your rights. The principles and position of the present administration of the United States—the Republican party—present some puzzling questions. While it is a fixed principle with them never to allow the increase of a foot of slave territory, they seem to be equally determined not to part with an inch "of the accursed soil." Notwithstanding their clamor against the institution, they seemed to be equally opposed to getting more, or letting go what they have got. They were ready to fight on the accession of Texas, and are equally ready to fight now on her secession. Why is this? How can this strange paradox be accounted for? There seems to be but one rational solution—and that is, notwithstanding their professions of humanity, they are disinclined to give up the benefits they derive from slave labor. Their philanthropy yields to their interest. The idea of enforcing the laws, has but one object, and that is a collection of the taxes, raised by slave labor to swell the fund, necessary to meet their heavy appropriations. The spoils is what they are after—though they come from the labor of the slave. . . . [Continued applause]

1. *According to Vice President Alexander H. Stephens, what was is the cornerstone of the Confederacy? What other explanations (cornerstones) might have been articulated by Confederate politicians for the establishment of the new nation?*
2. *President Jefferson Davis was greatly disturbed by Stephens's remarks, even though the two men shared basically the same beliefs. Why do you think this was so? How had Stephens shifted the focus of the political debate over the "creed" of the Confederacy?*

15-3 Mary Boykin Chesnut, A Confederate Lady's Diary (1861)

Born into the political and social elite of southern society, Chesnut was the daughter of a Senator and Governor of South Carolina. She married James Chesnut, one of the largest land owners in the state and soon to be Senator. After secession, he became a confederate congressman and later aide to Jefferson Davis. Mary Chesnut's house became a salon for leading members of Confederate society. During the war, Chesnut kept a diary that became famous for its portrayal of the Confederacy. This selection reveals the ambivalence that many in the South had towards slavery.

I wonder if it be a sin to think slavery a curse to any land. Sumner said not one word of this hated institution which is not true. Men & women are punished when their masters & mistresses are brutes & not when they do wrong-& then we live surrounded by prostitutes. An abandoned woman is sent out of any decent house elsewhere. Who thinks any worse of a Negro or Mulatto woman for being a thing we can't name. God forgive *us*, but ours is a *monstrous* system & wrong & iniquity. Perhaps the rest of the world is as bad. This is *only* what I see: like the patriarchs of old, our men live all in one house with their wives & their concubines, & the Mulattos one sees in every family exactly resemble the white children-& every lady tells you who is the father of all the Mulatto children in everybody's household, but those in her own, she seems to think drop from the clouds or pretends so to think-. Good women we have, *but* they talk of *nastiness tho* they never do wrong; they talk day & night of -. My disgust sometimes is boiling over-but they are, I believe, in conduct the purest women God ever made. Thank God for my countrywomen-alas for the men! No worse than men everywhere, but the lower their mistresses, the more degraded they must be.

My mother-in-law told me when I was first married not to send my female servants in the street on errands. They were there tempted, led astray-& then she said placidly, "So they told *me* when I came here-& I was very particular, *but you see with what* result." Mr. Harris said it was so patriarchal. So it is-flocks & herds & slaves-& wife Leah does not suffice. Rachel must be *added*, if not *married* & all the time they seem to think themselves patterns-models of husbands & fathers.

Mrs. Davis told me "everybody described my husband's father as an odd character, a Millionaire who did nothing for his son whatever, left him to struggle with poverty," &c. I replied, "Mr. Chesnut Senior thinks himself the best of fathers-& his son thinks likewise. I have nothing to say-but it is true, he has no money but what he makes as a lawyer," &c. Again I say, my countrywomen are as pure as angels-tho surrounded by another race who are-the social evil!

1. *What are Chesnut's sentiments and chief concerns in this account? In what ways does this diary entry reveal a "pre-war" sense of awareness? In other words, identify the events and thoughts that make up this entry? How might these concerns change in the coming months?*

15-4   Why They Fought (1861)

Samuel Storrow was born in Boston, Massachusetts, July 24, 1843. When the war broke out, Samuel was seventeen years old and in college. Although desiring to join the army, his wish met with objections from his parents, who considered him too young for military service. In the spring of 1862, Storrow was forced to obtain a leave of absence from college to recover from an eye infection and sailed for the Azores. He found, on his return, that his father was in Europe, and that his elder brother, Charles, had just entered the army with a commission as captain in the Forty-Fourth Massachusetts—then mustering for immediate service. Samuel returned to college, but immediately wrote the following letter to his father to ask his permission to join the regiment.

Captain George E. Pickett was stationed at Fort Bellingham on Puget Sound in the northwest when the news came about his native Virginia's secession from the Union. Faced with the need to make a quick decision about his future, Pickett's destiny was determined by his notion of loyalty. Writing to his fiancé, Sally Corbell, the future Confederate general explained his decision to resign his commission and cast his lot with the Confederacy. Pickett would later participate in the fateful charge at the Battle of Gettysburg that today bears his name.

> **Source:** Harvard Memorial Biographies
> http://www.geocities.com/Pentagon/2126/hmb.storrow.html
> George Edward Pickett, *The Heart of a Soldier, As Revealed in the Intimate Letters of Genl. George E. Pickett C.S.A.:* Electronic Edition.
> http://docsouth.unc.edu/pickett/pickett.html#pick33

As soon as I landed I heard of the formation of the 44th, and Charles's commission. I at once wished to join this; but mother and Charles both opposed it, saying that it was your intention and desire that I should rejoin my Class at once, and expressed themselves so strongly against my enlisting, that on the following Monday I went to Cambridge, and resumed my studies with what zeal I could. . . .The excitement and intensity of feeling, the daily agony of doubt and suspense, is a thing scarcely to be appreciated in full by one who was not here at the time, and who did not pass through it. I assure you, my dear father, I know nothing in the course of my life which has caused me such deep and serious thought as this trying crisis in the history of our nation. What is the worth of this man's life or of that man's education, if this great and glorious fabric of our Union, raised with such toil and labor by our forefathers, and transmitted to us in value increased tenfold, is to be shattered to pieces by traitorous hands, and allowed to fall crumbling into the dust? If our country and our nationality is to perish, better that we should all perish with it, and not survive to see it a laughing-stock for all posterity to be pointed at as the unsuccessful trial of republicanism. It seems to me the part of a coward to stay at home and allow others to fight my battles and incur dangers for me. What shame, what mortification would it cause me years hence to be obliged to confess that, in the great struggle for our national existence, I stood aloof, an idle spectator, without any peculiar ties to retain me at home, and yet not caring or not daring to do anything in the defense of my country. . . .The only reason which could at all deter me from enlisting was your absence. I felt reluctant to take so important a step without your advice and consent; and yet I felt that, had you been here, you would have given me your blessing and bade me go.

Here was a regiment formed and commanded by friends and kinsmen, and surpassing others in the material of which it was composed. If I embraced this opportunity, I should be among friends and equals, instead of being forced to accept as my associates any with whom I might be placed. If I did not make my decision quickly, the chance would be lost; and I knew that if I went, you would agree with mother in much preferring that Charles and I should be together in the same regiment. At that time, too, a draft seemed almost certain; and, as several thousand were said to be wanting to complete the quota of Boston, the chance of being drawn was by no means small. . . .

Poor mother, she has had a hard time during your absence, especially in coming to a decision about me. . . .Assure her fully of your approval of the course she has taken, and I shall be happy too. . . .Everybody thinks that she has acted nobly, and that you have reason to be proud of your wife was we have of our mother.

I have tried as well as I can, and I find that it is but poorly to give you some idea of my feelings on this subject. I feel well satisfied that I have done what, upon careful deliberation, has seemed to me most in accordance with all my duties. I have looked at the matter from every point of view; and if I shall seem to you to have arrived at a wrong conclusion, believe me, it was not from any hasty impulse of the moment, but from the sober dictates of my best judgment. If I have unwittingly made the wrong choice, God forgive me; I did what I thought was for the best.

Ever you affectionate son,
Samuel Storrow

SEVERAL weeks ago I wrote quite a long letter from far-away San Francisco to a very dear little girl, and told her that a certain soldier who wears one of her long, silken ringlets next his heart was homeward bound and that he hoped a line of welcome would meet him on his arrival in his native state. He told her of the difficulties he had experienced in being relieved from his post, of how sorry he was to sheathe the sword which had helped to bring victory to the country for which he had fought, and how sorry he was to say good-by to his little command and to part from his faithful and closest companion, his dog, and his many dear friends; but sorrier still for the existing circumstances which made this severance necessary. He told her many things for which, with him, she will be sorry, and some of which he hopes will make her glad. He is troubled by finding no answer to this long letter which, having at that time no notion of the real conditions here, he is afraid was written too freely by far.

No, my child, I had no conception of the intensity of feeling, the bitterness and hatred toward those who were so lately our friends and are now our enemies. I, of course, have always strenuously opposed disunion, not as doubting the right of secession, which was taught in our text-book at West Point, but as gravely questioning its expediency. I believed that the revolutionary spirit which infected both North and South was but a passing phase of fanaticism which would perish under the rebuke of all good citizens, who would surely unite in upholding the Constitution; but when that great assembly, composed of ministers, lawyers, judges, chancellors, statesmen, mostly white haired men of thought, met in South Carolina and when their districts were called crept noiselessly to the table in the center of the room and affixed their signatures to the parchment on which the ordinance of secession was inscribed, and when in deathly silence, spite of the gathered multitude, General Jamison arose and without preamble read: "The ordinance of secession has been signed and ratified; I proclaim the State of South Carolina an independent sovereignty," and lastly, when my old boyhood's friend called for an invasion, it was evident that both the advocates and opponents of secession had read the portents aright.

You know, my little lady, some of those cross-stitched mottoes on the cardboard samplers which used to hang on my nursery wall, such as, "He who provides not for his own household is worse than an infidel" and "Charity begins at home," made a lasting impression upon me; and while I love my neighbor, i.e., my country, I love my household, i.e., my state, more, and I could not be an infidel and lift my sword against my own kith and kin, even though I do believe, my most wise little counselor and confidante, that the measure of American greatness can be achieved only under one flag, and I fear, alas, there can never again reign for either of us the true spirit of national unity whether divided under two flags or united under one.

We did not tarry even for a day in 'Frisco, but under assumed names my friend, Sam Barron, and I sailed for New York, where we arrived on the very day that Sam's father, Commodore Barron, was brought there a prisoner, which fact was proclaimed aloud by the pilot amid cheers of the passengers and upon our landing heralded by the newsboys with more cheers. Poor Sam had a hard fight to hide his feelings and to avoid arrest. We separated as mere ship acquaintances, and went by different routes to meet again, as arranged, at the house of Doctor Paxton, a Southern sympathizer and our friend.

On the next day we left for Canada by the earliest train. Thence we made our perilous way back south again, barely escaping arrest several times, and finally arrived in dear old Richmond, September 13th, just four days ago. I at once enlisted in the army and the following day was commissioned Captain. But so bitter is the feeling here that my being unavoidably delayed so long in avowing my allegiance to my state has been most cruelly and severely criticized by friends—yes, and even relatives, too.

Now, little one, if you had the very faintest idea how happy a certain captain in the C.S.A. (My, but that "C" looks queer!) would be to look into your beautiful, soul-speaking eyes and hear your wonderfully musical voice, I think you would let him know by wire where he could find you. I shall almost listen for the electricity which says, "I am at —. Come." I know that you will have mercy on your devoted SOLDIER.

---

1. *What factors led Samuel Storrow to desire military service? Why do you think his parents submitted in 1862 when they had refused to grant their permission the previous year?*
2. *What made George E. Pickett, who was personally opposed to disunion, resign his commission and side with the Confederacy? How do you think he would define "loyalty"? How do Pickett's motives differ from Storrow's?*

15-5   A Confederate General Assesses First Bull Run (1861)

The first major land battle of the American Civil War was fought near Manassas, Virginia, on July 21, 1861. In many ways, the battle served to dispel assumptions on both sides about the brevity of the conflict. The Confederate victory also gave the South the initiative in terms of the war's momentum—at least in the eastern theater of operations. General Joseph E. Johnston, commander of all Confederate troops in Virginia, brought reinforcements by railroad to General P. G. T. Beauregard's threatened army at Manassas at the outset the battle and remained on the field to participate in the action. The following excerpt is from his memoir published in 1874.

> **Source:** Joseph Eggleston Johnston, *Narrative of Military Operations During the Civil War* (New York: D. Appleton and Company, 1874), pp. 48–51, 56, 84–85.

We came upon the field not a moment too soon. The long contest against great odds, and the heavy losses, especially of field-officers, had discouraged Bee's troops, and destroyed or dispersed those of Evans—for we found him apparently without a command. The Fourth Alabama Regiment, of Bee's brigade, had lost all its field-officers, and was without a commander. Colonel S. R. Gist,[1] a volunteer on General Bee's staff, was requested to take command of it.

Our presence with the troops under fire, and the assurance it gave of more material aid, had the happiest effect on their spirits. Order was easily and quietly restored, and the battle well reestablished. It was during the efforts for this that Jackson and his brigade are said to have acquired the name they have since borne—by Bee's calling to his men to observe how Jackson and his brigade[2] stood "like a stone-wall," a name made still more glorious in every battle in which general and brigade afterward fought.

After assigning General Beauregard to the command of the troops immediately engaged, which he properly suggested belonged to the second in rank, not to the commander of the army, I returned to the supervision of the whole field. The aspect of affairs was not encouraging, yet I had strong hope that Beauregard's capacity and courage, the high soldierly qualities of Bee and Jackson, and the patriotic enthusiasm of our Southern volunteers, would maintain the fight until adequate reinforcements could be brought to their aid. . . .

* * *

After these additions to the forces engaged, we had nine regiments and two companies of infantry, two hundred and fifty cavalry, and five field-batteries (twenty guns) of the Army of the Shenandoah, and twenty-seven companies of infantry, six companies of cavalry, and six pieces of artillery of the Army of the Potomac, contending with three divisions of the United States army and superior forces of cavalry and artillery; yet the brave Southern volunteers lost not a foot of ground, but repelled the repeated attacks of the heavy masses of the enemy, whose numbers enabled them to bring forward fresh troops after each repulse. Colonel Stuart contributed materially to one of these repulses, by a well-timed and vigorous charge upon the Federal right flank with two of his companies, those of Captains Welby Carter and J. B. Hoge.

It must not be supposed that such successful resistance by the Southern troops was due in any degree to want of prowess in their assailants. The army they fought belonged to a people who had often contended on the field on *at least* equal terms with the nation that had long claimed to be the most martial in Europe. The Northern army had the disadvantage, a great one to such undisciplined troops as were engaged on both sides, of being the assailants, and advancing under fire to the attack, which can be well done only by trained soldiers. They were much more liable to confusion, therefore, than the generally stationary ranks of the Confederates.

About two o'clock an officer of General Beauregard's adjutant-general's office galloped from Manassas Junction to report to me that a Federal army had reached the Manassas Gap Railroad, was marching toward us, and was then but three or four miles from our left flank. Although it seemed to me impossible that General Patterson could have come up so soon, and from that direction, I fixed on a new field upon which to concentrate our whole force should the report prove to be true—one nearly equidistant from Manassas Junction, the troops engaged, and those on the right—and sent orders to the commanders of the latter to gather their respective brigades south of the stream, that they might be ready to move to it promptly.

On the appearance of Fisher's (Sixth North Carolina) regiment soon after (at half-past two o'clock), approaching from the direction of Manassas Junction, Colonel Cocke was desired to lead his brigade into action on the right; which he did with alacrity. When Fisher's regiment came up, the Federal general seemed to be strengthening his right. It was ordered to the left, therefore. Kershaw's and Cash's regiments of Bonham's brigade, then in sight, received similar orders on arriving.

Soon after three o'clock, while General McDowell seemed to be striving, by strengthening his right, to drive back our left, and thus separate us from Manassas Junction, Brigadier-General Kirby Smith, hastening with Elzey's brigade from that railroad-station, arrived by the route Fisher had followed. He was instructed, by a staff-officer sent forward to meet him, to form on the left of the line, with his left thrown forward, and to assail the enemy's right flank. At his request I joined him, directed his march, and gave these instructions in person. . . .

* * *

The Southern infantry had great advantage over the Northern in their greater familiarity with firearms. It was the reverse however, in relation to the artillery; for that of the South had had neither time nor ammunition for practice while much of that of the North belonged to the regular service. Still, ours, directed principally by Colonel Pendleton, was more effective even than the regular batteries of the United States army, in that battle.

The pursuit was pressed as long as it was effective. But when the main column of retreating infantry was encountered, after the parties in its rear and on the flanks had been dispersed or captured, our cavalry found itself too weak to make any serious impression, and returned with the prisoners already taken. The infantry was not required to pursue far from the field, because by doing so it would have been harassed to no purpose. It is well known that infantry, unencumbered by baggage-trains, can easily escape pursuing infantry.

The victory was as complete as one gained by infantry and artillery only can be. . . .

* * *

Until the end of December, military operations were practicable; but, from that time to the beginning of spring, the condition of the country south of the Potomac and east of the Blue Ridge would have made them extremely difficult—indeed, almost impossible. The quantity of rain that fell, and of snow, always melting quickly, made a depth of mud rarely equaled.

The Confederate troops fought bravely and well wherever they encountered those of the United States, in 1861. At Bethel, under Magruder and D. H. Hill; at Oakhill, under Price and McCulloch; on the Gauley, under Floyd; on the Greenbrier, under H. R. Jackson; on Santa Rosa Island, under R. H. Anderson; at Belmont, under Polk and Pillow; on the Alleghany, under Edward Johnson, and at Chastenallah, under McIntosh. On all these occasions they were superior to their adversaries, from greater zeal and more familiarity with the use of fire-arms. The thorough system of instruction introduced into the United States army gradually established equality in the use of fire-arms, and our greater zeal finally encountered better discipline.

1. *To what does General Johnston attribute Confederate success in the battle of First Bull Run? What advantage, if any, did he ascribe to the Union army?*
2. *What does General Johnston say about the ability of Union soldiers? From what disadvantage did they suffer?*

15-6 Charles Harvey Brewster, Three Letters from the Civil War Front (1862)

Charles Brewster was born and raised in Northampton Massachusetts and enlisted in the 10th Massachusetts Volunteers at the age of 27. His family was poor and his father had died leaving his mother and sisters. Brewster had been, at the time of his enlistment, a store clerk. He was commissioned in the Mass. Volunteers in 1862. His letters, written to his mother and sisters, reveal the ambitions he hoped would be realized by serving and the day to day drudgeries of war. Brewster left the army in 1864 and eventually became a successful store and greenhouse proprietor. His letter provide a priceless glimpse into the attitudes, beliefs and experiences of an average union soldier.

Thursday Morning.

I feel some better this morning. I had the Doctor last evening and he gave me something which carried off my headache. We had more marching orders yesterday in so far as to be ready to start at any moment, with 2 days rations and 100 rounds of Cartridges, and everybody thinks we shall go in less than a week. I don't know but I shall be discharged, as the whole Regiment is almost in a state of mutiny on the Nigger question. Capt Miller the pro slavery Captain of the Shelburne Falls Co undertook with Major Marsh to back him to drive all the Contraband out of camp, he came to me and I had quite a blow up with him. Major Marsh took the Regiment off the camp to drill yesterday while they were gone Capt Miller searched the camp for niggers, but did not find any, this morning they are all here again, this morning placards were found posted around the camp threatening direful things if they persisted in driving them off, which is a most foolish thing, but the men did not come down here to oppress Niggers and they are not quite brutes yet, as some of their officers are. I have nothing to do with any of the trouble except that I refuse to order off my own servant, in this I am not alone, as Capt Walkly of the Westfield Co has done the same thing, the Officers are divided into two parties on the question, and most bitter and rancorous feelings have been excited which will never be allayed. I do not know how it will all end but I should not be all surprised if they made a fuss about it and should prefer charges against me, Capt Parsons, Lieut Weatherill, the Adjutant, Capt Walkley, Capt Lombard, Lieut Shurtleff, + our one or two others hold the same opinion that I do in the matter. I should hate to have to leave now just as the Regiment is going into active service, but I never will be instrumental in returning a slave to his master in any way shape or manner, I'll die first. Major Marsh well knows that the slaves masters are waiting outside of camp ready to snap them up, and it is inhuman to drive them into their hands, if you could have seen strong men crying like children, at the very thought as I did yesterday you would not blame me for standing out about it nor can one blame the men for showing sympathy for them, for they are from Massachusetts and are entirely unused to such scenes, and cannot recognize this property in human flesh and blood.

You may wonder where the Col. is in all this and I do also, we have all offered to give our servants up if he gives the order, but nobody knows that he has given any such order, and he is off camp all the while, attending a Court Martial, and the whole thing seems to be the doing of Maj Marsh Lieut Col Decker and Capt Miller, the last has been threatening to have the men sent to the Tortugas for mutiny, and perhaps he can do it, but I doubt it. I must close now and send this to the office in order to get it off by this mornings mail. please write again as soon as you get this, as I do not know as we shall be in this camp to receive more than one more letter. Give my love to all. I shall write to Mattie some time to day.

With much love Your aff son Charlie.

Dear Mattie

I received your most welcome letter accompanying the stockings, and also the pictures for which I cannot find words to express my thanks. I have to look at them fifty times a day. I am in camp alone to day as the Company is out on Grand Guard to day and as I went both of the last two times with them I managed to stay in this time. I have been slightly unwell for two or three days but have got pretty much over it now.

We have had another grand excitement over orders to march which we received last week. They were positive and we were to start at 3 o'clock in the morning but they were countermanded before 8 o'clock the same afternoon, and we are still here, but we are under standing orders to be ready at a moments notice, and to have 100 rounds of ammunition per man, and two days rations cooked all the time, and daily expecting orders to start, every man also is ordered to take an extra pair of shoes in his knapsack so it looks as if we were to have a long pull when we do move. Capt Lombard got a furlough the other day and started for home, and got as far as Washington where he got such information as convinced him that we should march in less than a week and he came back and gave it up. We were intended the other day to reinforce Gen Banks but the Rebels made no resistance to his advance and consequently we were not needed, and when it is proposed to send us next I am sure I cannot imagine.

We have had quite a row about giving up slaves and about the secessionists in this neighborhood and it threatened to be quite a serious affair for a time but things are quieter now. Capt Miller of Shelbourne Falls undertook to put all the Contrabands out of camp and myself and several other officers refused to give up our servants, at his order for we doubted his authority in the matter, as the Col had heretofor given us to understand that he was not opposed to our keeping them, and had appeared to be quite anti Slavery in his views, but he took the matter in hand and read the order for thier expulsion at the head of the Regt and pretended to consider it a mutiny and altogether got himself into a terrible rage about it, and went over to the pro Slavery side body and soul. so it seems that the prime object of our being in this country is to return niggers to thier masters. I don't think Massachusetts blood was ever quite so riled nor quite so humbled before, but we had to submit. I was mad enough to resign, if I had not thought it would please our slave catching brutes too much, we have a good many of that class among our officers, and I believe Major Marsh would go further to return a fugitive slave than he would to save the Union.

The stockings you sent were first rate. I have not put them on yet, but they look like just the thing I want

Dear Mother

I received your welcome letter to night and I think you must have received two from me before this time as I have written regularly though one of mine was delayed in consequence of your last (before this) having been sent by Captain and I was on Guard when I got it, and so I could not write in time to send it Monday morning. I expected you would be in fever when the news from here reached you but we have not gone yet, but we are expecting our orders every day. part of our division has already gone and we shall soon follow. we have had 2 Regiments of Regulars added to our Division, and they are the ones that have marched, but where they have gone to or where we are to go to nobody knows. You must not be alarmed at any reports that come from here as you cannot possibly hear any truth unless you have it from me, and you know we have got to go and take our part in the struggle. that's what we came for and we aught to be thankful that we did not have to meet the enemy while we were raw and undisciplined and not ready for battle. it is said that we are now about as well trained as well as can be for Volunteers and certainly we know everything that is in the book for Infantry tactics. The weather is getting warmer and the ground begins to settle and it seems as if the army must make an advance very soon if it ever does. We are as ready as we ever can be, and perfectly willing, and if God rules shall I truly believe render a good account of ourselves when the time comes. I am more concerned about the reports that will go home when the Army does move, and you cannot have even a shadow of truth to guide you and yet you will believe everything that comes. I could almost wish for your sakes that, all communication of every kind was cut off between here and the north.

We have not been paid off yet, and I don't know as we ever shall be again. The government has no money, and it takes three weeks just to sign enough paper money to pay 4 days expenses, and how they are ever going to catch up at that rate I am sure I do not know. . . .

1. *What various attitudes are revealed in these letters regarding "contrabands" and the prospect of returning them to their masters?*
2. *Characterize the author's mood and attitude toward future engagement in battle. What do these letters reveal regarding outfitting and financing the war effort?*

15-7 Clara Barton, Medical Life at the Battlefield (1862)

Born in Massachusetts, Clare Barton was a teacher and clerk in the U.S. Patent Office. Upon the arrival of the Civil War, she organized a network, separate from the government, to get food, supplies and nursing aid to the soldiers. She served as a nurse on several battlefields including Fredricksburg and Antietam. After the war, Barton went to Europe for a time where she became involved in the International Red Cross. Upon her return she worked for the establishment of the American Red Cross. Though she had much government opposition to her efforts, in 1882 the Senate ratified the Geneva Convention and the American Red Cross was born. At the age of 77 Barton again served conflict during the Spanish-American war. These letters reveal the horrific nature of the Civil War battlefield.

I was strong and thought I might go to the rescue of the men who fell. . . . What could I do but go with them, or work for them and my country? The patriot blood of my father was warm in my veins. The country which he had fought for, I might at least work for. . . .

But I struggled long and hard with my sense of propriety-with the appalling fact that I was only a woman whispering in one ear, and thundering in the other the groans of suffering men dying like dogs-unfed and unsheltered, for the life of every institution which had protected and educated me!

I said that I struggled with my sense of propriety and I say it with humiliation and shame. I am ashamed that I thought of such a thing.

When our armies fought on Cedar Mountain, I broke the shackles and went to the field. . . .

Five days and nights with three hours sleep-a narrow escape from capture-and some days of getting the wounded into hospitals at Washington, brought Saturday, August 30. And if you chance to feel, that the positions I occupied were rough and unseemly for a *woman*-I can only reply that they were rough and unseemly for *men*. But under all, lay the life of the nation. I had inherited the rich blessing of health and strength of constitution-such as are seldom given to woman-and I felt that some return was due from me and that I ought to be there. . . .

. . . . Our coaches were not elegant or commodious; they had no seats, no platforms, no steps, a slide door on the side the only entrance, and this higher than my head. For my man attaining my elevated position, I must beg of you to draw on your imaginations and spare me the labor of reproducing the boxes, boards, and rails, which in those days, seemed to help me up and down the world. We did not criticize the unsightly helpers and were thankful that the stiff springs did not quite jostle us out. This need not be limited to this particular trip or train, but will for all that I have known in Army life. This is the kind of conveyance which your tons of generous gifts have reached the field with the freights. These trains through day and night, sunshine and heat and cold, have thundered over heights, across plains, the ravines, and over hastily built army bridges 90 feet across the stream beneath.

At 10 o'clock Sunday (August 31) our train drew up at Fairfax Station. The ground, for acres, was a thinly wooded slope-and among the trees on the leaves and grass, were laid the wounded who pouring in by scores of wagon loads, as picked up on the field the flag of truce. All day they came and the whole hillside was red. Bales of hay were broken open and scattered over the ground littering of cattle, and the sore, famishing men were laid upon it.

And when the night shut in, in the mist and darkness about us, we knew that standing apart from the world of anxious hearts, throbbing over the whole country, we were a little band of almost empty handed workers literally by ourselves in the wild woods of Virginia, with 3,000 suffering men crowded upon the few acres within our reach.

After gathering up every available implement or convenience for our work, our domestic inventory stood 2 water buckets, 5 tin cups, 1 camp kettle, 1 stew pan, 2 lanterns, 4 bread knives, 3 plates, and a 2-quart tin dish, and 3,000 guest to serve.

You will perceive by this, that I had not yet learned to equip myself, for I was no Pallas, ready armed, but grew into my work by hard thinking and sad experience. It may serve to relieve your apprehension for the future of my labors if I assure you that I was never caught so again.

But the most fearful scene was reserved for the night. I have said that the ground was littered with dry hay and that we had only two lanterns, but there were plenty of candles. The wounded were laid so close that it was impossible to move about in the dark. The slightest misstep brought a torrent of groans from some poor mangled fellow in your path.

Consequently here were seen persons of all grades from the careful man of God who walked with a prayer upon his lips to the careless driver hunting for his lost whip,-each wandering about among this hay with an open flaming candle in his hands.

The slightest accident, the mere dropping of a light could have enveloped in flames this whole mass of helpless men.

How we watched and pleaded and cautioned as we worked and wept that night! How we put socks and slippers upon their cold feet, wrapped your blankets and quilts about them, and when we no longer these to give, how we covered them in the hay and left them to their rest! . . .

The slight, naked chest of a fair-haired lad caught my eye, dropping down beside him, I bent low to draw the remnant of his blouse about him, when with a quick cry he threw his left arm across my neck and, burying his face in the folds of my dress, wept like a child at his mother's knee. I took his head in my hands and held it until great burst of grief passed away. "And do you know me?" he asked at length, "I am Charley Hamilton, we used to carry your satchel home from school!" My faithful pupil, poor Charley. That mangled right hand would never carry a satchel again.

About three o'clock in the morning I observed a surgeon with a little flickering candle in hand approaching me with cautious step up in the wood. "Lady," he said as he drew near, "will you go with me? Out on the hills is a poor distressed lad, mortally wounded, and dying. His piteous cries for his sister have touched all our hearts none of us can relieve him but rather seem to distress him by presence."

By this time I was following him back over the bloody track, with great beseeching eyes of anguish on every side looking up into our faces, saying so plainly, "Don't step on us."

1. *What does Barton's account reveal about the difficulties and obstacles facing army nurses and medical personnel during the war?*
2. *Given the description presented by Barton, what conclusions can be made regarding the conditions of battle for the soldiers. How effective was the care given to the injured?*

15-8   James Henry Gooding, Letter to President Lincoln (1863)

James Henry Gooding was a 26 year old corporal in the 54th Massachusetts Infantry Regiment (Volunteers) when he wrote to President Lincoln on September 28, 1863, complaining that African American soldiers were paid three dollars a month less than their white counterparts. Only two months before, hundreds of the men of the 54th Massachusetts had lost their lives in the heroic storming of Fort Wagner in South Carolina. At war's end, Congress finally equalized the pay of black and white soldiers, but by that time Gooding had died a prisoner of war at the notorious Andersonville prison camp in Georgia.

Morris Island, S.C.
September 28, 1863
Your Excellency, Abraham Lincoln:
Your Excellency will pardon the presumption of an humble individual like myself, in addressing you, but the earnest solicitation of my comrades in arms besides the genuine interest felt by myself in the matter is my excuse, for placing before the Executive head of the Nation our Common Grievance.

On the 6th of the last Month, the Paymaster of the Department informed us, that if we would decide to receive the sum of $10 (ten dollars) per month, he would come and pay us that sum, but that, on the sitting of Congress, the Regt. [regiment] would, in his opinion, be allowed the other 3 (three). He did not give us any guarantee that this would be, as he hoped; certainly he had no authority for making any such guarantee, and we cannot suppose him acting in any way interested.

Now the main question is, are we Soldiers, or are we Laborers? We are fully armed, and equipped, have done all the various duties pertaining to a Soldier's life, have conducted ourselves to the complete satisfaction of General Officers, who were, if anything, prejudiced against us, but who now accord us all the encouragement and honors due us; have shared the perils an labor of reducing the first strong-hold that flaunted a Traitor Flag; and more, Mr. President, to-day the Anglo-Saxon Mother, Wife, or Sister are not alone in tears for departed Sons, Husbands, and Brothers. The patient, trusting descendant of Afric's Clime have dyed the ground with blood, in defence of the Union, and Democracy. Men, too, your Excellency, who know in a measure the cruelties of the iron heel of oppression, which in years gone by, the very power their blood is now being spilled to maintain, ever ground them in the dust.

But when the war trumpet sounded o'er the land, when men knew not the Friend from the Traitor, the black man laid his life at the altar of the Nation,-and he was refused. When the arms of the Union were beaten, in the first year of the war, and the Executive called for more food for its ravenous maw, again the black man begged the privilege of aiding his country in her need, to be again refused.

And now he is in the War, and how has he conducted himself? Let their dusky forms rise up, out of the mires of James Island, and give the answer. Let the rich mould around Wagner's parapet be upturned, and there will be found an eloquent answer. Obedient and patient and solid as a wall are they. All we lack is a paler hue and a better acquaintance with the alphabet.

Now your Excellency, we have done a Soldier's duty. Why can't we have a Soldier's pay? You caution the Rebel chieftain, that the United States knows no distinction in her soldiers. She insists on having all her soldiers of whatever creed or color, to be treated according to the usages of War. Now if the United States exacts uniformity of treatment of her soldiers from the insurgents, would it not be well and consistent to set the example herself by paying all her soldiers alike?

We of this Regt. were not enlisted under any "contraband" act. But we do not wish to be understood as rating our service of more value to the Government than the service of the ex-slave. Their service is undoubtedly worth much to the Nation, but Congress made express provision touching their case, as slaves freed by military necessity, and assuming the Government to be their temporary Guardian. Not so with us. Freemen by birth and consequently having the advantage of thinking and acting for ourselves so far as the Laws would allow us, we do not consider ourselves fit subjects for the Contraband act.

We appeal to you, Sir, as the Executive of the Nation, to have us justly dealt with. The Regt. do pray that they be assured their service will be fairly appreciated by paying them as American Soldiers, not as menial hirelings. Black men, you may well know, are poor; three dollars per month, for a year, will supply their needy wives and little ones with fuel. If you, as Chief Magistrate of the Nation, will assure us of our whole pay, we are content. Our Patriotism, our enthusiasm will have a new impetus, to exert our energy more and more to aid our Country. Not that our hearts ever flagged in devotion, spite the evident apathy displayed in our behalf, but we feel as though our country spurned us, now we are sworn to serve her. Please give this a moment's attention.

1. *Against what perceived prejudice is this complaint lodged? What is Gooding's argument in this letter?*
2. *Assess the effectiveness of this plea. What aspects of its style and content are particularly persuasive?*

15-9 Abraham Lincoln, Gettysburg Address (1863)

Perhaps the most famous speech in American history, the Gettysburg Address was considered a failure by many at the time it was given. Presented at the dedication of the Battlefield at Gettysburg, Lincoln was not even the featured speaker. His very short speech (only 10 sentences) was overlooked by many. Edward Everett (who gave a two hour oration just before) summed up the power of Lincoln's speech, however, when he said "I should be glad if I could flatter myself that I came as near to the central idea of the occasion in two hours as you did in two minutes."

Four score and seven years ago our fathers brought forth on this continent a new nation, conceived in liberty, and dedicated to the proposition that all men are created equal.

Now we are engaged in a great civil war, testing whether that nation, or any nation so conceived and so dedicated, can long endure. We are met on a great battlefield of that war. We have come to dedicate a portion of that field as a final resting-place for those who here gave their lives that nation might live. It is altogether fitting and proper that we should do this.

But, in a larger sense, we cannot dedicate-we cannot consecrate-we cannot hallow-this ground. The brave men, living and dead, who struggled here, have consecrated it far above our poor power to add or detract. The world will little note nor long remember what we say here, but it can never forget what they did here. It is for us, the living, rather, to be dedicated here to the unfinished work which they who fought here have thus far so nobly advanced. It is rather for us to be here dedicated to the great task remaining before us-that from these honored dead we take increased devotion to that cause for which they gave the last full measure of devotion; that we here highly resolve that these dead shall not have died in vain; that this nation, under God, shall have a new birth of freedom; and that government of the people, by the people, for the people, shall not perish from the earth.

1. *How does Lincoln honor the battle of Gettysburg in his address? What did the soldiers fight for in his opinion?*
2. *How does Lincoln connect the Battle of Gettysburg, the civil war, and the independence of America? How does his view of America in this speech differ from that of the southern leadership?*

15-10   John Dooley, Passages from a Journal (1863)

John Dooley was a young confederate soldier who served with General Pickett. He was wounded at Gettysburg. His accounts of the war provide an intimate glimpse at the common Confederate soldiers life.

Unpleasantly for myself, I am today in command of the rear guard, whose duty it is to urge forward stragglers and to keep up in fact all who desert their ranks under any pretense whatever. This is at times a painful duty, for frequently it happens-especially when the Division is moving rapidly, as today-that many soldiers leave their ranks through necessity, and, weakened by diarrhoea, can scarcely with all their efforts rejoin the ranks. Others fall by the roadside either deadly sick or pretending to be so (and who can be sure that they are only pretending?); others are barefoot, and although they may have thrown away their shoes purposely so as to have an excuse for desertion and straggling, still their feet are bruised and even bleeding, and it is a hard thing to keep these men upon the move.

Many good persons during the war seem to have the idea that any man who wears the confederate uniform and hails from a confederate regiment must of necessity be the very essence of all that is truly brave and chivalrous; and they receive, as a general thing, all their accounts of battles and their knowledge of heroic deeds of war from men who, far from having performed the deeds of daring they so vividly describe, have never seen witnessed the noble exploits of their brave companions in arms. For the true soldier has no time to stop by the wayside and recount his brave deeds to persons whom he does not know, and then devour their *buttermilk*, apple butter, and chickens in payment for the beautiful and thrilling tales he has fabricated. But he keeps in his ranks, is found in his camp, in the charge and the retreat, and leaves to the straggling coward the grateful task of glorifying his actions, who at the same time adopts them and makes them his own.

Between five and six o'clock in the evening we come within sight of the town of Gettysburg, and are marched into a small copse of woods to the right of the road. Here we must bivouac for the night, for although orders from the front have been received urging our Division forward, still, owing to representations (as we understand) made by our General (Pickett) regarding the jaded condition of his men, we are allowed a respite of a few hours, and our part in the action will not be executed until tomorrow.

The second day's fighting (the fiercest portion of which was the storming of Cemetery heights) is now at its height, and we can hear distinctly the roar of the cannon in our front and to the right of the town. It is a stubborn and bloody conflict and we are sure if we escape tonight, tomorrow we will have our full share.

July 3rd. Before the day was fully dawned we are on our way to occupy the position assigned to us for the conflict of the third day. As we turn from the main road to the right, Gen. Lee, or better known as Uncle Robert, silent and motionless, awaits our passing by, and anxiously does he gaze upon the only division of his army whose numbers have not been thinned by the terrible fires of Gettysburg. I must confess that the Genl's face does not look as bright as tho' he were certain of success. But yet it is impossible for us to be any otherwise than victorious and we press forward with beating hearts, hundreds of which will throb their last today.

How long we take to gain our position, what delays, what suspense! We are soon passing over the battlefield of yesterday, and the details of burying parties are digging graves to receive the freshly fallen comrades, and, in many instances, they have only the ghastly and mangled remnants of their gallant friends to deposit in these hastily dug pits. I pass very close to a headless body; the boy's head being torn off by a shell is lying around in bloody fragments on the ground. . . .

Now Genls. Lee, Longstreet, and Pickett are advising together and the work of the day is arranged. Soon we are ordered to ascend the rising slope and pull down a fence in our front, and this begins to look like work.

Farther to our right is posted a division of North Carolina troops who should have charged simultaneously or immediately following us, thus overlapping our flank (right) and preventing our force from being surrounded in that direction. Unfortunately, owing to bad management (I am sure not to want of bravery) they were of no assistance to us in the charge; and, advancing either in the wrong direction or when too late, two thousand of them fell into the enemy's hands.

Again, orders come for us to lie down in line of battle; *that all the cannon* on our side will open at a given signal, will continue for an hour and upon their ceasing we are to charge straight ahead over the open field and *sweep from our path* any thing in the shape of a Yankee that attempts to oppose our progress. This order is transmitted from Regt. to Regt., from Brigade to Brigade, and we rest a long time awaiting the signal.

At last it sounds away to the right and the echoes have scarcely rebounded from the rocks of the mountain when the earth, mountains and sky seem to open and darken the air with smoke and death dealing missiles. Never will I forget those scenes and sounds. The earth seems unsteady beneath this furious cannonading, and the air might be said to be agitated by the wings of death. Over 400 guns nearly every minute being discharged!

We are immediately in rear of Genl. Dearing's batteries and receive nearly all the missiles intended for his gallant troops. In one of our Regts. alone the killed and wounded, even before going into the charge, amounted to 88 men; and men lay bleeding and gasping in the agonies of death all around, and we unable to help them in the least. Ever and anon some companion would raise his head disfigured and unrecognizable, streaming with blood, or would stretch his full length, his limbs quivering in the pangs of death. Orders were to lie as closely as possible to the ground, and *I like a good soldier* never got closer to the earth than on the present occasion.

The sun poured down his fiercest beams and added to our discomfort. Genl. Dearing was out in front with his flag waving defiance at the Yankees and now and then rushing forward to take the place of some unfortunate gunner stricken down at his post. The ammunition wagons fly back and forth bringing up fresh supplies of ammunition, and still the air is shaking from earth to sky with every missile of death fired from the cannon's mouth. Around, above, beneath, and on all sides they schreech, sing, scream, whistle, roar, whirr, buzz, bang and whizz, and we are obliged to lie quietly tho' frightened out of our wits and unable to do any thing in our own defence or any injury to our enemies. . . .

Our artillery has now ceased to roar and the enemy have checked their fury, too. The time appointed for our charge is come.

I tell you, there is no romance in making one of these charges. You might think so from reading 'Charlies O'Malley,' that prodigy of valour, or in reading of any other gallant knight who would as little think of riding over *gunners and such like* as they would of eating a dozen oysters. But when you rise to your feet as we did today, I tell you the enthusiasm of ardent breasts in many cases *ain't there,* and instead of burning to avenge the insults of our country, families and altars and firesides, and the thought is most frequently, *Oh.* if I could just come out of this charge safely how thankful *would I be!*

1. Describe the battle conditions faced by many of the soldiers noted in this passage.
2. Summarize Dooley's assessment of the Battle of Gettysburg as it is represented in this document.

15-11   A Firsthand Account of the New York Draft Riots (1863)

The announcement of a draft lottery in New York City on July 11, 1863, led to a week-long riot during which wandering bands of working class immigrants took to the streets to protest a war for which they reasoned blacks were responsible. Fearing that liberated slaves would move north and commandeer jobs for unskilled labor, these dissidents were unwilling to participate in military service associated with emancipation. The violence was witnessed by John Torrey, one of the foremost botanists of the nineteenth century. In a letter to fellow botanist Asa Gray, Torrey describes the destruction inherent in the riot.

> **Source:** The New York City Historical Society, *A City in Chaos: Eyewitness Accounts of the New York City Draft Riots of 1863;*
> http://www.nyhistory.org/teachers/jtorrey.html

New York, July 13th, 1863

Dear Doctor,

We have had great riots in New York to-day & they are still in progress. They were reported to us at the Assay office about noon, but I thought they were exaggerated. Fresh accounts came in every half hour, & some of our Treasury officers (occupying the same building with us) were alarmed. I had made arrangements for visiting Eliza, at Snedens, this afternoon, but just as I was starting Mr. Mason came in & said that he saw a mob stop two 3rd. Avenue cars to take out some negros & maltreat them. This decided me to return home, so as to protect my colored servants. I could go neither by the 3rd nor 6th Avenue, as the cars had stopped. Taking the 4th Av. I found the streets full of people, & when I reached the terminus [now 34th St.] I found the whole road way and sidewalks filled with rough fellows (& some equally rough women) who were tearing up rails, cutting down telegraph poles, & setting fire to buildings. I walked quietly along through the midst of them, without being molested. In 49 St. they were numerous, & made, as I was passing near College, an attack upon one of a row of new houses in our street. The rioters were induced to go away by one or two Catholic priests, who made pacific speeches to them. I found Jane and Maggie a little alarmed, but not frightened. The mob had been in the College Grounds, & came to our house—wishing to know if a republican lived there, & what the College building was used for. They were going to burn Pres. King's house, as he was rich, & a decided republican. They barely desisted when addressed by the Catholic priests. The furious bareheaded & coatless men assembled under windows & shouted aloud for Jeff Davis'. We have some of the most valuable articles of small bulk, all packed & ready for removal at a moment's warning. All the family will remain the whole night with our clothes on, for there is no telling when they may return.

Towards evening the mob, furious as demons, went yelling over to the Colored-Orphan Asylum in 5th Avenue a little below where we live—& rolling a barrel of kerosine in it, the whole structure was soon in a blaze, & is now a smoking ruin. What has become of the 300 poor innocent orphans I could not learn. They must have had some warning of what the rioters intended; & I trust the children were removed in time to escape a cruel death. Before this fire was extinguished, or rather burned out, for the wicked wretches who caused it would not permit the engines to be used, the northern sky was brilliantly illuminated, probably by the burning of the Aged-Colored Woman's Home in 65th Street.—or the Harlem R. Road Bridge—both of which places were threatened by rioters. Just before dusk I took a walk a short distance down 5th Avenue, & seeing a group of rowdies in the grounds of Dr. Ward's large & superb mansion, I found they had gone there with the intention of setting fire to the building, which is filled with costly works of art! The family were all out, entreating the scamps to desist, as "they were all Brackenridge democrats & opposed to the draft". They finally went off, but may return before morning. I conversed with one of the ring-leaders who told me they would burn the whole city before they got through. He said they were to take Wall St. in hand tomorrow! We will be ready for them at the Assay Office & Treasury. Strange to say the military were nowhere to be seen at my latest investigations. They may be bloody times tomorrow.

Wednesday, July 15.

You doubtless learn from the newspapers that our city is still in the power of a brutal mob. We were not molested on Monday night, & I slept well, partly undressed. We are all quite calm & are chiefly concerned about our servants. Yesterday there were cars only on the lower part of 4th Avenue—all the others in the city, & the omnibuses were withdrawn. I was obliged to walk up from Wall St. in the heat of the day. On reaching home I found that we had been warned that all the College buildings were to be destroyed at night. Jane and Maggie had some of their most valuable articles packed, but we did not know where to send them. A friend took our basket of silver to her house. I look about to see what few articles I could put in a small traveling bag, but it was very difficult to make a selection. There were so many (to me) precious little souvenirs that it grieved me to think they would probably be destroyed. Then it did go hard with me to feel pretty well assured that the Herbarium & Botanical Books were to be given up! Yet we had a reprieve. Just as we were expecting the mob to come howling along, a person came in with a confidential message from a Catholic priest, that Gov. Seymour had taken the responsibility of stopping the draft, & the chief rioters were to be informed of this measure. So we made up our minds to take a good sleep, I was, however, mortified to find that the mob had, at least temporarily, triumphed. But we shall have to finish the business with saltpetre.

This morning I was obliged to ride down to the office in a hired coach. A friend who rode with me had seen a poor negro hung an hour or two before. The man had, in a frenzy, shot an Irish fireman, and they immediately strung up the unhappy African. At our office there had been no disturbance in the battery of about 25 rifle barrels, carrying 3 balls each & mounted on a guncarriage. It could be loaded & fired with rapidity. We had also 10-inch shells, to be lighted & thrown out of the windows. Likewise quantities of SO, with arrangements for projecting it on the mob. Walking home we found that a large number of soldiers—infantry, artillery & cavalry are moving about, & bodies of armed citizens. The worst mobs are on the 1st & 2nd & 7th Avenues. Many have been killed there. They are very hostile to the negros, & scarcely one of them is to be seen. A person who called at our house this afternoon saw three of them hanging together. The Central Park has been a kind of refuge to them. Hundreds were there to-day, with no protection in a very severe shower. The Station Houses of the police are crowed with them.

Walking out on 5th Avenue near 48th St., a man who lives there told me that a few minutes before, in broad sunlight, three ruffians seized the horses of a gentleman's carriage & demanded money. By whipping up, they barely escaped. Immediately afterwards they stopped another carriage, turned the persons out of it, & then got in themselves, shouting & brandishing their clubs. So that concessions have not yet quieted the mob, & the soldiers cannot be every where. reinforcements will doubtless arrive, & we shall have law & order. Thieves are going about in gangs, calling at houses & demanding money—threatening the torch if denied. They have been across the street this afternoon, & I saw them myself. Perhaps they will give a call; but we are all going to bed in a few minutes.

This evening there was a great light north of us—& I found, on looking with a spyglass, that it was from the burning a fine bridge over the Harlem valley—used by one of the railroads. There was some cannon-firing in the 1st Avenue, with what result I don't know.

The city looks very strangely. Nothing in Broadway but a few coaches. Most of the stores closed, but the side walks are full of people—& not a few ladies are out. It is half past 10 o'clock, & I must go to bed.

Thursday—U.S. Assay Office. The cars are running this morning, but the stores are closed in the greater part of 3rd avenue. Herb. came up to breakfast. He had been up all night at the Assay Office, & had been drilling, under a U.S. officer, as an artillerist. They had 4 cannon & a rifle battery ready for the mob, at the office. I found a body of marines there this morning. —Just at this moment there was a false alarm, "every man at his post." The great doors were slammed too [sic] in a moment, & the arms were seized. I was amused to see an old tar quietly light his match rope, & swing it about to get it well on fire. He had the shells, to be thrown from the windows, in charge. Quiet was soon restored.—Passing down the Avenue, I saw the 7th Regiment at their armory, ready to go wherever they were needed. They will be as impartial as veterans. Thurber & young Etheredge have been at the Tribune Office all the week,—ready for service.

I shall try & do up some botany at the College to-day, as there is little to keep us at the Office. We feel that our chief danger is past. We are now afraid only of the small gangs of thieves.

Here I have given you a long account of what has been on our minds this week. I suppose you have been somewhat concerned about us. We were in the most dangerous part of the city, & have been kept more or less anxious on account of colored servants, but I trust we shall not be driven from our home. A friend (Mr. Gibbons) who visits us almost every week, & is known to be an abolitionist, had his house smashed up yesterday.

Jane is going to spend a few days at Springfield, with Miss Day. She will probably leave home tomorrow. Eliza is still at her farm. Give my love to your own good Jane.

Ever yours —
John Torrey

1. Describe the destruction caused by the rioters in New York City as witnessed by John Torrey. How fearful was Torrey for his own safety?
2. How rational were the fears of these working-class ruffians? What other factors might have mobilized them into action other than employment anxiety?

15-12 Susie King Taylor, Reminiscences of an Army Laundress (1902)

Susie King Taylor traveled with the Thirty-third U.S. Colored Regiment in which her husband served. She and her husband were two of five thousand slaves who escaped to the Union army. This excerpt describes some of the daily life of a soldier and a soldier◊s wife and the special indignities suffered by African-American fighting men.

From Susie King Taylor, *Reminiscences of My Life in Camp with the 33rd United States Colored Troops* (Boston: 1902), 15-16, 26- 28, 32-35

I was enrolled as company laundress, but I did very little of it, because I was always busy doing other things through camp, and was employed all the time doing something for the officers and comrades....

The first colored troops did not receive any pay for eighteen months, and the men had to depend wholly on what they received from the commissary, established by Gen. Saxton. A great many of these men had large families, and as they had no money to give them, their wives were obliged to support themselves and children by washing for the officers of the gunboats and the soldiers, and making cakes and pies, which they sold to the boys in camp. Finally, in 1863, the government decided to give them half pay, but the men would not accept this. They wanted "full pay or nothing." They preferred rather to give their services to the state, which they did until 1864, when the government granted them full pay with all the back pay due. . .

I learned to handle a musket very well while in the regiment and could shoot straight and often hit the target. I assisted in cleaning the guns and used to fire them off, to see if the cartridges were dry, before cleaning and re-loading, each day. I thought this was great fun. I was also able to take a gun all apart and put it together again....

We had fresh beef once in a while, and we would have soup, and the vegetables they put in the soup were dried and pressed; they looked like hops. Salt beef was our standby. Sometimes the men would have what we called slap-jacks. This was flour made into bread and spread thin on the bottom of the mess-pan to cook; each man had one of them with a pint of tea for his supper, or a pint of tea and five or six hardtack. I often got my own meals and would fix some dishes for the noncommissioned officers also.

About the first of June, 1864, the regiment was ordered to Folly Island, staying there until the latter part of the month, when it was ordered to Morris Island. We landed on Morris Island between June and July, 1864. This island was a narrow strip of sandy soil, nothing growing on it but a few bushes and shrubs. The camp was one mile from the boat landing, called Pawnell Landing, and the landing one mile from Fort Wagner....

About four o'clock, July 2, the charge was made. The firing could be plainly heard in camp. I hastened down to the landing and remained there until eight o'clock that morning. When the wounded arrived, or rather began to arrive, the first one brought in was Samuel Anderson of our company. He was badly wounded. Then others of our boys, some with their legs off, arm gone, foot off, and wounds of all kinds imaginable. They had to wade through creeks and marshes, as they were discovered by the enemy and shelled very badly. A number of the men were lost, some got fastened in the mud and had to cut off the legs of their pants, to free themselves. The 103rd New York suffered the most, as their men were very badly wounded.

My work now began. I gave my assistance to try to alleviate their sufferings. I asked the doctor at the hospital what I could get for them to eat. They wanted soup, but that I could not get; but I had a few cans of condensed milk and some turtle eggs, so I thought I would try to make some custard. I had doubts as to my success, for cooking with turtle eggs was something new to me, but the adage has it, "Nothing ventured, nothing done," so I made a venture and the result was a very delicious custard. This I carried to the men, who enjoyed it very much. My services were given at all times for the comfort of these men. I was on hand to assist whenever needed.

1. *According to Taylor's account, what were the battlefield conditions for the black regiments? Describe their experiences in the war.*
2. *What does the account of the black soldiers' insistence on full pay reveal about their attitudes toward the war and their involvement in it? Characterize the soldiers as they are represented in this account.*

15-13   General William Tecumseh Sherman on War (1864)

Following the withdrawal of Confederate troops from Atlanta, Georgia, on September 1, 1864, General William Tecumseh Sherman issued Special Field Order No. 67 directing that Atlanta be evacuated by all civilians except those necessary for "the proper departments of government." The order met with a chorus of disapproval. Mayor James Calhoun and the city council asked the general to reconsider on the grounds that many citizens were too weak or infirm to travel and assume the role of refugee. Although sympathetic to a degree, Sherman was unyielding. In his response to Calhoun (included below), Sherman put into words his view of war and, in the months to come, further translated his ideas into practice during his "March to the Sea." In so doing, Sherman became the personification of "hard war."

> **Source:** The United States War Department, *The War of the Rebellion: A Compilation of the Official Records of the Union and Confederate Armies*, 128 vols. (Washington: Government Printing Office, 1880–1901), Series I, vol. 39, pt. II, pp. 837-838; The Sage Page for American History and Literature, http://www.nv.cc.va.us/home/nvsageh/Hist121/Part4/ShermanAtl.htm

Special Field Orders, No. 67.
Hdqrs. Mil. Div. of the Mississippi,
In the Field, Atlanta, Ga.,
September 8, 1864.

I. The city of Atlanta, being exclusively required for warlike purposes, will at once be vacated by all except the armies of the United States and such civilian employés as may be retained by the proper departments of government.

II. The chief quartermaster, Colonel Easton, will at once take possession of buildings of all kinds, and of all staple articles, such as cotton, tobacco, & c., and will make such disposition of them as is required by existing regulations, or such orders as he may receive from time to time from the proper authorities.

III. The chief engineer will promptly reconnoiter the city and suburbs, and indicate the sites needed for the permanent defense of the place, together with any houses, sheds, or shanties that stand in his way, that they may be set apart for destruction. Colonel Easton will then, on consultation with the proper officers of the ordinance, quartermaster, commissary, medical, and railroad departments, set aside such buildings and lots of ground as will be needed for them, and have them suitably marked and set apart. He will then, on consultation with Generals Thomas and Slocum, set apart such as may be necessary to the proper administration of the military duties of the Department of the Cumberland and of the post of Atlanta, and all buildings and materials not thus embraced will be held subject to the use of the Government as may hereafter arise, according to the just rules of the quartermaster's department.

IV. No general, staff, or other officers, or any soldier will on any pretense occupy any house or shanty, unless it be embraced in the limits assigned as the camp of the troops to which such general or staff belongs, but the chief quartermaster may allow the troops to use boards, shingles, or materials of buildings, barns, sheds, warehouses, and shanties, not needed by the proper departments of government, to be used in the reconstruction of such shanties and bivouacs as the troops and officers serving with them require, and he will also provide as early as practicable the proper allowance of tents for the use of the officers and men in their encampments.

V. In proper time just arrangements will be made for the supply to the troops of all articles they may need over and above the clothing, provisions, & c., furnished by Government, and on no pretense whatever will traders, manufacturers, or sutlers be allowed to settle in the limits of fortified places, and if these manage to come in spite of this notice, the quartermaster will seize their stores and appropriate them to the use of the troops, and deliver the parties or other unauthorized citizens who thus place their individual interests above that of the United States, in the hands of some provost marshal, to be put to labor on the forts or conscripted into one of the regiments or batteries already in service.

VI. The same general principles will apply to all military posts south of Chattanooga.

By order of Maj. Gen. W. T. Sherman:

L. M. DAYTON,
Aide-de-Camp.

Notice.   Atlanta, Ga., *September 8, 1864.*
To the Citizens of Atlanta:

Major-General Sherman instructs me to say to you that you must all leave Atlanta; that as many of you as want to go North can do so, and that as many as want to go South can do so, and that all can take with them their movable property, servants included, if they want to go, but that no force is to be used, and that he will furnish transportation for persons and property as far as Rough and Ready, from whence it is expected General Hood will assist in carrying it on. Like transportation will be furnished for people and property going North, and it is required that all things contemplated by this notice will be carried into execution as soon as possible.

All persons are requested to leave their names and number in their families with the undersigned as early as possible, that estimates may be made of the quantity of transportation required.

JAMES M. CALHOUN,
Mayor.

HEADQUARTERS MILITARY DIVISION OF THE MISSISSIPPI, IN THE FIELD, ATLANTA, GEORGIA

September 12, 1864

JAMES M. CALHOUN, Mayor, E. E. PAWSON and S. C. WELLS, representing City Council of Atlanta.

GENTLEMEN: I have your letter of the 11th, in the nature of a petition to revoke my orders removing all the inhabitants from Atlanta. I have read it carefully, and give full credit to your statements of the distress that will be occasioned, and yet shall not revoke my orders, because they were not designed to meet the humanities of the case, but to prepare for the future struggles in which millions of good people outside of Atlanta have a deep interest. We must have peace, not only at Atlanta, but in all America. To secure this, we must stop the war that now desolates our once happy and favored country. To stop war, we must defeat the rebel armies which are arrayed against the laws and Constitution that all must respect and obey. To defeat those armies, we must prepare the way to reach them in their recesses, provided with the arms and instruments which enable us to accomplish our purpose.

Now, I know the vindictive nature of our enemy, that we may have many years of military operations from this quarter; and, therefore, deem it wise and prudent to prepare in time. The use of Atlanta for warlike purposes is inconsistent with its character as a home for families. There will be no manufactures, commerce, or agriculture here, for the maintenance of families, and sooner or later want will compel the inhabitants to go. Why not go now, when all the arrangements are completed for the transfer, instead of waiting till the plunging shot of contending armies will renew the scenes of the past month? Of course, I do not apprehend any such thing at this moment, but you do not suppose this army will be here until the war is over. I cannot discuss this subject with you fairly, because I cannot impart to you what we propose to do, but I assert that our military plans make it necessary for the inhabitants to go away, and I can only renew my offer of services to make their exodus in any direction as easy and comfortable as possible.

You cannot qualify war in harsher terms than I will. War is cruelty, and you cannot refine it; and those who brought war into our country deserve all the curses and maledictions a people can pour out. I know I had no hand in making this war, and I know I will make more sacrifices today than any of you to secure peace. But you cannot have peace and a division of our country. If the United States submits to a division now, it will not stop, but will go on until we reap the fate of Mexico, which is eternal war. The United States does and must assert its authority, wherever it once had power; for, if it relaxes one bit to pressure, it is gone, and I believe that such is the national feeling. This feeling assumes various shapes, but always comes back to that of Union. Once admit the Union, once more acknowledge the authority of the national Government, and, instead of devoting your houses and streets and roads to the dread uses of war, I and this army become at once your protectors and supporters, shielding you from danger, let it come from what quarter it may. I know that a few individuals cannot resist a torrent of error and passion, such as swept the South into rebellion, but you can point out, so that we may know those who desire a government, and those who insist on war and its desolation.

You might as well appeal against the thunderstorm as against these terrible hardships of war. They are inevitable, and the only way the people of Atlanta can hope once more to live in peace and quiet at home, is to stop the war, which can only be done by admitting that it began in error and is perpetuated in pride.

We don't want your negroes, or your horses, or your houses, or your lands, or any thing you have, but we do want and will have a just obedience to the laws of the United States. That we will have, and, if it involves the destruction of your improvements, we cannot help it.

You have heretofore read public sentiment in your newspapers, that live by falsehood and excitement; and the quicker you seek for truth in other quarters, the better. I repeat then that, by the original compact of Government, the United States had certain rights in Georgia, which have never been relinquished and never will be; that the South began war by seizing forts, arsenals, mints, customhouses, etc., etc., long before Mr. Lincoln was installed, and before the South had one jot or tittle of provocation. I myself have seen in Missouri, Kentucky, Tennessee, and Mississippi, hundreds and thousands of women and children fleeing from your armies and desperadoes, hungry and with bleeding feet. In Memphis, Vicksburg, and Mississippi, we fed thousands upon thousands of the families of rebel soldiers left on our hands, and whom we could not see starve.

Now that war comes home to you, you feel very different. You deprecate its horrors, but did not feel them when you sent car-loads of soldiers and ammunition, and moulded shells and shot, to carry war into Kentucky and Tennessee, to desolate the homes of hundreds and thousands of good people who only asked to live in peace at their old homes, and under the Government of their inheritance. But these comparisons are idle. I want peace, and believe it can only be reached through union and war, and I will ever conduct war with a view to perfect and early success.

But, my dear sirs, when peace does come, you may call on me for any thing. Then will I share with you the last cracker, and watch with you to shield your homes and families against danger from every quarter.

Now you must go, and take with you the old and feeble, feed and nurse them, and build for them, in more quiet places, proper habitations to shield them against the weather until the mad passions of men cool down, and allow the Union and peace once more to settle over your old homes at Atlanta.

Yours in haste,

W. T. SHERMAN, Major-General commanding.

---

1. What was General Sherman's justification for demanding the evacuation of civilians from Atlanta? Do you find his explanation reasonable? What rights should civilians have in times of war?

2. How does Sherman define war? What was his goal in warfare other than victory?

PART SIXTEEN
RECONSTRUCTION

16-1 "Address from the Colored Citizens of Norfolk, Virginia, to the People of the United States" (1865)

The end of the Civil War left African Americans in a state of uncertainty. The Emancipation Proclamation and the impending Thirteenth Amendment to the Constitution promised legal abolition of slavery, but this Address shows that freedom remained more a dream than a reality for the ex-slaves who asked for protection against discriminatory action by state and local governments.

We believe our present position is by no means so well understood among the loyal masses of the country, otherwise there would be no delay in granting us the express relief which the nature of the case demands. It must not be forgotten that it is the general assumption, in the South, that the effects of the immortal Emancipation Proclamation of President Lincoln go no further than the emancipation of the Negroes then in slavery, and that it is only constructively even, that that Proclamation can be said, in any legal sense, to have abolished slavery, and even the late constitutional amendment, if duly ratified, can go no further; neither touch, nor can touch, the slave codes of the various southern States, and the laws respecting free people of color consequent therefrom, which, having been passed before the act of secession, are presumed to have lost none of their vitality, but exist, as a convenient engine for our oppression, until repealed by special acts of the State legislature. By these laws, in many of the southern States, it is still a crime for colored men to learn or be taught to read, and their children are doomed to ignorance; there is no provision for insuring the legality of our marriages; we have no right to hold real estate; the public streets and the exercise of our ordinary occupations are forbidden us unless we can produce passes from our employers, or licenses from certain officials; in some States the whole free Negro population is legally liable to exile from the place of its birth, for no crime but that of color; we have no means of legally making or enforcing contracts of any description; we have no right to testify before the courts in any case in which a white man is one of the parties to the suit, we are taxed without representation, and, in short, so far as legal safeguards of our rights are concerned, we are defenceless before our enemies. While this is our position as regards our legal status, before the State laws, we are still more unfortunately situated as regards our late masters. The people of the North, owing to the greater interest excited by war, have heard little or nothing, for the past four years, of the blasphemous and horrible theories formerly propounded for the defence and glorification of human slavery, in the press, the pulpit and legislatures of the southern States; but, though they may have forgotten them, let them be assured that these doctrines have by no means faded from the minds of the people of the South; they cling to these delusions still, and only hug them closer for their recent defeat. Worse than all, they have returned to their homes, with all their old pride and contempt for the Negro transformed into bitter hate for the new-made freeman, who aspires for the suppression of their rebellion. That this charge is not unfounded, the manner in which it has been recently attempted to enforce the laws above referred to proves. In Richmond, during the three days sway of the rebel Mayor Mayo, over 800 colored people were arrested, simply for walking the streets without a pass; in the neighboring city of Portsmouth, a Mayor has just been elected, on the avowed platform that this is a white man's government, and our enemies have been heard to boast openly, that soon not a colored man shall be left in the city; in the greater number of counties in this State, county meetings have been held, at which resolutions have been adopted *deploring*, while accepting, the abolition of slavery, but going on to pledge the planters composing the meeting, to employ no Negroes save such as were formerly owned by themselves, without a written recommendation from their late employers, and threatening violence towards those who should do so, thereby keeping us in a state of serfdom, and preventing our free selection of our employers; they have also pledged themselves, in no event, to pay their late adult slaves more than $60 per year for their labor. In the future, out of which, with characteristic generosity, they have decided that we are to find clothes for ourselves and families, and pay our taxes and doctors' bills; in many of the more remote districts individual planters are to be found who still refuse to recognize their Negroes as free, forcibly retaining the wives and children of their late escaped slaves; cases have occurred, not far from Richmond itself, in which an attempt to leave the plantation has been punished by shooting to death; and finally, there are numbers of cases, known to ourselves, in the immediate vicinity of this city, in which a faithful performance, by colored men, of the duties or labor contracted for, has been met by a contemptuous and violent refusal of the stipulated compensation. These are facts, and yet the men doing these things are, in many cases, loud in their professions of attachment to the restored Union, while committing these outrages on the most faithful friends that Union can ever have. Even well known Union men have often been found among our oppressors; witness the action of the Tennessee legislature in imposing unheard of disabilities upon us, taking away from us, and giving to the County Courts, the right of disposing of our children, by apprenticing them to such occupations as the court, not their parents, may see fit to adopt for them, and in this very city, and under the protection of military law, some of our white friends who have nobly distinguished themselves by their efforts in our behalf, have been threatened with arrest by a Union Mayor of this city, for their advocacy of the cause of freedom.

Fellow citizens, the performance of a simple act of justice on your part will reverse all this; we ask for no expensive aid from military forces, stationed throughout the South, overbearing State action, and rendering our government republican only in name; give us the suffrage, and you may rely upon us to secure justice for ourselves, and all Union men, and to keep the State forever in the Union.

While we urge you to this act of simple justice to ourselves, there are many reasons why you should concede us this right in your own interest. It cannot be that you contemplate with satisfaction a prolonged military occupation of the southern States, and yet, without the existence of a larger loyal constituency than, at present, exists in these States, a military occupation will be absolutely necessary, to protect the white Union men of the South, as well as ourselves, and if not absolutely to keep the States in the Union, it will be necessary to prevent treasonable legislation. . . .

You have not unreasonably complained of the operation of that clause of the Constitution which has hitherto permitted the slaveocracy of the South to wield the political influence which would be represented by a white population equal to three-fifths of the whole Negro population; but slavery is now abolished, and henceforth the representation will be in proportion to the enumeration of the whole population of the South, *including people of color*, and it is worth your consideration if it is desirable or politic that the fomentors of this rebellion against the Union, which has been crushed at the expense of so much blood and treasure, should find themselves, after defeat, more powerful than ever, their political influence enhanced by the additional voting power of the other two-fifths of the colored population, by which means four Southern votes will balance in the Congressional and Presidential elections at least seven Northern ones. The honor of your country should be dear to you, as it is, but is that honor advanced, in the eyes of the Christian world, when America alone, of all Christian nations, sustains an unjust distinction against four millions and a half of her most loyal people, on the senseless ground of a difference in color? You are anxious that the attention of every man, of every State legislature, and of Congress, should be exclusively directed to redressing the injuries sustained by the country in the late contest; are these objects more likely to be effected amid the political distractions of an embarrassing Negro agitation? You are, above all, desirous that no future intestine wars should mar the prosperity and destroy the happiness of the country; will your perfect security from such evils be promoted by the existence of a colored population of four millions and a half, placed, by your enactments, outside the pale of the Constitution, discontented by oppression, with an army of 200,000 colored soldiers, whom you have drilled, disciplined, and armed, but whose attachment to the State you have failed to secure by refusing them citizenship? You are further anxious that your government should be an example to the world of true Republican institutions; but how can you avoid the charge of inconsistency if you leave one eighth of the population of the whole country without any political rights, while bestowing these rights on every immigrant who comes to these shores, perhaps from a despotism, under which he could never exercise the least political right, and had no means of forming any conception of their proper use? . . .

It is hardly necessary here to refute any of the slanders with which our enemies seek to prove our unfitness for the exercise of the right of suffrage. It is true, that many of our people are ignorant, but for *that* these very men are responsible, and decency should prevent *their* use of such an argument. But if our people are ignorant, no people were ever more orderly and obedient to the laws; and no people ever displayed greater earnestness in the acquisition of knowledge. Among no other people could such a revolution have taken place without scenes of license and bloodshed; but in this case, and we say it advisedly, full information of the facts will show that no single disturbance, however slight, has occurred which has not resulted from the unprovoked aggression of white people, and, if any one doubts how fast the ignorance, which has hitherto cursed our people, is disappearing, 'mid the light of freedom, let him visit the colored schools of this city and neighborhood, in which between two and three thousand pupils are being taught, while, in the evening, in colored schools may be seen, after the labors of the day, hundreds of our adult population from budding manhood to hoary age, toiling, with intensest eagerness, to acquire the invaluable arts of reading and writing, and the rudimentary branches of knowledge. One other objection only will we notice; it is that our people are lazy and idle; and, in support of this allegation, the objectors refer to the crowds of colored people subsisting on Government rations, and flocking into the towns. To the first statement we reply that we are poor, and that thousands of our young and able-bodied men, having been enlisted in the army to fight the battles of their country, it is but reasonable that that country should contribute something to the support of those whose natural protectors that country has taken away. With reference to the crowds collected round the military posts and in the cities, we say that though some may have come there under misapprehensions as to the nature of the freedom they have just received, yet this is not the case with the majority; the colored man knows that freedom means freedom to labor, and to enjoy its fruits, and in that respect evinces at least an equal appreciation of his new position with his late owners; if he is not to be found laboring for these late owners, it is because he cannot trust them, and feels safe, in his new-found freedom, nowhere out of the immediate presence of the national forces; if the planters want his labor (and they do) fair wages and fair treatment will not fail to secure it.

In conclusion, we wish to advise our colored brethren of the State and nation, that the settlement of this question is to a great extent dependent on them, and that supineness on their part will do as much to delay if not defeat the full recognition of their rights as the open opposition of avowed enemies. Then be up and active, and everywhere let associations be formed having for their object the agitation, discussion and enforcement of your claims to equality before the law, and equal rights of suffrage. Your opponents are active; be prepared, and organize to resist their efforts. We would further advise that all political associations of colored men, formed within the limits of the State of Virginia, should communicate the fact of their existence, with the names and post office addresses of their officers, to Joseph T. Wilson, Norfolk, Va., in order that communication and friendly cooperation may be kept up between the different organizations, and facili-ties afforded for common and united State action, should occasion require it.

1. According to this document, what have been the effects of the Emancipation Proclamation upon the lives of African Americans in America?
2. What "simple act of justice" is requested? What would be the results of granting this plea?

16-2 Carl Schurz, Report on the Condition of the South (1865)

At the end of the Civil War, the issue of the reconstruction of the South stimulated animated discussion among northerners. For some, including Carl Schurz, reconstruction had initiated a social revolution in a land experiencing severe economic distress. Especially regarding developing a free labor systems, the question arose over who would control the process of change for what ends.

We ought to keep in view, above all, the nature of the problem which is to be solved. As to what is commonly termed "reconstruction," it is not only the political machinery of the States and their constitutional relations to the general government, but the whole organism of southern society that must be reconstructed, or rather constructed anew, so as to bring it in harmony with the rest of American society. The difficulties of this task are not to be considered overcome when the people of the south take the oath of allegiance and elect governors and legislatures and members of Congress, and militia captains. That this would be done had become certain as soon as the surrenders of the southern armies had made further resistance impossible, and nothing in the world was left, even to the most uncompromising rebel, but to submit or to emigrate. It was also natural that they should avail themselves of every chance offered them to resume control of their home affairs and to regain their influence in the Union. But this can hardly be called the first step towards the solution of the true problem, and it is a fair question to ask, whether the hasty gratification of their desire to resume such control would not create new embarrassments.

The true nature of the difficulties of the situation is this: The general government of the republic has, by proclaiming the emancipation of the slaves, commenced a great social revolution in the south, but has, as yet, not completed it. Only the negative part of it is accomplished. The slaves are emancipated in point of form, but free labor has not yet been put in the place of slavery in point of fact. And now, in the midst of this critical period of transition, the power which originated the revolution is expected to turn over its whole future development to another power which from the beginning was hostile to it and has never yet entered into its spirit, leaving the class in whose favor it was made completely without power to protect itself and to take an influential part in that development. The history of the world will be searched in vain for a proceeding similar to this which did not lead either to a rapid and violent reaction, or to the most serious trouble and civil disorder. It cannot be said that the conduct of the southern people since the close of the war has exhibited such extraordinary wisdom and self-abnegation as to make them an exception to the rule.

In my despatches from the south I repeatedly expressed the opinion that the people were not yet in a frame of mind to legislate calmly and understandingly upon the subject of free negro labor. And this I reported to be the opinion of some of our most prominent military commanders and other observing men. It is, indeed, difficult to imagine circumstances more unfavorable for the development of a calm and unprejudiced public opinion than those under which the southern people are at present laboring. The war has not only defeated their political aspirations, but it has broken up their whole social organization. When the rebellion was put down they found themselves not only conquered in a political and military sense, but economically ruined. The planters, who represented the wealth of the southern country, are partly laboring under the severest embarrassments, partly reduced to absolute poverty. Many who are stripped of all available means, and have nothing but their land, cross their arms in gloomy despondency, incapable of rising to a manly resolution. Others, who still possess means, are at a loss how to use them, as their old way of doing things is, by the abolition of slavery, rendered impracticable, at least where the military arm of the government has enforced emancipation. Others are still trying to go on in the old way, and that old way is in fact the only one they understand, and in which they have any confidence. Only a minority is trying to adopt the new order of things. A large number of the plantations, probably a considerable majority of the more valuable estates, is under heavy mortgages, and the owners know that, unless they retrieve their fortunes in a comparatively short space of time, their property will pass out of their hands. Almost all are, to some extent, embarrassed. The nervous anxiety which such a state of things produces extends also to those classes of society which, although not composed of planters, were always in close business connexion with the planting interest, and there was hardly a branch of commerce or industry in the south which was not directly or indirectly so connected. Besides, the southern soldiers, when returning from the war, did not, like the northern soldiers, find a prosperous community which merely waited for their arrival to give them remunerative employment. They found, many of them, their homesteads destroyed, their farms devastated, their families in distress; and those that were less unfortunate found, at all events, an impoverished and exhausted community which had but little to offer them. Thus a great many have been thrown upon the world to shift as best they can. They must do something honest or dishonest, and must do it soon, to make a living, and their prospects are, at present, not very bright. Thus that nervous anxiety to hastily repair broken fortunes, and to prevent still greater ruin and distress, embraces nearly all classes, and imprints upon all the movements of the social body a morbid character.

In which direction will these people be most apt to turn their eyes? Leaving the prejudice of race out of the question, from early youth they have been acquainted with but one system of labor, and with that one system they have been in the habit of identifying all their interests. They know of no way to help themselves but the one they are accustomed to. Another system of labor is presented to them, which, however, owing to circumstances which they do not appreciate, appears at first in an unpromising light. To try it they consider an experiment which they cannot afford to make while their wants are urgent. They have not reasoned calmly enough to convince themselves that the trial must be made. It is, indeed, not wonderful that, under such circumstances, they should study, not how to introduce and develop free labor, but how to avoid its introduction, and how to return as much and as quickly as possible to something like the old order of things. Nor is it wonderful that such studies should find an expression in their attempts at legislation. But the circumstance that this tendency is natural does not render it less dangerous and objectionable. The practical question presents itself: Is the immediate restoration of the late rebel States to absolute self-control so necessary that it must be done even at the risk of endangering one of the great results of the war, and of bringing on in those States insurrection or anarchy, or would it not be better to postpone that restoration until such dangers are passed? If, as long as the change from slavery to free labor is known to the southern people only by its destructive results, these people must be expected to throw obstacles in its way, would it not seem necessary that the movement of social "reconstruction" be kept in the right channel by the hand of the power which originated the change, until that change can have disclosed some of its beneficial effects?

It is certain that every success of free negro labor will augment the number of its friends, and disarm some of the prejudices and assumptions of its opponents. I am convinced one good harvest made by unadulterated free labor in the south would have a far better effect than all the oaths that have been taken, and all the ordinances that have as yet been passed by southern conventions. But how can such a result be attained? The facts enumerated in this report, as well as the news we receive from the south from day to day, must make it evident to every unbiased observer that unadulterated free labor cannot be had at present, unless the national government holds its protective and controlling hand over it. It appears, also, that the more efficient this protection of free labor against all disturbing and reactionary influences, the sooner may such a satisfactory result be looked for. One reason why the southern people are so slow in accommodating themselves to the new order of things is, that they confidently expect soon to be permitted to regulate matters according to their own notions. Every concession made to them by the government has been taken as an encouragement to persevere in this hope, and, unfortunately for them, this hope is nourished by influences from other parts of the country. Hence their anxiety to have their State governments restored *at once*, to have the troops withdrawn, and the Freedmen's Bureau abolished, although a good many discerning men know well that, in view of the lawless spirit still prevailing, it would be far better for them to have the general order of society firmly maintained by the federal power until things have arrived at a final settlement. Had, from the beginning, the conviction been forced upon them that the adulteration of the new order of things by the admixture of elements belonging to the system of slavery would under no circumstances be permitted, a much larger number would have launched their energies into the new channel, and, seeing that they could do "no better," faithfully co-operated with the government. It is hope which fixes them in their perverse notions. That hope nourished or fully gratified, they will persevere in the same direction. That hope destroyed, a great many will, by the force of necessity, at once accommodate themselves to the logic of the change. If, therefore, the national government firmly and unequivocally announces its policy not to give up the control of the free-labor reform until it is finally accomplished, the progress of that reform will undoubtedly be far more rapid and far less difficult than it will be if the attitude of the government is such as to permit contrary hopes to be indulged in.

The machinery by which the government has so far exercised its protection of the negro and of free labor in the south-the Freedmen's Bureau-is very unpopular in that part of the country, as every institution placed there as a barrier to reactionary aspirations would be. That abuses were committed with the management of freedmen's affairs; that some of the officers of the bureau were men of more enthusiasm than discretion, and in many cases went beyond their authority: all this is certainly true. But, while the southern people are always ready to expatiate upon the shortcomings of the Freedmen's Bureau, they are not so ready to recognize the services it has rendered. I feel warranted in saying that not half of the labor that has been done in the south this year, or will be done there next year, would have been or would be done but for the exertions of the Freedmen's Bureau. The confusion and disorder of the transition period would have been infinitely greater had not an agency interfered which possessed the confidence of the emancipated slaves; which could disabuse them of any extravagant notions and expectations and be trusted; which could administer to them good advice and be voluntarily obeyed. No other agency, except one placed there by the national government, could have wielded that moral power whose interposition was so necessary to prevent southern society from falling at once into the chaos of a general collision between its different elements. That the success achieved by the Freedmen's Bureau is as yet very incomplete cannot be disputed. A more perfect organization and a more carefully selected personnel may be desirable; but it is doubtful whether a more suitable machinery can be devised to secure to free labor in the south that protection against disturbing influences which the nature of the situation still imperatively demands.

1. *Summarize Schurz's opinion of the state of the South. How is the South dealing with reconstruction?*
2. *What difficulties and dangers are present as the South attempts to make the transition from slavery to free labor?*

16-3   Clinton B. Fisk, Plain Counsels for Freedmen (1865)

After emancipation, questions arose about African American labor. In this document, Clinton B. Fisk counsels African Americans on the value of free labor and the judicious use of the income generated by work.

I come to speak to you this evening about work; yes, work, good, honest, hard work. Do not turn away, and say you will not hear me,-that you know all about it, and that it is not a good subject for a lecture.

Listen! The very first verse of the Holy Bible tells us that God is a worker,-that in six days he made all this great world on which we dwell, and the sun and moon and stars.

All the holy angels in heaven are very busy. They go forth to do the will of the Great Being, and find their greatest bliss in action.

Good and great men are all hard workers. And do you know what it is that makes a free state so rich and strong? It is, above all things save God's blessing, *patient, honest work.*

There is nothing degrading in *free* labor,-nay, it is most honorable. Why, when God placed Adam and Eve in the garden of Eden, before either of them had ever done any wrong thing, and while they were as pure as the angels, he made gardeners of them. He required them to dress the garden and keep it nice and in good condition.

The blessed Saviour himself worked at the bench, at the carpenter's trade, until he was about thirty years of age.

And yet, some very silly people are above work,-are ashamed to have hard hands,-and do their best to get through the world without honest toil.

But this was not the case with Abraham Lincoln, the man who wrote the Proclamation of Emancipation. He used the hoe, the ax, and the maul, cleared ground, and fenced it with the rails he had split, and was ready to turn his hands to any honest work.

I know that it is quite natural that you should associate work with slavery, and freedom with idleness, because you have seen slaves working all their lives, and free people doing little or nothing. And I should not blame you if you should ask, "What have we gained by freedom, if we are to work, work, work!"

Now, let me explain. A slave works all his life for others. A free man works for himself,-that is, he gets pay for his labor; and if he saves what he earns and manages well, he can get on so well that he may spend the afternoon of his life in his own pleasant home, and never want for any thing. . . .

If you earn twelve dollars in a month, and spend thirteen, you are on the road to misery, for you will get into debt, deeper and deeper, until after awhile it will be a load you can not carry.

You should make it a rule, therefore, to spend less each month and each year than you make. If you do this, you will become well to do in the world.

A free man should always consider before he buys an article, whether he can afford it. He would like a new hat,-price five dollars,-but if he needs the five for other and more pressing uses, to make a payment, for example, for something he has bought, then he should deny himself the pleasure of the new hat, and brush up the old one. A new coat might be very desirable, but if its purchase would create a debt, better keep the old one in good repair as possible, and stick to it another season. It is much pleasanter to wear the old clothes than to have the constable chasing you in the new ones.

Many a poor man has been driven almost out of his wits by constables, who were pursuing him for the payment of debts made to gratify the vanity of his wife. She wanted a handsome breastpin, and begged him to buy it. He could not resist, and bought it with the proceeds of a week's hard toil, and, as a consequence, was obliged to go in debt for meat and bread. Then she wanted a fine dress; then this, and then that; and so he sank into debt, step by step, until he was ruined.

A wife can soon destroy her husband's good name, by urging him to buy her things she could do without, and for which he is unable to pay.

It is a good plan for a man and woman who are just setting out as you are to make a living, to balance their accounts-that is count up what they earn and what they spend, and see how they compare-a great many times in the year. It will not take them long to do it, and the task will be both pleasant and useful.

Resolve that you will, by the blessing of God, live within your means. This is one of the most important secrets of success. It may cost you a struggle, but stick to it resolutely, and the day will come when you will be able to purchase not only the necessaries, but the luxuries of life.

I am not counseling you to be mean and stingy,-by no means; but no man has a right to be liberal with another man's money and at another man's expense.

For the sake of your good name, do not make a splurge in society with jewelry and fine clothes which have not been paid for, and for which you will never be able to pay. That is almost as mean as theft.

"The borrower," says the Bible, "is servant to the lender," and, let me assure you, a creditor is a very hard master. Do not put your necks in his iron yoke.

I am acquainted with many white persons who commenced married life twenty-five years ago with as little as you have now, and who worked with their hands for less than is given to you, who are now owners of handsome houses and farms, and are in very easy circumstances. They made it a rule to spend less than they earned.

1. *What are the rewards of work in the opinion of the author?*
2. *What advice does the author have for those who may be earning wages and handling money for the first time in their lives?*

16-4   Mississippi Black Code (1865)

In the aftermath of Emancipation, southern states passed a variety of laws known as "Black Codes". Although these codes varied from state to state, they were all aimed at tightly controlling the lives and labor of newly freed people. The codes angered Congress and the northern pubic, who viewed them as southern attempts to roll back Emancipation and subvert Reconstruction. The Civil Rights Act of 1866, the Fourteenth Amendment, and the Military Reconstitution Act of 1867 were all designed in part to counter the Black Codes.

The Civil Rights of Freedmen in Mississippi

Section 1. Be it enacted by the legislature of the State of Mississippi, That all freedmen, free Negroes, and mulattoes may sue and be sued, implead and be impleaded in all the courts of law and equity of this state, and may acquire personal property and choses in action, by descent or purchase, any may dispose of the same, in the same manner, and to the same extent that white persons may: Provided that the provisions of this section shall not be so construed as to allow any freedman, free Negro, or mulatto to rent or lease any lands or tenements, except in incorporated town or cities in which places the corporate authorities shall control the same.

Sec. 2. Be it further enacted, That all freedmen, free Negroes, and mulattoes may intermarry with each other, in the same manner and under the same regulations that are provided by law for white persons: Provided, that the clerk of probate shall keep separate records of the same.

Sec. 3. Be it further enacted, That all freedmen, free Negroes, and mulattoes, who do now and have heretofore lived and cohabited together as husband and wife shall be taken and held in law as legally married, and the issue shall be taken and held as legitimate for all purposes. That it shall not be lawful for any freedman, free Negro, or mulatto to intermarry with any white person; nor for any white person to intermarry with any freedman, free Negro, or mulatto; any person who shall so intermarry shall be deemed guilty of felony and, on conviction thereof, shall be confined in the state penitentiary for life; and those shall be deemed freedmen, free Negroes, and mulattoes who are of pure Negro blood, and those descended from a Negro to the third generation inclusive, though one ancestor of each generation may have been a white person.

Sec. 4. Be it further enacted, That in addition to cases in which freedmen, free Negroes, and mulattoes are now by law competent witnesses, freedmen, free Negroes, or mulattoes shall be competent in civil cases when a party or parties to the suit, either plaintiff or plaintiffs, defendant or defendants, also in cases where freedmen, free Negroes, and mulattoes is or are either plaintiff or plaintiffs, defendant or defendants, and a white person or white persons is or are the opposing party or parties, plaintiff or plaintiffs, defendant or defendants. They shall also be competent witnesses in all criminal prosecutions where the crime charged is alleged to have been committed by a white person upon or against the person or property of a freedman, free Negro, or mulatto: Provided that in all cases said witnesses shall be examined in open court on the stand, except, however, they may be examined before the grand jury, and shall in all cases be subject to the rules and tests of the common law as to competency and credibility.

Sec. 5. Be it further enacted, That every freedman, free Negro, and mulatto shall, on the second Monday of January, one thousand eight hundred and sixty-six, and annually thereafter, have a lawful home or employment. . . .

Sec. 6. Be it further enacted, That all contracts for labor made with freedmen, free Negroes, and mulattoes for a longer period than one month shall be in writing and in duplicate, attested and read to said freedman, free Negro, or mulatto, by a beat, city or county officers, or two disinterested white persons of the country in which the labor is to be performed, of which each party shall have one; and said contracts shall be taken and held as entire contracts, and if the laborer shall quit the service of the employer, before expiration of his term of service, without good cause, he shall forfeit his wages for that year, up to the time of quitting.

Sec. 7. Be it further enacted, That every civil officer shall, and every person may, arrest and carry back to his or her legal employer any freedman, free Negro, or mulatto who shall have quit the service of his or her employer before the expiration of his or her term of service without good cause, and said officer and person shall be entitled to receive for arresting and carrying back every deserting employee aforesaid, the sum of five dollars, and ten cents per mile from the place of arrest to the place of delivery, and the same shall be paid by the employer, and held as a set-off for so much against the wages of said deserting employee.

Sec. 8. Be it further enacted, That upon affidavit made by the employer of any freedman, free Negro, or mulatto, or other credible person, before any justice of the peace or member of the board of police, that any freedman, free Negro, or mulatto, legally employed by said employer, has illegally deserted said employment, such justice of the peace or member of the board of police shall issue his warrant or warrants, returnable before himself, or other such officer, directed to any sheriff, constable, or special deputy, commanding him to arrest said deserter and return him or her to said employer, and the like proceedings shall be had as provided in the preceding section. . . .

Sec. 9. Be it further enacted, That if any person shall persuade or attempt to persuade, entice, or cause any freedman, free Negro, or mulatto to desert from the legal employment of any person, before the expiration of his or her term of service, or shall knowingly employ any such deserting freedman, free Negro, or mulatto, or shall knowingly give or sell to any such deserting freedman, free Negro, or mulatto, any food, raiment, or other thing, he or she shall be guilty of a misdemeanor and, upon conviction, shall be fined not less than twenty-five dollars and not more then two hundred dollars and the costs, and, if said fine and costs shall not be immediately paid, the court shall sentence said convict to not exceeding two months' imprisonment in the county jail, and he or she shall moreover be liable to the party injured in damages: . . . .

Sec. 10. Be it further enacted, That it shall be lawful for any freedman, free Negro, or mulatto to charge any white person, freedman, free Negro, or mulatto, by affidavit, with any criminal offense against his or her person or property and upon such affidavit the proper process shall be issued and executed as if said affidavit was made by a white person, and it shall be lawful for any freedman, free Negro, or mulatto, in any action, suit, or controversy pending, or about to be instituted, in any court of law or equity of this state, to make all needful and lawful affidavits, as shall be necessary for the institution, prosecution, or defense of such suit or controversy.

Sec. 11. Be it further enacted, That the penal laws of this state, in all cases not otherwise specially provided for, shall apply and extend to all freedmen, free Negroes, and mulattoes. . . .

Approved November 25, 1865

1. Identify and explain the actual freedoms and rights that are granted under the Mississippi Black Code.
2. What restrictions and laws enacted by the Black Code effectively extend the racist doctrines of pre-Civil War slavery? What freedoms are notably denied under the Code?

16-5   James C. Beecher, Report on Land Reform in the South Carolina Islands (1865, 1866)

The controversial Reconstruction of the South after the Civil War was a difficult time for African Americans. Though given the right to voice political opinions for the first time, their voices often went unheeded. As southern whites regained control of political offices after Reconstruction, African Americans slowly lost much of their newfound political freedom.

November 29, 1865
Maj. Gen. R. Saxton

General:

I am to leave for Edisto Island in the morning. It seems that some of the planters whose lands have been restored were driven off by the freed people. Gen. Sickles immediately ordered that a company of white troops be sent there. Gen. Devens agreed with me that my troops were the ones to send if any and so I take a company with me.

I have apprehended trouble ever since the Govt determined to rescind the authority to occupy those lands. It is true that the War Dept. did not, in so many words, approve Gen. Sherman's order, but it certainly did *act* upon it, and there is an apparent bad faith in the matter which I am sure the freed people will feel. I cannot refrain from expressing grave fears of collisions on the island. The same difficulty is affecting the Combahee plantations. I hope to visit that section by Monday next.

James C. Beecher
National Archives

January 9, 1866

I . . . called the people together and carefully instructed them in their rights and duties. They said they had been assured by certain parties that Mr. Heyward [a local white planter] would be obliged to lease his land to them, and that they would not work for him at any price. They were perfectly good natured about it but firm. I then announced Mr. Heyward's offer:

That they were to retain their houses and gardens, with the privilege of raising hogs, poultry, etc. That he would pay for full hands, men $12, women $8 per month. They to find themselves-or he would pay $10 per month to men, $4 to women and ration them.

I am satisfied that no higher wages will be offered this year. Therefore I told the people that they could take it or leave it, and that if they declined to work the plantation the houses must be vacated. I proceeded to call the roll of all the able bodied men and women, each of whom responded "no." I then notified them that every house must be vacated on or before the 18th inst. I propose to remain and see everyone outside the plantation lines on that date.

Today I have pursued the same course on another large plantation, with the same results. Of course I anticipated this. It could not be otherwise considering the instructions which these people have received. I do not blame them in the slightest degree, and so long as they show no violence, shall treat them with all possible kindness. But it is better to stop the error they are laboring under, at once.

January 31, 1866

I am informed that on or about 12th inst a meeting was called on Wadmalaw Island to take measures to prevent white persons from visiting the island-that the Captain Commanding (very properly) forbade the proceeding, and notified the actors that in future no meetings could be held until notice of the same should be given him.

I am further informed that certain parties immediately proceeded to Charleston and returned with a document signed "By order Maj. Gen. Saxton" stating that the military authorities had nothing to do with them and they were at liberty to hold meetings when and where they pleased. This document was brought by three colored men calling themselves Commissioners from Edisto Island, attended by an escort of forty or fifty freedmen, and exhibited to the Officer. They then proceeded to Rockville, and held the meeting.

It is to be regretted that the Bureau should seem to bring the freed people in collision with the Military Police of the islands. Already in two instances the freed people have committed themselves seriously by acts of stupid violence and I have record of hurtful advice given by speakers at the meeting in question. I shall be exceedingly grieved to find myself in collision with the [Bureau] but being responsible for the military police of these islands cannot do otherwise than prevent disorder by any means in my power.

I respectfully request that instruction be sent to the same "Commissioners" to the effect that the order in question must be respected on Wadmalaw and Johns Island. Such instructions will prevent collision between the [freedmen] and the U.S. forces.

1. What difficulties are reported by Beecher regarding the settling of land disputes in the South Carolina Islands? Describe the two different views of the dispute.

16-6   The Memphis Riot (1866)

The Memphis riot began on May 1, 1866, when the horse-drawn carriages of a black man and a white man collided. Fighting broke out as a group of black soldiers from nearby Fort Pickering tried to intervene to stop the arrest of the black man by the mainly Irish-American police. Passions escalated into three days of racially motivated violence between the police and black residents of Memphis. When peace was restored, forty-six blacks and two whites had been killed, five black women raped, and hundreds of black homes, schools, and churches had been vandalized or destroyed. The following is the report of an investigation into the riot prepared for General Oliver Otis Howard, Commissioner of the Bureau of Refugees, Freedmen and Abandoned Lands.

> **Source:** The Freedmen's Bureau Online, *Records of the Assistant Commissioner for the State of Tennessee, Bureau of Refugees, Freedmen, and Abandoned Lands, 1865–1869.* National Archives Microfilm Publication M999, roll 34 "Reports of Outrages, Riots and Murders, Jan. 15, 1866–Aug. 12, 1868".
> http://www.freedmensbureau.com/tennessee/outrages/memphisriot.htm

Memphis, Tenn. May 22 '66

Maj. Genl. O.O. Howard
Commissioner B.R.F. & A. L.
Washington, D.C.

General,

In accordance with the instructions contained in S. O. No. 64, Ex. II, War Dept., B. R. F. & A. L. dated Washington, D. C. May 7, 1866 and your letter of "confidential instructions" of the same date, I have the honor herewith to submit a report of an investigation of the late riots in Memphis.

I reached Memphis May 11th and I found General Fisk, the Asst. Commissioner for Ky. and Tenn, here. He had already directed his Inspector General Col. C. T. Johnson to institute an investigation and I found the Colonel had commenced his work and was well advanced.

At the suggestion of General Fisk I immediately conferred with Colonel Johnson and we determined to make a joint investigation and report. We have taken some affidavits and as many more could have been procured if we could have taken the time.

I have the honor to be
Very Respectfully
Your Obdt. Servant
(sd) T. W. Gilbreth
Aid-de-Camp

Report of an investigation of the cause, origin, and results of the late riots in the city of Memphis made by Col. Charles F. Johnson, Inspector General States of Ky. and Tennessee and Major T. W. Gilbreth, A. D. C. to Maj. Genl. Howard, Commissioner Bureau R. F. & A. Lands.

The remote cause of the riot as it appears to us is a bitterness of feeling which has always existed between the low whites & blacks, both of whom have long advanced rival claims for superiority, both being as degraded as human beings can possibly be.

In addition to this general feeling of hostility there was an especial hatred among the city police for the Colored Soldiers, who were stationed here for a long time and had recently been discharged from the service of the U.S., which was most cordially reciprocated by the soldiers.

This has frequently resulted in minor affrays not considered worthy of notice by the authorities. These causes combined produced a state of feeling between whites and blacks, which would require only the slightest provocation to bring about an open rupture.

The Immediate Cause

On the evening of the 30th April 1866 several policemen (4) came down Causey Street, and meeting a number of Negroes forced them off the sidewalk. In doing so a Negro fell and a policeman stumbled over him. The police then drew their revolvers and attacked the Negroes, beating them with their pistols. Both parties then separated, deferring the settlement by mutual consent to some future time (see affidavit marked "A"). On the following day, May 1st, during the afternoon, between the hours of 3 and 5, a crowd of colored men, principally discharged soldiers, many of whom were more or less intoxicated, were assembled on South Street in South Memphis.

Three or four of these were very noisy and boisterous. Six policemen appeared on South Street, two of them arrested two of the Negroes and conducted them from the ground. The others remained behind to keep back the crowd, when the attempt was made by several Negroes to rescue their comrades. The police fell back when a promiscuous fight was indulged in by both parties.

During this affray one police officer was wounded in the finger, another (Stephens) was shot by the accidental discharge of his pistol in his own hand, and afterward died.

About this time the police fired upon unoffending Negroes remote from the riotous quarter. Colored soldiers with whom the police first had trouble had returned in the meantime to Fort Pickering. The police was soon reinforced and commenced firing on the colored people, men, women and children, in that locality, killing and wounding several.

Shortly after, the City Recorder (John C. Creighton) arrived upon the ground (corner of Causey and Vance Streets) and in a speech which received three hearty cheers from the crowd there assembled, councilled and urged the whites to arm and kill every Negro and drive the last one from the city. Then during this night the Negroes were hunted down by police, firemen and other white citizens, shot, assaulted, robbed, and in many instances their houses searched under the pretense of hunting for concealed arms, plundered, and then set on fire, during which no resistance so far as we can learn was offered by the Negroes.

A white man by the name of Dunn, a fireman, was shot and killed by another white man through mistake (reference is here made to accompanying affidavit mkd "B").

During the morning of the 2nd inst. (Wednesday) everything was perfectly quiet in the district of the disturbances of the previous day. A very few Negroes were in the streets, and none of them appeared with arms, or in any way excited except through fear. About 11 o'clock A.M. a posse of police and citizens again appeared in South Memphis and commenced an indiscriminate attack upon the Negroes, they were shot down without mercy, women suffered alike with the men, and in several instances little children were killed by these miscreants. During this day and night, with various intervals of quiet, the nuisance continued.

The city seemed to be under the control of a lawless mob during this and the two succeeding days (3rd & 4th). All crimes imaginable were committed from simple larceny to rape and murder. Several women and children were shot in bed. One woman (Rachel Johnson) was shot and then thrown into the flames of a burning house and consumed. Another was forced twice through the flames and finally escaped. In some instances houses were fired and armed men guarded them to prevent the escape of those inside. A number of men whose loyalty is undoubted, long residents of Memphis, who deprecated the riot during its progress, were denominated Yankees and Abolitionists, and were informed in language more emphatic than gentlemanly, that their presence here was unnecessary. To particularize further as to individual acts of inhumanity would extend the report to too great a length. But attention is respectfully called for further instances to affidavits accompanying marked C, E, F & G.

The riot lasted until and including the 4th of May but during all this time the disturbances were not continual as there were different times of greater or less length in each day, in which the city was perfectly quiet, attacks occurring generally after sunset each day.

The rioters ceased their violence either of their own accord or from want of material to work on, the Negroes having hid themselves, many fleeing into the country.

Conduct of the Civil Authorities

The Hon. John Park, Mayor of Memphis, seemed to have lost entire control of his subordinates and either through lack of inclination and sympathy with the mob, or on utter want of capacity, completely failed to suppress the riot and preserve the peace of the city. His friends offer in extenuation of his conduct, that he was in a state of intoxication during a part or most of the time and was therefore unable to perform the high and responsible functions of his office. Since the riot no official notice has been taken of the occurrence either by the Mayor or the Board of Aldermen, neither have the City Courts taken cognizance of the numerous crimes committed.

Although many of the perpetrators are known, no arrests have been made, nor is there now any indication on the part of the Civil Authorities that any are meditated by them.

It appears the Sheriff of this County (P. M. Minters) endeavored to oppose the mob on the evening of the 1st of May, but his good intentions were thwarted by a violent speech delivered by John C. Creighton, City Recorder, who urged and directed the arming of the whites and the wholesale slaughter of blacks.

This speech was delivered on the evening of the 1st of May to a large crowd of police and citizens on the corner of Vance and Causey streets, and to it can be attributed in a great measure the continuance of the disturbances. The following is the speech as extracted from the affidavits herewith forwarded marked "B" . . . "That everyone of the citizens should get arms, organize and go through the Negro districts," and that he "was in favor of killing every God damned nigger" . . . "We are not prepared now, but let us prepare and clean out every damned son of a bitch of a nigger out of town . . . "Boys, I want you to go ahead and kill every damned one of the nigger race and burn up the cradle."

The effect of such language delivered by a municipal office so high in authority, to a promiscuous and excited assemblage can be easily perceived. From that time they seemed to act as though vested with full authority to kill, burn and plunder at will. The conduct of a great number of the city police, who are generally composed of the lowest class of whites selected without reference to their qualifications for the position, was brutal in the extreme. Instead of protecting the rights of persons and property as is their duty, they were chiefly concerned as murderers, incendiaries and robbers. At times they even protected the rest of the mob in their acts of violence.

No public meeting has been held by the citizens, although three weeks have now elapsed since the riot, thus by their silence appearing to approve of the conduct of the mob. The only regrets that are expressed by the mass of the people are purely financial. There are, however, very many honorable exceptions, chiefly among men who have fought against the Government in the late rebellion, who deprecate in strong terms, both the Civil Authorities and the rioters.

Action of Bvt. Brig. Genl. Ben P. Runkle, Chief Supt., Bureau R.F. and A.L. Sub-District of Memphis

General Runkle was waited upon every hour in the day during the riot, by colored men who begged of him protection for themselves and families, and he, an officer of the Army detailed as Agent of the Freedmen's Bureau was suffered the humiliation of acknowledging his utter inability to protect them in any respect. His personal appearance at the scenes of the riot had no affect on the mob, and he had no troops at his disposal.

He was obliged to put his Headquarters in a defensive state, and we believe it was only owing to the preparations made, that they were not burned down. Threats had been openly made that the Bureau office would be burned, and the General driven from the town. He, with his officers and a small squad of soldiers and some loyal citizens who volunteered were obliged to remain there during Thursday and Friday nights.

The origin and results of the riot may be summed up briefly as follows:

The remote cause was the feeling of bitterness which as always existed between the two classes. The minor affrays which occurred daily, especially between the police and colored persons.

The general tone of certain city papers which in articles that have appeared almost daily, have councilled the low whites to open hostilities with the blacks.

The immediate cause was the collision heretofore spoken of between a few policemen and Negroes on the evening of the 30th of April in which both parties may be equally culpable, followed on the evening of the 1st May by another collision of a more serious nature and subsequently by an indiscriminate attack upon inoffensive colored men and women.

Three Negro churches were burned, also eight (8) school houses, five (5) of which belonged to the United States Government, and about fifty (50) private dwellings, owned, occupied or inhabited by freedmen as homes, and in which they had all their personal property, scanty though it be, yet valuable to them and in many instances containing the hard earnings of months of labor.

Large sums of money were taken by police and others, the amounts varying five (5) to five hundred (500) dollars, the latter being quite frequent owing to the fact that many of the colored men had just been paid off and discharged from the Army.

No dwellings occupied by white men exclusively were destroyed and we have no evidence of any white men having been robbed.

From the present disturbed condition of the freedmen in the districts where the riot occurred it is impossible to determine the exact number of Negroes killed and wounded. The number already ascertained as killed is about (30) thirty; and the number wounded about fifty (50). Two white men were killed, viz., Stephens, a policeman and Dunn of the Fire Department.

The Surgeon who attended Stephens gives it as his professional opinion that the wound which resulted in his death was caused by the accidental discharge of a pistol in his hands (see affidavit marked "B"). Dunn was killed May 1st by a white man through mistake (see affidavit marked "B"). Two others (both Policemen) were wounded, one slightly in the finger, the other (Slattersly) seriously.

The losses sustained by the Government and Negroes as per affidavits received up to date amount to the sum of ninety eight thousand, three hundred and nineteen dollars and fifty five cents ($98,319.55). Subsequent investigations will in all probability increase the amount to one hundred and twenty thousand dollars ($120,00.00).

> (signed) Chas. F. Jackson
> Col. And Insptr. Genl. Ky. & Tenn.
> T. W. Gilbreth
> Aide-de-Camp.

1. *According to the investigation, how widespread was white animosity toward the black community in Memphis in 1866? In addition to outright violence, how was this animosity manifested? Why do you think Irish-Americans in Memphis might have felt particularly threatened by freedmen?*
2. *According to the investigation, who should be held accountable for the death and destruction during the riot? Although not directly addressed in the report, how might future incidents such as this be prevented?*

16-7 The Fourteenth Amendment (1868)

Southern attempts to deprive African Americans of their rights stimulated constitutional remedies. Congressional radical reconstruction hoped that constitutional guarantees of citizenship and federal protection of rights would alleviate oppressive state laws.

Sec. 1. All persons born or naturalized in the United States, and subject to the jurisdiction thereof, are citizens of the United States and of the State wherein they reside. No State shall make or enforce any law which shall abridge the privileges or immunities of citizens of the United States; nor shall any State deprive any person of life, liberty, or property, without due process of law; nor deny to any person within its jurisdiction the equal protection of the laws.

Sec. 2. Representatives shall be apportioned among the several States according to their respective numbers, counting the whole number of persons in each State, excluding Indians not taxed. But when the right to vote at any election for the choice of electors for President and Vice President of the United States, Representatives in Congress, the Executive and Judicial officers of a State, or the members of the Legislature thereof, is denied to any of the male inhabitants of such State, being twenty-one years of age, and citizens of the United States, or in any way abridged, except for participation in rebellion, or other crime, the basis of representation therein shall be reduced in the proportion which the number of such male citizens shall bear to the whole number of male citizens twenty-one years of age in such State.

Sec. 3. No person shall be a Senator or Representative in Congress, or elector of President and Vice President, or hold any office, civil or military, under the United States, or under any State, who, having previously taken an oath, as a member of Congress, or as an officer of the United States, or as a member of any State legislature, or as an executive or judicial officer of any State, to support the Constitution of the United States, shall have engaged in insurrection or rebellion against the same, or given aid or comfort to the enemies thereof. But Congress may by a vote of two-thirds of each House, remove such disability.

Sec. 4. The validity of the public debt of the United States, authorized by law, including debts incurred for payment of pensions and bounties for services in suppressing insurrection or rebellion, shall not be questioned. But neither the United States nor any State shall assume or pay any debt or obligation incurred in aid of insurrection or rebellion against the united States, or any claim for the loss or emancipation of any slave; but all such debts, obligations and claims shall be held illegal and void.

Sec. 5. The Congress shall have power to enforce, by appropriate legislation, the provisions of this article.

1. Explain the focus, scope, and effect of the Fourteenth Amendment.

16-8   Albion W. Tourgee, Letter on Ku Klux Klan Activities (1870)

Founded by former Confederate general Nathan Bedford Forrest in Tennessee, the Ku Klux Klan spread across the South. As this excerpt shows, southern whites in the Ku Klux Klan used brutality and violence against those who supported Reconstruction governments and efforts to improve conditions for African Americans.

Some of the Outrages-Letter from Judge Tourgee to Senator Abbott

Greensboro, N.C. May 24, 1870.
Gen. Jos. C. Abbott

My Dear General:

It is my mournful duty to inform you that our friend John W. Stephens, State Senator from Caswell, is dead. He was foully murdered by the Ku-Klux in the Grand Jury room of the Court House on Saturday or Saturday night last. The circumstances attending his murder have not yet fully come to light there. So far as I can learn, I judge these to have been the circumstances: He was one of the Justices of the Peace in that township, and was accustomed to hold court in that room on Saturdays. It is evident that he was set upon by some one while holding this court, or immediately after its close, and disabled by a sudden attack, otherwise there would have been a very sharp resistance, as he was a man, and always went armed to the teeth. He was stabbed five or six times, and then hanged on a hook in the Grand Jury room, where he was found on Sunday morning. Another brave, honest Republican citizen has met his fate at the hands of these fiends. Warned of his danger, and fully cognizant of the terrible risk which surrounded him, he still manfully refused to quit the field. Against the advice of his friends, against the entreaties of his family, he constantly refused to leave those who had stood by him in the day of his disgrace and peril. He was accustomed to say that 3,000 poor, ignorant, colored Republican voters in that county had stood by him and elected him, at the risk of persecution and starvation, and that he had no idea of abandoning them to the Ku-Klux. He was determined to stay with them, and either put an end to these outrages, or die with the other victims of Rebel hate and national apathy: Nearly six months ago I declared my belief that before the election in August next the Ku-Klux would have killed more men in the State than there would be members to be elected to the Legislature. A good beginning has been made toward the fulfillment of this prophecy. The following counties have already filled, or nearly so, their respective "quotas:" Jones County, quota full, excess 1; Orange County quota full; excess, 1. Caswell County quota full; excess, 2; Alamance County quota full; excess, 1. Chatham County quota nearly full. Or, to state the matter differently, there have been twelve murders in five counties of the district during the past eighteen months, by bands of disguised villains. In addition to this, from the best information I can derive, I am of the opinion that in this district alone there have been 1,000 outrages of a less serious nature perpetrated by the same masked fiends. Of course this estimate is not made from any absolute record, nor is it possible to ascertain with accuracy the entire number of beatings and other outrages which have been perpetrated. The uselessness, the utter futility of complaint from the lack of ability in the laws to punish is fully known to all. The danger of making such complaint is also well understood. It is therefore not unfrequently by accident that the outrage is found out, and unquestionably it is frequently absolutely concealed. Thus, a respectable, hard working white carpenter was working for a neighbor, when accidentally his shirt was torn, and disclosed his back scarred and beaten. The poor fellow begged for the sake of his wife and children that nothing might be said about it, as the Ku-Klux had threatened to kill him if he disclosed how he had been outraged. Hundreds of cases have come to my notice and that of my solicitor. . . .

Men and women come scarred, mangled, and bruised, and say: "The Ku-Klux came to my house last night and beat me almost to death, and my old woman right smart, and shot into the house, 'bust' the door down, and told me they would kill me if I made complaint;" and the bloody mangled forms attest the truth of their declarations. On being asked if any one knew any of the party it will be ascertained that there was no recognition, or only the most uncertain and doubtful one. In such cases as these nothing can be done by the court. We have not been accustomed to enter them on record. A man of the best standing in Chatham told me that he could count up 200 and upward in that county. In Alamance County, a citizen in conversation one evening enumerated upward of 50 cases which had occurred within his own knowledge, and in one section of the county. He gave it as his opinion that there had been 200 cases in that county. I have no idea that he exceeded the proper estimate. That was six months ago, and I am satisfied that another hundred would not cover the work done in that time.

These crimes have been of every character imaginable. Perhaps the most usual has been the dragging of men and women from their beds, and beating their naked bodies with hickory switches, or as witnesses in an examination the other day said, "sticks" between a "switch" and a "club." From 50 to 100 blows is the usual allowance, sometimes 200 and 300 blows are administered. Occasionally an instrument of torture is owned. Thus in one case two women, one 74 years old, were taken out, stripped naked, and beaten with a paddle, with several holes bored through it. The paddle was about 30 inches long, 3 or 4 inches wide, and 1/4 of an inch thick, of oak. Their bodies were so bruised and beaten that they were sickening to behold. They were white women and of good character until the younger was seduced, and swore her child to its father. Previous to that and so far as others were concerned her character was good.

Again, there is sometimes a fiendish malignity and cunning displayed in the form and character of the outrages. For instance, a colored man was placed astride of a log, and an iron staple driven through his person into the log. In another case, after a band of them had in turn violated a young negro girl, she was forced into bed with a colored man, their bodies were bound together face to face, and the fire from the hearth piled upon them. The K. K. K. rode off and left them, with shouts of laughter. Of course the bed was soon in flames, and somehow they managed to crawl out, though terribly burned and scarred. The house was burned.

I could give other incidents of cruelty, such as hanging up a boy of nine years old until he was nearly dead, to make him tell where his father was hidden, and beating an old negress of 103 years old with garden pallings because she would not own that she was afraid of the Ku-Klux. But it is unnecessary to go into further detail. In this district I estimate their offenses as follows, in the past ten months: Twelve murders, 9 rapes, 11 arsons, 7 mutilations, ascertained and most of them on record. In some no identification could be made.

Four thousand or 5,000 houses have been broken open, and property or persons taken out. In all cases all arms are taken and destroyed. Seven hundred or 800 persons have been beaten or otherwise maltreated. These of course are partly persons living in the houses which were broken into.

And yet the Government sleeps. The poor disarmed nurses of the Republican party-those men by whose ballots the Republican party holds power-who took their lives in their hands when they cast their ballots for U.S. Grant and other officials-all of us who happen to be beyond the pale of the Governmental regard-must be sacrificed, murdered, scourged, mangled, because some contemptible party scheme might be foiled by doing us justice. I could stand it very well to fight for Uncle Sam, and was never known to refuse an invitation on such an occasion; but this lying down, tied hand and foot with the shackles of the law, to be killed by the very dregs of the rebellion, the scum of the earth, and not allowed either the consolation of fighting or the satisfaction that our "fall" will be noted by the Government, and protection given to others thereby, is somewhat too hard. I am ashamed of the nation that will let its citizens be slain by scores, and scourged by thousands, and offer no remedy or protection. I am ashamed of a State which has not sufficient strength to protect its own officers in the discharge of their duties, nor guarantee the safety of any man's domicile throughout its length and breadth. I am ashamed of a party which, with the reins of power in its hands, has not nerve or decision enough to arm its own adherents, or to protect them from assassinations at the hands of their opponents. A General who in time of war would permit 2,000 or 3,000 of his men to be bushwhacked and destroyed by private treachery even in an enemy's country without any one being punished for it would be worthy of universal execration, and would get it, too. How much more worthy of detestation is a Government which in time of peace will permit such wholesale slaughter of its citizens? It is simple cowardice, inertness, and wholesale demoralization. The wholesale slaughter of the war has dulled our Nation's sense of horror at the shedding of blood, and the habit of regarding the South as simply a laboratory, where every demagogue may carry on his reconstructionary experiments at will, and not as an integral party of the Nation itself, has led our Government to shut its eyes to the atrocities of these times. Unless these evils are speedily remedied, I tell you, General, the Republican party has signed its death warrant. It is a party of cowards or idiots-I don't care which alternative is chosen. The remedy is in our hands, and we are afraid or too dull to bestir ourselves and use it.

But you will tell me that Congress is ready and willing to act if it only knew what to do. Like the old Irish woman it wrings its hands and cries, "O Lawk, O Lawk; if I only knew which way." And yet this same Congress has the control of the militia and can organize its own force in every county in the United States, and arm more or less of it. This same Congress has the undoubted right to guarantee and provide a republican government, and protect every citizen in "life, liberty, and the pursuit of happiness," as well as the power conferred by the XVth Amendment. And yet we suffer and die in peace and murderers walk abroad with the blood yet fresh upon their garments, unharmed, unquestioned and unchecked. Fifty thousand dollars given to good detectives would secure, if well used, a complete knowledge of all this gigantic organization of murderers. In connection with an organized and armed militia, it would result in the apprehension of any number of these Thugs *en masque* and with blood on their hands. What then is the remedy? *First:* Let Congress give to the U. S. Courts, or to Courts of the States under its own laws, cognizance of this class of crimes, as crimes against the nation, and let it provide that this legislation be enforced. Why not, for instance, make going armed and masked or disguised, or masked or disguised in the night time, an act of insurrection or sedition? *Second:* Organize militia, National-State militia is a nuisance-and arm as many as may be necessary in each county to enforce its laws. *Third:* Put detectives at work to get hold of this whole organization. Its ultimate aim is unquestionably to revolutionize the Government. If we have not pluck enough for this, why then let us just offer our throats to the knife, emasculate ourselves, and be a nation of self-subjugated slaves at once.

And now, Abbott, I have but one thing to say to you. I have very little doubt that I shall be one of the next victims. My steps have been dogged for months, and only a good opportunity has been wanting to secure to me the fate which Stephens has just met, and I speak earnestly upon this matter. I feel that I have a right to do so, and a right to be heard as well, and with this conviction I say to you plainly that any member of Congress who, especially if from the South, does not support, advocate, and urge immediate, active, and thorough measures to put an end to these outrages, and make citizenship a privilege, is a coward, a traitor, or a fool. The time for action has come, and the man who has now only speeches to make over some Constitutional scarecrow, deserves to be damned.

1. *Summarize some of the actions described in this letter that are attributed to the KKK? Why, do you think, Tourgee goes into such detail?*
2. *What is the tone of this letter? To whom does Tourgee turn in his plea?*
3. *Explain Tourgee's ultimate purpose in this letter. What remedy is suggested?*

16-9 The Nation, "The State of the South" (1872)

The end of the Civil War left the South in dire economic straits. Despite efforts to revive the southern economy, by 1872, conditions had improved little. The Nation suggested the corrupt actions of carpet-baggers were exacerbating the situation.

The indolent excuse for our failure to understand the condition of the South is that nobody can very accurately comprehend it who has not been there to see for himself. With regard to troubles of a social character, this excuse is valid; but there are some plain statistical facts recently brought to light and published which it is our duty to recognize and confront. We must acknowledge that the condition of the South from almost every point of view is extremely wretched. The property of the eleven States in 1860, exclusive of slaves, was valued at $2,728,825,006. At the end of the war their increased liabilities and loss, exclusive of slaves, was $1,272,900,390, nearly one-half the assessed value of their property at the beginning of the war. This, however, was only the State loss. Secretary Belknap fixes the rebel debt, on the 1st of April, 1865, at $2,345,297,823. This estimate would make the total loss of the rebellious States by the war $5,262,303,554. This sum, it will be seen, is about twice the assessed value of all Southern property in 1860, exclusive of slaves. Five-eighths of Southern property is gone, and the taxes upon the remainder are four times that upon the original property before the war. How much of the money wrung from this impoverished country is expended upon public improvements, it is difficult to tell; but it is likely that most of it, and certain that much of it, goes to feed the vulgar and rapacious rogues who rob and rule a people helpless and utterly exhausted.

With the exception of Virginia and Tennessee, the debts of all the States have been increased since the end of the war. The near neighborhood of those communities to the Ohio may have had some influence in driving rogues further south. The real reason, however, is the comparative fewness of the negroes. The debt of Alabama in 1866 was $5,000,000; under the rule of the enlightened and disinterested economists who have undertaken to repair her finances, that debt has been increased to $24,000,000. In North Carolina the new government was established in 1868. In 1860, the State debt was $14,000,000; in 1865, $20,000,000; in 1868, $24,000,000; and in 1871, $34,000,000. Thus the increase of debt since the war has been more than twice the increase during the war-which looks as if war were a cheaper and more prosperous condition than peace. At any rate, reconstruction seems to be morally a more disastrous process than rebellion. Guile is the strength of the weak, and the carpet-baggers have taught the Southern people to meet rogues with trickery. The Ku-klux Committee, commenting upon their dreadful poverty at the close of the war, says that manifestly they must have at once succumbed under their loss of $5,000,000,000 had it not been for the benefactions of the North. It states that the Freedmen's Bureau has spent $13,000,000 upon Southern sufferers of both colors. This does not seem a considerable sum when we think that the increased debt since the war in North Carolina has been $14,000,000. Certainly, our charities have done less good than our carpet-baggers have done damage. The theory, of course, is that something remains from the enormous sums raised by taxation, that they have been expended upon needed public improvements. In North Carolina, it was alleged, the large subsidies given to railroads would encourage immigration. There has been no immigration, however; the bonds have been sold at a disadvantage; some of the money has been stolen, and a few of the rogues have been indicted. It is impossible to say how much of the sums raised remain to the States. The carpet-baggers have had it pretty much their own way. If they chose to rob, there was nothing to prevent them. Give men a chance to be tyrants or scamps, and there is no fear that some will not be found who will avail themselves of it. Here in New York, where we have all the rascals and all the plunderers within a radius of five miles, we know how long we have been in bringing the Ring to bay. The carpet-baggers have an immense extent of country to rifle; they do not buy the legislatures, they constitute them; they enact their own registration acts and vote their own supplies. The persons they rob are not of that apathetic and well-to-do class too indifferent to go to the polls, but people who could not go if they would.

All accounts agree as to the widespread misery and penury. In Mississippi, a large planter testified that it took all his cotton for the year 1871 to pay his taxes. It is South Carolina, however, that enjoys the unenviable eminence of being the worst-robbed State of the whole eleven. In the single county of Kershaw, possessing a population of only 11,000, there were 3,600 tax-executions issued. The taxation during 1870, $2,365,047, was more than the whole taxation on double the property for five years before the war. In order to change the fiscal year, they proposed to double this, and, in 1871, to levy a tax of $4,730,094; whether this law was executed we do not know, but the fact remains that it was enacted. Peculation and corruption are as universal as poverty and distress. In 1860, South Carolina paid for offices and salaries, $123,800; in 1871, the State expended on these $581,640. In two years, $1,208,577 67 have been paid out, for which no vouchers are to be found in the Treasury. According to the minority report of the Ku-klux Committee, the disbursements exceed the appropriations by $170,683. This report, though spoiled by some rather low allusions to "ebony legislators," "men and brothers," etc., brings to light some amusing facts. Money voted with which to fit up committee-rooms has been expended on the private apartments of the colored members of the legislatures. Their rooms were furnished with Brussels carpets, sofas, mirrors, etc. About seventy-five imported porcelain spittoons, bought for the South Carolina State-House, likewise adorned their private apartments. This fact seemed to affect the democratic minority of the committee even more profoundly than the vast robberies and excessive taxations. They remark, with rugged, Spartan simplicity, that they themselves, in "the splendid capital of the nation," had never had anything but "an article of common, plain brown earthenware, of domestic manufacture." This striking disparity between fortune and desert does not excite in us any feeling of indignation against the negroes. Emerging from a long night of slavery and cruel bondage, who can grudge them their fantastic lease of liberty and luxury? Did not graver considerations check us, our humor would be to vote them State barbers and the most delightful of oriental baths. We suspect the truth to be that in the distribution of spoils the poor African gets the gilt and plush, the porcelain spittoons, the barbaric upholstery, while the astuter Caucasian clings to the solider and more durable advantages. The negroes by themselves would be but little to be feared; yet, in the hands of the carpet-baggers, they have been the unwitting instruments of most of the harm that has been done. The swindlers could not have so got the control of things without the help of the negroes. They have made numerically the largest part of the conventions and legislatures in South Carolina. The Convention of 1868, which drew up a State constitution, was composed of 72 negroes and 49 white men. This convention made provision for a levy of $2,230,950 upon the State, which would necessitate taxation at the rate of 6 per cent; yet but 13 of the 72 negroes paid taxes. In the Legislature of 1869, there were twelve black and twenty white senators; eight of the twelve black senators paid no taxes. In the House, there were 86 black and 37 white members; 68 of the 86 black members paid no taxes. As things are at present, there seems to be no limit to the power of the carpet-baggers to plunder the South as they choose. The only ray of hope is in the passage of an act of universal amnesty. We have given the negro the ballot to protect him against his old master; we need now to give the white citizen the vote to protect him against the carpet-bagger.

Seven years have gone over us since the close of the war, and, instead of occupying this precious season with endeavors to re-establish prosperity and to sow the seeds of a peace which, in another generation, would ripen into good-will and forgetfulness, we have averted our eyes from the whole problem, refused to listen to the complaints of men whose hands we have tied, and have fallen back upon the lazy belief that in some way this great country is bound to go through. The unconscious syllogism working in the indolent Northern mind seems to be: "Things are no doubt very bad-how bad, we haven't the time or the inclination to ascertain. Examination of such unpleasant matters, if a duty at all, is a disagreeable one. After all, the rebels have made their own bed, and they must lie in it." Perhaps their sufferings are only the just punishment of their crimes; but at any rate, there can be no reason for giving over the criminals into the hands of the carpet-baggers. What services have these persons rendered the country that we should grant them the monopoly of robbing rebels? It would be better to levy tribute-money, and get some national advantage from the merciless exactions inflicted upon the Southern people. Let us make up our minds one way or the other-do we or do we not propose further to punish the rebel States for their rebellion? If we do, let us at once proceed to devise some intelligent means for that purpose. If we do not, let us make haste to protect society from the ravages of ignorance and rapacity, or give society the means to protect itself. We thought it worth four years of war to retain the Southern States in the Union, now we hardly deem it worth an act of Congress to preserve them.

1. *Summarize the South's economic situation as it is represented in this document.*
2. *What, in the opinion of the author, has been the effect of Reconstruction policies upon the South? What attitude is voiced in this document toward carpetbaggers? What have carpetbaggers done? What is the solution to this problem?*

16-10 Susan B. Anthony and the "New Departure" for Women (1873)

During the early 1870s, Susan B. Anthony and Elizabeth Cady Stanton engaged in a strategy that they believed would secure the right to vote for women. This "New Departure" was based on the belief that the Fourteenth and Fifteenth Amendments guaranteed all citizens the right to vote regardless of gender. Anthony tested its constitutionality by casting a ballot in the 1872 presidential election. Anthony was arrested, indicted by a grand jury and placed on trial in June 1873 in Canandaigua, New York. The judge ordered the all-male jury to return a guilty verdict. In her comments to the court, Anthony exposed the trial for the travesty it was. She was fined $100 but refused to pay.

Source: Ken Burns and Paul Barnes, *"Not For Ourselves Alone"*: The Story of Elizabeth Cady Stanton and Susan B. Anthony.
http://www.pbs.org/stantonanthony/resources/index.html?body=04activity.html

Friends and Fellow-citizens: I stand before you to-night, under indictment for the alleged crime of having voted at the last Presidential election, without having a lawful right to vote. It shall be my work this evening to prove to you that in thus voting, I not only committed no crime, but, instead, simply exercised my citizen's right, guaranteed to me and all United States citizens by the National Constitution, beyond the power of any State to deny.

Our democratic-republican government is based on the idea of the natural right of every individual member thereof to a voice and a vote in making and executing the laws. We assert the province of government to be to secure the people in the enjoyment of their unalienable rights. We throw to the winds the old dogma that governments can give rights. Before governments were organized, no one denies that each individual possessed the right to protect his own life, liberty and property. And when 100 or 1,000,000 people enter into a free government, they do not barter away their natural rights; they simply pledge themselves to protect each other in the enjoyment of them, through prescribed judicial and legislative tribunals. They agree to abandon the methods of brute force in the adjustment of their differences, and adopt those of civilization.

Nor can you find a word in any of the grand documents left us by the fathers that assumes for government the power to create or to confer rights. The Declaration of Independence, the United States Constitution, the constitutions of the several states and the organic laws of the territories, all alike propose to protect the people in the exercise of their God-given rights. Not one of them pretends to bestow rights.

"All men are created equal, and endowed by their Creator with certain unalienable rights. Among these are life, liberty and the pursuit of happiness. That to secure these, governments are instituted among men, deriving their just powers from the consent of the governed."

Here is no shadow of government authority over rights, nor exclusion of any from their full and equal enjoyment. Here is pronounced the right of all men, and "consequently," as the Quaker preacher said, "of all women," to a voice in the government. And here, in this very first paragraph of the declaration, is the assertion of the natural right of all to the ballot; for, how can "the consent of the governed" be given, if the right to vote be denied. Again:

"That whenever any form of government becomes destructive of these ends, it is the right of the people to alter or abolish it, and to institute a new government, laying its foundations on such principles, and organizing its powers in such forms as to them shall seem most likely to effect their safety and happiness."

Surely, the right of the whole people to vote is here clearly implied, for however destructive in their happiness this government might become, a disfranchised class could neither alter nor abolish it, nor institute a new one, except by the old brute force method of insurrection and rebellion. One-half of the people of this nation to-day are utterly powerless to blot from the statute books an unjust law, or to write there a new and a just one. The women, dissatisfied as they are with this form of government, that enforces taxation without representation,—that compels them to obey laws to which they have never given their consent,—that imprisons and hangs them without a trial by a jury of their peers, that robs them, in marriage, of the custody of their own persons, wages and children,—are this half of the people left wholly at the mercy of the other half, in direct violation of the spirit and letter of the declarations of the framers of this government, every one of which was based on the immutable principle of equal rights to all. By those declarations, kings, priests, popes, aristocrats, were all alike dethroned, and placed on a common level politically, with the lowliest born subject or serf. By them, too, me, as such, were deprived of their divine right to rule, and placed on a political level with women. By the practice of those declarations all class and caste distinction will be abolished; and slave, serf, plebeian, wife, woman, all alike, bound from their subject position to the proud platform of equality. . . .

The preamble of the federal constitution says:

"We, the people of the United States, in order to form a more perfect union, establish justice, insure domestic tranquility, provide for the common defense, promote the general welfare and secure the blessings of liberty to ourselves and our posterity, do ordain and established this constitution for the United States of America."

It was we, the people, not we, the white male citizens, nor yet we, the male citizens; but we, the whole people, who formed this Union. And we formed it, not to give the blessings of liberty, but to secure them; not to the half of ourselves and the half of our posterity, but to the whole people-women as well as men. And it is downright mockery to talk to women of their enjoyment of the blessings of liberty while they are denied the use of the only means of securing them provided by this democratic-republican government-the ballot. . . .

For any State to make sex a qualification that must ever result in the disfranchisement of one entire half of the people, is to pass a bill of attainder, or an ex post facto law, and is therefore a violation of the supreme law of the land. By it, the blessings of liberty are forever withheld from women and their female posterity. . . .

There is no she, or her, or hers, in the tax laws. . . .

The same is true of all the criminal laws. . . .

The only question left to be settled, now, is: Are women persons? And I hardly believe any of our opponents will have the hardihood to say they are not. Being persons, then, women are citizens, and no state has a right to make any new law, or to enforce any old law, that shall abridge their privileges or immunities. Hence, every discrimination against women in the constitutions and laws of the several states, is to-day null and void, precisely as is every one against negroes.

Is the right to vote one of the privileges or immunities of citizens? I think the disfranchised ex-rebels, and the ex-state prisoners will agree with me, that it is not only one of the them, but the one without which all the others are nothing. Seek the first kingdom of the ballot, and all things else shall be given thee, is the political injunction.

Webster, Worcester and Bouvier all define citizen to be a person, in the United States, entitled to vote and hold office. . . .

Prior to the adoption of the thirteenth amendment, by which slavery was forever abolished, and black men transformed from property to persons, the judicial opinions of the country had always been in harmony with these definitions. To be a person was to be a citizen, and to be a citizen was to be a voter. . . .

If the fourteenth amendment does not secure to all citizens the right to vote, for what purpose was the grand old charter of the fathers lumbered with its unwieldy proportions? The republican party, and Judges Howard and Bingham, who drafted the document, pretended it was to do something for black men; and if that something was not to secure them in their right to vote and hold office, what could it have been? For, by the thirteenth amendment, black men had become people, and hence were entitled to all the privileges and immunities of the government, precisely as were the women of the country, and foreign men not naturalized. According to Associate Justice Washington, they already had the "Protection of the government, the enjoyment of life and liberty, with the right to acquire and possess property of every kind, and to pursue and obtain happiness and safety, subject to such restraints as the government may justly prescribe for the general welfare of the whole; the right of a citizen of one state to pass through or to reside in any other state for the purpose of trade, agriculture, professional pursuit, or otherwise; to claim the benefit of the writ of habeas corpus, to institute and maintain actions of any kind in the courts of the state; to take, hold, and dispose of property, either real or personal, and an exemption from higher taxes or impositions than are paid by the other citizens of the state."

Thus, you see, those newly freed men were in possession of every possible right, privilege and immunity of the government, except that of suffrage, and hence, needed no constitutional amendment for any other purpose. What right, I ask you, has the Irishman the day after he receives his naturalization papers that he did not possess the day before, save the right to vote and hold office? And the Chinamen, now crowding our Pacific coast, are in precisely the same position. What privilege or immunity has California or Oregon the constitutional right to deny them, save that of the ballot? Clearly, then if the fourteenth amendment was not to secure to black men their right to vote, it did nothing for them, since they possessed everything else before. But, if it was meant to be a prohibition of the states, to deny or abridge their right to vote-which I fully believe-then it did the same for all persons, white women included, born or naturalized in the United States; for the amendment does not say all male persons of African descent, but all persons are citizens. . . .

Clearly, then, the national government must not only define the rights of citizens, but it must stretch out its powerful hand and protect them in every state in this Union. . . .

But if you will insist that the fifteenth amendment's emphatic interdiction against robbing United States citizens of their right to vote," on account of race, color, or previous condition of servitude," is a recognition of the right, either of the United States, or any state, to rob citizens of that right, for any or all other reason, I will prove to you that the class of citizens for which I now plead, and to which I belong, may be, and sure, by all the principles of our government, and many of the laws of the states, included under the term "previous condition of servitude."

First, the married women and their legal status. What is servitude? "The condition of a slave," What is a slave? "A person who is robbed of the proceeds of his labor; a person who is subject to the will of another."

By the law of Georgia, South Carolina, and all the states of the South, the negro had no right to the custody and control of his person. He belonged to his master. If he was disobedient, the master had the right to use correction. If the negro didn't like the correction, and attempted to run away, the master had a right to use coercion to bring him back.

By the law of every state in this Union to-day, North as well as South, the married woman has no right to the custody and control of her person. The wife belongs to her husband; and if she refuses obedience to his will, he may use moderate correction, and if she doesn't like his moderate correction, and attempts to leave his "bed and board," the husband may use moderate coercion to bring her back. The little word "moderate," you see, is the saving clause for the wife, and would doubtless be overstepped should offended husband administer his correction with the "cat-o'-nine-tails," or accomplish his coercion with blood-hounds.

Again, the slave had no right to the earnings of his hands, they belonged to his master; no right to the custody of his children, they belonged to his master; no right to sue or be sued, or testify in the courts. If he committed a crime, it was the master who must sue or be sued.

In many of the states there has been special legislation, giving to married women the right to property inherited, or received by bequest, or earned by the pursuit of any avocation outside of the home; also, giving her the right to sue and be sued in matters pertaining to such separate property; but not a single state of this Union has ever secured the wife in the enjoyment of her right to the joint ownership of the joint earnings of the marriage copartnership. And since, in the nature of things, the vast majority of married women never earn a dollar, by work outside of their families, nor inherit a dollar from their fathers, it follows that from the day of their marriage to the day of the death of their husbands, not one of them ever has a dollar, except it shall please her husband to let her have it.

Is anything further needed to prove woman's condition of servitude sufficiently orthodox to entitle her to the guaranties of the fifteenth amendment?

Is there a man who will not agree with me, that to talk of freedom without the ballot, is mockery-is slavery-to the women of this Republic, precisely as New England's orator Wendell Phillips, at the close of the late war, declared it to be to the newly emancipated black men?

I admit that prior to the rebellion, by common consent, the right to enslave, as well as to disfranchise both native and foreign born citizens, was conceded to the States. But the one grand principle, settled by the war and the reconstruction legislation, is the supremacy of national power to protect the citizens of the United States in their right to freedom and the elective franchise, against any and every interference on the part of the several States. And again and again, have the American people asserted the triumph of this principle, by their overwhelming majorities for Lincoln and Grant.

The one issue of the last two Presidential elections was, whether the fourteenth and fifteenth amendments should be considered the irrevocable will of the people; and the decision was, they shall be—and that it is only the right, but the duty of the National Government to protect all United States citizens in the full enjoyment and free exercise of all their privileges and immunities against any attempt of any State to deny or abridge.

And in this conclusion Republican and Democrats alike agree.

Senator Frelinghuysen said:

"The heresy of State rights has been completely buried in these amendments, that as amended, the constitution confers not only national but State citizenship upon all persons born or naturalized within our limits."

The Call for the national Republican convention said:

"Equal suffrage has been engrafted on the national constitution; the privileges and immunities of American citizenship have become a part of the organic law."

The national Republican platform said:

"Complete liberty and exact quality in the enjoyment of all civil, political and public rights, should be established and maintained throughout the union by efficient and appropriate State and federal legislation."

If that means anything, it is that Congress should pass a law to require the States to protect women in their equal political rights, and that the States should enact laws making it the duty of inspectors of elections to receive women's votes on precisely the same conditions they do those of men.

Judge Stanley Mathews—a substantial Ohio democrat—in his preliminary speech at the Cincinnati convention, said most emphatically.

"The constitutional amendments have established the political equality of all citizens before the law."

President Grant, in his message to Congress March 30th 1870, on the adoption of the fifteenth amendment, said:

"A measure which makes at once four millions of people voters, is indeed a measure of greater importance than any act of the kind from the foundation of the Government to the present time."

How could four million negroes be made voter if two million were not included?

The California State Republican convention said:

"Among the many practical and substantial triumphs of the principles achieved by the Republican party during the past twelve years, it enumerated with pride and pleasure, the prohibiting of any State from abridging the privileges of any citizen of the Republic, the declaring the civil and political equality of every citizen, and the establishing all these principles in the federal constitution by amendments thereto, as the permanent law."

Benjamin F. Butler, in a recent letter to me, said:

"I do not believe anybody in Congress doubts that the Constitution authorizes the right of women to vote, precisely as it authorizes trial by jury and many other like rights guaranteed to citizens."

And again, General Butler said:

"It is not laws we want; there are plenty of laws—good enough, too. Administrative ability to enforce law is the great want of the age, in this country especially. Everybody talks of law, law. If everybody would insist on the enforcement of law, the government would stand on a firmer basis, and question would settle themselves."

And it is upon this just interpretation of the United States Constitution that our National Woman Suffrage Association which celebrates the twenty-fifth anniversary of the woman's rights movement in New York on the 6th of May next, has based all its arguments and action the past five years.

We no longer petition Legislature or Congress to give us the right to vote. We appeal to the women everywhere to exercise their too long neglected "citizen's right to vote." We appeal to the inspectors of election everywhere to receive the votes of all United States citizens as it is their duty to do. We appeal to United States commissioners and marshals to arrest the inspectors who reject the names and votes of United States citizens, as it is their duty to do, and leave those alone who, like our eighth ward inspectors, perform their duties faithfully and well.

We ask the juries to fail to return verdicts of "guilty" against honest, law-abiding, tax-paying United States citizens for offering their votes at our elections. Or against intelligent, worthy young men, inspectors of elections, for receiving and counting such citizens votes.

We ask the judges to render true and unprejudiced opinions of the law, and wherever there is room for a doubt to give its benefit on the side of liberty and equal rights to women, remembering that "the true rule of interpretation under our national constitution, especially since its amendments, is that anything for human rights is constitutional, everything against human right unconstitutional."

And it is on this line that we propose to fight our battle for the ballot-all peaceably, but nevertheless persistently through to complete triumph, when all United States citizens shall be recognized as equals before the law.

1. *According to Anthony, what is the connection between citizenship and the right to vote? What example(s) did she use to prove her point?*
2. *According to Anthony, how do the Fourteenth and Fifteenth Amendments address the rights of women? How does she support her assertions?*

16-11 James T. Rapier, Testimony Before U.S. Senate Regarding the Agricultural Labor Force in the South (1880)

An essential freedom African Americans gained in the post-Civil War era was the ability to move freely around the country. Seeking improvement of their situation, many African Americans emigrated to other states. As this excerpt shows, a variety of forces combined to push African Americans to emigrate.

A. Well, sir, there are several reasons why the colored people desire to emigrate from Alabama; one among them is the poverty of the South. On a large part of it a man cannot make a decent living. Another is their want of school privileges in the State: and there is a majority of the people who believe that they cannot any longer get justice in the courts; and another and the greatest reason is found in the local laws that we have, and which are very oppressive to that class of people in the black belt.

Q. State what some of them are.

A. First, we have only schools about three months in the year, and I suppose I need not say anything more on that head. In reference to the poverty of the soil, 33 to 40 per cent of the lands in Alabama is about all on which a man can make a living.

Q. Do you mean the parts that are subdued?

A. Yes, sir; the arable land. The average is one-third of a bale of cotton to the acre, not making three bales to the hand; and a hundred bushels of corn to the hand, on an average. Then take the price of cotton for the last two years; it has not netted more than $45 to $47.50 to the bale; and I suppose it would not be amiss for me to state something of the plans of working the land in Alabama.

Mr. Vance. It will be very proper.

The Witness. The general plan is that the landlord furnishes the land and the teams and feed for the teams and the implements, for which he draws one half of the crop. I remarked that the three bales of cotton and a hundred bushels of corn is about all that you can make to a hand. We allow in Alabama that much, for that is as much as a man can get out of it, and that is not enough to support his family, including himself and the feed of his family; $95 to $100 is as much as a hand can make, and that is not enough to feed any man in a Christian country. . . .

A. . . . Now, it is very clear that a man cannot live on such terms, and hence the conclusion of many of these people, that there is not a decent living for them in that State. They are like the white people, and their living no better. Numbers of them, probably not less than 20,000 whites, have left Alabama since the war and gone to Texas to better their condition, and the blacks are doing the same thing, and that is the whole there is of it. So far as the negroes are concerned now they have a high desire to submit their fate to their own keeping in another country. Now here is one of the laws which also affects us, to which I will call attention. It is found in the acts of Alabama for 1878-'79, page 63, act No. 57, section 1.

Section 1. *Be it enacted by the general assembly of Alabama,* That section 4369 of the Code be, and the same is hereby, amended so as to read as follows: Any person who shall buy, sell, receive, barter, or dispose of any cotton, corn, wheat, oats, pease, or potatoes after the hour of sunset and before the hour of sunrise of the next succeeding day, and any person who shall in any manner move, carry, convey, or transport, except within the limits of the farm or plantation on which it is raised or grown, any seed cotton between the hours of sunset and sunrise of the next succeeding day, shall be guilty of a misdemeanor, and, on conviction, shall be fined not less than ten nor more five hundred dollars, and may also be imprisoned in the county jail, or put to hard labor for the county, for not more than twelve months. But this section shall not effect the right of municipal corporations to establish and regulate under their charters public markets within their limits for the sale of commodities for culinary purposes, nor the right of any proprietor or owner of any plantation or premises to sell on such plantation or premises the necessary grain and provisions for the subsistence of man and beast for the night to traveling or transient persons, or for the use of agricultural laborers in his own employment on such plantation or premises: *Provided,* That the provisions of such section shall not apply to any person carrying seed cotton to a gin for the purpose of having the same ginned.

Now, the effect of this upon the labor of the South is this: A great many laborers work by the month, but all of them are under contract. If I live three miles from a store, and I must work from sunup to sundown, I cannot go where I can do my trading to the best advantage. A man is prevented, no matter whether his family is sick from sundown to sunrise, from going and selling anything that he has, as the landlord will not give them time between sunrise and sundown.

Q. What was the purpose of this law?

A. It was, as appears from the debates, to keep the negroes from going to stores and taking off seed cotton from the plantation. Certainly it was to have that effect, but it goes further and prevents a man from selling what he has raised and has a right to sell. If a man commits a crime he ought to be punished, but every man ought to have a right to dispose of his own property.

Q. Is there any particular limitation of time to which this law applies?

A. No, sir.

Q. It runs all the year round?

A. Yes, sir.

Q. After the division of the crops as well as before?

A. Yes, sir; it operates so that a man cannot sell his crop at all in many cases.

Q. Do you say that the landlord will not let him sell his crop or that he can prevent it?

A. I say he will not let him do it, because the landlord will not let him take two or three hours out of the time due him in the day to sell it, and the law prevents him from selling at night.

Q. You say the effect of it is not to let him sell his crop at all?

A. I do; for if a man agrees to work from sunup to sundown he is made to do it. I work them that way myself, and I believe all the rest do. . . .

Q. It shall not be lawful to buy or sell seed cotton?

A. Yes, sir.

Q. At any time?

A. Yes, sir; night or day.

Q. From nobody?

A. From nobody.

Q. White or black?-A. White or black; but you see it applies wholly to black counties.

Q. But there are some white people there, are there not?

A. Yes, sir; but I do not know many who raise seed cotton.

Q. I thought something, may be, was left out of that act?

A. No, sir; that is to say, the gist of the matter is this: I may raise as much cotton as I please in the seed, but I am prohibited by law from selling it to anybody but the landlord, who can buy it because he has advanced to me on the crop. One of the rules is this: I have people working for me to day, but I give them an outside patch. If a man makes outside 1,200 pounds of seed cotton, which is worth $2.50 per 100 pounds, he cannot sell it unless to me. I may say I will give him $1.50 per 100 pounds for it, and he will be forced to take it; but I cannot sell it again unless I have a merchantable bale, which is 500 pounds, or 450 pounds by the cotton congress.

Q. Then the effect of that law is to place all the seed cotton into the hands of the landlord?

A. Yes, sir.

Q. He is the only purchaser who is allowed by law to buy it?

A. Yes, sir; nobody else can buy it. . . .

Q. I thought the law said that grand larceny should consist of as much as $235 worth?

A. No, sir; you have not got it right yet. Two ears or a stalk of corn is a part of an outstanding crop, and any man who sells any part of an outstanding crop can be prosecuted and convicted of grand larceny. . . .

The Witness. The point is this: Under the laws of Alabama the probate judge, the clerk, and the sheriff have had the drawing of jurors, and have had since Alabama was admitted as a State; but this bill comes in and covers those counties where the Republicans are likely to have a majority, and where they would draw the jurors. The proper heading of the law might have been, "An act to keep negroes off the juries." I want to state that it is the general opinion of the colored people in Alabama, and I will say of some of the judges, that it is a difficult matter for a colored man to get justice when there is a case between him and a white man. I will cite one of those cases: There was a case in Montgomery in which Judge J.

Q. Smith presided. It was a civil suit. A white man had a black man's crop attached, and he had lost it. The colored man sued him on the attachment bond, and employed Judge Gardiner to defend or prosecute it for him. Soon after the case was given to the jury they brought in a verdict for the defendant. Judge Gardiner moved for a new trial, on the ground that the verdict was not in accordance with the facts; and the judge said, "I have observed that where an issue is between a white and a black man before a jury the verdict is almost invariably against the black man. The grounds on which the judge said he would not grant a new trial would be because he thinks the next verdict would not be different from that rendered, and as I do not think there would be a different verdict, I decline to give the new trial."

1. *What is the plight of the free southern black farmer according to this testimony? What particular challenges face the black farmer in this account?*
2. *In what ways is a black farmer in the south barely better off than he was under slavery?*
3. *What prejudices against blacks in the legal system are revealed by this testimony?*

16-12   A Sharecrop Contract (1882)

During the Reconstruction era, sharecropping emerged as the most common method of organizing and financing southern agriculture. Large plantations, no longer worked by gangs of slaves, were broken up into small plots worked by individual families. the following contract typifies the sort of formal arrangements that many thousands of poor black and white farmers made with local landowners

To every one applying to rent land upon shares, the following conditions must be read, and agreed to.

To every 30 and 35 acres, I agree to furnish the team, plow, and farming implements, except cotton planters, and I do not agree to furnish a cart to every cropper. The croppers are to have half of the cotton, corn, and fodder (and peas and pumpkins and potatoes if any are planted) if the following conditions are complied with, but-if not-they are to have only two-fifths ($^2/_5$). Croppers are to have no part or interest in the cotton seed raised from the crop planted and worked by them. No vine crops of any description, that is, no watermelons, muskmelons, . . . squashes or anything of that kind, except peas and pumpkins, and potatoes, are to be planted in the cotton or corn. All must work under my direction. All plantation work to be done by the croppers. My part of the crop to be housed by them, and the fodder and oats to be hauled and put in the house. All the cotton must be topped about 1st August. If any cropper fails from any cause to save all the fodder from his crop, I am to have enough fodder to make it equal to one-half of the whole if the whole amount of fodder had been saved.

For every mule or horse furnished by me there must be 1000 good sized rails. . . hauled, and the fence repaired as far as they will go, the fence to be torn down and put up from the bottom if I so direct. All croppers to haul rails and work on fence whenever I may order. Rails to be split when I may say. Each cropper to clean out every ditch in his crop, and where a ditch runs between two croppers, the cleaning out of that ditch is to be divided equally between them. Every ditch bank in the crop must be shrubbed down and cleaned off before the crop is planted and must be cut down every time the land is worked with his hoe and when the crop is "laid by," the ditch banks must be left clean of bushes, weeds, and seeds. The cleaning out of all ditches must be done by the first of October. The rails must be split and the fence repaired before corn is planted.

Each cropper must keep in good repair all bridges in his crop or over ditches that he has to clean out and when a bridge needs repairing that is outside of all their crops, then any one that I call on must repair it.

Fence jams to be done as ditch banks. If any cotton is planted on the land outside of the plantation fence, I am to have three-fourths of all the cotton made in those patches, that is to say, no cotton must be planted by croppers in their home patches.

All croppers must clean out stable and fill them with straw, and haul straw in front of stable whenever I direct. All the cotton must be manured, and enough fertilizer must be brought to manure each crop highly, the croppers to pay for one-half of all manure bought, the quantity to be purchased for each crop must be left to me.

No cropper is to work off the plantation when there is any work to be done on the land he has rented, or when his work is needed by me or other croppers. Trees to be cut down on Orchard, house field, & Evanson fences, leaving such as I may designate.

Road field is to be planted from the very edge of the ditch to the fence, and all the land to be planted close up to the ditches and fences. No stock of any kind belonging to croppers to run in the plantation after crops are gathered.

If the fence should be blown down, or if trees should fall on the fence outside of the land planted by any of the croppers, any one or all that I may call upon must put it up and repair it. Every cropper must feed or have fed, the team he works, Saturday nights, Sundays, and every morning before going to work, beginning to feed his team (morning, noon, and night every day in the week) on the day he rents and feeding it to including the 31st day of December. If any cropper shall from any cause fail to repair his fence as far as 1000 rails will go, or shall fail to clean out any part of his ditches, or shall fail to leave his ditch banks, any part of them, well shrubbed and clean when his crop is laid by, or shall fail to clean out stables, fill them up and haul straw in front of them whenever he is told, he shall have only two-fifths ($^2/_5$) of the cotton, corn, fodder, peas, and pumpkins made on the land he cultivates.

If any cropper shall fail to feed his team Saturday nights, all day Sunday and all the rest of the week, morning/noon, and night, for every time he so fails he must pay me five cents.

No corn or cotton stalks must be burned, but must be cut down, cut up and plowed in. Nothing must be burned off the land except when it is impossible to plow it in.

Every cropper must be responsible for all gear and farming implements placed in his hands, and if not returned must be paid for unless it is worn out by use.

Croppers must sow & plow in oats and haul them to the crib, but must have no part of them. Nothing to be sold from their crops, nor fodder nor corn to be carried out of the fields until my rent is all paid, and all amounts they owe me and for which I am responsible are paid in full.

I am to gin & pack all the cotton and charge every cropper an eighteenth of his part, the cropper to furnish his part of the bagging, ties, & twine. The sale of every cropper's part of the cotton to be made by me when and where I choose to sell, and after deducting all they owe me and all sums that I may be responsible for on their accounts, to pay them their half of the net proceeds. Work of every description, particularly the work on fences and ditches, to be done to my satisfaction, and must be done over until I am satisfied that it is done as it should be.

No wood to burn, nor light wood, nor poles, nor timber for boards, nor wood for any purpose whatever must be gotten above the house occupied by Henry Beasley-nor must any trees be cut down nor any wood used for any purpose, except for firewood, without my permission.

1. *Identify and explain the stipulations of this contract that result in virtual slavery for the sharecropper.*